TURBULENCE IN THE EASTERN MEDITERRANEAN

Federal Foreign Office — IISS–Europe acknowledges the financial support of the German Federal Foreign Office in producing this strategic dossier.

an **IISS** *strategic dossier*

TURBULENCE IN THE EASTERN MEDITERRANEAN

GEOPOLITICAL, SECURITY AND ENERGY DYNAMICS

published by

The International Institute for Strategic Studies

ARUNDEL HOUSE | 6 TEMPLE PLACE | LONDON | WC2R 2PG | UK

an **IISS** *strategic dossier*

TURBULENCE IN THE EASTERN MEDITERRANEAN

GEOPOLITICAL, SECURITY AND ENERGY DYNAMICS

The International Institute for Strategic Studies
ARUNDEL HOUSE | 6 TEMPLE PLACE | LONDON | WC2R 2PG | UK

DIRECTOR-GENERAL AND CHIEF EXECUTIVE **Dr Bastian Giegerich**
EDITORS **Emile Hokayem, Rym Momtaz**
CONTRIBUTORS **Dr Hasan Alhasan, John V. Bowlus, Nicholas Crawford, Shiloh Fetzek, Maximilian Hess, Emile Hokayem, Gareth Jenkins, Jacob Judah, Camille Lons, Francesca Maremonti, Gabriel Mitchell, Rym Momtaz, Carole Nakhle, Erica Pepe, Umberto Profazio, John Psaropoulos, Yara Saab, Ester Sabatino, Heba Taha, Julien Théron, Kévin Thiévon, Tom Waldwyn**
ASSOCIATE EDITOR **Katie Holland**
EDITORIAL **Alice Aveson, Gregory Brooks, Marcos Economides, Nicholas Fargher, Christopher Harder, Katie Holland, Jill Lally, Gráinne Lucey-Tremblay, Michael Marsden, Adam Walters, Lauren Whelan, Nicholas Woodroof**
GRAPHICS COORDINATOR **Nicholas Woodroof**
DESIGN **Alessandra Beluffi, Ravi Gopar, Jade Panganiban, James Parker, Kelly Verity**

This publication has been prepared by the Director-General and Chief Executive of the Institute and his staff. It incorporates commissioned contributions from recognised subject experts, which were reviewed by a range of experts in the field. The IISS would like to thank the various individuals who contributed their expertise to the compilation of this dossier. The responsibility for the contents is ours alone. The views expressed herein do not, and indeed cannot, represent a consensus of views among the worldwide membership of the Institute as a whole.

First published December 2024 by The International Institute for Strategic Studies.

© 2024 The International Institute for Strategic Studies

All rights reserved. No part of this book may be reprinted or reproduced or utilised in any form or by any electronic, mechanical, or other means, now known or hereafter invented, including photocopying and recording, or in any information storage or retrieval system, without the prior permission in writing from the publishers.

British Library Cataloguing in Publication Data | A catalogue record for this book is available from the British Library

Library of Congress Cataloging in Publication Data | A catalog record for this book has been requested

ISBN PAPERBACK 978-1-032-99463-5 | E-BOOK 978-1-003-60428-0

About The International Institute for Strategic Studies
The International Institute for Strategic Studies is an independent centre for research, information and debate on the problems of conflict, however caused, that have, or potentially have, an important military content. The Council and Staff of the Institute are international and its membership is drawn from over 100 countries. The Institute is independent and it alone decides what activities to conduct. It owes no allegiance to any government, any group of governments or any political or other organisation. The IISS stresses rigorous research with a forward-looking policy orientation that can improve wider public understanding of international security problems and influence the development of sounder public policy.

CONTENTS

FLAG GLOSSARY	6
EXECUTIVE SUMMARY	8

THEMES — 10

CHAPTER ONE	GEOPOLITICS: FRAGMENTATION, COMPETITION AND THE PERSISTENCE OF CONFLICT	12
CHAPTER TWO	MARITIME DISPUTES: THE COMPLEX INTERSECTION OF HISTORY, LAW AND GEOPOLITICS	40
CHAPTER THREE	ENERGY IN THE EASTERN MEDITERRANEAN: POTENTIAL MEETS GEOPOLITICS	62
CHAPTER FOUR	ARMED FORCES: DEFENCE POLICY, CAPABILITY, COOPERATION AND MODERNISATION	88

REGIONAL ACTORS — 128

CHAPTER FIVE	TURKIYE: ERDOĞAN'S STATECRAFT, REGIONAL AMBITIONS AND STRUCTURAL LIMITATIONS	130
CHAPTER SIX	TURKISH COERCIVE DIPLOMACY: SYRIA AND LIBYA AS LABORATORIES	146
CHAPTER SEVEN	GREECE: REGIONAL COOPERATION AS GRAND STRATEGY	156
CHAPTER EIGHT	CYPRUS: PROTRACTED DIVISION, INCREASED STRATEGIC DEPTH AND AN ISRAELI GAMBLE	170
CHAPTER NINE	LIBYA: INTERNAL DIVISIONS, FOREIGN INTERVENTION AND OIL	184
CHAPTER TEN	EGYPT: REGIONAL AMBITIONS AND DOMESTIC WEAKNESS	192
CHAPTER ELEVEN	ISRAEL: BETWEEN THE AMBITION OF REGIONAL INTEGRATION AND THE REALITY OF CONFLICT	204
CHAPTER TWELVE	LEBANON: ENDURING POLYCRISIS AND ON THE BRINK OF WAR	222
CHAPTER THIRTEEN	SYRIA: A BROKEN STATE AND AN ARENA FOR COMPETITION	230

GLOBAL ACTORS — 238

CHAPTER FOURTEEN	UNITED STATES: BETWEEN RETRENCHMENT AND ENTANGLEMENT	240
CHAPTER FIFTEEN	FRANCE: HIGH AMBITIONS, REDUCED INFLUENCE	252
CHAPTER SIXTEEN	THE SOUTHERN FLANK: A CHALLENGE FOR NATO AND THE EU	260
CHAPTER SEVENTEEN	THE GULF STATES IN THE EASTERN MEDITERRANEAN: FROM GEOPOLITICS TO GEO-ECONOMICS	270
CHAPTER EIGHTEEN	RUSSIA: MAXIMISING THE POLITICAL RETURNS OF ITS INTERVENTIONS	284
CHAPTER NINETEEN	CHINA IN THE EASTERN MEDITERRANEAN: SMALL BUT GROWING PRESENCE	296

FLAG GLOSSARY

- Albania
- Arab League
- Armenia
- Azerbaijan
- Bahrain
- Bulgaria
- Canada
- China
- Croatia
- Cyprus
- Denmark
- Egypt
- European Union

- France
- Georgia
- Germany
- Greece
- Hamas
- Iran
- Iraq
- Israel
- Italy
- Kuwait
- Lebanon
- Libya
- Luxembourg

FLAG GLOSSARY

- Morocco
- NATO
- the Netherlands
- Occupied Palestinian Territories/*State of Palestine*
- Oman
- Pakistan
- Poland
- Portugal
- Qatar
- Romania
- Russia
- Saudi Arabia
- Serbia

- Somalia
- South Korea
- Spain
- Sudan
- Syria
- *Turkish Republic of Northern Cyprus*
- Turkiye
- Ukraine
- United Arab Emirates
- United Kingdom
- United Nations
- United States

Note: Entities in italics lack recognition, statehood or full UN membership.

TURBULENCE IN THE EASTERN MEDITERRANEAN: GEOPOLITICAL, SECURITY AND ENERGY DYNAMICS   AN IISS STRATEGIC DOSSIER

THEMES

CHAPTER ONE | GEOPOLITICS: FRAGMENTATION, COMPETITION AND THE PERSISTENCE OF CONFLICT	12
CHAPTER TWO | MARITIME DISPUTES: THE COMPLEX INTERSECTION OF HISTORY, LAW AND GEOPOLITICS	40
CHAPTER THREE | ENERGY IN THE EASTERN MEDITERRANEAN: POTENTIAL MEETS GEOPOLITICS	62
CHAPTER FOUR | ARMED FORCES: DEFENCE POLICY, CAPABILITY, COOPERATION AND MODERNISATION	88

↑

(top to bottom) Turkish Naval Forces conducting the *Sea Wolf* (*Denizkurdu*) exercise in the Aegean Sea on 23 May 2017; Egyptian foreign minister Sameh Shoukry (C-R), in the presence of Greek foreign minister Nikos Dendias (L), French foreign minister Jean-Yves Le Drian (C-L) and Cypriot foreign minister Nikos Christodoulides (R), speaks to the press following a meeting to discuss developments in Libya held in Cairo, Egypt, on 8 January 2020; the drillship Stena *DrillMAX* near the port of Limassol, Cyprus, on 21 July 2023. (Photos: Ahmet Izgi/Anadolu Agency via Getty Images; Mohamed el-Shahed/AFP via Getty Images; Danil Shamkin/NurPhoto via Getty Images)

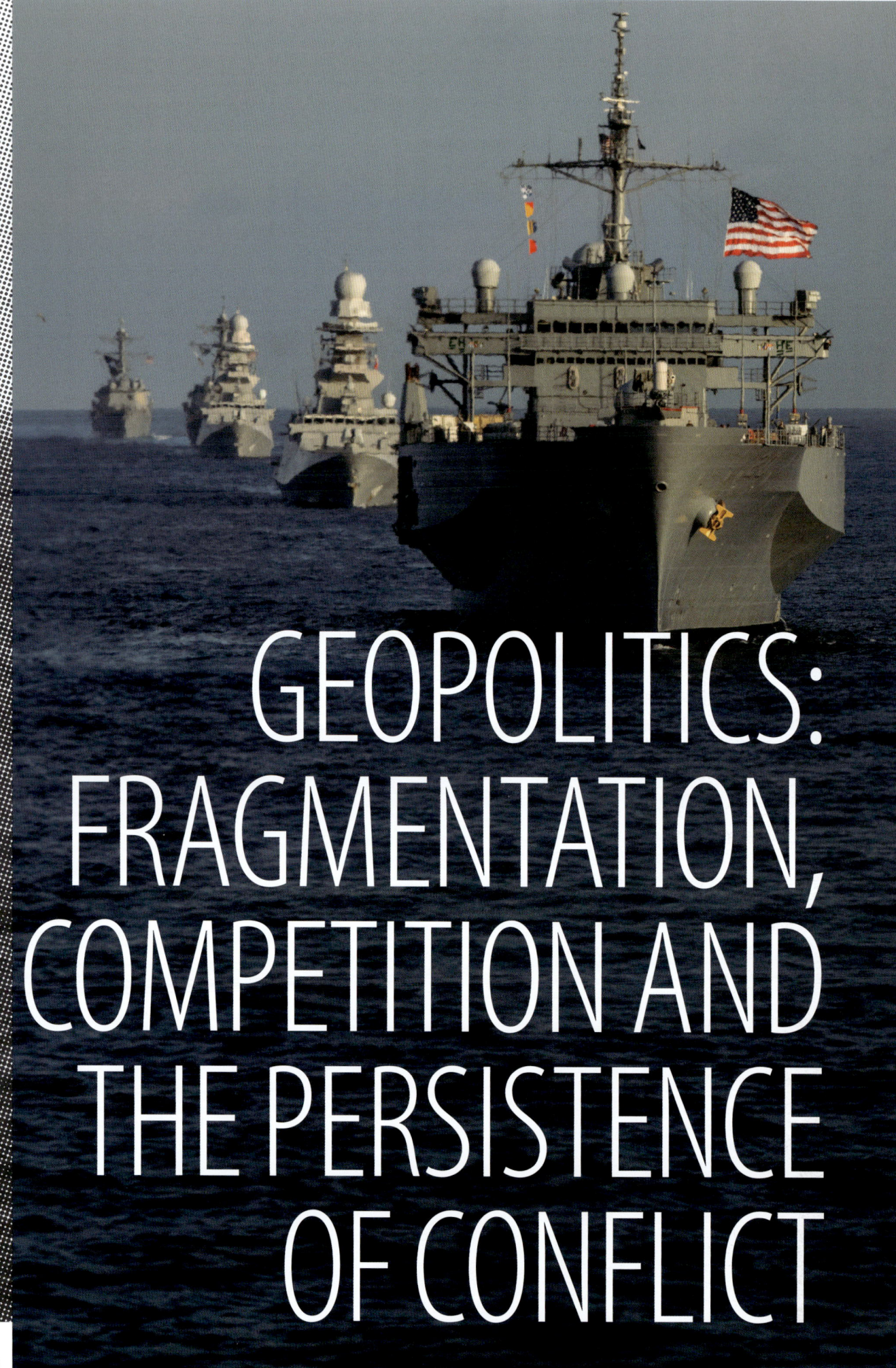

GEOPOLITICS: FRAGMENTATION, COMPETITION AND THE PERSISTENCE OF CONFLICT

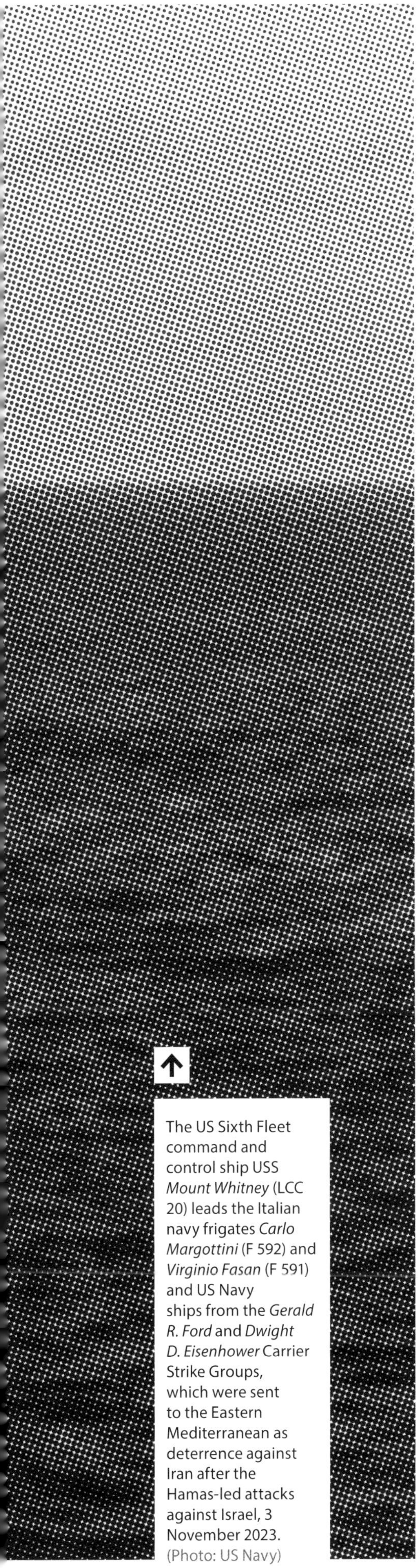

THEMES | GEOPOLITICS: FRAGMENTATION, COMPETITION AND THE PERSISTENCE OF CONFLICT

CHAPTER ONE

The US Sixth Fleet command and control ship USS *Mount Whitney* (LCC 20) leads the Italian navy frigates *Carlo Margottini* (F 592) and *Virginio Fasan* (F 591) and US Navy ships from the *Gerald R. Ford* and *Dwight D. Eisenhower* Carrier Strike Groups, which were sent to the Eastern Mediterranean as deterrence against Iran after the Hamas-led attacks against Israel, 3 November 2023. (Photo: US Navy)

THE EASTERN MEDITERRANEAN remains politically and strategically fragmented. While brinkmanship and external interference are rife, no single actor can shape or dominate it. The cyclical resumption of conflicts is likely and there is a serious possibility of a multi-front war for the first time since 1973.

THE ISRAEL–HAMAS WAR illustrates the limits of Eastern Mediterranean cooperation centred on energy, connectivity and regional defence. Geopolitics and concerns about domestic stability remain the main drivers of policy, not integration or commercial considerations.

TURKIYE HAS BEEN AN ACTIVE REGIONAL SHAPER, but faced pushback from Cyprus, Egypt, Greece and Israel throughout the 2010s. With an ailing economy and limited gains from its brinkmanship at sea, Ankara has had to engage in a de-escalation process with Egypt, Greece and the United States.

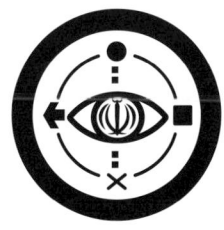

IRAN HAS BECOME A DE FACTO LOCAL POWER in the Eastern Mediterranean through its networks of powerful non-state militias in Lebanon, the Occupied Palestinian Territories and Syria. But Tehran's influence is under pressure as it struggles to maintain credible deterrence.

THE HAMAS-LED ATTACKS ON 7 OCTOBER 2023 shattered Israel's security doctrine and its approach towards the Occupied Palestinian Territories. Whether Israel can avoid regional isolation will depend on its domestic politics, the course of the war in Gaza and against Hizbullah, and its management of relations with existing regional partners.

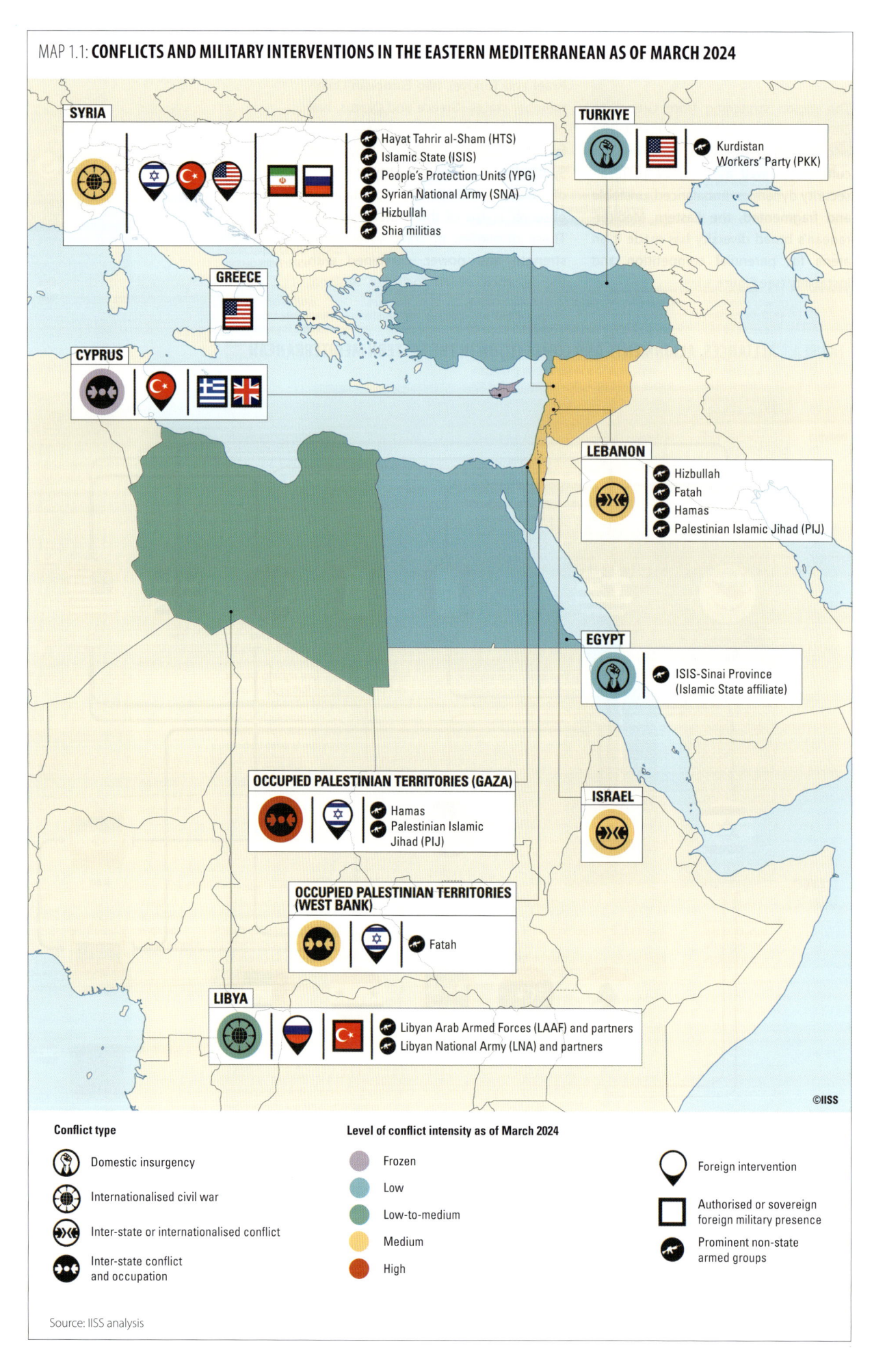

MAP 1.1: CONFLICTS AND MILITARY INTERVENTIONS IN THE EASTERN MEDITERRANEAN AS OF MARCH 2024

SYRIA
- Hayat Tahrir al-Sham (HTS)
- Islamic State (ISIS)
- People's Protection Units (YPG)
- Syrian National Army (SNA)
- Hizbullah
- Shia militias

Foreign involvement: Israel, Türkiye, USA, Iran, Russia

TURKIYE
- Kurdistan Workers' Party (PKK)

Foreign involvement: USA

GREECE
Foreign involvement: USA

CYPRUS
Foreign involvement: Türkiye, Greece, UK

LEBANON
- Hizbullah
- Fatah
- Hamas
- Palestinian Islamic Jihad (PIJ)

EGYPT
- ISIS-Sinai Province (Islamic State affiliate)

OCCUPIED PALESTINIAN TERRITORIES (GAZA)
- Hamas
- Palestinian Islamic Jihad (PIJ)

Foreign involvement: Israel

ISRAEL

OCCUPIED PALESTINIAN TERRITORIES (WEST BANK)
- Fatah

Foreign involvement: Israel

LIBYA
- Libyan Arab Armed Forces (LAAF) and partners
- Libyan National Army (LNA) and partners

Foreign involvement: Russia, Türkiye

©IISS

Conflict type
- Domestic insurgency
- Internationalised civil war
- Inter-state or internationalised conflict
- Inter-state conflict and occupation

Level of conflict intensity as of March 2024
- Frozen
- Low
- Low-to-medium
- Medium
- High

- Foreign intervention
- Authorised or sovereign foreign military presence
- Prominent non-state armed groups

Source: IISS analysis

architecture able to contain conflicts and facilitate dialogue, have exacerbated political disputes, competition and belligerence (see Table 1.1).

The research for this dossier was launched in early 2023, at a time of relative hopefulness for the Middle East. It was precisely such optimistic beliefs that motivated the International Institute for Strategic Studies to conduct a wide-ranging study to identify and assess the drivers of instability in the region beyond circumstantial developments. This mood was best captured by US National Security Advisor Jake Sullivan, who asserted that 'although the Middle East remains beset with perennial challenges, the region is quieter than it has been for decades' in the November–December 2023 issue of Foreign Affairs, which was written in September.[1] This sense of optimism was disrupted on 7 October 2023. That day, the armed branch of the Palestinian Islamist group Hamas and Palestinian Islamic Jihad, both relatively small and contained non-state armed groups, carried out ambitious and deadly attacks against Israel. Israel had thought its military dominance, economic success and increasing regional integration meant it had neutralised the Palestinian issue. This view was shared by other states in the region and had formed the basis of a growing regional convergence.

The war that followed the Hamas-led attacks is ongoing. The full extent of its local and regional repercussions and outcomes remains unclear at the time of writing. The war, however, exposed the fragile foundations of regional detente, notably how unresolved conflicts can threaten the whole edifice. The Israel–Hamas war also quickly became a multi-front conflict as it provided an opportunity for the Iran-backed 'Axis of Resistance' to mobilise in Iraq, Lebanon, Syria and Yemen in a show of solidarity with their Palestinian partner. Although this conflict has yet to evolve into an all-out inter-state war, it has exposed enduring regional fragmentation, misalignments and lack of cohesion, with no local actor or set of local actors able or willing to contain the conflict.

Israel Defense Forces infantry fighting vehicles deploy along the border with Gaza in southern Israel on 13 October 2023. (Photo: Jack Guez/AFP via Getty Images)

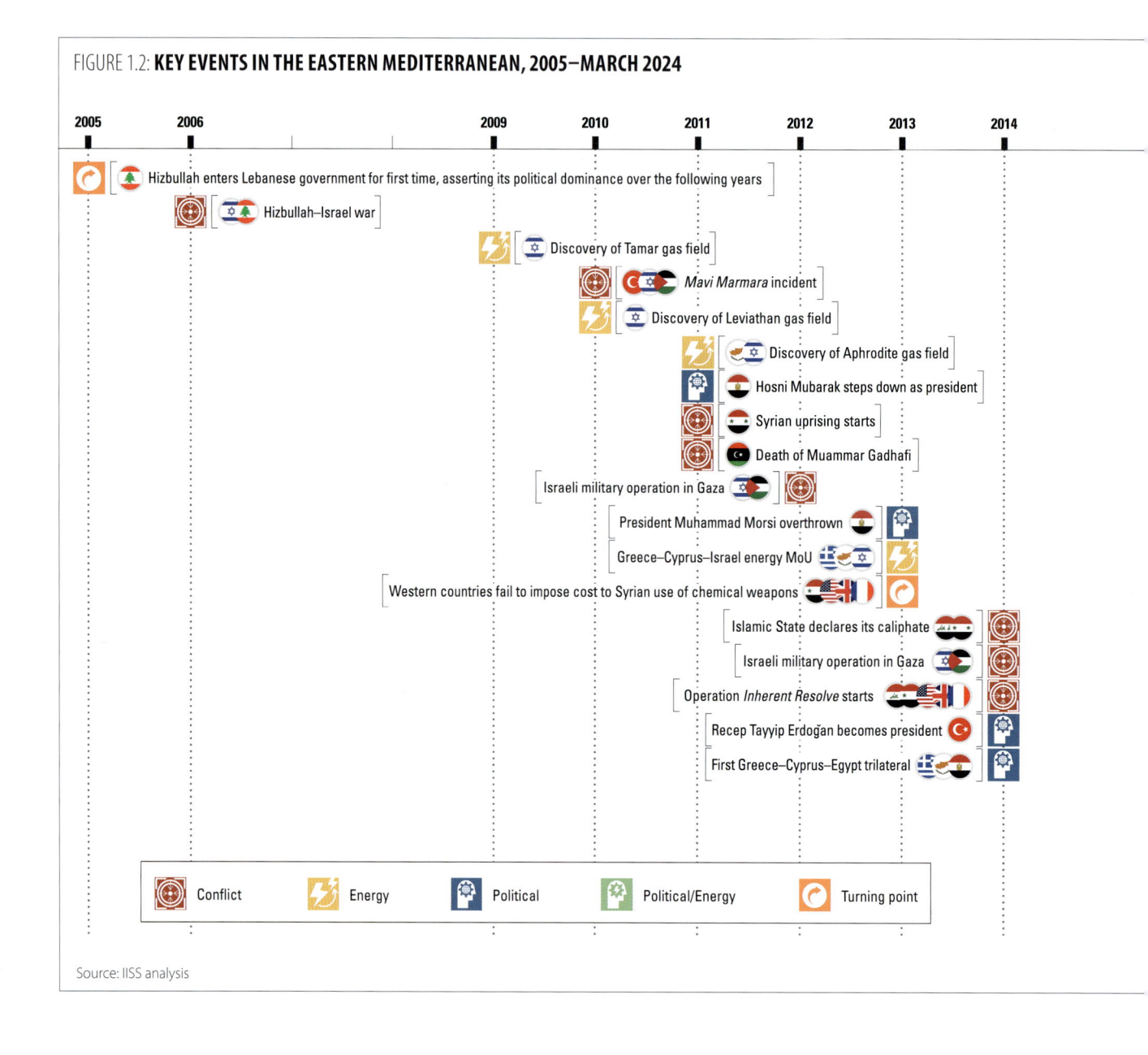

FIGURE 1.2: KEY EVENTS IN THE EASTERN MEDITERRANEAN, 2005–MARCH 2024

Timeline (2005–2014):

- **2005:** Hizbullah enters Lebanese government for first time, asserting its political dominance over the following years *(Turning point)*
- **2006:** Hizbullah–Israel war *(Conflict)*
- **2009:** Discovery of Tamar gas field *(Energy)*
- **2010:** *Mavi Marmara* incident *(Conflict)*; Discovery of Leviathan gas field *(Energy)*
- **2011:** Discovery of Aphrodite gas field *(Energy)*; Hosni Mubarak steps down as president *(Political)*; Syrian uprising starts *(Political)*; Death of Muammar Gadhafi *(Political)*
- **2012:** Israeli military operation in Gaza *(Conflict)*
- **2013:** President Muhammad Morsi overthrown *(Political)*; Greece–Cyprus–Israel energy MoU *(Political/Energy)*; Western countries fail to impose cost to Syrian use of chemical weapons *(Turning point)*
- **2014:** Islamic State declares its caliphate *(Conflict)*; Israeli military operation in Gaza *(Conflict)*; Operation *Inherent Resolve* starts *(Conflict)*; Recep Tayyip Erdoğan becomes president *(Political)*; First Greece–Cyprus–Egypt trilateral *(Political)*

Legend: Conflict | Energy | Political | Political/Energy | Turning point

Source: IISS analysis

THE EVOLVING GEOPOLITICS OF THE EASTERN MEDITERRANEAN

The 2010s were a particularly turbulent decade defined by the Arab uprisings (see Figure 1.2). The failure of political and economic governance in several Arab countries led to revolutions, counter-revolutions, external interference, civil wars and other forms of instability. The Arab uprisings were also accompanied by the intense competition between conservative monarchies and countries that supported Islamist movements; the spread of transnational jihadism, whose most advanced form, the Islamic State in Iraq and Syria, disrupted the Middle East at great cost; and Iranian regional ascendancy, which Gulf states and Western partners have unsuccessfully tried to contain.

During this period, a main strategic driver of regional relations was the attempted containment of Turkiye. Indeed, at least seven local actors (Greece, Cyprus, Israel, post-2013 Egypt, the Assad government in Syria, eastern Libyan factions and, to a lesser extent, the Palestinian Authority governing the West Bank) were embroiled in separate rivalries with Ankara. A growing alignment between Egypt, Cyprus, Greece and Israel began to take shape, sustained by extra-regional powers such as the United States, France, the United Arab Emirates and, to a lesser extent, Saudi Arabia. The emergence in Athens of a pro-US governing elite and the cooling of relations between Cyprus and Russia sped up a process of rapprochement with the US and Israel that had been progressing slowly since the 1990s. This fostered regional defence cooperation, with the Cypriot, Egyptian, Greek and Israeli militaries engaging in exercises and intelligence sharing with US and French support. The discovery and exploitation of offshore energy reserves presented the tantalising possibility of regional integration between Egypt, Israel, Cyprus and Greece based on shared economic interests.

In parallel, the Turkish leadership saw the Arab popular movements as an opportunity to expand its influence. Early on,

Timeline

- 2015: Discovery of Zohr gas field
- 2015: Russia intervenes militarily in Syria
- 2016: Failed attempted coup in Turkiye
- 2016: Turkiye–EU migration agreement
- 2017: Crans-Montana talks fail
- 2019: Turkiye–Libya EEZ MoU
- 2020: Qasem Soleimani assassinated
- 2020: Post-agreement Turkiye–EU migration crisis
- 2020: End of siege of Tripoli by forces of Khalifa Haftar
- 2020: Naval incidents between France, Greece and Turkiye
- 2020: Egyptian threat to intervene in Libya
- 2020: Beirut explosion
- 2020: Greece–Egypt maritime-delimitation agreement
- 2020: US sanctions on Turkiye over purchase of Russian S-400 air-defence system
- 2020: US-backed German mediation de-escalates Turkish–Greek–Cypriot tensions
- 2021: Greece–France Strategic Partnership
- 2022: US lifts arms embargo on Cyprus
- 2022: Israel–Lebanon maritime deal
- 2023: Erdoğan re-elected president
- 2023: Greece and Turkiye help each other in their respective natural disasters
- 2023: Hamas-led attacks against Israel
- 2023: Israeli military operation against Gaza

©IISS

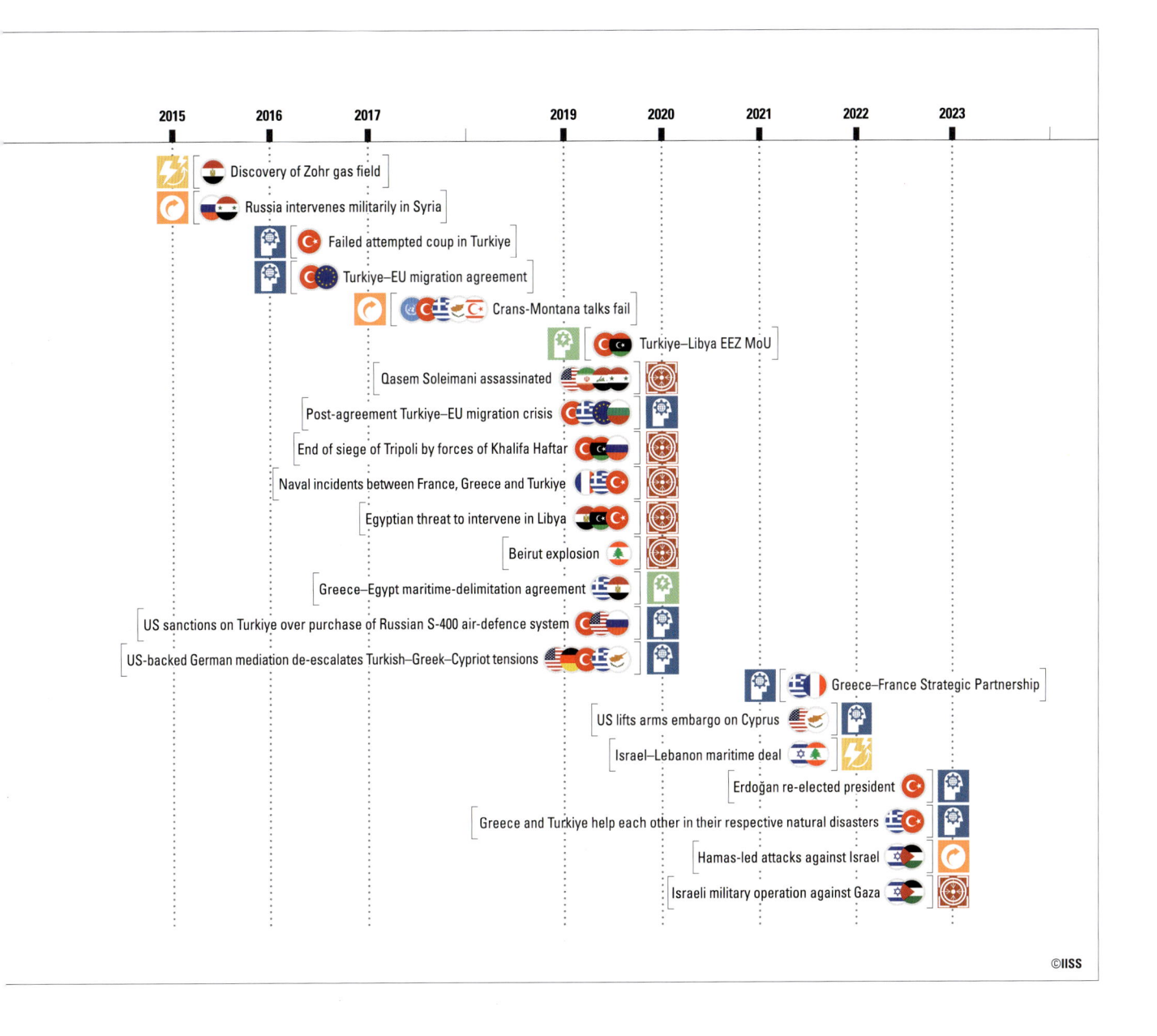

it seemed that Turkiye could achieve significant inroads in Egypt, Libya and Syria. Turkiye's ambitions were undercut, however, by setbacks suffered by its local partners. Cyprus and Greece worried that Egyptian president Muhammad Morsi's Muslim Brotherhood government in Cairo would side with Ankara on regional matters, including border delineations, while Israel saw President Recep Tayyip Erdoğan's support for Hamas as part of its regional Islamist outreach. In an effort to curtail Ankara, Turkiye's many rivals across the region supported Egypt's 2013 military coup, resulting in the removal of Morsi. As part of this intensifying competition, Turkiye's rivals also supported anti-Turkish factions in Syria's civil war and in the conflict over legitimacy and authority in Libya.

Apart from these setbacks, two events stoked Ankara's revanchism: the July 2016 attempted coup against Erdoğan and the failure of the UN-led negotiations for the reunification of Cyprus at Crans-Montana in 2017, for which Turkish and other negotiators placed the blame on Nicosia. In response, Turkiye sought to check its rivals through a series of daring moves: military interventions in Libya and Syria, where factions backed by its rivals were stopped, and maritime brinkmanship that riled Cyprus, Egypt and Greece. By the end of the decade, the high cost and risk of this intense and unbridled competition were evident to all, as was the impossibility of there being any one 'winner'.

Enthusiastic plans for greater integration and cooperation in the region ignored the potentially explosive consequences of a rapidly failing Lebanon, a war-ravaged Syria and Libya, and a divided and occupied Palestine. By 2024, three of these four theatres were active fronts, each involving Israel against non-state armed groups backed by Iran.

Nevertheless, some geopolitical tensions in the region began to ease in the early 2020s. By 2023, Greece and Turkiye had resumed dialogue, fuelling expectations that elections in both countries would further improve relations. Ankara and Cairo jump-started their own de-escalation process, leading to diplomatic normalisation. Unresolved conflicts in Syria and Libya seemed effectively frozen and no longer disruptive for regional priorities. Arab normalisation with the Assad regime in Syria, though discouraged by Western states, proceeded with the assent of most Eastern Mediterranean countries. The Abraham Accords and Negev Forum showed an ostensible desire among the regional elite to integrate Israel regardless of the final status of the State of Palestine. Improbably, Lebanon and Israel also signed a maritime agreement despite being officially at war. Political progress gave momentum to discussions on connectivity and energy cooperation. In September 2023, leaders met on the sidelines of the G20 summit in India to announce the creation of the India–Middle East–Europe Economic Corridor, a logistical and geo-economic artery that would include the Eastern Mediterranean, notably Israel and Cyprus (but neither Turkiye nor Egypt).

The Hamas-led attacks against Israel and the ensuing war upended this hopeful (if quixotic) regional agenda. The war illustrated the vulnerability of state-driven geo-economic and integration projects to conflict, and to non-state armed groups, when fundamental political disagreements remain unresolved. It also highlighted the complacency of governments especially when it came to the Israeli–Palestinian conflict. No major state had dedicated serious attention to it since 2014, but it has dominated the region since October 2023 and is likely to have wide-ranging consequences for regional dynamics.

At the time of writing, major war fighting has remained contained to the Gaza Strip. However, the prospect of a multi-front war is high (see Map 1.1). Lebanon and Syria have become arenas for escalating tit-for-tat clashes between Israel and Iranian-backed militias, which carry a high risk of miscalculation. By March 2024, more than 300 Hizbullah commanders and fighters and more than a dozen Islamic Revolutionary Guard Corps (IRGC) commanders and officers had been killed by the Israeli air force in Lebanon and Syria. Over 80,000 residents of northern Israel had fled south, and a similar number of southern Lebanese had fled north, putting immense political pressure on their respective governments.

Up until March 2024, the war's direct adverse effects on regional dynamics have been limited. Prior regional de-escalation undeniably helped to manage the post-7 October shockwaves. The war compelled greater diplomatic activity because it made more tangible the risks of mass displacement, transnational terrorism, a breakdown in regional relations and even inter-state war. Some countries sped up their rapprochement to immunise themselves against such instability. This was the case for Egypt and Turkiye, Greece and Turkiye and, further away, Iran and Saudi Arabia. Several Arab states pursued the normalisation of their relations with Syria despite its government being an ally of Iran and a co-sponsor of its partners. Notably, while the Negev Forum and other Abraham Accords-centric activities have been suspended, Israel's 2020 normalisation agreements have unsurprisingly been ring-fenced and, so far, have survived the crisis. The peace accords with Jordan and Egypt have also withstood the crisis, although deep anxiety about Israel's strategy has emerged in both countries. Greece and Cyprus, which have been increasingly invested in their relations with Israel, have watched with concern Israel's management of the conflict. While they have shown sympathy with Tel Aviv since the October attacks, both countries voted for UN General Assembly resolutions in support of a ceasefire in Gaza, Palestinian sovereignty and self-determination as well as humanitarian access in Gaza, which Israel forcefully opposed (see Figure 1.3). This reflected in part the fact that their other Mediterranean partners have all been more supportive of the Palestinian cause.

In effect, the region appears to be waiting to see what Israel's decisions will be on the future of Gaza, on the possible widening of the war, on a potential resumption of peace talks and on the recalibration of its security policies.

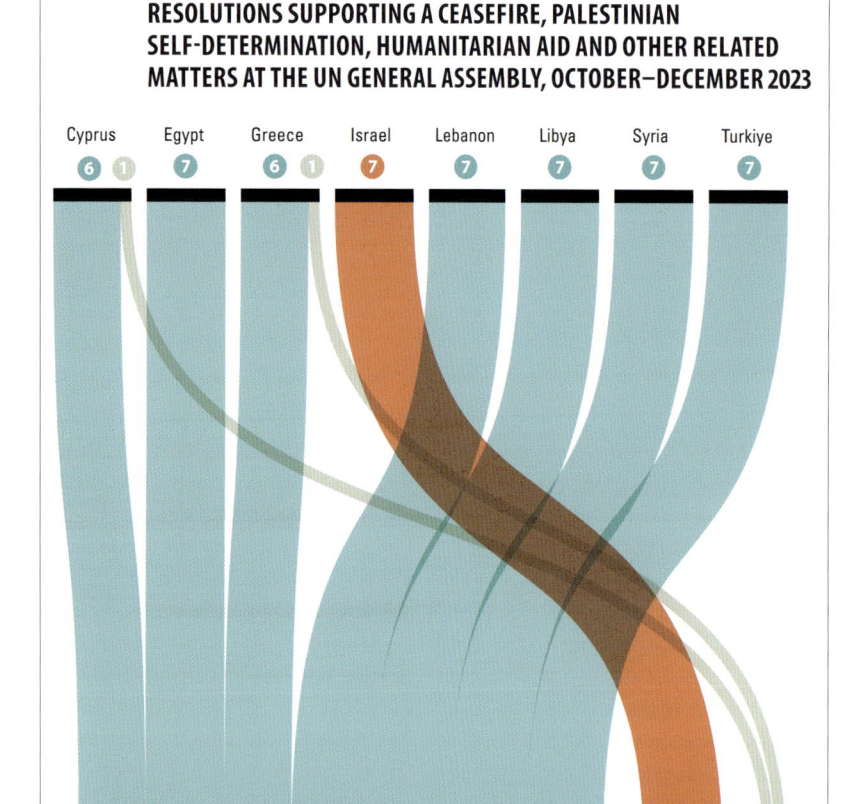

FIGURE 1.3: VOTING DECISIONS BY EASTERN MEDITERRANEAN COUNTRIES ON RESOLUTIONS SUPPORTING A CEASEFIRE, PALESTINIAN SELF-DETERMINATION, HUMANITARIAN AID AND OTHER RELATED MATTERS AT THE UN GENERAL ASSEMBLY, OCTOBER–DECEMBER 2023

Country	Yes	Abstained	No
Cyprus	6	1	
Egypt	7		
Greece	6	1	
Israel			7
Lebanon	7		
Libya	7		
Syria	7		
Turkiye	7		

Note: Cyprus and Greece abstained on the resolution 'Work of the Special Committee to Investigate Israeli Practices Affecting the Human Rights of the Palestinian People and Other Arabs of the Occupied Territories', but voted 'Yes' on all resolutions concerning humanitarian efforts and self-governance.
Source: United Nations Digital Library
©IISS

CYPRUS'S GROWING REGIONAL PROFILE

Strategically situated to offer an alternative platform for humanitarian delivery into Gaza, Cyprus has deftly capitalised on logistical and security needs arising from the ongoing Israel–Hamas war to deepen its relationship with both Israel and the US, and to raise its diplomatic profile within the EU. Nicosia sees such a rapprochement as raising its leverage and profile in its decades-long conflict with Turkiye.

Since the 7 October Hamas-led attacks, Cyprus has intensified its already deepening security and intelligence cooperation with Tel Aviv. Furthermore, it became a safe haven for thousands of Israelis who sought temporary refuge from the conflict on the island.

Simultaneously, it positioned itself as the natural logistical hub for large-scale operations to deliver humanitarian aid to Gaza and, in the immediate aftermath of the Israeli offensive in Gaza, proposed a maritime corridor to deliver aid. It took five months to get the initiative off the ground, but in March 2024, the European Commission announced the launch of the Cyprus-led Amalthea plan. It aims to set up a maritime corridor to ship aid to Gaza with the backing of Germany, Greece, Italy, the Netherlands, the UAE, the United Kingdom and the US.

Yet the limits of such an effort soon became apparent. Barely three weeks after the first large shipment sailed from the port of Larnaca in mid-March, humanitarian deliveries had to be suspended after Israeli forces killed seven team members from the US non-governmental organisation World Central Kitchen while they were delivering aid inside Gaza.

At the time of writing, it remains unclear when and how aid efforts can resume; it will depend on assurances from the Israeli government on operational security and the lifting of its restrictions on aid.

Cyprus, as well as the British Sovereign Base Area of Akrotiri, have become major hubs for Western logistics and

Israeli foreign minister Eli Cohen (R) and his Cypriot counterpart Constantinos Kombos (L) give a press conference in Nicosia, Cyprus, on 20 December 2023 on the Amalthea plan to provide a maritime corridor for humanitarian aid to Gaza. (Photo: Elisa Amouret/AFP via Getty Images)

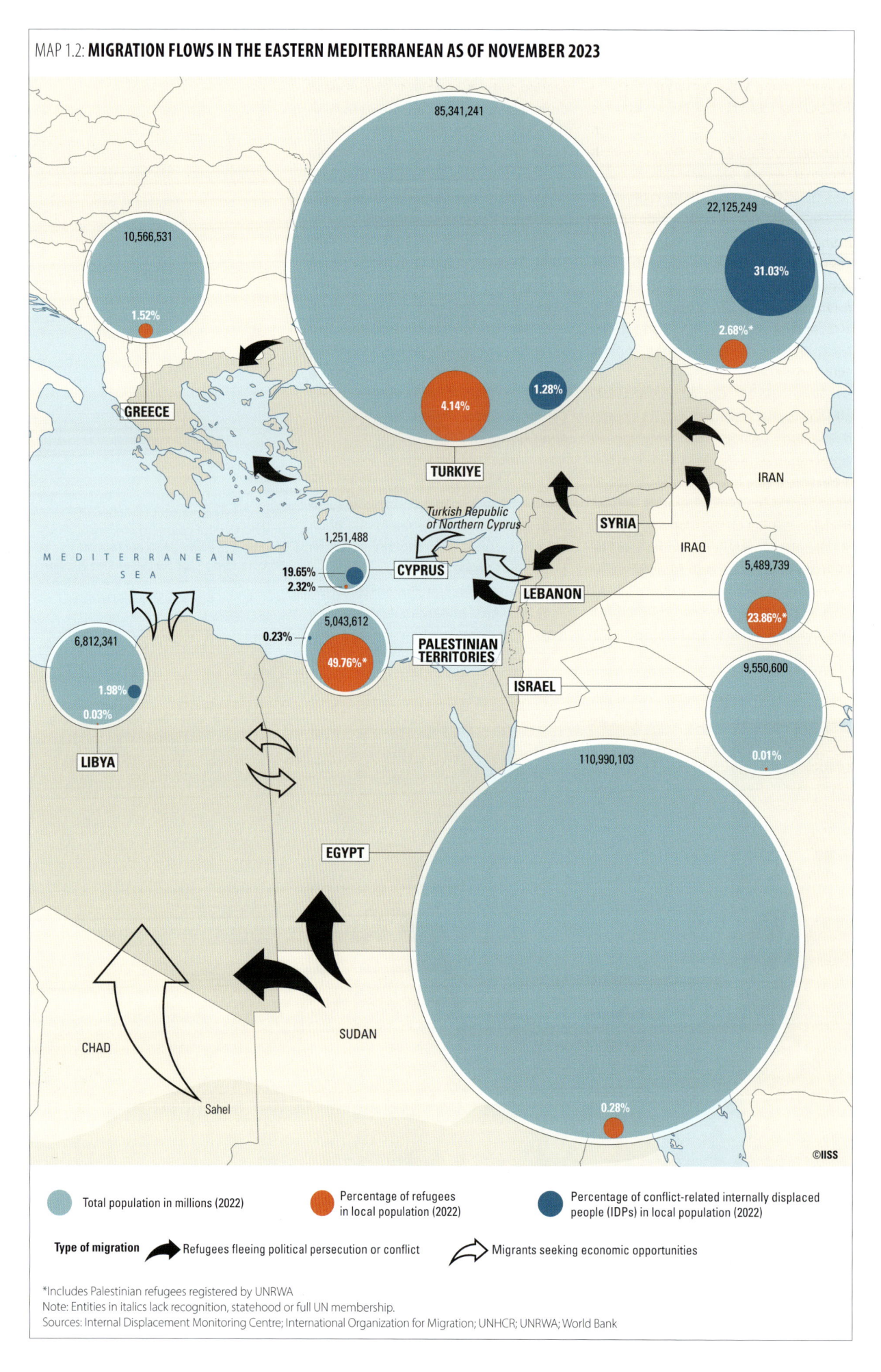

MAP 1.2: MIGRATION FLOWS IN THE EASTERN MEDITERRANEAN AS OF NOVEMBER 2023

GREECE — 10,566,531 — 1.52%

TURKIYE — 85,341,241 — 4.14% — 1.28%

Turkish Republic of Northern Cyprus

CYPRUS — 1,251,488 — 19.65% — 2.32%

SYRIA — 22,125,249 — 31.03% — 2.68%*

IRAQ — 5,489,739 — 23.86%*

LEBANON

PALESTINIAN TERRITORIES — 5,043,612 — 49.76%* — 0.23%

ISRAEL — 9,550,600 — 0.01%

LIBYA — 6,812,341 — 1.98% — 0.03%

EGYPT — 110,990,103 — 0.28%

CHAD

SUDAN

Sahel

IRAN

MEDITERRANEAN SEA

Legend

- ⬤ Total population in millions (2022)
- ⬤ Percentage of refugees in local population (2022)
- ⬤ Percentage of conflict-related internally displaced people (IDPs) in local population (2022)

Type of migration
- ⬛➡ Refugees fleeing political persecution or conflict
- ⬜➡ Migrants seeking economic opportunities

*Includes Palestinian refugees registered by UNRWA
Note: Entities in italics lack recognition, statehood or full UN membership.
Sources: Internal Displacement Monitoring Centre; International Organization for Migration; UNHCR; UNRWA; World Bank

©IISS

contingency planning. Dozens of military transport aircraft have been stationed in both, along with personnel. Akrotiri has been used by the UK for surveillance gathering and as a launch pad for British *Typhoon* fighter jets striking Ansarullah (Houthis) targets.

As concern over the potential spread of the conflict to Lebanon and the wider region increased among Western countries, some of them, such as Germany, the UK and the US, dispatched military personnel to Cyprus to prepare for evacuation contingencies based on their past experience of evacuating tens of thousands of their citizens from Lebanon through Cyprus during the 2006 Hizbullah–Israel war.

Cyprus's humanitarian-aid initiative embodies the crux of Cypriot strategic positioning in the region over recent years. It aims to overcome the perception that it is a nuisance or a complication in the wheel of EU–Turkish and EU–NATO cooperation, and instead to leverage its geography to demonstrate how it can be an asset for the EU and US in the Eastern Mediterranean. 'We felt compelled to try to add the maritime route. It's our moral duty', President Nikos Christodoulides said at the time. He added, 'it gives flesh and bone to what we always say that we are: an EU member state that is an integral part of the region, a reliable partner'.[2]

It is in that context that Cyprus's participation in trilateral formats with Greece and Israel, and Greece and Egypt, as well as in the East Mediterranean Gas Forum (EMGF) should be seen. However, the current momentum it has gathered risks being short-lived. It is highly vulnerable to the fluctuations of US policy in the region, the magnitude of EU–Turkish trade and other imperatives tied to migration and security.

Before the war in Gaza, Cyprus had already deepened its cooperation with Israel on energy projects. Both are keen for the EuroAsia Interconnector undersea cable to become active in order to connect the electricity grids of Cyprus, Greece and Israel. Israeli gas companies are also involved in the development of the biggest Cypriot offshore gas field, known as Aphrodite, and both countries are considering the development of infrastructure to transfer gas to Europe.

Larnaca achieved a major objective when the US lifted in September 2022 the last part of its weapons embargo. Washington enacted the embargo in 1987 to stave off a potential arms race between Cyprus and the breakaway self-declared Turkish Republic of Northern Cyprus (TRNC) and to support peace talks. The suspension of the embargo was extended for 2024 and looks set to continue. How much further the US–Cyprus relationship will develop will depend on how the regional situation progresses. The Israel–Hamas war and its potential escalation into a wider conflict have compelled Washington to increase its military footprint and rethink its regional posture after years of disinterest. Cyprus may be seen as a convenient platform, though a lasting military presence would create new challenges, notably in terms of US–Turkish relations. Nevertheless, Larnaca must continue balancing its position. It is vulnerable to migration movements from Lebanon, Syria and the TRNC (see Map 1.2) as well as terror attacks, especially with the increased Israeli presence on the island. It is also still hamstrung by its unresolved conflict with Turkiye, which has had a chilling effect both on foreign direct investment and on Cyprus's place within the EU. Indeed, several member states, keen to increase cooperation and trade with Turkiye, have seen Nicosia as both uncompromising and obstructive.

TURKIYE: RESETTING REGIONAL RELATIONS

Although Turkiye has been a very effective strategic shaper, with decisive interventions in Syria and Libya, and brinkmanship at sea, it is hampered by its struggling economy and an isolated regional position. It has therefore been reinvesting in diplomacy and warming relations in order to best capitalise on its geostrategic potential.

Beginning in 2022, and in part driven by its economic challenges, Turkiye set aside its policy of brinkmanship in the region and began to improve relations with Egypt and Greece, its two main regional rivals. If the current dynamic is sustained, the resumption of these relations could be transformative for the region. With Athens and Cairo being two of the major actors in the EMGF, improved relations could pave the way to Turkish inclusion and be a lifeline for Ankara's struggling economy, which

> THE ISRAEL–HAMAS WAR ILLUSTRATED THE VULNERABILITY OF STATE-DRIVEN GEO-ECONOMIC AND INTEGRATION PROJECTS TO CONFLICT, AND TO NON-STATE ARMED GROUPS, WHEN FUNDAMENTAL POLITICAL DISAGREEMENTS REMAIN UNRESOLVED.

is saddled with 65% inflation and high unemployment. Ankara has also made progress in lowering tensions with the US, though major issues remain.

At the same time, Turkiye was even on track to reset its relationship with Israel, after extended periods of severe tension. At the UN General Assembly in September 2023, Erdoğan met Israeli Prime Minister Benjamin Netanyahu for the first time. Buoyed by their recent electoral victories, they set out to thaw the ties that had been fraught since nine pro-Palestinian activists were killed in the 2010 Israeli raid on a Turkish ship attempting to break the Israeli blockade on Gaza. Both recalled their ambassadors at the time and only reinstated them in 2016. They withdrew them again just two years later in 2018, when clashes occurred in Gaza and Turkiye offered refuge to Hamas leaders. Diplomatic ties were only fully renewed in 2022. The 2023 meeting was therefore upbeat and hopeful. The two leaders reportedly discussed advancing trade and energy ties; cooperation on technology, innovation and artificial intelligence; and a possible visit by Erdoğan to Jerusalem for the 100th anniversary of the Turkish republic.

The Hamas-led attacks and the war in Gaza have now derailed the relationship. Initially, Erdoğan was conciliatory and measured, stating, 'we openly oppose the killing of civilians on Israeli territories. Likewise, we can never accept the massacre of defenceless innocents in Gaza by indiscriminate, constant bombardments.'[3] But once the Israeli ground offensive began, Erdoğan changed his tone, affirming that Hamas was 'defending their land', and called Israel a 'terrorist state', accusing it of perpetrating a 'genocide' and saying that 'what this Netanyahu is doing' is not 'less than what Hitler did'. Netanyahu responded by saying Erdoğan 'commits genocide against the Kurds, [and] … holds a world record for imprisoning journalists who oppose his rule'.[4]

Both countries have again recalled their ambassadors over the Israel–Hamas war. Though this episode has solidified Erdoğan's street credibility among Arab Sunni populations that appreciate his outspokenness – a public the president often appeals to – Turkiye has played a marginal role during what is arguably the most consequential armed conflict in the region in decades. Erdoğan's

Turkish President Recep Tayyip Erdoğan (R) receives Israeli Prime Minister Benjamin Netanyahu (L) at the Turkish House in New York, United States, where they arrived to attend the 78th session of the United Nations General Assembly on 19 September 2023. (Photo: TUR Presidency/ Murat Cetinmuhurdar/ Handout/Anadolu Agency via Getty Images)

verbal attacks and Turkiye's economic woes, from high inflation and unemployment to persistent current-account deficits, have undermined Ankara's potential diplomatic role. Instead, it is Qatar that has been leading mediation talks to release Israeli hostages held by Hamas and other armed groups in Gaza, to reach a ceasefire, and to secure the release of Palestinian prisoners held in Israeli jails.

Relations between Ankara and Tel Aviv could resume at a later date, depending on how the Israel–Hamas war ends. Erdoğan himself has admitted that 'completely severing ties is not possible' and economic incentives for rapprochement remain strong. Yet the break appears deeper this time around, including in trade, with Turkiye halting the export of 54 types of goods to Israel, including aluminium and cement, and Israel threatening to lobby the US Congress for sanctions on Ankara. Erdoğan's successful reset with Egyptian President Abdel Fattah al-Sisi – capped by a visit to Cairo in February 2024 after a decade of entrenched political confrontation – may offer a model for the future of the Turkish–Israeli relationship. Both countries' economic imperatives, and potentially lucrative cooperation in the fields of energy, defence and industry, have pushed them to compromise and look past ideological conflict. A couple of months before the visit, Turkish authorities reportedly nullified the citizenship of the acting supreme guide of the Muslim Brotherhood, as well as four other Egyptian nationals who had been residing in Turkiye. This move illustrated how Turkiye could subordinate its ideological and Islamist leanings to its strategic and economic interests.

DETENTE BETWEEN GREECE AND TURKIYE

Turkiye has also worked to improve its relationship with Greece, after tensions nearly boiled over during its maritime brinkmanship in 2018–20. Calm was restored thanks to US-backed German mediation, but it wasn't until the devastating February 2023 earthquake in Turkiye that relations were put on a positive track again. Greece was the first country to express solidarity and deployed humanitarian aid, which, in line with previous disaster diplomacy, was appreciated by the Turkish side. In the summer of 2023, Turkiye reciprocated by providing valuable assistance to Greece to fight record wildfires. Officials on both sides acknowledge that these gestures facilitated reciprocal openings.

With both leaders comfortably re-elected in 2023, Erdoğan paid his first visit to Athens in six years, on 7 December 2023, and met his counterpart Prime Minister Kyriakos Mitsotakis. It was a visit that had been 'designed to succeed', according to a Greek official. Erdoğan hailed a new era of friendship with Athens and expressed hope for the Aegean to become a 'sea of peace'. Mitsotakis behaved similarly and stressed the historical responsibility incumbent on both parties to resolve their differences. Erdoğan insisted that a 'glass half-full perspective' was the best practical approach to talks, while stressing to Mitsotakis that 'there is no issue between us that is unsolvable'.[5]

This remarkable change in tone stems from both leaders' more comfortable domestic political situation, conducive economic imperatives and their desire to forge their legacies. Both were also strongly encouraged by the US and Germany to improve relations and build on the positive dynamic created by the disaster diplomacy they had mutually engaged in. Washington and Berlin are seen as the only effective mediators in the relationship, although Erdoğan and Mitsotakis have established direct communication and met without third-party mediation. In contrast, Ankara has spurned the EU, seen as obedient to Cypriot interests and as unwilling to accommodate Turkish demands for accession, and has especially shunned France, which is perceived as overly belligerent in most Eastern Mediterranean theatres.

The mostly symbolic 'Athens Declaration' which both countries signed in 2023 included a substantial agreement on migration and called for better deconfliction through enhanced communication. Trafficking has remained a challenge given lucrative revenue streams, but, reflecting better cooperation between the Greek and Turkish coastguards, illegal migration was reduced by about 60% from October–December 2023. The two countries also established a hotline and placed coastguard liaisons in several of each other's ports.

The rapprochement between Ankara and Athens remains fragile and tentative, dependent on both sides' goodwill, as the agreement is not binding. Both sides are therefore proceeding with caution and gradualism.

Yet with Greece still rebuilding its financial health and Turkiye trying to recover from years of economic struggle, pragmatic motivations could force a more realistic partnership. Mitsotakis has set a 'realistic goal' to increase trade relations between the two states to US$10.8 billion in the next five years, a more than twofold increase from its current level.[6] Greek exports to Turkiye will help mitigate their trade deficit of US$3.59bn as of November 2023. Turkiye's devalued currency, as a silver lining, should make its products competitive to foreign consumers such as Greece in this new trade agreement. This will aid a reduction in the country's current-account deficit which stood at US$2.1bn in December 2023, and foreign debt of around US$480bn.

Both countries are also being urged, in particular by the US, to increase regional cooperation especially on energy issues, given the region only has a limited window of opportunity to benefit from its recently discovered reserves before the EU completes its transition to green energies. Yet the regional hydrocarbon potential will be massively curtailed as long as Cyprus, Greece and Turkiye do not at least reach an agreement to ring-fence the issue from the rest of their historic conflict. At their meeting in Athens, Erdoğan and Mitsotakis agreed to disagree about the Cyprus question. As much as Greece may want to improve its relationship with Turkiye, it cannot decouple from Cyprus. Cyprus has always been a friction frontier for Turkiye and Greece, with significant hardline constituencies in both countries unwilling to explore compromises. Cyprus's Western alignment, both with its membership in the EU and its burgeoning relationship with Washington, has weakened Turkish power and influence on the

Turkish President Recep Tayyip Erdoğan (L) and Greek Prime Minister Kyriakos Mitsotakis (R) during a press conference in Athens, Greece, on 7 December 2023 after signing the Athens Declaration and deals on areas including tourism and migration. (Photo: Yorgos Karahalis/Bloomberg via Getty Images)

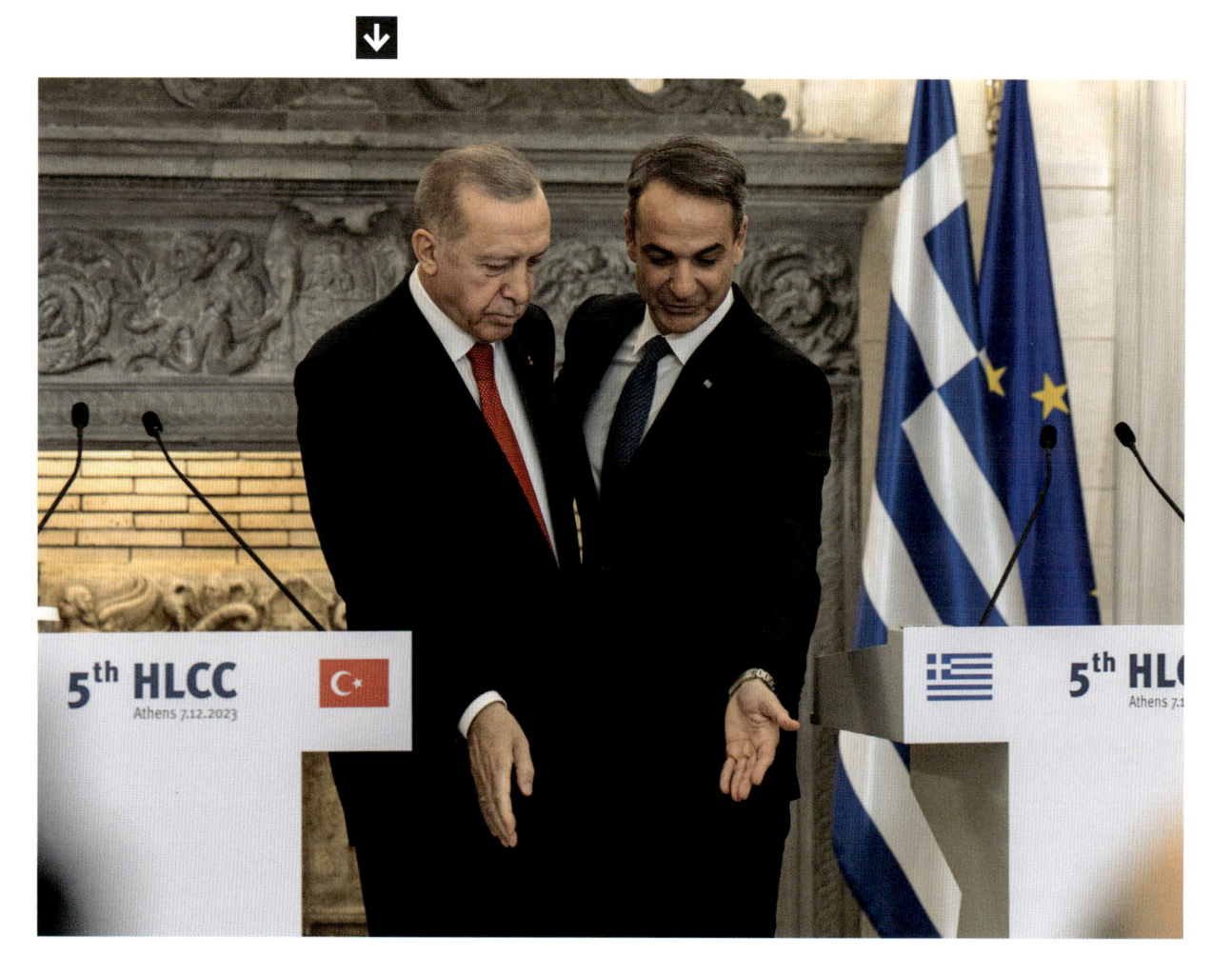

island. Cyprus's prosperity contrasts with the TRNC's economic isolation and dependence on Turkiye, fuelling Cypriot disinterest in a resolution and Northern Cypriot resentment.

US–TURKISH RELATIONS: ON THE MEND?

US–Turkish relations never fully recovered from the Turkish purchase of Russian S400 air-defence systems and the 2016 attempted coup in Turkiye that Erdoğan accused Washington of being involved in.

The relationship is hamstrung by tensions in key theatres. From the Turkish perspective, the US has made hostile policy choices in the Eastern Mediterranean, a region Turkiye considers to be of utmost strategic interest. US cooperation with the Syrian Democratic Forces, a Kurdish armed group linked to the US foreign terrorist organisation-designated transnational Kurdistan Workers' Party, and the US-backed energy partnerships that have developed in the Eastern Mediterranean between Cyprus, Egypt, Greece and Israel have been perceived by Ankara as means to encircle and isolate it.

The two countries' NATO membership has been crucial in stabilising their relationship. US–Turkish relations further improved in 2022 and 2023 out of necessity. In exchange for Ankara approving Sweden and Finland joining NATO – in response to the Russian invasion of Ukraine – the US finally agreed to a major aircraft deal which Turkiye has been requesting since being denied access to F-35 *Lightning* II aircraft in 2019. The US$23bn agreement that was approved in January 2024 includes 40 new F-16 *Fighting Falcon* jets and equipment to modernise a further 79 already owned by Turkiye. This had been a central point of friction between the two capitals, especially as the US has been increasing its defence cooperation with Greece and Cyprus. The State Department notification of the F-16 deal also included a simultaneous US$8.6bn sale of up to 40 F-35 *Lightning* II jets to Greece.

Turkish President Recep Tayyip Erdoğan (L), British Prime Minister Rishi Sunak (2nd L), US President Joe Biden (1st R) and NATO Secretary-General Jens Stoltenberg (2nd R) on the first day of the 2023 NATO Summit on 11 July 2023 in Vilnius, Lithuania.
(Photo: Paul Ellis - Pool via Getty Images)

EGYPT'S MOMENT OF DANGER AND OPPORTUNITY

Egypt has looked at the war between Israel and Hamas with serious concern. The prospect of a lasting conflict on its border with Israel seeping into the Sinai Peninsula, an underdeveloped and unstable region, has raised alarm in Cairo. The security establishment is united in support of the peace agreement with Israel, but has voiced significant concern over Israeli plans to conquer Rafah and re-establish control over the Philadelphi Corridor, which separates Egypt from Gaza, and over a potentially entrenched Israeli occupation and a Hamas-led insurgency on its borders. Such developments would pose security challenges for Egypt: how to safeguard its security interests and how to provide a safe haven for Palestinians without being perceived as complicit with or resigned to Israeli policy. Cairo is concerned that the increasingly powerful Israeli political far right, which has advocated for the forced expulsion of the Gazan population, pays no heed to Israeli security officials, who have been keen to reassure their Egyptian counterparts.

In previous years, domestic instability, economic travails, an enthusiasm for the Abraham Accords and Saudi Arabia's increasing influence had sidelined Egypt as a regional power. Cairo's security problems in Ethiopia, Libya and Sudan received limited international support. While the US was central to Egyptian security policy, the relationship remained fraught. To compensate, Cairo cultivated relations with Greece and Cyprus (as well as Italy and France) as useful partners for developing influence within the EU (it also maintained a strong relationship with Moscow, which provided weapons systems and built Egypt's first-ever nuclear plant). The two Eastern Mediterranean countries were mostly in alignment with Cairo on Libya, Turkiye and the Levant and were reassured by the non-Islamist character of the Egyptian regime. They also had concerns that instability in Egypt would lead to large-scale migration. Those partnerships therefore were key in developing pro-Egypt constituencies in Athens and Nicosia that advocated for EU political and economic support at a time when major donors were sceptical about the country's economic trajectory.

(L–R) Austrian Federal Chancellor Karl Nehammer, Greek Prime Minister Kyriakos Mitsotakis, European Commission President Ursula von der Leyen, Egyptian President Abdel Fattah al-Sisi, Cypriot President Nikos Christodoulides, Belgian Prime Minister Alexander De Croo and Italian Prime Minister Giorgia Meloni meet in Cairo, Egypt, on 17 March 2024 to agree a support package for Egypt. (Photo: Dirk Waem/Belga MAG/AFP via Getty Images)

The Israel–Hamas war has elevated Egypt's profile, placing it at the centre of the diplomatic map after years of international disinterest. Cairo is seen as a mediator for the release of Israeli hostages and for negotiations with Hamas over Gaza's future and for containing aftershocks of the war. Its centrality to the humanitarian response has contributed to muting criticism of its own restrictions on Gaza, poor human-rights record and mismanagement of the economy.

Cairo has also been able to capitalise on US and European fears of a catastrophic domino effect. By March 2024, Egypt's gamble that it was 'too big to fail' paid off. To reward Cairo for its diplomatic role and to stem potential ripple effects of its acute economic crisis (due to rising debt and severe domestic pressures), major donors announced significant financial assistance, hoping to secure a few years of respite. In rapid succession, Egypt obtained a US$35bn investment from the UAE, the EU offered an US$8bn assistance package, the IMF provided an US$8bn loan and the World Bank US$6bn in grants and projects, a total of US$57bn in fresh financial support.

IRAN AS AN EASTERN MEDITERRANEAN POWER

The Hamas-led attacks starkly illustrated how Iran's nurturing of armed non-state actors in the Eastern Mediterranean has anchored it in the region and transformed its role. Its presence there is so embedded, pervasive and multifarious that it has arguably become a de facto local power.

Iran's regional reach is the product of a patient, opportunistic strategy that has relied on a long-standing alliance with the Assad government in Syria and an investment in non-state armed groups in Lebanon, the Occupied Palestinian Territories and Syria. However, Iran's relationships with these groups vary significantly.

At the top of the spectrum is Lebanese Hizbullah, the crown jewel with organic and ideological ties to the Khomeinist regime and its ultimate instrument of deterrence and punishment against the US and Israel. Iran has helped elevate Hizbullah as a major military force equipped with advanced missile capabilities and the ability to

Leaders pose for a family photo during the Cairo Peace Summit in Cairo, Egypt, on 21 October 2023. International and Arab participants met to discuss the latest developments in the Israel–Hamas war.
(Photo: EU Council/Pool/Handout/Anadolu via Getty Images)

project force. It provided crucial military and financial support to the Assad regime during the Syrian civil war.

While to a lesser degree, Iran has also supported Hamas. However, Hamas's Sunni Islamist identity has made relations complex given conflicted loyalties and opposition to the Assad regime during the Syrian civil war. Ties improved considerably once a hardline Hamas leadership, more interested in fighting Israel than in governing Gaza, took over in 2017 and began soliciting Iranian military, logistical and financial support.

By 2023, Iran was confident enough in this network that it proclaimed a 'unity of fronts' against the US and Israel, indicating strategic and operational coordination among the various militias it backed. An operations room was established in Beirut which reportedly comprised IRGC commanders alongside representatives of Yemen's Ansarullah, Palestinian Hamas and Islamic Jihad, Iraq's Kataib Hizbullah and other groups, and Lebanese Hizbullah, as well as junior Syrian factions.

That security doctrine and Iran's vaunted 'strategic patience' have been tested since the 7 October attacks. Beginning 8 October, Hizbullah launched rocket attacks on Israel out of solidarity. Iraqi and Syrian militias targeted US facilities in their respective countries and the Yemeni Houthis targeted Israel with uninhabited aerial vehicles and missiles, and disrupted maritime traffic in the Red Sea. Iran and its militia partners did not necessarily approve, or were even aware of, the attacks' details or the decision to conduct them. Western and Middle East governments have since recognised that Iran neither ordered nor was aware of Hamas's decision to strike Israel in October, although Iran undoubtedly enabled Hamas.

Instead, Iran showed a mix of opportunism and caution. It sought to benefit politically from Arab and international outrage at the Israeli campaign in Gaza while relying on its affiliated armed groups to harass US forces in Syria and Iraq. However, at the time of writing, Iran has resisted being pulled into a direct all-out war in which it would be at a serious disadvantage. This meant adjusting and at times restraining the activities of its partners to avoid an unwanted escalation. The most important aspect of this conflict management was the calibration of Hizbullah's attacks on Israel so as not to escalate into a full-blown war.

This posture has proven difficult to maintain. By proving reluctant to support Hamas in its all-out conflict with Israel, Iran has telegraphed its risk profile and the limits of its resistance agenda against Western powers, which has put its reliability in times of conflict into doubt amongst its partners. This also gave Israel escalation dominance, the ability to push the pre-established rules of engagement and leeway to degrade Iranian as well as Hizbullah's capabilities across Syria and Lebanon, with limited consequences so far. By March 2024, confident that it had effectively deterred Tehran, Israel had killed many senior IRGC commanders inside Syria. Whether this calculation holds true will be critical to future regional dynamics. Iran has been concerned that Israel's actions would trap it by compelling it to counter-escalate, thereby drawing it into a confrontation with the US. Iran's and Hizbullah's standings have suffered from this calculated restraint and it has led to questions about their very purpose in Lebanon and Syria.

THE US IN THE EASTERN MEDITERRANEAN

The Israel–Hamas war represents a strategic and costly distraction for the US. The 2022 US National Security Strategy had sought to de-emphasise the Middle East and focus US resources and priorities on power competition in the European and Indo-Pacific theatres. US policy in the Middle East under President Joe Biden was therefore deliberately minimalist, seeking to preserve its smaller footprint and mainly focused on delivering a major legacy piece: the normalisation of relations between Saudi Arabia and Israel. Where possible, the US engaged in de-escalation, for example working with Germany to move Greece and Turkiye towards dialogue, and mediation, such as that between Israel and Lebanon over their maritime borders.

The war exposed the lack of a cohesive US strategy for the region, while the Hamas-led attacks pointed to a failure of intelligence and forecasting. However, despite the perception of declining US influence in the region, it soon became obvious that Washington remained at the centre of the region's dynamics. The US was also the only actor that could provide the necessary deterrence to avoid an expansion of the conflict. Within days of the attacks, the US forcefully lobbied Israel to refrain from attacking Hizbullah in Lebanon, which would have led to an inter-state war and possibly regional escalation.

By deploying significant military capabilities, including two carrier strike groups, the US was able to reassure Israel and to deter Iran and its allies. This – as well as steadfast US support for Israel during its Gaza campaign – meant, however, that the US was once again deeply entangled in a Middle Eastern war with no obvious endgame.

In parallel, the US has been compelled to allay Egyptian and Jordanian concerns about Israeli intentions. The numerous Israeli statements about expelling Gazans to Egypt have raised concerns in Cairo about an Israeli desire to offload the problem onto its shoulders, regardless of international law, US policy and Egyptian political and security considerations. Jordan, meanwhile, saw Gaza as a potential template for future Israeli action in the West Bank. In an attempt to reassure them, US Secretary of State Antony Blinken issued specific conditions in November: 'No forcible displacement of Palestinians from Gaza – not now, not after the war. No use of Gaza as a platform for terrorism or other violent attacks. No reoccupation of Gaza after the conflict ends. No attempt to blockade or besiege Gaza.'[7] The question of whether Israel will abide by any of these parameters will affect US regional standing at a time of significant doubt over its credibility and influence.

Further, it seems likely that the United States' focus on the region will be difficult to sustain. US strategic priorities demand attention in other theatres and the Israeli–Palestinian peace track which it has been advocating will now need a level of diplomatic investment that the US may not be willing to fulfil. Importantly, the expected policy volatility should Donald Trump win a second term as president in November 2024 is likely to deter any courageous move by the Israeli, Palestinian or broader Arab leaderships in the coming months.

For US defence planners, the question of a post-war defence posture will be raised once the fighting subsides. In addition to supporting the Israeli war effort, the multi-front war imposed heavy demands on an already stretched US military, which has used naval capabilities instead of al-Udeid, its main air base in the Middle East, to conduct air operations during the conflict.

US President Joe Biden (L) and Israeli Prime Minister Benjamin Netanyahu (R) meet in Tel Aviv, Israel, on 18 October 2023. (Photo: Israeli government press office/Handout/Anadolu via Getty Images)

ENERGY: NEUTRAL EFFECTS?

The war in Gaza has had a limited impact on the natural-gas sector in the region. There was no significant or noteworthy effect on the price of either Brent-oil futures or natural gas, reflecting the marginality of Eastern Mediterranean gas on world markets. Between September 2023 and February 2024, Brent futures traded for an average price of around US$83.5 per barrel, and natural gas traded for around US$2.75 per metric million British thermal unit (MMBtu, a unit to measure gas) for the same period, which is lower than what natural-gas prices were before the 7 October attacks.

Israel, one of the main gas exporters in the region, temporarily suspended some exports for a few weeks in the immediate aftermath of the attacks, only to resume them by mid-November. During October, it managed to export 82% of the monthly contract quantity that it was committed to exporting to Egyptian processing facilities, through which it is in turn exported to the rest of the world. In February, Chevron approved a US$24 million investment to boost gas production at the Israeli Tamar offshore gas field, in part to increase its exports to Egypt by a reported 6bn cubic feet per year.

The biggest consequence of the Israel–Hamas war for the energy sector has been the suspension of the British Petroleum–Abu Dhabi National Oil Company (BP–ADNOC) bid to acquire a 50% stake in Israeli gas producer NewMed Energy for US$2bn, due to take place mid-March 2024. NewMed is the largest stakeholder in Israel's Leviathan gas field – Chevron being the other major stakeholder (with a 45.3% share). NewMed's statement blamed 'uncertainty created by the external environment', in reference to the months-long war.[8] But industry insiders also reported that, in addition to the deteriorated geopolitical context, the two sides of the potential deal had disagreed on financial terms. An independent committee convened by NewMed recommended, in early October 2023, that the offer price should be raised by 10–20% from the initial US$2bn, based on the rise in commodity prices and fluctuations in the shekel.

The potential deal was seen as significant evidence of improving Israeli–UAE relations in the wake of their 2020 normalisation. At the time of writing, there was uncertainty about whether the deal was simply suspended while the two sides worked out their differences over the pricing, or while they waited to see what the fallout would be from the war. Emirati investments in Israel's hydrocarbon sector have withstood previous rounds of fighting in Gaza. In May 2021, the UAE's sovereign wealth fund Mubadala delayed the purchase of a 22% stake in Israel's Tamar gas field from Delek Drilling (which in 2022 became NewMed Energy) because of an ongoing conflict, but the deal did ultimately close months later.

This time around, the economic and political stakes are high. The UAE – like Bahrain and Morocco – have worked on ring-fencing their normalisation agreements with Israel despite popular outrage at the brutality of some of Israel's actions. If the war were to cause a loss as significant as the BP–ADNOC deal, however, it could have a chilling effect on any further consolidation of the natural-gas sector at a moment when it needs to be amplified.

Apart from this deal, the energy landscape has largely held steady, despite the intensity and length of the ongoing war. Gas flows between Israel and Egypt were only suspended for a couple of weeks and were restored shortly thereafter. Despite a cooling in the political relationship between the two countries over the conduct of the war, both need to maintain their energy cooperation given their respective economic situations.

Ultimately, however, the longer the war lasts and the wider the fallout, the more it will delay the region's ability to fully capitalise on its energy potential in a timely fashion, especially when the EU is planning a shift in policy to green energy and it therefore only has a short window to export to Europe.

Rubble lies on the ground from buildings hit by *Storm Daniel*, which struck Libya's eastern city of Derna on 10 September 2023. (Photo: AFP via Getty Images)

EXTREME CLIMATE: FORECAST, IMPACTS AND REQUIREMENTS

As a result of rising global temperatures, the Eastern Mediterranean region appears increasingly exposed to extreme climate events. Heatwaves, wildfires, droughts and floods will disrupt natural and human systems, with social, economic and security ramifications that regional governments are underprepared for (see Figure 1.4). This is compounded by the rudimentary level of regional cooperation and integration of capabilities to anticipate, prevent and manage natural disasters.

IMPACTS OF EXPECTED CLIMATE CHANGE

The Eastern Mediterranean basin is projected to experience heat and aridity extremes significantly exceeding global averages, due to a unique high-pressure dry zone created by a combination of the region's topography and a decreasing differential between sea and land temperatures.[I]

The Eastern Mediterranean is warming at nearly twice the global average rate, projected to reach up to 5°C by the end of the twenty-first century in a business-as-usual emissions scenario. Precipitation is projected to decline significantly over the same period, decreasing between 20% and 40% in winter.[II] Heat and drought will have wide-ranging impacts for hydropower generation, food security, livelihoods and economies.[III] Among other challenges, this is likely to make transboundary natural-resource management increasingly necessary but potentially fraught, while opening opportunities for non-state armed groups (NSAGs) to weaponise scarcer natural resources.

Ocean warming is also projected to increase the intensity of Mediterranean cyclones, or 'medicanes', leading to the recurrence of extreme precipitation events such as *Storm Daniel* in September 2023, which caused floods in Greece and Libya. The consequences in Libya were particularly severe: dams burst, 4,345 people were killed and more than 8,500 were reported missing, with another 43,400 internally displaced as of mid-October 2023.[IV]

[I] Alexandre Tuel and Elfatih Eltahir, 'Why Is the Mediterranean a Climate Change Hot Spot?', *Journal of Climate*, vol. 33, no. 14, May 2020, pp. 5829–5843, https://journals.ametsoc.org/view/journals/clim/33/14/JCLI-D-19-0910.1.xml.

[II] Giorgos Zittis et al., 'Climate Change and Weather Extremes in the Eastern Mediterranean and Middle East', *Reviews of Geophysics*, vol. 60, no. 3, June 2022, https://agupubs.onlinelibrary.wiley.com/doi/full/10.1029/2021RG000762.

[III] Ibid.

[IV] OCHA, 'Libya: Flood Response Humanitarian Update (as of 17 October 2023)', 19 October 2023, https://www.unocha.org/publications/report/libya/libya-flood-response-humanitarian-update-17-october-2023-enar.

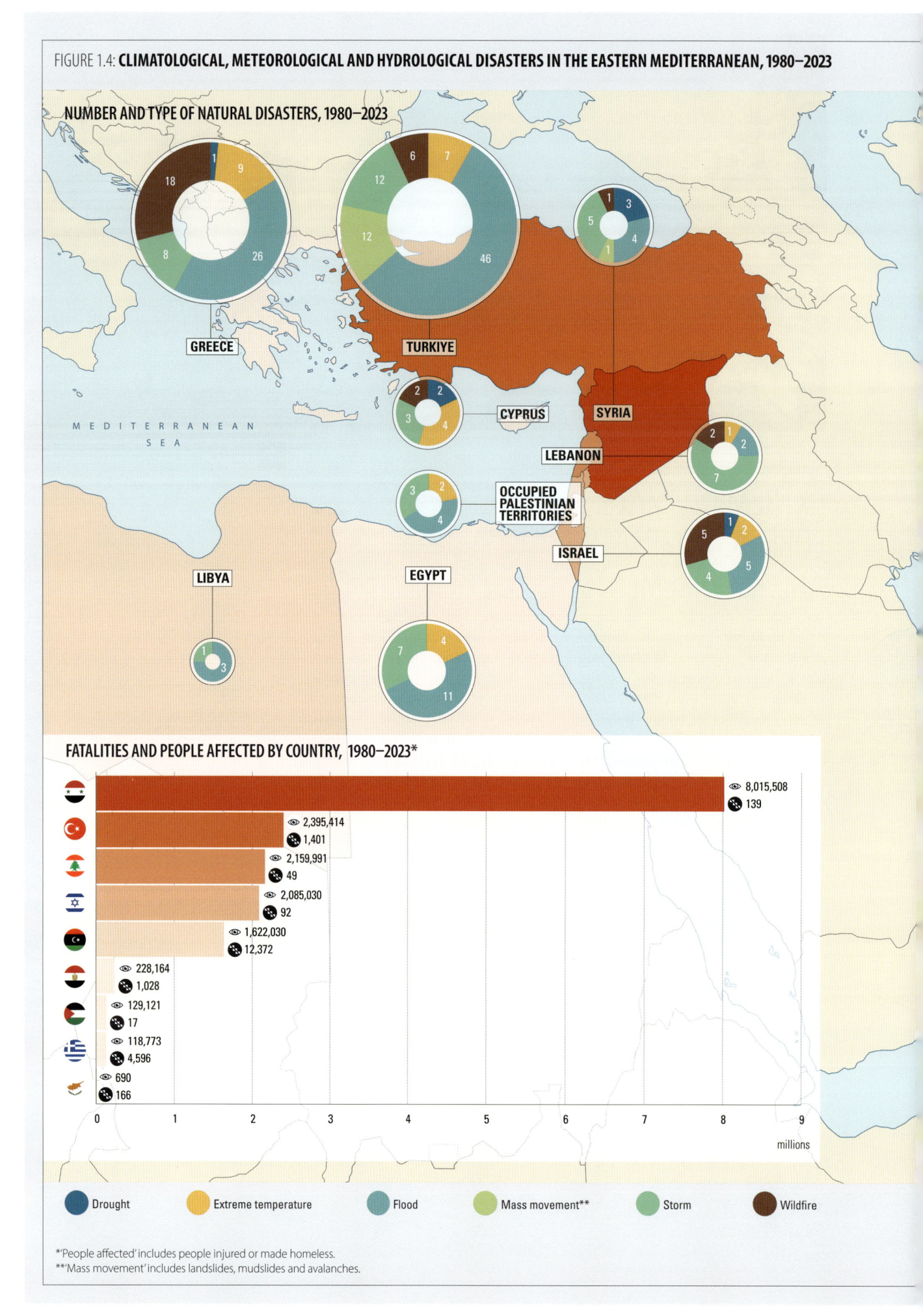

FIGURE 1.4: **CLIMATOLOGICAL, METEOROLOGICAL AND HYDROLOGICAL DISASTERS IN THE EASTERN MEDITERRANEAN, 1980–2023**

NUMBER AND TYPE OF NATURAL DISASTERS, 1980–2023

GREECE: Wildfire 18, Drought 1, Extreme temperature 9, Flood 26, Storm 8

TURKIYE: Wildfire 6, Extreme temperature 7, Flood 46, Storm 12, Mass movement 12

CYPRUS: Drought 1, Extreme temperature 3, Flood 4, Storm 1, Mass movement 5

SYRIA (shown on map)

LEBANON: Drought 2, Extreme temperature 2, Flood 4, Storm 3

OCCUPIED PALESTINIAN TERRITORIES

ISRAEL: Wildfire 2, Extreme temperature 1, Flood 2, Storm 7

LIBYA: Drought 1, Flood 3

EGYPT: Extreme temperature 4, Flood 7, Storm 11

(Jordan pie): Drought 1, Extreme temperature 2, Flood 5, Storm 4, Wildfire 5

FATALITIES AND PEOPLE AFFECTED BY COUNTRY, 1980–2023*

Country	People affected 👁	Fatalities 💀
Syria	8,015,508	139
Türkiye	2,395,414	1,401
Lebanon	2,159,991	49
Israel	2,085,030	92
Libya	1,622,030	12,372
Egypt	228,164	1,028
Jordan	129,121	17
Greece	118,773	4,596
Cyprus	690	166

Legend: ● Drought ● Extreme temperature ● Flood ● Mass movement** ● Storm ● Wildfire

*'People affected' includes people injured or made homeless.
**'Mass movement' includes landslides, mudslides and avalanches.

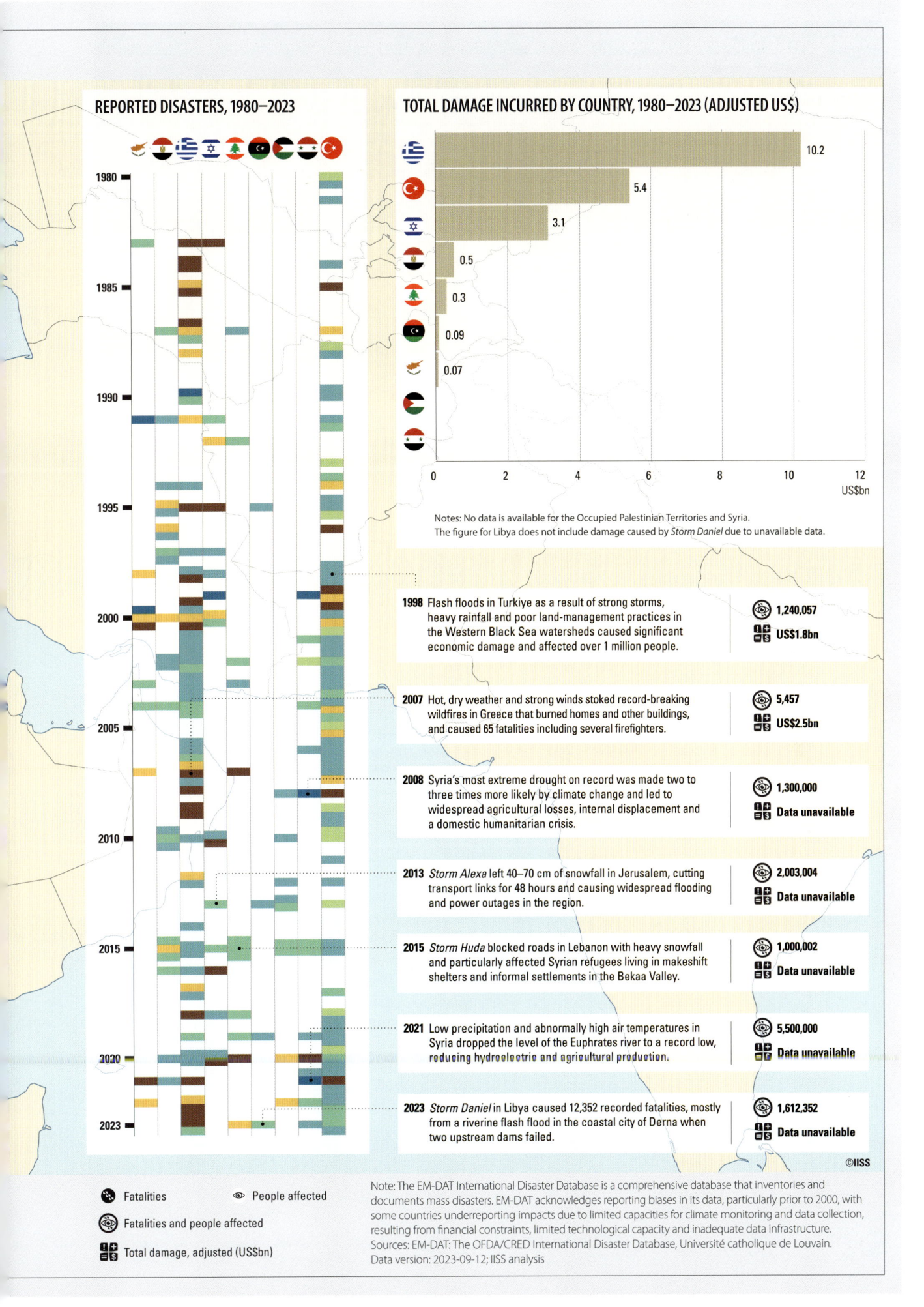

THEMES — GEOPOLITICS: FRAGMENTATION, COMPETITION AND THE PERSISTENCE OF CONFLICT

REPORTED DISASTERS, 1980–2023

TOTAL DAMAGE INCURRED BY COUNTRY, 1980–2023 (ADJUSTED US$)

Country	US$bn
Greece	10.2
Türkiye	5.4
Israel	3.1
Egypt	0.5
Lebanon	0.3
Libya	0.09
Cyprus	0.07
Jordan	—
Syria	—

Notes: No data is available for the Occupied Palestinian Territories and Syria.
The figure for Libya does not include damage caused by *Storm Daniel* due to unavailable data.

1998 Flash floods in Türkiye as a result of strong storms, heavy rainfall and poor land-management practices in the Western Black Sea watersheds caused significant economic damage and affected over 1 million people.
- People affected: 1,240,057
- Total damage: US$1.8bn

2007 Hot, dry weather and strong winds stoked record-breaking wildfires in Greece that burned homes and other buildings, and caused 65 fatalities including several firefighters.
- People affected: 5,457
- Total damage: US$2.5bn

2008 Syria's most extreme drought on record was made two to three times more likely by climate change and led to widespread agricultural losses, internal displacement and a domestic humanitarian crisis.
- People affected: 1,300,000
- Total damage: Data unavailable

2013 *Storm Alexa* left 40–70 cm of snowfall in Jerusalem, cutting transport links for 48 hours and causing widespread flooding and power outages in the region.
- People affected: 2,003,004
- Total damage: Data unavailable

2015 *Storm Huda* blocked roads in Lebanon with heavy snowfall and particularly affected Syrian refugees living in makeshift shelters and informal settlements in the Bekaa Valley.
- People affected: 1,000,002
- Total damage: Data unavailable

2021 Low precipitation and abnormally high air temperatures in Syria dropped the level of the Euphrates river to a record low, reducing hydroelectric and agricultural production.
- People affected: 5,500,000
- Total damage: Data unavailable

2023 *Storm Daniel* in Libya caused 12,352 recorded fatalities, mostly from a riverine flash flood in the coastal city of Derna when two upstream dams failed.
- People affected: 1,612,352
- Total damage: Data unavailable

Legend:
- Fatalities
- People affected
- Fatalities and people affected
- Total damage, adjusted (US$bn)

Note: The EM-DAT International Disaster Database is a comprehensive database that inventories and documents mass disasters. EM-DAT acknowledges reporting biases in its data, particularly prior to 2000, with some countries underreporting impacts due to limited capacities for climate monitoring and data collection, resulting from financial constraints, limited technological capacity and inadequate data infrastructure.
Sources: EM-DAT: The OFDA/CRED International Disaster Database, Université catholique de Louvain.
Data version: 2023-09-12; IISS analysis

©IISS

Cypriot minister of agriculture Costas Kadis speaks during the 2nd Ministerial Meeting of the Cyprus Government Initiative for Coordinating Climate Change Actions in the Eastern Mediterranean and Middle East in Limassol, Cyprus, on 7 June 2022. (Photo: Kostas Pikoulas/NurPhoto via Getty Images)

Extreme weather will likely continue to overwhelm regional disaster-response capabilities, the limitations of which have recently been evident in Greece, Libya, Syria, Turkiye and elsewhere. The expected growing frequency and severity of fires, floods and droughts underscore the need for greater regional cooperation on disaster management, including firefighting, early-warning systems and coordination with the international community.

Rising sea levels could threaten critical economic infrastructure, including floating liquefied-natural-gas facilities (FLNG) and floating production storage and offloading (FPSO) vessels that are central to energy exports from the region.

These threats make it likely that there will be more protracted humanitarian emergencies and deteriorating security situations in conflict-affected countries such as Syria and Libya. Similar risks are present for unstable areas further south and east that indirectly affect Eastern Mediterranean states.

Climate impacts will also be one of the drivers of rural–urban migration, contributing to rapid urban population growth in countries lacking the required infrastructure to adjust. Migration towards Europe is also expected to be fuelled by climate-related events.

GOVERNANCE WILL BE KEY

Managing the scale of the projected climate impacts in the region, alongside a rapid energy transition in line with countries' United Nations Framework Convention on Climate Change (UNFCCC) commitments, will require improvements in governance given the disparate regional levels of readiness to manage climate vulnerabilities.

Israel, Greece and Cyprus have the highest levels of readiness, while Lebanon, Libya and Syria are particularly lacking in capabilities.[v] Moreover, a significant proportion of the populations of Egypt and Libya – 39% and 17% respectively – live in highly climate-exposed areas.[vi]

The need to strengthen infrastructure to achieve greater climate resilience is a major financial and governance challenge, as highlighted by the burst dams in Libya (see Figure 1.4 ('Reported disasters, 1980–2023')). But there may be hard limits to adaptation, with no obvious technical solutions to problems such as rising sea levels. Major infrastructure projects that meet climate-adaptation needs, such as dams, have also begun to lose value, as heat and declining precipitation decrease river discharge.

Although the level of cooperation across the region has been low, some

---

[v] See, for example, Notre Dame Global Adaptation Initiative (ND-GAIN), 'Country Index Rankings', 2021, https://gain.nd.edu/our-work/country-index/rankings/. The country index measured vulnerability to climate impacts and readiness to improve resilience. Out of 183 countries, the rankings for the Eastern Mediterranean countries, in descending order, were Israel 27th, Greece 32nd, Cyprus 43rd, Turkiye 48th, Tunisia 67th, Egypt 107th, Lebanon 117th, Libya 125th and Syria 153rd. The Occupied Palestinian Territories were not evaluated.

[vi] Ashley Moran et al., 'The Intersection of Global Fragility and Climate Risks', USAID, September 2018, https://www.strausscenter.org/wp-content/uploads/The-Intersection-of-Global-Fragility-and-Climate-Risks-2018.pdf.

The Akkuyu Nuclear Power Plant under construction in Mersin province, Turkiye, on 26 April 2023. (Photo: Ozan Kose/AFP via Getty Images)

coordination efforts are under way, mainly through the Eastern Mediterranean and Middle East Climate Change Initiative. This is a Cyprus-led project, launched in 2018 to assess climate risks and develop an action plan for regional governments to tackle climate mitigation and adaptation.[VII] Following a high-level declaration at COP27 in November 2022, it has now moved into the implementation phase, focusing on transnational coordination of projects ranging from hydro-diplomacy to energy-transition financing.[VIII] Cyprus continues to lead partner countries in a dialogue and stocktaking process around joint adaptation and mitigation projects, and is convening a regional conference in September 2024.[IX] In the longer term, the success of the initiative will depend on the broader political will to implement projects at the scale and pace needed.

There have already been instances of cooperation of a more ad hoc nature, such as the mutual assistance in 2023 between Turkiye and Greece, despite their tense geopolitical relations, to manage the impacts of the Gaziantep earthquake and the floods from *Storm Daniel*.

ENERGY TRANSITIONS: STRATEGIC RISKS AND OPPORTUNITIES

In addition to the physical impacts of climate change, the required energy transition also presents strategic risks and opportunities.

The cost of transitioning to a greener energy mix will further pressure already tight national budgets, increasing the risk of social unrest.

Civil nuclear programmes in Egypt and Turkiye are expected to meet demand for lower-carbon energy diversification. This, however, may give rise to other challenges around safeguarding nuclear installations from climate impacts, such as ensuring the safety of their water-cooling systems if river discharge is decreasing and sea levels rising.[X]

At present, several countries in the region are moving toward integrating

---

[VII] Eastern Mediterranean and Middle East Climate Change Initiative, 'Sharm El-Sheikh Declaration of the Eastern Mediterranean and Middle East Climate Change Initiative at the 27th Conference of the Parties of the UNFCCC (COP 27)', 8 November 2022, https://emme-cci.org/cop-27/. The declaration signatories are Bahrain, Cyprus, Egypt, Greece, Iraq, Israel, Jordan, Lebanon, Oman and the State of Palestine.

[VIII] Eastern Mediterranean and Middle East Climate Change Initiative, 'Declaration', Sharm al-Sheikh, 8 November 2022, https://emme-cci.org/wp-content/uploads/Final-declaration_EMME_CCI_.pdf; and Costas Kadis, 'Eastern Mediterranean and Middle East Climate Change Initiative', presentation at COP27, 8 November 2022, https://emme-cci.org/wp-content/uploads/Kadis_Summit_221108-.pdf.

[IX] Government of Cyprus, Press and Information Office, 'National Statement (Brief Intervention) by the President of the Republic, Mr Nikos Christodoulides, at the COP28 Summit, in Dubai', 1 December 2023, https://www.pio.gov.cy/en/press-releases-article.html?id=38602#flat; and The Cyprus Institute, 'Climate Crisis in the Eastern Mediterranean and the Middle East', https://emmeclimate2024.cyi.ac.cy/.

[X] Nilsu Goren, 'Nuclear Energy Developments, Climate Change and Security in Turkey', Council on Strategic Risks, Briefer no. 7, 27 April 2020, https://councilonstrategicrisks.org/wp-content/uploads/2020/04/Nuclear-Energy-Climate-Change-and-Security-in-Turkey_BRIEFER-7_2020_4_27-1.pdf.

Egyptian foreign minister Sameh Shoukry speaks during COP27 in Sharm al-Sheikh, Egypt, on 18 November 2022. (Photo: Mohamed Abdel Hamid/Anadolu Agency via Getty Images)

nuclear power as part of their energy mix. Reactors are under construction in Turkiye, which received its first fuel delivery at Akkuyu Nuclear Power Plant in April 2023; a nuclear power plant is under construction in Egypt; Jordan is considering nuclear power to produce energy and drinking water; and there are discussions on nuclear power in Israel, Libya and Tunisia.[xi]

Investments in renewable energy could act as a stabilising factor in the Eastern Mediterranean, strengthening interdependencies and cooperation as countries reshape or integrate their energy grids, if pre-existing geopolitical disputes can be contained. Examples include the EuroAsia Interconnector undersea cables between Cyprus, Greece and Israel. Exploiting the region's abundant renewables potential could increase GDP and provide jobs, for example through exports of green hydrogen to European markets.

Such initiatives could provide proofs of concept for projects that increase regional integration and climate resilience, promote the energy transition, and leverage relevant technologies – such as in the Israeli water sector – for wider regional climate adaptation.

THE WAY FORWARD

It is possible that fallout from the accelerating climate crisis will stress local economies and challenge the legitimacy of governments. Building up regional cooperation and pooling capabilities will be crucial, given that none of the countries in the Eastern Mediterranean has the necessary resources and capabilities to meet the climate challenge alone.

Road maps identifying projects that meet the goals of climate adaptation, mitigation and stability are emerging, but countries need the vision, political will and resources to take a regional approach to stability and prosperity in a climate-changed future. Linking or pursuing complementarity on regional investments, and aligning external climate finance with these objectives, will be essential.

This narrative is gaining some traction, with more governments recognising climate as a cross-cutting issue and greater regional participation at COP27 in Sharm al-Sheikh in 2022 than at previous UN climate conferences. However, this will also require a significant move away from business-as-usual regional politics, including diplomatic progress on long-standing disputes, and a demonstration of the benefits of a mutual-interests regional approach to climate-risk management before the climate vulnerabilities reinforce trends toward hardline nationalist governments.

[xi] 'Putin, Sisi Mark New Phase of Egypt's Russian-built Nuclear Plant', Reuters, 23 January 2024, https://www.reuters.com/business/energy/putin-sisi-mark-new-phase-egypts-russian-built-nuclear-plant-2024-01-23/; Lucy Ashby, 'Jordan Advances Nuclear Power Programme with Support from IAEA SMR', International Atomic Energy Agency, 4 October 2023, https://www.iaea.org/newscenter/news/jordan-advances-nuclear-power-programme-with-support-from-iaea-smr-platform; and World Nuclear Association, 'Emerging Nuclear Energy Countries', April 2023, https://world-nuclear.org/information-library/country-profiles/others/emerging-nuclear-energy-countries.aspx.

ENDNOTES

1. See Katie Rogers, 'Jake Sullivan's "Quieter" Middle East Comments Did Not Age Well', *New York Times*, 26 October 2023, https://www.nytimes.com/2023/10/26/us/politics/jake-sullivan-foreign-affairs-israel-middle-east.html.

2. Henry Foy, 'How Diplomacy Succeeded in Sending the First Aid Ship to Gaza', *Financial Times*, 14 March 2024, https://www.ft.com/content/bca2720c-b761-4b41-a742-74effea74123.

3. 'Turkey's Erdogan Calls Israeli Siege and Bombing of Gaza "A Massacre"', 11 October 2023, https://www.aljazeera.com/news/2023/10/11/turkeys-erdogan-calls-israeli-siege-and-bombing-of-gaza-a-massacre.

4. 'Turkey's Erdogan Says Israeli PM Netanyahu No Different from Hitler', Reuters, 27 December 2023, https://www.reuters.com/world/middle-east/turkeys-erdogan-says-israeli-pm-netanyahu-no-different-hitler-2023-12-27/.

5. Angeliki Koutantou and Tuvan Gumrukcu, 'Turning a Page, Greece and Turkey Agree To Mend Ties', Reuters, 7 December 2023, https://www.reuters.com/world/greece-turkey-seek-restart-relations-with-meetings-athens-2023-12-06/.

6. 'Leaders of Greece and Turkey Agree To Increase Cooperation', 7 December 2023, https://www.voanews.com/a/leaders-of-turkey-and-greece-agree-to-increase-cooperation/7388473.html.

7. United States, Department of State, 'Secretary Antony J. Blinken at a Press Availability', 8 November 2023, https://www.state.gov/secretary-antony-j-blinken-at-a-press-availability-41/.

8. NewMed Energy, 'Update Re Offer To Purchase Participation Units of the Partnership', 13 March 2024, https://newmedenergy.com/wp-content/uploads/2024/03/NewMed-IR-10.3.24-%D7%9E%D7%95%D7%A0%D7%92%D7%A9.pdf.

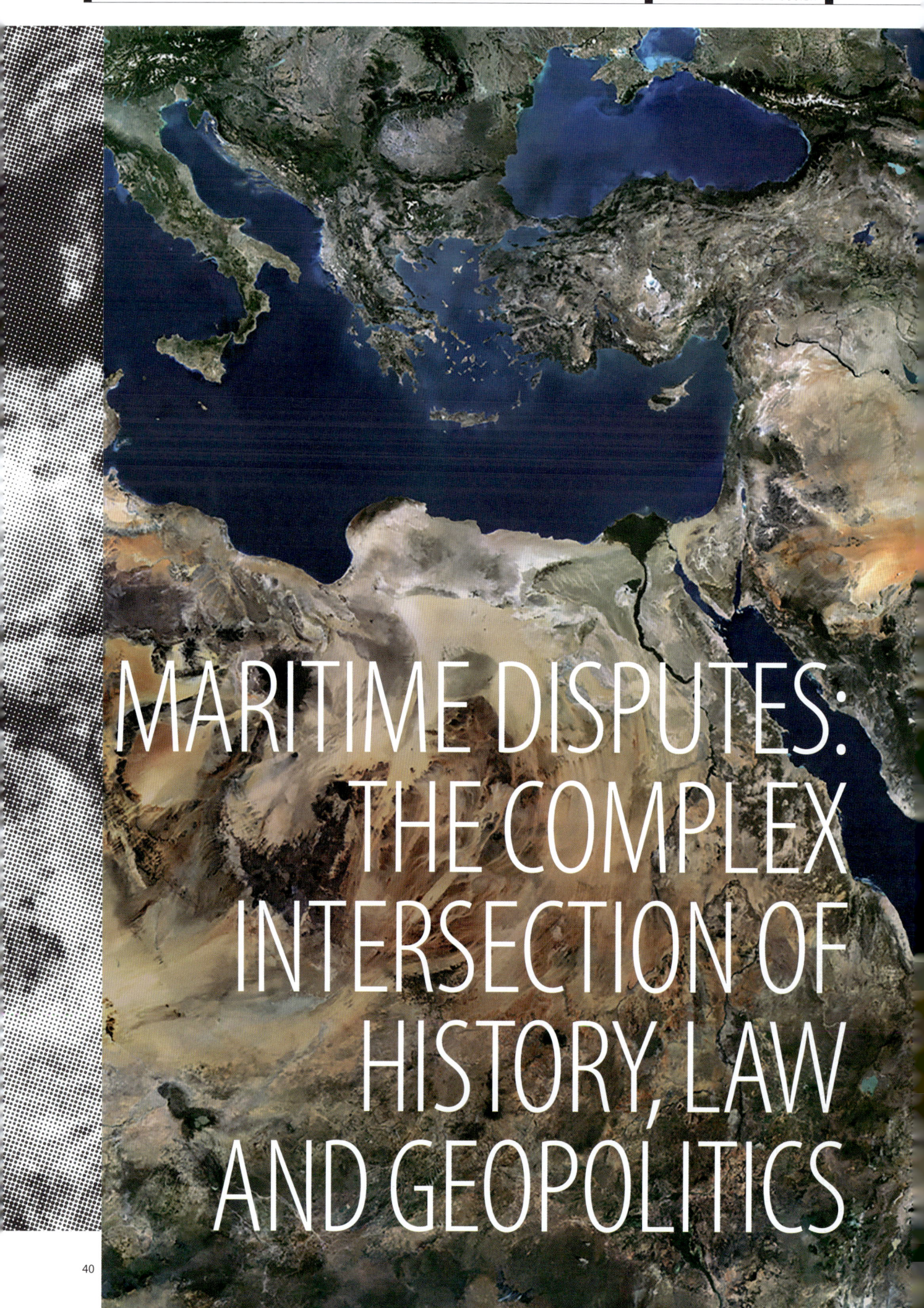

MARITIME DISPUTES: THE COMPLEX INTERSECTION OF HISTORY, LAW AND GEOPOLITICS

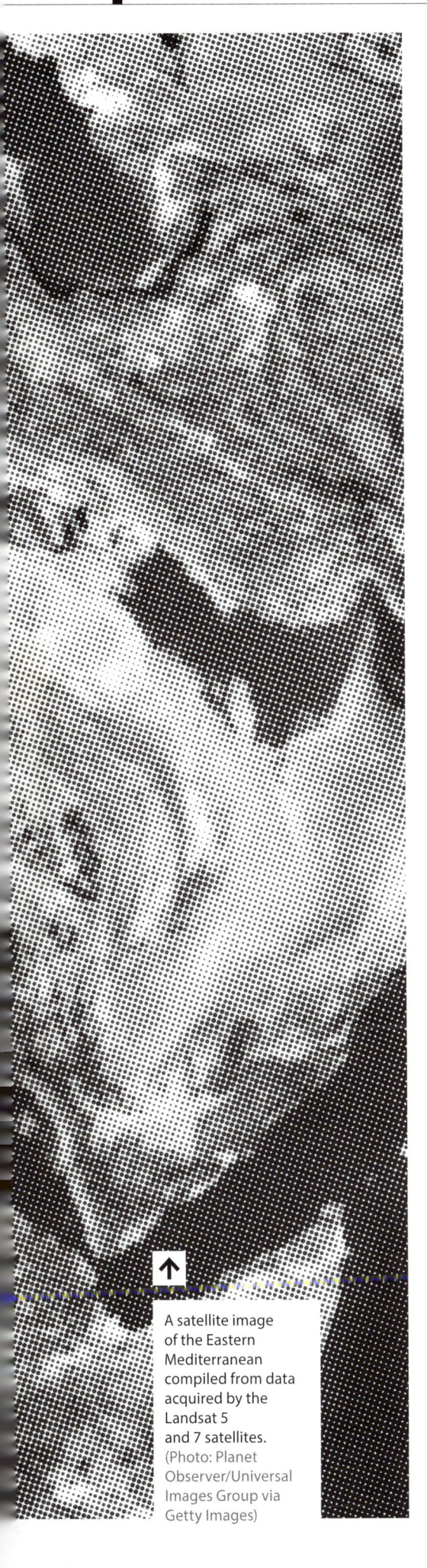

THEMES | MARITIME DISPUTES: THE COMPLEX INTERSECTION OF HISTORY, LAW AND GEOPOLITICS

CHAPTER TWO

BORDER DISPUTES emanating from the collapse of empires and the formation of modern states throughout the twentieth century have evolved into geopolitical contests with political, economic, commercial and nationalistic stakes.

IN THE EASTERN MEDITERRANEAN, the apparent intractability of historical disagreements and the lack of political will of parties to resolve their disputes have paralysed the application of international law pertaining to maritime borders.

MAXIMALIST CLAIMS and zero-sum bargaining have given primacy to power politics in attempts to resolve outstanding disputes.

EGYPT AND ISRAEL, each leveraging their status as the only current major gas producers in the region and their pre-existing infrastructure, could shape the landscape towards solutions that ultimately favour their gas-exporting and geopolitical interests.

COMMERCIAL DRIVERS have catalysed both disputes, such as around Cyprus, and piecemeal resolutions, such as between Israel and Lebanon. They are not sufficient to settle disputes without domestic political will, attention from outside powers and investment by international energy companies.

↑ A satellite image of the Eastern Mediterranean compiled from data acquired by the Landsat 5 and 7 satellites. (Photo: Planet Observer/Universal Images Group via Getty Images)

INTRODUCTION

The Eastern Mediterranean is the locus of several long-standing border disputes that have amplified geopolitical tensions. Maritime borders between several countries remain undelineated and involve competing claims either between the two sides or from third countries. These include Greece and Turkiye, Turkiye and Cyprus, Turkiye and Egypt, Greece and Libya, Syria and Lebanon, Syria and Cyprus, and Egypt and Libya. (This chapter does not cover in depth the many dimensions of the conflict between Israel and the State of Palestine.)

The situation is made more complex by the fact that Turkiye is one of only two countries (alongside Azerbaijan) that do not recognise the Republic of Cyprus and instead have relations with the self-declared Turkish Republic of Northern Cyprus (TRNC), itself only recognised by Turkiye at the time of writing. As such, throughout this study, 'Cyprus' refers to the Republic of Cyprus.

In this chapter, and throughout this study, 'the State of Palestine' is the entity with non-member observer status at the United Nations; 'the Occupied Palestinian Territories' refers to the regions of the West Bank and Gaza; and 'the Palestinian Authority' refers to the internationally recognised Palestinian interlocutor and entity governing parts of the West Bank.

Maritime-border disputes emanate from states seeking to delineate their continental shelves and exclusive economic zones (EEZs). (In this Strategic Dossier, 'delineate', 'delimit' and 'demarcate' are used interchangeably.) Continental shelves are the areas extending beyond a state's territorial sea through the natural prolongation of its land territory that typically extend to 200 nautical miles from the shoreline. An EEZ is restricted to 200 nautical miles off a state's coast.

Over recent years, international law has taken a back seat as geopolitics, power dynamics and commercial interests have informed efforts to resolve inter-state disputes.

Maritime disputes are as much geopolitical and geo-economic problems as they are disputes over sovereignty. As such, they are difficult to solve because they are multifaceted. Nationalism, history, and strategic and economic competition, as well as the concerned parties' regional and global relations, come into play. Nevertheless, in some cases, commercial considerations and the prospect of considerable hydrocarbon revenues for otherwise cash-strapped countries can also create a positive dynamic and help find a resolution.

Major transcontinental infrastructure projects, as well as the growing need for European Union member states to diversify their gas sources since committing in 2022 to ending Russian gas imports, have created new prospective commercial and strategic incentives for a resolution to the main disputes that involve Cyprus and Turkiye, and Greece and Turkiye.

Resolving the disputes and allowing pipelines and other infrastructure investments would allow all littoral countries to capitalise on their most valuable asset: their geographic location. Gas-exporting countries Egypt and Israel would gain new markets for their production. Gas-transit and gas-importing countries Greece and Turkiye would respectively earn revenues and secure gas supply. Weaker gas importers and potential gas producers such as Cyprus, Lebanon and the Occupied Palestinian Territories would improve their financial and gas-supply security. Yet geopolitics has so far largely stymied these potentially strong commercial incentives.

Turkiye considers the maritime-delimitation agreement that Cyprus and Egypt reached in 2003 the starting point for the past two decades of tensions over maritime borders in the region. Recognising neither Cyprus nor its right to a continental shelf or EEZ, it protested the entire premise of the deal.

The disputes related to maritime borders and maritime zones, including territorial seas and EEZs, in which countries can legally explore and produce natural resources intensified in the 2010s. It was then that Israel discovered major viable natural-gas fields in the Eastern Mediterranean and international energy companies began exploring for gas in offshore waters around Cyprus.

The formation of the East Mediterranean Gas Forum (EMGF) in 2019 by Cyprus, Egypt, Greece, Israel, Italy, Jordan and the State of Palestine, and its upgrading into a membership organisation in 2021 (which France then joined) to cooperate on developing regional gas resources exacerbated divisions because it excluded Turkiye, which many saw as the main regional troublemaker. In response to the EMGF proposal to build the EastMed Gas Pipeline to ship Israeli and potentially Cypriot gas through Cypriot and Greek waters to Italy, Turkiye reached a delimitation agreement with Libya in 2019 that contradicted Greece's maritime claim and therefore posed legal and security risks that would undermine the development of the potential pipeline.

This chapter outlines the evolution of international law pertaining to the Eastern

GLOSSARY

Territorial sea: The sovereign coastal waters of a state that extend beyond its land territory, generally accepted as 12 nautical miles from the baseline, or low-water line, of a coast. Sovereign jurisdiction applies to the sea, airspace, seabed and subsoil.[i]

Exclusive economic zone: The area of coastal waters that extends a certain distance, no further than 200 nautical miles from the baseline, in which states have rights to explore, sustainably exploit, manage and conserve living or non-living resources but do not have sovereign jurisdiction.[ii]

Continental shelf: The seabed and subsoil of the submarine areas extending beyond a state's territorial sea through the natural prolongation of its land territory. This can stretch beyond 200 nautical miles up to a maximum of 350 nautical miles, if certain conditions are satisfied.[iii]

---

i UN Convention on the Law of the Sea, 'Part II: Territorial Sea and Contiguous Zone', United Nations, https://www.un.org/depts/los/convention_agreements/texts/unclos/part2.htm.
ii UN Convention on the Law of the Sea, 'Part V: Exclusive Economic Zone', United Nations, https://www.un.org/depts/los/convention_agreements/texts/unclos/part5.htm.
iii UN Convention on the Law of the Sea, 'Part VI: Continental Shelf', United Nations, https://www.un.org/depts/los/convention_agreements/texts/unclos/part6.htm#:~:text=The%20continental%20shelf%20of%20a,baselines%20from%20which%20the%20breadth.

Mediterranean maritime-border disputes before shifting to a discussion of existing maritime disputes and agreements between the Eastern Mediterranean's eight coastal states – Cyprus, Egypt, Greece, Israel, Lebanon, Libya, Syria and Turkiye – as well as the State of Palestine.

It also explains how disputes and countries' diplomatic and military strategies have evolved over time, and evaluates the risks of these leading to conflict as well as potential pathways for peaceful resolution.

INTERNATIONAL LAW GOVERNING MARITIME BORDERS

Among the nine actors in the Eastern Mediterranean, four (Israel, Libya, Syria and Turkiye) do not adhere to the jurisprudence on maritime delimitation developed by international adjudicatory bodies such as the International Tribunal for the Law of the Sea (ITLOS), the International Court of Justice (ICJ) and arbitral tribunals.[1] This has allowed conflicts to fester and crystallise in the region.

The League of Nations Codification Conference held in The Hague in 1930 was the first attempt to codify maritime law. It produced draft articles on the legal status of territorial waters and other questions pertaining to maritime issues, but it ultimately did not have significant support from the international community. Nevertheless, these articles formed the basis for the International Law Commission, which the UN established in 1947.[2] The commission produced the draft articles on the Law of the Sea in 1956. These were in turn presented and discussed at the 1958 UN Conference on the Law of the Sea in Geneva (see pages 44–45).[3]

HISTORICAL FOUNDATIONS

Greece and Turkiye have been locked in disputes that span the Aegean Sea and Eastern Mediterranean for a century. Though somewhat separate seas with distinct histories, both countries take them as a whole. For Greece, the priority is resolving the dispute over the continental shelf in both seas. For Turkiye, resolving the continental-shelf dispute is only one of several issues, including territorial seas and the status of islands in the Aegean. The two countries' inability to agree on which issues are still contentious and how to address them is a major impediment to a resolution.

The issues begin with the 1923 Treaty of Lausanne that ceded the islands under dispute in the eastern Aegean Sea to either Greece or Turkiye. It determined

The Treaty of Lausanne is ratified by representatives from France, Greece, Italy, Japan, Romania, Turkiye, the United Kingdom and Yugoslavia in Lausanne, Switzerland, on 24 July 1923. (Photo: Keystone-France/Gamma-Keystone via Getty Images)

MAP 2.1: DEMILITARISED ISLANDS IN THE AEGEAN SEA

Legend:
- Demilitarised islands according to the Treaty of Lausanne, 1923
- Partially demilitarised islands according to the Treaty of Lausanne, 1923
- Demilitarised islands according to the Treaty of Peace with Italy, 1947

····· Median line*
▬ Greek territorial sea**
▨ Turkish territorial sea***
--- Exclusive economic zone (EEZ)

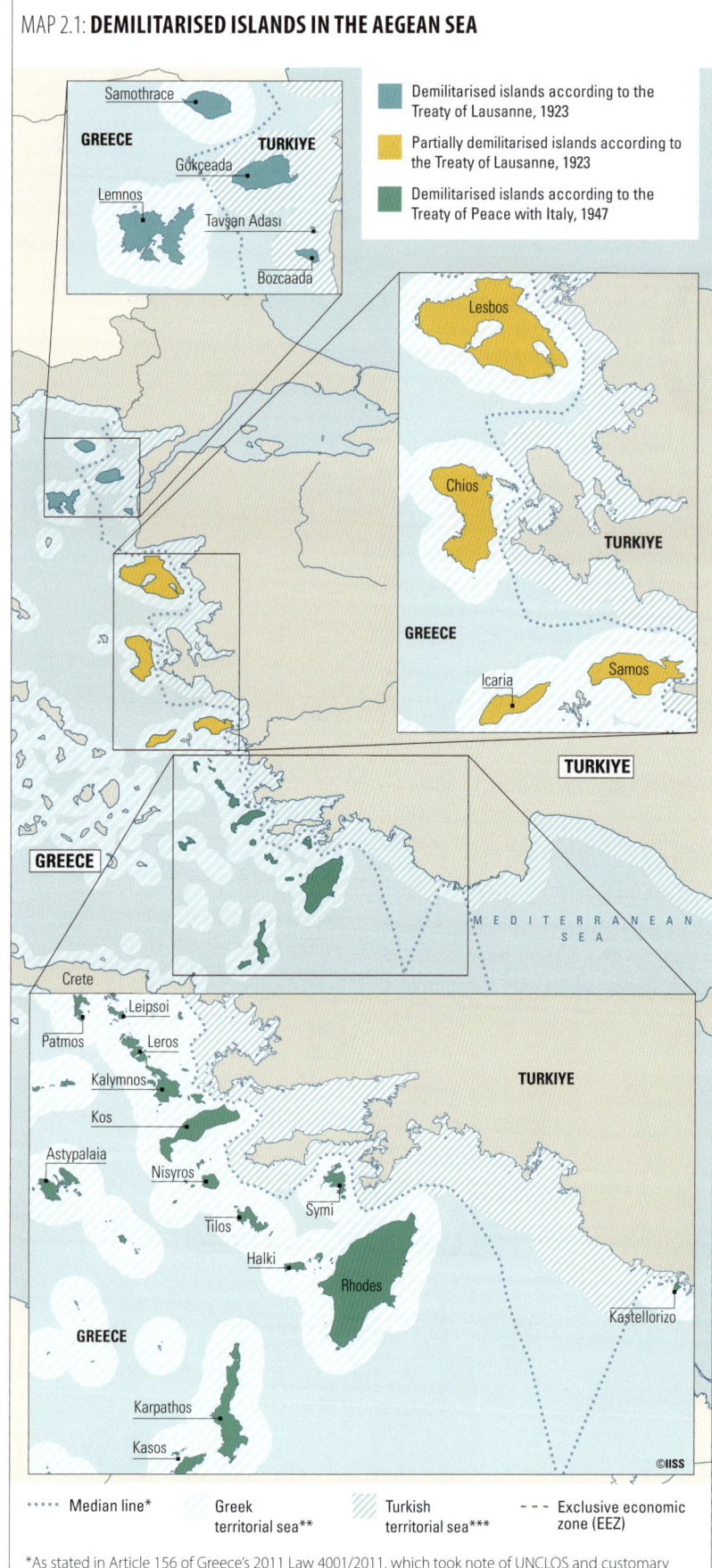

*As stated in Article 156 of Greece's 2011 Law 4001/2011, which took note of UNCLOS and customary international law, in the absence of a delineation agreement the outer limit of the Greek continental shelf and EEZ is the median line. **Greece maintains a six-nautical-mile limit to its territorial sea in the Aegean. ***Türkiye maintains a six-nautical-mile limit to its territorial sea in the Aegean and a 12-nautical-mile limit to its territorial sea in the Eastern Mediterranean.
Note: Türkiye has not submitted a claim for a continental shelf or an EEZ in the Aegean Sea.
Sources: Government documents; IISS analysis

that islands within three miles of the coastal states are considered part of that country's frontier, established territorial waters for all islands as three nautical miles, and imposed a demilitarised zone on Greek islands in the eastern Aegean (see Map 2.1).[4]

Two other relevant maritime legal agreements that went into force prior to 1958 also affected the Aegean. The first was the 1936 Montreux Convention Regarding the Regime of the [Turkish] Straits (the Dardanelles and the Bosporus). This gave Türkiye responsibility for overseeing traffic through these critical military and trade choke points rather than the International Straits Commission of the League of Nations, which had assumed responsibility under the Treaty of Lausanne.

Signed by ten countries including Greece, the convention guaranteed freedom of transit and navigation for civilian shipping vessels and limited the passage of warships during peacetime. It also gave Türkiye the right to block the passage of warships through the straits at its discretion during wartime. Türkiye used this right to block Axis warships during the Second World War.[5]

A second development also emerged from the Second World War. As a losing power, Italy was forced to cede the Dodecanese islands in the southeastern Aegean, which include Rhodes and 24 additional smaller islands, to the United Kingdom. (Türkiye had ceded control of these islands to Italy in the Treaty of Lausanne.) Then, Article 14 of the 1947 Paris peace treaty between Italy and the Allied Powers (Treaty of Peace with Italy) ceded the islands to Greece with the stipulation that they would remain demilitarised, overcoming Turkish objections to the cession (see Map 2.1). During the Greek–Turkish crises in the 1960s, however, Greece remilitarised some of the islands, which remains a source of contention, especially regarding the island of Kastellorizo, which lies roughly two nautical miles off the Turkish coast.[6] A dispute emerged over the definitions of 'demilitarisation' and 'militarisation' (including the type and number of installations and troops).

UNCLOS

After these agreements, the 1958 UN Conference on the Law of the Sea formed the foundation for the codification of today's international law pertaining to territorial-sea rights and responsibilities. Attended by 86 states, the conference adopted two conventions that established the principles later reflected in the UN Convention on the Law of the Sea (UNCLOS).

The first, the Convention on the Territorial Sea and the Contiguous Zone, included rules on baselines, bays, adjacent or frontal maritime borders, innocent passage and the contiguous zone, but it failed to produce agreement on 12 nautical miles as the breadth of the territorial sea.

The second, the Convention on the Continental Shelf, established that states have sovereign rights to the resources of an area that extends beyond the external limit of their territorial sea, without agreeing on specifics.

The Second UN Conference on the Law of the Sea was held in 1960 to address outstanding issues related to the law of the sea, building upon the work of the first conference in 1958, but also failed to adopt a comprehensive convention to resolve these issues.[7]

Two factors prompted the UN to renew its push for a holistic agreement and led to the Third Conference on the Law of the Sea: the 1967 Arab–Israeli War, which highlighted uncertainties about territorial seas in the Gulf of Aqaba, and the increasing range and depth at which oil could be exploited offshore.[8]

While only 86 countries had participated in the first and second conferences, states that had gained their independence post-colonisation pushed the total number of participants in the third conference to 160.[9] Stretching from 1973 to 1982, the conference achieved notable breakthroughs in delimiting maritime zones in five relevant categories (see box and Figure 2.1): internal waters; territorial sea (12 nautical miles from the baseline); contiguous zone (additional 12 nautical miles beyond the territorial sea); EEZs (200 nautical miles from the baseline); and continental shelf (the seabed and subsoil of the submarine areas extending beyond the territorial sea through the natural prolongation of a state's land territory).

UNCLOS did not enter into force until 1994 due to a series of issues including the entry-into-force conditions and national ratification processes that required modifying domestic legislation.

MAJOR AGREEMENTS RELATING TO EASTERN MEDITERRANEAN MARITIME BORDERS

Treaty of Lausanne, 1923
Ceded the islands under dispute in the eastern Aegean to either Greece or Turkiye, with the overwhelming majority going to Greece except for the islands that lay within three nautical miles of Turkiye's coast. Also imposed a demilitarised zone on Greek islands in the eastern Aegean.

Montreux Convention Regarding the Regime of the Straits, 1936
Gave Turkiye responsibility for overseeing traffic through the Dardanelles and the Bosporus, guaranteed free passage of civilian ships and placed provisions on the flow of warships in peacetime. It also gave Turkiye the ability to close the straits to warships during wartime.

Treaty of Peace with Italy, 1947
Ceded the Dodecanese islands in the southeastern Aegean Sea, including Rhodes and 24 additional smaller islands, to Greece and demilitarised them.

First and Second UN Conference on the Law of the Sea, 1958 and 1960
These first attempts to codify the international law of the sea established common rules, but reached no lasting agreement on the breadth of territorial seas. The 86 states in attendance forged the foundations for UNCLOS, which codified principles for how to delimit frontal and adjacent borders of territorial seas, EEZs and continental shelves.

Third UN Conference on the Law of the Sea, 1973–82
This third conference concluded with the adoption of UNCLOS, which entered into force in 1994. This conference included 160 countries and codified the rules for delimiting maritime boundaries. Parties to UNCLOS can submit disputes to a wide variety of dispute-settlement mechanisms, including conciliation, arbitration and judicial settlement by the ICJ or the ITLOS, where particular conditions are satisfied.

EQUITY VERSUS EQUIDISTANCE

The resolution of disputes in the Eastern Mediterranean is further complicated by the high concentration of littoral countries – Israel, Syria and Turkiye – that have not ratified UNCLOS and that hold diverging views on what the applicable rules should be. And while international law requires negotiations between coastal states to reach agreement on the borders of relevant maritime zones, that has not been possible given the fraught political relations that exist among parties. These differences have unsurprisingly grown more rigid since the Eastern Mediterranean gas discoveries in the 2010s, with countries vying for more acreage to explore, especially around Cyprus.[10]

Technically speaking, two kinds of border exist and two guiding principles can be applied to help draw maritime-boundary lines. If countries disagree on which principle to apply, but have the political will to resolve the dispute, they can do so through dispute settlement. Disputes become more complicated when states lack that will.

Countries that have coasts facing each other are said to have 'frontal' borders, while countries with coasts next to each other are said to have 'adjacent' borders.

The equidistance principle involves drawing a median line between coasts, every point of which is equidistant from the nearest points of the baselines from which the breadth of each state's territorial sea is measured.

The equity principle considers whether the line produces a situation that is equitable for both parties. Factors that

FIGURE 2.1: UN CONVENTION ON THE LAW OF THE SEA

National airspace — International airspace

12nm | 24nm | 200nm

Territorial sea | Contiguous zone

Exclusive economic zone | High seas

BASELINE

Continental shelf — To a maximum of 350nm from the baseline or 100nm beyond the 2,500 metre isobath, whichever is greatest

Deep seabed area

Notes: Not drawn to scale; nm = nautical mile.
Source: *Asia-Pacific Regional Security Assessment 2022*, IISS

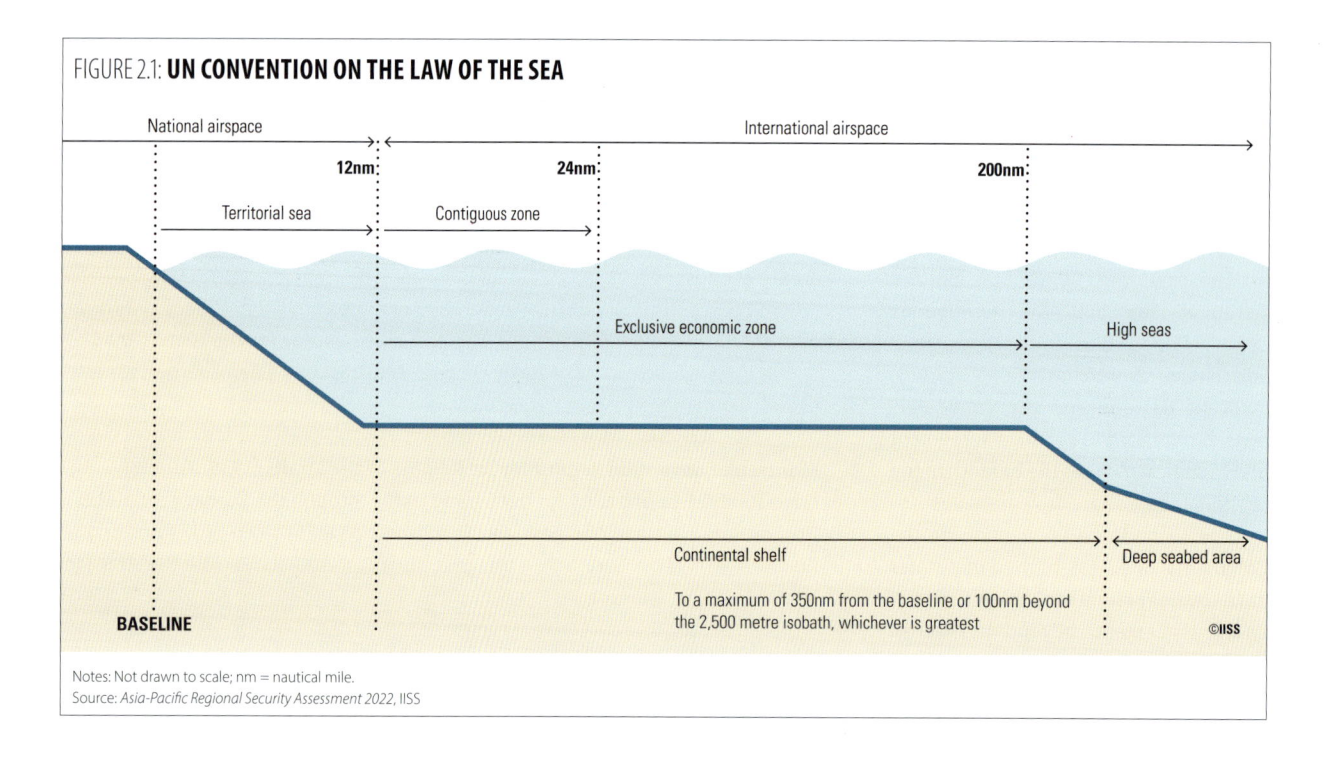

influence equity include, for example, adjustments to the equidistance line if special circumstances justifying deviation exist, such as islands that generate full or partial maritime zones; historic title claims; economic factors, such as a state's dependence on resources; traditional fishing rights; and conservation and environmental factors.

One of the most long-standing frontal-border cases is that which pits Greece and Cyprus on the one hand against Turkiye on the other. Addled by the political conflict over the Cyprus question, the parties have been at odds for decades over how to define borders around the island. This has had repercussions for their border delimitations with Egypt and Libya (see Map 2.2).

One of the most contentious adjacent borders in the region used to be the one separating Israel and Lebanon. The dispute was resolved in 2022 through the confluence of three factors: US mediation, political will for a resolution, and the promise of a sizeable economic windfall from the exploitation of offshore gas.

In relation to the EEZ and the continental shelf, UNCLOS declared equidistance a non-binding principle and allowed states to argue for 'equity' in delimiting an adjacent border, an ill-defined principle that UNCLOS outlined in Articles 74 and 83. Thus, states are allowed to pursue agreement under international law to achieve an equitable result.

Around the world, the equidistance principle has solved many adjacent-border disputes in a straightforward fashion, but many others remain unsolved because of the ambiguity of the equity principle.[11] In the Eastern Mediterranean, it has proven equally problematic. During the UN Conference on the Law of the Sea, Syria and Turkiye supported the principle of equity, while Cyprus and Greece supported the principle of equidistance. These divides remain in place today.[12]

More recent jurisprudence from the ITLOS and the ICJ has framed delimitation methodology in what is now called a three-step approach. This approach first draws an equidistance line, and then considers whether or not the situation it produces creates a situation of equity. If states disagree over the application of equidistance or whether to bring in principles of equity, they either negotiate or go through dispute settlement (conciliation, arbitration, adjudication, etc.).

Ultimately, given the historical and geopolitical acrimony that characterises relations between the parties to the major border disputes in the region, littoral countries have struggled to engage in good-faith negotiations to resolve their disputes through the available dispute-settlement mechanisms, be they at the ICJ, ITLOS or through arbitration.

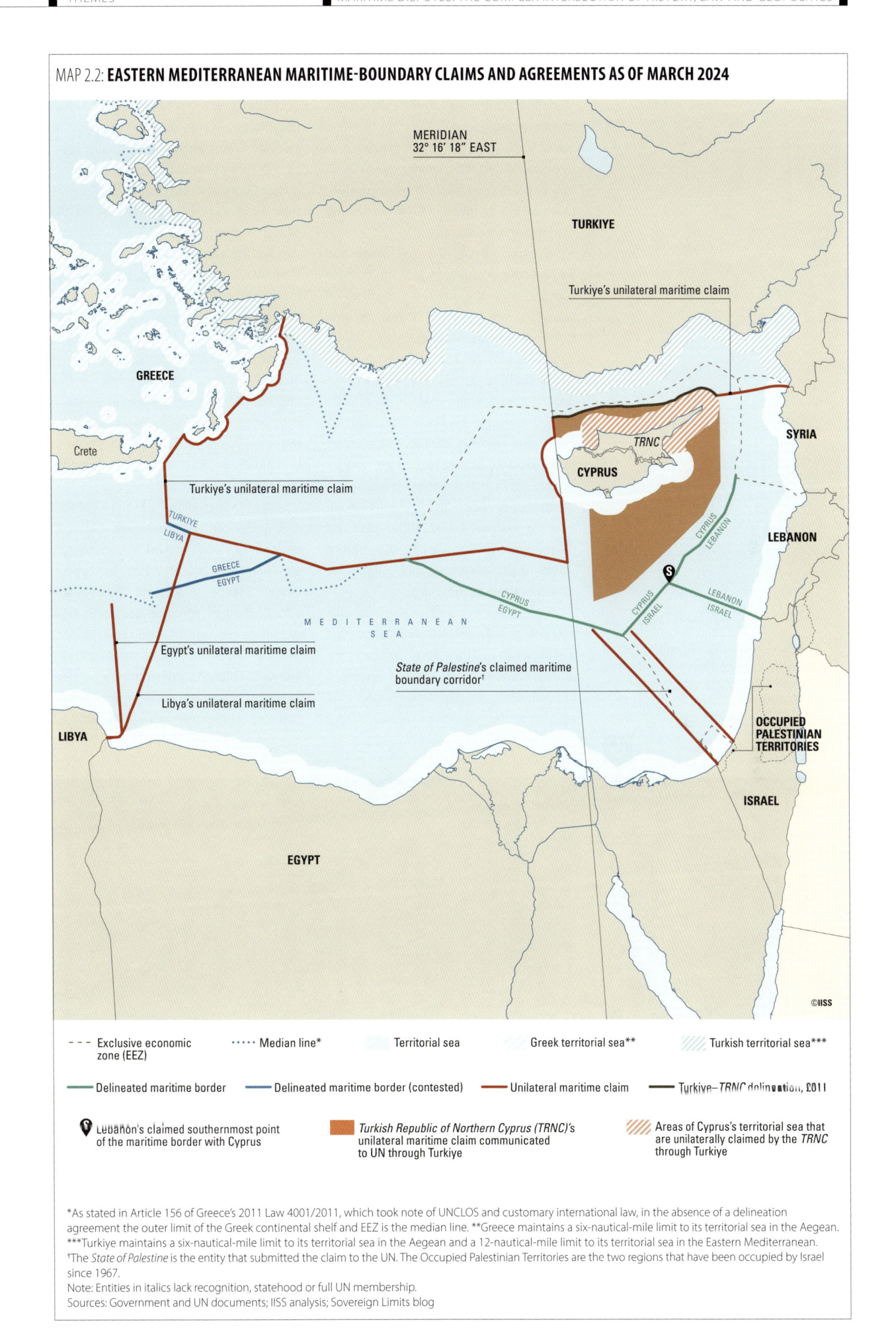

THEMES — MARITIME DISPUTES: THE COMPLEX INTERSECTION OF HISTORY, LAW AND GEOPOLITICS

MAP 2.2: EASTERN MEDITERRANEAN MARITIME-BOUNDARY CLAIMS AND AGREEMENTS AS OF MARCH 2024

Legend:
- – – – Exclusive economic zone (EEZ)
- ····· Median line*
- Territorial sea
- Greek territorial sea**
- Turkish territorial sea***
- ——— Delineated maritime border
- ——— Delineated maritime border (contested)
- ——— Unilateral maritime claim
- ——— Turkiye–TRNC delineation, 2011
- 📍 Lebanon's claimed southernmost point of the maritime border with Cyprus
- Turkish Republic of Northern Cyprus (TRNC)'s unilateral maritime claim communicated to UN through Turkiye
- Areas of Cyprus's territorial sea that are unilaterally claimed by the TRNC through Turkiye

*As stated in Article 156 of Greece's 2011 Law 4001/2011, which took note of UNCLOS and customary international law, in the absence of a delineation agreement the outer limit of the Greek continental shelf and EEZ is the median line. **Greece maintains a six-nautical-mile limit to its territorial sea in the Aegean. ***Turkiye maintains a six-nautical-mile limit to its territorial sea in the Aegean and a 12-nautical-mile limit to its territorial sea in the Eastern Mediterranean.
†The *State of Palestine* is the entity that submitted the claim to the UN. The Occupied Palestinian Territories are the two regions that have been occupied by Israel since 1967.
Note: Entities in italics lack recognition, statehood or full UN membership.
Sources: Government and UN documents; IISS analysis; Sovereign Limits blog

LAWFARE AND BRINKMANSHIP

Given this context, a kind of 'lawfare' – defined here as states' diplomatic manoeuvring and narrative-building about their rights over maritime space, as opposed to asserting claims via litigation in the courts – has been increasingly used by countries involved in disputes around the Eastern Mediterranean.

Cyprus, Egypt, Greece, Israel and Turkiye have an advantage in this domain compared to the limited capacities of Lebanon, the State of Palestine, and Syria. Israel notably deploys a formidable arsenal to build a narrative to justify the legality of force and occupation. In contrast, the State of Palestine's limited resources and lack of standing as a UN non-member observer state have obstructed its ability to counter Israel's arguments in international arenas.[13]

Both Greece and Cyprus have leveraged their EU membership and deepening relations with the United States to pursue 'maximalist' claims for their maritime-border rights.

Turkiye, for its part, has also pushed a maximalist position and tried to support it with lawfare. Since 2004, it has assiduously responded to Cypriot attempts to delineate its maritime borders or explore for hydrocarbons by submitting its objections to the UN, arguing for its interpretation of its continental shelf 'in accordance with the outcome of future delimitation agreements among all relevant States, and with equitable principles'.[14] Turkiye's most essential argument is that Cyprus cannot determine its maritime borders until a resolution on the island's status is reached.[15]

Additionally, parties to disputes, and their supporting partners, have increasingly used military means to assert legal claims. In 2019 and 2020, Turkiye sent warships to escort its hydrocarbon-exploration vessels in disputed waters around Cyprus. Turkiye's brinkmanship limited international vessels' freedom of navigation.[16] In 2020, France sent warships to the region to support Greece's right to unilaterally exploit maritime acreage that UNCLOS bestows to it.[17]

The intractability of the political and historical disagreements between regional powers makes it increasingly possible that powers such as Cyprus, Egypt, Greece, Israel and Turkiye will either adopt or continue using this kind of lawfare and brinkmanship to legitimate their political, economic and security interests. This will render maritime borders more difficult to adjudicate upon unless a diplomatic breakthrough is achieved.[18]

A Hellenic Navy ship enters the port of the Greek island of Kastellorizo, located approximately two nautical miles off the coast of Turkiye. (Photo: Diego Cupolo/NurPhoto Agency via Getty Images)

STATUS OF BILATERAL MARITIME-BORDER AGREEMENTS OR DISPUTES

Bilateral maritime borders in the Eastern Mediterranean (see Map 2.2 and Table 2.1) fall into four categories based on their status and the likelihood of any dispute developing into a flashpoint for kinetic conflict:

1. Resolved: bilateral agreement in place applying UNCLOS principles

2. Ongoing talks towards resolution: ongoing talks and unlikely flashpoint given both sides' interest in a quick resolution

3. Unresolved: undelineated, but unlikely flashpoint

4. Potential flashpoint: open dispute between countries that have opposing views on the application of international maritime law and are geopolitical rivals

RESOLVED

CYPRUS'S AGREEMENTS WITH EGYPT AND ISRAEL

Offshore-gas discoveries and prospective discoveries have been a major catalyst in delimiting many borders in the Eastern Mediterranean.

Cyprus was the prime mover in this field in its quest to promote regional integration and initiate gas exploration in its offshore waters. Between 2003 and 2010, it reached agreements with Egypt and Israel, though its ongoing conflict with Turkiye casts a long shadow over its diplomacy.

Cyprus reached its first delimitation agreement on its frontal border with Egypt in 2003; this used the median-line principle and served as a model for others in the region. The text for the 2010 Cyprus–Israel agreement was virtually identical to it.[19]

For Turkiye, the Cypriot agreement with Egypt is generally considered the starting point for the past two decades of tensions regarding maritime borders in the region. Ankara protested the move, arguing that Greece's islands in the southeastern Aegean and Cyprus can claim neither a continental shelf nor an EEZ in the maritime area between them. Moreover, it argued that the Turkish continental-shelf limit should extend to a median line with Egypt's EEZ and that Cyprus should put its exploration activities on hold until a larger solution to the dispute between Greece and Greek Cypriots on the one hand, and Turkiye and Turkish Cypriots on the other, over the island can be reached.[20]

Creating an environment conducive to offshore exploration of hydrocarbon fields often located at or near borders was a main driver of the Cypriot agreements with Egypt and Israel. Cyprus and Egypt

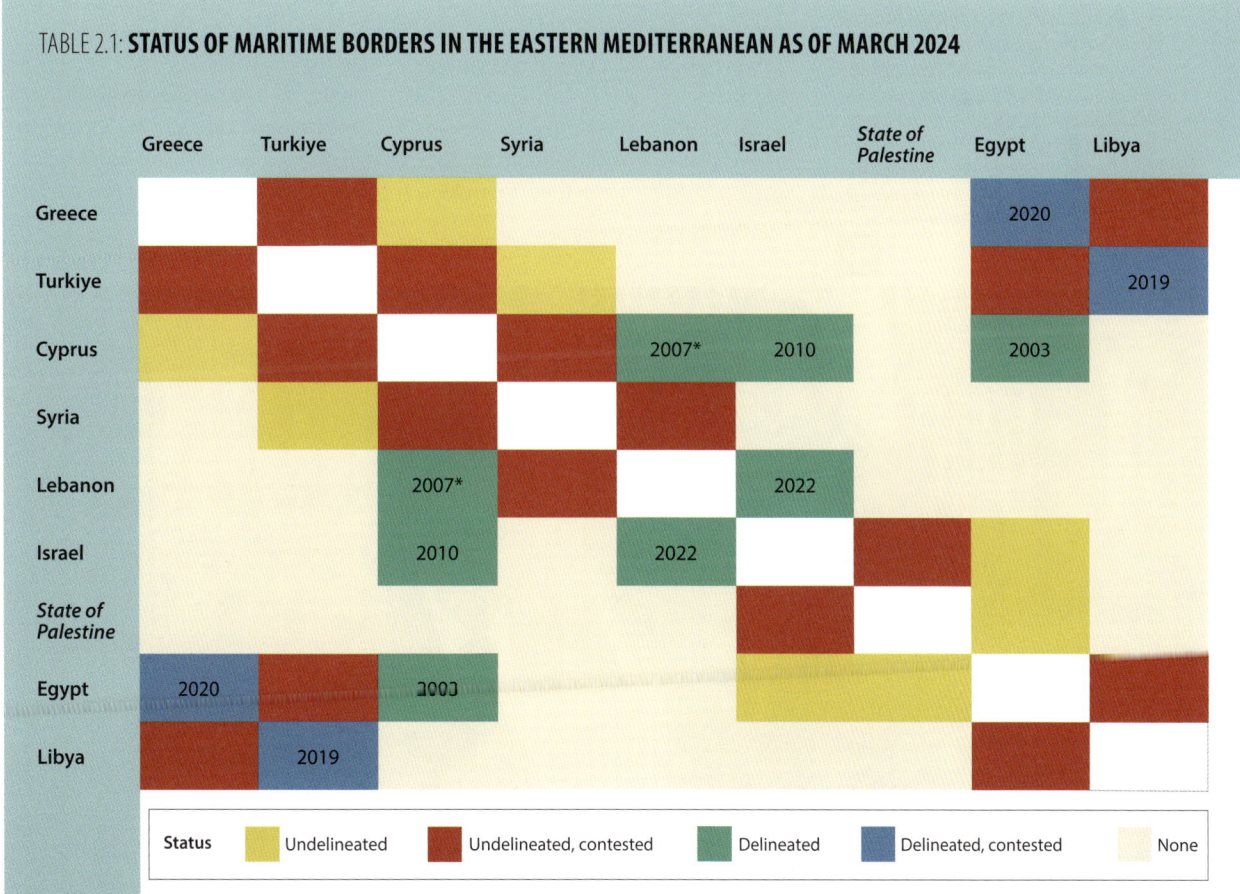

TABLE 2.1: STATUS OF MARITIME BORDERS IN THE EASTERN MEDITERRANEAN AS OF MARCH 2024

	Greece	Turkiye	Cyprus	Syria	Lebanon	Israel	State of Palestine	Egypt	Libya
Greece		Undelineated, contested	Undelineated					Delineated, contested 2020	Undelineated, contested
Turkiye	Undelineated, contested		Undelineated, contested	Undelineated				Undelineated, contested	Delineated, contested 2019
Cyprus	Undelineated	Undelineated, contested			Delineated 2007*	Delineated 2010		Delineated 2003	
Syria		Undelineated			Undelineated, contested				
Lebanon			Delineated 2007*	Undelineated, contested		Delineated 2022			
Israel			Delineated 2010		Delineated 2022		Undelineated, contested	Undelineated	
State of Palestine						Undelineated, contested		Undelineated, contested	
Egypt	Delineated, contested 2020	Undelineated, contested	Delineated 2003			Undelineated	Undelineated, contested		Undelineated, contested
Libya	Undelineated, contested	Delineated, contested 2019						Undelineated, contested	

Status: Undelineated (yellow) | Undelineated, contested (red) | Delineated (green) | Delineated, contested (blue) | None (cream)

*Talks are ongoing to amend in accordance with the 2022 Lebanon–Israel delineation agreement.
Notes: Entities in italics lack recognition, statehood or full UN membership. 'Contested' refers to situations in which the two parties have competing claims, and/or a third party is challenging the delineation. The status of the Egypt–Israel and Egypt–*State of Palestine* maritime borders is contingent upon the resolution of the Israeli–Palestinian conflict.
Source: IISS analysis

©IISS

inked an agreement on the development of cross-median-line hydrocarbon resources in 2013, built on a 2005 memorandum of understanding (MoU). Egypt's giant Zohr gas field is located six kilometres[21] from the median line between the two countries. In 2014, Cyprus and Israel signed an agreement to exchange information on hydrocarbons pertaining to adjacent gas-exploration blocks in their respective EEZs.[22]

EGYPT AND GREECE

EMGF members Egypt and Greece finalised the delimitation of their respective EEZs in 2020, clearing the way for rapprochement on energy and defence cooperation.

Egypt and Greece began negotiating their boundary delimitation in 2005. Their bilateral agreement in August 2020 to partially delimit their EEZs in adherence with UNCLOS included a reference in Article 2 to jointly pursuing an agreement on the exploitation of gas. Article 1, section 5 added that if one of the parties begins negotiations with a third state sharing maritime borders with both parties, it must inform and consult the other.[23]

Geopolitical hedging also features in the delimitations of maritime borders. Egypt and Israel have tried to strike a balance in their approach to the ongoing dispute between Greece and Turkiye in an attempt to preserve their respective interests and relations with both. Cyprus, Egypt and Israel have been careful not to launch gas-production operations in waters around Cyprus that Turkiye claims. Moreover, Turkiye does not claim waters that would interfere with either Egypt's or Israel's borders with Cyprus. It was notably careful in its 2019 MoU with Libya to only demarcate waters that overlapped with Greece's claim. Despite its own tensions with Cairo, it did not want to aggravate Egypt or violate Egypt's maritime-border agreement with Athens.

In other words, regional powers – Egypt, Greece, Israel and Turkiye – want to balance claims over their maritime zones with their respective regional and bilateral interests. Thus, while the competition inherent in geopolitics catalyses disputes over maritime borders, it also helps constrain countries from prosecuting their maximalist positions in this domain, or any other one for that matter.

LEBANON AND ISRAEL

In 2022, US mediation enabled an agreement between Lebanon and Israel, even though the two states do not have diplomatic relations. The maritime-border

Lebanese president Michel Aoun (R) receives US mediator Amos Hochstein (L) after Aoun signed the maritime-border delineation agreement with Israel mediated by the US in Beirut, Lebanon, on 27 October 2022. (Photo: Lebanese Presidency/Handout/Anadolu Agency via Getty Images)

delimitation agreement aims to use the potential windfall from still-unproven Lebanese gas reserves to disincentivise a new eruption of war between the two sides. The agreement stipulates that Israel will receive about 17% of the revenues from the prospective Qana gas field that straddles both sides of the border.[24] But the Hamas-led 7 October attacks against Israel, Israel's subsequent war in Gaza and the reignition of conflict on the Lebanese–Israeli front have shown the vulnerability of such agreements to geopolitics.

The dispute had been driven by a divergence in approaches: Israel argued for the equidistance principle, while Lebanon advocated the equity principle. Against the backdrop of a financial collapse of historic proportions in Lebanon, and despite the ongoing military conflict between the two sides, they reached an agreement in large part thanks to US mediation.

While the agreement was a breakthrough and included a model for revenue-sharing, it requires continuous negotiation between the two countries over the Qana field's development. Given the historic distrust between the two states, it has the potential to unravel.[25] This fragile dynamic is exacerbated by an imbalance between the two countries in their ability to harness legal expertise and diplomatic know-how. This was reflected in the way Lebanon determined its delineation lines on the basis of low-quality topographical and hydrographic studies. In 2011, Beirut put forward a line called Line 23. A subsequent, more developed study showed, however, that Lebanon could claim a line further south, called Line 29; this line intersected with the lucrative Karish gas field, which extends into Israeli waters. But the study was conducted too late, as negotiations between both sides had already begun based on Line 23 (which Israel had initially rejected, but later accepted). As such, Israel obtained a satisfactory deal on the basis of equidistance that also gave it full rights to the most lucrative gas field discovered in the area to date.

ONGOING TALKS TOWARDS RESOLUTION

Lebanon has open talks on EEZ delimitation with Cyprus that do not constitute a trigger for conflict. Lebanon signed an EEZ delimitation agreement with Cyprus in 2007 according to the equidistance principle, but the agreement was never ratified by the Lebanese parliament. When countries delineate their borders, they draw a line connecting multiple points between their coasts. In a 2011 letter to the UN, Lebanon disputed one of these points – known as point 1 – from the 2010 Israel–Cyprus agreement.[26] Talks to reach legal agreement with Cyprus, however, restarted in 2022.[27] These ongoing talks are part of Lebanon's broader diplomatic push to resolve its maritime borders, which included the agreement with Israel reached in October 2022 (see above).

UNRESOLVED

Libya, the State of Palestine (with the Palestinian Authority as the negotiating party), and Syria each have open disputes that, although unlikely to be resolved in the near term, do not constitute potential flashpoints.

LIBYA

Libya's unresolved disputes are with Egypt and Greece, and their resolution is hampered by the division of the country between the UN-recognised Government of National Unity (GNU) in the west and the Government of National Stability in the east, both of which claim legitimacy to run the country. Divided in this way, Libya cannot resort to international law to solve its disputes with either Egypt or Greece and must rely on controversial diplomatic agreements such as the one the GNU signed with Turkiye in 2019 at a time when it was courting Ankara's political and military support. This agreement is controversial and faced domestic legal and political challenges. Nevertheless, the Libya–Egypt and Libya–Greece disputes are unlikely to escalate into a military conflict. Libya resolved its disputes with Tunisia in 1982 and Malta in 1985 through ICJ arbitration rulings based on UNCLOS principles, demonstrating its willingness, at that time, to operate within the UNCLOS-based legal framework.[28]

The Egypt–Libya maritime border became a focus of dispute after the fall of Libyan leader Muammar Gadhafi in 2011. Like with Lebanon and Israel, the two countries disagree on the applicable principle of international law. Egypt claims, based on the equidistance principle, that its maritime boundary with Libya should run along a line that extends from the land border between the two countries to the point where the 25th parallel north intersects with the Egyptian coastline.[29] Libya, on the other hand, embraces the equity principle and claims that the boundary should extend along a line that runs parallel to its coast. In December 2022, Egyptian President Abdel Fattah al-Sisi issued a presidential decree that unilaterally demarcated his country's maritime border with Libya. Cairo defended the decision on the grounds that the divided state of Libya – with presidential elections postponed indefinitely – makes it impossible to resolve the matter and develop gas resources expeditiously, while Egypt needs to move fast to develop potential gas assets. After the announcement, Turkiye called on both countries to negotiate to resolve the matter.[30] In February 2023, the GNU formally rejected Egypt's unilateral demarcation in a letter[31] to the UN and laid out the coordinates of its claim to the border (see Map 2.2).

Libya also lacks an EEZ agreement with Greece. The two share a maritime boundary but have not made progress towards delimiting their maritime zones, despite maintaining cordial relations. Tripoli and Athens are at odds over Libya's claim to the Gulf of Sirte and the delimitation of the eastern limits of Libya's contiguous zone which, in Greece's view, encroach on the maritime zone of the Greek island of Crete. Reaching a resolution has been further hampered by Libya's MoU with Turkiye. Libya and Greece have never held formal talks, largely complicated by the GNU's close relationship with Turkiye and Athens's resulting rapprochement with eastern Libyan factions. After a presidential visit held in Athens in 2021, the Greek government and the GNU agreed to resume talks on delineating their maritime borders, but these have not resulted in concrete progress.[32] For Athens, obtaining a Libyan abrogation of the 2019 agreement with Turkiye, either through a political or a judicial decision, would represent a significant diplomatic success. However, inertia in Libya as well as Turkish influence make this prospect unlikely at present. In May 2024, the GNU in Tripoli sent a *note verbale* to the Greek ambassador to Libya objecting to what it deemed illegal Greek prospecting south of Crete.[33]

STATE OF PALESTINE

The State of Palestine (the entity nominally in charge of the Occupied Palestinian Territories) has two maritime borders with Israel and Egypt and, like Cyprus, is eager to delineate them to participate in the joint development of gas fields. Neither border is likely to be a trigger for a conflict, though their sustainable resolution is contingent on the resolution of the wider Israeli–Palestinian conflict.

Israel and the Palestinian Authority (as the interlocutor for the State of Palestine) have had maritime-border discussions in recent years that have seen little progress. The fact that the Palestinian Authority has not ruled Gaza since 2007 has weakened its negotiating position. In June 2023, Israel gave preliminary approval to allow the Palestinian Authority to develop the Gaza Marine offshore gas field with Egypt, but an agreement on borders has not been reached.[34] After Egypt's successful deal with Greece in August 2020, it had appeared possible that it might negotiate with the State of Palestine,[35] but nothing came of initial talks.

However, in October 2022, Egypt's petroleum minister confirmed that a framework agreement had been reached for Egypt's state-owned gas company EGAS to develop the Gaza Marine field and share revenues with the State of Palestine.[36] But in any case, the status of Gaza after the Israel–Hamas war is fraught with so much uncertainty that the question appears moot at the time of writing.

SYRIA

As a fractured country whose government does not exert full control over its territory, Syria will struggle to resolve its maritime-border disputes with Cyprus, Lebanon and Turkiye, which will therefore remain frozen for the foreseeable future. Moreover, Syria's offshore waters are not expected to be geologically rich, unlike the southern Eastern Mediterranean basin, meaning that there is less urgency to explore them. Despite efforts prior to 2011, Syria and Cyprus have never held bilateral talks, partly because of Turkiye's and the unrecognised TRNC's claimed borders. Syria and Turkiye have likewise failed to reach agreement on their adjacent maritime border. Syria claims this should be based on an equidistant line extending out from its land border in a way that encroaches on the rights of Turkiye's Hatay Province, to which Syria has not abandoned its claim since France ceded it to Turkiye in 1939. Meanwhile, Turkiye argues that the maritime border should be drawn in an equitable fashion. Nevertheless, this border dispute is unlikely to be a flashpoint between two countries that have other significant points of friction.

Syria has, however, taken unilateral steps towards offshore-gas development. This has created tension with Lebanon at various stages, though it is unlikely to boil over into a full-blown conflict. In 2011, Lebanon unilaterally delimited its EEZ boundary with Syria through a letter to the UN, a move Syria rejected in 2014.[37] Lebanon claims that the equidistance principle should apply to delimit the adjacent border, whereas Syria argues for the equity principle. Russia has made timid efforts to mediate this dispute since 2019.[38] Lebanon's 2022 agreement with Israel, however, has renewed interest in delineating its other maritime borders, including with Syria, which it must delimit in order to finalise its talks with Cyprus.[39]

POTENTIAL FLASHPOINTS

CYPRUS, GREECE AND TURKIYE

Greece and Turkiye are locked in disputes that span two overlapping, interconnected geographies – the Aegean Sea on the one hand and the eastern Mediterranean Sea (including Cyprus) on the other. It is the latter that came close to being the scene of hot confrontations in 2019 and 2020.

The two countries disagree over the delimitation of continental shelves and EEZs, territorial waters and airspaces, demilitarisation of islands and sovereignty over islands. A combination of the geopolitics of gas, history and geography render the maritime-border disputes between Greece and Turkiye that centre on Cyprus the most intractable to solve.

The history of the Greece–Turkiye maritime-border disputes makes them difficult to solve. The 1973–74 crisis over Cyprus, which resulted in the Turkish occupation of northern Cyprus, and current Cypriot exploration in waters that Turkiye disputes, have built high levels of distrust that make getting to the negotiating table challenging.

The geography of the Greece–Turkiye maritime border may be the most significant challenge, with some islands located extremely close to the Turkish coast. Greece has thousands of islands and islets, with 1.65 million people living on 227 of them,[40] many of which fall within both Greece's and Turkiye's 200-nautical-mile EEZs as outlined by UNCLOS. There are few geographies in the world that resemble this complicated scenario, with the South China Sea

The Turkish drillship *Yavuz*, accompanied by a Turkish Naval Forces ship, carries out drilling operations offshore Cyprus on 11 July 2019.(Photo: Turkish National Defence Ministry/Handout/Anadolu Agency via Getty Images)

providing the most similar example. All of the aforementioned factors have made the disputes intractable in the context of strained political relations between the two sides. A thawing that started in late 2023 may eventually lead to constructive talks and dispute resolution. At the time of writing, Greece and Turkiye are still building up confidence by working on less contentious issues.

In addition, new competition between the two countries over their ambitions to become Eastern Mediterranean energy hubs that feed into Europe has further complicated the resolution of these disputes (see Chapter Three).

AEGEAN SEA

The disputes in the Aegean have a far longer history than those in the Mediterranean, but are less likely to trigger conflict at this stage because an understanding has taken hold that territorial seas must not interfere with innocent passage in this critical sea.

In 1936, Greece unilaterally extended its territorial sea to six nautical miles, something Turkiye also did in 1964. By the time of the third UN law-of-the-sea conference in 1982, a 12-nautical-mile limit had become customary around the world, which UNCLOS later enshrined. Turkiye only accepts that Greek islands have territorial waters up to six nautical miles in a way that ensures that these coastlines do not reach Turkiye's waters and allows for free navigation. Greece reserves the right, as UNCLOS permits, to expand this out to 12 nautical miles and has publicly expressed interest in doing so, but has nevertheless so far kept its limit to six nautical miles (which also constitutes its national airspace).

Turkiye's frequent violations of Greece's 10-nautical-mile airspace limit has been another point of contention, as have attendant disputes pertaining to the limits of Greece's flight-information regions and search-and-rescue zones.[41]

Cyprus's turbulent independence in 1960 and subsequent tensions over the island launched a new chapter in the maritime-border disputes. Greece began issuing exploration permits to international oil companies from 1969. Turkiye did not oppose these until 1973, when oil was discovered off the coast of the Greek island of Thasos in the Aegean in waters disputed by Turkiye. Turkiye began issuing exploration permits to the Turkish Petroleum Corporation (TPAO) until July 1974.[42] These moves reopened the continental-shelf question, with Turkiye claiming half of the Aegean,

Turkiye and the unrecognised Turkish Republic of Northern Cyprus conduct the *Martyr Lieutenant Caner Gönyeli* 2023 search-and-rescue exercise offshore the Turkish Republic of Northern Cyprus between 24 and 25 October 2023.
(Photo: Harun Ozalp/Anadolu via Getty Images)

and helped trigger the Greek–Turkish crisis over Cyprus in 1974, which ultimately resulted in the Turkish invasion of northern Cyprus. Turkiye also requested in 1975 that Greece reduce the limit of its national airspace to six nautical miles, which Greece did not accept.

The 1976 Bern agreement, however, marked the end of this crisis period and included a moratorium on offshore activities. It also forged an 'agree to disagree' approach in the Aegean, even if the question of territorial-sea delimitation remains at the core of today's dispute.

According to the Turkish Ministry of Foreign Affairs:

> Turkish policy is based on respect for the status quo whereas Greece appears determined to alter it in its favor. The threat of extending Greek territorial waters beyond their present width of 6 miles … the remilitarization of the Eastern Aegean Islands placed under demilitarized status by virtue of the very agreements ceding them to Greece, a 10 mile 'national air space' over territorial waters of 6 [nautical miles] … can be counted among these efforts which are the real underlying causes of the Turco-Greek conflict.[43]

To this day, Greece and Turkiye maintain a six-nautical-mile limit to the territorial sea in the Aegean, but Turkiye asserts a 12-nautical-mile limit in the Eastern Mediterranean.[44]

From 1974 to 1995, Greek–Turkish maritime-border disputes remained relatively quiet, but the entry into force of UNCLOS in 1994 and the enshrinement of the 12-nautical-mile limit prompted Greece to submit legislation to extend its territorial sea. Turkiye responded by adopting a resolution in 1995 that would treat such an extension as a *casus belli*. In December 1995, a Turkish cargo ship ran aground at Imia and refused help from Greek tugboats because it claimed the ship was in Turkish waters, setting off a diplomatic crisis that ultimately had to be settled through US diplomatic intervention.

This episode led Turkiye to launch in 1996 a 'grey area' policy that strategically questions Greek sovereignty over rocks, islets and islands in the Aegean and beyond to include islands such as Gavdos to the south of Crete, which Turkiye argues were not legally ceded to Greece through international treaties. According to Turkish officials, Turkiye has kept the exact number of islands vague in order to preserve good faith for an eventual resolution through negotiations.

The 'grey area' policy underscored two fundamentally different approaches to reaching agreement on how to delimit continental shelves. Turkiye seeks all-encompassing talks that review all bilateral problems in the Aegean and Eastern Mediterranean seas, including territorial waters, demilitarisation of Greek islands and ownership rights, whereas Greece considers that the dispute over the delineation of the continental shelves is the main one.[45]

CYPRUS

The next round of Greek–Turkish tensions started in 2003, after Cyprus and Egypt concluded an agreement to delimit their EEZs. Turkiye lodged a formal objection with the UN, maintaining that the agreement violated its continental shelf.[46] It responded similarly to Cyprus's agreements with Lebanon in 2007 and Israel in 2010.

Since international law does not allow a third party to interfere with two countries reaching an EEZ delimitation agreement, Turkiye's approach was fruitless. It therefore took a new approach. Starting in 2004, Turkiye claimed that the territorial sea to the west of the 32° 16' 18'' meridian belonged to it based on relative coastal length, proportionality, distance and non-encroachment (see Map 2.3).[47]

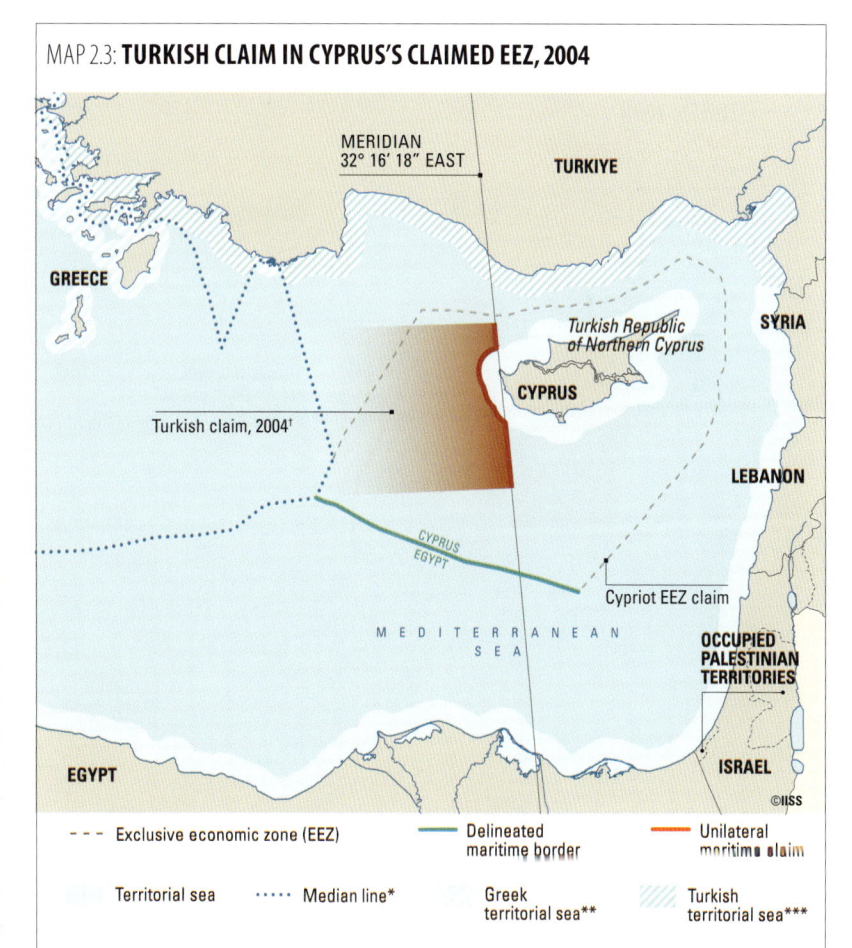

MAP 2.3: **TURKISH CLAIM IN CYPRUS'S CLAIMED EEZ, 2004**

*Prior to the 2011 passing of Law 4001/2011, Greece based its unilateral claim to a continental shelf and EEZ on the median line, as outlined in UNCLOS and customary international law. **Greece maintains a six-nautical-mile limit to its territorial sea in the Aegean. ***Turkiye maintains a six-nautical-mile limit to its territorial sea in the Aegean and a 12-nautical-mile limit to its territorial sea in the Eastern Mediterranean.
†The claim made by Turkiye, published by the UN in the Law of the Sea Bulletin No. 54, intended to reserve 'all its legal rights related to the delimitation of the maritime areas including the seabed and subsoil and the superjacent waters in the west of the longitude 32° 16' 18'' but gave no indication of the western terminus of the claim.
Note: Entities in italics lack recognition, statehood or full UN membership.
Sources: Government and UN documents; IISS analysis; Sovereign Limits blog

The Cyprus dispute intensified in 2004 after Cyprus became a full member of the EU, which gave the country the right to apply EU legislation to exploration for hydrocarbons and, more importantly, to expect the diplomatic backing of EU member states while pursuing its interests.

In 2007, the publication of an EU-commissioned map that was prepared by the University of Seville in 2003, the so-called Seville Map, drew maximalist maritime borders for Cyprus and Greece and ignored Turkish claims.

Though the map was originally drawn up for environmental assessments and the US and EU later disavowed it, it heightened tensions as Turkiye considered it a Western plot to back Greece in their maritime-border dispute. Some observers identify the map's publication as the starting point of the current crisis.[48]

The increase in tensions, however, mostly resulted from the Cypriot government promulgating its 2007 Hydrocarbon Law in January and then, in February 2007, issuing its first licensing round for hydrocarbons exploration in 11 offshore blocks in waters south of the island that Turkiye disputed.[49]

The licensing round only attracted three bids, a low number reflecting the chilling effect of the geopolitical risk tied to the maritime dispute, and only one licence was awarded in 2008: to US medium-sized oil-and-gas exploration and production company Noble Energy, now part of energy giant Chevron. Noble Energy later became the most prominent operator in Israeli offshore-gas exploration and development, discovering the Tamar gas field in 2009 and Leviathan in 2010.

To counter Cyprus's moves, the self-proclaimed TRNC president Mehmet Ali Talat registered objections in April 2009 with the UN, but he did so through Turkiye as the TRNC lacks UN membership and international recognition. Talat noted that such unilateral activities before a settlement 'are aimed at prejudging and violating the fundamental rights and interests of the Turkish Cypriot people'.[50] Turkiye also became more proactive in asserting its rights to its own continental-shelf claims and blocking Cyprus's exploration plans by granting TPAO exploration licences in areas within this zone in 2008, which were published in Turkiye's *Official Gazette* in 2009 (see Map 2.4).[51]

In 2011, Turkiye announced a continental-shelf delineation agreement with the unrecognised TRNC in violation of the median-line principle and the Cypriot EEZ claim. Turkiye expanded its claims in 2012 (see Map 2.5), announcing TPAO concessions in areas claimed by Cyprus to the north and west of the island.

Moreover, Turkiye encouraged the TRNC to make claims south of the island even though, as an entity lacking international recognition, the TRNC is not entitled to offer any concessions. The TRNC proceeded and granted concessions to the TPAO in April 2012,[52] two months after Cyprus launched its second licensing round.[53]

Cyprus's licensing round in 2012 was an act of defiance intended to assert its sovereignty. It was launched in an area that Turkiye had claimed as part of its

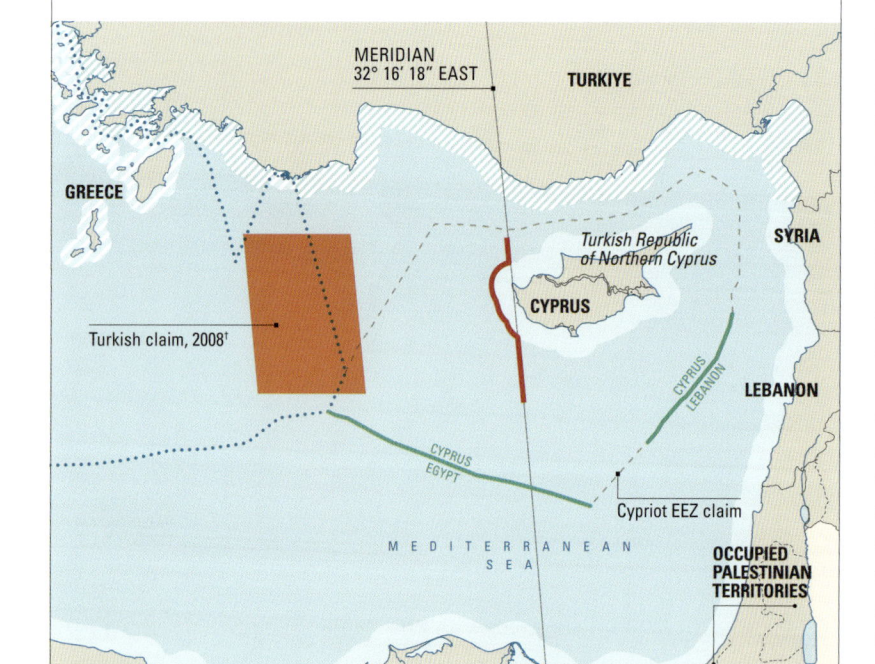

MAP 2.4: TURKISH CLAIMS IN CYPRUS'S AND GREECE'S CLAIMED MARITIME ZONES, 2008

- - - Exclusive economic zone (EEZ)
— Delineated maritime border
— Unilateral maritime claim
Territorial sea
····· Median line*
Greek territorial sea**
Turkish territorial sea***

*Prior to the 2011 passing of Law 4001/2011, Greece based its unilateral claim to a continental shelf and EEZ on the median line, as outlined in UNCLOS and customary international law. **Greece maintains a six-nautical-mile limit to its territorial sea in the Aegean. ***Turkiye maintains a six-nautical-mile limit to its territorial sea in the Aegean and a 12-nautical-mile limit to its territorial sea in the Eastern Mediterranean.
†The claim is based upon hydrocarbon-exploration licences granted to TPAO in 2008 and published in the Turkish *Official Gazette* on 16 July 2009.
Note: Entities in italics lack recognition, statehood or full UN membership.
Sources: Government and UN documents; IISS analysis; Sovereign Limits blog

own continental shelf, a position it has maintained since the 2003 Cyprus–Egypt border delimitation. By this stage, the battle lines in the dispute had become openly political. Whereas Greece and Turkiye had publicly discussed resolving their disputes through legal channels and in good faith at various stages before 2012, the allure of gas revenues made these issues political red lines for both countries.

There was brief hope in 2014 that an agreement regarding Cyprus could be reached, highlighted by then-vice president of the United States Joe Biden's visit to the island to support energy cooperation and unification, but this did not alter Greece–Turkiye dynamics. That hope has since faded due to the deterioration in US–Turkish relations since 2016; failed negotiations over the Cyprus question in 2017 at Crans-Montana, Switzerland; the heated confrontations over exploration ships from 2018 to 2020; and the warming of relations between the US on the one hand, and Greece and Cyprus on the other.

TURKIYE'S 'BLUE HOMELAND' STRATEGY

In response to the acceleration of exploration activities around Cyprus, Turkiye has turned to maritime brinkmanship to jolt and drive away international companies exploring for gas by raising the risk.

In 2019, the Turkish navy undertook large-scale exercises which invoked a strategic doctrine that had been years in the making: the so-called *Mavi Vatan* ('Blue Homeland'). Blue Homeland was first conceived in 2006 by then-head of Turkish naval planning Admiral Cem Gürdeniz as a way for Turkiye to assert its foreign-policy ambitions. The doctrine informs all of Turkiye's maritime claims to date. It expresses the country's maximalist vision for an expansion of Turkish maritime rights and power by encroaching on Greece's and Cyprus's arguably maximalist claims to their respective EEZs and extending Turkiye's maritime rights to the eastern half of the Aegean. It stops short of encroaching on the six-mile territorial waters of Greek islands.[54]

The most high-profile demonstration of this doctrine occurred in August–September 2020 when the *Oruç Reis* exploration vessel, accompanied by Turkish navy vessels, explored for hydrocarbons in disputed waters. The policy is consistent with Turkiye's historical stance of defending its claims to a continental-shelf limit

MAP 2.5: TURKISH CLAIMS IN CYPRUS'S AND GREECE'S CLAIMED MARITIME ZONES, 2011–12

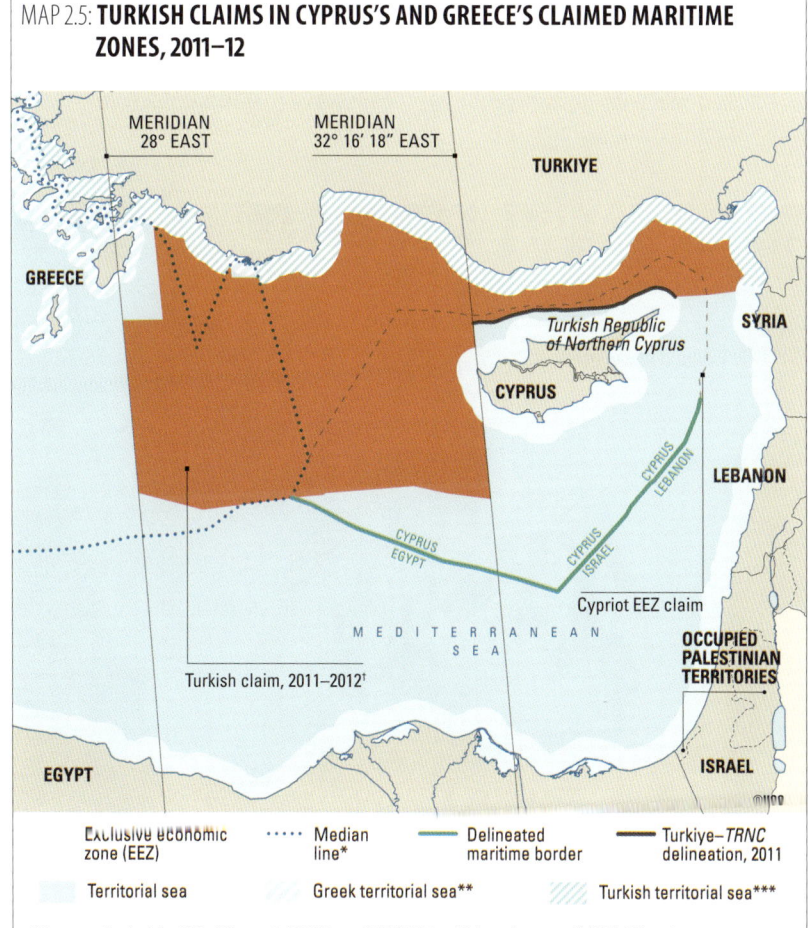

*As stated in Article 156 of Greece's 2011 Law 4001/2011, which took note of UNCLOS and customary international law, in the absence of a delineation agreement the outer limit of the Greek continental shelf and EEZ is the median line. **Greece maintains a six-nautical-mile limit to its territorial sea in the Aegean. ***Turkiye maintains a six-nautical-mile limit to its territorial sea in the Aegean and a 12-nautical-mile limit to its territorial sea in the Eastern Mediterranean. †The claim is based upon hydrocarbon-exploration licences granted to TPAO in 2012 and published in the Turkish *Official Gazette* on 27 April 2012, and the Turkiye–TRNC delineation signed on 21 September 2011.
Note: Entities in italics lack recognition, statehood or full UN membership.
Sources: Government and UN documents; IISS analysis; Sovereign Limits blog

> THE RESOLUTION OF THE CYPRUS QUESTION IS AN EXPLICIT PRECONDITION FOR TURKIYE JOINING THE EAST MEDITERRANEAN GAS FORUM. WERE THAT TO HAPPEN, IT WOULD GO A LONG WAY IN DE-ESCALATING GREECE–TURKIYE DISPUTES OVER MARITIME BORDERS.

that extends up to a median line with the Egyptian EEZ, upon which Cyprus's offshore blocks encroach. In Ankara's view, hydrocarbon activities are unacceptable unless they consider the rights of Turkish Cypriots, which requires a solution to the Cyprus question more broadly.[55] A change in leadership in Turkiye would not alter these claims, as they have cross-partisan support among Turkish parties.

Meanwhile, Turkiye has continued to issue verbal threats towards Greece and Cyprus. In December 2022, then-foreign minister of Turkiye Mevlüt Çavuşoğlu again reiterated the 1995 policy: a Greek move to extend its territorial seas out to 12 nautical miles would constitute a reason for war.[56] In 2022, Turkish President Recep Tayyip Erdoğan repeatedly threatened to invade Greece overnight.[57]

The likelihood that these threats will turn kinetic without additional aggravating events or brinkmanship remains low. Tensions have mostly cooled since late 2020, when the EU agreed to impose only limited sanctions on Turkiye for its brinkmanship and Germany successfully mediated a de-escalation. Also, the discovery of large gas reserves in Turkiye's undisputed waters in the Black Sea since this crisis has shifted Ankara's energy-policy focus, as these fields make it easier to produce and export gas, including through existing infrastructure.

In December 2023, Erdoğan and his Greek counterpart Prime Minister Kyriakos Mitsotakis furthered a warming of relations that had started when the two countries assisted each other in their mutual responses to natural disasters earlier that year.[58]

Despite these improving relations, Greece and Turkiye have remained consistent in how they pursue their maritime-border claims. Turkiye has sought a holistic solution that is not strictly in line with UNCLOS determinations but operates within UNCLOS equity principles. However, it also demonstrated in 1974 and again in 2019–20 a willingness to exert military force to pursue its interests in the Eastern Mediterranean when it feels it must respond to what it perceives as Greek provocations.

Youth members of a Turkish political group distribute literature about Turkiye's *Mavi Vatan* ('Blue Homeland') doctrine, which expresses the country's maximalist vision for an expansion of maritime rights and power in the Aegean Sea, Black Sea and Eastern Mediterranean, in the Kadıköy district of Istanbul, Turkiye, in October 2020. (Photo: Diego Cupolo/ NurPhoto via Getty Images)

Greece has little reason to shift its policy approach while it continues to rely on international law to pursue its claims. In fact, it seems as though both sides use the conflict to score political points at home. Given these dynamics, it is reasonable to conclude that a frozen disagreement is unlikely to transform into a kinetic conflict, unless Cyprus starts exploiting gas in waters where Turkiye believes it has a claim.

PATHWAYS TO RESOLUTION, AND OUTLOOK

With political tensions paralysing dispute resolution through international legal forums, the trend in the Eastern Mediterranean has increasingly moved in favour of agreements based not on the law but rather on compromises reflecting geopolitical and commercial considerations, which may not have taken into account the legal rights of third parties. This seems set to remain the case, at least as long as Turkiye does not become a party to UNCLOS.

The fraying of the US-backed rules-based international order and the rise of regional and international power dynamics further support this general outlook. Countries are now searching for more local and regional solutions in a fragmenting world.[59]

Nevertheless, the legal framework set out by UNCLOS serves as an invaluable baseline for discussion instead of kinetic engagement. UNCLOS, and dispute settlement under its regime, have value in de-escalating tensions in some circumstances and its rules have been applied in the successful negotiation of numerous bilateral maritime borders around the world.

Yet the window of opportunity to pragmatically resolve outstanding disputes in the Eastern Mediterranean could be narrow. This is due in part to the limited time for littoral countries to reap the potential economic benefits of offshore-gas discoveries, either for domestic consumption or exporting to Europe, given the ongoing energy transition. While commercial drivers have facilitated some deals, they also need powerful outside sponsors and domestic political support.

In the linchpin case of Greece–Turkiye, the commercial advantages each stands to obtain from a major infrastructural integration of the region are clear, even though the domestic political headwinds remain hard to overcome. Whether they can achieve the breakthrough needed remains hard to predict.

The EMGF provides the regional architecture in which members who are already exploiting offshore assets can work on further integration to open new export routes and markets. The resolution of the Cyprus question is an explicit precondition for Turkiye joining the EMGF. Were that to happen, it would go a long way in resolving the problems of the last decade and de-escalating Greece–Turkiye disputes over maritime borders.

Commercial incentives and support from hydrocarbon majors capable of investing in finding and processing the gas, coupled with a conducive domestic political situation, could bring Turkiye into the fold and turn a seemingly unsolvable legal and diplomatic situation into a win–win for the region.

This could take the form of a regional revenue-sharing agreement for energy exploration and production that assumes an 'agree to disagree' policy on maritime borders, produces bilateral deals or, better yet, sees Turkiye join the EMGF. Prior to the Hamas-led 7 October attacks against Israel and the subsequent Israel–Hamas war, many saw the US-brokered deal between Israel and Lebanon, in which political and private commercial interests aligned to produce a positive result, as a possible model for the region.

Geopolitics will remain the dominant force shaping regional dynamics, including energy choices. Whether and how the US re-engages in the region could have consequences for the chances of a resolution of the Greek–Turkish–Cypriot disputes. An increased American investment in the relationship with Cyprus and Greece, if not accompanied by a reset in relations with Turkiye, may lead to more brinkmanship and maximalist lawfare. How European countries such as Germany and France emerge from the geopolitical challenge of the Russia–Ukraine war will also have repercussions for their ability to mediate a resolution.

ENDNOTES

1. This jurisprudence recalls the wording of UNCLOS reflecting customary international law, which requires delimitation between states with opposite or adjacent coasts by agreement, or in its absence by resorting to peaceful dispute-settlement mechanisms such as mediation, arbitration or adjudication.

2. The commission was established to advance the development and codification of international law and to address the evolving needs and challenges of the international community.

3. Nicholas A. Ioannides, *Maritime Claims and Boundary Delimitation: Tensions and Trends in the Eastern Mediterranean Sea* (New York: Routledge, 2020), p. 5.

4. Angelo Syrigos and Thanos Dokos, *Atlas of Greek-Turkish Relations* (Piraeus, Greece: Kathimerini, 2020), pp. 19, 21, 41.

5. '1936 Convention Regarding the Regime of the Straits', https://cil.nus.edu.sg/wp-content/uploads/2019/02/1936-Convention-Regarding-the-Regime-of-the-Straits-1.pdf.

6. 'Turkey-Greece: From Maritime Brinkmanship to Dialogue', International Crisis Group, 31 May 2021, pp. 38–39, https://www.crisisgroup.org/europe-central-asia/western-europemediterranean-turkiye-cyprus/turkey-greece-maritime-brinkmanship.

7. Tullio Treves, '1958 Geneva Conventions on the Law of the Sea: Introductory Note', UN Audiovisual Library of International Law, September 2008, https://legal.un.org/avl/ha/gclos/gclos.html.

8. Ioannides, *Maritime Claims and Boundary Delimitation*, p. 9.

9. Surabhi Ranganathan, 'Decolonization and International Law: Putting the Ocean on the Map', *Journal of the History of International Law*, vol. 23, no. 1, December 2020, pp. 161–83.

10. Alexander Loengarov, 'Between Maritime Law and Politics in the East Mediterranean', Washington Institute for Near East Policy, 24 March 2022.

11. Andreas Østhagen, 'Maritime Boundary Disputes: What are They and Why do They Matter?' *Marine Policy*, vol. 120, October 2020.

12. Ioannides, *Maritime Claims and Boundary Delimitation*, pp. 19, 37.

13. Ibid.

14. 'Letter Dated 18 March 2020 from the Permanent Representative of Turkey to the United Nations Addressed to the Secretary-General', UN Digital Library, 18 March 2020, https://digitallibrary.un.org/record/3856643?ln=en.

15. Ergun Olgun, 'Turkish Cypriot View: A Confederation for the "Island of Cyprus"?', Republic of Turkiye, Ministry of Foreign Affairs, https://www.mfa.gov.tr/turkish-cypriot-view_-a-confederation-for-the-_island-of-cyprus__.en.mfa.

16. 'Freedom of Navigation in the East Med Sea', *MariTimesCrimes*, 22 March 2022, https://maritimescrimes.com/2022/03/22/freedom-of-navigation-in-the-east-med-sea/.

17. Anthee Carassava, 'France Sends Forces to Mediterranean as Greece, Turkey Dispute Territory', Voice of America, 14 August 2020, https://www.voanews.com/a/rance_france-sends-forces-mediterranean-greece-Turkiye-dispute-territory/6194437.html.

18. Loengarov, 'Between Maritime Law and Politics in the East Mediterranean'.

19. Ioannides, *Maritime Claims and Boundary Delimitation*, pp. 93–94.

20. Syrigos and Dokos, *Atlas of Greek-Turkish Relations*, p. 102.

21. Ibid., p. 101.

22. 'Cyprus and Israel Sign Additional Natgas Info Deal', *Financial Mirror*, 28 April 2014, https://www.financialmirror.com/2014/04/28/cyprus-and-israel-sign-additional-natgas-info-deal/.

23. Ioannis N. Grigoriadis and Lennart T. Belke, 'UNCLOS and the Delimitation of Maritime Zones in the Eastern Mediterranean', ELIAMEP, 17 September 2020, https://www.eliamep.gr/en/publication/η-σύμβαση-των-ηνωμένων-εθνών-για-το-δίκ/.

24. Dan Williams and Maya Gebeily, 'Israel's Lapid to Fast-track Lebanon Maritime Border Deal', Reuters, 12 October 2022, https://www.reuters.com/world/middle-east/us-brokered-deal-is-permanent-equitable-resolution-maritime-dispute-between-2022-10-12/.

25. Constantinos Yiallourides, Nicholas A. Ioannides and Roy Andrew Partain, 'Some Observations on the Agreement Between Lebanon and Israel on the Delimitation of the Exclusive Economic Zone', *European Journal of International Law*, 26 October 2022, https://www.ejiltalk.org/some-observations-on-the-agreement-between-lebanon-and-israel-on-the-delimitation-of-the-exclusive-economic-zone/.

26. Letter from Lebanon to UN, 3 September 2011, https://www.un.org/depts/los/LEGISLATIONANDTREATIES/PDFFILES/communications/lbn_re_isr__listofcoordinates_e.pdf.

27. 'Cypriot Envoy Says Any Maritime Border Dispute with Lebanon "Easily" Resolved', Reuters, 28 October 2022, https://www.reuters.com/world/middle-east/cypriot-envoy-says-any-maritime-border-dispute-with-lebanon-easily-resolved-2022-10-28/.

28. Grigoriadis and Belke, 'UNCLOS and the Delimitation of Maritime Zones in the Eastern Mediterranean'.

29. United Nations, 'Decree of the President of the Arab Republic of Egypt No. 595 (2022) Concerning the Delimitation of the Western Maritime Boundaries of the Arab Republic of Egypt in the Mediterranean Sea', chrome-extension://efaidnbmnnnibpcajpcglclefindmkaj/https://www.un.org/depts/los/LEGISLATIONANDTREATIES/PDFFILES/DEPOSIT/MZN162EDecree595.pdf.

30. Edward Yeranian, 'Egypt Draws Maritime Border, Ignites Tensions Among Regional Gas Alliances', Voice of America, 19 December 2022, https://www.voanews.com/a/egypt-draws-maritime-border-ignites-tensions-among-regional-gas-alliances/6883639.html.

31. Note verbale from Libya to the UN, 13 February 2023, https://digitallibrary.un.org/record/4004589?ln=en&v=pdf.

32. 'Greece, Libya to Hold Talks over Maritime Border Demarcation', Al-Jazeera, 14 April 2021, https://www.aljazeera.com/news/2021/4/14/greece-libya-to-hold-talks-over-maritime-border-demarcation.

33. Vassilis Nedos, 'Tripoli Protests Prospecting South of Crete', *Ekathimerini*, 22 May 2024, https://www.ekathimerini.com/politics/foreign-policy/1239318/tripoli-protests-prospecting-south-of-crete/.

34. 'Israel Gives Nod to Gaza Marine Gas Development', Reuters, 18 June 2023, https://www.reuters.com/business/energy/israel-gives-nod-gaza-marine-gas-development-wants-security-assurances-2023-06-18/.

35. Ahmad Abu Amer, 'Egypt to Negotiate Sea Border with Palestine', Al-Monitor, 3 November 2020, https://www.al-monitor.com/originals/2020/11/palestine-egypt-negotiations-maritime-border-demarcation.html.

36. 'Egypt Oil Min Says Framework Agreement in Place on Gaza Marine Field', Reuters, 25 October 2022, https://www.reuters.com/business/energy/egypt-oil-min-says-framework-agreement-place-gaza-marine-field-2022-10-25/.

37. Letter from Syria to UN, 2014, https://www.un.org/depts/los/LEGISLATIONANDTREATIES/PDFFILES/communications/syria_note_eng.pdf.

38. Anton Mardasov, 'Russia Offers to Mediate in Syria-Lebanon Maritime Border Dispute', Al-Monitor, 21 June 2019, https://www.al-monitor.com/originals/2019/06/russia-lebanon-syria-maritime-dispute.html.

39. Rouba El Husseini and Aya Iskandarani, 'After Israel, Lebanon Eyes Maritime Border Talks with Syria', Al-Monitor, 9 November 2022, https://www.al-monitor.com/originals/2022/11/after-israel-lebanon-eyes-maritime-border-talks-syria#ixzz7wIrnJlZP.

40. 'Clean Energy for EU Islands – Greece', European Commission, https://clean-energy-islands.ec.europa.eu/countries/greece.

41. Syrigos and Dokos, *Atlas of Greek-Turkish Relations*, pp. 25–26.

42 *Ibid.*, p. 46.

43 Republic of Turkiye, Ministry of Foreign Affairs, 'Background Note on Aegean Dispute', https://www.mfa.gov.tr/background-note-on-aegean-dispute.en.mfa.

44 Ioannides, *Maritime Claims and Boundary Delimitation*, pp. 16–17, 75–76.

45 Serhat S. Çubukçuoğlu, 'A Maritime Dispute in the Mediterranean: Assessing the Greece-Turkiye Relationship Through the Lens of Neorealism', *Fletcher Forum of World Affairs*, vol. 45, no. 2, 2021, pp. 65–74.

46 Loengarov, 'Between Maritime Law and Politics in the East Mediterranean'.

47 Çubukçuoğlu, 'A Maritime Dispute in the Mediterranean'.

48 Michaël Tanchum, 'Where to Draw the Line in the Eastern Mediterranean', *Foreign Policy*, 24 March 2021, https://foreignpolicy.com/2021/03/24/where-to-draw-the-line-in-the-eastern-mediterranean/.

49 Anastasios Giamouridis, 'The Offshore Discovery in the Republic of Republic of Cyprus: Monetisation Prospects and Challenges', Oxford Institute for Energy Studies, July 2012, p. 18, https://www.oxfordenergy.org/wpcms/wp-content/uploads/2012/07/NG_65.pdf.

50 'Letter Dated 17 April 2009 from the Permanent Representative of Turkey to the United Nations Addressed to the Secretary-General', UN Digital Library, 17 April 2009, https://digitallibrary.un.org/record/653077?ln=es.

51 Ayla Gürel, Fiona Mullen and Harry Tzimitras, 'The Cyprus Hydrocarbons Issue: Context, Positions and Future Scenarios', Peace Research Institute Oslo, 2013, https://www.prio.org/publications/7365; and Turkiye, Directorate of Administrative Affairs, *Official Gazette*, no. 27290, 16 July 2009, https://www.resmigazete.gov.tr/eskiler/2009/07/20090716.htm.

52 Syrigos and Dokos, *Atlas of Greek-Turkish Relations*, pp. 68–69.

53 'Cyprus Opens Second Hydrocarbons Licensing Round', Reuters, 13 February 2012, https://www.reuters.com/article/idUSL5E8DD2W4/.

54 Cem Gürdeniz, 'What Is the Blue Homeland in the 21st Century?', United World International, 31 July 2020, https://uwidata.com/12952-what-is-the-blue-homeland-in-the-21st-century/.

55 Ioannides, *Maritime Claims and Boundary Delimitation*, p. 109.

56 Nektaria Stamouli, 'Turkey Renews Threat of War over Greek Territorial Sea Dispute', Politico, 29 December 2022, https://www.politico.eu/article/turkey-mevlut-cavusoglu-threat-war-greece-territorial-sea-dispute/.

57 Tristan Fiedler, 'Erdoğan Repeats Threat Against Greece During G20', Politico, 16 November 2022, https://www.politico.eu/article/recep-erdogan-Turkiye-threat-against-greece-g20/.

58 Helena Smith, 'Erdoğan Hails "New Era" of Friendship with Greece in Historic Visit to Athens', *Guardian*, 7 December 2023, https://www.theguardian.com/world/2023/dec/07/erdogan-hails-new-era-of-friendship-with-greece-during-historic-visit-to-athens#:~:text=%E2%80%9CIt%20is%20part%20of%20rapprochement,Turkish%20president%20in%2065%20years.

59 'What Think Tanks Are Thinking: "Deglobalisation"', European Parliament, 29 November 2022, https://www.europarl.europa.eu/RegData/etudes/BRIE/2022/739219/EPRS_BRIE_TT_739219_Deglobalisation_final.pdf.

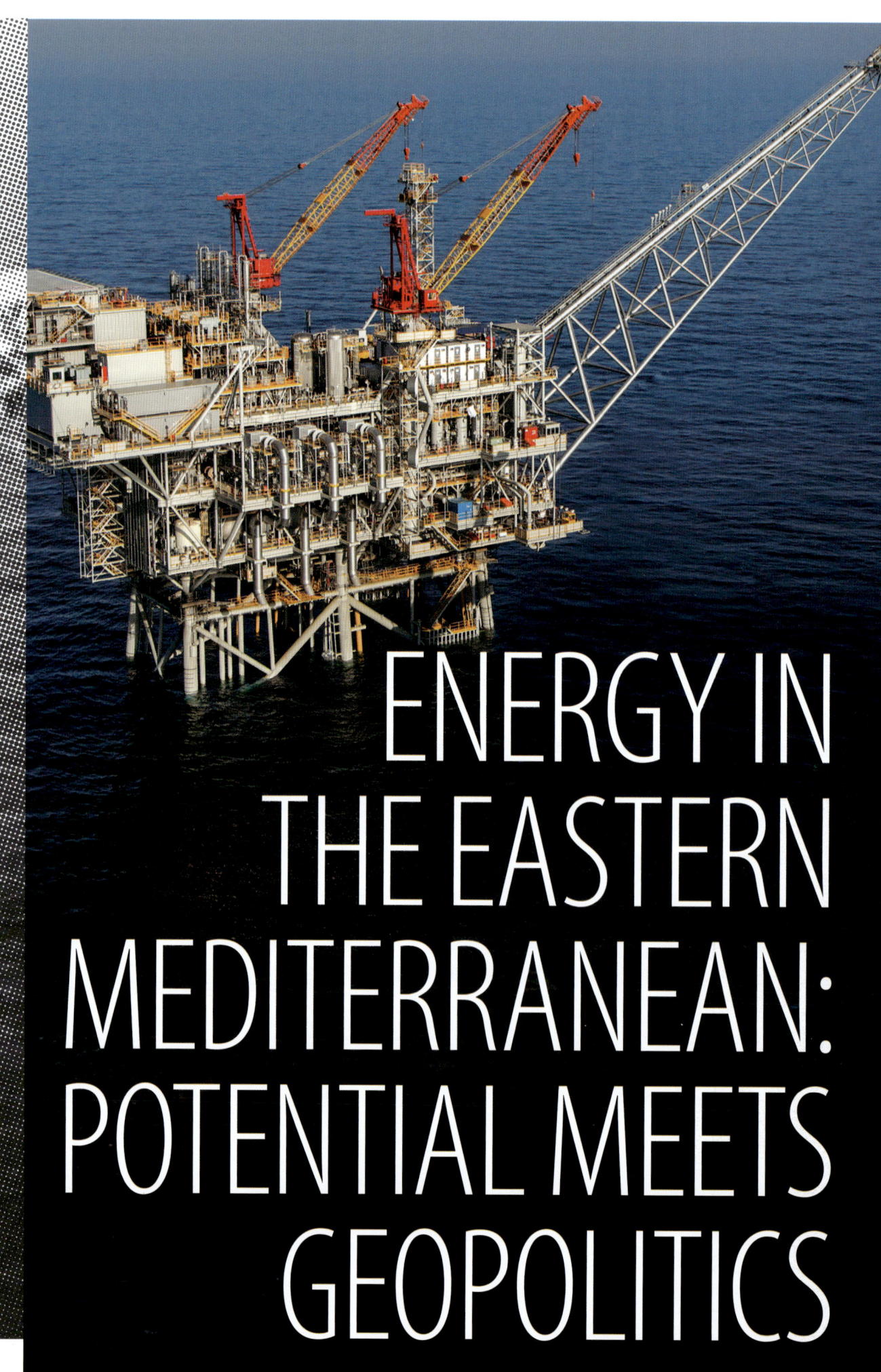

ENERGY IN THE EASTERN MEDITERRANEAN: POTENTIAL MEETS GEOPOLITICS

THEMES | ENERGY IN THE EASTERN MEDITERRANEAN: POTENTIAL MEETS GEOPOLITICS

CHAPTER THREE

GAS DISCOVERIES in the Eastern Mediterranean basin have catalysed regional cooperation among friendly nations, but have not had a transformative effect on a region where geopolitical drivers and domestic concerns dominate decision-making.

GAS REVENUES are crucially important for producing countries, but the Eastern Mediterranean gas stock remains small on the global scale and negligible in terms of current and future global market needs.

DOMESTIC AND REGIONAL DEMAND has underpinned most gas investment in the region to date, but reliable export routes to profitable markets are required to de-risk future investments, in particular for Israel and Cyprus.

ISRAEL IS THE ENERGY-EXPORTING POWERHOUSE of the region, but the full impact of the Israel–Hamas war remains unclear. While it has not disrupted production and export of gas, it has increased the political risk for companies operating in the region.

INTERNATIONAL OIL COMPANIES prefer to use pre-existing liquefied-natural-gas (LNG) infrastructure in Egypt over building new pipelines to the European markets. This has given Egypt a first-mover advantage over Greece and Turkiye, which are also vying to become the region's energy hub.

↑ The Tamar gas field's production platform is seen 24 kilometres west of Ashkelon, Israel, on 28 March 2013. (Photo: Albatross via Getty Images)

INTRODUCTION

The Eastern Mediterranean is a relative newcomer to international trade in natural gas. Whereas Algeria, in the Western Mediterranean, has exported large volumes of gas to Europe since the 1980s, the Eastern Mediterranean has always been a smaller player. Egypt has long produced gas but its domestic market, rather than international markets, has underpinned the sector's growth.

Periodic developments have raised expectations that the Eastern Mediterranean could become a bigger energy player. Egypt was a small but regionally significant gas exporter for a short, ten-year period between 2004 and 2014, and it built the infrastructure necessary to export liquefied natural gas (LNG). But domestic consumption soon surpassed its gas-production capacity and eroded its export potential. A string of gas discoveries in the early 2010s – of the Tamar and especially Leviathan gas fields in Israeli waters, the Aphrodite field offshore Cyprus, and the giant Zohr field in Egypt – were seen by some as a game changer for the region. Egypt was able to quickly commercialise its discoveries. At first, Israel faced more challenges, notably because of its dependency on Egypt's LNG export capacity. The full-fledged development of the sector in Cyprus remains hamstrung by its ongoing territorial disputes with Turkiye.

More recently, Europe's need to diversify its energy sources, having moved away from Russian supplies in the wake of Moscow's 2022 invasion of Ukraine, revived interest in the Eastern Mediterranean as an additional source of natural gas. While every bit counts when diversifying, the Eastern Mediterranean's export capacities cannot rival those of the bigger players.

Cyprus's and Israel's significant gas reserves and relatively modest consumption mean that both could become global

TABLE 3.1: SIGNIFICANT GAS FIELDS IN THE EASTERN MEDITERRANEAN

Country	Gas field	Remaining reserves (billion cubic metres)
Cyprus	Aphrodite/Yishai	127
	Glaucus	85–113
	Zeus	57–85
	Cronos	70
	Calypso	28–57
Egypt	Zohr	652
	West Nile Delta	117
	Nargis	99
	Great Nooros Area	75
	Nour	56
	North Damietta	37
	Disouq	28
	Abu El-Gharadig	20
	Abu Qir	20
	West Delta Deep Marine	14
	Northeast Abu Gharadig	13
	Khalda	13
	Harmattan Deep	11
	El-Manzala and West El-Manzala	10
Israel	Leviathan	412
	Tamar and Tamar Southwest	337
	Karish and Karish North	74
	Katlan (formerly Olympus)	31
	Tanin	29
Occupied Palestinian Territories	Gaza Marine	28

Notes: Gas fields with remaining reserves of ≤10 billion cubic metres have been excluded. Data correct as of December 2023.
Source: IISS analysis

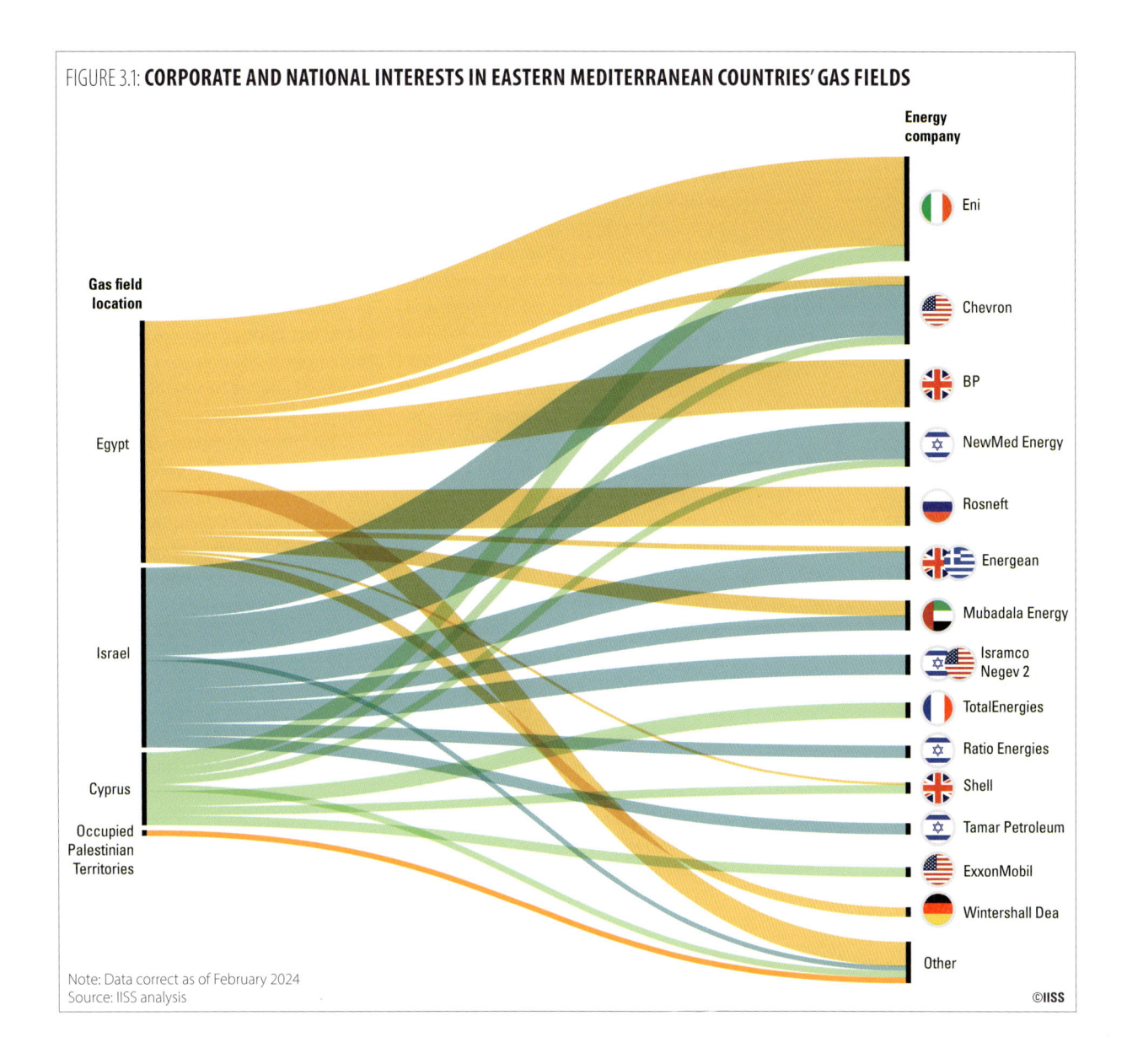

FIGURE 3.1: CORPORATE AND NATIONAL INTERESTS IN EASTERN MEDITERRANEAN COUNTRIES' GAS FIELDS

Gas field location: Egypt, Israel, Cyprus, Occupied Palestinian Territories

Energy company: Eni, Chevron, BP, NewMed Energy, Rosneft, Energean, Mubadala Energy, Isramco Negev 2, TotalEnergies, Ratio Energies, Shell, Tamar Petroleum, ExxonMobil, Wintershall Dea, Other

Note: Data correct as of February 2024
Source: IISS analysis
©IISS

exporters of natural gas, though considerably smaller players than Qatar, Algeria, the United States and other producers of LNG. But decisions about natural-gas infrastructure will determine whether Cyprus and Israel play a part in global or only regional gas markets. Egypt's existing LNG infrastructure has so far been the key to unlocking exports from its neighbours and the country aspires to be the regional hub for Eastern Mediterranean gas. All gas exported from the region has been dispatched from Egypt as LNG, but both of its onshore liquefaction plants currently only have the capacity to export the equivalent of 5% of Europe's gas consumption. That could increase to 13% of Europe's current gas consumption if further infrastructure investments are made. However, other proposals abound, including for long-distance pipelines to Europe and alternative LNG facilities elsewhere in the region, such as the Cyprus Gateway project. Ultimately, geopolitical and geo-economic considerations will play a big part in determining how the region's gas landscape pans out. There is a cautiousness among both Israeli and Cypriot stakeholders about tying themselves too closely to Egypt. There is also a recognition that in the long term all exporters will need to look eastward to Asia, and therefore LNG is their best option.

This chapter will explore the big questions facing the Eastern Mediterranean around whether and how it can surmount the geopolitical, political and commercial obstacles it faces in bringing new gas discoveries onstream, getting that gas to market, and establishing the region as a serious energy player.

EXPLORATION AND PRODUCTION

The Eastern Mediterranean could hold as much as 8 trillion cubic metres (tcm) in discovered and undiscovered recoverable natural-gas reserves. Although these are small compared to the global leader Russia, with its 47 tcm of proven reserves (and potentially 6 tcm more undiscovered),[1] the Eastern Mediterranean's resources are big enough that it could become a moderately important player in the global gas market.[2] However, Cyprus, Egypt and Israel have had varying degrees of success in commercialising the gas discoveries made within their borders; indeed, as of late 2023, Cyprus had yet to produce any gas at all. Lebanon also harbours hopes of finding significant gas reserves, but no discoveries have yet been made.

EGYPT

Egypt is the Eastern Mediterranean's most established and largest gas producer (see Table 3.1 and Figure 3.1). It has produced gas since 1975, initially from gas finds in the Western Desert, and then from gas discoveries in the Nile Delta in the late 1990s and further offshore in the Levantine Basin in the 2000s, which increased production significantly, turning the country into a net producer of gas between 2004 and 2014 (see Figure 3.2). But production fell in the early 2010s and Egypt became a net consumer of gas once again.

It was the discovery of the large Zohr gas field in 2015 that changed Egypt's fortunes, with proven reserves of 849 billion cubic metres (bcm). Zohr came onstream in 2017 and reversed the decline in Egypt's production. By 2022, Egypt produced 64.5 bcm, 7% more than its previous peak and equivalent to 1.6% of global and 25.9% of Africa's gas production. Since the discovery of Zohr, further gas fields have been found, but none is on the same scale. Chevron's discovery of Nargis in 2022 was the largest discovery since Zohr, but is reportedly estimated at only 99 bcm (see Table 3.1).[3] Reflecting concern about falling production, Tarek El-Molla, the Egyptian petroleum minister, stated in December 2022 that Egypt was set to invest a total of US$2.1bn in oil and natural-gas exploration plans and drill more than 300 exploration wells by 2025.[4]

Without further discoveries on a similar scale to Zohr, gas production in Egypt is expected to peak soon. Experts at the Center on Global Energy Policy (CGEP) have forecast production to peak in 2028 at below 80 bcm before declining to around 60 bcm by 2035, close to the output of 2022.[5] The International Energy Agency has suggested similarly that production will be at around 74 bcm in 2030, but then fall more slowly by 1.2% per year until 2050 (reaching 58 bcm), although more ambitious climate policies in Egypt could see production decrease faster.[6]

Nevertheless, Egypt's well-developed gas infrastructure, including for exports, has enabled it to monetise new gas discoveries much more quickly than its neighbours, where infrastructure is lacking. This helped Italy's Eni bring Zohr, the biggest gas field in the Eastern Mediterranean region, onstream in less than two and a half years from discovery – a record time for a field of this size in deep waters.[7] The government has also gradually improved the regulatory framework for gas exploration in Egypt to encourage new investment. From around 2015, it awarded higher-risk areas for exploration and made favourable modifications to its production-sharing agreements and to the gas price companies would get.[8] This successfully bolstered investment sentiment and led to several discoveries, including Eni's discovery of Zohr.

The main challenges for investors in Egypt's gas production have been the country's failure to liberalise fully its gas market and its recurring economic crises. The government made some progress towards liberalisation, particularly through significant 2017 reforms granting third-party access to the national pipelines, and announced that the market would be fully liberalised by 2022. This progress has stalled, however, with the state continuing to intervene in the gas market and publish prices for natural gas in various uses such as steel, ammonia and electricity generation.[9] Moreover, the government's 2022 road map for the regulation of the gas industry, with an appendix listing 'Justifications for Maintaining/Increasing State's Investments in Some Economic Activities and Sectors', signalled this approach will continue. As Mathios Rigas, CEO of Energean, an investor in Egypt, stated in a 2022 interview, companies like his own will prioritise investment elsewhere if the Egyptian government forces them to sell gas at almost a tenth of global prices.[10] Additionally, Egypt's rising domestic consumption has eroded its export potential, compelling the authorities to ship gas from Israel via a pipeline. This has been politically embarrassing for the government, though it helped consolidate the relationship with Israel at a time of high regional volatility and deteriorating US–Egypt ties.

Moreover, Egypt's economic crises have caused the government and the state-owned Egyptian General Petroleum Company (EGPC) to accumulate arrears to international oil and gas companies. Amid the economic chaos caused by the 2011 Egyptian revolution, the government's arrears shot up to US$6.3bn, and these persisted, being gradually paid until 2021.[11] The failure to make timely payments led investors including Shell to demur on the further development of Egyptian gas fields.[12]

Egypt's economy has recently run into new troubles. Despite the development of Zohr, Egypt's gas exports remain minimal, depriving the government of much-needed revenues, while foreign investors have withdrawn from Egyptian debt. At the same time, Russia's full-scale invasion of Ukraine led to rising food-import prices and the loss of tourism revenue from Russia and Ukraine, which previously accounted for a large share of the country's inbound tourism. All this has taken place against the backdrop of rapidly rising government debt due to excessive state spending on infrastructure megaprojects, with public debt reaching almost 90% of GDP. Together, these factors have caused the current-account deficit to surge and have placed pressure on the value of the Egyptian pound. Forced by the IMF to float its exchange rate in October 2022, the value of the Egyptian pound had fallen by around 50% by July 2023 and the country faces a severe shortage of US dollars.[13] A new US$8bn IMF loan package was announced in March 2024, with Egypt agreeing to adopt a flexible exchange rate, tighten its monetary and fiscal policies and reduce its infrastructure spending.[14] In the two years leading up to March 2024, the Egyptian lira has lost 68% of its value against the dollar.

In the meantime, the Egyptian government has once again failed to make payments owed to foreign gas producers in the country. (It has also failed to clear imports at its ports due to its dollar shortages.) Moreover, with the cash-strapped bureaucracy increasingly strained,[15] and qualified labour expected to leave Egypt in search of jobs elsewhere, foreign investors are likely to face growing problems operating in the country.

Economic and political grievances ensure an underlying risk of social and political unrest. The chaotic experience of the Arab uprisings in Egypt in 2011, the military coup of 2013, and the return of authoritarian rule under Field Marshal Abdel Fattah al-Sisi since 2014 has instilled a wariness about the prospect of political instability. The military's control of the country's institutions also provides a superficial stability. But other risk factors abound. In particular, the

Egyptian Minister of Petroleum and Mineral Resources Tarek El-Molla (C) speaks during the opening session of the 24th ministerial meeting of the Gas Exporting Countries Forum in Cairo, Egypt, on 25 October 2022. (Photo: Khaled Desouki/AFP via Getty Images)

share of Egypt's youth (aged 15–24) not in education, employment or training remains high at around 30%, and the lack of opportunities ensures lingering discontent among this growing segment of the population.[16] Stubbornly high headline inflation hovered around 30% in 2022–23, with food inflation even higher at around 60%, causing serious erosion of Egyptians' living standards.[17] An outbreak of social unrest, leading to a violent crackdown, a new revolution or new terrorist challenges, is unlikely in the near future but remains a risk.

ISRAEL

Israel's gas production has increased steadily since 2004, with the discovery and development of new and larger fields (see figures 3.3 and 3.5). The two small offshore discoveries in 1999–2000, Noa and Mari-B, confirmed the presence of gas reserves,[18] but it was the discovery of the Tamar field in 2009 and especially Leviathan in 2010 that opened the door to the development of a significant gas industry. Once the Tamar gas field came onstream in 2013, Israel became self-sufficient in natural gas. And with the start of production from Leviathan in 2020, the country began producing gas well in excess of domestic demand, becoming a net producer. Israel has discovered several more gas fields since, including Karish, which borders Lebanese waters, but these more recent discoveries have all been a fraction of the size of Tamar and Leviathan (see Table 3.1). Although Israel has just 0.6 tcm of proved gas reserves currently – equivalent to 0.3% of global reserves – the Israeli government hopes to identify additional gas resources of 0.5 to 1 tcm over the next decade.[19]

The outlook for Israeli gas production is supported by plans for the further expansion of the Leviathan and Tamar fields, and the likelihood of other discoveries coming onstream. Currently, Leviathan is producing at a maximum capacity of 12 bcm per year (bcm/y); however, there are plans to increase its capacity to 14 bcm/y by 2025 and 21 bcm/y in the longer term, according to NewMed Energy, one of the licensees.[20] Production from Tamar

European Commissioner for Energy Kadri Simson (L), European Commission President Ursula von der Leyen (2nd L), Egyptian Minister of Petroleum and Mineral Resources Tarek El-Molla (2nd R) and Israeli energy minister Karine Elharrar (R) at the signing of an MoU between Egypt, the EU and Israel at the 7th ministerial meeting of the East Mediterranean Gas Forum in Cairo, Egypt, on 15 June 2022. (Photo: Khaled Desouki/ AFP via Getty Images)

will also increase to 12.3 bcm/y by 2025, up from 11 bcm/y, with a second phase of expansion taking place after 2025 with an undeclared target to date.[21] According to the CGEP, Israel's gas supply is forecasted to reach 42.6 bcm/y by 2027, nearly double its current output, and then continue at that level, unless further major discoveries are made.

One of the main obstacles to the expansion of Israel's gas production is the continued enforcement of a strict cap on gas exports. Securing supplies for the domestic market has been Israel's priority, whereas exporting gas has been a controversial issue as some feared it would increase the country's dependence on foreign states.[22] Therefore, in 2013, the government required that 60% of the gas reserves be made exclusively available for the domestic market. With domestic demand now fully met, this has been an obstacle to scaling up production further. In 2022, Israel produced around 22 bcm – nearly 10 bcm more than domestic consumption. A debate is ongoing over whether to increase the country's export quota. The government first proposed to lower the limit to 40% in 2021,[23] and in August 2023, Israel's energy minister came out in favour of increasing exports, but opposition to such a change remains.[24] The Hamas-led 7 October attacks against Israel and the Israel–Hamas war that ensued may push the government to adopt an even more conservative approach to its energy security.

Besides the cap, the potential export routes for Israeli gas are an issue for the further ramp-up of Israel's gas production too. The direct pipeline to Egypt has a capacity of 7 bcm/y, and deliveries to Egypt via Jordan are limited both by the size of the Israel–Jordan pipelines (3 bcm/y) and by Jordan's own consumption of Israeli gas. Therefore, new pipelines or alternative export routes are essential to scale up Israel's gas production further.

Aside from these regulatory restrictions, geopolitical factors, including international companies' concerns that investing in Israel might harm their investments in the Arab region, hindered the development of Israel's gas reserves. Large international oil and gas companies appeared to shy away from investing in Israel even after large discoveries were made in the country. Instead, Israel's gas sector has long been dominated by small companies, both local and international. US firm Noble Energy and Israeli entity Delek Drilling (now known as NewMed Energy) were the main investors at first, developing the small Mari-B and Noa fields, and then the larger Tamar and Leviathan fields. More recently, Energean, a British–Greek company, acquired a large number of blocks in Israel, along with various small Indian and local companies, following government interventions to disrupt Noble Energy and NewMed Energy's monopoly in the sector.

However, the normalisation agreement signed by Israel and the United Arab Emirates in 2020, known as the Abraham Accords, significantly reduced the geopolitical risks of investing in Israel. That same year, Chevron entered the Israeli gas sector through its acquisition of Noble Energy, and the following year UAE state-owned enterprise Mubadala Energy (then Mubadala Petroleum) acquired a 22% stake in Israel's Tamar gas field for US$1bn (see Figure 3.1). The Mubadala Energy investment was the largest deal between the UAE and Israel at that time. Illustrative of global interest in Israeli gas, five out of the nine companies that bid for exploration during Israel's fourth licensing round in December 2022 were new to the Israeli market.

Despite significant improvements in Israel's geopolitical position pre-7 October, Israel's increasingly fractious domestic politics introduced risks for gas investors in the country. Instability in Israeli politics has caused repeated disruptions in decision-making in recent years.[25] In 2023, prior to the Hamas-led attacks, the IMF had warned that 'absent the emergence of a durable and politically sustainable solution, continued uncertainty could significantly increase the price of risk in the economy, tightening financial conditions and hindering investment and consumption, with potential repercussions for growth, also in the longer term'.[26] For instance, this has resulted in delays in resolving the unitisation of the Aphrodite/Yishai gas field between Israel and Cyprus.

How the 7 October attacks will shape Israel's energy future is unclear at the time of writing. Energy diplomacy has been a major plank of Israel's regional-integration strategy, embedding the country in regional networks such as the East Mediterranean Gas Forum. This has contributed to improved relations with Cyprus, Egypt, Greece and Jordan and fostered the perhaps unrealistic sense that energy interests could stabilise the area's politics. The 2022 US-mediated maritime-demarcation deal between Israel and Lebanon was seen as an example of this. The 2023 war between Israel and Hamas and the regional escalation that ensued shattered this thinking, though without dealing a setback to existing projects and investments.

In the immediate aftermath of the attacks, the energy sector proved resilient. The war in Gaza has had a minimal impact on Israeli gas production and exploration, and only a momentary effect on gas exports to Egypt. While some companies temporarily shut down some exploration and production operations at the request of the Israeli government, others have continued to supply Israel with energy during the war.[27] For instance, while Chevron suspended the operations on a platform in the Tamar gas field off the coast of Gaza for just over a month, Chevron's other operations continued normally, while Energean provided up to 60% of all of Israel's gas demand.[28] Israel was also keen to demonstrate steadiness. For example, only three weeks after the attacks, it awarded 12 exploration concessions to six companies, including BP and Eni. However, in March 2024, Israel's NewMed Energy announced that BP and the UAE's national oil company ADNOC had suspended discussions over a much-anticipated acquisition of 50% of NewMed Energy due to 'uncertainty created by the external environment'. NewMed's statement added that 'there can be no certainty that discussions will resume or that an agreement will be reached in the future, nor as to the terms of an agreement should one be reached'.[29] The suspension illustrated starkly investors' concern over the exposure to regional conflict and political spillover. But industry insiders also reported that, in addition to the deteriorated geopolitical context, the parties to the potential deal had disagreed on financial terms.

Over the longer term, the conflict has highlighted other latent security and geopolitical risks, and by extension raised concerns about regional integration. In November, Jordan froze but did not cancel the signing of a much-awaited water-for-energy deal to protest against Israel's campaign in Gaza. Egyptians, both in the elite and among the general public, have called for a suspension of energy and economic relations; however, the government dismissed such measures given Egypt's financial and energy dependency on Israeli gas, reluctance to antagonise its partners, notably the US, and continued attachment to the peace agreement with Israel.

While Hamas did not hit offshore gas facilities, likely due to a lack of appropriate weapons systems, the possibility of such attacks is now more prominent in investors' minds in this heightened risk environment. Importantly, Lebanese Hizbullah is known to have more advanced capabilities, including uninhabited aerial vehicles, unmanned underwater vehicles and anti-ship cruise missiles, though the distance from Lebanon to Israeli facilities is greater.

An additional risk relates to gas fields located within maritime zones off the coast of Gaza claimed by the State of Palestine, notably Gaza Marine, which is estimated roughly to contain over 1trn cubic feet of natural gas. Some contract licences awarded to international energy companies in October 2023 may violate international law as they reach into the maritime zones of the Palestinian Gaza Strip, according to Palestinian officials and human-rights organisations.[30] The licences granted include zone G adjacent to Gaza, which overlaps with 62% of the State of Palestine's declared maritime boundaries. Zones H and E also include Palestinian claims (73% and 5% respectively). These maritime zones were claimed in 2019 by the State of Palestine based on the United Nations Convention on the Law of the Sea (UNCLOS). However, Israel is not a signatory to UNCLOS, rejects Palestinian maritime claims and argues that the State of Palestine lacks the standing to declare boundaries or to refer the case to the International Court of Justice because it is not a UN-recognised member state.

In this more complex environment, the relationship between Israel and Cyprus continues to thrive. Cyprus may ultimately benefit from a rethink of Israel's energy policies, which so far have

The Leviathan gas field's production platform is pictured from the beach at Nahsholim, northern Israel, on 29 August 2022. (Photo: Jack Guez/AFP via Getty Images)

prioritised exports through Egypt, in part to bind Cairo politically and strategically but also because of cost and efficiency. Should Cyprus develop the necessary infrastructure as part of the Cyprus Gateway vision, Israel would have an alternative option, although this would still come with complicated policy and economic ramifications.

CYPRUS

Cyprus is yet to develop any of its gas fields, despite making its first discovery, the Aphrodite field, in 2011. Since then, gas exploration has stalled and experienced fits and starts. The first phase of enthusiastic exploration in Cyprus took place between 2007 and 2011 and proved the presence of hydrocarbons in its waters. Between 2012 and 2017 there were no discoveries, despite significant licensing activity. But since 2018, four new discoveries have been made: Calypso, Glaucus, Cronos and Zeus.

Initially, there was little interest in the prospect of gas in Cyprus: in the country's first licensing round in 2007, only three bids were submitted despite the government offering 11 of its 13 offshore blocks. This reflected both the political risk tied to the ongoing territorial dispute with Turkiye and geological risk. At the time, no major discoveries had been made previously in the offshore Levantine Basin.[31] However, Noble Energy, later acquired by Chevron, bid for and received a licence for Block 12, suspecting that hydrocarbon accumulations offshore Israel could extend northwards to Cyprus. The company's discovery of Aphrodite in 2011 proved this suspicion right.

Geological risk thereafter diminished, especially following Eni's discovery of Zohr in Egypt and Noble's discovery of Leviathan and Tamar in Israel, in both cases close to the Cypriot maritime border. The Cypriot government sought to build on the Aphrodite discovery with a second licensing round in 2012, and a third licensing round was launched in 2016. However, it wasn't until 2018 that another discovery was made, when Eni found the Calypso field in Block 6. ExxonMobil then found the Glaucus field in Block 10 in 2019; and Eni found two further fields, Cronos and Zeus, in Block 6 in 2022. Further drilling is planned in several other blocks.

Once Cyprus's discoveries become productive, CGEP expects the island's

Greek Prime Minister Kyriakos Mitsotakis (C), his Israeli counterpart Benjamin Netanyahu (R) and Cypriot president Nicos Anastasiades (L) shake hands in Athens, Greece, on 2 January 2020 at the signing of the agreement to build the EastMed Gas Pipeline. (Photo: Aris Messinis/AFP via Getty Images)

gas output to reach around 32 bcm/y. However, the pace of development of the fields will dictate when Cyprus would reach such a level. To date, the pace has been slow. Aphrodite, the longest-known and largest discovery, is the field closest to production. In May 2023, the licensees, Chevron (following its acquisition of Noble Energy), Shell and NewMed Energy, submitted a development plan for the field for government approval. Should approval be granted, the field could be online in 2027–28, 17 years after its discovery.[32] But by late 2023, no Cypriot discovery had been developed or monetised, for various technical, commercial and political reasons.

Geopolitical risk has also played an important part in investors' wariness about investing in Cyprus, due to competing maritime-border claims and rival licensing of exploration blocks around the island. Turkiye does not recognise the Republic of Cyprus and disputes its claim to a continental shelf. It therefore contests all of Cyprus's claimed maritime borders – despite recognition of these borders by the European Union, Egypt, Israel and Lebanon. At the time of the first licensing round in 2007, Turkiye protested against the legitimacy of Cyprus's licensing of blocks within waters contested by the two countries and by the unrecognised Turkish Republic of Northern Cyprus (TRNC), which likely deterred some prospective bidders.[33] Turkiye's claims particularly affect exploration blocks to the southwest of Cyprus, two of which are licensed to Eni and Total. In 2019, Turkiye sent the drillship *Yavuz* to Block 7, licensed to TotalEnergies, and it later deployed the drillship *Fatih* to a contested area west of Cyprus.[34]

In addition, the TRNC has attempted to license areas to the south and east of the island in waters recognised internationally as under the Republic of Cyprus's authority. No multinational company will pursue licences from the TRNC government, but the entity has granted licences to the Turkish state-owned company Turkish Petroleum Corporation which, in 2019, sent *Yavuz* to the east of Cyprus to drill in one such area.[35] Turkiye also attempted to enforce the TRNC's claims in 2018 by sending a Turkish naval vessel to prevent a drillship chartered by Eni from travelling to Block 3 under a Republic of Cyprus exploration licence.[36]

However, the main gas fields identified in Cypriot waters so far – Aphrodite, Glaucus and Calypso – are not in contested areas, and the Cyprus–Turkiye tensions do not explain the long delay between Aphrodite's discovery and its development.

Probably the most important reason for the delay in developing Aphrodite has been the challenge of commercialising the reserves. Cyprus itself is a tiny market for natural gas. Until 2022, it used no natural gas in its energy system, and even though it has now installed a floating import terminal for LNG, it will still be able to use very little. Therefore, exports are essential to the commercialisation of the Aphrodite field, but it is far from straightforward to determine the most economical means of getting this gas to market. Its options include tying the field back to gas-production platforms in Egypt and selling it into the Egyptian market or international markets via Egypt's liquefaction terminals, or installing liquefaction facilities in Cyprus, either onshore or floating. But to justify the installation of liquefaction facilities in Cyprus, additional gas fields besides Aphrodite will need to feed in (see pages 82–83).

Another reason for the delay in developing the Aphrodite field has been the need to agree with Israel how much of the field lies within Israeli waters, where it is known as the Yishai prospect. The field largely lies on the Cypriot side of the agreed maritime border between the two countries, and will thus be developed under Cypriot licence, so Israel wants guarantees that it will, nonetheless, reap some benefit. In 2018, Israel stated that it expected to benefit from at least 5% of the field's production,[37] and it advised the Cypriot licensees not to proceed with the field's development until agreement has been reached,[38] despite promises from the Cypriot government that Israel would be compensated.[39]

This process has proven difficult. In March 2021, the respective governments assigned the Cypriot and Israeli licensees one year to negotiate a solution – potentially involving the Cypriot licensees (Chevron, Shell and NewMed Energy) buying the Israeli licence – but by March 2022, no agreement had been reached.[40] Instead, the task of resolving the issue reverted to the governments. Although they claimed in September 2022 that progress had been made, no resolution had been found at the time of writing, with both governments likely preoccupied with national elections in the intervening year, but also a political crisis and a war for Israel.[41]

LEBANON

Discoveries of gas in Israel have prompted interest among major companies in the prospect of gas in neighbouring Lebanon. When Lebanon announced its first offshore licensing round in 2017, 52 international oil and gas companies submitted pre-qualification applications and 46 were short-listed, including major oil companies such as Shell and ExxonMobil, having met the country's relatively strict financial and technical pre-qualification requirements. In the end, two of the five available blocks were licensed in 2017, both to a consortium comprised of Eni, TotalEnergies and Russian firm Novatek. Following Russia's invasion of Ukraine, Novatek exited the consortium to be replaced by Qatar Energy.

The maritime-border agreement that was signed by Israel and Lebanon in 2022 settles the long-contested maritime border between the two countries and has unlocked previously disputed blocks. Although Israel will maintain a small equity stake in the Qana prospect in Lebanese waters, TotalEnergies, the operator of Block 9, is now free to proceed in earnest with its exploration activities.

However, no gas has yet been discovered in the licensed blocks and interest in Lebanon has waned due to a combined political and economic crisis. Moreover, the country's poor performance on governance indicators means it ranks unfavourably from an investment perspective. Lebanon's dire economic situation has developed over many years, but it came to a head in 2019. The IMF's conservative estimate put the country's gross government debt at 174% of GDP in 2019,[42] which subsequently rose to 350% of GDP by 2021.[43] Protests in 2019 led to withdrawal of US dollars from Lebanon, triggering a combined debt, liquidity and balance-of-payments crisis, and the Lebanese lira, which had been pegged to the US dollar, collapsed in value by 98% on the parallel market and 90% officially.[44]

The World Bank described the crisis as 'one of the top ten, possibly top three most severe economic collapses worldwide since the 1850s'.[45]

Political turmoil has prevented any Lebanese government from addressing the economic crisis. Since 2019, the country has had four prime ministers, and has had a caretaker government without a president since 2022. The IMF has offered a package of support, but the government is unable to deliver the political agreement necessary to accept it and implement the demanded reforms.

For investors in the oil and gas sector, the chaos is an obstacle to any new project in the country. Lebanon's political and economic crisis is crippling the policymaking and bureaucratic capacity of the country and prompting many of its educated and qualified citizens to leave. Endemic corruption and the breakdown of governance will complicate approvals for gas investments, and US-dollar shortages create a high risk of non-payment for any gas produced in Lebanon and sold domestically. Lebanon performs poorly on every governance indicator and is ahead of only Syria in the region on several such indicators. Should any sizeable discovery be made in Lebanon, significant domestic reforms will still be needed to bring the gas onstream.

OCCUPIED PALESTINIAN TERRITORIES

In 1999, British BG Group announced the discovery of the Gaza Marine gas field in the waters claimed by the State of Palestine, but the discovery remains undeveloped due to political disputes between Palestinian factions as well as the conflict with Israel. Gaza Marine is the only potential domestic source of energy for the Occupied Palestinian Territories, which for decades have been starved of sufficient resources. A 2019 UN Conference on Trade and Development report estimated the size of the energy reservoir at 1.4trn cubic feet (less than 40 bcm).[46]

Following the Hamas-led 7 October 2023 attacks on Israel, there is no prospect for agreement between the Palestinian Authority and the Israeli government on the exploitation of Gaza Marine in the near future. International energy companies have shown no interest in the field as long as Palestine's and Gaza's final statuses are not settled.

However, the US recognises Palestinian maritime claims over offshore gas fields off of Gaza. During a November 2023 visit to Israel, Amos Hochstein, US President Joe Biden's senior energy-security advisor, said unambiguously that 'the gas belongs to the Palestinian people', noting Israel may not have any say in the use of future revenues from the field.

(L–R) CEO of Italian energy company Eni Claudio Descalzi, Qatari Minister of State for Energy Affairs and CEO of QatarEnergy Saad Sherida Al-Kaabi, Lebanese Prime Minister Najib Mikati, Lebanese Minister of Energy and Water Walid Fayad, and Patrick Pouyanné, CEO of TotalEnergies, meet in Beirut, Lebanon, on 29 January 2023 to sign an agreement to start gas exploration in Lebanon's blocks 9 and 4.
(Photo: Hussam Shbaro/Anadolu Agency via Getty Images)

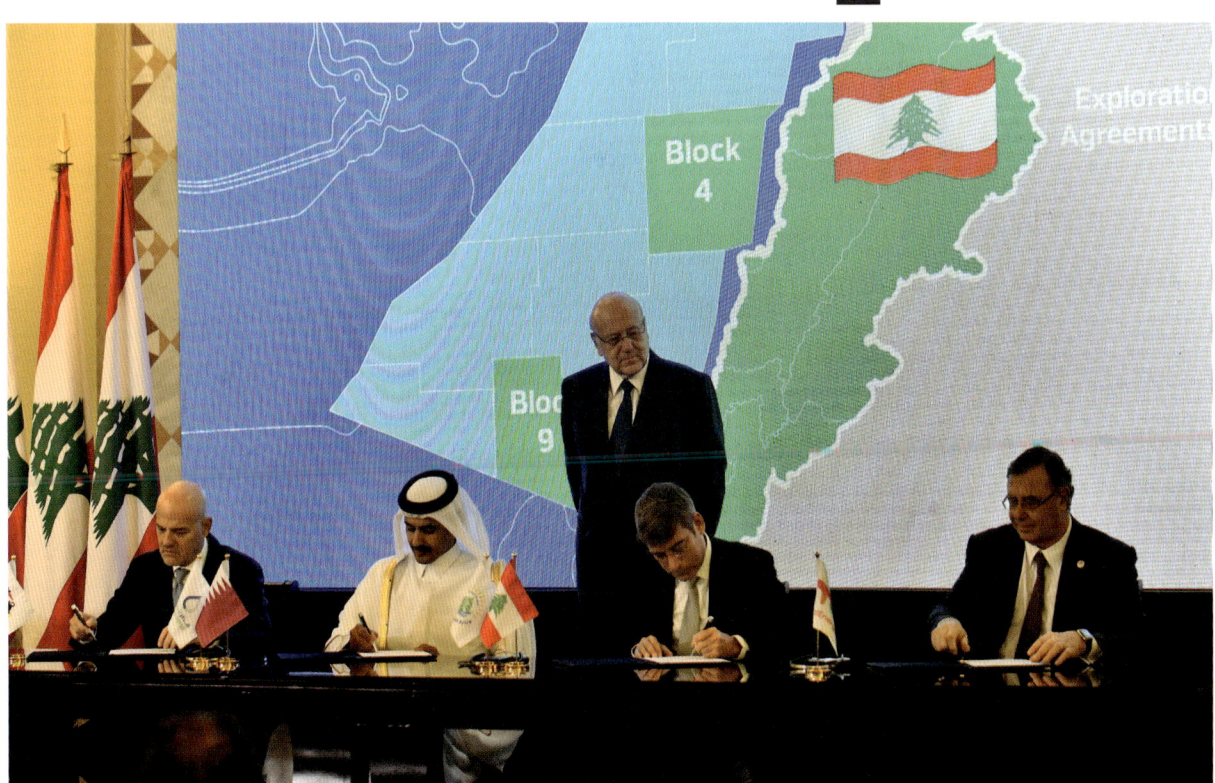

REGIONAL DEMAND AND EXPORT POTENTIAL

The prospects for the Eastern Mediterranean as a player in the global natural-gas market are strongly shaped by the region's own gas consumption and how much remains available for wider export.

Although Egypt is the Eastern Mediterranean's largest gas producer, it is also the region's largest natural-gas market. Its demand for gas has grown rapidly since the late 1990s (see Figure 3.4), despite efforts by the Egyptian government to curtail demand growth, reaching 62 bcm in 2021. Between 2002 and 2012, demand grew at 7.1% on average per year, outpacing production, due to generous subsidies and government support for the fuel's use in industry and power generation. This prompted the government to begin phasing out gas subsidies in 2014, and it pledged, under the terms of an IMF Extended Fund Facility Agreement in 2016, to end energy subsidies altogether.[47] However, seven years on the country still has not fully adopted market-based pricing.

Egypt's gas demand is expected to rise much further in the years ahead, driven in part by the expected increase in electricity generation from gas due

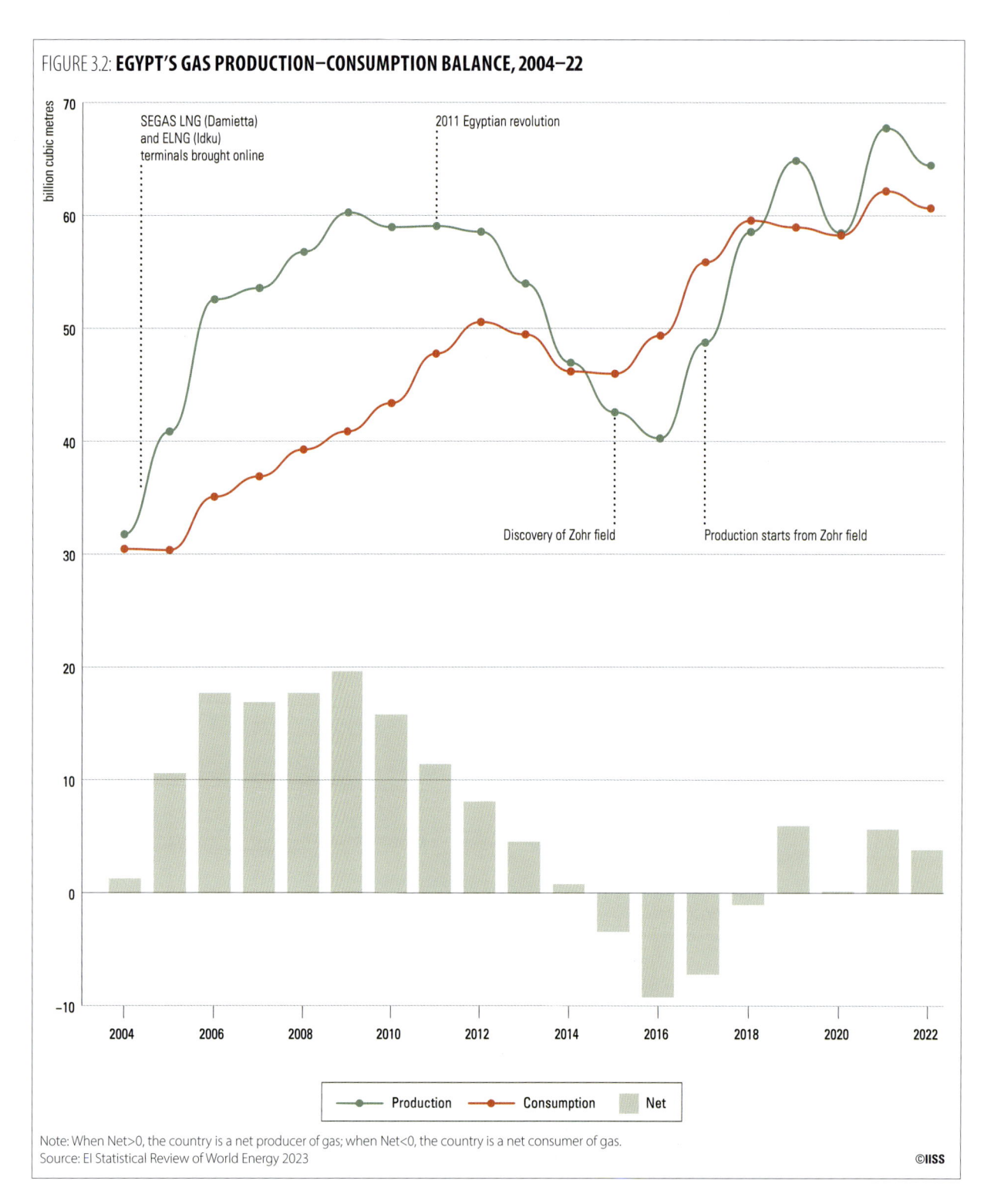

FIGURE 3.2: EGYPT'S GAS PRODUCTION–CONSUMPTION BALANCE, 2004–22

Note: When Net>0, the country is a net producer of gas; when Net<0, the country is a net consumer of gas.
Source: EI Statistical Review of World Energy 2023

to rapid population growth (Egypt's population stood at 110 million as of 2023). Both the International Renewable Energy Agency and an academic study expect demand from the power-generation sector to increase from 37 bcm in 2021 to around 60 bcm in 2030 (adding 23 bcm of demand); and the latter study expects demand from power generation to increase further to 93 bcm by 2040.[48] Heavy industry and transportation are also expected to consume more gas in future. It is likely therefore that domestic gas consumption will outpace national gas production, which is due to peak at around 74 bcm in 2030, with Egypt becoming a net importer of gas in the coming years. Fitch Ratings, a research firm, forecast that Egyptian LNG exports would peak in 2023 at 13.6 bcm and decline thereafter as domestic demand growth weighs down exports;[49] others expect the natural-gas balance in Egypt to turn negative by 2024.[50] Egypt's hopes for continued gas exports depend on cutting demand by transitioning rapidly to renewable energy generation (see box on page 77).

Currently, only Israel produces gas significantly in excess of domestic demand, and will likely continue to do so for many years. According to the Israeli Ministry of Energy and Infrastructure, gas exports reached 10 bcm in 2022 – nearly 50% of the country's output in that year.[51] The Israeli government expects domestic gas demand to increase steadily from 11.9 bcm in 2021 to 16.9 bcm in 2030 and 27.5 bcm by 2045, with electricity generation, petrochemicals industry and compressed natural gas for transportation all accounting for the growing consumption.[52] However, this falls well short of predicted production. The country's output may exceed domestic demand by around 25 bcm/y by 2030, which closely aligns with the government's goal of doubling its gas-export capacity to 25–30 bcm by the end of the decade. Israel therefore stands a much better chance than Egypt of expanding its exports further.

However, if Cyprus can commercialise its gas discoveries, it too will produce much more gas than it can consume. As a small country with a population of just 1.2m people (including territories outside the control of the government in Nicosia), the Cypriot government expects gas consumption of just 0.9 bcm/y in 2030 after completing the construction of its new LNG terminal.[53] By comparison, Cyprus's potential gas production is around 32 bcm/y.

Jordan consumes natural gas produced by Egypt and Israel thanks to the Eastern Mediterranean's existing pipeline infrastructure. In the 2000s, the Arab Gas Pipeline was built to connect Egypt to Jordan (from 2003), but later also connected Syria (from 2008) and Lebanon (from 2009). Egypt intended to export up to 10 bcm/y to its neighbours via the pipeline. However, damage to the pipeline by militants in the Sinai Peninsula and then by warring factions in Syria amid the country's civil war have disrupted the flow of gas. The other major pipeline, the offshore East Mediterranean Gas Pipeline, links Arish in Egypt with Ashkelon in Israel. Completed in 2008, the pipeline was initially intended to carry up to 8 bcm/y of gas from Egypt to Israel. Besides

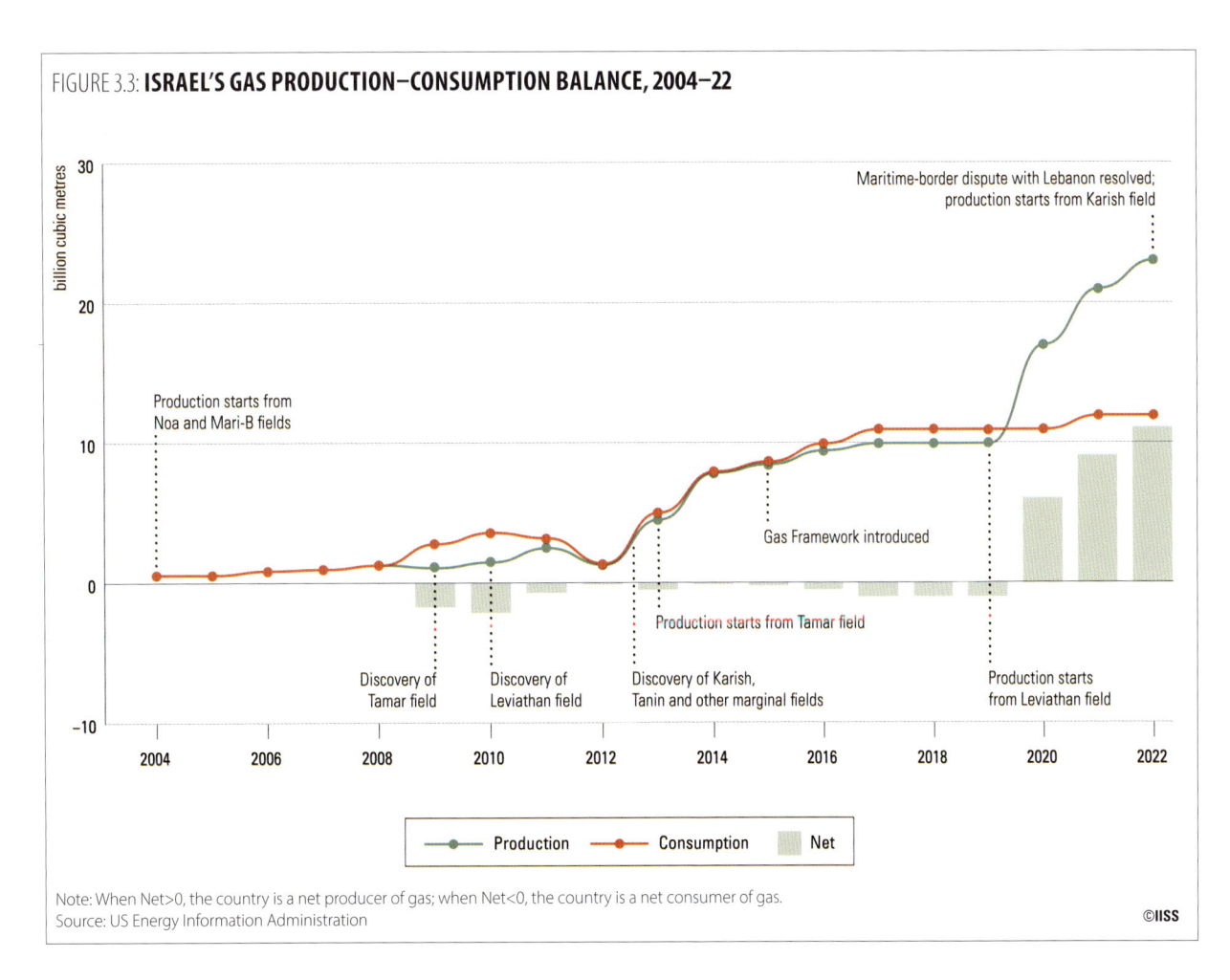

FIGURE 3.3: **ISRAEL'S GAS PRODUCTION–CONSUMPTION BALANCE, 2004–22**

Note: When Net>0, the country is a net producer of gas; when Net<0, the country is a net consumer of gas.
Source: US Energy Information Administration

©IISS

these, a smaller pipeline links Israel's gas-transmission grid with the Arab Gas Pipeline in the north of Jordan, and another even smaller pipeline connects a Jordanian industrial cluster with Israel at the Dead Sea.

Although these pipelines were originally intended to deliver Egyptian gas across the region, Egypt's gas consumption has meant that little or no Egyptian gas has been available for export. Instead, the flow of gas through the East Mediterranean Gas Pipeline has been reversed, with Israel sending gas to Egypt to supply the Egyptian market or for re-export from Egypt's liquefaction terminals. Likewise, Israel has used the pipeline network to export gas to Jordan via Arish and the Arab Gas Pipeline (see Map 3.1). Jordan's gas consumption currently stands at around 2.5 bcm/y and its projected need by 2030 at 3.4 bcm/y. It produces only around 0.16 bcm/y domestically so its gas demand will, most likely, be met either through the LNG terminal at Aqaba or by pipeline from Israel.[54]

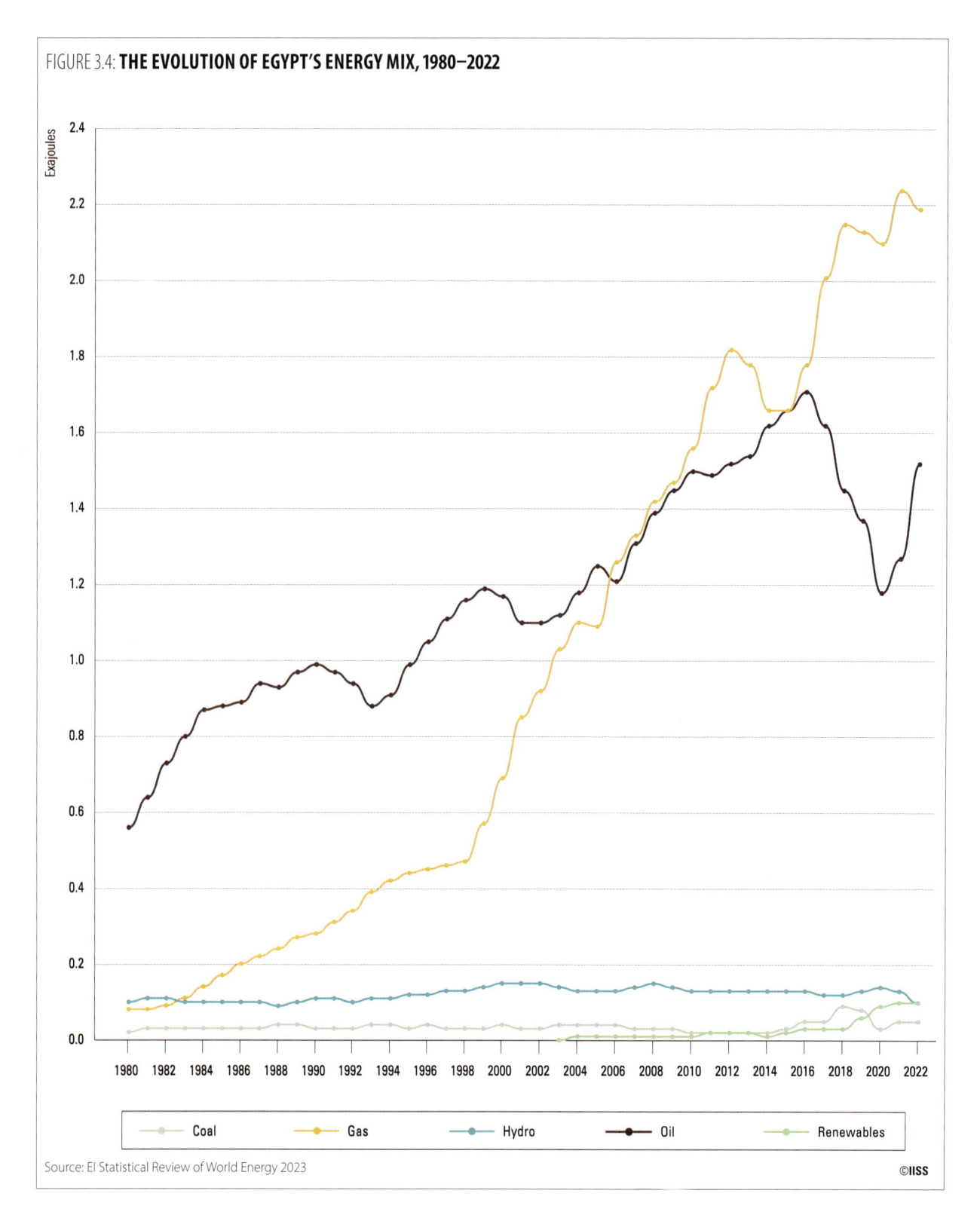

FIGURE 3.4: **THE EVOLUTION OF EGYPT'S ENERGY MIX, 1980–2022**

Source: EI Statistical Review of World Energy 2023

©IISS

EGYPT'S ENERGY TRANSITION

Moderating Egypt's domestic demand for natural gas is essential to its ability to export the fuel. In 2022, it did so by substituting fuel oil (mazut) for natural gas for a portion of its power generation. The share of mazut in electricity generation increased from 11% to 19% in 2022, while the share of electricity generation from natural gas fell correspondingly from 65% to 57%.[I] However, mazut is highly polluting and harmful, and the government has been trying to phase out its use.[II]

The only politically and environmentally sustainable way to reduce natural-gas consumption is to instead expedite the country's roll-out of renewables. The Egyptian government has therefore targeted a dramatic increase in renewable power generation, up to 33% by 2025, 48% by 2030, 55% by 2035 and 61% by 2040.[III] Although the government's plans look optimistic – renewables currently account for just 12% of power generation and 5.3% of primary energy demand[IV] – the country has abundant resources to tap. Large parts of the country have high stable wind speeds averaging eight to ten metres per second at 100m, and are among the areas with the highest potential in the world for solar-power generation.

The involvement of partner countries and foreign investors is critical to this rapid roll-out of renewables in Egypt. Gulf investors are playing an important role. Emirati state-owned energy company Masdar has invested significantly in Benban Solar Park – the largest solar park in Egypt and Africa. In addition, a Masdar-led consortium and the Saudi Arabian state-owned investor ACWA Power have both announced plans to build ten-gigawatt (GW) wind farms in Egypt,[V] and the Norwegian firm Scatec is planning a five-GW wind farm. Together, these three wind-power investments mark a huge step up from the 1.1 GW of wind capacity currently installed in the country, adding around 89 terawatt hours of generation per year, or around 23% of the electricity demand forecast by the International Renewable Energy Agency for 2030.[VI]

International investors are also exploring opportunities to produce green hydrogen in Egypt, primarily for export. Although these projects would not free up significant volumes of natural gas, exports of green hydrogen and its derivatives could contribute to rebalancing Egypt's current account and boosting the availability of foreign exchange, reducing the pressure on the government to prioritise gas exports. In 2022, British, Chinese, French, German, Indian, Saudi and US companies were all studying potential hydrogen projects in the country.[VII]

I   Sarah El Safety, 'Egypt Burns More Heavy Fuel Oil to Free Gas for Export', Reuters, 13 December 2022, https://www.reuters.com/business/energy/egypt-burns-more-heavy-fuel-oil-free-gas-export-2022-12-13/; and Ember, 'Egypt', May 2023, https://ember-climate.org/countries-and-regions/countries/egypt/.

II Sebastian Rodriguez, '"Complete Contradiction": Egypt Burns Dirtier Fuel to Sell More Gas to Europe', Climate Home News, 15 November 2022, https://www.climatechangenews.com/2022/11/15/complete-contradiction-cop27-host-egypt-dirty-fuels-sell-more-gas-to-europe/.

III Jason Mitchell, 'Egyptian Equilibrium: How Can the Country Balance Renewables and Fossil Fuels?', Power Technology, 2 August 2022, https://www.power-technology.com/features/egypt-fossil-renewable-power-balance-egyptian/.

IV US Energy Information Administration, International data: Electricity generation, Egypt, https://www.eia.gov/international/data/world/electricity/more-electricity-data?pd=2&p=0000000000000000000000000000b&u=0&f=A&v=mapbubble&a=-&i=none&vo=value&&t=C&g=none&l=249--64&s=315532800000&e=160945920000.

V   'Egypt Has Just Lined Up as Much as 25 GW Worth of Wind Projects', Enterprise, 9 November 2022, https://enterprise.press/stories/2022/11/09/egypt-has-just-lined-up-as-much-as-25-gw-worth-of-wind-projects-86669/.

VI Assuming a 40.6% capacity factor, in line with Egypt's existing Zafarana wind farm. See IRENA, 'Renewable Energy Outlook: Egypt'.

VII Nada El Sawy, 'Egypt–Europe Alliance Aims to Make Green Hydrogen Hype a Reality', National, 8 December 2022, https://www.thenationalnews.com/business/energy/2022/12/08/egypt-europe-alliance-aims-to-make-green-hydrogen-hype-a-reality/.

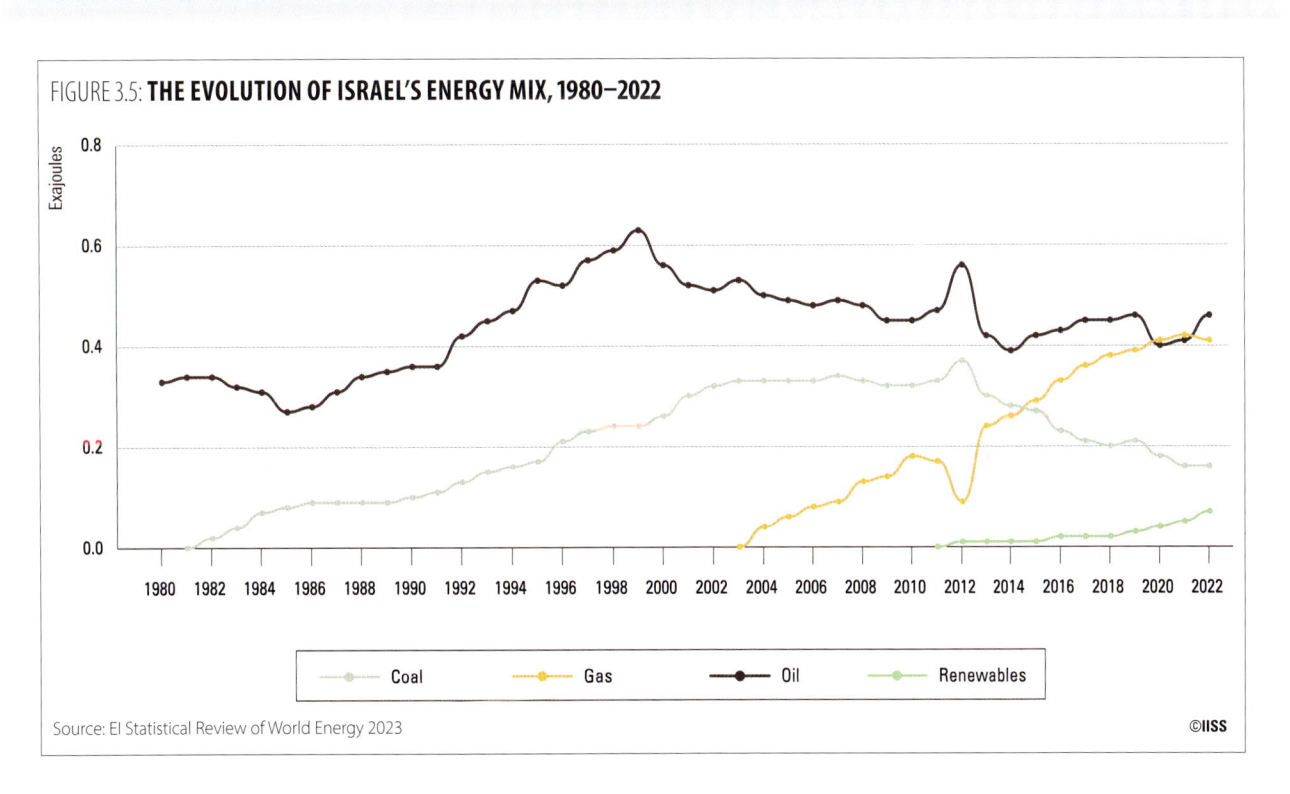

FIGURE 3.5: **THE EVOLUTION OF ISRAEL'S ENERGY MIX, 1980–2022**

Source: EI Statistical Review of World Energy 2023

©IISS

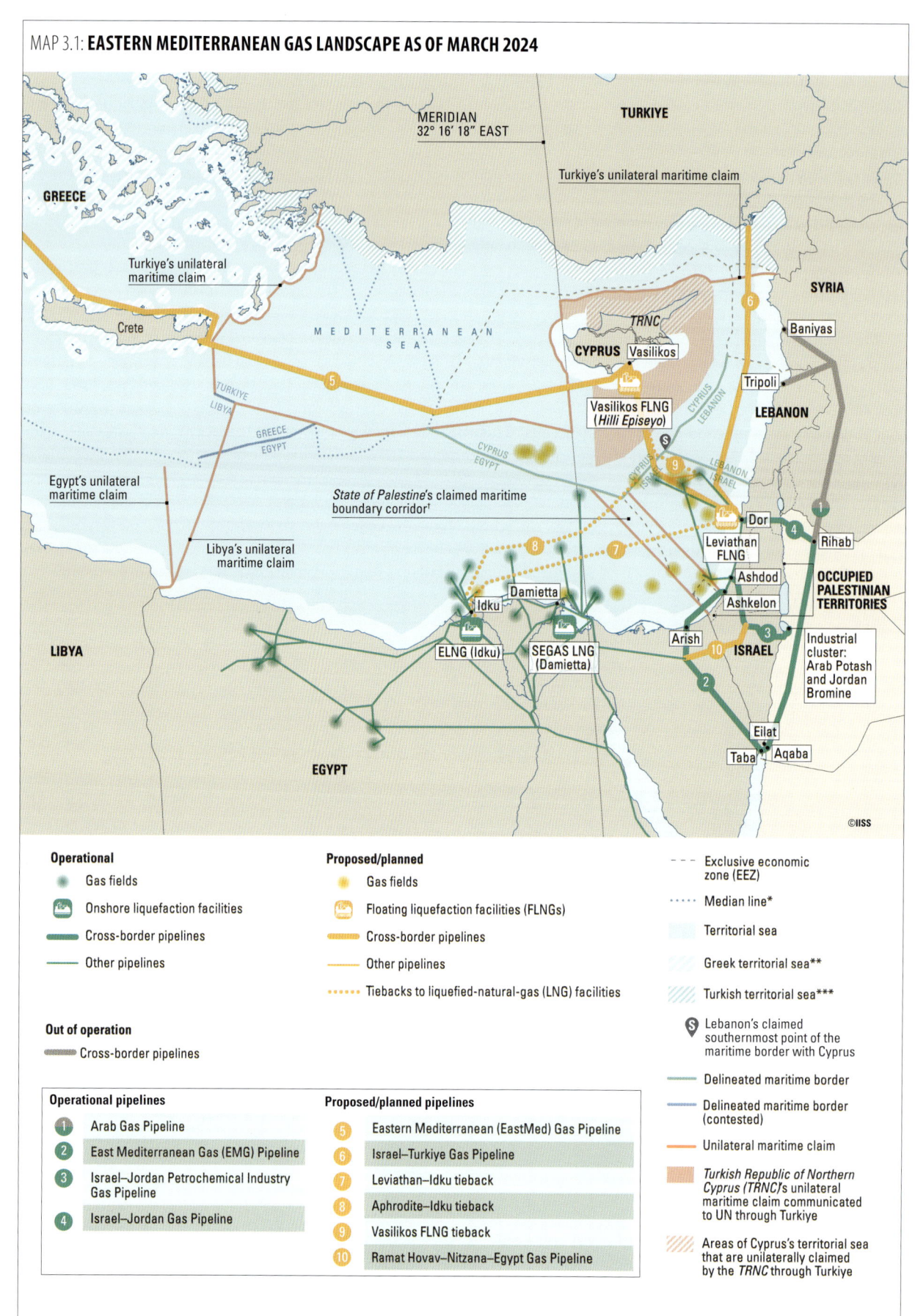

MAP 3.1: EASTERN MEDITERRANEAN GAS LANDSCAPE AS OF MARCH 2024

Operational
- Gas fields
- Onshore liquefaction facilities
- Cross-border pipelines
- Other pipelines

Out of operation
- Cross-border pipelines

Proposed/planned
- Gas fields
- Floating liquefaction facilities (FLNGs)
- Cross-border pipelines
- Other pipelines
- Tiebacks to liquefied-natural-gas (LNG) facilities

- --- Exclusive economic zone (EEZ)
- ····· Median line*
- Territorial sea
- Greek territorial sea**
- Turkish territorial sea***
- Ⓢ Lebanon's claimed southernmost point of the maritime border with Cyprus
- Delineated maritime border
- Delineated maritime border (contested)
- Unilateral maritime claim
- *Turkish Republic of Northern Cyprus (TRNC)'s unilateral maritime claim communicated to UN through Turkiye*
- Areas of Cyprus's territorial sea that are unilaterally claimed by the *TRNC* through Turkiye

Operational pipelines
1. Arab Gas Pipeline
2. East Mediterranean Gas (EMG) Pipeline
3. Israel–Jordan Petrochemical Industry Gas Pipeline
4. Israel–Jordan Gas Pipeline

Proposed/planned pipelines
5. Eastern Mediterranean (EastMed) Gas Pipeline
6. Israel–Turkiye Gas Pipeline
7. Leviathan–Idku tieback
8. Aphrodite–Idku tieback
9. Vasilikos FLNG tieback
10. Ramat Hovav–Nitzana–Egypt Gas Pipeline

*As stated in Article 156 of Greece's 2011 Law 4001/2011, which took note of UNCLOS and customary international law, in the absence of a delineation agreement the outer limit of the Greek continental shelf and EEZ is the median line. **Greece maintains a six-nautical-mile limit to its territorial sea in the Aegean. ***Turkiye maintains a six-nautical-mile limit to its territorial sea in the Aegean and a 12-nautical-mile limit to its territorial sea in the Eastern Mediterranean. †The *State of Palestine* is the entity that submitted the claim to the UN. The Occupied Palestinian Territories are the two regions that have been occupied by Israel since 1967.
Note: Entities in italics lack recognition, statehood or full UN membership.
Sources: Government and UN documents; IISS analysis; Sovereign Limits blog

Due to the damage to the Arab Gas Pipeline in Syria and concerns about US sanctions on the country, no gas has been delivered to Lebanon, which therefore consumes no natural gas at present. Conservative estimates of the potential size of Lebanon's market suggest that if gas becomes widely used in industry and power generation, total gas demand could reach 2 bcm/y by 2035, but more ambitious estimates have put potential demand at 7 bcm/y even sooner (2032). There is therefore little consensus on the market's potential size, but both estimates indicate that the local market will be small.

Other countries in the wider Eastern Mediterranean region draw less directly on gas production in Egypt and Israel. Any gas exports to Greece or Turkiye are delivered as LNG and so consumption in these countries has little impact on the Eastern Mediterranean's prospects as a player in global gas markets. And although Syria's gas demand stands currently at around 3.4 bcm, its plans and prospects for the post-war redevelopment of its energy sector are unclear.[55]

Together, Israel and Cyprus may be able to export as much as 60 bcm/y. But whether this will make them players on the global gas market will depend both on how much of their gas is consumed in Egypt and (to a much lesser extent) Jordan and Lebanon, and on the routes to market chosen by the governments and licensees in Israel and Cyprus.

EXPORT ROUTES

There are three main risks related to exporting gas to Egypt: firstly, that the price Egypt pays is not competitive with global LNG prices; secondly, that Egypt's economic mismanagement results in non-payment for gas; thirdly, that Egypt leverages its position as Cyprus's and Israel's only export route to exert commercial or political pressure on them. Cyprus and Israel are likely to direct more gas to Egypt if they can mitigate the former risks through bilateral and commercial agreements, but they are likely to pursue alternative routes to market, by developing new floating or onshore LNG facilities, as well.

To date, all gas exported from the region has been dispatched from Egypt as LNG. In 2022, the country exported 8.9 bcm of Egyptian and Israeli gas to world markets, accounting for 1.6% of global LNG trade. This has typically been sold on short-term contracts, unlike many other LNG exporters that sell most gas on long-term contracts, which has given Egypt destination flexibility and the ability to take advantage of higher gas prices in Europe in the wake of Russia's 2022 invasion of Ukraine.

EXPORT MARKETS

The Eastern Mediterranean is seen as having the potential to contribute to the diversification of Europe's gas supply as it moves towards ending its energy imports from Russia. Even now, despite ceasing almost all its imports of Russian pipeline gas, Europe continues to import Russian LNG. Many want to see this LNG trade with Russia come to an end, and argue Eastern Mediterranean gas could go some way to fill the gap.

The energy crisis prompted by Russia's invasion of Ukraine – and by subsequent Western sanctions on Russian energy exports – has certainly boosted Europe's demand for gas from new suppliers. It also prompted the European Commission to negotiate an agreement with Israel and Egypt to secure deliveries of Israeli gas to Europe via Egypt's LNG export terminals. Whereas in 2021, 71% of Egyptian LNG went to Asia, in 2022, 73% went to Europe. Turkiye, Spain and France were the top three destinations.

The Eastern Mediterranean has geographic advantages as an LNG exporter to Europe. It is cheaper on average to send gas from North Africa and the Levant to Europe than it is from the rest of Africa. And East Africa (Mozambique) and North Africa and the Levant complement each other: based on shipping costs, East Africa can focus on supplying India and Northeast Asia, whereas North Africa can focus on supplying Europe. Although the region's export capacity is marginal on the global market (compared to Qatar, the US and Australia, which together account for 61% of global LNG trade), the supply economics from the region, via Egypt, are relatively competitive.

However, the Eastern Mediterranean's gas producers cannot rely on Europe as their primary export market in the long run. The European Commission has no intention of entering into further arrangements with Egypt and Israel to secure gas deliveries to Europe. Rather, it is determined that Europe should quickly reduce its gas demand as part of its climate-transition policies. Energy consultancy DNV expects annual European gas consumption to fall from 580 bcm in 2020 to 170 bcm (less than the region's present gas production) by 2050, a much faster decline than predicted before the Russia–Ukraine war.[56] According to European governments' announced pledges, the EU's gas consumption will fall even further, by around 80% from 2020, to just 122 bcm in 2050.

By contrast, the Asian market for LNG will continue to grow – at least until 2030 – and then shrink only gradually through to 2050, with much less ambitious greenhouse-gas-emissions targets than Europe. Therefore, for Eastern Mediterranean gas producers, the flexibility to serve the Asian market in the long run, as well as the European market in the shorter term, is central to their choice of infrastructure for exports from the region. The Eastern Mediterranean may be less ideally located to serve the Asian market than East Africa or the Gulf but the appetite for gas means that exporting is still a promising prospect. Gas-export infrastructure therefore needs to position the region for exports to the east, not just north to Europe.

EGYPT AS A REGIONAL HUB

Egypt offers probably the most obvious route to export natural gas from the Eastern Mediterranean. The country has two onshore liquefaction plants which together have the capacity to export the equivalent of 5% of Europe's gas consumption. The larger plant, Egypt LNG (ELNG) in Idku, is jointly owned by Egyptian Natural Gas Holding Company (EGAS), EGPC, Shell and Petronas, and has existing capacity to export 9.8 bcm/y of gas (7.2 megatons per annum [mtpa] of LNG). The slightly smaller plant, SEGAS LNG in Damietta, is owned jointly by EGAS, Eni and BP, and has capacity of 6.5 bcm/y (4.8 mtpa). Currently, these plants are under-utilised. After Egypt became a net gas importer in the early 2010s, Damietta closed in 2013 and Idku followed suit in 2015, liquefying minimal volumes to keep equipment running. Although the production of gas at Egypt's large Zohr field and the import of gas from Israel into Egypt enabled the operators to reopen Idku in 2020 and Damietta in 2021, spare capacity remains. There is, moreover, an opportunity to expand these plants, adding four trains at Idku and one at

Damietta, potentially reaching a total capacity of 44 bcm of exports (32 mtpa) – the equivalent of 13% of Europe's current gas consumption.[57]

Exports from the Eastern Mediterranean could be increased quickly and significantly by sending gas to Egypt from Israel in larger volumes, either by building additional pipelines for processed gas or by tying new wells back to processing plants in Egypt. There are two existing pipeline routes for transporting gas from Israel to Egypt, namely the East Mediterranean Gas Pipeline that runs directly offshore between Ashkelon and Arish, and the Arab Gas Pipeline which Israel can feed into via Jordan. Israel and Egypt plan to construct an additional, onshore pipeline – from Ramat Hovav to Nitzana and into Egypt – to add 6 bcm/y capacity for transmission between the two countries. The Israeli Ministry of Energy and Infrastructure approved the plan in May 2023, but the final investment decision has not been made. The impact of the ongoing war between Israel and Hamas on the two countries' readiness to pursue this project is also unclear. There are also proposals to tie back Israel's Leviathan gas field directly to ELNG at Idku.

Cyprus too could direct gas to Egypt. This option is favoured by Chevron, Shell and NewMed Energy in the development plan they submitted to the Cypriot government in June 2023 for the Aphrodite field. Their proposal was to transport untreated gas from Aphrodite via a subsea pipeline to Shell's under-utilised West Delta Deep Marine (WDDM) facilities offshore Egypt, where it would be treated. This would save the partners building an expensive new dedicated processing and production facility in Cyprus, thereby significantly reducing development costs. The treated gas would then be transported to the Idku LNG plant, also operated by Shell, and either liquefied for export or used domestically to meet Egypt's growing gas demand. The plan appears to be the most commercially attractive option for Aphrodite's development. Likewise, Eni could tie back the Calypso, Cronos and Zeus fields it has discovered in Cyprus to the company's existing production platform at Zohr in nearby Egyptian waters.

(L-R) Cypriot energy minister Georgios Lakkotrypis, Italian economy minister Carlo Calenda, Israeli energy minister Yuval Steinitz, Greek environment and energy minister Giorgos Stathakis and EU commissioner for climate action and energy Miguel Arias Cañete present a map of the EastMed Gas Pipeline Project during a joint press conference following an energy summit in Tel Aviv, Israel, on 3 April 2017. (Photo: Jack Guez/AFP via Getty Images)

Were Lebanon to discover gas, and the Arab Gas Pipeline repaired, it too could export to Egypt. However, without obtaining a waiver or exemption, the United States' Caesar Act sanctions on Syria would prevent companies from working with the Syrian government to carry out the repairs or from engaging in a commercial relationship,[58] and the pipeline's 2.2 bcm/y capacity would severely limit exports from the country.[59]

Egypt has proactively pitched itself as a regional gas hub in this vein. Egypt's Ministry of Petroleum and Mineral Resources presented its strategy to become a hub in the sixth programme of its petroleum-sector modernisation plan.[60] And among government and military stakeholders, there are strong vested interests in achieving this. Egyptian state-owned energy companies and the Egyptian General Intelligence Service (GIS) are currently influential stakeholders in the import of gas from Israel – the GIS through its ownership of East Gas. The immediate buyer for Israeli gas exports to Egypt is Blue Ocean Energy, but it serves only as an intermediary.[61] It sells Israeli gas on to East Gas for transmission, and East Gas then sells the gas on to the state-owned EGAS. Via East Gas, the GIS also has a stake in pipeline infrastructure through its ownership of the Egyptian stretch of the Arab Gas Pipeline, and its stake in the Arish–Ashkelon pipeline both directly (9%) and indirectly (18.5%) as a 50% shareholder in the Noble Energy–NewMed–East Gas joint venture EMED.[62]

However, there are three key prerequisites for Egypt to establish itself as a hub: a well-connected market with diverse gas suppliers and consumers, political will, and a liberalised gas market with minimal government intervention, and on market liberalisation Egypt fares poorly (see pages 66–68). To date, Egypt's gas imports from Israel have been linked to Brent crude oil prices, which offers a form of indexation but does not fully reflect international gas prices.[63]

Egypt's own soaring gas consumption, and inability to produce enough gas to meet domestic demand, could mean that little gas makes its way to the country's LNG facilities. In 2014, Shell declared *force majeure* at the ELNG plant in Idku due to the government's diversion of gas from its WDDM fields to meet domestic demand.[64] Ultimately, government interference creates substantial risk and uncertainty about the country's prospects as a gas hub.

There are also security risks for infrastructure connecting other Eastern Mediterranean states with Egypt. In 2011, for example, Islamist groups in Sinai attacked the East Mediterranean Gas Pipeline, taking it offline for a short period of time. Similarly, other groups had previously put the Arab Gas Pipeline out of action.

The Cypriot government and several companies are therefore wary of relying entirely on Egypt as their route to market, which would leave them heavily exposed to Egypt's political and economic instability and domestic gas pricing, and to manoeuvring by the Egyptian government. Cyprus has so far blocked the Chevron-led consortium's plans to tie back Aphrodite to Egyptian facilities; it remains keen on developing export infrastructure domestically. The country's gas minister insists that Cypriot gas should not be directed to Egyptian LNG terminals.[65] Other investors in Cyprus and Israel, including both ExxonMobil and Energean, are working towards alternative routes.

The commercial rationale for tying back Cypriot and Israeli gas fields to Egypt and building up the latter as the regional gas hub looks strong. But in practice, this option carries big risks for Egypt's neighbours, which would become significantly exposed to unfavourable developments in Egypt and its high political risk.

PIPELINES TO EUROPE

Two main pipeline routes have been mooted to transport Eastern Mediterranean gas to Europe, but both proposals have been hampered by geopolitical and economic obstacles. Neither is likely to proceed in the foreseeable future.

The best-known proposal is the Eastern Mediterranean Pipeline (EastMed), promoted by IGI Poseidon, a joint venture between the Italian and Greek utility companies Edison and DEPA. The proposal envisages a pipeline from Israeli and Cypriot gas fields to Cyprus, onwards to Crete and then the Greek mainland before joining the existing Poseidon pipeline across the Ionian Sea to Italy. The European Commission designated the proposal a 'Project of Common Interest' in 2013 and since then the relevant governments have signed a raft of agreements on the project. In 2017, Cyprus, Greece, Israel and Italy signed a memorandum of understanding for the construction of the pipeline and in 2020, the Cypriot and Israeli governments gave construction the go-ahead with backing from the United States' then-secretary of state Mike Pompeo.

The rationale for EastMed has always been partly geopolitical. Even before Russia's invasion of Ukraine in 2022, the pipeline was envisaged as contributing to Europe's efforts to diversify its gas imports away from Russia, and this view was encouraged by the US, which offered its backing to the project. Among Eastern Mediterranean governments, the project was an opportunity to strengthen political ties. The Israeli government saw it as a way of strengthening ties to Europe, and any European reliance on Israeli gas could be beneficial in the event of future tensions over Israeli–Palestinian relations. In turn, the Greek and Cypriot governments wanted to strengthen their relationship with Israel.

However, the EastMed project has lived up to its 'pipedream' moniker. It remains stranded at the feasibility-study stage, having failed to raise the necessary €6bn in funding; and, in early 2022, the US retracted its support.[66] Although the Biden administration has issued no public statements about the United States' change of position, it is understood to be motivated by its wish to improve relations with Ankara, given Turkiye's opposition to the project and the importance of bolstering US–Turkiye relations against the backdrop of the Russia–Ukraine war. The proposed route traverses maritime territory contested by Turkiye on one side and Cyprus and Greece on the other. The risk of Turkish interference with the project meant that the parties relied on US backing as a tacit security guarantee, so the lack of US support casts a shadow on its prospects. Eni, among others, sees the project as unviable without an agreement on Turkiye's participation.[67]

The EastMed's questionable long-term commercial prospects also contribute to the project's paralysis. Pipeline projects usually have a lifespan of around 40 years, with the initial investment costs paid back over that period,[68] but the EU is pushing for a global pledge to phase out unabated fossil fuels by 2050 and plans to reduce gas consumption by 35% by 2035 (from 2019 levels).[69] There is therefore considerable uncertainty about the return on any pipeline investment.

The project's proponents have tried to rescue EastMed by proposing that it could, in future, transport hydrogen rather than natural gas, but the technical requirements for converting pipelines from gas to hydrogen remain highly uncertain. Pipeline projects have also fallen out of favour in Europe in the wake of Russia's invasion of Ukraine, with LNG having the advantage that it can be sourced flexibly from a range of gas exports.

The second option for long-distance pipelines is an offshore pipeline from Israel to Turkiye, connecting there with the existing pipeline network between Turkiye and Europe. Technically, the proposal is much simpler than EastMed – the seabed is much shallower and less rugged and the distance much shorter, so the cost should be lower. Turkish President Recep Tayyip Erdoğan has supported the idea and early-stage discussions have taken place between the Israeli and Turkish governments.[70]

However, the construction of an Israel–Turkiye pipeline is also unlikely. For Israeli exporters, the proposal comes with two main risks. Just as with EastMed, the pipeline would commit Israel to selling its gas into European markets (plus Turkiye) over a period long enough to justify the construction cost, while Europe is actively working on decreasing its gas needs and moving towards a greener energy mix. Moreover, it would expose Israeli energy exports to Turkish influence amid long-standing uneasy relations between the two countries. During Erdoğan's tenure as Turkiye's leader, the Turkish and Israeli governments have clashed frequently over Israeli actions in Gaza, resulting in the countries mutually withdrawing their ambassadors between 2018 and 2022.[71] The Israeli offensive in Gaza has led to a new deep diplomatic rift between Turkiye and Israel. For Europe, another pipeline via Turkiye is also an unappealing prospect. Europe is keen to avoid depending excessively on imports via a single route, and given the various geopolitical frictions between Europe and Turkiye there is little appetite among European governments to give Ankara greater influence over the region's gas supply.

In the event of large gas discoveries in Lebanon, it too could look to develop an offshore pipeline to Turkiye. But building such a pipeline would require cooperation with Syria, and the two countries are yet to agree their maritime borders. This is further complicated by the US Caesar Act sanctions on Syria and domestic Lebanese political difficulties with Syria.

LNG ALTERNATIVES

The alternative to accepting Egypt as the Eastern Mediterranean's gas hub and to building long-distance pipelines is for the region's other gas producers – currently Israel and in the future likely Cyprus – to invest in their own LNG export terminals, whether onshore or floating offshore. The Cypriot government expects this to become the optimum option for the country's gas sector and has contracted the building of an LNG terminal.[72]

Unlike pipelines (whether to Egypt, Greece-to-Italy or Turkiye) which force the producer and the customer to enter into a rigid, long-term relationship, LNG offers both players greater flexibility and optionality. They can diversify their natural-gas exports, gain access to new markets not connected to existing pipeline infrastructure, manage their natural-gas supply and respond more swiftly to changes in demand, and gain greater leverage in negotiations with gas importers.

ONSHORE LNG

Israel is likely to produce enough gas to justify investment in an onshore gas terminal, but physical constraints are hard to surmount. The two main options for the location of such a plant both come with major challenges. The first would be to find a site on Israel's Mediterranean coast, but the significant land requirements and need for a jetty for an onshore terminal make this difficult. The coast is densely populated and there are environmental obstacles to building on any available land. The second would be a plant at Eilat on the Gulf of Aqaba fed by a pipeline from Ashkelon. However, the large size and turning circle of LNG tankers would result in a large isolation zone that would impact marine life, leisure activities and tourism – an important local industry[73] – so the idea appears to have been dismissed.[74] There is an additional factor for Israel to consider: non-state armed groups in the Occupied Palestinian Territories, Lebanon and Syria see energy infrastructure as legitimate targets and have announced their readiness to hit such facilities.[75] In the current war, Hamas has failed to do so, likely lacking adequate capabilities, but Hizbullah is more likely to hold unmanned air systems, anti-ship missiles and sea drones in its arsenal.

> THE EASTERN MEDITERRANEAN'S GAS-EXPORT POTENTIAL WILL PRIMARILY RELY ON ISRAEL AND CYPRUS.

Cyprus does not face the same physical constraints and an onshore terminal there is a long-term possibility. However, its limited (discovered) domestic gas reserves are a major hurdle. The proposed ideas for Cyprus include a terminal at Vasilikos with up to three LNG trains, each with a nominal capacity of 5 mtpa (or 6.8 bcm/y), giving the country an export capacity of nearly 20 bcm. However, according to the Cypriot Ministry of Energy, the unsuccessful exploration in Block 9 and lower reserves estimates for the Aphrodite field cast doubts on the viability of an onshore plant, and it is currently on hold.[76] It appears that initial estimates for the Calypso and Glaucus fields were also optimistic.[77]

To compensate for its limited domestic supplies, Cyprus could bring in gas by pipeline from neighbouring countries for liquefaction and export. A 2011 study by a British oil-and-gas consulting company found that bringing gas through subsea pipelines from Israel to Cyprus would be 'very favourable' from an engineering perspective.[78] ExxonMobil has also entertained the possibility of developing a liquefaction facility in Cyprus not only for its gas finds in Cypriot waters (Glaucus) but also for its exploration blocks in Egypt that border Cypriot waters; however, it is yet to announce any major discoveries in those Egyptian blocks.[79] Lebanon could also tie back any discoveries it makes to an onshore facility in Cyprus, although it may be unable, on political grounds, to cooperate with any liquefaction project in Cyprus that involves Israeli parties.

Ultimately, building an onshore terminal in Cyprus and pipelines to it will be expensive, and uncertainty about how much gas Cyprus can produce domestically leaves it hard to justify commercially. The country needs to find intermediate export solutions until it can more clearly demonstrate that Cypriot gas fields and nearby fields in Israel and, potentially, Egypt can feed an onshore terminal with sufficient gas.

FLOATING LNG

The alternative to an onshore liquefaction facility is a floating LNG plant (FLNG). Unlike onshore terminals, FLNGs do not require the liquefaction of large volumes of gas over long periods in a single location to justify the investment cost; they are vessels moored temporarily near a gas field, and can be either leased for a time or owned outright and moved from country to country. FLNGs are expensive to run in the long term and for large volumes of gas, as they have much smaller capacity than onshore facilities. (The largest FLNG to date, Prelude FLNG in Australia, has a maximum liquefaction capacity of 4.9 bcm/y.) But they are a realistic operation for the commercialisation of modest gas finds in Cyprus and Israel, especially as an intermediate solution.

Energean, a small UK-headquartered gas investor in Israel, has proposed sending gas from offshore Israeli fields

The SEGAS LNG complex in Damietta, Egypt. (Photo: Barry Iverson via Alamy Stock Photo)

(Karish, Katlan[80] and Tamar), via their Karish processing platform, through a 200 kilometre pipeline with a capacity of 4 bcm/y, to an FLNG moored near Vasilikos in Cyprus.[81] Rather than commissioning a new FLNG of its own, Energean has an option to lease the existing Hilli Episeyo FLNG, owned by Golar LNG and currently moored off Cameroon, which has a capacity of 3.2 bcm/y.[82] The vessel is due to be available by 2026, coinciding with the projected timeline for the development of Energean's natural-gas fields in Israel. It is unclear who would fund the FLNG, although Vitol, a commodity-trading company, has expressed interest in being the recipient of LNG for exports to Europe and other destinations.

The proposal seems to have captured the interest of both the Israeli and Cypriot governments, and the two are drafting a formal agreement.[83] Sending gas to an FLNG in Cyprus would decrease the risks of depending entirely on exports to Egypt and would reinforce the bilateral relationship between Cyprus and Israel. Moreover, mooring the FLNG in Cyprus may avoid some of the security risk associated with deploying such a vessel in Israeli waters. As accounting and consultancy firm KPMG reports, 'peace of mind from security concerns' is among the top reasons companies choose FLNGs, since the offshore location makes it less accessible to would-be attackers or saboteurs.[84] Defensive measures such as remote monitoring and barriers can also make it difficult to scale the vessel.

Chevron, which operates the Leviathan field in Israel, is also exploring the possible use of FLNG to expand its exports from the field, and has commissioned shipyards to undertake front-end engineering and design studies for a new-build vessel.[85] But unlike Energean, Chevron expects any FLNG to be moored in Israeli waters, close to the processing platform for its Leviathan field.[86]

OUTLOOK

Inevitably, the outlook for the Eastern Mediterranean's gas exports depends on several factors that remain uncertain, including whether new discoveries will be made, where and how big they are, how the region's domestic markets are reformed, and how quickly it rolls out renewables. External factors, including the expansion of other producer countries and changing demand in key markets, will shape the region's prospects too. As Europe's 2022 energy crisis revealed, other big gas producers can respond quickly to changing demand, presenting stiff competition for Eastern Mediterranean gas.

It is nevertheless clear that the region's export potential will primarily rely on Israel and Cyprus. Currently, Israel is the only country with a significant surplus to export, and its export potential is likely to increase significantly in the decade ahead. And although Cypriot gas fields have not yet come onstream, they are likely to be developed in the next few years and the country will look to export the majority of the gas it produces. By contrast, Egypt is likely to consume all the gas it can produce, and Lebanon is yet to make a discovery.

In the short term, Cyprus and Israel will need to settle for whichever export infrastructure allows them to bring new gas fields onstream quickly but limits as little as possible their long-term export options. This means mooring FLNGs and using pipelines and tie-backs to Egypt for a ramp-up period until gas production is on a large enough scale in Cyprus and Israel to justify investment in their own onshore LNG export terminal. There is no guarantee that they will ever produce gas in sufficient volumes to make that leap, but the upshot is that in the interim and in the long term, the Eastern Mediterranean is likely to have a more flexible patchwork of export infrastructure, rather than tying the whole region to the development of Egypt as a hub or a common long-distance pipeline project, with its associated risks. For the Eastern Mediterranean, LNG has a clear advantage over pipelines, enabling it to service growth markets in Asia as well as the shrinking European markets.

Economics aside, the fragmented political situation in the Eastern Mediterranean will continue to be an obstacle and could stop any project from proceeding, irrespective of the commercial rationale. To date, this has enabled other new gas producers, such as Mozambique, to surge ahead of Eastern Mediterranean states and climb the ranks of the world's largest LNG exporters. Unless the political impasse significantly changes, the Eastern Mediterranean will not be able to play a notable role in regional and global gas trade.

ENDNOTES

1. 'Worldwide Reserves and Production', *Oil & Gas Journal*, 6 December 2022, https://www.ogj.com/ogj-survey-downloads/worldwide-production/document/14287591/worldwide-reserves-and-production; and Christopher J. Schenk, 'An Estimate of Undiscovered Conventional Oil and Gas Resources of the World, 2012', US Geological Survey, 2012, https://pubs.usgs.gov/fs/2012/3042/fs2012-3042.pdf.

2. Christopher J. Schenk et al., 'Assessment of Undiscovered Conventional Oil and Gas Resources in the Eastern Mediterranean Area, 2020', US Geological Survey, 2021, https://pubs.usgs.gov/fs/2021/3032/fs20213032.pdf.

3. Bartolomej Tomic, 'Report: Chevron Hits Gas Offshore Egypt', *Offshore Engineer*, 5 December 2022, https://www.oedigital.com/news/501376-report-chevron-hits-gas-offshore-egypt.

4. Ahmad El-Assasy, 'Egypt Makes 53 New Oil and Gas Discoveries in 2022', Sada Elbalad English, 30 December 2022, https://see.news/egypt-makes-53-new-oil-and-gas-discoveries-in-2022.

5. Shangyou Nie and Robin Mills, 'Eastern Mediterranean Deepwater Gas to Europe: Not Too Little, but Perhaps Too Late', Center on Global Energy Policy, March 2023, https://www.energypolicy.columbia.edu/wp-content/uploads/2023/03/East-Med-Gas-CGEP_Report_030923-2.pdf.

6. International Energy Agency, 'World Energy Outlook 2022', November 2022, https://iea.blob.core.windows.net/assets/830fe099-5530-48f2-a7c1-11f35d510983/WorldEnergyOutlook2022.pdf; the Stated Policies Scenario (STEPS) shows the trajectory implied by today's policy settings, while the Announced Pledges Scenario (APS) assumes that all aspirational targets announced by governments are met on time and in full, including their long-term net-zero and energy-access goals.

7. Eni, 'Eni Begins Producing from Zohr, the Largest Ever Discovery of Gas in the Mediterranean Sea', 20 December 2017, https://www.eni.com/en-IT/media/press-release/2017/12/eni-begins-producing-from-zohr-the-largest-ever-discovery-of-gas-in-the-mediterranean-sea.html.

8. Mohamed Fouad, 'Production Sharing Agreements: Overview', Egypt Oil & Gas, 9 March 2015, https://egyptoil-gas.com/features/production-sharing-agreements-overview/.

9. Gas Regulatory Authority, Egypt, 'Natural Gas Pricing', https://www.gasreg.org.eg/natural-gas-pricing/.

10. Peter Ramsay, 'East Med Aims to Reap Renewed Gas Appetite Dividend', *Petroleum Economist*, 29 April 2022, https://pemedianetwork.com/petroleum-economist/articles/gas-lng/2022/east-med-aims-to-reap-renewed-gas-appetite-dividend/.

11. US International Trade Administration, 'Egypt – Country Commercial Guide', 8 August 2022, https://www.trade.gov/country-commercial-guides/egypt-oil-and-gas-equipment.

12. Mohamed Adel, 'Production from Rosetta Gas Field to Cease in July', *Daily News Egypt*, 11 December 2016, https://www.dailynewsegypt.com/2016/12/11/production-rosetta-gas-field-cease-july/.

13. Heba Saleh, 'Egypt's Exchange Rate Uncertainty Stifling Business, Say Entrepreneurs', *Financial Times*, 16 May 2023, https://www.ft.com/content/b69bbce2-11e1-4da8-9608-b7af2a6fd329.

14. Mirette Magdy, Abdel Latif Wahba and Tarek El-Tablawy, 'Egypt Unlocks $8 Billion IMF Loan to Ease Crisis with FX Float', Bloomberg, 6 March 2024, https://www.bloomberg.com/news/articles/2024-03-06/egypt-gets-breakthrough-imf-deal-to-lift-loan-size-to-8-billion.

15. 'Egypt Orders Ministries to Curb Spending amid Foreign Currency Crunch', Reuters, 10 January 2023, https://www.reuters.com/world/africa/egypt-orders-ministries-curb-spending-amid-foreign-currency-crunch-2023-01-10/.

16. International Labour Organization, 'Egypt', Labour Force Statistics database (LFS): Share of youth aged 15–24 years not in employment, education or training (NEET) by sec (%), Total, 2021, https://www.ilo.org/ilostat-files/Country_Dashboard/EGY.html.

17. Alvin R. Cabral, 'Egypt's Inflation Accelerates to Nearly 33% in May as Food and Beverage Prices Soar', *National*, 10 June 2023, https://www.thenationalnews.com/business/economy/2023/06/10/egypts-inflation-accelerates-to-nearly-33-in-may-as-food-and-beverage-prices-soar/.

18. Tethys Sea Partnership, a consortium between Delek Drilling and Noble Energy, made the two discoveries.

19. Israel, Ministry of Energy and Infrastructure, 'Overview', https://www.energy-sea.gov.il/home/policy-regulation-overview/.

20. NewMed Energy, 'Leviathan – Phase B', https://newmedenergy.com/operations/leviathan-phase-b/.

21. 'Chevron and Partners to Proceed with Tamar Field Expansion Project', *Offshore Technology*, 9 December 2022, https://www.offshore-technology.com/news/chevron-tamar-expansion/.

22. Michael Ratner, 'Israel's Offshore Natural Gas Discoveries Enhance Its Economic and Energy Outlook', Congressional Research Service, 4 May 2011, https://crsreports.congress.gov/product/pdf/R/R41618/12.

23. Tom Pepper, 'Israel Weighs Gas Export Policy Reforms', Energy Intelligence, 5 July 2022, https://www.energyintel.com/00000181-cda7-d598-a183-fdafbbdb0000.

24. Ari Rabinovitch, 'Israel Energy Minister Backs More Natural Gas Exports', Reuters, 2 August 2023, https://www.reuters.com/business/energy/israels-energy-minister-favors-more-natural-gas-exports-2023-08-02/.

25. Israel experienced five general elections and four governments in 2019–23, and the Knesset (parliament) remains finely balanced between the right-wing, six-party bloc governing coalition and the opposition parties. Coalition disputes could quickly precipitate new elections and coalition negotiations.

26. IMF, 'Israel: Staff Concluding Statement of the 2023 Article IV Mission', 10 May 2023, https://www.imf.org/en/News/Articles/2023/05/10/israel-staff-concluding-statement-of-the-2023-article-iv-mission.

27. Collin Eaton, 'Israel Orders Chevron to Shut Down Gas Platform Near Gaza', *Wall Street Journal*, 9 October 2023, https://www.wsj.com/business/energy-oil/israel-orders-chevron-to-shut-down-gas-platform-near-gaza-b93c2add.

28. Shotaro Tani and David Sheppard, 'How One Gas Producer Kept Israel's Lights On', *Financial Times*, 28 November 2023, https://www.ft.com/content/a45e366d-8193-4243-9ea5-a79db82f28dd.

29. NewMed Energy, 'Update re Offer to Purchase Participation Units of the Partnership', 13 March 2024, https://newmedenergy.com/wp-content/uploads/2024/03/NewMed-IR-10.3.24-מגנום.pdf.

30. Al-Haq, 'Israeli Gas Exploration Licenses in Palestine's Maritime Areas Are Illegal and Violate International Law', 8 February 2024, https://www.alhaq.org/advocacy/22619.html.

31. S&P Global Market Intelligence, 'Cyprus Attracts Just Three Bids in First Phase of Licensing Round', 17 August 2007, https://www.spglobal.com/marketintelligence/en/mi/country-industry-forecasting.html?ID=106597757.

32. Michele Kambas, 'Cyprus in Renewed Push to Extract Natural Gas as Shortages Loom in EU', Reuters, 7 October 2022, https://www.reuters.com/business/energy/cyprus-renewed-push-extract-natgas-shortages-loom-eu-2022-10-07/.

33. See Chapter Two, 'Maritime Disputes'.

34. Stuart Elliott, David O'Byrne and Gary Lakes, 'Turkey Raises Stakes in East Mediterranean Gas with Move into Cyprus' Block 7', S&P Global Commodity Insights, 7 October 2019, https://www.spglobal.com/commodityinsights/en/market-insights/latest-news/natural-gas/100719-turkey-raises-stakes-in-east-mediterranean-gas-with-move-into-cyprus-block-7.

35. Hannah L. Smith, 'Turkey Defies EU Sanctions by Sending Fourth Ship to Hunt for Gas Off Cyprus', *The Times*, 17 July 2019,

https://www.thetimes.co.uk/article/turkey-defies-eu-sanctions-by-sending-fourth-ship-to-hunt-for-gas-off-cyprus-d6hf88wsp.

36 'Turkish Blockade of Ship Off Cyprus Is Out of Eni's Control: CEO', Reuters, 16 February 2018, https://www.reuters.com/article/us-cyprus-natgas-turkey-eni-idUSKCN1G01K0; and 'Eni's Drillship Blocked by Turkish Armed Forces', *Maritime Executive*, 13 February 2018, https://www.maritime-executive.com/article/eni-s-drillship-blocked-by-turkish-armed-forces.

37 Ora Coren, 'Israel's 5% Claim on Gas in Cypriot Field Causes Dispute with Nicosia', *Haaretz*, 11 May 2018, https://www.haaretz.com/israel-news/business/2018-05-11/ty-article/israels-5-claim-on-gas-in-cypriot-field-causes-dispute-with-nicosia/0000017f-f6ae-d318-afff-f7ef4bc80000.

38 'Israel Tells Energy Companies to Hold Fire on Cyprus Gas Project', Reuters, 9 December 2019, https://www.reuters.com/article/us-israel-cyprus-natgas-idUSKBN1YD1HC/.

39 Stuart Elliott, 'Cyprus Gas Field Project Still on Despite Israeli Claim: Minister', S&P Global Commodity Insights, 10 December 2019, https://www.spglobal.com/commodityinsights/en/market-insights/latest-news/natural-gas/121019-cyprus-gas-field-project-still-on-despite-israeli-claim-minister.

40 Michael Harari, 'Israel, Cyprus Face an Opportunity for Shared Economic Reservoir – Opinion', *Jerusalem Post*, 10 March 2022, https://www.jpost.com/opinion/article-700949.

41 Elias Hazou, 'Progress Made on Splitting Proceeds of Natural Gas', *Cyprus Mail*, 20 September 2022, https://cyprus-mail.com/2022/09/20/progress-made-on-splitting-proceeds-of-natural-gas/.

42 Emilie Madi and Mohamed Azakir, 'As Economy Worsens, Lebanese Juggle Dizzying Rates for Devalued Pound', Reuters, 19 March 2023, https://www.reuters.com/world/middle-east/economy-worsens-lebanese-juggle-dizzying-rates-devalued-pound-2023-03-19/.

43 IMF, 'Lebanon: 2023 Article IV Consultation – Press Release; Staff Report; and Statement by the Executive Director for Lebanon', 29 June 2023, https://www.imf.org/en/Publications/CR/Issues/2023/06/28/Lebanon-2023-Article-IV-Consultation-Press-Release-Staff-Report-and-Statement-by-the-535372.

44 Madi and Azakir, 'As Economy Worsens, Lebanese Juggle Dizzying Rates for Devalued Pound'.

45 World Bank, 'Lebanon's Crisis: Great Denial in the Deliberate Depression', 25 January 2022, https://www.worldbank.org/en/news/press-release/2022/01/24/lebanon-s-crisis-great-denial-in-the-deliberate-depression.

46 UN Conference on Trade and Development, 'The Economic Costs of the Israeli Occupation for the Palestinian People: The Unrealized Oil and Natural Gas Potential', 2019, https://unctad.org/system/files/official-document/gdsapp2019d1_en.pdf.

47 IMF, 'IMF Executive Board Approves US$12 Billion Extended Arrangement Under the Extended Fund Facility for Egypt', 11 November 2016, https://www.imf.org/en/News/Articles/2016/11/11/PR16501-Egypt-Executive-Board-Approves-12-billion-Extended-Arrangement#:~:text=On%20November%2011%2C%202016%2C%20the,quota)%20to%20support%20the%-20authorities.

48 Both forecasts from the International Renewable Energy Agency (IRENA)'s reference scenario and from Mondal et al.'s study are based on the TIMES energy-systems model. IRENA forecasts that electricity output will increase from just over 200 terawatt hours (TWh) in 2021 to 385 TWh, and that 75% of this electricity will be generated from fossil fuels in 2030. Assuming only minor efficiency improvements, this will account for 60 bcm of natural-gas demand. See IRENA, 'Renewable Energy Outlook: Egypt', 2018, https://www.irena.org/-/media/Files/IRENA/Agency/Publication/2018/Oct/IRENA_Outlook_Egypt_2018_En.pdf; and Md. Alam Hossain Mondal et al., 'Long-term Optimization of Egypt's Power Sector: Policy Implications', *Energy*, vol. 166, January 2019, pp. 1063–73, https://doi.org/10.1016/j.energy.2018.10.158.

49 Fitch Solutions, 'Egypt's LNG Exports Set to Peak in 2023', 24 January 2023, https://www.fitchsolutions.com/bmi/oil-gas/egypts-lng-exports-set-peak-2023-24-01-2023#:~:text=the%20past%20quarter.-,We%20forecast%20Egypt's%20LNG%20exports%20to%20grow%20by%20 30%25%20y%2Do%2Dy,more%20gas%20 for%20export%20availability.

50 Nie and Mills, 'Eastern Mediterranean Deepwater Gas to Europe: Not Too Little, but Perhaps Too Late'.

51 Israel, Ministry of Energy and Infrastructure, 'Export', https://www.energy-sea.gov.il/home/export/#:~:text=It%20is%20 estimated%20that%20in,million)%20 for%20the%20Israeli%20government.

52 Israel, Ministry of Energy and Infrastructure, 'Domestic Demand: Natural Gas Demand in Israel', accessed 5 January 2023, https://www.energy-sea.gov.il/home/domestic-demand/.

53 Government of Cyprus, 'Cyprus' Integrated National Energy and Climate Plan', January 2020, https://energy.ec.europa.eu/system/files/2020-01/cy_final_necp_main_en_0.pdf.

54 Kingdom of Jordan, Ministry of Energy & Mineral Resources, 'Summary of Jordan Energy Strategy 2020–2030', 2020, https://www.memr.gov.jo/EBV4.0/Root_Storage/EN/EB_Info_Page/StrategyEN2020.pdf.

55 IRENA, 'Energy Profile: Syrian Arab Republic', 8 August 2023, https://www.irena.org/-/media/Files/IRENA/Agency/Statistics/Statistical_Profiles/Middle%20 East/Syrian%20Arab%20Republic_ Middle%20East_RE_SP.pdf.

56 DNV, 'Energy Transition Outlook 2022', October 2022, https://www.connaissancedesenergies.org/sites/default/files/pdf-actualites/DNV_Energy_Transition_Outlook_2022_main_report.pdf.

57 'Factbox: Egypt's Push to Be East Mediterranean Gas Hub', Reuters, 15 January 2020, https://www.reuters.com/article/us-egypt-israel-gas-factbox-idUSKBN1ZE1ON; and Eni, 'ENI Inks Deal with Egypt for 2nd LNG Train in Damietta', press release via Rigzone, 27 March 2005, https://www.rigzone.com/news/oil_gas/a/21356/eni_inks_deal_with_egypt_for_2nd_lng_train_in_damietta/.

58 'Syria Says Pipeline Blast that Caused Blackout Was Terrorist Attack', *Arab News*, 24 August 2020, https://www.arabnews.com/node/1723726/middle-east.

59 UN Development Programme, 'Sustainable Oil and Gas Development in Lebanon, "SODEL"', 1 November 2016, https://procurement-notices.undp.org/view_file.cfm?doc_id=107786.

60 Egypt, Ministry of Petroleum and Mineral Resources, 'Program 6: Oil and Gas Hub Strategy', https://www.petroleum.gov.eg/en/update-project/programs/Documents/P6_En.pdf.

61 Hossam Bahgat, 'Who's Buying Israeli Gas? A Company Owned by the General Intelligence Service', *Mada Masr*, 23 October 2018, https://www.madamasr.com/en/2018/10/23/feature/politics/whos-buying-israeli-gas-a-company-owned-by-the-general-intelligence-service/.

62 *Ibid.*; 'PTT Buys 25% of East Mediterranean Gas Co', *Oil & Gas Journal*, 7 December 2007, https://www.ogj.com/pipelines-transportation/article/17286904/ptt-buys-25-of-east-mediterranean-gas-co; and NewMed Energy, '2022 Financial Statements as of 31.03.2022', p. 25, https://newmedenergy.com/wp-content/uploads/2022/05/FS31032022ENG.pdf.

63 'Leviathan Gas Field', Delek Drilling, July 2020, https://newmedenergy.com/wp-content/uploads/2021/12/DD_Leviathan_Presentation_13072020_VF1_0.pdf.

64 Shell, 'Annual Report', 2016, p. 35, https://reports.shell.com/annual-report/2016/servicepages/downloads/files/entire_shell_ar16.pdf.

65 'Cyprus to Go Ahead with Importing Natural Gas, Despite Geopolitics – Minister', In-Cyprus, 25 May 2023, https://in-cyprus.philenews.com/local/cyprus-to-go-ahead-with-importing-natural-gas-despite-geopolitics-minister/.

66 'U.S. Voices Misgivings on EastMed Gas Pipeline – Greek Officials', Reuters, 11 January 2022, https://www.reuters.com/business/energy/us-voices-misgivings-eastmed-gas-pipeline-greek-officials-2022-01-11/.

67 'Eni's Descalzi Says Ankara Is Needed to Resume EastMed Efforts', *Decode39*, 18 May 2023, https://decode39.com/6761/eni-descalzi-turkey-needed-eastmed/.

68. Gergely Molnar, 'Economics of Gas Transportation by Pipeline and LNG', in Manfred Hafner and Giacomo Luciani (eds.), *The Palgrave Handbook of International Energy Economics* (Cham, Switzerland: Palgrave Macmillan, 2022), p. 27.

69. Kate Abnett, 'EU Agrees to Push for Fossil Fuel Phaseout Ahead of COP28', Reuters, 9 March 2023, https://www.reuters.com/business/environment/eu-agrees-push-fossil-fuel-phaseout-ahead-cop28-2023-03-09/; and Rheanna Johnston et al., 'Repowering Towards EU Gas Demand Reduction', E3G, 21 October 2022, https://www.e3g.org/publications/repowering-towards-eu-gas-demand-reduction/.

70. Orhan Coskun and Ari Rabinovitch, 'Israel–Turkey Gas Pipeline Discussed as European Alternative to Russian Energy', Reuters, 29 March 2022, https://www.reuters.com/business/energy/israel-turkey-gas-pipeline-an-option-russia-wary-europe-sources-2022-03-29/.

71. James Mackenzie and Ece Toksabay, 'Turkey, Israel to Re-appoint Ambassadors After Four-year Chill', Reuters, 18 August 2022, https://www.reuters.com/world/middle-east/israel-says-restore-full-diplomatic-relations-with-turkey-2022-08-17/.

72. 'Cyprus Wants Shipping Corridor to Export Natgas – President', Reuters, 29 May 2023, https://www.reuters.com/article/cyprus-energy/cyprus-wants-shipping-corridor-to-export-natgas-president-idINL8N37Q14X/.

73. Petroleum Development Consultants, 'PDC Response on LNG', https://www.gov.il/BlobFolder/reports/ng_commitee/he/PDCResponseonLNG.pdf.

74. Global Energy Monitor Wiki, 'Eilat FLNG Terminal', https://www.gem.wiki/Eilat_LNG_Terminal.

75. 'Hezbollah Threatens to Target Israel's Offshore Gas Platforms', *Times of Israel*, 7 February 2018, https://www.timesofisrael.com/hezbollah-threatens-to-target-israels-offshore-gas-platforms/.

76. Cyprus, Ministry of Energy, Commerce and Industry, 'LNG Terminal', https://hydrocarbons.gov.cy/en/energy-infrastructures/lng-terminal.

77. Peter Stevenson, 'Cyprus Gas Ambitions: From Dreams to Reality in 2023?', *MEES*, vol. 66, no. 4, 27 January 2023, https://www.mees.com/2023/1/27/oil-gas/cyprus-gas-ambitions-from-dreams-to-reality-in-2023/f0154a20-9e43-11ed-b50a-fbcb54be70bc.

78. Petroleum Development Consultants, 'PDC Response on LNG'.

79. Nassir Shirkhani, 'LNG on Radar for ExxonMobil After Cyprus Success', Upstream Online, 7 March 2019, https://www.upstreamonline.com/weekly/lng-on-radar-for-exxonmobil-after-cyprus-success/2-1-556700.

80. Known until recently as Olympus.

81. 'Cyprus: A Transforming Hub for Natural Gas Transport to Europe', Fast Forward, 6 June 2023, https://fastforward.com.cy/business/cyprus-transforming-hub-natural-gas-transport-europe.

82. Golar LNG, 'Fleet', https://www.golarlng.com/fleet.aspx.

83. Menelaos Hadjicostis, 'Cyprus, Israel Working on Deal for Natural Gas Pipeline, Processing Plant in Cyprus', Associated Press, 15 May 2023, https://apnews.com/article/cyprus-israel-natural-gas-pipeline-liquefaction-mediterranean-3d74bbc70e512e6aa1dba70aadb1c6e0.

84. KPMG, 'Floating LNG: Revolution and Evolution for the Global Industry?', 2014, https://assets.kpmg.com/content/dam/kpmg/pdf/2014/11/floating-LNG-evolution-and-revolution-for-the-global-industry.pdf.

85. Lucy Hine, 'Chevron and NewMed Select Yards for Leviathan FLNG Dual FEED Contracts', TradeWinds, 4 April 2023, https://www.tradewindsnews.com/gas/chevron-and-newmed-select-yards-for-leviathan-flng-dual-feed-contracts/2-1-1430070.

86. Iain Esau, 'Chevron Set to Light Touchpaper on FLNG Contest', Upstream Online, 22 March 2023, https://www.upstreamonline.com/exclusive/chevron-set-to-light-touchpaper-on-flng-contest/2-1-1423065.

ARMED FORCES: DEFENCE POLICY, CAPABILITY, COOPERATION AND MODERNISATION

THEMES | ARMED FORCES: DEFENCE POLICY, CAPABILITY, COOPERATION AND MODERNISATION

CHAPTER FOUR

DEFENCE COOPERATION has thickened links between key Eastern Mediterranean powers in recent years, but it has not translated into formal alliances.

THE RISK OF WAR between the adversarial states of the region is generally low, but protracted conflicts, significant investments in defence modernisation and an appetite for brinkmanship may lead to miscalculation in the maritime and aerospace domains.

ALONGSIDE THE ISRAEL–HAMAS WAR, in March 2024 the biggest risk of major conflict involves Israel, Iran and Lebanese Hizbullah, with a possible extension to Syria. Below that threshold, Israel carries out regular military operations in the West Bank, Lebanon and Syria, while Turkiye intervenes militarily in Cyprus, Libya and Syria.

TURKIYE AND ISRAEL are the region's most militarily powerful and capable states but are also those with the most foes or rivals. Their defence policies and regional ambitions are major drivers of the overall regional landscape.

THE US remains the most significant external security partner in the region even as states diversify their relationships.

A photo taken on 7 August 2019 shows the French anti-submarine frigate *Auvergne* (R), the US Navy USS *Donald Cook* guided-missile destroyer (2R) and the Greek HS *Aigaion* frigate (2L) during an exercise simulating a humanitarian response to a powerful earthquake and significant movement of IDF and foreign vessels in the Mediterranean Sea. (Photo: Jack Guez/AFP via Getty Images)

LIST OF ACRONYMS

AFV	armoured fighting vehicle
APC	armoured personnel carrier
AShM	anti-ship missile
ASW	anti-submarine warfare
AUV	armoured utility vehicle
CAC	Chengdu Aircraft Industrial Group
CISR	combat, intelligence, surveillance and reconnaissance
CNG	Cypriot National Guard
EAF	Egyptian Armed Forces
EEZ	Exclusive Economic Zone
EMPAE	Single Medium-Term Modernization Development Program
FDI HN	*Frégate de Défense et d'Intervention* – Hellenic Navy (defence and intervention frigate – Hellenic Navy)
FGA	fighter-ground attack
FMF	Foreign Military Financing
FREMM	*Frégate Européenne Multi-Mission* (European multi-purpose frigate)
G2G	government-to-government
GMYP	Gideon Multi-Year Plan
HAF	Hellenic Armed Forces
IDF	Israel Defense Forces
IFV	infantry fighting vehicle
IMF	International Monetary Fund
ISIS	Islamic State
ISR	intelligence, surveillance and reconnaissance
LHD	amphibious assault ship
LoI	Letter of Intent
MBT	main battle tank
MDCA	Mutual Defense Cooperation Agreement
MoU	Memorandum of Understanding
MRH	multi-role helicopter
n.k.	not known
OMN	Oman
OPV	offshore patrol vessel
PKK	Kurdistan Workers' Party
PPV	protected patrol vehicle
QME	Qualitative Military Edge
ROK	Republic of Korea
SAM	surface-to-air missile
SAR	search and rescue
SoI	Statement of Intent
TAF	Turkish Armed Forces
TAI	Turkish Aerospace Industries
TKMS	ThyssenKrupp Marine Systems
UAE	United Arab Emirates
UAV	uninhabited aerial vehicle
UCAV	uninhabited combat air vehicle

INTRODUCTION

This chapter analyses the defence policy, relationships, capability, economics and procurement of the five Eastern Mediterranean countries with the most significant defence cooperation and modernisation policies: Cyprus, Egypt, Greece, Israel and Turkiye (see Figure 4.1). Although a war between some of these states with adversarial relations is unlikely, there is a risk of miscalculation, especially in the maritime and aerospace domains. In particular, Cyprus, Egypt, Greece and Israel have shared similar concerns about Turkish ambitions since the 2010s, which their security policies have sought to contain.

All five nations rely on conscription with plans for the mobilisation of substantial reserves in the event of a major conflict. While several of these countries are still oriented towards a large-scale land conflict, they all recognise that there is a need to address other threats, such as in the maritime domain and those brought by non-state armed groups. Israel's technological capability is substantially greater than that of the other states, notably in the air domain (see Figure 4.9). However, its relatively small, and littoral-focused, navy puts it at a disadvantage in the maritime domain compared to some of the other nations (see Figure 4.12).

The United States has been and will continue to be the most significant defence partner for most states in the region. While Russia successfully projected military power into Syria in 2015, improved its defence relations with Egypt and Turkiye, and has a military footprint in Syria and Libya, its overall defence profile pales in comparison with that of the US. No other external power has been or will be able to offer the same level of security assurances, training, funding and equipment in the near term as the US. The lifting of the US arms embargo on Cyprus in 2022 creates the possibility that Nicosia will also align with this trend (see Figure 4.5). However, all five countries have made efforts to diversify their defence relationships and as the US seeks to direct more of its effort to the Indo-Pacific region, the US relationship could become less central to these countries' security, albeit to very different degrees. The United States' key role in deterring

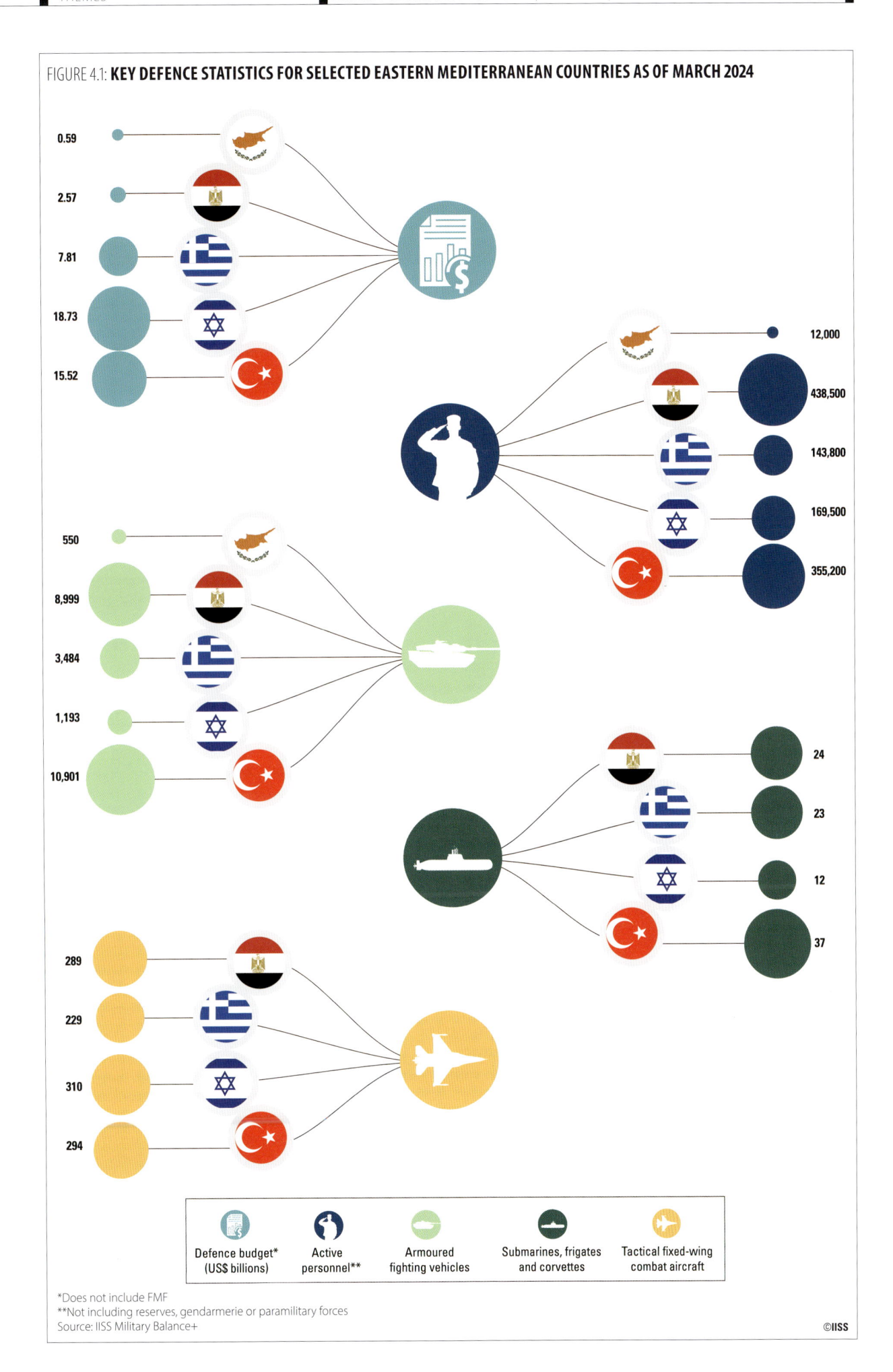

FIGURE 4.1: KEY DEFENCE STATISTICS FOR SELECTED EASTERN MEDITERRANEAN COUNTRIES AS OF MARCH 2024

Defence budget* (US$ billions)
- Cyprus: 0.59
- Egypt: 2.57
- Greece: 7.81
- Israel: 18.73
- Türkiye: 15.52

Active personnel
- Cyprus: 12,000
- Egypt: 438,500
- Greece: 143,800
- Israel: 169,500
- Türkiye: 355,200

Armoured fighting vehicles
- Cyprus: 550
- Egypt: 8,999
- Greece: 3,484
- Israel: 1,193
- Türkiye: 10,901

Submarines, frigates and corvettes
- Egypt: 24
- Greece: 23
- Israel: 12
- Türkiye: 37

Tactical fixed-wing combat aircraft
- Egypt: 289
- Greece: 229
- Israel: 310
- Türkiye: 294

*Does not include FMF
**Not including reserves, gendarmerie or paramilitary forces
Source: IISS Military Balance+

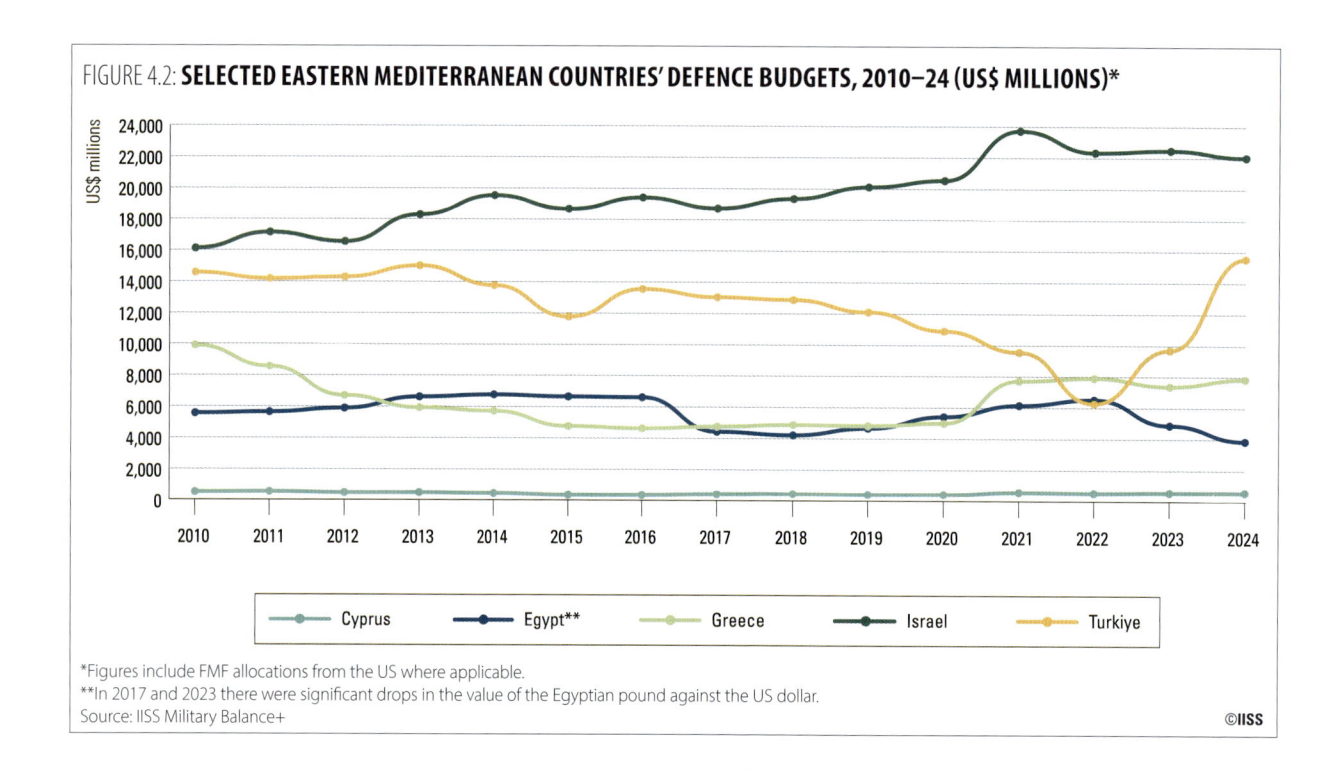

FIGURE 4.2: **SELECTED EASTERN MEDITERRANEAN COUNTRIES' DEFENCE BUDGETS, 2010–24 (US$ MILLIONS)***

*Figures include FMF allocations from the US where applicable.
**In 2017 and 2023 there were significant drops in the value of the Egyptian pound against the US dollar.
Source: IISS Military Balance+

regional escalation at the beginning of the 2023 Israel–Hamas war, as well as Israel's reliance on the US for its defence needs, illustrates its enduring centrality.

The 7 October Hamas-led attacks on Israel and the ensuing war demonstrate the Israeli dilemma. Israel has invested significantly in modernising its forces to meet new threats, with domestic defence spending bolstered by annual US Foreign Military Funding (FMF) allocations that currently come to US$3.3 billion. However, its overreliance on and over-confidence in superior technology and intelligence, and its strategy of degrading rivals through targeted assassinations and destruction of weapons arsenals, have caused it to dismiss enduring security and political realities. The country has yet to conduct a comprehensive review of the failures that led to the October attacks and to rethink its defence strategy accordingly. More immediately, its armed forces are focused on defeating Hamas, degrading Lebanese Hizbullah and deterring Iran. These are complex and resource-intensive missions that will shape the future of Israeli grand strategy.

Egypt, with the largest military in the region by personnel, has made heavy investments in the 'sharp end' of the navy's and air force's capability over the past decade. However, this has not been matched by comparable investment in combat 'enabling' capabilities. The bulk of its large army and separate air-defence command are probably no more capable than they were before the 2013 coup, having received less equipment recapitalisation than the other two services. The growth of the armed forces' role in the economy has also had a negative impact on capability and readiness.

Turkish foreign policy has become increasingly assertive during President Recep Tayyip Erdoğan's tenure at the helm of the Turkish Republic. The counter-insurgency campaign against the Kurdish Workers' Party (PKK) in Turkiye has been accompanied by cross-border action and large-scale interventions against PKK-associated Kurdish groups in northern Syria and Iraq. Military support to Libya and Azerbaijan has also been substantial. Despite the risks, these operations have achieved political objectives and demonstrated a level of expeditionary military capability that the other states in this study either do not have or have certainly not demonstrated recently. However, this independent and militarised approach has produced regional animosity and has conflicted with the interests of NATO allies. Turkiye's expulsion from the F-35 programme in 2019 due to its acquisition of a Russian surface-to-air missile (SAM) system is the most significant consequence of this so far. Mass purges of personnel from the Turkish military following a coup attempt in 2016 have had a negative impact on operational capability, although the extent to which

FIGURE 4.3: **NOMINAL CHANGE IN LOCAL CURRENCY UNIT OF SELECTED EASTERN MEDITERRANEAN COUNTRIES' DEFENCE BUDGETS, 2010–24 (2010=100)**

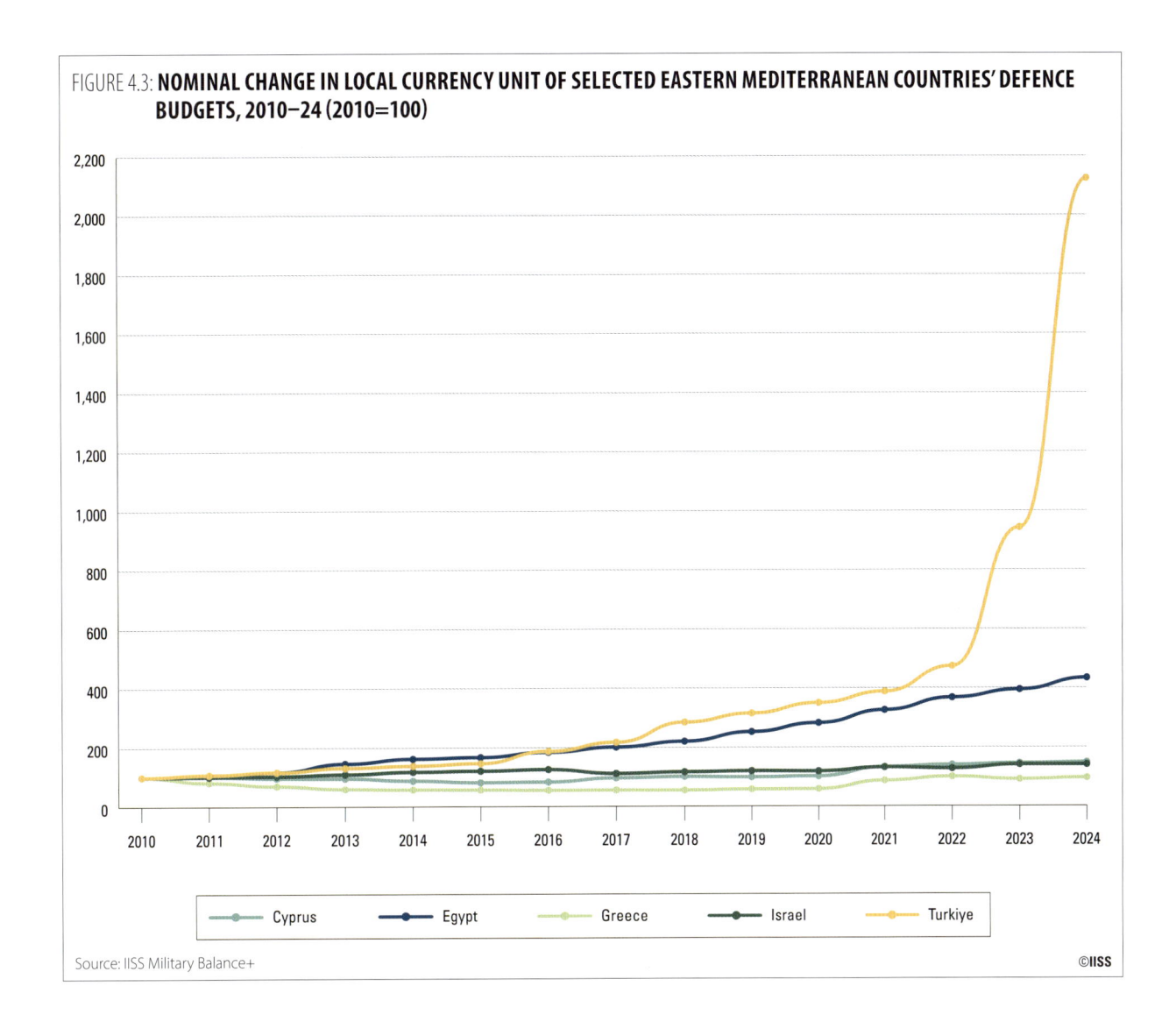

Source: IISS Military Balance+

©IISS

FIGURE 4.4: **REAL CHANGE IN SELECTED EASTERN MEDITERRANEAN COUNTRIES' DEFENCE BUDGETS, 2010–24 (2010=100)**

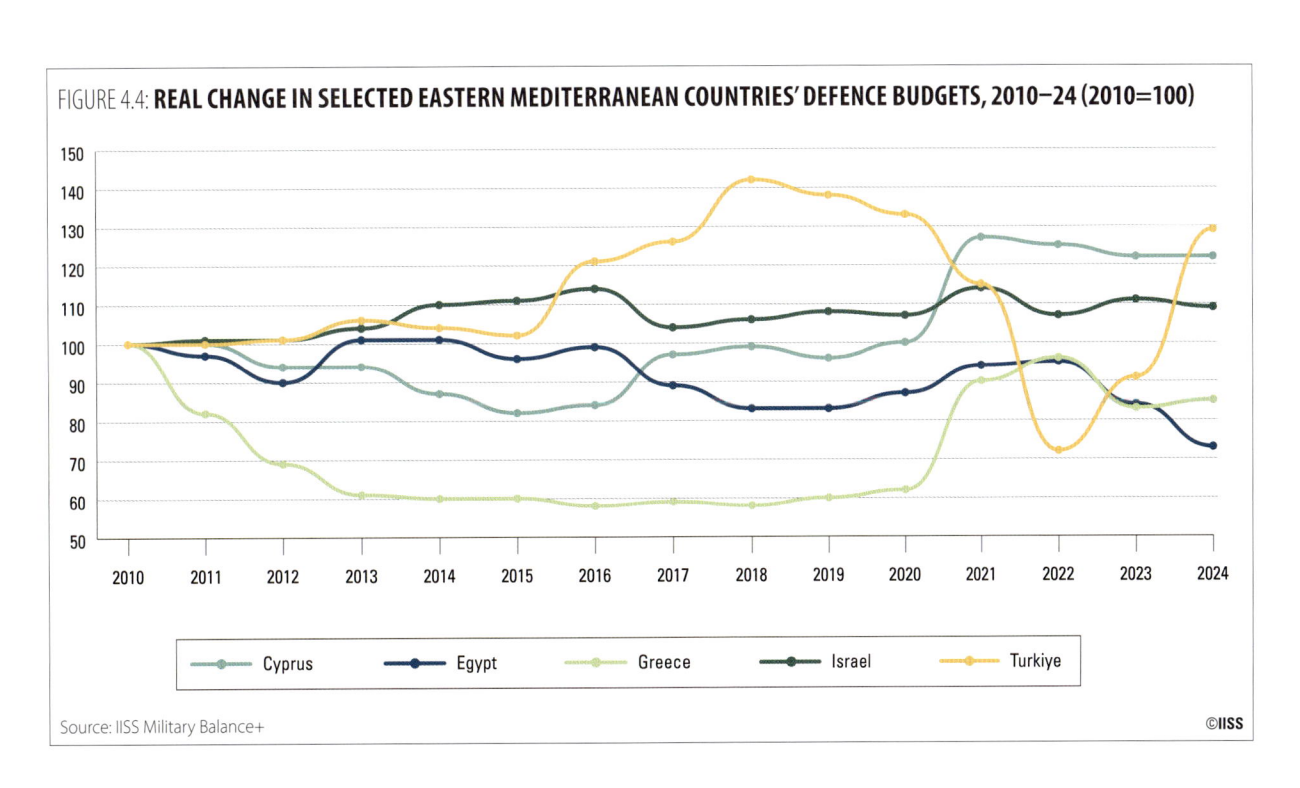

Source: IISS Military Balance+

©IISS

this is still the case is unclear. Substantial investment in the local defence industry has enabled the production of a broad range of equipment, most notably armed uninhabited aerial vehicles (UAVs) (see Table 4.5). It has also partly offset the decreasing value of the lira against the dollar as well as the effect of embargoes placed on Turkiye by other states.

As relations with its Turkish neighbour have deteriorated, Greece has sought to strengthen its relationship with the US and France as well as newer partners such as Israel. The impact of the 2008 global financial crisis on Greek public finances forced a pause in modernisation efforts until the late 2010s; defence spending has yet to return to the 2010 level, in real terms, despite a dramatic uplift in spending since 2021. Ambitious plans to modernise the navy and the air force will require this to continue and, on the current trajectory, will give Greece a qualitative combat-air advantage over rival Turkiye by the end of the decade.

Knowing that it would struggle to resist a Turkish offensive by itself, Cyprus has invested in developing defence ties with other countries as well as strengthening its own capabilities. Even before the lifting of the US embargo in 2022, Nicosia had sought to cultivate ties with the US while developing them with neighbouring Israel and maintaining them with its ally Greece. Efforts to professionalise the national guard are under way, with the defence budget now holding steady following a significant uplift in 2021.

As exploitation of undersea resources develops over the 2020s, all five countries will require greater capabilities in the maritime domain even as traditional threats remain or take precedence, such as Israel's concern with Iran's nuclear programme and the activities of non-state armed groups in its near abroad. All five countries have recently made, or begun to make, substantial investments to modernise and enlarge (in tonnage if not overall ship numbers) their navies. Defence ties between Cyprus, Egypt, Greece and Israel have developed rapidly just as Turkiye has questioned maritime boundaries allocated under international law, for example through its 2019 memorandum of understanding (MoU) signed with Libya. Whether this convergence will end due to the current detente between Egypt, Greece and Turkiye or survive the repercussions of the Israel–Hamas war or a potential regional war remains uncertain.

CYPRUS

DEFENCE POLICIES AND PRIORITIES

Following Turkiye's invasion in 1974 and support for the breakaway state of the Turkish Republic of Northern Cyprus (TRNC), Cyprus's security priority is protecting its territorial integrity. Efforts to achieve reunification have failed and, at the time of writing, the prospect of holding new negotiations remains low.[1] Turkiye maintains a substantial deployment of forces in that territory and, should hostilities resume, the Cypriot National Guard (CNG) is tasked with stalling an advance until allied forces can arrive.[2] A modernisation effort, launched in 2016, seeks to increase professionalisation and reduce conscript liability.[3] Cyprus has no public defence white papers or strategy documents, although there have been calls to create one.[4] More recently, ministers have talked of a 'six pillar' strategy which includes strengthening defence relations with other states, participating in European Union (EU) defence initiatives and cracking down on 'draft dodging'.[5]

DEFENCE RELATIONSHIPS

Since Cyprus gained independence from the United Kingdom in 1960, Greece has been its primary security partner. Athens has forward-deployed troops to Cyprus ever since and fought alongside the CNG during the Turkish invasion in 1974. Unable to join NATO because of Turkish opposition, Cyprus has had to find its own way.

Cyprus has emerged as a key nerve centre during the ongoing Israel–Hamas war, serving as a logistical hub for the US, while the UK has conducted air operations from its sovereign bases and Germany has established an evacuation force there.[6] Today, Cyprus has 17 defence-cooperation agreements (bilateral, tripartite and quadripartite) with both regional and international actors, including with Egypt, France, Germany, Israel, the UK and the US (see Figure 4.5).[7] Cyprus views the EU as a significant component of its security

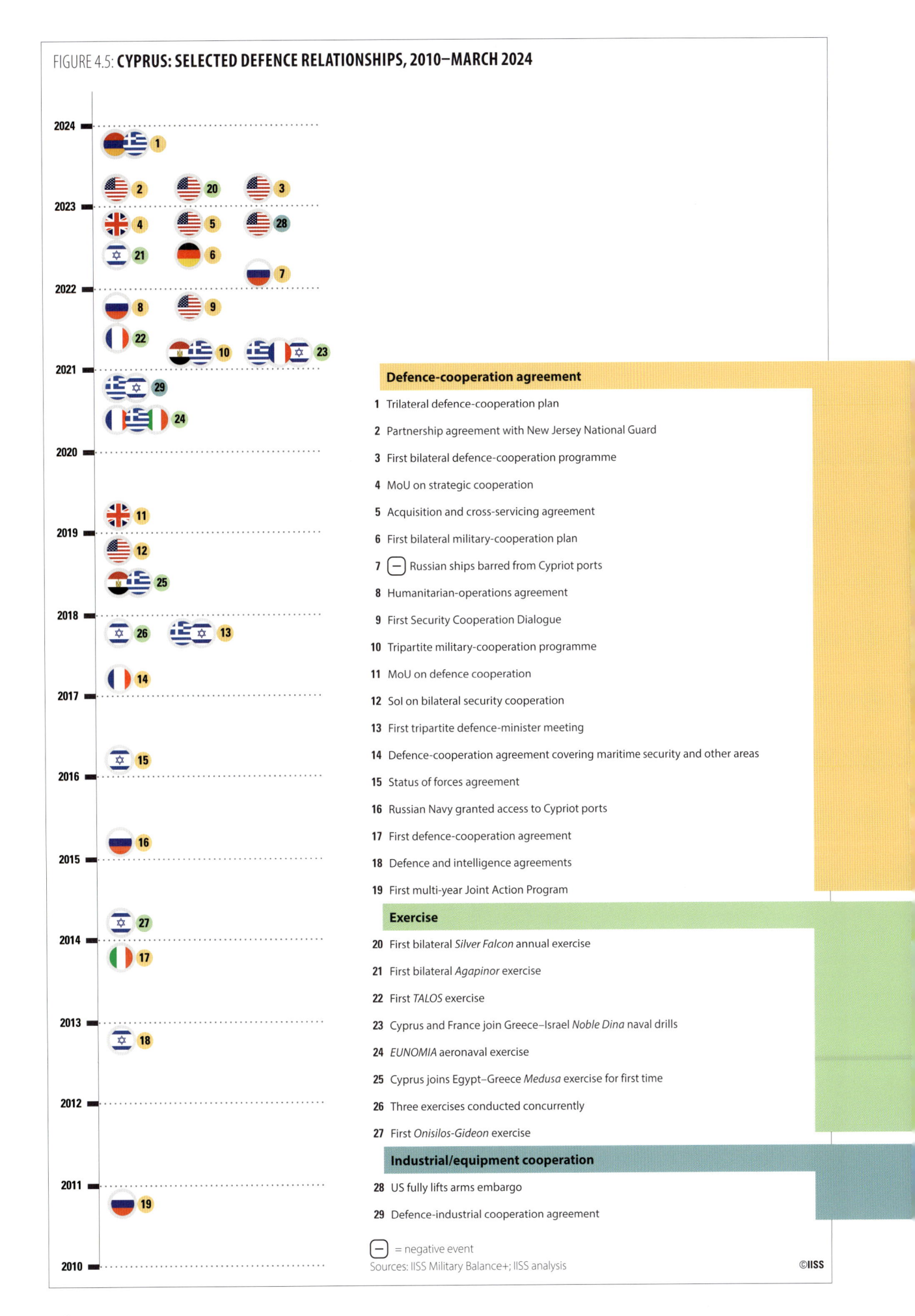

THEMES — ARMED FORCES: DEFENCE POLICY, CAPABILITY, COOPERATION AND MODERNISATION

FIGURE 4.5: CYPRUS: SELECTED DEFENCE RELATIONSHIPS, 2010–MARCH 2024

Defence-cooperation agreement

1. Trilateral defence-cooperation plan
2. Partnership agreement with New Jersey National Guard
3. First bilateral defence-cooperation programme
4. MoU on strategic cooperation
5. Acquisition and cross-servicing agreement
6. First bilateral military-cooperation plan
7. (−) Russian ships barred from Cypriot ports
8. Humanitarian-operations agreement
9. First Security Cooperation Dialogue
10. Tripartite military-cooperation programme
11. MoU on defence cooperation
12. SoI on bilateral security cooperation
13. First tripartite defence-minister meeting
14. Defence-cooperation agreement covering maritime security and other areas
15. Status of forces agreement
16. Russian Navy granted access to Cypriot ports
17. First defence-cooperation agreement
18. Defence and intelligence agreements
19. First multi-year Joint Action Program

Exercise

20. First bilateral *Silver Falcon* annual exercise
21. First bilateral *Agapinor* exercise
22. First *TALOS* exercise
23. Cyprus and France join Greece–Israel *Noble Dina* naval drills
24. *EUNOMIA* aeronaval exercise
25. Cyprus joins Egypt–Greece *Medusa* exercise for first time
26. Three exercises conducted concurrently
27. First *Onisilos-Gideon* exercise

Industrial/equipment cooperation

28. US fully lifts arms embargo
29. Defence-industrial cooperation agreement

(−) = negative event
Sources: IISS Military Balance+; IISS analysis

©IISS

framework and hopes that its participation in the EU Permanent Structured Cooperation and the European Defence Fund will contribute to continental security and enable Cyprus to achieve its own modernisation objectives.[8]

In 2022, the US lifted an arms embargo that had been in place since 1987,[9] with Congress requesting an increase in security cooperation with Cyprus and Greece.[10] Deepened defence relations with Cyprus were defined in the 2024 annual Bilateral Defence Cooperation Programme.[11] The embargo, however, had forced Cyprus to pursue other relationships, notably with Russia, whose navy enjoyed access to Cypriot ports.[12] However, a combination of US and EU pressure, the legacy of the Cypriot banking crisis and the 2021 elections forced a change in policy and prevented an expansion in access to ports and airports by the Russian military.[13] Russia's full-scale invasion of Ukraine in early 2022 altered the relationship further: Cyprus has barred all Russian vessels from its ports since March 2022,[14] granting entry instead to US vessels in exchange for military logistic support.[15]

Cyprus participates in a range of multi-domain military exercises with Eastern Mediterranean states. These include the *Onisilos-Gideon* and *Iadon* exercises with Israel, which involve Cypriot air-defence systems,[16] and the Egypt-led *Tams-Heracles* special-operations drills.[17] Similarly, Cyprus participates in the *Medusa* drills, held since 2019, with Egypt, Greece and others.[18] In 2022, the CNG sent troops, for the first time, to the US–Jordanian *Eager Lion* exercise in Jordan.[19] Cypriot and Jordanian special forces held a smaller bilateral exercise in Cyprus.[20]

MILITARY CAPABILITY

The CNG is comprised of a relatively small active component of 12,000 personnel, most of whom are conscripts, which would then be supplemented by a reserve pool of 50,000 during wartime. Since 2016, the CNG has sought to become a more professional force, reducing national service from 24 to 14 months.[21] The CNG is oriented towards territorial defence and the land element consists of a mix of armoured, mechanised and infantry brigades with supporting battalions of artillery. The small air wing of rotary-wing platforms provides fire support to ground units, with a small search and rescue (SAR) component. The CNG's maritime wing is tasked with exclusive economic zone (EEZ) patrol and coastal defence: it is small but will likely grow, certainly in tonnage, over the next decade as resource exploitation in Cyprus's EEZ develops further.[22] The CNG's armoured-vehicle and artillery fleet is ageing and is a mix of Soviet/Russian and French equipment in need of recapitalisation.

ECONOMICS, PROCUREMENT AND MODERNISATION

After years of cuts between 2010 and 2015 that averaged 3.9% annually in

TABLE 4.1: CYPRUS: SELECTED PROCUREMENT PROGRAMMES, 2010–MARCH 2024

Contract date	Equipment	Type	Quantity	Value (US$ millions)	Contractor	Delivery	Service
c. 2014	*Alasia* (ex-OMN *Al Mabrukha*)	Coastal patrol craft	1	Donation	Omani government	2017	Navy
c. 2016	*Commodore Andreas Ioannides* (OPV 62)	Coastal patrol craft	1	49	Israel Shipyards	2018	Navy
December 2018	*Aerostar*	Medium ISR UAV	4	13	Aeronautics	2019	Air Force
2019	• NORA B-52 • BOV M16 *Milos*	• 155mm self-propelled howitzer • AUV	• 24 • 8	86	Yugoimport	2019–21	Army
December 2019	MM40 *Exocet*	Land-based AShM	n.k.	101	M MBDA	n.k.	Navy
December 2019	*Mistral*	Point defence SAM	n.k.	168	M MBDA	n.k.	Army
July 2022	H145M	MRH	6	156	M Airbus	By 2026	Air Force

Ⓜ = Multinational

Sources: IISS Military Balance+; IISS analysis

©IISS

Picture taken from Cyprus's coastal patrol craft *Commodore Andreas Ioannides* shows a UK Royal Navy *Lynx* helicopter taking part in the *Argonaut* 2019 exercise, in which the militaries of Cyprus, France, Germany, Greece, Israel, the UK and the US participated from 28–30 May 2019 offshore Cyprus. (Photo: Iakovos Hatzistavrou/AFP via Getty Images)

real terms, the Cypriot defence budget gradually recovered before a significant increase was implemented in 2021, followed by more moderate annual increases (see Figure 4.2). The budget grew from €362 million in 2010 to €525m in 2023, an increase of 45%. In dollar terms, however, the increase is much smaller. For example, when measured in constant US dollars, funding went from US$402m in 2010 to US$499m in 2023, an increase of approximately 24%. The budget uplifts in recent years are likely in response to falls in the value of the euro against the dollar as well as to higher inflation, which soared to 8.1% in 2022.

According to Cyprus's draft 2024 budget, funding for the Ministry of Defence will increase again but by a more modest amount than in recent years to reach €535m (US$585m). Official projections are less positive still, with the budgets set to contract to €529m for 2025 and remain at this level in 2026. Such a funding profile will result in cuts in real terms, although inflation is expected by the IMF to steadily drop from 3.5% in 2023 to 2.1% by 2026.[23] The economic outlook for Cyprus is fairly stable; however, the current war between Israel and Hamas might generate further economic pressure on countries in the region.

During the Cold War and the decades immediately after, Cyprus largely sourced equipment from France, Greece and the Soviet Union and later Russia, although cuts in defence spending in the first half of the 2010s impacted modernisation efforts. The improvement in Cypriot–Israeli relations over the past decade has had a defence-procurement element,[24] while the recent acquisition of Serbian howitzers[25] and German armed helicopters[26] suggests a further broadening of the sources of equipment (see Table 4.1). The end of the United States' 35-year-long arms embargo on Cyprus in 2022[27] is a major development and will reinforce this trend.

EGYPT

DEFENCE POLICIES AND PRIORITIES

Egypt does not publish formal defence white papers or strategy documents, which makes assessing its priorities difficult. Since the 2013 coup, much effort has gone into regime consolidation and expanding the military's role in the civilian economy, likely at the expense of operational capability. In a 2020 speech, President Abdel Fattah al-Sisi stated that the Egyptian Armed Forces' (EAF) mission was 'to protect our country, secure our people, safeguard our destiny and preserve our homeland against all … threats that aim at destabilising the … security of our nation by attempting to approach its land, sea and air borders'.[28]

Despite such multi-domain threat assessments, modernisation efforts of the last decade have prioritised the air force and navy (see figures 4.9 and 4.12), with the army and the air-defence command undergoing more limited equipment recapitalisation (see Figure 4.6).

At the time of writing, the war in Gaza is Egypt's highest national-security priority. The prospect of a lasting medium- to high-intensity conflict in Gaza and the potential forced displacement of the Gazan population into Egypt has mobilised Egyptian diplomacy and security forces. Cairo has been part of the diplomatic efforts to secure a ceasefire and to facilitate humanitarian assistance to stave off a potential societal collapse that would put pressure on Egypt to open its borders. Egyptian authorities are concerned that the war could re-energise Islamic State (ISIS)-affiliated groups in northern Sinai. These continue to be the main internal threat, even though the Egyptian military largely defeated them in the 2010s.

The war has also sparked Egyptian concerns about its relationship with Israel. Cairo is committed to the peace treaty with Tel Aviv, though it worries that Israel's maximalist ambitions in Gaza could threaten Egypt's stability. A related concern has been Red Sea security. The war has disrupted traffic so much that by February 2024 Egypt had seen a 50% drop[29] in revenue from the Suez Canal compared to the same period in 2023, with an outsized impact on its access to critical foreign currency. Yet Egypt has been unwilling to lead or take part in a maritime response to the threat despite the fact that protecting these maritime choke points and offshore natural-gas fields in the Mediterranean is a core responsibility of the revitalised Egyptian navy. For the Egyptian defence establishment, Israel's military-modernisation plans based on the lessons of the Israel–Hamas war may also be challenging. Cairo will likely be unable to match Israel's probably greater defence spending or access to advanced weaponry, deepening the military imbalance between the two countries. And while defence cooperation has thus far withstood the crisis, it may be politically problematic for Cairo to hold exercises or share information with Israel as it did in the past if no diplomatic progress is made.

On its western flank, Egypt sees Libya as particularly unstable. In a highly unusual move, it threatened to intervene militarily in order to counter Turkish influence before a ceasefire with the United Nations-backed Libyan interim authority was signed in August 2020.[30] Turkiye's growing influence has indeed been a major concern for Cairo. It saw Ankara's support for Islamist forces, power projection in Syria and Libya, and revisionist policies as an ideological and strategic challenge. Cairo has therefore sought to organise a regional front to contain Turkish power, with mixed results. The sluggish Egyptian economy has jeopardised such ambition.[31] Since 2022, however, relations between the two countries have improved. Egypt reportedly facilitated the transfer of Turkish armed UAVs to Sudan in 2023 and approved the acquisition of its own shortly before President Erdoğan visited Cairo in February 2024.[32]

The ongoing civil war in Sudan is another source of concern in Cairo. It has backed the Sudanese Armed Forces against the Rapid Support Force, a paramilitary group that is backed by the United Arab Emirates (UAE). Large-scale atrocities and famine have created large numbers of internally displaced persons, raising fears in Cairo of large refugee flows moving north.

Further south, Egypt is concerned that Ethiopia's Grand Ethiopian Renaissance Dam could severely cut into the Nile River's water discharge and reduce

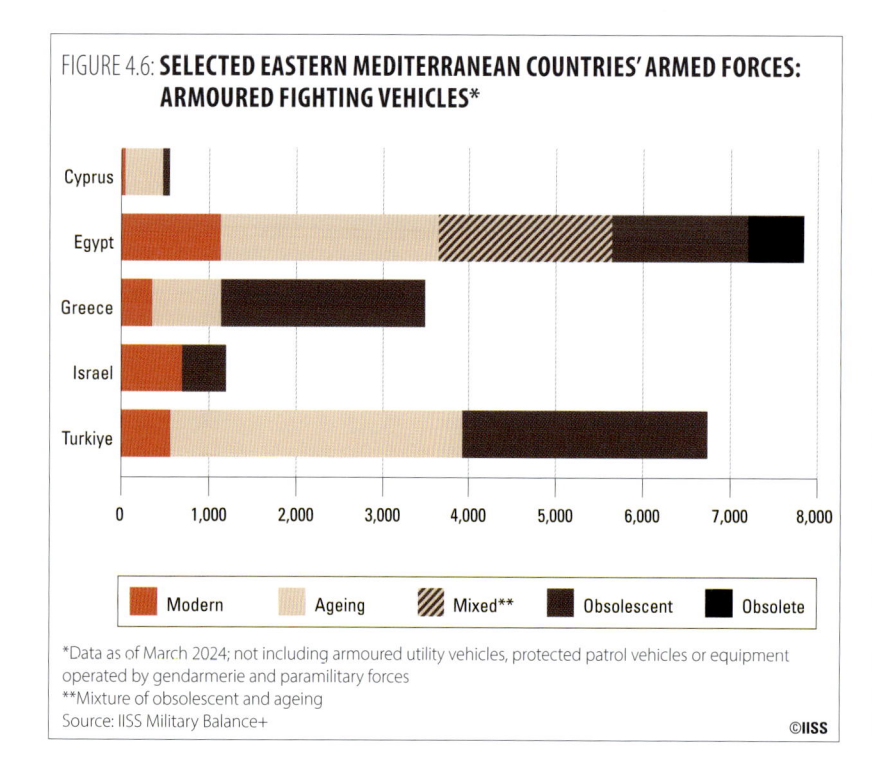

FIGURE 4.6: **SELECTED EASTERN MEDITERRANEAN COUNTRIES' ARMED FORCES: ARMOURED FIGHTING VEHICLES***

Legend: Modern | Ageing | Mixed** | Obsolescent | Obsolete

*Data as of March 2024; not including armoured utility vehicles, protected patrol vehicles or equipment operated by gendarmerie and paramilitary forces
**Mixture of obsolescent and ageing
Source: IISS Military Balance+

An Egyptian Army M60 *Patton* MBT (L) and a YPR-765 PRI IFV (R) are deployed near the Egyptian side of the Rafah border crossing with Gaza on 23 March 2024. (Photo:Khaled Desouki/AFP via Getty Images)

the volume of water available to Egypt. Egypt has alluded to a military option in the form of an airstrike to destroy the dam, but this threat is assessed to be low and designed to provide leverage for a diplomatic agreement.

DEFENCE RELATIONSHIPS

Egypt's major defence partner is the US, which has provided over US$50bn and US$30bn in military and economic assistance, respectively, since 1978.[33] Cooperation has included strategic coordination, training and defence equipment,[34] with the two countries holding regular high-level meetings (see Figure 4.7).[35] Nonetheless, this did not prevent Egypt from signing cooperation agreements with Russia in 2018[36] and 2020.[37] Egypt's desire to diversify its relationships is also reflected in the defence-acquisition sphere, with Russian imports representing the third-largest foreign source of defence equipment between 2019 and 2023 by some measures.[38]

Highly significant is the Egyptian relationship with Gulf states Saudi Arabia and the UAE, which supported the Egyptian government politically and financially following the 2013 coup.[39] This has likely included funding for major defence acquisitions (see page 103). In turn, Egypt took a more junior role in defence and security terms in the region in recent decades due to its economic woes and domestic instability.[40] Egypt contributed naval forces to the Saudi-led intervention in Yemen but resisted sending ground forces (see page 100).

Egyptian–Israeli relations have moved a long way since the two countries signed a peace treaty in 1979, with reports of each country allowing the other to deploy troops or conduct operations in or near the Sinai Peninsula.[41] However, despite this behind-the-scenes cooperation, there are no formal agreements in the defence sphere as there are for energy exploitation.[42]

Since 2014, Cyprus, Egypt and Greece have strengthened diplomatic and defence ties, driven in part by the discovery of offshore energy resources.[43] While this cooperation is currently limited to exercises, training and exchange of expertise,[44] the trilateral format is reinforced by Egypt's bilateral agreements with Cyprus[45] and Greece.[46] The agreements with Greece are defined on an annual basis[47] and include cooperation on SAR.[48]

Although it is difficult to assess the effectiveness of domestic training exercises, Egyptian operational readiness is likely improved through participation in international exercises. The longest-standing of these is the US–Egyptian

Bright Star exercise, which has been held in Egypt since 1980, with the 18th iteration taking place in 2023.[49] Over time, the exercise has evolved to include more countries – the 2021 iteration included personnel from 21 countries[50] – although recent drills are smaller than in the past.[51] The Egyptian Navy also conducts exercises with other Mediterranean navies such as France[52] and Greece[53] as well as drills with Russia[54] and China.[55]

MILITARY CAPABILITY

Whilst Egypt has one of the largest militaries in the region, the operational capability of most of the armed forces, particularly in the army, is unclear. Efforts to professionalise the EAF by providing regular joint and combined-arms training are likely undermined by overly scripted exercises, a continuing reliance on conscripted personnel and a relatively rigid command structure. This offers junior and non-commissioned officers little opportunity for initiative.[56] Reports of relatively low spending on support packages when acquiring US systems likely reflect a wider issue in the EAF's approach to equipment planning. It is probable that the availability rate (the average percentage of the fleet that is ready for use at any time) of non-Western equipment, for which the same level of in-service support is not typically offered at the point of sale, is lower. A growing skills gap between active and reserve personnel, with the latter being assigned menial roles, will further reduce the overall capability of the EAF in the event of a major conflict.[57] The bulk of the army is unlikely to be more capable or operationally ready compared with a decade ago. In fact, it may be worse off due to the relatively anaemic defence budget (see 'Economics, procurement and modernisation' section), the trend of making promotions based on political loyalty and its greater involvement in the civilian economy.

Initially defensive by nature, most of the Egyptian Army remains oriented towards the Sinai Peninsula and Israel. Around half of the army's armoured and mechanised divisions are deployed along the Suez Canal as part of the 2nd and 3rd armies. Strengthened elements (units that were reorganised, fully staffed and better equipped) were pushed forward into the Sinai for security operations.[58] A smaller number of divisions are assigned to the Libyan border in the west, with the remainder held in reserve around Cairo and Alexandria.[59] To protect its coastline and the Suez Canal choke point, the navy is divided between a large Northern Fleet in the Mediterranean and a more recently established Southern Fleet in the Red Sea. Spearheaded by the two French-built *Mistral*-class amphibious assault ships (LHDs), the navy has developed a regional deployment capacity but still lacks maritime helicopters to utilise fully these vessels' capabilities. The air force is generally viewed as the most capable branch of the armed forces. Nevertheless, the wide variety of aircraft types, ages and origins undoubtedly complicates maintenance, a problem faced by the other services as well.

Recent military deployments have been limited, and Cairo remains cautious in using forces beyond its borders. After a heavy-handed approach against the Sinai insurgency, with 88 battalions deployed in the peninsula in early 2018, Egypt adopted a more effective counter-insurgency strategy.[60] Abroad, the EAF takes part in UN missions and has conducted airstrikes in Libya, mainly against ISIS positions. It also contributed a small contingent to the Saudi-led intervention in Yemen by sending four vessels and some F-16s.[61]

ECONOMICS, PROCUREMENT AND MODERNISATION

Since 2010, the Egyptian defence budget has grown by 11.1% annually on average in nominal terms, with significant growth evident in 2013 and 2014 following the overthrow of President Muhammad Morsi by the armed forces. In Egyptian pounds, the budget in 2024 is nominally around four times the level it was in 2010 (see Figure 4.3). However, high and volatile rates of inflation – which is projected to exceed 30% in 2024 – combined with a faltering exchange rate mean that in real US-dollar terms, the growth in defence budgets has been much smaller. Indeed, the 2024 budget is 27% lower in real terms than in 2010 (see Figure 4.4).

However, Egypt receives US$1.3bn annually in FMF from the US, which helps to shore up the increasingly eroded domestic defence budget. This funding is for the procurement of equipment and services from US companies. With major procurement programmes projected to remain a priority, Egypt will likely

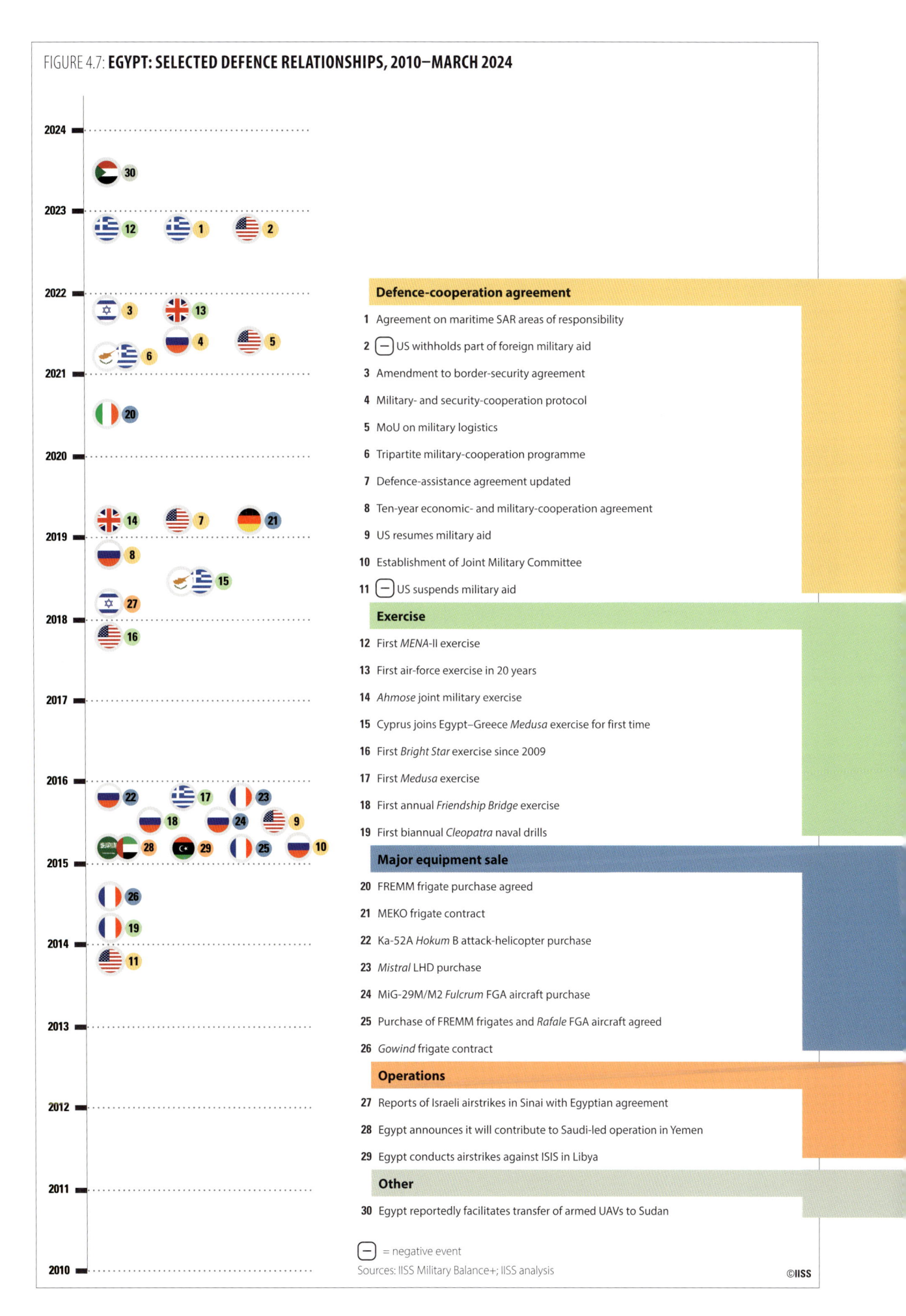

FIGURE 4.7: EGYPT: SELECTED DEFENCE RELATIONSHIPS, 2010–MARCH 2024

Timeline of events (2010–2024):

- 2023: Sudan (30)
- 2022: Greece (12), Greece (1), US (2)
- 2021: Israel (3), UK (13), Cyprus (6), Russia (4), US (5)
- 2020: Italy (20)
- 2019: UK (14), US (7), Germany (21), Russia (8), Israel (27), Cyprus/Greece (15), US (16)
- 2015: Russia (22), Greece (17), France (23), Russia (18), Russia (24), US (9), Saudi Arabia (28), UAE, Libya (29), France (25), Russia (10)
- 2014: France (26), France (19)
- 2013: US (11)

Defence-cooperation agreement

1. Agreement on maritime SAR areas of responsibility
2. (−) US withholds part of foreign military aid
3. Amendment to border-security agreement
4. Military- and security-cooperation protocol
5. MoU on military logistics
6. Tripartite military-cooperation programme
7. Defence-assistance agreement updated
8. Ten-year economic- and military-cooperation agreement
9. US resumes military aid
10. Establishment of Joint Military Committee
11. (−) US suspends military aid

Exercise

12. First *MENA*-II exercise
13. First air-force exercise in 20 years
14. *Ahmose* joint military exercise
15. Cyprus joins Egypt–Greece *Medusa* exercise for first time
16. First *Bright Star* exercise since 2009
17. First *Medusa* exercise
18. First annual *Friendship Bridge* exercise
19. First biannual *Cleopatra* naval drills

Major equipment sale

20. FREMM frigate purchase agreed
21. MEKO frigate contract
22. Ka-52A *Hokum* B attack-helicopter purchase
23. *Mistral* LHD purchase
24. MiG-29M/M2 *Fulcrum* FGA aircraft purchase
25. Purchase of FREMM frigates and *Rafale* FGA aircraft agreed
26. *Gowind* frigate contract

Operations

27. Reports of Israeli airstrikes in Sinai with Egyptian agreement
28. Egypt announces it will contribute to Saudi-led operation in Yemen
29. Egypt conducts airstrikes against ISIS in Libya

Other

30. Egypt reportedly facilitates transfer of armed UAVs to Sudan

(−) = negative event

Sources: IISS Military Balance+; IISS analysis

©IISS

TABLE 4.2: **EGYPT: SELECTED PROCUREMENT PROGRAMMES, 2010–MARCH 2024**

Contract date	Equipment	Type	Quantity	Value (US$ millions)	Contractor		Delivery	Service
October 2010	C295M	Light transport aircraft	3	n.k.	M	Airbus	2011	Air Force
c. 2012	Type-209/1400	Attack submarine	4	n.k.		TKMS	2017–21	Navy
March 2012	C295M	Light transport aircraft	3	n.k.	M	Airbus	2012–13	Air Force
January 2013	C295M	Light transport aircraft	6	n.k.	M	Airbus	2013–14	Air Force
December 2013	S-300VM	Long-range SAM	Approximately 18	500		Almaz-Antey	2015–17	Air Defence Command
July 2014	Al-Fateh (FRA Gowind)	Frigate	4	1,328		Naval Group	2017–ongoing	Navy
July 2014	C295M	Light transport aircraft	8	n.k.	M	Airbus	2015–16	Air Force
c. 2015	Wing Loong	Heavy CISR UAV	n.k.	n.k.		CAC	By 2016	Air Force
2015	C295M	Light transport aircraft	4	n.k.	M	Airbus	2016	Air Force
February 2015	Rafale	FGA aircraft	24	3,881		Dassault Aviation	2015–19	Air Force
February 2015	Tahya Misr (FRA Aquitaine FREMM)	Frigate	1	1,109		Naval Group	2016	Navy
April 2015	MiG-29M/M2 Fulcrum	FGA aircraft	Approximately 46	n.k.		MiG	2017–20	Air Force
September 2015	• Caiman • RG-33	• PPV • PPV	• 400 • 350	Donation		US government	2016–18	Army
September 2015	Gamal Abdel Nasser (FRA Mistral)	LHD	2	1,053		Naval Group	2016	Navy
December 2015	Ka-52A Hokum B	Attack helicopter	46	n.k.		Russian Helicopters	2017–19	Air Force
April 2016	TIBA-1	Communications satellite	1	663	M	Airbus	2019	Egyptian government
2017	• Caiman • RG-33	• PPV • PPV	• 100 • 68	Donation		US government	2018–19	Army
September 2017	Shabab Misr (ex-ROK Po Hang)	Corvette	1	Donation		South Korean government	2017	Navy
2018	Su-35 Flanker M	FGA aircraft	Approximately 24	2,000		Sukhoi	Cancelled	Air Force
November 2018	Wing Loong 1D	Heavy CISR UAV	32	60.46		CAC	n.k.	Air Force
c. 2019	Al-Aziz (GER MEKO A200)	Frigate	4	n.k.		TKMS	2022–ongoing	Navy
c. 2019	IRIS-T SLM	Medium-range SAM	7 batteries	859		Diehl Defence	n.k.	Air Defence Command
2019	• AW149 • AW189	• MRH • MRH	• 24 • 8	975		Leonardo	2020–ongoing	Air Force
August 2020	Al-Galala (ITA FREMM)	Frigate	2	1,371		Fincantieri	2020–21	Navy
c. 2021	AH-64E Apache	Attack helicopter upgrade	Up to 43	n.k.		Boeing	n.k.	Air Force
c. 2021	IRIS-T SLS/X	Medium-range SAM	16 batteries	n.k.		Diehl Defence	n.k.	Air Defence Command
October 2021	Fort Rosalie (ex-UK)	Logistics ship	2	n.k.		UK government	n.k.	Navy
November 2021	Rafale	FGA aircraft	30	4,674		Dassault Aviation	n.k.	Air Force
February 2022	K9 Thunder	155mm self-propelled howitzer	200	1,662		Hanwha Aerospace	n.k.	Army
December 2022	CH-47F Chinook	Heavy transport helicopter	12	426		Boeing	2026	Air Force

(M) = Multinational

Sources: IISS Military Balance+; IISS analysis

©IISS

continue to make strong increases to the defence budget. However, until inflation abates and the pound stabilises against the dollar, the value of these increases will continue to falter and Egypt may struggle with ongoing recapitalisation efforts.

The lack of transparency in defence planning makes it difficult to assess whether Egypt is meeting its own modernisation objectives. Several large procurement decisions seem to have been made with the aim of strengthening political relationships or because an opportunity arose to acquire advanced platforms very quickly.[62] The US has been Egypt's primary source for defence equipment since the peace treaty with Israel in 1979. This led to the US providing Egypt with FMF and the acquisition of seven batches of F-16 fighter aircraft.[63] Although the cessation of US aid in 2013 following the military coup[64] was short-lived,[65] it seems to have prompted Cairo to diversify its sources of equipment. France has been the most significant beneficiary of this and has sold Egypt over 50 *Rafale* fighter aircraft, five frigates, a communications satellite and two LHDs worth US$12.7bn (see Table 4.2). Several acquisitions were reportedly at least partly funded by allies Saudi Arabia and the UAE.[66] The two LHDs had been built for Russia before France cancelled the deal in 2014, which indicates that the acquisition was opportunistic rather than part of a strategic modernisation plan.

Despite the impressive modernisation of the navy, the army and air force still operate large numbers of obsolete platforms. Despite signing contracts for approximately 100 new fighter aircraft over the last decade (not including the almost certainly cancelled deal for the Su-35 *Flanker* M from Russia), Egypt will be hard pressed to recapitalise its combat-aircraft fleet on a one-for-one basis. The separate air-defence command service has one of the most diverse inventories of systems in the world, likely coming with a host of maintenance, training and inter-operability problems. Most of these systems are decades old and approaching obsolescence. The army has seen even less investment: the donation of surplus American patrol vehicles and the assembly of the last of the 1,130 M1A1 main battle tanks (MBTs) are the most significant examples of recapitalisation during the last decade. As with the air force, large numbers of legacy platforms mean a one-for-one replacement will be difficult.

The *Gamal Abdel Nasser* (R), the first of two LHDs sold by France to Egypt based on the former's *Mistral* class, leaves the harbour of Saint-Nazaire, France, on 6 May 2016 for a one-week training session. (Photo: Loic Venance/AFP via Getty Images)

GREECE

DEFENCE POLICIES AND PRIORITIES

The Hellenic Armed Forces (HAF) are a defensive force focused on protecting territorial integrity. Relations with neighbour and NATO ally Turkiye have been marked by persistent tension and competition, illustrated by Turkish brinkmanship at sea in 2019 and 2020 and the MoU it signed with Libya in 2019. However, relations started to improve in 2023.[67]

Greece's latest Defence White Paper was published in 2015[68] and an update is long overdue, particularly as the country's economic performance has improved significantly since then. Some of its warnings have become outdated: the document cites the global economic crisis as a significant cause of uncertainty in southern Europe, which was hit particularly hard. But others remain relevant, such as Russia's annexation of Crimea, nationalist tensions, corruption and transnational organised crime, as well as the continuing deployment of Turkish troops in the TRNC. The paper also lists the exploitation of energy resources in the Mediterranean as a significant element of the country's security.

Greek defence planning was formerly based on five-yearly Single Medium-Term Modernization Development Programs (EMPAEs).[69] However, an expanded ten-year EMPAE, approved in 2006, was effectively ended by the 2008 global financial crisis.[70] Since then, Greece has authorised two classified Force Structure plans. The first, approved in 2013, sought to make the Hellenic Army less top-heavy.[71] As part of this, two corps-level commands were disbanded and their units subordinated directly to 1st Army headquarters.[72] Fewer details of the more recent Force Structure (2020–34) have been released beyond the establishment of the US SOCOM-style Special Warfare Command[73] and ambitions to create new units with a higher level of readiness.[74]

DEFENCE RELATIONSHIPS

NATO membership, and in particular the relationship with the US, forms the backbone of Greek security (see Figure 4.8). Greece gives the US military access to four bases including its naval base in Crete.[75] Amendments to the US–Greece Mutual Defense Cooperation Agreement in 2019 and 2021 now allow the US to use Greek ports to reinforce the NATO eastern flank and

Greek Prime Minister Kyriakos Mitsotakis (L) shakes hands with French President Emmanuel Macron (R) following the signing ceremony of a new defence deal at the Élysée Palace in Paris, France, on 28 September 2021. Greece agreed to buy three frigates from France as part of the strategic partnership agreed between the two countries. (Photo: Ludovic Marin/AFP via Getty Images)

bypass the Bosporus strait through the port of Alexandroupolis.[76] France and the UK are two other privileged partners. Greece's relationship with Paris dates to Greek independence,[77] and was significantly upgraded through the strategic partnership signed in 2021. That agreement included a mutual-assistance[78] clause and paved the way for the acquisition of frigates for the Hellenic Navy. The two countries regularly conduct bilateral military exercises such as the *ARGO*[79] drill, which includes amphibious operations. Greece signed a Joint Vision Statement with the UK in early 2023, which seeks to strengthen defence relations and inter-operability between the two armed forces.[80]

Shared concerns about Turkiye's actions in the region have catalysed Egyptian–Greek defence cooperation. An agreement signed in 2022 allows for officers to attend the two countries' respective military academies.[81] It was followed by an agreement to cooperate on SAR.[82] Greek–Israeli relations have improved since 2010 in part because of worsening Israeli–Turkish ties. This has included a military dimension, such as holding joint military exercises,[83] and Israeli company Elbit Systems establishing a flight-training centre in Greece.[84] The acquisition by Israeli defence companies SK Group and Plasan of Greece's Hellenic Vehicle Industry (ELVO) went ahead in part because of these growing ties.[85] Since the 7 October Hamas-led attacks against Israel, Greece has supported Israel's response to the attack, though it voiced concerns over the proportionality of the response and the lack of a political strategy.[86] Cyprus, with which Greece has maintained strong and sustained defence links since 1960, is often a third partner in this relationship,[87] and this format is expected to grow through the 2020s.

With the emergence of its more confident defence profile, Greece has provided the operational command for the EU's *Aspides* maritime-security operation as well as contributing its frigate *Hydra*. The operation aims to restore freedom of navigation in the Red Sea in response to Ansarullah (Houthis) attacks against shipping vessels.[88]

Elsewhere, Greece is investing in deepening ties with other countries. It entered a strategic partnership with the UAE in 2020, its first formal defence agreement with a country outside of NATO or the EU.[89] Greece has also begun establishing defence ties with Saudi Arabia, although there is no formal agreement in place. Greece deployed a *Patriot* SAM battery to the country in 2021 (see page 106) and the two countries held their first joint bilateral exercise, *Falcon-Eye*, in 2021,[90] which is expected to become a regular exercise.[91]

Since the late 1980s, Greece has organised the *Iniochos* 'medium scale' air-force exercise.[92] The 2023 iteration saw a record participation from the air forces of 12 countries.[93] Cyprus, France, Greece and Italy have engaged in the quadripartite *EUNOMIA* aeronaval exercises since 2020, with the aim of improving inter-operability.[94] The regular *MEDUSA* maritime exercise held between Cyprus, Egypt and Greece has been conducted since 2017 and was extended to France and the UAE in 2020.[95]

MILITARY CAPABILITY

As the HAF was gradually reduced in size over the past two decades, it sought to increase the proportion of professionals serving and reduce conscript liability. However, the HAF, and the army in particular, would still be heavily reliant on reserves in the event of a major conflict. Most of the army is based in the north of the country, with the bulk of the fighting capability located under D Corps on the Turkish border. The army's organisation mirrors that of the Turkish army across the border and the Aegean Sea, with an army-level command coordinating Greek operations in the event of a major conflict but also doubling up as one of the EU National Operational Headquarters.[96] The independent Supreme Military Command of the Interior and the Islands controls formations on Aegean islands, including National Guard units, on islands covered by the Lausanne and Paris treaties.

The HAF maintains a wide variety of capabilities, although much of this is ageing following a hiatus in major procurement efforts which lasted until the late 2010s (see page 108), and certain key capabilities are lacking. For example, while the Hellenic Air Force operates modern tactical combat aircraft and a handful of airborne early-warning aircraft (see Figure 4.9), the service does

> **TURKIYE HAS COMMITTED SIGNIFICANT RESOURCES TO LOCALLY DEVELOPED SYSTEMS, ALTHOUGH IT OFTEN RELIES ON KEY FOREIGN SUBSYSTEMS.**

not possess tanker aircraft that would increase the range and mission time of these aircraft. Similarly, the navy only recently obtained the funds for major procurement. Efforts in the years prior to this focused on improving the lethality of existing platforms, both maritime and aviation, through mid-life upgrades.[97]

The HAF has forward-deployed the Hellenic Force in Cyprus (ELDYK) formation to the island since 1960 to support Cypriot territorial integrity.[98] It is Greece's largest foreign deployment and currently consists of a mechanised brigade, albeit one with ageing equipment. Elsewhere, the HAF contributes small contingents to EU and UN peacekeeping missions such as Kosovo Force (KFOR) and the United Nations Interim Force in Lebanon (UNIFIL). The deployment in 2021 of a *Patriot* SAM battery to Saudi Arabia to help the kingdom counter missile attacks from Yemen was a significant milestone in Greek–Saudi relations.[99]

ECONOMICS, PROCUREMENT AND MODERNISATION

The Greek defence budget experienced severe cuts between 2010 and 2013 due to the economic impact of the 2007–08 global financial crisis and the Greek debt crisis (see Figure 4.2). Greece's real GDP contracted by 6.3% annually on average between 2010 and 2013 as the country struggled to service its high debt levels when borrowing costs increased. The Greek defence budget fell from €7.43bn (US$9.86bn) in 2010 to €4.44bn (US$5.90bn) in 2013, with reductions averaging 15.8% annually in real terms. After stagnating between 2014 and 2020, the defence budget dramatically increased in 2021 and 2022, recovering to €7.44bn (US$7.88bn) before falling back slightly in 2023, followed by only a moderate increase in 2024. The 2021 and 2022 increases were primarily driven by major weapons acquisitions, including the purchase of *Rafale* fighter aircraft from France.[100] However, with the purchase of up to 40 F-35A *Lightning*-II fighter aircraft alongside planned naval acquisitions, the drivers behind further uplifts in the short term are still pressing.

Greece has typically acquired defence equipment from NATO allies, although there has been some procurement from other countries since the end of the Cold War. This has included Russia and Sweden in the 1990s and early 2000s and more recently Israel. France and the US continue to be the key sources of equipment and Washington has donated relatively large numbers of equipment from its stocks over the last decade (see Table 4.3). Germany transferred hundreds of armoured fighting vehicles (AFVs) in the 1990s and 2000s in

(L–R) A Hellenic Air Force F-16 *Fighting Falcon* assigned to the 115 Combat Wing, four US Air Force F-15E *Strike Eagles* assigned to the 494th Fighter Squadron and two F-35A *Lightning* IIs assigned to the 495th Fighter Squadron fly in formation during the *Poseidon's Rage* exercise on 11 July 2022. The exercise focused on the partnership between the US and Hellenic air forces in order to validate F-35 and F-15E deployment capabilities and was the first iteration of the exercise to feature the F-35.
(Courtesy photo by Hellenic Air Force)

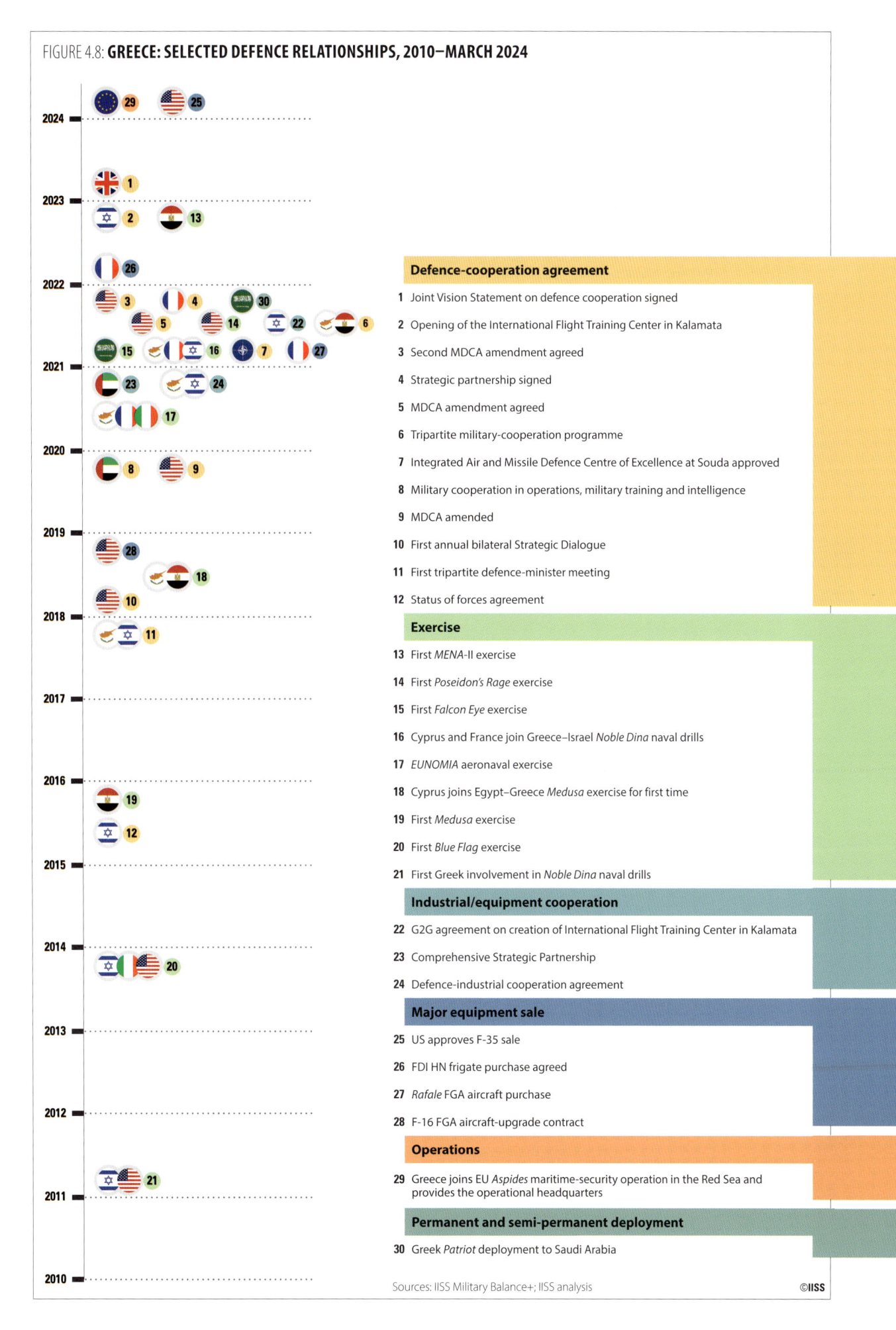

FIGURE 4.8: GREECE: SELECTED DEFENCE RELATIONSHIPS, 2010–MARCH 2024

Defence-cooperation agreement
1. Joint Vision Statement on defence cooperation signed
2. Opening of the International Flight Training Center in Kalamata
3. Second MDCA amendment agreed
4. Strategic partnership signed
5. MDCA amendment agreed
6. Tripartite military-cooperation programme
7. Integrated Air and Missile Defence Centre of Excellence at Souda approved
8. Military cooperation in operations, military training and intelligence
9. MDCA amended
10. First annual bilateral Strategic Dialogue
11. First tripartite defence-minister meeting
12. Status of forces agreement

Exercise
13. First *MENA*-II exercise
14. First *Poseidon's Rage* exercise
15. First *Falcon Eye* exercise
16. Cyprus and France join Greece–Israel *Noble Dina* naval drills
17. *EUNOMIA* aeronaval exercise
18. Cyprus joins Egypt–Greece *Medusa* exercise for first time
19. First *Medusa* exercise
20. First *Blue Flag* exercise
21. First Greek involvement in *Noble Dina* naval drills

Industrial/equipment cooperation
22. G2G agreement on creation of International Flight Training Center in Kalamata
23. Comprehensive Strategic Partnership
24. Defence-industrial cooperation agreement

Major equipment sale
25. US approves F-35 sale
26. FDI HN frigate purchase agreed
27. *Rafale* FGA aircraft purchase
28. F-16 FGA aircraft-upgrade contract

Operations
29. Greece joins EU *Aspides* maritime-security operation in the Red Sea and provides the operational headquarters

Permanent and semi-permanent deployment
30. Greek *Patriot* deployment to Saudi Arabia

Sources: IISS Military Balance+; IISS analysis
©IISS

order to meet its obligations under the Treaty on Conventional Armed Forces in Europe.[101] This was followed in the early 2000s by the acquisition of Leopard 2 tanks, PzH 2000 howitzers and four submarines (see below). However, since then Greece has opted to acquire little defence materiel from Germany. Berlin's willingness to sell equipment to Turkiye, as well as the legacy of the 2008 financial crisis, may have hurt German companies' competitiveness in Athens. However, an agreement to transfer Marder infantry fighting vehicles to Greece in exchange for Athens delivering BMP-1s to Ukraine could help improve the relationship.[102]

Cuts to defence spending after 2009 meant few major modernisation efforts could proceed, with the cancellation of plans to buy six FREMM frigates from France being the most notable example.[103] Instead, agreements with the United States for the transfer of second-hand armoured vehicles, helicopters and patrol boats have comprised the extent of army equipment modernisation over the past decade (see Table 4.3).

The Hellenic Air Force and Navy, however, have begun to see the benefits of increased defence spending, with several major contracts signed since 2018. Deliveries of the first of 24 Rafales began in 2021 under a 2018 contract.[104] Alongside this, the modernisation of 84 F-16s, signed in 2018, to the latest Viper standard is under way,[105] and more recently Greece has requested to acquire up to two F-35 squadrons.[106] This investment in combat air capability will likely result in the Hellenic Air Force having a significantly greater capability in this domain than its rival Turkiye by the end of the decade, assuming Turkish upgrade efforts and domestic programmes do not proceed.

The Hellenic Navy's most significant procurement of the last 25 years was the acquisition of four Type-214 submarines from Germany in 2000. Suffering from technical difficulties, changes in shipyard ownership and corruption prosecutions,[107] the first boat was not delivered until ten years after the contract signing, while the three locally assembled boats did not follow until the mid-2010s. Ambitious plans for the 2020s include new frigates, corvettes, helicopters, UAVs and submarines.[108] A contract for three new frigates from France, based on the French navy's Frégate de Défense et d'Intervention (FDI) (Defence and Intervention Frigate) design, represents the most expensive element of this portfolio, and deliveries are planned to begin in the middle of the decade.

TABLE 4.3: GREECE: SELECTED PROCUREMENT PROGRAMMES, 2010–MARCH 2024

Contract date	Equipment	Type	Quantity	Value (US$ millions)	Contractor	Delivery	Service
c. 2013	• M113A2 • M577 • M106A2 • M901	• Tracked APC • Tracked APC • 107mm self-propelled mortar • Self-propelled anti-tank system	• 196 • 145 • 1 • 72	Donation	US government	2014	Army
c. 2016	CH-47D Chinook	Heavy transport helicopter	10	150 (estimate)	US government	2016–19	Army
2018	Mk V	Fast patrol boat	4	Donation	US government	2020	Navy
2018	OH-58D Kiowa Warrior	MRH	70	Donation	US government	2019	Army
July 2018	P2002JF	Training aircraft	12	3	Tecnam	2018–19	Air Force
December 2018	F-16V (Block 72) Fighting Falcon	FGA aircraft upgrade	84	997	Lockheed Martin	2022–27	Air Force
c. 2020	M1117	AUV	1,200	Donation	US government	2021–ongoing	Army
May 2020	Heron	Heavy ISR UAV*	2	51	Israel Aerospace Industries	From June 2021	Air Force
October 2020	MH-60R Seahawk	ASW helicopter	7	n.k.	Lockheed Martin	By 2025	Navy
January 2021	Rafale	FGA aircraft	24	4,193	Dassault Aviation	2021–ongoing	Air Force
April 2021	M-346	Training aircraft	10	See Notes**	Elbit Systems with Leonardo	n.k.	Air Force
November 2021	A900	Light ISR UAV	5	2	Alpha Unmanned Systems	2022	Navy
March 2022	Kimon (FDI HN)	Frigate	3	3,681	Naval Group	2025–26	Navy
September 2022	Marder 1A3	IFV	40	Donation	Rheinmetall	2022–23	Army
April 2023	Spike	Anti-tank missile	n.k.	408	Rafael Advanced Defense Systems	n.k.	Army; Navy

*3+ year lease
**Part of US$1.6bn contract with Elbit Systems for establishment of flight training centre
Sources: IISS Military Balance+; IISS analysis

©IISS

ISRAEL

DEFENCE POLICIES AND PRIORITIES

Israel published its first public defence strategy document in 2015 as part of the Gideon Multi-Year Plan (GMYP), a five-year programme that aimed to modernise the Israel Defense Forces (IDF). Articulated around the principles of deterrence, early warning, defence and victory, the policy identified three types of threats: states (Iran, Lebanon, Syria), 'substates' (Hizbullah, Hamas) and terrorist organisations (e.g. Palestinian Islamic Jihad, Islamic State).[109] Accordingly, it refocused the IDF on asymmetric warfare, with urban warfare, airpower and air defence considered key priorities. Concerns over Hizbullah's ability to overwhelm Israel's defences with rockets and missiles have in part driven Israeli defence strategy towards a territorial-defence focus.[110]

In 2020, Israel launched the Tnufa (Momentum) five-year plan which follows and builds on the GMYP. Through it, the IDF underlines the need to be multi-dimensional, combining 'air, sea, land, cyberspace and electronic warfare' to fight multi-front wars and shorten the time to victory.[111] The underlying ambition is to surpass enemies' capabilities while relying on advanced technology, intelligence, airpower and limited on-the-ground operations.[112] But, in light of the 7 October Hamas-led attacks, elements of this approach now require reconsideration. Tel Aviv has also not announced a new policy regarding Iran's pursuit of nuclear capabilities since drawing a literal 'red line' at 90% enrichment at the UN General Assembly in 2012.[113] The IDF Official Strategy states that strategic and tactical deterrence relies on cyber warfare, early-warning intelligence and pre-emptive strikes.[114]

To support this defence policy and its swift-victory approach, Israel seeks to preserve its military superiority – which the US labels Qualitative Military Edge (QME) – by having better weapons and being better trained than its neighbours. To keep the upper hand, Tel Aviv launched a project dubbed 'Edge of Tomorrow' in May 2022. This technology-driven programme aims to improve key infantry capabilities such as lethality, situational awareness, stamina and survivability.[115]

These defence concepts and advances are being tested by the war with Hamas. The Hamas-led attacks amounted to a strategic, military and intelligence failure for Israel's armed and security forces and political leadership. The policy of containment through remote surveillance, border fences and assassinating key individuals, known as 'mowing the grass', has led to an overconfidence that meant intelligence warnings regarding Hamas activity were not taken as seriously as they should have been.[116] It shattered Israeli citizens' trust in their military and in their political establishment. The IDF was compelled to fight a ground war in Gaza it had not planned for, as the driving assumption was that Hamas was effectively contained in Gaza. That failure is sure to have extensive repercussions on Israeli defence thinking and planning. IDF and defence officials, as well as the Knesset, have announced that in-depth reviews will be launched at the end of the war.

In the early months of the war, the IDF demonstrated a high level of operational effectiveness, killing large numbers of Hamas militants and suffering limited casualties, through an intensive bombing and ground campaign that led to a high civilian-casualty count. It also succeeded in largely suppressing Hamas rocket-firing, debilitating its organisation and degrading its power-projection capabilities.

However, at the time of writing, the war is in its sixth month, while Israel's defence doctrine demanded overwhelming force and swift victory. Hamas's transformation into an insurgency will affect its ability to cross into Israeli territory, but ensures a persistent presence across the Gaza Strip, despite Israel's stated goal of annihilating it. The conflict simultaneously opened several other low- to medium-intensity fronts, requiring the IDF to deploy air assets, air defences, ground forces, intelligence capabilities and artillery along its northern borders.

Israel's ability to mobilise and equip quickly 360,000 reservists for high-intensity combat is something that few states could replicate. However, six months into the war, it has also opted to demobilise a significant portion of these reservists, not least because of how costly the mobilisation has been. In November 2023, the central bank estimated that the war would cost US$53bn through to 2025.[117] By February 2024, it was estimated that the Israeli economy had contracted by nearly 20%.[118] Prolonging the mobilisation longer, for example for an offensive in Rafah or to fight Hizbullah in the north, would put further strain on the Israeli economy and the government's domestic civilian support. The IDF has announced plans to lengthen military service to three years and increase both the number of training days per year and the age limit for reservist liability.[119] These plans would require the Knesset's approval and could provoke domestic criticism, given the resistance of religious segments of the population to military service.

For the first time, Israel's military conduct has led to considerable criticism, resulting in a careful examination of its objectives, targeting practices, rules of engagement, orders and discipline. A case against Israel on the charge of genocide was heard by the International Court of Justice, which called on Israel to 'take all measures within its power to prevent and punish the direct and public incitement to commit genocide' in Gaza.[120] Talk of sanctions or denial of arms sales has become frequent. For example, a court in the Netherlands ordered the government to stop the supply of parts for F-35 aircraft to Israel.[121]

DEFENCE RELATIONSHIPS

Israel's most important security relationship is and will continue to be with the US, with the latter committed financially and diplomatically to ensuring that Israel maintains its QME. The alliance is backed up by regular military exercises, defence-industrial cooperation and intelligence sharing (see Figure 4.10). The two countries signed a joint declaration on strategic partnership in 2022 which reiterated these objectives and included a US commitment to never 'allow Iran to acquire a nuclear weapon'.[122]

The intensity and complexity of the Israel–Hamas war underscored the importance of US support for Israel. The US sped up ammunition supply, provided intelligence, deployed two carrier strike groups to deter Israel's enemies and sent a US$14bn military-aid package. The US has also deployed substantial forces to the Red Sea to protect commercial shipping and intercept missiles aimed at Israel by the Houthis in Yemen. However, as the war has continued, several congressional leaders have suggested conditioning some US lethal aid over violations of US laws in the use of weaponry and to punish Israel for restricting humanitarian assistance to civilians in need in Gaza. Although these views represent a minority, at the time of writing, there is a growing concern among increasingly senior US officials regarding Israel's unwillingness to agree on a ceasefire and to present a plan for Gaza's future governance.[123]

The US mediated the signing of the Abraham Accords in 2020, which allows for the normalisation of relations between Israel and some Arab states. So far this has led to agreements with the UAE,[124] Bahrain[125] and Morocco,[126] with some reports suggesting this has facilitated the first equipment sales to these countries.[127] A shared concern with Iran's nuclear programme and support for militant groups in Gaza, Lebanon, Western Sahara and Yemen encouraged strategic convergence.[128] While there has yet to be an equivalent agreement with Saudi Arabia, in June 2022 then-defense minister Benny Gantz told the Knesset that an initiative with the US and Arab countries, possibly including Saudi Arabia,[129] called the Middle East Air Defense system was 'already operating', although it is unclear exactly what this entails and whether it is still functioning due to the war.[130] Similarly, in January 2023 Israel hosted the inaugural meeting of the Negev Forum with Bahrain, Egypt, Morocco, the UAE and the US. The forum is non-binding in nature, but countries have committed to increase cooperation in several fields, including regional security, through coordination, capacity-building and training activities.[131]

The strength of these relationships is being tested by the Israel–Hamas war. All the Arab countries that have signed peace deals with Israel have condemned its campaign in Gaza and have cooled their relationships with Tel Aviv. Saudi Arabia, seen as the biggest prize, has clearly stated that a condition for normalisation was the announcement of irreversible steps towards Palestinian statehood. Washington has been keen to keep these prospects alive, but the war is a setback to Israel's and the United States' hopes of regional defence integration. For example, Egypt and Saudi Arabia declined to play a role against the Houthis' actions in Yemen out of concern they would be accused of siding with Israel.

Israel signed a Status of Forces Agreement with Greece in 2015,[132] the first Israel had signed with a country other than the US. Formal agreements are in place with Cyprus,[133] which is also included in tripartite Cyprus–Greece–Israel cooperation arrangements. This format foresees annual action plans and joint training.[134] The agreements were partly driven by the deterioration of Israeli–Turkish relations

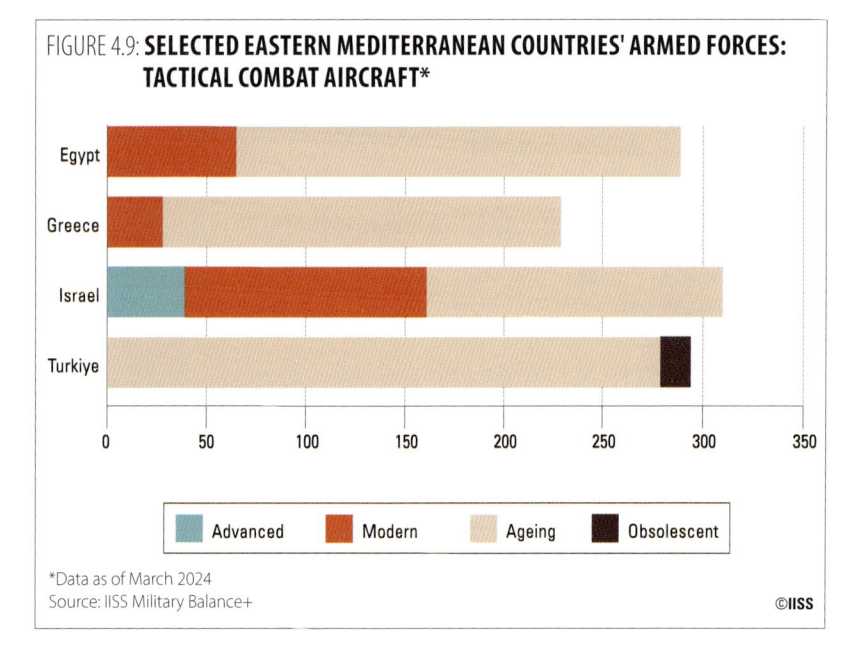

FIGURE 4.9: **SELECTED EASTERN MEDITERRANEAN COUNTRIES' ARMED FORCES: TACTICAL COMBAT AIRCRAFT***

Legend: Advanced, Modern, Ageing, Obsolescent

*Data as of March 2024
Source: IISS Military Balance+

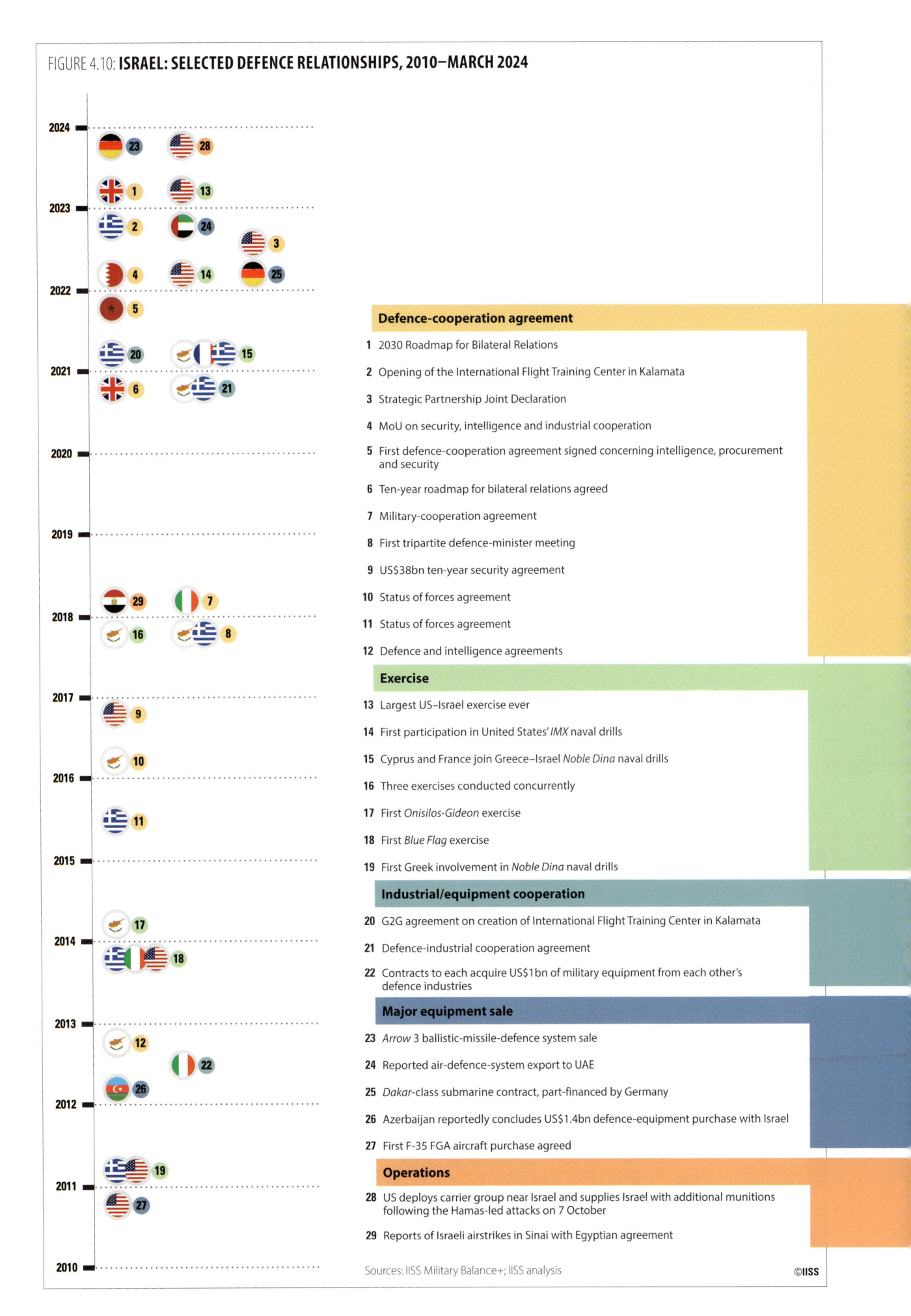

FIGURE 4.10: ISRAEL: SELECTED DEFENCE RELATIONSHIPS, 2010–MARCH 2024

Defence-cooperation agreement

1. 2030 Roadmap for Bilateral Relations
2. Opening of the International Flight Training Center in Kalamata
3. Strategic Partnership Joint Declaration
4. MoU on security, intelligence and industrial cooperation
5. First defence-cooperation agreement signed concerning intelligence, procurement and security
6. Ten-year roadmap for bilateral relations agreed
7. Military-cooperation agreement
8. First tripartite defence-minister meeting
9. US$38bn ten-year security agreement
10. Status of forces agreement
11. Status of forces agreement
12. Defence and intelligence agreements

Exercise

13. Largest US–Israel exercise ever
14. First participation in United States' *IMX* naval drills
15. Cyprus and France join Greece–Israel *Noble Dina* naval drills
16. Three exercises conducted concurrently
17. First *Onisilos-Gideon* exercise
18. First *Blue Flag* exercise
19. First Greek involvement in *Noble Dina* naval drills

Industrial/equipment cooperation

20. G2G agreement on creation of International Flight Training Center in Kalamata
21. Defence-industrial cooperation agreement
22. Contracts to each acquire US$1bn of military equipment from each other's defence industries

Major equipment sale

23. *Arrow* 3 ballistic-missile-defence system sale
24. Reported air-defence-system export to UAE
25. *Dakar*-class submarine contract, part-financed by Germany
26. Azerbaijan reportedly concludes US$1.4bn defence-equipment purchase with Israel
27. First F-35 FGA aircraft purchase agreed

Operations

28. US deploys carrier group near Israel and supplies Israel with additional munitions following the Hamas-led attacks on 7 October
29. Reports of Israeli airstrikes in Sinai with Egyptian agreement

Sources: IISS Military Balance+; IISS analysis

©IISS

in 2010 following the killing of ten Turkish activists on the *Mavi Marmara* vessel by Israeli special forces.[135]

Israel regularly participates in and hosts exercises with regional and international actors and, since 2011, has organised the *Noble Dina* naval exercise. Initially conducted with the US and Greece, it has now been opened to France and Cyprus.[136] In the air domain, Israel has hosted the biannual *Blue Flag* air-forces exercise since 2013.[137] The latest iteration in 2021 saw the participation of France, Germany, Greece, India, Italy, the UK and the US and practised the combined operation of fourth- and fifth-generation fighter aircraft.[138] In early 2023, Israel and the US conducted *Juniper Oak*, their largest-ever bilateral exercise.[139] Around 6,400 US and 1,500 Israeli troops, 140 aircraft, 12 naval vessels and a number of HIMARS artillery systems tested complex operational scenarios.[140]

MILITARY CAPABILITY

The IDF is recognised as a competent and well-equipped force. But with at least 102,500 conscripts, almost double the 67,000 professional personnel, the IDF remains heavily dependent on reserves to fight in a major conflict.[141] This was clearly illustrated by the mobilisation of 360,000 reservists after the 7 October Hamas-led attacks. Concerns that divisions in Israeli society over the government's judicial-reform plans could mean reservists would not mobilise proved to be unfounded. Reserve units that have been deployed into Gaza generally appear to have achieved battlefield objectives, albeit with reports of poor discipline.[142] Reported underinvestment in reservist training and equipment prior to the war is highly likely to be rectified in the near future.

In general, military capabilities align with defence policy. Following the GMYP, conventional-warfare capabilities, such as infantry and armoured forces, have been downsized but remain pivotal, although the importance of these echelons will likely be reconsidered in the next defence review.[143] As part of the plan's multidimensional approach, the IDF favoured small battlegroups with combined capabilities and independent battle plans.[144]

The Israeli Air Force (IAF) is designed to carry out massive and stealthy bombardment, which has given it an edge over its adversaries but has proven insufficient in delivering the swift victories Israel's defence doctrine aims for. The IDF maintains a multi-layered approach to air defence which

An IDF M109 155mm self-propelled howitzer fires rounds near the border with Gaza in southern Israel on 11 October 2023. (Photo: Jack Guez/AFP via Getty Images)

has largely proven effective against the scale and type of threats faced to date.[145] Deterrence is supported by Israel's assumed nuclear capability based on a triad of platforms, although Israel has never officially confirmed its existence.[146]

Given its defence policy, Israel's logistics and maintenance support are focused towards sustaining operations within its territory or in immediately neighbouring states. The IAF's ten ageing tanker aircraft help the air force conduct airstrikes abroad but have limited availability.[147] In terms of industrial support, a strong and innovative local defence industry contributes to maintaining Israel's QME. Three large companies – Rafael Advanced Defense Systems, Israel Aerospace Industries and Elbit Systems – spearhead this ecosystem along with organic maintenance, repair and overhaul capabilities within the IDF. However, despite its sophisticated industrial capability, Israel has been reliant on US resupply efforts to sustain its offensive in Gaza. It is plausible that Israel may re-evaluate the scale of some industrial capabilities, such as artillery ammunition and precision-guided munition production, to make the country more self-reliant in future operations.

Prior to the current war, Israel's last two major conflicts were fought against Hamas in 2014 and 2021 and involved the combined use of ground and air forces. Until the 2023 war, it frequently conducted intelligence operations in the Occupied Palestinian Territories and airstrikes on Gaza during periods between wars. Elsewhere, Israel undertakes air-to-ground missions in Syria and also provides sporadic tactical air support in Egypt's Sinai.[148] Moreover, cyber attacks on Iranian nuclear facilities have been attributed to Israel, while the air force maintains the capacity to launch conventional strikes against such infrastructure.[149] The navy, for its part, operates in territorial waters to protect littoral areas and interdict illicit shipments, although there are indications that it has also started to expand its maritime footprint, deploying more vessels to the Red Sea in response to Iranian activities. A *Dolphin*-class submarine was even reported to have headed towards the Gulf.[150] Due to the ongoing war, Israel's plan to join the NAVCENT-led Combined Maritime Forces that operate in the Gulf and surrounding waters is almost certainly on hold.

ECONOMICS, PROCUREMENT AND MODERNISATION

Despite regional security concerns, growth in Israeli defence spending between 2010 and 2023 was moderated by political and economic constraints. In recent years, political upheaval has prevented budgets from being agreed, while there have long been highly public debates between the Ministry of Defense and Ministry of Finance over the balance between defence investments and other government spending. In 2010, the budget came to 49.8bn shekels (US$13.3bn), with total defence funding reaching US$16.1bn once FMF is included. By 2022, the budget had reached 663.9bn shekels (US$19.0bn, or US$22.3bn including FMF; see Figure 4.2). Between 2020 and 2022, domestic budgets averaged nominal growth of 2.2%, with real growth averaging 0.6%. The 2023 budget implemented a sizeable 9.6% nominal (4.3% real) increase for the defence budget, up to 70.1bn shekels (US$19.2bn, US$22.5bn including FMF). This increase was sustained in the 2024 budget, although future increases in defence spending can be expected in the wake of the Hamas-led October 2023 attacks.

The vast majority of US aid to Israel is in the form of military assistance, which has served to transform the IDF and Israel's industrial base into one of the most sophisticated globally.[151] The outlook for Israeli defence spending will continue to be driven by ongoing security concerns and strategic ambitions as outlined in the IDF's 2020 multi-year plan.[152]

Israel's defence planning documents do not give specific procurement requirements but do outline broad modernisation objectives (see page 109). Because of the close relationship with the US and accompanying FMF allocations, major Israeli purchases, particularly in the aerospace domain, are made with US companies (see Table 4.4). Israel has committed to buy 50 F-35 aircraft to outfit two squadrons. These are modified to a unique F-35I *Adir* standard with an Israeli electronic-warfare package,[153] and Israel has sought greater in-country maintenance capabilities.[154] Israel approved the acquisition of a third squadron in 2023 and is also negotiating the acquisition of a squadron of Boeing F-15s based on the latest US Air Force design.[155]

> THE BULK OF EGYPT'S LARGE ARMY AND SEPARATE AIR-DEFENCE COMMAND ARE PROBABLY NO MORE CAPABLE THAN THEY WERE BEFORE THE 2013 COUP, HAVING RECEIVED LESS EQUIPMENT RECAPITALISATION THAN THE OTHER TWO SERVICES.

Germany, which is Israel's second-biggest weapons supplier, has subsidised Israel's acquisition of German systems as part of its Second World War reparations.[156] Recently this has been used to fund new submarines and corvettes, platforms that Israel cannot build locally. Once delivered, however, these are then outfitted with local sensors and weaponry. A mutual-procurement agreement with Italy in 2011 saw Israel buy training aircraft in exchange for Italy acquiring an intelligence, surveillance and reconnaissance satellite and two airborne early-warning aircraft. Both deals were worth US$1bn and this agreement has now been extended further.[157]

The Israeli defence industry is capable of manufacturing most land systems, although chassis and propulsion systems are supplied by foreign, typically US, subcontractors. Israel has produced several hundred Namer tracked armoured personnel carriers (APCs), which utilise the Merkava MkIV tank chassis. The Eitan wheeled APC is replacing legacy M113s, and IDF units began operating the system in 2023. Israel maintains armoured-vehicle production as a state-owned capability while private companies provide the IDF with UAVs, artillery, air-defence systems and sensors which, in contrast to armoured vehicles, are exported widely.

TABLE 4.4: ISRAEL: SELECTED PROCUREMENT PROGRAMMES, 2010–MARCH 2024

Contract date	Equipment	Type	Quantity	Value (US$ millions)	Contractor	Delivery	Service
March 2010	C-130J-30 Hercules	Medium transport aircraft	7	500	Lockheed Martin	2014–18	Air Force
September 2010	F-35I Adir	FGA aircraft	50	7,800	Lockheed Martin	2016–24*	Air Force
2011	Namer	Tracked APC	290+	n.k.	Tank Rehabilitation and Maintenance Center	2012–ongoing	Army
March 2012	Tanin	Attack submarine**	1	514	TKMS	2024*	Navy
July 2012	M-346 (Lavi)	Training aircraft	30	1,000	Leonardo	2014–16	Air Force
2013	M270 MLRS	227mm multiple rocket launcher	15	n.k.	US government	2015	Army
September 2013	Super Dvora Mk III	Fast patrol boat	3	n.k.	IAI RAMTA	2016–17	Navy
Mid-2010s	Lynx (Lahav)	Multiple rocket launcher	n.k.	n.k.	IMI Systems (formerly Israel Military Industries)	Mid-2010s	Army
2015	F-15D Eagle (Baz)	FGA aircraft	9	n.k.	US government	2016–17	Air Force
May 2015	Magen (Sa'ar 6)	Corvette	4	477***	TKMS	2020–21	Navy
c. 2018	Merkava MkIV Barak	MBT	n.k.	n.k.	Tank Rehabilitation and Maintenance Center	From 2023	Army
March 2018	Eitan	• IFV • Wheeled APC	n.k.	n.k.	Tank Rehabilitation and Maintenance Center	From 2023	Army
March 2019	SIGMA	155mm self-propelled howitzer	n.k.	125	Elbit Systems	By end of 2031*	Army
December 2019	AW119Kx	Light transport helicopter	12	67	Leonardo	By end of 2024*	Air Force
January 2020	Dror 1	Communications satellite	1	n.k.	Israel Aerospace Industries	n.k.	Israeli government
July 2021	Shaldag V	Fast patrol boat	4	n.k.	Israel Shipyards	n.k.	Navy
August 2021	Reshef	Corvette	R&D	n.k.	Israel Shipyards	n.k.	Navy
January 2022	Dakar	Attack submarine	3	3,160	TKMS	From 2031	Navy
February 2022	CH-53K King Stallion	Heavy transport helicopter	12	2,000	Sikorsky	2025–27	Air Force
August 2022	KC-46A Pegasus	Tanker/transport aircraft	4	n.k.	Boeing	2025–26	Air Force
November 2023	JLTV	AUV	75+	n.k.	Oshkosh Defense	n.k.	Army

*Planned
**Third of class
***Part-funded by German government. Value likely does not include weapons and radars later installed in Israel
Sources: IISS Military Balance+; IISS analysis

©IISS

TURKIYE

DEFENCE POLICIES AND PRIORITIES

In the last decade Turkish defence policy and efforts have increasingly focused southwards, resting on three pillars: the eradication of the PKK and its affiliates in Syria and Iraq, greater assertiveness using a forward military posture in the near abroad, and a growing diplomatic and military presence in friendly countries further afield such as Qatar and Somalia. These priorities are not new: the country's last white paper, published in 2000, identified the PKK, instability in the Middle East and international terrorism as the major threats to its national security.[158] The 2000 policy implies a proactive military approach and seeks to make Turkiye an independent power with a strong diplomatic voice.[159] Turkiye's *Mavi Vatan* ('Blue Homeland') concept provides a strategic framework for its ambitions, reflecting Ankara's will to assert its regional influence in its surrounding seas (see Chapter Two, pages 57–58).[160]

Relations with Cyprus, the northern part of which Turkiye has occupied since 1974, continue to be conflictual with few prospects for improvement. Those with rival Greece fluctuate constantly, although the meeting between President Erdoğan and Greek Prime Minister Kyriakos Mitsotakis in Athens in December 2023 suggests that the relationship may have turned a corner.[161] As well as causing tension in the region, the status quo will continue to block Turkish ambitions to cooperate with the EU on defence and security as well as the official goal of becoming a member of the organisation. On the other hand, Turkiye uses its NATO membership to assert its power and prevent multilateral defence cooperation with Cyprus. Overall, Ankara's goal is to be recognised as a significant military power, strategically autonomous and regionally dominant.[162]

The Turkish Armed Forces (TAF) are the spearhead of these ambitions and have played an increasingly important part in achieving foreign-policy goals over the last eight years. This has been supported by prioritising indigenous equipment development with a view to achieving self-sufficiency, although some key subsystems are still imported.[163] For example, Ankara completed the first flight of its domestically developed *Kaan* (TF-X) fifth-generation combat aircraft in February 2024, but the programme is dependent on foreign engines.[164] Ankara seeks to become a significant exporter of military materiel to make its defence-industrial development more sustainable as well as develop and improve relations with other states.[165]

DEFENCE RELATIONSHIPS

Turkiye's independent and assertive foreign policy under President Erdoğan has created tensions with NATO allies. This has come at a cost for some of the country's ambitious defence-modernisation plans, compelling Ankara to seek alternatives to systems denied by the US or to engage in political brinkmanship to obtain them. Ankara's controversial acquisition of a Russian SAM system led to Turkiye being ejected from the F-35 programme in 2019 (see page 120). Ankara held up ratification of Sweden's accession to NATO[166] not only to obtain concessions from Stockholm over the presence of Kurdish movements there, but also to compel the US to agree to modernise its F-16 fleet. Concerns in Washington over Turkish foreign and domestic policies, both within the Biden administration and among key legislators, had held up this programme.[167] This was only the latest in a number of disagreements with allies that include interventions in Syria and Libya and the continued occupation of northern Cyprus. However, despite difficulties, it is highly likely that NATO will continue to be fundamental to Turkish security going forward.

Turkiye has been the main backer of the internationally recognised Government of National Accord in Libya and deployed troops there to support it in 2020 (see Figure 4.11).[168] Turkiye has delivered military equipment to Libya and also committed to improving the training and operational capabilities of the air force.[169] However, the controversial 2019 agreement on the delineation of maritime boundaries between it and Libya[170] cut through Greece's EEZ, further fuelling tensions between the two countries. In the Gulf, Turkiye and Qatar agreed a strategic military partnership on industry, intelligence and operational readiness[171] that includes a Turkish military base in the country.[172] Major defence sales to Saudi Arabia and the UAE in 2023 mark a rapprochement in Turkiye's relations with both countries.[173]

Turkiye's close ties with neighbour Azerbaijan are informed by cultural links as well as an alignment of interests. Turkiye, already a supplier of military equipment, transferred armed UAVs to Azerbaijan during the second Nagorno-Karabakh war, which likely had a significant influence on the outcome of the conflict. Following the defeat of Armenia, Azerbaijan and Turkiye signed the Shusha Declaration, which contains a mutual-defence clause in case of 'a threat or an act of aggression'.[174] Following the conflict, the two countries' militaries have conducted joint exercises.[175]

Defence-industrial elements are common in Turkish agreements, including with states with advanced defence industries, such as the UK. A framework agreement on military cooperation with that country was updated in 2019,[176] and BAE Systems has provided assistance to Turkiye's *Kaan* next-generation fighter programme.[177] Similar agreements exist with France and Italy,[178] and all three cooperate on air-defence systems.[179] The establishment of new production facilities in partner countries, such as Kazakhstan, Qatar and Ukraine, will deepen relationships and increase exports further.[180]

The Turkish military organises regular multi-domain exercises with partners. The 2022 edition of the *EFES* exercise was the largest-ever Turkish joint exercise, with the participation of 13 regional and allied countries and 24 observers from Africa, Asia and Europe.[181] The exercise, initially an annual national joint exercise, was expanded to include eight other countries in 2016.[182] The first *Anatolian Eagle* exercise was held in 2001 with the aim of increasing the inter-operability and air-combat capacity of the Turkish, US and Israeli armed forces.[183] The 2022 edition had a 'limited link' to the NATO *Ramstein Dust*-II 2022 (RADU-II/22) air command-and-control exercise and involved Azerbaijani, Jordanian, Pakistani and NATO air forces.[184]

MILITARY CAPABILITY

The professionalisation of the TAF has been improved over recent years through regular training of personnel and reducing the proportion of conscripts.

Turkish President Recep Tayyip Erdoğan at the presentation ceremony of the *Kaan* next-generation fighter programme in Ankara, Turkiye, on 1 May 2023. (Photo: Yavuz Ozden/Dia images via Getty Images)

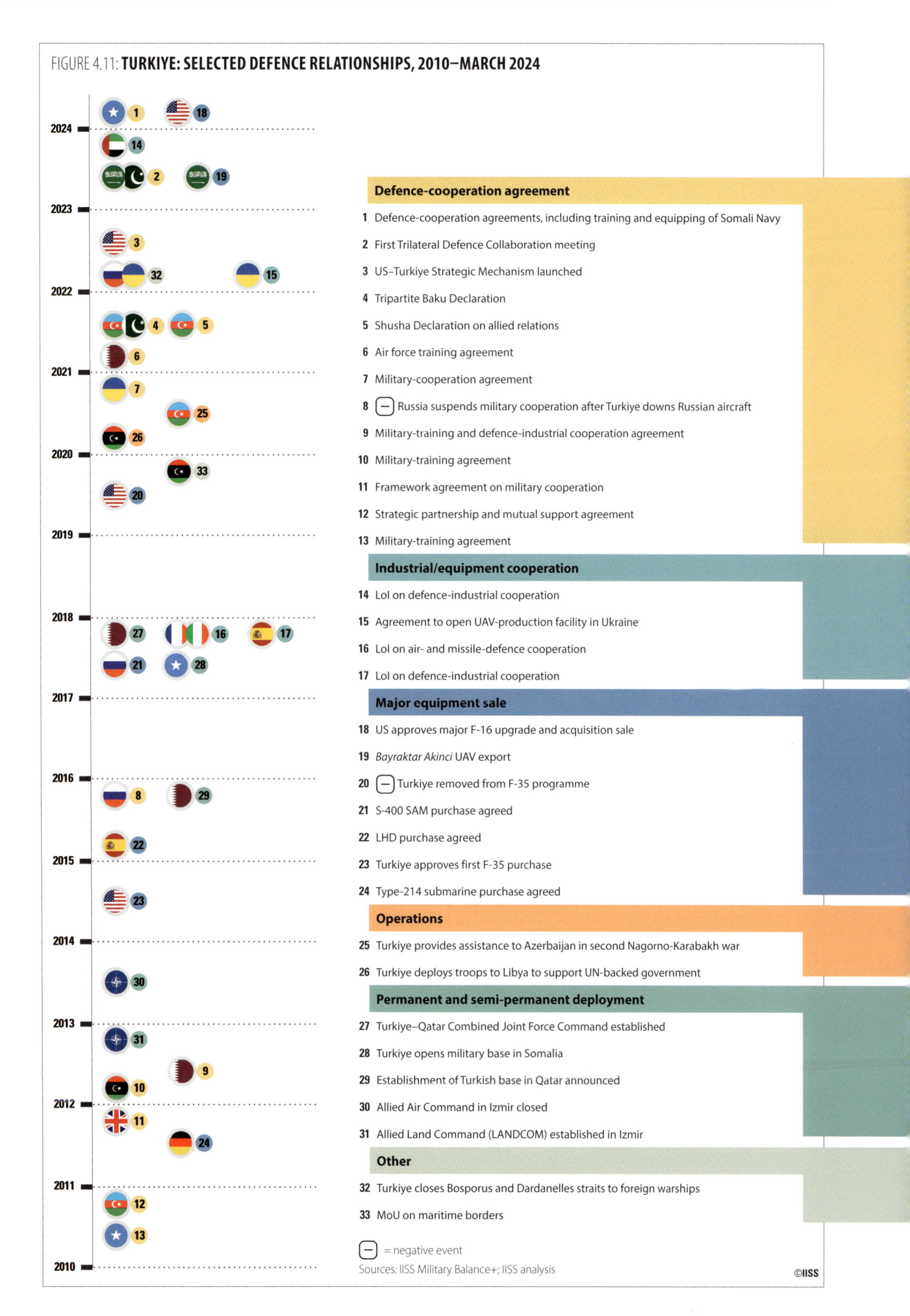

FIGURE 4.11: TURKIYE: SELECTED DEFENCE RELATIONSHIPS, 2010–MARCH 2024

Defence-cooperation agreement
1. Defence-cooperation agreements, including training and equipping of Somali Navy
2. First Trilateral Defence Collaboration meeting
3. US–Turkiye Strategic Mechanism launched
4. Tripartite Baku Declaration
5. Shusha Declaration on allied relations
6. Air force training agreement
7. Military-cooperation agreement
8. (−) Russia suspends military cooperation after Turkiye downs Russian aircraft
9. Military-training and defence-industrial cooperation agreement
10. Military-training agreement
11. Framework agreement on military cooperation
12. Strategic partnership and mutual support agreement
13. Military-training agreement

Industrial/equipment cooperation
14. LoI on defence-industrial cooperation
15. Agreement to open UAV-production facility in Ukraine
16. LoI on air- and missile-defence cooperation
17. LoI on defence-industrial cooperation

Major equipment sale
18. US approves major F-16 upgrade and acquisition sale
19. *Bayraktar Akinci* UAV export
20. (−) Turkiye removed from F-35 programme
21. S-400 SAM purchase agreed
22. LHD purchase agreed
23. Turkiye approves first F-35 purchase
24. Type-214 submarine purchase agreed

Operations
25. Turkiye provides assistance to Azerbaijan in second Nagorno-Karabakh war
26. Turkiye deploys troops to Libya to support UN-backed government

Permanent and semi-permanent deployment
27. Turkiye–Qatar Combined Joint Force Command established
28. Turkiye opens military base in Somalia
29. Establishment of Turkish base in Qatar announced
30. Allied Air Command in Izmir closed
31. Allied Land Command (LANDCOM) established in Izmir

Other
32. Turkiye closes Bosporus and Dardanelles straits to foreign warships
33. MoU on maritime borders

(−) = negative event

Sources: IISS Military Balance+; IISS analysis

In 2019, President Erdoğan modified the length of compulsory military service from six to 12 months.[185] On fee payment, conscription can be reduced to one month.[186] Following the failure of a military coup in July 2016, a large number of senior officers, over 24,000 military personnel in total, were either arrested or fired, including personnel posted to NATO headquarters.[187] Although these postings have reportedly been quickly filled with politically acceptable replacements, there was an impact on the military's overall capability and it is unclear the extent to which that persists today.

The TAF is one of the largest armed forces, in terms of equipment, in the Eastern Mediterranean region.[188] It is structured for national defence and is generally well equipped. The navy is being modernised with blue-water operations in mind: a new LHD, *Anadolu*, will significantly expand Turkiye's maritime reach, and Ankara is developing armed UAVs to be operated from the vessel. But many AFVs and combat aircraft are ageing (see figures 4.6 and 4.9), and Ankara depends on US approval to modernise its F-16 fleet and replace older aircraft before the *Kaan* programme can bear fruit.[189]

Turkiye's largest foreign deployment continues to be to northern Cyprus, where Ankara stations more than 33,000 troops, but more recent operations have taken place further afield, as well as across Turkiye's southeastern border. Turkiye has developed impressive autonomous expeditionary capabilities, deploying troops to Iraq, Libya and Syria. In these operations, Turkiye has utilised different approaches, including counter-terrorism tactics, airstrikes and train-and-equip missions, with success. It has also set up military bases in Qatar and Somalia with permanent troops deployed there; in February 2024 Somalia announced that Turkiye will provide training to the navy.[190] But Syria is the main theatre where the TAF operates: Ankara occupies large areas in the north and in early 2024 hinted at a possible widening of the campaign in the country, as well as in Iraq.[191] The navy, for its part, is mostly used to support Ankara's assertiveness in the Eastern Mediterranean, notably as part of the border-delimitation disputes with Cyprus and Greece, as well as operations in Libya.[192]

ECONOMICS, PROCUREMENT AND MODERNISATION

Since 2010, the Turkish defence budget has seen significant rates of nominal growth aimed to counter the impact of soaring rates of inflation and a weakening currency (see Figure 4.3). In lira, the defence budget in 2022 was nearly five times the size of the 2010 budget, with nominal growth averaging 14.1% annually over the time frame. The defence budget then doubled in 2023 and again in 2024.

However, sizeable nominal increases were often eroded in real terms and the impact of erosion became more severe from 2018, when inflation rates began to climb higher (see Figure 4.4). Since 2022, the issue has become acute, with the inflation rate reaching 72.3% that year, 51.2% in 2023 and 62.5% in 2024.[193] The 2023 and 2024 surges in the defence budget did result in increases in real terms, but are perhaps better seen as symptomatic of the country's high inflation rate and a desire to maintain recent trends, rather than a real uplift in capability.

President Erdoğan's pursuit of high rates of economic growth meant that the Turkish central bank had been reluctant to raise interest rates. However, the persistence of excessive inflation rates and a shift in political stance saw a hike in the interest rate to 50% in March 2024.[194] Such a move may work to ease inflation rates; however, Turkiye faces wider economic pressures, including extensive reconstruction costs following the devastating earthquakes in the southeast of the country on 6 February 2023.[195] The outlook for the Turkish defence budget is therefore constrained. Nominal increases are likely to continue but the current rate of increase is unsustainable. Therefore, repeated increases in dollar or real terms will be difficult to repeat in the short term. The fall in the value of the lira against the dollar, and indeed other key currencies including the euro and British pound, is a further driver of Turkish self-sufficiency goals in the defence domain.

In 2015, President Erdoğan outlined a desire to achieve an autarkic defence industry by 2023.[196] Although this ambitious goal has not been achieved, Turkiye has made significant progress across all domains and seen steady growth in its defence exports. Turkiye's foreign policy can be at odds with those of key partners and Ankara has had arms embargoes placed on it at different times during the last 50 years. The government's desire for a more sovereign defence-industrial capability is aimed at lessening or removing the embargoes' impacts and giving Turkiye greater freedom of manoeuvre in its foreign policy.[197]

Although 'autarky' is a hazy objective, modernisation efforts have been impressive in some areas and Turkiye has committed significant resources to locally developed systems, although it often relies on key foreign subsystems. This has included surface combatants, guided-weapons and air-defence systems, armoured vehicles and UAVs (see Table 4.5). The successful development of these systems has contributed to a major growth in defence exports,[198] and some platforms have been operated in combat by both Turkiye and other states. Although the ambitious export targets (US$25bn in

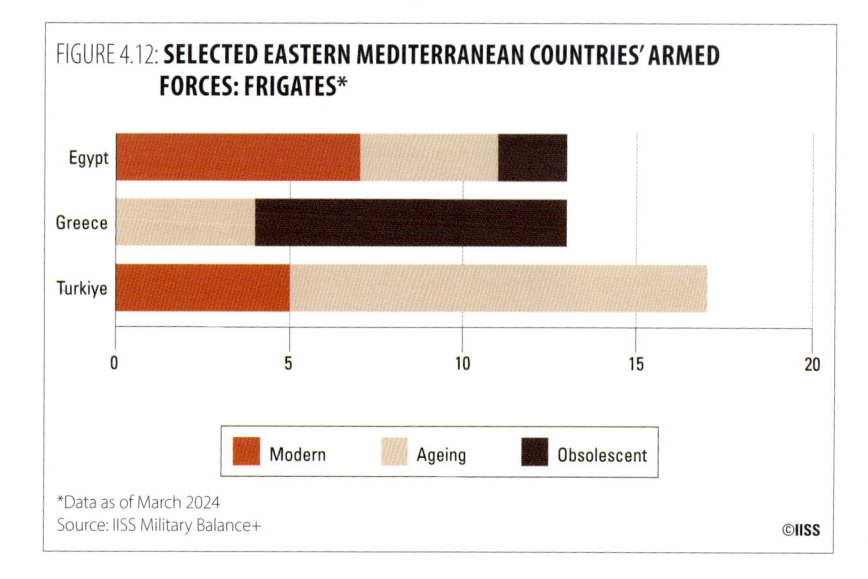

FIGURE 4.12: SELECTED EASTERN MEDITERRANEAN COUNTRIES' ARMED FORCES: FRIGATES*

Legend: Modern | Ageing | Obsolescent

*Data as of March 2024
Source: IISS Military Balance+

TABLE 4.5: TURKIYE: SELECTED PROCUREMENT PROGRAMMES, 2010–MARCH 2024

Contract date	Equipment	Type	Quantity	Value (US$ millions)	Contractor	Delivery	Service
July 2010	CH-47F *Chinook*	Heavy transport helicopter	11	403	🇺🇸 Boeing	2016–19	Army
November 2010	T129A	Attack helicopter	9	199	🇹🇷 TAI*	2014–15	Army
June 2011	*Bayraktar*	Landing ship tank	2	n.k.	🇹🇷 Anadolu Shipyard	2017–18	Navy
July 2011	*Reis* (Type-214)	Attack submarine	6	2,783	🇩🇪 TKMS**	2023–27	Navy
November 2011	*Bayraktar* TB2	Medium CISR UAV	200+	n.k.	🇹🇷 Baykar	2014–ongoing	Various
October 2013	*Anka*-S	Heavy CISR UAV	33+	n.k.	🇹🇷 TAI	2018–ongoing	Air Force; Navy; Gendarmerie
December 2013	*Hurkus*-B	Training aircraft	15	n.k.	🇹🇷 TAI	2018–ongoing	Air Force
May 2015	*Anadolu* (*Juan Carlos* I mod)	LHD	1	999	🇪🇸 SEDEF with Navantia	2023	Navy
May 2016	*Korkut*	35mm self-propelled air-defence artillery	n.k.	n.k.	🇹🇷 ASELSAN	2019–ongoing	Army
June 2016	• *Kaplan* STA • *Pars* STA 4x4	• Self-propelled anti-tank system • Self-propelled anti-tank system	• 208 • 136	n.k.	🇹🇷 FNSS	2019–ongoing	Army
June 2016	S-70i *Black Hawk* (T-70)	Medium transport helicopter	109	3,500	🇹🇷🇺🇸 TAI with Sikorsky	From 2022	Army; Air Force; Gendarmerie et al.
August 2016	*Kaan* (TF-X)	FGA aircraft development	n.k.	n.k.	🇹🇷 TAI	By 2028	Air Force
December 2016	*Ufuk* (MILGEM)	Intelligence-collection vessel	1	n.k.	🇹🇷 STM	2022	Navy
February 2017	F-35A *Lightning* II	FGA aircraft	6	n.k.	🇺🇸 Lockheed Martin	Cancelled***	Air Force
March 2017	ZAHA	Amphibious assault vehicle	27	n.k.	🇹🇷 FNSS	2023	Navy
May 2017	*Bayraktar Akinci*	Heavy CISR UAV	15+	n.k.	🇹🇷 Baykar	2019–ongoing	Army; Air Force
May 2017	*Hurkus*-C	Ground-attack aircraft	12	n.k.	🇹🇷 TAI	n.k.	Air Force
September 2017	*Aksungur*	Heavy CISR UAV	6+	n.k.	🇹🇷 TAI	2021–ongoing	Navy
September 2017	S-400 (RS-SA-21 *Growler*)	Long-range SAM	8 batteries	2,500	🇷🇺 Almaz-Antey	2019	Air Force
December 2017	T129B	Attack helicopter	27	n.k.	🇹🇷 TAI	2018–ongoing	Gendarmerie
2018	T-155 *Firtina* II	155mm self-propelled howitzer	140	n.k.	🇹🇷 BMC	2021–27	Army
July 2018	*Derya*	Fleet-replenishment oiler	1	n.k.	🇹🇷 Sefine Shipyard	2024	Navy
August 2018	HAVA SOJ	Electronic-warfare aircraft	4	667	🇹🇷 ASELSAN; TAI	By 2025	Air Force
November 2018	*Altay*	MBT	250	n.k.	🇹🇷 BMC	n.k.	Army
2019	HISAR	Short-range SAM	n.k.	n.k.	🇹🇷 ASELSAN; Roketsan	From 2021	Army; Air Force
April 2019	*Istif* (MILGEM)	Frigate	4	n.k.	🇹🇷 STM	From 2024	Navy
November 2020	*Akhisar* (MILGEM)	Offshore-patrol ship	2	n.k.	🇹🇷 Istanbul Naval Shipyard	From 2024	Navy
2022	*Anka*-3	UCAV development	n.k.	n.k.	🇹🇷 TAI	n.k.	Air Force
December 2023	SIPER	Long-range SAM	n.k.	n.k.	🇹🇷 ASELSAN; Roketsan; TUBITAK SAGE	From 2026	Air Force

*With AgustaWestland
**Licence-built in Turkiye
***Turkiye expelled from F-35 programme in 2019
Sources: IISS Military Balance+; IISS analysis

©IISS

defence and aerospace by 2023) outlined in 2014[199] have not been fully achieved, this should not detract from the overall positive trend. This growth is due to a number of factors, including a willingness to export certain technologies where the US and others were unwilling such as armed UAVs, political relationships, quality and cost competitiveness. Over the last five years, Turkish companies have also begun to have success in competitions against foreign firms, indicating that the quality of Turkish systems is reasonably competitive.[200]

Yet real challenges remain. Although an increasing amount of the equipment budget goes to local companies, Turkish industry is currently unable to produce certain key systems. This is particularly an issue with complex aerospace and maritime platforms, for which Turkiye has often opted to licence-produce a foreign design with increased localisation over time. Examples of this include German submarines, a Spanish LHD and Italian attack helicopters. Although wholesale imports are now increasingly rare, Turkiye has acquired US CH-47F *Chinook* heavy transport helicopters and Russian S-400 (RS-SA-21 *Growler*) long-range SAM systems, as local industry cannot currently supply an alternative.

Turkiye has struggled to modernise certain elements of its military including its large fleet of US-origin combat aircraft. Turkiye's removal in 2019 from the F-35 programme in retaliation for acquiring the Russian S-400s was a significant blow to modernisation efforts.[201] Turkiye had been a member of the Joint Strike Fighter programme since its creation in 1999, and Turkish companies were integrated into the F-35 supply chain. The 100 F-35A aircraft that Turkiye had planned to acquire would have replaced approximately one-third of the current fighter-aircraft fleet.[202] More recently, Congress approved a mid-life upgrade programme for elements of the F-16 fleet and the supply of new aircraft following Turkish ratification of Sweden's[203] NATO membership. The planned production of a first batch of *Altay* MBTs has been delayed by a halt in German defence exports to Turkiye following the latter's military actions in Syria.[204] Although replacements are being sourced from South Korea,[205] that country has struggled to develop its own power pack for the K2, upon which the *Altay* is based.[206]

Turkish Naval Forces conducting the *Denizkurdu*-1 exercise in the Black Sea, Aegean Sea and Eastern Mediterranean simultaneously on 15 January 2024. (Photo: Avuz Ozden/Dia images via Getty Images)

ENDNOTES

1. Nektaria Stamouli, '5 Things to Know About the Latest Cyprus Talks', Politico, 27 April 2021, https://www.politico.eu/article/5-things-to-know-about-latest-cyprus-talks/.

2. Evie Andreou, 'National Guard Will Remain a Defensive, Not Offensive Force, President Says', Cyprus Mail, 7 March 2018, https://web.archive.org/web/20180322043455/https://cyprus-mail.com/2018/03/07/national-guard-will-remain-defensive-not-offensive-force-president-says/; and AP NEWS, 'Cyprus to UN: Turkey Seeks Full Control of Breakaway North', 6 June 2022, https://apnews.com/article/united-nations-recep-tayyip-erdogan-nicos-anastasiades-cyprus-abc11b3093895f326bdb356b66ad0429.

3. Michali Papadopoulos Μιχάλη Παπαδόπουλου, '«Ipó mális» stin Epitropí Áminas' «Υπό μάλης» στην Επιτροπή Άμυνας ['Under dispute' at the Defence Committee], Simerini η σημερινή, 26 February 2016, https://simerini.sigmalive.com/article/2016/2/26/upo-males-sten-epitrope-amunas/.

4. Ilias Hatzikoumis Ηλίας Χατζηκουμής, 'Lefkí Vívlos yia tin Ámina kai tin Asphália tis Kíprou' Λευκή Βίβλος για την Άμυνα και την Ασφάλεια της Κύπρου [White Paper on the Defence and Security of Cyprus], Philenews, 7 July 2022, https://www.philenews.com/f-me-apopsi/paremvaseis-ston-f/article/1506539/lefki-biblos-ga-tin-amyna-kai-tin-asfaleia-tis-kyproy; and Nikos Christodoulides, 'Enískhisi Apotreptikís Iskhíos – Ámina kai Asphália' Ενίσχυση Αποτρεπτικής Ισχύος – Άμυνα και Ασφάλεια' [Strengthening Deterrence – Defense and Security], Nikos Christodoulides 2023 presidential candidacy website, https://web.archive.org/web/20230207150959/https://www.christodoulides2023.com/pylones/planitis/amyna/.

5. 'IPAM: Katéthese nomoskhédio pou tha epitrépi stous SIOP na paraménoun stin ipiresía mékhri ta 42 éti' ΥΠΑΜ: Κατέθεσε νομοσχέδιο που θα επιτρέπει στους ΣΥΟΠ να παραμένουν στην υπηρεσία μέχρι τα 42 έτη [Ministry of Defence: Filed a bill that will allow SYOPs to remain in service until 42 years], ANT1LIVE, 26 November 2022, https://www.ant1live.com/politiki/528612_ypam-katethese-nomoshedio-poy-tha-epitrepei-stoys-syop-na-paramenoyn-stin-ypiresia; and Gina Agapiou, 'National Guard Is Constantly Improving and Adapting Says Minister', Cyprus Mail, 24 January 2023, https://cyprus-mail.com/2023/01/24/national-guard-is-constantly-improving-and-adapting-says-minister/.

6. Germany, Federal Foreign Office, 'The Federal Foreign Office and the Federal Ministry of Defence on the Bundeswehr's Military Evacuation Force in Cyprus', 21 November 2023, https://www.auswaertiges-amt.de/en/newsroom/news/-/2632638.

7. Cyprus, Ministry of Defence, 'Welcome Speech by Minister of Defence for the "Battlefield Redefined Conference 2023" - The Cyprus International Defence and Security Conference', 23 January 2023, https://mod.gov.cy/en/announcements/2023/01/23/welcome-speech-by-minister-of-defenceon-battlefield-redefined-2023/.

8. Yvonni-Stefania Efstathiou, 'PeSCo: The Cyprus Perspective', IRIS/Armament Industry European Research Group, February 2019, https://www.iris-france.org/wp-content/uploads/2019/02/Ares-35.pdf.

9. Ned Price, 'Lifting of Defense Trade Restrictions on the Republic of Cyprus for Fiscal Year 2023', US, Department of State, 16 September 2022, https://www.state.gov/lifting-of-defense-trade-restrictions-on-the-republic-of-cyprus-for-fiscal-year-2023/.

10. US, Senate Foreign Relations Committee, 'Congress Passes Menendez-Rubio Bill Reshaping U.S. Policy in Eastern Mediterranean', 20 December 2019, https://www.foreign.senate.gov/press/dem/release/congress-passes-menendez-rubio-bill-reshaping-us-policy-in-eastern-mediterranean_-.

11. 'Cyprus: The New Epicenter of U.S. Military Strategy in the Mediterranean', KNews, 25 February 2024, https://knews.kathimerini.com.cy/en/news/cyprus-the-new-epicenter-of-u-s-military-strategy-in-the-mediterranean.

12. 'Cyprus Signs Deal to Allow Russian Navy to Use Ports', BBC News, 26 February 2015, https://www.bbc.co.uk/news/world-europe-31632259.

13. Cyprus, Ministry of Foreign Affairs, 'Statement to the Press by the Minister of Foreign Affairs of the Republic of Cyprus, Mr. Nikos Christodoulides, Following His Meeting with the Minister of Foreign Affairs of the Russian Federation, Mr. Sergey Lavrov', 21 October 2021, https://mfa.gov.cy/press-releases/2021/10/21/fm-christodoulides-press-statement-moscow/.

14. Kyriacos Iacovides, '"Humanitarian" Deal Allowing Russian Ships in Cyprus Jeopardised Lifting of US Arms Embargo', Cyprus Mail, 29 January 2023, https://cyprus-mail.com/2023/01/29/a-crafty-but-risky-humanitarian-deal-with-moscow/; and 'Cyprus Minister Reportedly Offered Russian Warships Ports Under Deal', National Herald, 30 January 2023, https://www.thenationalherald.com/cyprus-minister-reportedly-offered-russian-warships-ports-under-deal/.

15. 'Cyprus to Provide Logistical Support and Services to US Naval Vessels', KNews, 20 September 2022, https://knews.kathimerini.com.cy/en/news/cyprus-to-provide-logistical-support-and-services-to-us-naval-vessels-video.

16. 'Cyprus-Israel Military Exercise an "Absolute Success"', Financial Mirror, 19 November 2020, https://www.financialmirror.com/2020/11/19/cyprus-israel-military-exercise-an-absolute-success/; Sharon Wrobel, 'Israel and Cyprus Kick off Two-day "Onisilos-Gideon" Military Air Defense Drill', Algemeiner, 5 April 2021, https://www.algemeiner.com/2021/04/05/israel-and-cyprus-kick-off-two-day-onisilos-gideon-military-air-defense-drill/; Cyprus, Ministry of Defence, 'Oloklírosi áskisis «ONISILOS – YEDEON 2021»' Ολοκλήρωση άσκησης «ΟΝΗΣΙΛΟΣ – ΓΕΔΕΩΝ 2021» [Completion of 'Onisilos-Gideon Exercise 2021'], 6 April 2021, https://mod.gov.cy/announcements/2021/04/06/%CE%BF%CE%BB%CE%BF%CE%BA%CE%BB%CE%AE%CF%81%CF%89%CF%83%CE%B7-%CE%AC%CF%83%CE%BA%CE%B7%CF%83%CE%B7%CF%82-%CE%BF%CE%BD%CE%B7%CF%83%CE%B9%CE%BB%CE%BF%CF%82/; and Ohav Turgeman, '"Onisilos Gedeon" Joint Exercise in Cyprus', Israeli Air Force, 19 November 2020, https://www.iaf.org.il/9204-52582-en/IAF.aspx; Cyprus, Ministry of Defence, 'Exercise "IASON-2020"', 27 October 2020, https://mod.gov.cy/en/announcements/2020/10/27/%CE%BF%CE%BB%CE%BF%CE%BA%CE%BB%CE%AE%CF%81%CF%89%CF%83%CE%B7-%CE%AC%CF%83%CE%BA%CE%B7%CF%83%CE%B7%CF%82-%C2%AB%CE%B9%CE%B1%CF%83%CF%89%CE%BD-2020%C2%BB/.

17. 'National Guard Completes Joint Exercise in Egypt', Cyprus Mail, 26 August 2022, https://cyprus-mail.com/2022/08/26/national-guard-completes-joint-exercise-in-egypt/.

18. France, Ministry of the Armed Forces, 'Méditerranée orientale – La France représentée lors de l'exercice tripartite MEDUSA 21' [Eastern Mediterranean – France represented during the MEDUSA 21 tripartite exercise], 25 November 2021, https://www.defense.gouv.fr/operations/actualites/mediterranee-orientale-france-representee-lors-lexercice-tripartite-medusa-21.

19. Katy Turner, 'National Guard Takes Part in Multi-national Exercise', Cyprus Mail, 18 September 2022, https://cyprus-mail.com/2022/09/18/national-guard-takes-part-in-multi-national-exercise-video/.

20. 'National Guard Takes Part at Military Exercise with Jordanian and US Forces', In-cyprus, 18 September 2022, https://in-cyprus.philenews.com/news/local/national-guard-takes-part-at-military-exercise-with-jordanian-and-us-forces-video/.

21. Kerry Kolasa-Sikiaridi, 'Cyprus Drastically Reduces Mandatory Army Service to 14 Months', Greek Reporter, 15 July 2016, https://greekreporter.com/2016/07/15/cyprus-drastically-reduces-mandatory-army-service-to-14-months/; and Philip Mark, 'Professional Army Era Begins', Cyprus Mail, 29 July 2016, https://web.archive.org/web/20160730225251/https://cyprus-mail.com/2016/07/29/professional-army-era-begins/.

22 'Cyprus Signs $9 Billion Gas Extraction Deal with Israel's Delek, Other Firms', *Times of Israel*, 8 November 2019, https://www.timesofisrael.com/cyprus-signs-9-billion-gas-extraction-deal-with-israels-delek-other-firms/.

23 IMF, 'Inflation Rate, Average Consumer Prices', 5 June 2023, https://www.imf.org/external/datamapper/PCPIPCH@WEO/OEMDC/.

24 Apostolos Tomaras Απόστολου Τομαρά, '«Arkhipliarkhos A. Ioannidis» to stolidi tou P. Naftikoú (vínteo)' «Αρχιπλοίαρχος Α. Ιωαννίδης» το στολίδι του Π. Ναυτικού (βίντεο) ["Archpilot A. Ioannidis" the jewel of the navy (video)], *Kathimerini* Η καθημερινή, 4 January 2018, https://www.kathimerini.com.cy/gr/kypros/arxiploiarxos-a-ioannidis-to-stolidi-toy-p-naytikoy-binteo; and Savvas Vlassis Σάββας βλάσσης, 'Próti dimósia emphánisi tou Aerostar tis Ethnikís Phrourás' Πρώτη δημόσια εμφάνιση του Aerostar της Εθνικής Φρουράς [First public appearance of the National Guard's Aerostar], *Doureios Ippos ΔΟΥΡΕΙΟΣ ΙΠΠΟΣ*, 8 November 2021, https://doureios.com/proti-dimosia-emfanisi-tou-aerostar-tis-ethnikis-frouras/.

25 'Self-propelled Howitzer "NORA B-52" and Armored Vehicle "MILOS" Presented at Military Parade in Cyprus', Yugoimport, 2 October 2019, https://www.yugoimport.com/en/actualities/news/self-propelled-howitzer-nora-b-52-and-armored-vehicle-milos-presented-military-parade-cyprus.

26 Airbus, 'Cyprus Orders Six H145Ms for Its National Guard', 24 June 2022, https://www.airbus.com/en/newsroom/press-releases/2022-06-cyprus-orders-six-h145ms-for-its-national-guard.

27 'Cyprus Hails US Decision to Fully Lift Weapons Embargo', Voice of America, 17 September 2022, https://www.voanews.com/a/cyprus-hails-us-decision-to-fully-lift-weapons-embargo/6751628.html.

28 Egypt, State Information Service, 'Speech by H.E. President Abdel Fattah El Sisi at the Western Military Zone', 23 June 2020, https://www.sis.gov.eg/Story/147756/Speech-by-by-H.E.-President-Abdel-Fattah-El-Sisi-at-the-Western-Military-Zone?lang=en-us.

29 Parisa Kamali et al., 'Red Sea Attacks Disrupt Global Trade', IMF, 7 March 2024, https://www.imf.org/en/Blogs/Articles/2024/03/07/Red-Sea-Attacks-Disrupt-Global-Trade.

30 See Alessia Melcangi, 'Egypt Recalibrated Its Strategy in Libya Because of Turkey', Atlantic Council, 1 June 2021, https://www.atlanticcouncil.org/blogs/menasource/egypt-recalibrated-its-strategy-in-libya-because-of-turkey/.

31 Khalil Al-Anani, 'Egypt-Turkey Strained Relations: Implications for Regional Security', Arab Center Washington DC, 18 March 2020, https://arabcenterdc.org/resource/egypt-turkey-strained-relations-implications-for-regional-security/.

32 Benoit Faucon, Nicholas Bariyo and Summer Said, 'Ignoring U.S. Calls for Peace, Egypt Delivered Drones to Sudan's Military', *Wall Street Journal*, 14 October 2023, https://www.wsj.com/world/africa/ignoring-u-s-calls-for-peace-egypt-delivered-drones-to-sudans-military-6f7fdcda; Giorgio Cafiero, 'Why Egypt and Turkey are Ending a Decade of Tension', The New Arab, 22 February 2024, https://www.newarab.com/analysis/why-egypt-and-turkey-are-ending-decade-tension.

33 US, Department of State, 'U.S. Relations With Egypt: Bilateral Relations Fact Sheet', 29 April 2022, https://www.state.gov/u-s-relations-with-egypt/.

34 'Egypt Keen to Boost Military Cooperation with US: Defence Minister to CENTCOM Commander', *Ahram Online*, 11 September 2022, https://english.ahram.org.eg/NewsContent/1/1237/475870/Egypt/Defence/Egypt-keen-to-boost-military-cooperation-with-US-D.aspx.

35 US, Department of Defense, '33rd U.S.-Egypt Military Cooperation Committee (MCC)', 15 September 2022, https://www.defense.gov/News/Releases/Release/Article/3160169/33rd-us-egypt-military-cooperation-committee-mcc/.

36 'Strategic Cooperation Agreement Between Russia and Egypt Comes Into Force', *Egypt Independent*, 12 January 2021, https://egyptindependent.com/strategic-cooperation-agreement-between-russia-and-egypt-comes-into-force/.

37 Khalil Al-Anani, 'Growing Relations Between Egypt and Russia: Strategic Alliance or Marriage of Convenience?', Arab Center Washington DC, 27 September 2021, https://arabcenterdc.org/resource/growing-relations-between-egypt-and-russia-strategic-alliance-or-marriage-of-convenience/#_ftn2.

38 Pieter D. Wezeman et al., 'Trends in International Arms Transfers, 2023', SIPRI, March 2024, p. 12, https://www.sipri.org/sites/default/files/2024-03/fs_2403_at_2023.pdf.

39 Gregory Aftandilian, 'Egyptian-Saudi Relations: Strategic Ties with Some Political Strains', Arab Center Washington DC, 9 February 2021, https://arabcenterdc.org/resource/egyptian-saudi-relations-strategic-ties-with-some-political-strains/.

40 David Butter, 'Egypt and the Gulf: Allies and Rivals', Chatham House, April 2020, https://www.chathamhouse.org/sites/default/files/CHHJ8102-Egypt-and-Gulf-RP-WEB_0.pdf.

41 Gregory Aftandilian, 'Egypt's Ties to Israel Deepen Despite Public Misgivings', Arab Center Washington DC, 19 March 2021, https://arabcenterdc.org/resource/egypts-ties-to-israel-deepen-despite-public-misgivings/.

42 Sarah El Safty and Ari Rabinovitch, 'EU, Israel and Egypt Sign Deal To Boost East Med Gas Exports to Europe', Reuters, 15 June 2022, https://www.reuters.com/business/energy/eu-israel-egypt-sign-deal-boost-east-med-gas-exports-europe-2022-06-15/.

43 Egypt, State Information Service, 'The 9th Tripartite Summit Between Egypt, Greece, and Cyprus in Athens', 19 October 2021, https://www.sis.gov.eg/Story/159635/The-9th-Tripartite-Summit-between-Egypt%2C-Greece%2C-and-Cyprus-in-Athens?lang=en-us.

44 Nael Shama, 'Between Alliance and Entente: The Egyptian-Greek-Cypriot Partnership', in Zenonas Tziarras (ed.), *The New Geopolitics of the Eastern Mediterranean: Trilateral Partnerships and Regional Security* (Nicosia: Peace Research Institute Oslo/Friedrich-Ebert-Stiftung, 2019), pp. 105–106, https://library.fes.de/pdf-files/bueros/zypern/15662.pdf.

45 Athanasios Koutoupas, 'Egypt Signs Military Agreement with Cyprus', Greek Community of Alexandria, 6 March 2016, https://ekalexandria.org/en/2016/03/06/egypt-signsmilitary-cooperation-agreementcyprus/#.Y-oxc3aZOUl.

46 Greece, General Staff of National Defence, 'Ipographi «Programmatos Stratiotikis Sinergasias Ellados – Aiyiptou» yia to Etos 2022 Υπογραφή «Προγράμματος Στρατιωτικής Συνεργασίας Ελλάδος – Αιγύπτου» για το Έτος 2022 [Signing of the 'Greece-Egypt Military Cooperation Programme' for the year 2022], 28 March 2022, https://geetha.mil.gr/ypografi-programmatosstratiotikis-synergasias-ellados-aigyptoygia-to-etos-2022/; and Greece, General Staff of National Defence, 'Episimi Episkepsi Arkhigou YEETHA stin Araviki Dimokratia tis Aiyiptou' Επίσημη Επίσκεψη Αρχηγού ΓΕΕΘΑ στην Αραβική Δημοκρατία της Αιγύπτου [Official visit of the Head of GEETHA to the Arab Republic of Egypt], 1 September 2022, https://geetha.mil.gr/episimi-episkepsi-archigoy-geetha-stinaraviki-dimokratia-tis-aigyptoy-2/.

47 Hellenic Army General Staff, 'Greece – Egypt 2022 Military Cooperation Programme', 22 June 2022, http://army.gr/en/content/greece-egypt-2022-military-cooperation-programme.

48 Sami Hegazi, 'Egypt, Greece Sign Agreement on Maritime Rescue', *Daily News Egypt*, 22 November 2022, https://dailynewsegypt.com/2022/11/22/egyptgreece-sign-agreement-on-maritimerescue/; and 'Greece, Egypt sign MoU on Aeronautics, Maritime Search and Rescue – Says FM Nikos Dendias', The Libya Update, 23 November 2022, https://libyaupdate.com/greece-egypt-sign-mou-on-aeronautics-maritime-search-and-rescue-says-fm-nikos-dendias/.

49 US Central Command, 'Bright Star 2023 Highlights the Long-standing Egyptian-American Ties', 8 September 2023, https://www.centcom.mil/MEDIA/NEWS-ARTICLES/News-Article-View/Article/3520694/bright-star-2023-highlights-the-long-standing-egyptian-american-ties/.

50 US, Central Command Public Affairs, 'U.S. Forces Participate in Exercise Bright Star in Egypt', US Embassy in Egypt, 5 September 2021, https://eg.usembassy.gov/u-s-forces-participate-in-exercise-bright-star-in-egypt/; and US Comptroller General, 'Forging A New Defense Relationship With Egypt', 5 February 1982, https://www.gao.gov/assets/id-82-15.pdf.

51 Michael R. Gordon and Declan Walsh, 'General Says U.S. Wants to Resume Major Military Exercise with Egypt', *New York Times*, 26 February 2017,

52. Egypt, Ministry of Defense, 'The Commencement of the Egyptian-French Joint Naval Exercise (Cleopatra-2021)', 22 March 2021, https://www.mod.gov.eg/modwebsite/NewsDetails.aspx?id=40688.
53. Gobran Mohamed, 'Egyptian, Greek Naval Forces Carry Out Joint Exercises in Mediterranean', *Arab News*, 3 August 2022, https://www.arabnews.com/node/2135371/middle-east.
54. 'Russia and Egypt Hold First-ever Joint Naval Drills', *Defense News*, 10 June 2015, https://www.defensenews.com/home/2015/06/10/russia-and-egypt-hold-first-ever-joint-naval-drills/.
55. 'Egypt, China Conduct Joint Naval Drill In Mediterranean Sea', China Military, 21 August 2019, http://eng.chinamil.com.cn/view/2019-08/21/content_9597297.htm.
56. Robert Springborg and F. C. 'Pink' Williams, 'The Egyptian Military: A Slumbering Giant Awakes', Carnegie Middle East Center, 28 February 2019, https://carnegie-mec.org/2019/02/28/egyptian-military-slumbering-giant-awakes-pub-78238.
57. IISS, *The Military Balance 2021* (Abingdon: Routledge for the IISS, 2021), p. 322.
58. Ahmed Mohammed Hassan and Aidan Lewis, 'Egypt Steps Up Security on Border as Israeli Offensive in Gaza Nears', Reuters, 9 February 2024, https://www.reuters.com/world/middle-east/egypt-steps-up-security-border-israeli-offensive-gaza-nears-2024-02-09/.
59. IISS, *The Military Balance 2021*, p. 322.
60. Ido Levy, 'Egypt's Counterinsurgency Success in Sinai', The Washington Institute for Near East Policy, 9 December 2021, https://www.washingtoninstitute.org/policy-analysis/egypts-counterinsurgency-success-sinai.
61. Springborg and Williams, 'The Egyptian Military: A Slumbering Giant Awakes'.
62. Khalil Al-Anani, 'Sisi Intensifies Arms Imports to Secure External Support for His Policies', Arab Center Washington DC, 28 February 2022, https://arabcenterdc.org/resource/sisi-intensifies-arms-imports-to-secure-external-support-for-his-policies/.
63. 'Egyptian Air Force', F-16.net, https://www.f-16.net/f-16_users_article4.html.
64. Steve Holland and Jeff Mason, 'Obama Cancels Military Exercises, Condemns Violence in Egypt', Reuters, 16 August 2013, https://www.reuters.com/article/us-egypt-protests-obama-idUSBRE97E0N020130816.
65. 'US Unlocks Military Aid to Egypt, Backing President Sisi', BBC News, 22 June 2014, https://www.bbc.co.uk/news/world-middle-east-27961933.
66. Hélène Sallon, 'Mistral : l'Arabie saoudite et l'Egypte « sont prêtes à tout pour acheter les deux navires »' [Mistral: Saudi Arabia and Egypt 'are ready to do anything to buy the two ships'], *Le Monde*, 7 August 2015, https://www.lemonde.fr/afrique/article/2015/08/07/l-egypte-et-l-arabie-saoudite-candidates-au-rachat-des-mistrals_4715520_3212.html.
67. Nektaria Stamouli, 'Erdoğan Warns Greece That Turkish Missiles Can Reach Athens', Politico, 11 December 2022, https://www.politico.eu/article/erdogan-warns-greece-that-turkish-missiles-can-reach-athens%EF%BF%BC/; and 'Leaders of Turkey and Greece Vow to Repair Ties after Year of Tension', Reuters, 12 July 2023, https://www.reuters.com/world/leaders-turkey-greece-vow-repair-ties-after-year-tension-2023-07-12/.
68. Greece, Ministry of National Defence, 'White Paper', 23 January 2015, https://web.archive.org/web/20150628172915/http:/static2271.ovhcloudcdn.com/v1/AUTH_a4f5f2560789433da7bcbb5945bf92fa/default/sites/mod.mil.gr/White_Paper.pdf.
69. Yiannis Duniadakis, '«Agorés tou aióna» ta teleftaía 50 khrónia: Yia tin ámina tis khóras í yia to NATO kai tin EE?' «Αγορές του αιώνα» τα τελευταία 50 χρόνια: Για την άμυνα της χώρας ή για το NATO και την ΕΕ; ['Markets of the Century' in the Last 50 Years: For the Defence of the Country or for NATO and the EU?], ALT.GR, 6 March 2021, https://www.alt.gr/agores-toy-aiona-ta-teleytaia-50-chroni/.
70. '2005–2018: O exoplistikós «aftokhiriasmós» tis khóras' 2005–2018: Ο εξοπλιστικός «αυτοχειριασμός» της χώρας [2005–2018: The Armament 'Self Handling' of the Country], Defence Review, https://defencereview.gr/2005-2018-o-exoplistikos-aftochiriasmos-tis-choras/.
71. 'ES: Oloklírosi tis Domís Dinámeon 2013–2027 (1i STRATIA, Méros A')' ΕΣ: Ολοκλήρωση της Δομής Δυνάμεων 2013-2027 (1η ΣΤΡΑΤΙΑ, Μέρος Α') [Hellenic Army: Completion of the Force Structure 2013–2027 (1st Army, Part I)], Defencepoint, 29 April 2014, https://www.defence-point.gr/news/%CE%B5%CF%83-%CE%BF%CE%BB%CE%BF%CE%BA%CE%BB%CE%AE%CF%81%CF%89%CF%83%CE%B7-%CF%84%CE%B7%CF%82-%CE%B4%CE%BF%CE%BC%CE%AE%CF%82-%CE%B4%CF%85%CE%BD%CE%BD%CE%AC%CE%BC%CE%B5%CF%89%CE%BD-2013-2027-1%CE%B7-%CF%83.
72. 'Míosi anóταton axiomatikón ton ED, exortholoyismós' Μείωση ανώτατων αξιωματικών των ΕΔ, εξορθολογισμός [Reduction of Senior HAF Officers, Rationalisation], Defencepoint, 27 June 2014, https://www.defence-point.gr/news/%CE%BC%CE%B5%CE%B9%CF%8E%CE%BD%CE%BF%CE%BD%CF%84%CE%B1%CE%B9-%CE%BF%CE%B9-%CE%B1%CE%BD%CF%8E%CF%84%CE%B1%CF%84%CE%BF%CE%B9-%CE%B1%CE%BE%CE%B9%CF%89%CE%BC%CE%B1%CF%84%CE%B9%CE%BA%CE%BF%CE%AF-%CF%84.
73. 'Néa Domí Enóplon Dinámeon: Émmesi anasístasi V' SS kai ta krísima zitímata pou periplékontai' Νέα Δομή Ενόπλων Δυνάμεων: Έμμεση ανασύσταση Β' ΣΣ και τα κρίσιμα ζητήματα που περιπλέκονται [New Structure of the Armed Forces: Indirect Reconstitution of the Second Army Corps and the Critical Issues Involved], Defencepoint, 19 May 2021, https://www.defence-point.gr/news/nea-domi-enoplon-dynameon-emmesi-anasystasi-v-ss-kai-ta-krisima-zitimata-poy-periplekontai.
74. 'Allázoun i Énoples Dinámis: "Prásino phos" sti néa domí' Αλλάζουν οι Ένοπλες Δυνάμεις: "Πράσινο φως" στη νέα δομή [The Armed Forces are Changing: 'Green Light' on the New Structure], Capital, 23 September 2020, https://www.capital.gr/epikairotita/3482884/allazoun-oi-enoples-dunameis-prasino-fos-sti-nea-domi.
75. 'Greek Parliament Approves Defence Pact Change on Eve of PM's Visit to U.S.', Reuters, 12 May 2022, https://www.reuters.com/world/greek-parliament-approves-defence-pact-change-eve-pms-visit-us-2022-05-12/; 'Greece to Extend Base Access Deal with US Military', Defense News, Associated Press, 12 May 2022, https://www.defensenews.com/news/your-military/2022/05/12/greece-to-extend-base-access-deal-with-us-military/.
76. US, Department of State, 'Integrated Country Strategy: Greece', 28 March 2022, https://www.state.gov/wp-content/uploads/2022/06/ICS_EUR_Greece_Public.pdf.
77. Greece, Ministry of Foreign Affairs, 'France', https://www.mfa.gr/en/blog/greece-bilateral-relations/france/.
78. Sebastian Sprenger, 'Greece Signs Pact to Buy Three Frigates from France', *Defense News*, 28 September 2021, https://www.defensenews.com/global/europe/2021/09/28/greece-signs-pact-to-buy-three-frigates-from-france/.
79. France, Ministry of the Armed Forces, 'Méditerranée orientale – Bilan de la coopération franco-grecque lors de l'exercice ARGO 22' [Eastern Mediterranean – Assessment of Franco-Greek cooperation during the ARGO 22 exercise], 6 October 2022, https://www.defense.gouv.fr/marine/actualites/mediterranee-orientale-bilan-cooperation-franco-grecque-lors-lexercice-argo-22.
80. UK, Ministry of Defence, 'UK and Greece Seek Strengthened Defence Partnership', 7 February 2023, https://www.gov.uk/government/news/uk-and-greece-seek-strengthened-defence-partnership.
81. 'Egypt, Greece Sign Protocol to Support Bilateral Military Cooperation', Middle East Monitor, 2 September 2022, https://www.middleeastmonitor.com/20220902-egypt-greece-sign-protocol-to-support-bilateral-military-cooperation/; Hellenic Army General Staff, 'Greece – Egypt 2022 Military Cooperation Programme'.
82. Sami Hegazi, 'Egypt, Greece Sign MoU in Field of Air and Sea Search, Rescue', *Daily News Egypt*, 25 November 2022, https://dailynewsegypt.com/2022/11/24/egypt-greece-sign-mou-in-field-of-air-and-sea-search-rescue/.
83. Emanuel Fabian, 'Israeli and Greek Air Forces Hold Dogfighting and Refueling

Drill Over Israel', *Times of Israel*, 13 July 2022, https://www.timesofisrael.com/israeli-and-greek-air-forces-hold-dogfighting-and-refueling-drill-over-israel/.

84 Derek Gatopoulos, 'With Eye on Turkey, Greece Opens Israeli-built Flight School', AP News, 21 October 2022, https://apnews.com/article/middle-east-europe-Turkiye-greece-israel-8df1558d1c0b3ce0a9bb02df6475497f.

85 Plasan, 'SK Group and Plasan Acquired The Greek Company ELVO', 6 July 2023, https://plasan.com/news_posts/sk-group-and-plasan-acquired-the-greek-company-elvo/.

86 Anne McElvoy and Claudia Chiappa, 'Israel's Friends Must Give It 'Hard Truths' Over Gaza Assault, Says Greek PM', Politico, 9 November 2023, https://www.politico.eu/article/kyriakos-mitsotakis-greece-israel-allies-hamas-gaza-europe/.

87 Vassilis Kappis, 'Evaluating the Prospects of Greek-Israeli Military Cooperation', Cyprus Center for European and International Affairs, 6 June 2016, https://cceia.unic.ac.cy/wp-content/uploads/EMPN_7.pdf.

88 European External Action Service, 'EUNAVFOR Operation Aspides', February 2024, https://www.eeas.europa.eu/sites/default/files/documents/2024/EUNAVFOR%20OPERATION%20ASPIDES_2024_0.pdf.

89 'Greece Is Expanding Its Military Cooperation with the UAE', Geopolitiki, 14 May 2022, https://geopolitiki.com/greece-is-expanding-its-military-cooperation-uae/.

90 Paul Iddon, 'How Significant Is Greece's Growing Military Cooperation With the UAE and Saudi Arabia?', Forbes, 31 March 2021, https://www.forbes.com/sites/pauliddon/2021/03/31/how-significant-is-greeces-growing-military-cooperation-with-the-uae-and-saudi-arabia/?sh=df8866719ef6.

91 'Saudi Air Force Combat Aircraft Arrive in Greece to Participate in Falcon Eye 3 Air Drill', Saudi Press Agency, 4 November 2022, https://www.spa.gov.sa/2398283.

92 Hellenic Air Force, '«INIOCHOS» Exercise', https://www.haf.gr/en/structure/htaf/air-tactics-center/iniohos/.

93 Hellenic Air Force, 'Iniochos 2023', https://www.haf.gr/en/structure/htaf/air-tactics-center/iniohos/archives/iniochos-2023/.

94 Giovanni Prete, 'Aeronautical Exercise Between Greece, Cyprus, France, Italy Kicks Off', Greek Reporter, 4 October 2022, https://greekreporter.com/2022/10/04/aeronautical-exercise-eunomia-greece-cyprus-france-italy/.

95 'Greece-Egypt-Cyprus Sign Military Cooperation Deal', Greek City Times, 7 April 2021, https://greekcitytimes.com/2021/04/07/greece-egypt-cyprus-military-deal/; Paul Antonopoulos, 'France and UAE to Participate in MEDUSA Exercises with Trilateral Alliance for the First Time', Greek City Times, 29 November 2020, https://greekcitytimes.com/2020/11/29/france-egypt-medusa-exercises/.

96 Greece, Ministry of National Defence, 'Deputy Minister of National Defence Alkiviadis Stefanis Attends Exercise "MILEX-21"', 18 June 2021, https://www.mod.mil.gr/en/deputy-minister-of-national-defence-alkiviadis-stefanis-attends-exercise-milex/.

97 Lockheed Martin, 'Hellenic Navy Receives First Modernized P-3 Orion Maritime Patrol Aircraft', 17 May 2019, https://news.lockheedmartin.com/2019-05-17-Hellenic-Navy-Receives-First-Modernized-P-3-Orion-Maritime-Patrol-Aircraft.

98 Greece, Hellenic Army, 'ΕΛΔΥΚ' [ELDYK], http://army.gr/el/content/eldyk.

99 'Greece Deploys PATRIOT Missile Battery to Saudi Arabia', Greek City Times, 15 September 2021, https://greekcitytimes.com/2021/09/15/greece-deploys-patriot-missile-saudi/.

100 IISS, Military Balance+ database, accessed 6 June 2023.

101 United Nations Register of Conventional Arms (UNROCA), https://www.unroca.org/.

102 Greece, Ministry of National Defence, 'Transfer of 40 BMP-1 IFVs from Greece to Ukraine and Replacement with 40 MARDER IFVs from Germany', 18 September 2022, https://www.mod.mil.gr/en/transfer-of-40-bmp-1-ifvs-from-greece-to-ukraine/.

103 Michel Cabirol, 'La France propose à la Grèce deux frégates FDI via une vente de type FMS à la française' [France Offers Two FDI Frigates to Greece Via a French FMS-style Sale], *La Tribune*, 24 September 2019, https://www.latribune.fr/entreprises-finance/industrie/aeronautique-defense/la-france-propose-a-la-grece-deux-fregates-fdi-via-une-vente-de-type-fms-a-la-francaise-828715.html.

104 Dassault Aviation, 'DASSAULT AVIATION Delivers Its First Rafale to Greece', 21 July 2021, https://www.dassault-aviation.com/en/group/press/press-kits/dassault-aviation-delivers-its-first-rafale-to-greece/.

105 US, Department of Defense, 'Contracts For Dec. 20, 2018', 20 December 2018, https://dod.defense.gov/News/Contracts/Contract-View/Article/1719367/.

106 Prime Minister of Greece, 'Sinéntefxi Típou tou Prothipourgoú Kiriákou Mitsotáki metá ti líxi ton ergasión tis Sinódou Koriphís tou NATO sti Madríti' Συνέντευξη Τύπου του Πρωθυπουργού Κυριάκου Μητσοτάκη μετά τη λήξη των εργασιών της Συνόδου Κορυφής του ΝΑΤΟ στη Μαδρίτη [Press conference of prime minister Kyriakos Mitsotakis after the conclusion of the work of the NATO Summit in Madrid], 30 June 2022, https://primeminister.gr/2022/06/30/29685; and US Defense Security Cooperation Agency, 'Greece - F-35 Joint Strike Fighter Conventional Take Off and Landing (CTOL) Aircraft', 26 January 2024, https://www.dsca.mil/press-media/major-arms-sales/greece-f-35-joint-strike-fighter-conventional-take-and-landing-ctol.

107 Suzanne Daley, 'So Many Bribes, a Greek Official Can't Recall Them All', *New York Times*, 7 February 2014, https://www.nytimes.com/2014/02/08/world/europe/so-many-bribes-a-greek-official-cant-recall-all.html.

108 Dimitris Mitsopoulos, 'The Future of the Hellenic Navy Fleet', Naval News, 22 November 2022, https://www.navalnews.com/naval-news/2022/11/the-future-of-the-hellenic-navy-fleet/.

109 Belfer Center, 'Deterring Terror - How Israel Confronts the Next Generation of Threats: English Translation of the Official Strategy of the Israel Defense Forces', August 2016, p. 4, https://www.belfercenter.org/sites/default/files/legacy/files/IDF%20doctrine%20translation%20-%20web%20final2.pdf.

110 Ehud Eilam, 'How the Israel Defense Forces Seek to Defeat Non-state Actors', *RUSI Journal*, vol. 167, no. 4–5, December 2022, p. 109.

111 Amiram Barkat, 'Chief of Staff Launches Plan for "More Lethal" IDF', *Globes*, 13 February 2020, https://en.globes.co.il/en/article-chief-of-staff-launches-plan-for-more-lethal-idf-1001318466; and Seth J. Frantzman, 'Israel Rolls Out New Wartime Plan to Reform Armed Forces', *Defense News*, 18 February 2020, https://www.defensenews.com/global/mideast-africa/2020/02/18/israel-rolls-out-new-wartime-plan-to-reform-armed-forces/.

112 Eilam, 'How the Israel Defense Forces Seek to Defeat Non-state Actors', p. 111.

113 Jeffrey Heller, 'Netanyahu Draws "Red Line" on Iran's Nuclear Program', Reuters, 28 September 2012, https://www.reuters.com/article/idUSBRE88Q0GI/.

114 Belfer Center, 'Deterring Terror - How Israel Confronts the Next Generation of Threats: English Translation of the Official Strategy of the Israel Defense Forces', p. 48.

115 Seth J. Frantzman, 'Israel Launches Edge of Tomorrow Program to Improve Lethality, Bring in New Tech', *Defense News*, 19 May 2022, https://www.defensenews.com/global/mideast-africa/2022/05/19/israel-launches-edge-of-tomorrow-program-to-improve-lethality-bring-in-new-tech/.

116 Peter Beaumont, 'Israeli Intelligence Leak Details Extent of Warnings over Hamas Attack', *Guardian,* 28 November 2023, https://www.theguardian.com/world/2023/nov/28/israeli-military-had-warning-of-hamas-training-for-attack-reports-say; and Raphael S. Cohen et al., 'Lessons from Israel's Wars in Gaza', RAND, 18 October 2017, https://www.rand.org/pubs/research_briefs/RB9975.html.

117 Matthias Dietrich, 'Economic Fallout of Israel's Gaza Strip Operation Threatens Growth Prospects', IISS, Military Balance Blog, 16 February 2024, https://www.iiss.org/online-analysis/military-balance/2024/02/economic-fallout-of-israels-gaza-strip-operation-threatens-growth-prospects/.

118 'Israel's Economy Shrank at 20% Rate After Outbreak of War', *Financial Times*, https://www.ft.com/content/763bb384-a974-4222-996f-8aecfbc32074.

119 Emanuel Fabian, 'IDF Announces Plans To Increase Service Time for Conscripts and Reservists', *Times of Israel*, 7 February 2024, https://www.timesofisrael.com/liveblog_entry/idf-announces-plans-to-increase-service-time-for-conscripts-and-reservists/.

120 International Court of Justice, 'Summary of the Order of 26 January 2024', 26 January 2024, https://www.icj-cij.org/node/203454#:~:text=The%20Court%20is%20also%20of,group%20in%20the%20Gaza%20Strip.

121 George Wright, 'Dutch Court Orders Halt to F-35 Jet Parts Exports to Israel', BBC News, 12 February 2024, https://www.bbc.co.uk/news/world-europe-68272233.

122 Israel, Ministry of Foreign Affairs, 'Israel-US Sign Joint Declaration on Strategic Partnership', 14 July 2022, https://www.gov.il/en/departments/news/israel-us-sign-joint-declaration-on-strategic-partnership-14-jul-2022; and The White House, 'The Jerusalem U.S.-Israel Strategic Partnership Joint Declaration', 14 July 2022, https://www.whitehouse.gov/briefing-room/statements-releases/2022/07/14/the-jerusalem-u-s-israel-strategic-partnership-joint-declaration/.

123 'Blinken in Israel as US Supports Call for Immediate Ceasefire in Gaza Tied to Hostage Deal', BBC News YouTube channel, 22 March 2024, https://www.youtube.com/watch?v=E93Fnqy9WhQ.

124 Michaël Tanchum, 'The Geopolitics of the Eastern Mediterranean Crisis: A Regional System Perspective on the Mediterranean's New Great Game', in Michaël Tanchum (ed.), *Eastern Mediterranean in Uncharted Waters: Perspectives on Emerging Geopolitical Realities* (Ankara: Konrad Adenauer Stiftung, 2021), p. 17, https://www.kas.de/documents/283907/10938219/Publikation+Eastern+Mediterranean+in+Uncharted+Waters.pdf/4722827e-1091-bb20-5bdf-d9cb45734e34?version=1.0&t=1610522619923.

125 Israel, Ministry of Foreign Affairs, 'MOD Gantz Meets His Majesty King Hamad bin Isa bin Salman Al Khalifa of Bahrain and Signs Historic Defense MOU', 3 February 2022, https://www.gov.il/en/Departments/news/mod-gantz-meets-the-king-of-bahrain-3-feb-2022.

126 For Morocco, see IISS, 'The Defence Policy and Economics of the Middle East and North Africa', 2022, pp. 27–28, 73, https://www.iiss.org/globalassets/media-library---content--migration/files/research-papers/2022/05/the-defence-policy-and-economics-of-the-middle-east-and-north-africa1.pdf.

127 Alexander Cornwell and John Irish, 'Exclusive: Israel to Sell Air Defence System to United Arab Emirates', Reuters, 23 September 2022, https://www.reuters.com/world/middle-east/exclusive-israel-sell-air-defence-system-united-arab-emirates-sources-say-2022-09-22/.

128 Patrick Kingsley and Ronen Bergman, 'Israel Confirms Regional Military Project, Showing Its Growing Role', *New York Times*, 20 June 2022, https://www.nytimes.com/2022/06/20/world/middleeast/israel-arab-military-alliance.html.

129 Michael Gordon and David Cloud, 'U.S. Held Secret Meeting With Israeli, Arab Military Chiefs to Counter Iran Air Threat', *Wall Street Journal*, 26 June 2022, https://www.wsj.com/articles/u-s-held-secret-meeting-with-israeli-arab-military-chiefs-to-counter-iran-air-threat-11656235802; and David Schenker, 'Regional Security Cooperation Partnerships in the Middle East', The Washington Institute for Near East Policy, 21 September 2022, https://www.washingtoninstitute.org/policy-analysis/regional-security-cooperation-partnerships-middle-east.

130 'Israel's Unexpected Military Alliance in the Gulf', *The Economist*, 30 June 2022, https://www.economist.com/middle-east-and-africa/2022/06/30/israels-unexpected-military-alliance-in-the-gulf.

131 US, Department of State, 'The Negev Forum Working Groups and Regional Cooperation Framework', 10 January 2023, https://www.state.gov/the-negev-forum-working-groups-and-regional-cooperation-framework/.

132 Tanchum, 'The Geopolitics of the Eastern Mediterranean Crisis: A Regional System Perspective on the Mediterranean's New Great Game', p. 17.

133 'Cyprus and Israel Sign Two Defence and Intelligence Agreements', PIME asianews, 1 November 2012, https://www.asianews.it/news-en/Cyprus-and-Israel-sign-two-defence-and-intelligenceagreements--23662.html; Israel, Ministry of Foreign Affairs, 'Israel and Cyprus Sign Defense Exports Agreements', 30 June 2022, https://www.gov.il/en/departments/news/israel-and-cyprus-sign-defenseexports-agreements-30-jun-2022; and 'Cyprus and Israel Conclude Latest Military Drill', *Cyprus Mail*, 14 September 2022, https://cyprus-mail.com/2022/09/14/cyprus-and-israel-conclude-latest-military-drill/.

134 Cyprus, Ministry of Defence, 'Oloklirόthike me epitikhía i 2i Trimerís Sinántisi ton Ipourgón Áminas Kíprou, Elládas, Israíl' Ολοκληρώθηκε με επιτυχία η 2η Τριμερής Συνάντηση των Υπουργών Άμυνας Κύπρου, Ελλάδας, Ισραήλ [The 2nd Tripartite Meeting of the Ministers of Defense of Cyprus, Greece, Israel was successfully completed], 22 June 2018, https://mod.gov.cy/announcements/2018/06/22/%CE%BF%CE%BB%CE%BF%CE%BA%CE%BB%CE%B7%CF%81%CF%8E%CE%B8%CE%B7%CE%BA%CE%B5-%CE%BC%CE%B5-%CE%B5%CF%80%CE%B9%CF%84%CF%85%CF%87%CE%AF%CE%B1-%CE%B7-2%CE%B7-%CF%84%CF%81%CE%B9%CE%BC%CE%B5%CF%81%CE%AE%CF%82-%CF%83%CF%85%CE%BD%CE%AC%CE%BD%CF%84%CE%B7%CF%83%CE%B7-%CF%84%CF%89%CE%BD-%CF%85%CF%80%CE%BF%CF%85%CF%81%CE%B3%CF%8E%CE%BD-%CE%AC%CE%BC%CF%85%CE%BD%CE%B1%CF%82-%CE%BA%CF%8D%CF%80%CF%81%CE%BF%CF%85,-%CE%B5%CE%BB%CE%BB%CE%AC%CE%B4%CE%B1%CF%82,-%CE%B9%CF%83%CF%81%CE%B1%CE%AE%CE%BB/.

135 'Mavi Marmara: Why Did Israel Stop The Gaza Flotilla?', BBC News, 27 June 2016, https://www.bbc.co.uk/news/10203726.

136 Eugene Kogan, 'Israeli-Greek Naval, Air Force and Defence Industry Cooperation', Austria Institut für Europa- und Sicherheitspolitik, October 2021, https://www.aies.at/download/2021/AIES-Fokus-2021-10.pdf.

137 Senior Master Sgt. Dwayne Gordon, 'AF Participates in First Israeli Blue Flag Exercise', US Air Force, 3 December 2013, https://www.af.mil/News/Article-Display/Article/467653/af-participates-in-first-israeli-blue-flag-exercise/.

138 Israeli Air Force, 'Opening of the Blue Flag 2021 Exercise, the Largest and Most Advanced Held in Israel', 14 October 2021, https://www.idf.il/en/mini-sites/israeli-air-force/opening-of-the-blue-flag-2021-exercise-the-largest-and-most-advanced-held-in-israel/.

139 US Central Command (@CENTCOM), post on X, formerly Twitter, 26 January 2023, https://twitter.com/CENTCOM/status/1618601053083127811.

140 IISS, Military Balance+ database, accessed 6 June 2023.

141 *Ibid.*; see also Dotan Druck, 'The Reserves Will Hold', RUSI Journal, vol. 166, no. 4, 2021, pp. 40–50.

142 Raffi Berg, 'Israeli Soldiers' Mosque Behaviour Condemned by IDF', BBC News, 14 December 2023, https://www.bbc.co.uk/news/world-middle-east-67719820; and Merlyn Thomas and Jamie Ryan, 'Israel to Act on Soldier Misconduct After BBC Investigation', BBC News, 12 February 2024, https://www.bbc.co.uk/news/world-middle-east-68277124.

143 Eilam, 'How the Israel Defense Forces Seek to Defeat Non-state Actors', p. 109.

144 Avi Jager, 'The Transformation of the Israel Defense Forces', *Naval War College Review*, vol. 74, no. 2, Spring 2021, p. 13.

145 Eilam, 'How the Israel Defense Forces Seek to Defeat Non-state Actors', p. 109.

146 'Israel', Nuclear Threat Initiative, 16 February 2023, https://www.nti.org/countries/israel/#:~:text=Although%20Israel%20has%20possessed%20nuclear,has%20never%20signed%20the%20NPT.

147 IISS, Military Balance+ database, accessed 6 June 2023.

148 Mona Yacoubian, 'Ukraine's Consequences Are Finally Spreading to Syria', War On The Rocks, 10 January 2023, https://warontherocks.com/2023/01/ukraines-consequences-are-finally-spreading-to-syria/; and David Schenker, 'Egypt's Remilitarized Sinai Is a Future Powder Keg', *Foreign Policy*, 3 June 2022, https://foreignpolicy.com/2022/06/03/egypt-israel-peace-sinai-islamic-state-military-terrorism-treaty/.

149 Ismaeel Naar et al., 'Expect More Covert Israeli Operations Against Iran after Nuclear Talks Stall', *National*, 30 January 2023, https://www.thenationalnews.com/mena/iran/2023/01/30/expect-more-covert-israeli-operations-against-iran-after-nuclear-talks-stall-say-experts/; see also Schenker, 'Egypt's Remilitarized Sinai Is a Future Powder Keg'.

150 Farzin Nadimi, 'Submarine Movements on Iran's Doorstep: Military and Legal Implications', The Washington Institute for Near East Policy, 29 December 2020, https://www.washingtoninstitute.org/policy-analysis/submarine-movements-irans-doorstep-military-and-legal-implications.

151 Jeremy M. Sharp, 'U.S. Foreign Aid to Israel', Congressional Research Service, updated 1 March 2023, p. 2, https://sgp.fas.org/crs/mideast/RL33222.pdf.

152 Eran Ortal, 'Going on the Attack: The Theoretical Foundation of the Israel Defense Forces' Momentum Plan', Dado Center, 1 October 2020, https://www.idf.il/en/mini-sites/dado-center/vol-28-30-military-superiority-and-the-momentum-multi-year-plan/going-on-the-attack-the-theoretical-foundation-of-the-israel-defense-forces-momentum-plan-1.

153 Tzvi Ben Gedalyahu, 'Panetta's Visit Sealed F-35 Jet Sale to Israel', Israel National News, 5 August 2012, http://www.israelnationalnews.com/news/158594#.UTPFZzCG0j4.

154 Barbara Opall-Rome, 'Israel Seeks Greater Autonomy for F-35 Fighter Force', *Defense News*, 4 April 2016, https://www.defensenews.com/home/2016/04/04/israel-seeks-greater-autonomy-for-f-35-fighter-force/.

155 Emanuel Fabian, 'Israel Advancing Deals with US to Purchase Fighter Jets, Helicopters and Munitions', *Times of Israel*, 26 January 2024, https://www.timesofisrael.com/israel-advancing-deals-with-us-to-purchase-fighter-jets-helicopters-and-munitions/#:~:text=Defense%20sources%20told%20The%20Times,were%20advanced%20during%20the%20discussions.

156 Pieter D. Wezeman et al., 'Trends in International Arms Transfers, 2023', SIPRI, March 2024, p. 6, https://www.sipri.org/sites/default/files/2024-03/fs_2403_at_2023.pdf.

157 Seth J. Frantzman, 'Israel, Italy Swap Helicopters and Missiles in New Arms Deal', *Defense News*, 24 September 2020, https://www.defensenews.com/global/europe/2020/09/24/israel-italy-swap-helicopters-and-missiles-in-new-arms-deal/.

158 Turkiye, Ministry of National Defence (MND), 'Defense White Paper 2000', 2000, https://www.files.ethz.ch/isn/154907/Turkey_2000eng.pdf.

159 For example, Ankara's role in the Astana Process, alongside Iran and Russia, on the Syrian civil war; its implication in the Berlin conferences on Libya; and its attempts to mediate the Russia–Ukraine conflict.

160 Aurélien Denizeau, 'Mavi Vatan, the "Blue Homeland": The Origins, Influences and Limits of an Ambitious Doctrine for Turkey', Etudes de l'Ifri, 29 April 2021, https://www.ifri.org/en/publications/etudes-de-lifri/mavi-vatan-blue-homeland-origins-influences-and-limits-ambitious; and Ryan Gingeras, 'Blue Homeland: The Heated Politics Behind Turkey's New Maritime Strategy', War On the Rocks, 2 June 2020, https://warontherocks.com/2020/06/blue-homeland-the-heated-politics-behind-turkeys-new-maritime-strategy/.

161 Alexandros Diakopoulos and Nikos Stournaras, 'Turkey's Quest for Strategic Autonomy', ELIAMEP, policy paper no. 102, 9 June 2022, p. 17, https://www.eliamep.gr/en/publication/%CE%B7-%CF%84%CE%BF%CF%85%CF%81%CE%BA%CE%AF%CE%B1-%CF%83%CE%B5-%CE%B1%CE%BD%CE%B1%CE%B6%CE%AE%CF%84%CE%B7%CF%83%CE%B7-%CF%83%CF%84%CF%81%CE%B1%CF%84%CE%B7%CE%B3%CE%B9%CE%BA%CE%AE%CF%82-%CE%B1%CF%85%CF%85/; and Helena Smith, 'Erdoğan Hails "New Era" of Friendship with Greece on Historic Visit to Athens', *Guardian*, 7 December 2023, https://www.theguardian.com/world/2023/dec/07/erdogan-hails-new-era-of-friendship-with-greece-during-historic-visit-to-athens.

162 Hakan Mehmetcik and Arda Can Çelik, 'The Militarization of Turkish Foreign Policy', *Journal of Balkan and Near Eastern Studies*, vol. 24, no. 1, 2022, p. 25.

163 Émile Bouvier, 'Turkey. The Arms Industry on the Fast Track to Autonomy', Orient XXI, 27 October 2021, https://orientxxi.info/magazine/turkey-the-arms-industry-on-the-fast-track-to-autonomy,5142.

164 Paul Iddon, 'TF-X: Turkey Plans to Fly Its Homegrown Stealth Fighter in 2023, But It's Still Far From Finished', Forbes, 12 January 2023, https://www.forbes.com/sites/pauliddon/2023/01/12/tf-x-turkey-plans-to-fly-its-homegrown-stealth-fighter-in-2023-but-its-still-far-from-finished/?sh=62d99cb47b72.

165 The *Bayraktar* TB2 drone has reportedly been exported to 33 countries. See Goksel Yildirim, 'Bayraktar TB2: Türkiye's Flag Bearer Combat Drone', Anadolu Agency, 26 February 2024, https://www.aa.com.tr/en/science-technology/bayraktar-tb2-turkiyes-flag-bearer-combat-drone/3147999.

166 Gerard O'Dwyer, 'Turkey Frustrates Finland's and Sweden's NATO Bids', *Defense News*, 30 January 2023, https://www.defensenews.com/global/europe/2023/01/30/turkey-frustrates-finlands-and-swedens-nato-bids/.

167 Patricia Zengerle, 'Senior US Lawmaker Wants Change from Turkey Before F-16 Sale Approval', Reuters, 31 May 2023, https://www.reuters.com/world/senior-us-lawmaker-wants-change-turkey-before-f-16-sale-approval-2023-05-31/.

168 Patrick Wintour, 'Turkish Troops Deploy to Libya to Prop Up Embattled Government', *Guardian*, 5 January 2020, https://www.theguardian.com/world/2020/jan/05/turkish-troops-deploy-to-libya-to-prop-up-embattled-government.

169 Galip Dalay, 'Turkey, Europe, and the Eastern Mediterranean: Charting a Way Out of the Current Deadlock', Brookings Institution, 28 January 2021, https://www.brookings.edu/research/turkey-europe-and-the-eastern-mediterranean-charting-a-way-out-of-the-current-deadlock/; and 'Libya Secures Military Agreement with Turkey', Economist Intelligence Unit, 3 November 2022, https://country.eiu.com/article.aspx?articleid=632545246&Country=Libya&topic=Politics&subtopic=Forecast&subsubtopic=International+relations&oid=1902381173.

170 United Nations, 'Memorandum of Understanding Between the Government of the Republic of Turkey and the Government of National Accord-state of Libya on Delimitation of Maritime Jurisdiction Areas in the Mediterranean', 8 December 2019, https://www.un.org/depts/los/LEGISLATIONANDTREATIES/PDFFILES/TREATIES Turkey_11122019_%28HC%29_MoU_Libya-Delimitation-areas-Mediterranean.pdf.

171 Engin Yüksel and Haşim Tekineş, 'Turkey's Love-in with Qatar', Clingendael Institute, January 2021, https://www.clingendael.org/pub/2021/drivers-of-turkish-qatari-relations/4-turkish-and-qatari-cooperation-on-security-and-defence/.

172 Micha'el Tanchum, 'Turkey's String of Pearls: Turkey's Overseas Naval Installations Reconfigure the Security Architecture of Mediterranean-Red Sea Corridor', Austria Institut für Europa- und Sicherheitspolitik, April 2019, https://www.aies.at/download/2019/AIES-Fokus-2019-04.pdf.

173 Elisabeth Gosselin-Malo, 'Saudi Arabia Signs Major Order for Turkish Drones', *Defense News*, 18 July 2023, https://www.defensenews.com/global/mideast-africa/2023/07/18/saudi-arabia-signs-major-order-for-turkish-drones/; and Burak Ege Bekdil, 'Turkey, UAE Strengthen Defense Industry Ties with Dozens of Deals', *Defense News*, 13 October 2023, https://www.defensenews.com/industry/2023/10/13/turkey-uae-strengthen-defense-industry-ties-with-dozens-of-deals/.

174 Permanent Representation of the Republic of Azerbaijan to the Council of Europe, 'Shusha Declaration on Allied Relations Between the Republic of Azerbaijan and the Republic of Turkey', 21 June 2021, https://coe.mfa.gov.az/en/news/3509/shusha-declaration-on-allied-relations-between-the-republic-of-azerbaijan-and-the-republic-of-turkey.

175 Joshua Kucera, 'Azerbaijan and Turkey in Joint Military Exercises on Iranian Border', Eurasianet, 7 December 2022,

175 https://eurasianet.org/azerbaijan-and-turkey-in-joint-military-exercises-on-iranian-border.

176 UK Government, 'Framework Agreement Between the Government of the United Kingdom of Great Britain and Northern Ireland and the Government of the Republic of Turkey on Military Cooperation', 14 August 2019, https://assets.publishing.service.gov.uk/government/uploads/system/uploads/attachment_data/file/824813/TS_5.2019_UK_Turkey_Framework_Agreement_on_Military_Cooperation.pdf.

177 BAE Systems, 'BAE Systems Signs Heads of Agreement for a Future Contract with Turkish Aerospace Industries for TF-X Programme', 28 January 2017, https://www.baesystems.com/en-uk/article/bae-systems-signs-heads-of-agreement-for-a-future-contract-with-turkish-aerospace-industries-for-tf-x-programme.

178 Italy Government, 'Joint Declaration - 3rd Türkiye-Italy Intergovernmental Summit', 5 July 2022, https://www.governo.it/sites/governo.it/files/Joint_Declaration_3rd_Turkiye_Italy_Intergovernmental_Summit_5July2022_Ankara.pdf; Italy, Ministry of Foreign Affairs, 'Accordo tra il Governo della Repubblica Italiana e il governo della repubblica di Turchia sulla reciproca protezione delle informazioni classificate nell'industria della difesa' [Agreement Between the Government of the Italian Republic and the Government of the Republic of Turkey on the Mutual Protection of Classified Information in the Defence Industry], 5 July 2022, https://atrio.esteri.it/Search/Allegati/52842.

179 Eurosam, 'Turkey, France and Italy Sign an Agreement on Air Defense', 9 November 2017, https://eurosam.com/turkey-france-and-italy-sign-an-agreement-on-air-defense/. Dialogue on the potential acquisition of SAMP/T systems resumed in 2022 after a deadlock due to diverging positions in Syria.

180 See, for example, the ongoing construction of a UAV-production facility in Ukraine. For more information see Pesha Magid, 'Turkey's Drone Maker Baykar Begins To Build Plant in Ukraine', Reuters, 7 February 2024, https://www.reuters.com/business/aerospace-defense/turkeys-drone-maker-baykar-begins-build-plant-ukraine-2024-02-06/.

181 Cem Akalin, 'EFES-2022 Combined Joint Live-fire Exercise Successfully Completed', Defence Turkey, 14 August 2022, https://www.defenceturkey.com/en/content/efes-2022-combined-joint-live-fire-exercise-successfully-completed-5190.

182 Sgt. Whitney Hughes, 'Taking the Beach in Turkey,' US Army, 26 May 2016, https://www.army.mil/article/168652/Taking_the_beach_in_Turkey/.

183 Haluk Sahar, 'Anatolian Eagle Air Warfare Training', The Washington Institute for Near East Policy, 26 July 2005, https://www.washingtoninstitute.org/policy-analysis/anatolian-eagle-air-warfare-training-valuable-turkish-contribution-nato-united.

184 NATO, 'NATO Deployable Control Unit Supports Turkish-led Live-fly Exercise Anatolian Eagle', 28 June 2022, https://ac.nato.int/archive/2022/nato-deployable-control-unit-supports-turkishled-livefly-exercise-anatolian-eagle-22.

185 'New Military Service Law Approved', Hurriyet Daily News, 26 June 2019, https://www.hurriyetdailynews.com/turkish-parliament-ratifies-new-military-service-law-144475.

186 'Parliament Adopts Bill Reducing Conscription, Making Paid Military Service Exemption Permanent', Daily Sabah, 25 June 2019, https://www.dailysabah.com/turkey/2019/06/25/parliament-adopts-bill-reducing-conscription-making-paid-military-service-exemption-permanent.

187 Firat Tasdemir and Sarp Ozer, 'Turkey Neutralized 2,529 Terrorists in 2021: Defense Ministry', Anadolu Agency, 30 November 2021, https://www.aa.com.tr/en/turkey/turkey-neutralized-2-529-terrorists-in-2021-defense-ministry/2434903.

188 IISS, The Military Balance 2023 (Abingdon: Routledge for the IISS, 2023), p. 141.

189 Humeyra Pamuk, 'U.S. Congress Says F-16 Sale to Turkey Depends on NATO Approval', Reuters, 2 February 2023, https://www.reuters.com/business/aerospace-defense/us-congress-says-f-16-sale-turkey-depends-nato-approval-2023-02-02/.

190 Omar Faruk, 'Somalia Makes Deal with Turkey To Bolster Naval Force', Defence News, 21 February 2024, https://www.defensenews.com/global/mideast-africa/2024/02/21/somalia-makes-deal-with-turkey-to-bolster-naval-force/.

191 'Turkey's Erdogan Vows To Widen Operations Against Kurdish Groups in Syria and Iraq', Associated Press, 16 January 2024, https://apnews.com/article/erdogan-syria-iraq-kurdish-militants-c31b579cd8a487bbdf63861110560965.

192 Mehmetcik and Çelik, 'The Militarization of Turkish Foreign Policy', p. 28.

193 IMF World Economic Outlook Database, April 2024, https://www.imf.org/external/datamapper/datasets/WEO.

194 Adam Samson, 'Turkey Raises Interest Rates to 50% As It Seeks To Cool Runaway Inflation', Financial Times, 21 March 2024, https://www.ft.com/content/70ad468f-1fc7-4cdb-9920-14ff64f3c609.

195 M. Murat Kubilay, 'Already Vulnerable, Turkey's Economy Now Faces Massive Earthquake Recovery Costs', Middle East Institute, 13 February 2023, https://www.mei.edu/publications/already-vulnerable-turkeys-economy-now-faces-massive-earthquake-recovery-costs.

196 Presidency of the Republic of Türkiye (TCCB), 'Amacımız, 2023 Yılında Savunma Sanayimizi Dışa Bağımlılıktan Tamamen Kurtarmaktır' [Our Aim is to Completely Save our Defence Industry from Foreign Dependency in 2023], 5 May 2015, https://www.tccb.gov.tr/haberler/410/32257/amacimiz-2023-yilinda-savunma-sanayimizi-disa-bagimliliktan-tamamen-kurtarmaktir.

197 Çağlar Kurç, 'Between Defence Autarky and Dependency: The Dynamics of Turkish Defence Industrialization', Defence Studies, vol. 17, no. 3, 31 July 2017, p. 272.

198 Yvonni-Stefania Efstathiou and Tom Waldwyn, 'Turkish Defence Exports to 2023: Grand Ambitions', IISS Military Balance Blog, 10 April 2019, https://www.iiss.org/blogs/military-balance/2019/04/turkishdefence-exports.

199 'Savunma Sanayii Müsteşarı 2023 hedeflerini anlattı' [Undersecretary for Defence Industries explained 2023 targets], Memurlar, 24 October 2014, https://www.memurlar.net/haber/487626/savunma-sanayii-mustesari-2023-hedeflerini-anlatti.html.

200 'Estonia to Purchase Approximately €200 Million Worth of New Armoured Vehicles', Centre for Defence Investment (RKIK), 18 October 2023, https://www.kaitseinvesteeringud.ee/en/estonia-to-purchase-approximately-e200-million-worth-of-new-armoured-vehicles/.

201 Aaron Mehta, 'Turkey Officially Kicked Out of F-35 Program, Costing US Half a Billion Dollars', Defense News, 17 July 2019, https://www.defensenews.com/air/2019/07/17/turkey-officially-kicked-out-of-f-35-program/.

202 'Turkey', F35.com, archived 15 December 2018, https://web.archive.org/web/20181215071840/https://www.f35.com/global/participation/turkey.

203 US Defense Security Cooperation Agency, 'Türkiye – F-16 Aircraft Acquisition and Modernization', 26 January 2024, https://www.dsca.mil/press-media/major-arms-sales/turkiye-f-16-aircraft-acquisition-and-modernization.

204 Burak Ege Bekdil, 'Turkey in Talks with South Korea to Salvage Altay Tank Program', Defense News, 19 November 2020, https://www.defensenews.com/industry/2020/11/19/turkey-in-talks-with-south-korea-to-salvage-altay-tank-program/.

205 Korea Financial Supervisory Service (2023), 'Announcement of Hyundai Rotem's Altay Tank Mass Production Parts Supply Contracts', 1 February 2023, https://dart.fss.or.kr/dsaf001/main.do?rcpNo=20230202800044.

206 IISS, The Military Balance 2022 (Abingdon: Routledge for the IISS, 2022), p. 246.

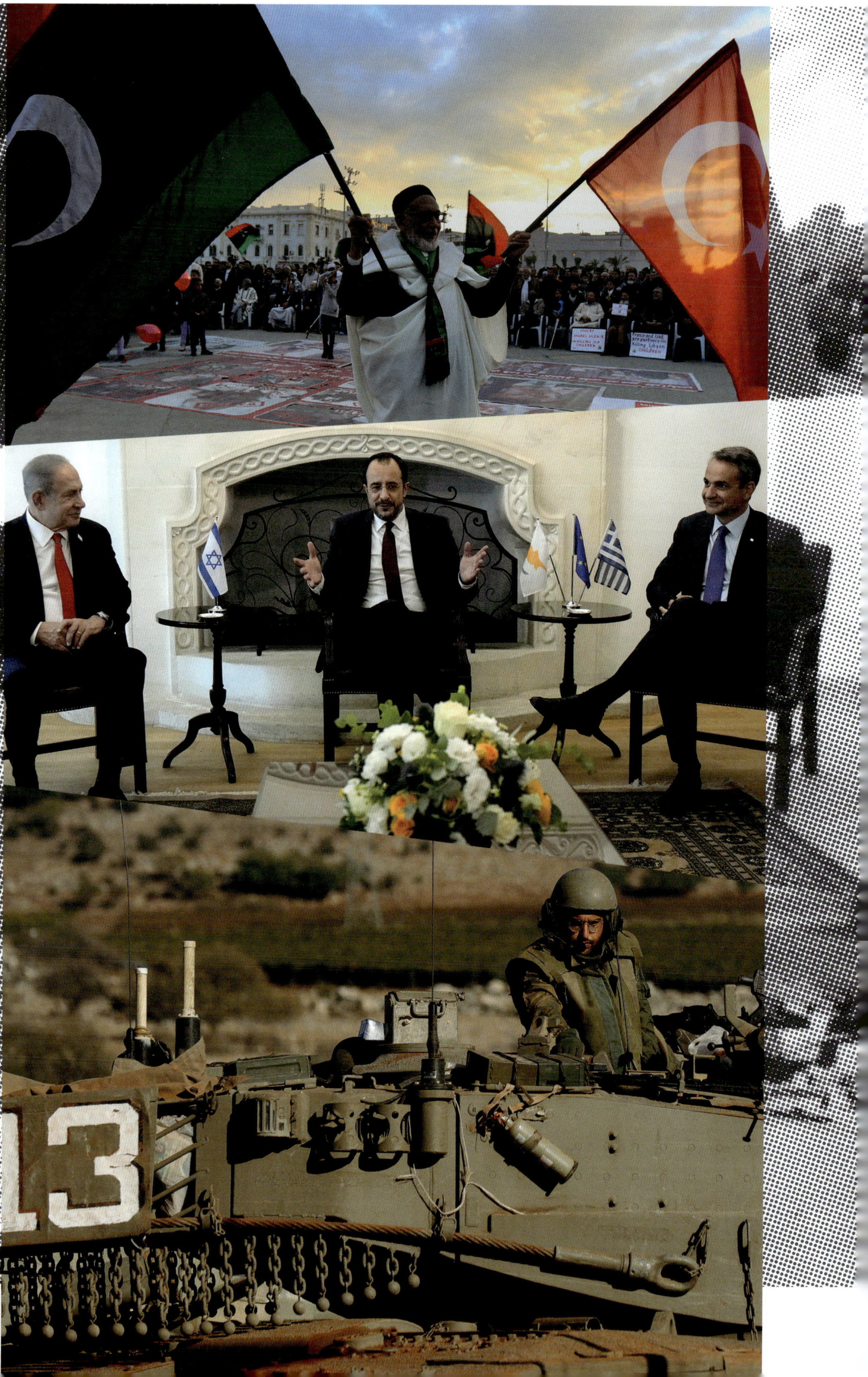
13

REGIONAL ACTORS

CHAPTER FIVE	TURKIYE: ERDOĞAN'S STATECRAFT, REGIONAL AMBITIONS AND STRUCTURAL LIMITATIONS	130
CHAPTER SIX	TURKISH COERCIVE DIPLOMACY: SYRIA AND LIBYA AS LABORATORIES	146
CHAPTER SEVEN	GREECE: REGIONAL COOPERATION AS GRAND STRATEGY	156
CHAPTER EIGHT	CYPRUS: PROTRACTED DIVISION, INCREASED STRATEGIC DEPTH AND AN ISRAELI GAMBLE	170
CHAPTER NINE	LIBYA: INTERNAL DIVISIONS, FOREIGN INTERVENTION AND OIL	184
CHAPTER TEN	EGYPT: REGIONAL AMBITIONS AND DOMESTIC WEAKNESS	192
CHAPTER ELEVEN	ISRAEL: BETWEEN THE AMBITION OF REGIONAL INTEGRATION AND THE REALITY OF CONFLICT	204
CHAPTER TWELVE	LEBANON: ENDURING POLYCRISIS AND ON THE BRINK OF WAR	222
CHAPTER THIRTEEN	SYRIA: A BROKEN STATE AND AN ARENA FOR COMPETITION	230

↑

(top to bottom) A man holds the flags of Libya and Turkiye during a demonstration against the Benghazi-based General Khalifa Haftar and in support of the UN-recognised Government of National Accord at Martyrs' Square in Tripoli, Libya, on 10 January 2020; Cypriot President Nikos Christodoulides (C) holds a trilateral summit with Greek Prime Minister Kyriakos Mitsotakis (R) and Israeli Prime Minister Benjamin Netanyahu (L) at the presidential palace in Nicosia, Cyprus, on 4 September 2023; Israeli soldiers take part in a military drill near the border with Lebanon in the upper Galilee region of northern Israel on 26 October 2023. (Photos: Hazem Turkia/Anadolu Agency via Getty Images; Petros Karadjias/POOL/AFP via Getty Images; Jalaa Marey/AFP via Getty Images)

TURBULENCE IN THE EASTERN MEDITERRANEAN: GEOPOLITICAL, SECURITY AND ENERGY DYNAMICS ■ AN IISS STRATEGIC DOSSIER

↑ An F-16 aircraft flies over the mausoleum of the founder of the Turkish republic, Mustafa Kemal Atatürk, during celebrations to mark the 100th anniversary of the Republic of Turkiye in Ankara, Turkiye, on 29 October 2023. (Photo: Adem Altan/AFP via Getty Images)

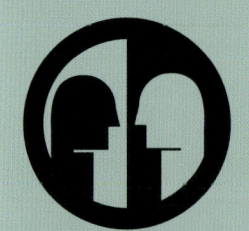

THE EASTERN MEDITERRANEAN is a theatre that Turkiye seeks to shape through diplomacy, influence networks and power projection. Its long coastline, military superiority and economic power are locally unrivalled, with Erdoğan's personal and ideological interest in the region fuelling wariness among neighbours.

ACROSS THE POLITICAL SPECTRUM and national-security establishment, Turkiye sees itself as being unfairly denied the maritime space it deserves and as unjustly blamed for diplomatic paralysis over Cyprus. In contrast, its neighbours see Turkish aims in the Eastern Mediterranean as fundamentally revisionist.

TURKIYE'S REGIONAL RIVALS attempted to isolate and contain it throughout the 2010s but struggled to do so due to their own misaligned priorities and risk profiles, geopolitical events, and Turkiye's aggressive pushback. Nevertheless, Ankara's enduring economic and domestic weaknesses contributed to an overall decline in Turkish power.

CHAPTER FIVE

TURKIYE: ERDOĞAN'S STATECRAFT, REGIONAL AMBITIONS AND STRUCTURAL LIMITATIONS

INTRODUCTION

Since the Justice and Development Party (AKP) first took office in November 2002, Turkiye has sought to establish itself as the dominant regional power in the Middle East. Initially, the emphasis was on winning over the predominantly Sunni Muslim populations of the region by providing a successful model of Islamist governance and leadership. By building such a sphere of influence, Ankara hoped it could gain leverage with the region's governments and their support for a favourable resolution of the Cyprus conflict, or at least more regional alignment on economic and security issues.

High-profile and sometimes high-risk regional gambits have been central to President Recep Tayyip Erdoğan's attempt to establish Turkiye as an independent power shaping the emerging multipolar world and to create a domestic legacy by elevating Turkiye's profile as a modern Muslim state (see Figure 5.1). He has deftly used foreign policy to capture conservative and nationalist votes and defeat his rivals. His electoral track record suggests that his often confrontational approach has played well with domestic audiences: he has been in power for more than two decades, first as prime minister, and since 2014 as president. As such, he has surpassed Mustafa Kemal Atatürk, the founder of modern Turkiye, who only spent 18 years in power.

The upheaval that followed the 2011 Arab uprisings created openings for Turkish influence across the Eastern Mediterranean but also generated geopolitical and local pushback that ultimately checked Turkish ambitions. In parallel, renewed interest in energy resources in the region supercharged this dynamic. The cost for Turkiye of a decade of intense competition and military deployments has been significant. Although the attempt by a constellation of regional rivals to contain it failed, it was ultimately a combination of domestic turbulence and economic weakness that restrained Ankara. From late 2020 onwards Turkiye turned to once-rival regional powers, such as Saudi Arabia and the United Arab Emirates (UAE), to bolster its ailing economy (see Figure 5.2). Starting in 2023, Turkiye normalised diplomatic relations with regional arch-rivals Greece and even, albeit very briefly, Israel.[1]

Erdoğan's ambitious statecraft has also been somewhat constrained by the country's need to preserve working relations with other international actors active in the region – such as the United States, traditionally its main defence partner; the European Union, its main trading partner; and Russia, its primary supplier of energy.

CHANGING BALANCES OF DOMESTIC POWER

There is wide support across the Turkish political spectrum, including among opponents of the AKP, for the push to transform Turkiye into the dominant power in the Eastern Mediterranean. The region has particular appeal because of Ottoman imperial history and its cultural and political legacies, as well as the continued rivalry with countries like Greece, which nationalist forces view as responsible for Turkiye's territorial

FIGURE 5.1: KEY EVENTS IN TURKISH REGIONAL POLICY, NOVEMBER 2002–DECEMBER 2023

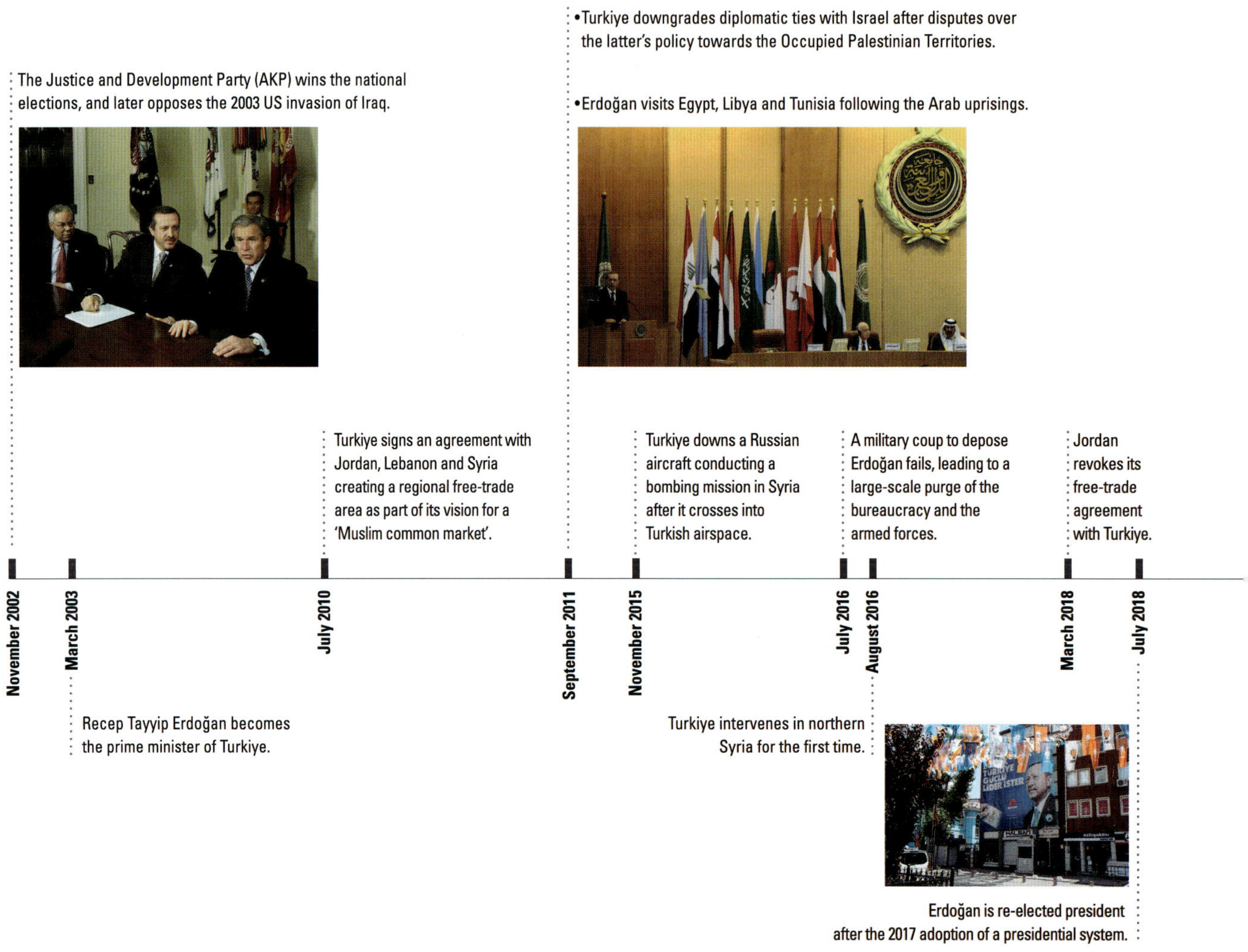

November 2002: The Justice and Development Party (AKP) wins the national elections, and later opposes the 2003 US invasion of Iraq.

March 2003: Recep Tayyip Erdoğan becomes the prime minister of Turkiye.

July 2010: Turkiye signs an agreement with Jordan, Lebanon and Syria creating a regional free-trade area as part of its vision for a 'Muslim common market'.

September 2011: Turkiye downgrades diplomatic ties with Israel after disputes over the latter's policy towards the Occupied Palestinian Territories. Erdoğan visits Egypt, Libya and Tunisia following the Arab uprisings.

November 2015: Turkiye downs a Russian aircraft conducting a bombing mission in Syria after it crosses into Turkish airspace.

July 2016: A military coup to depose Erdoğan fails, leading to a large-scale purge of the bureaucracy and the armed forces.

August 2016: Turkiye intervenes in northern Syria for the first time.

March 2018: Jordan revokes its free-trade agreement with Turkiye.

July 2018: Erdoğan is re-elected president after the 2017 adoption of a presidential system.

Source: IISS analysis

---

contraction in the early twentieth century. The main driver of Turkiye's increased engagement with the Middle East has been the AKP and Erdoğan himself. Other factors have also facilitated and shaped this engagement. These include shifts in the internal balances of power within the Turkish state, the rise and fall of individuals within the policymaking elite, the development of Turkiye's defence industry, fluctuations in the regional and global strategic environment, and changing economic needs and considerations.

As Erdoğan has consolidated power, he has also changed the way policymaking is done. During most of the twentieth century, the General Staff of the Turkish Armed Forces (TGS) formulated, or at least had to approve, Turkish security and foreign policy, setting policy parameters for the civilian government. The involvement of the TGS – often working closely with the Ministry of Foreign Affairs (MFA) – provided a measure of stability and continuity given that unstable and relatively short-lived political coalitions governed Turkiye. Foreign policy tended to be regarded as 'state' rather than 'government' policy.

The influence of the TGS over foreign policy had already begun to decline in both breadth and depth before the AKP took office, but the AKP accelerated and broadened this dynamic. Although the TGS retains a significant role in informing security and defence policy, it has played increasingly less of a role in areas such as the economy, energy and regional outreach. As the TGS's influence decreased, the input from the National Intelligence Organization (MİT) – headed from May 2010 until June 2023 by Hakan Fidan, an Erdoğan loyalist – increased, including in areas which had previously been the preserve of the TGS.

Along with the shift in emphasis under the AKP came a change in the way that Turkiye conducted its foreign policy. Not only was decision-making concentrated in the higher echelons of the government, but career diplomats in the MFA also started to play a less important role than political appointees and senior politicians in direct contacts with their foreign counterparts. Most importantly, Erdoğan's highly personalised transactional style meant that the nature and quality of his relationships with foreign leaders often dictated policy.

The transition to an executive presidential system in July 2018 further consolidated Erdoğan's control. Since then, he has made foreign-policy decisions largely in consultation with a small group of trusted advisers, which are then

Timeline

January 2019 — The *Fatih* drillship, accompanied by a Turkish naval escort, begins exploration activities off Cyprus's western coast.

January 2019 — Cyprus, Egypt, Greece, Israel, Italy, Jordan and the State of Palestine declare their intention to establish the East Mediterranean Gas Forum (EMGF). The EMGF is formally established in September 2020. Turkiye is purposely excluded.

May 2019 — The EU sanctions Turkiye over drilling in the Eastern Mediterranean.

November 2019 — Turkiye and Libya (Government of National Accord, GNA) sign a memorandum of understanding delineating their maritime border.

January 2020 — Turkiye deploys troops to Libya to support the GNA against the Libyan National Army (LNA).

April 2020 — Turkish-backed GNA forces push LNA forces back to eastern Libya.

July–August 2020 — The GNA and LNA reach a ceasefire agreement. A subsequent UN-mediated agreement in October stipulates that all foreign forces should leave Libya within three months.

August 2020 — Turkiye suspends drilling in the Eastern Mediterranean but then resumes following an agreement between Egypt and Greece that delineates their exclusive economic zones (EEZs).

October 2020 — Turkiye withdraws the *Yavuz* drillship from disputed waters off Cyprus after the EU threatens to impose further sanctions.

August 2022 — Turkiye resumes drilling in the Eastern Mediterranean outside disputed waters off Cyprus.

February 2023 — A devastating earthquake hits southeastern Turkiye.

July 2023 — Erdoğan embarks on a tour of the Gulf capitals, securing investment pledges.

September 2023 — Erdoğan meets Israel's Prime Minister Benjamin Netanyahu for the first time.

December 2023 — Erdoğan visits Athens and signs a non-binding 'Friendly Relations and Good-neighbourliness Declaration' with Greece's Prime Minister Kyriakos Mitsotakis.

---

communicated to the MFA for implementation. Tellingly, he appointed Fidan, a key member of his brain trust, foreign minister in 2023, which MFA bureaucrats have seen as elevating its role.

GLOBAL VISIONS, REGIONAL POWER BASE

The AKP's attraction to and focus on the Middle East is fuelled, but not solely dictated, by religious solidarity and nostalgia for the Ottoman past. The AKP aims to recapture and recreate the Ottoman Empire's combined political and religious authority as the region's pre-eminent military power that also claimed leadership of the world's Muslims. This was often subsumed into calls for redressing an imbalance in Turkiye's foreign policy. One of the most high-profile advocates of this 'redressing of balance' was the academic Ahmet Davutoğlu, who rose to become Erdoğan's foreign minister and ultimately, from 2014 to 2016, prime minister.[2] Davutoğlu provided Turkiye with a conceptual framework to promote increased engagement with the Middle East. In his writings and public speeches, he frequently referred to Turkiye's 'strategic depth': the belief that Turkiye is not merely a regional power but one of a small group of countries which he termed 'central powers' on a global scale.[3]

Interestingly, Davutoğlu's perspective had little to say about Greece and Cyprus, historical rivals that were, however, outside his areas of priority. This reflected in part the fact that the AKP generally does not have any concept of the 'Eastern Mediterranean' as such. Davutoğlu's focus was primarily on the Sunni Muslim-majority populations to Turkiye's south – including those in the littoral states of the Eastern Mediterranean – rather than the acquisition of territory or natural resources. His goal was to establish Turkiye as the dominant power in the region, to which other Sunni Muslims willingly looked for leadership rather than having it imposed upon them. Davutoğlu accordingly advocated the use of soft power to create Turkish regional and global spheres of influence. This vision of Turkish exceptionalism also resonated with non-AKP Turkish nationalists, who were otherwise suspicious of the AKP's Islamist orientation. In their minds, successive governments had subordinated Turkiye's own interests to the preservation of good relations

FIGURE 5.2: TURKIYE'S REAL GDP GROWTH, 2010–24

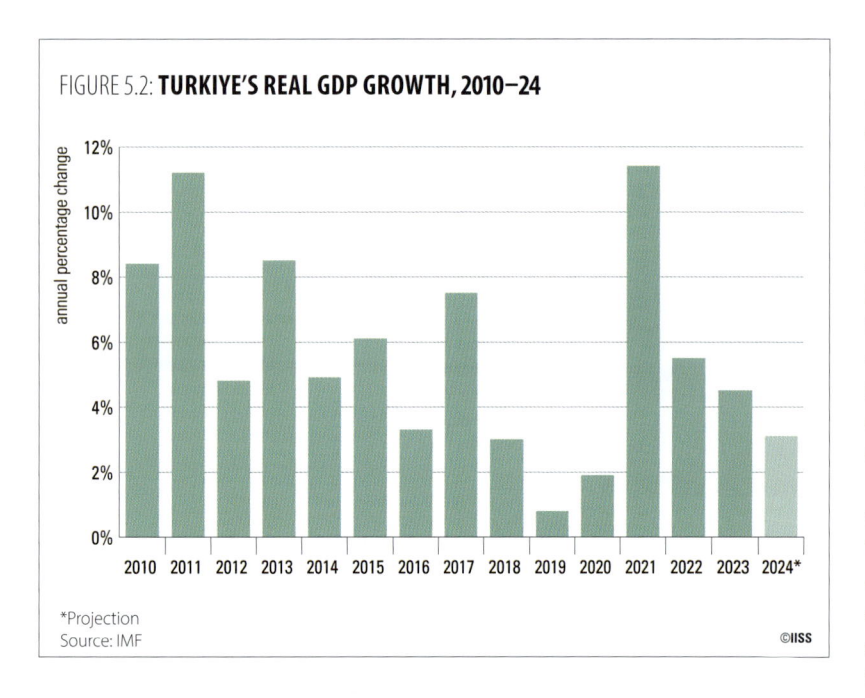

*Projection
Source: IMF

with the US and the EU, such as through acquiescing to Western constraints on Turkiye's long-running war against the Kurdistan Workers' Party (PKK).

Consequently, Davutoğlu's vision of Turkiye as a global actor, able to pursue policy and strategic goals independently – and, if necessary, in defiance – of Western powers, gained considerable traction across the political spectrum.

THE ERA OF SOFT POWER

After it took office in 2002, the AKP sought to deepen personal ties between Turkiye and the peoples of the region, including by abolishing visa requirements for citizens of several predominantly Sunni Muslim countries of the Middle East. Similarly, the AKP also sought to strengthen Turkiye's bonds with these countries through closer economic ties.

In 2004–05, Davutoğlu was a driving force behind Turkiye's free-trade agreements with Egypt, Morocco, Syria and Tunisia – the only ones that Turkiye signed during these years. In December 2009, after Davutoğlu became foreign minister, he expanded the policy by adding a free-trade agreement with Jordan and in 2010 with Lebanon. In July 2010, Turkiye signed an agreement with Jordan, Lebanon and Syria creating a free-trade area called the Close Neighbours Economic and Trade Association Council (CNETAC), a move the pro-AKP media hailed as laying the ground for a 'Muslim common market' – something that Davutoğlu had advocated in his writings.[4]

However, these perceptions of religious solidarity and ambitions to create a Turkish sphere of influence were also intertwined with more economic motives, including boosting both tourism revenue and Turkish exports.

The AKP and the successive Islamist parties that preceded it were bankrolled by conservative businesspeople, whose companies had grown in the Anatolian hinterland and were mostly from outside the traditional Istanbul-based Turkish business elite. They vigorously supported the AKP's outreach to other predominantly Sunni Muslim countries in the region, often forming large business delegations that accompanied government officials on visits.

Despite the EU remaining Turkiye's largest trading partner by total volume, in the AKP's first decade in office, trade with the 'Near and Middle East' grew faster than with any other region in the world. It doubled as a share of Turkiye's total foreign trade, from 9% in 2001 to 18% in 2012.[5] Although they remained suspicious of the AKP's long-term ideological agenda, the Istanbul-based Turkish business elite also supported the AKP's economic outreach to the Middle East, which they regarded as supplementing rather than replacing their main markets in the West.

In practice, ambition sometimes outstripped reality. The CNETAC did little to boost trade between the four member countries and effectively became moribund. Turkiye and Lebanon failed to ratify their free-trade agreement and Jordan revoked its own one with Turkiye in 2018, citing alleged unfair competition from Turkish textile manufacturers. The civil war in Syria and resulting tensions between Ankara and Damascus put economic cooperation between the two countries on hold for years to come.

Erdoğan's criticism of Israel's policy towards the Palestinians further boosted Turkiye's and the AKP's appeal among Arabs in the Middle East. He aggressively condemned the Israeli military operation in Gaza in 2008, clashed with then-president of Israel, Shimon Peres, at Davos in January 2009 and supported the *Mavi Marmara* flotilla that attempted to break the Israeli naval blockade of the Gaza Strip in 2010.[6] Turkiye cancelled a 1997 intelligence-cooperation agreement with Israel, told Mossad to close its liaison office in Ankara and, after a September 2011 United Nations report found that Israel had used excessive force when intercepting the flotilla, expelled the Israeli ambassador and downgraded bilateral diplomatic ties to second-secretary level. Similarly, defence-industrial ties between the two countries – which had been largely based on a 1996 bilateral defence-industrial cooperation agreement that the TGS had strongly supported – came to a halt.[7]

Turkiye's support for Muslim Brotherhood-affiliated groups which were viscerally hostile to Israel in the uprisings that swept the region starting in 2011 exacerbated tensions. Deep-rooted anti-Israel sentiments among the AKP's support base accompanied this, reflected in and fuelled by pro-government Turkish media.

Erdoğan's harsh criticism of Israel was primarily motivated by personal outrage at Israeli policies towards the Palestinians and undoubtedly increased his – and thus also Turkiye's – popularity among Arab publics, where many contrasted his bluntness with their own leaders' subdued positions. Insofar as he was playing to an audience at all, however, it was a domestic one. Erdoğan cited his popular support in the Middle East as proof that he had transformed Turkiye into a regional power and the de facto leader of the world's Sunni Muslims, name-checking cities in regional

Muslim-majority countries at domestic political rallies.

This public hostility towards Israel left Erdoğan with little room for an attempt at rapprochement. In the 1990s, there had been speculation that cooperation between the two countries would lead to a strategic alliance. But now, open hostility between the two governments invigorated Israel's attempts to forge closer ties with alternative partners in the region. The discovery of large reserves of natural gas in the Eastern Mediterranean, including off the Israeli coast, gave this added impetus. Nonetheless, despite the public antagonism, bilateral trade between Turkiye and Israel continued to grow, rising from US$3.4 billion in 2010 to US$7.1bn in 2023.[8]

HARD POWER AND THE ALLURE OF IDEOLOGY

The popular protests that swept through the Middle East from December 2010 through 2011 took the AKP by surprise, resulting in the recalibration of its policies towards the region and the deployment of new policy instruments.

In September 2011, Erdoğan embarked on a visit to Egypt, Libya and Tunisia – three predominantly Sunni Muslim countries that had recently undergone regime change. In Cairo he condemned Israel's policies towards the Palestinians and, in defiance of Washington, called for the State of Palestine to become a UN member. But he also antagonised the Muslim Brotherhood, which had been one of the prime movers in the street protests that had led to the overthrow of president Hosni Mubarak in February 2011, by calling on Egypt to look to Turkiye as a model to follow and thus claiming seniority in the relationship. The Muslim Brotherhood dominated Egypt's government for only one year, not enough time to develop an alliance with Ankara and deliver practical results. Nevertheless, ideological convergence meant that when the military coup of July 2013 overthrew the government, Erdoğan provided refuge to members of the organisation who had been able to flee Egypt. Istanbul became the Muslim Brotherhood's main organisational and propaganda hub.

The AKP government subsequently used its support for the Muslim Brotherhood as an instrument for pursuing its regional ambitions, forming close links with the organisation's affiliates, which actively opposed many of the region's incumbent governments. High-ranking officials in the AKP government and members of MİT, rather than the Turkish MFA or military, managed these links. Support for the Brotherhood and its affiliates exacerbated tensions with not only the new administration in Cairo but also

A person holds up an image of the former Egyptian president Muhammad Morsi with the Turkish President Recep Tayyip Erdoğan during funeral prayers held for Morsi at the Fatih Mosque in Istanbul, Turkiye, on 18 June 2019. (Photo: Orhan Akkanat/Anadolu Agency via Getty Images)

Israel, Greece, and Gulf powerhouses Saudi Arabia and the UAE. In Syria too, Turkiye's active support of the rebellion against President Bashar al-Assad's government rested on its relationship with the Brotherhood.

If this regional outreach departed from the TGS's conservative political agenda, the AKP supported the military's ambition to develop an indigenous defence industry. Beyond the economic benefits of such an endeavour, it strengthened Turkiye's strategic autonomy. By growing indigenous capabilities, at least in some domains like uninhabited aerial vehicles (UAVs), it reduced the leverage that Western countries, by restricting arms sales, could exert. They had done this after Turkiye's invasion of Cyprus in 1974, and again to pressure Ankara regarding alleged human-rights abuses in its war with Kurdish nationalists. Further, the development of the Turkish defence industry gave the AKP another instrument for bolstering ties with what it regarded as friendly states. Most recipients and clients have been Muslim-majority states. Qatar became a privileged buyer during its stand-off with Saudi Arabia and the UAE – which at the time were among Ankara's main rivals for influence in the Eastern Mediterranean.

From 2017, Turkish foreign policy in the region became not only more confrontational but also more diverse – applying different tools in different situations. Turkiye showed an increased willingness to be more assertive militarily, whether through brinkmanship in the Eastern Mediterranean, briefly facing off against Russia in Syria in 2015, or through direct involvement in Syria starting in 2016 and in the Libyan civil war starting in 2019.

NATURAL GAS AND THE BLUE HOMELAND DOCTRINE

Between 2015 and 2020, Turkiye's search for its own natural-gas sources became a main determinant of its policy towards the region in general and the Eastern Mediterranean in particular. This shift was partly overseen by Erdoğan's son-in-law Berat Albayrak, who served as energy minister from November 2015 to July 2018 and then effectively became economic tsar as trade and finance minister from July 2018 to November 2020.[9] Albayrak saw the discovery of natural-gas reserves as a way to reduce both Turkiye's dependence on foreign suppliers and its persistently high current-account deficit. The aim was also to transform Turkiye into an energy hub, moving gas – both from its own waters in the Eastern Mediterranean, onshore, and from other littoral countries as well as the Caucasus – through the natural-gas pipeline network connecting Turkiye with lucrative markets in Europe.

In 2015, Turkiye possessed only two vessels capable of exploring for hydrocarbons, both of which were named for Ottoman privateers but neither of which were capable of deep-sea drilling. Albayrak oversaw the purchase of four deep-sea drillships between 2017 and 2021.[10] In keeping with the AKP's reverence for the Ottoman past, three were named after Ottoman sultans renowned for expanding the boundaries of their empire and the fourth after Sultan Abdülhamid II (1842–1918), the pan-Islamist autocrat whom Erdoğan often cites admiringly.

State-owned Turkish Petroleum Corporation's (TPAO) purchase of drillships marked a new phase in Turkiye's reaction to the discovery of large natural-gas reserves in the Eastern Mediterranean in 2009–11, and to Cyprus's announcement in February 2012 of a second round of licensing for natural-gas exploration in waters within its claimed exclusive economic zone (EEZ). Initially, Turkish efforts had focused on pressuring other littoral states into recognising the rights of the breakaway Turkish Republic of Northern Cyprus (TRNC), which only Ankara recognises, to the natural-gas fields off the island.

The drillship purchase also allowed Turkiye to pursue a more aggressive policy, conducting its own exploration activities and staking its own claim to any natural gas subsequently discovered. In October 2018, after undergoing tests, *Fatih* was dispatched to conduct exploration activities off the coast of the Turkish Mediterranean resort city of Antalya. In May 2019, *Fatih* began conducting exploration activities – with a Turkish naval escort – in waters within Cyprus's EEZ off the island's western coast.

In 2020, Turkish drillships, accompanied by Turkish naval escorts, continued to conduct exploration activities within Cyprus's claimed EEZ, triggering an EU protest. In February 2020, the EU sanctioned two leading TPAO officials and warned Turkiye that further and more severe sanctions would follow if it continued to explore for natural gas in waters regarded as forming part of a member state's EEZ. Rather than risk a severe crisis with its largest trading partner, and as part of a broader de-escalation strategy that also coincided with gas discoveries in the Black Sea, Turkiye suspended exploration activities in disputed waters in the Eastern Mediterranean. Instead, it turned its focus towards the Black Sea, in waters the other littoral states recognised as being within Turkiye's EEZ.

But Ankara did not relinquish its claim to a large proportion of the Eastern Mediterranean, including waters claimed by Cyprus, instead reinforcing them through a 2011 agreement with the TRNC.[11] It justified the claims with what came to be known as the *Mavi Vatan* ('Blue Homeland') doctrine. This maintained that, in addition to the land of the Turkish Republic, whose integrity the land forces and the air force were fighting to protect, the country also had a 'blue homeland' in the waters off its coasts – and needed a well-equipped navy to defend it. Controversially, Turkiye defined the outer limits of its maritime zone by only taking into account the mainland coasts of other countries, and ignoring the islands – including Greek islands like Crete – in the zone. In the Black Sea the limits of the Blue Homeland broadly corresponded with the maritime zone the other littoral states regarded as forming Turkiye's EEZ. But in the Aegean and Eastern Mediterranean, it crossed into areas other littoral states – most notably Greece and Cyprus – claimed as forming part of their EEZs.

The doctrine originated in the Turkish navy, and one of its earliest and most enthusiastic proponents was Admiral Cem Gürdeniz.[12] It became known to the Turkish public after the media appearances of the then navy chief of staff, Admiral Cihat Yaycı. Even though many in the AKP had been suspicious of the Turkish military, the doctrine overlapped with its vision of Turkiye being the dominant power in the Eastern Mediterranean; the ruling party therefore adopted it.

In February–March 2019, the Turkish navy carried out its largest-ever exercise and, in a demonstration that it was prepared to put theory into practice,

Turkish President Recep Tayyip Erdoğan (2nd R) attends a ceremony in Yalova, Turkiye, to mark the delivery of four new naval platforms to the Turkish navy on 19 January 2024. (Photo: TUR Presidency/Murat Cetinmuhurdar/Anadolu via Getty Images)

named it *Blue Homeland*. Erdoğan not only approved the name but attended the exercise. In September 2019 he was photographed in front of a wall map of the Blue Homeland at the National Defence University in Istanbul. The map included the Turkish claim to large areas of the Aegean and Eastern Mediterranean seas which Greece and Cyprus regard as forming part of their own EEZs.

Yet, to the Turkish public, the appeal of the Blue Homeland doctrine lay in its portrayal of Turkiye as the dominant maritime power in the region. Although the main opposition Republican People's Party (CHP) expressed concerns, these were more about the aggressive way in which the doctrine was presented than its substance or overarching goal.

Crucially, both Gürdeniz and Yaycı had argued that the Blue Homeland required an increase in the capabilities of the Turkish navy. This corresponded with Erdoğan's vision of Turkiye becoming the pre-eminent power in the region.

Although the AKP advocated for the development of all the armed services, it had introduced plans to boost the capabilities of the Turkish navy before the concept of the Blue Homeland had entered the public domain. The navy had previously lagged behind the air and land forces in terms of defence-spending priorities and prestige. In 2004, the AKP government had launched the *MilGem* project which resulted in the building of four *Ada*-class corvettes by 2019 and foresaw the commissioning of four frigates by 2027, followed by up to seven destroyers.[13] The AKP also supported the construction under licence in Turkish shipyards of six submarines, the first of which carried out sea trials in December 2022.[14] In addition, the AKP oversaw the building of the country's first-ever amphibious assault ship, the TCG *Anadolu*, which was commissioned in April 2023. Originally expected to carry F-35B *Lightning* II aircraft, it was converted to accommodate Turkish-produced UAVs when Turkiye was removed from the F-35 programme in July 2019 after purchasing Russian S-400 air-defence systems.[15]

If completed, the warship programme could result in Turkiye's naval capabilities dwarfing those of the other littoral states of the Eastern Mediterranean, except perhaps for Egypt. Although the build-up has fuelled foreign anxieties about Turkish intentions, it was presented to a domestic audience not as aggression but as a necessity for the defence of the now-established doctrine of the Blue Homeland. Conveniently, Turkish officials have cited the enforced conversion of the TCG *Anadolu* as proof of the vulnerability of being reliant on foreign defence suppliers.

LIBYA AND PUTTING THE BLUE HOMELAND DOCTRINE INTO PRACTICE

The Turkish government used the Blue Homeland doctrine as a justification – not least to the Turkish public – for increased involvement in Libya after the overthrow of Libyan leader Muammar Gadhafi and the ensuing civil war that has split the country since 2014 between a Tripoli-based authority (then known as the Government of National Accord or GNA) and a rival Tobruk-based House of Representatives (HoR) which has appointed several governments. In November 2019, Turkiye signed a memorandum of understanding with the GNA delimiting their maritime border along the lines of the Blue Homeland's maximalist vision, before deepening its involvement two months later when it lent military support to the GNA as it resisted an attack on Tripoli by the eastern-based rival Libyan National Army (LNA, though UN experts also refer to it as the Haftar Armed Forces or HAF).[16] In 2021, after the LNA attack was repelled and a reconciliation process launched with UN encouragement, a Tripoli-based Government of National Unity (GNU) was formed, though the split with the HoR persisted.

Emboldened by the success of its military projection of power, Turkiye signed an energy-cooperation agreement with the GNU in October 2022, which foresaw oil and gas exploration in the two countries' EEZs as delineated in the November 2019 agreement. But there had long been unease about the November 2019 agreement even among some elements in the GNA, who felt that Ankara had exploited the precarious military situation in which the GNA found itself at the time. By February 2024, the Tripoli-based Libyan Court of Appeal had annulled the 2022 energy agreement.[17] The setback came amid a decrease in Turkish influence in Libya: as the fear of imminent military defeat diminished, so did the potential benefits of Turkish military assistance for its local partners. The regional de-escalation in the following years, with Ankara normalising relations with Egypt, the Gulf states and other local powers, further pushed Libya down on the Turkish agenda.

Rather than cowing the other littoral states of the Eastern Mediterranean into acceptance, the vigorous promotion of the Blue Homeland doctrine had the opposite effect, spurring them into greater cooperation while intensifying Turkiye's regional isolation. In January 2019, Cyprus, Egypt, Greece, Israel, Italy, Jordan and the State of Palestine announced their intention to form the East Mediterranean Gas Forum (EMGF), which created a framework for regional energy cooperation and became a membership organisation in 2020. France became a member while the EU, US and World Bank became permanent observers. This effectively pitted a powerful coalition of countries, including Turkiye's main economic partners, against its ambitions in the Eastern Mediterranean. While Turkish officials publicly showed disdain and disinterest towards the EMGF, Turkiye perceived its exclusion as another move to contain its power and ambitions. The implicit prerequisite before being welcomed into the Forum – to resolve its maritime disputes with members Cyprus and Greece – only reinforced that view.

By then, Ankara was facing the limits of its ability to unilaterally impose the Blue Homeland. The Turkish economy was also increasingly in need of an injection of foreign funding, not least to support the vulnerable Turkish lira (see Figure 5.3).

The Turkish government was spared a humiliating climbdown by the discovery – amid much fanfare in the pro-government media – of substantial recoverable natural-gas reserves in the Black Sea in August 2020. Although officials continued to advocate the Blue Homeland doctrine, in practice the government shifted its focus to the Black Sea. When, in August 2022, the ship *Abdülhamid Han* was dispatched to carry out exploratory drilling activities in the Eastern Mediterranean soon after being commissioned, it was in waters generally regarded as being within Turkiye's EEZ.

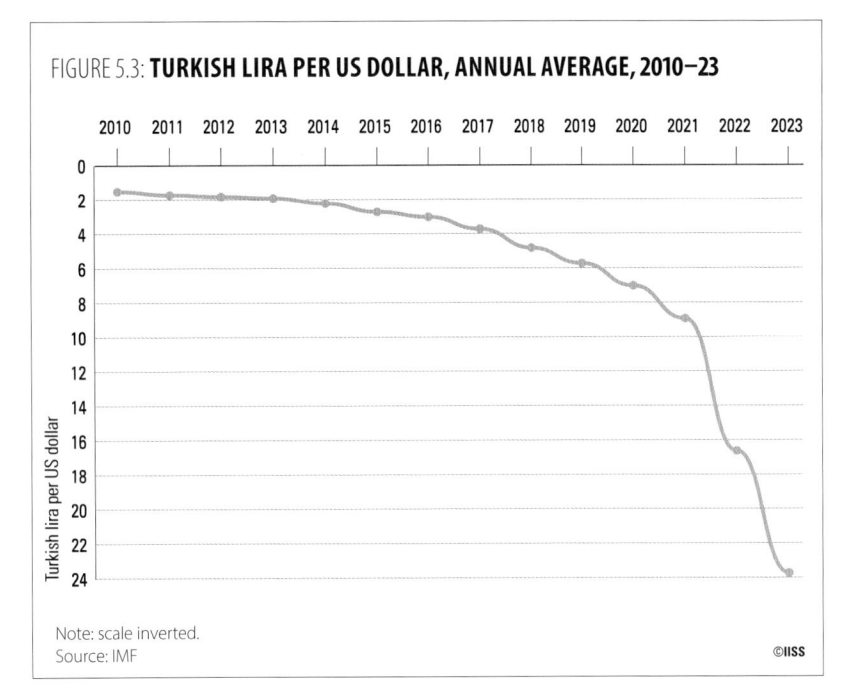

FIGURE 5.3: **TURKISH LIRA PER US DOLLAR, ANNUAL AVERAGE, 2010–23**

Note: scale inverted.
Source: IMF

CYPRUS

Before the AKP gradually took over Turkiye's foreign policy, the military had regarded Cyprus as one of its main policy prerogatives. Its invasion in 1974 resulted in the creation of a Turkish Cypriot polity in the north of the island. Turkiye has treated the self-proclaimed TRNC as a de facto protectorate ever since, guarding it with an estimated military presence of up to 33,800 ground troops backed by artillery and armour.[18] These are further backed up by an air base at Geçitkale/Lefkoniko that can host aircraft and UAVs, providing Turkiye greater reach into the Eastern Mediterranean.

The AKP has tended to see the Cyprus issue primarily in the context of relations with the West. The EU remains opposed to Turkiye's role in the continued division of the island, but its members are divided over how much priority to give this matter and how to manage Turkish claims. As a result, Turkish policy has been to try to persuade Western countries to recognise a discrete Turkish Cypriot polity in the north of the island, whether as part of or instead of the island's reunification.

Turkish support for the UN-drafted 2004 agreement (commonly known as the 'Annan Plan') to reunite the island was underpinned by an expectation that, if Greek Cypriots rejected the plan, the West would then become more sympathetic to the Turkish position. But this bet ultimately failed. Despite Greek Cypriots rejecting the plan in an April 2004 referendum, the Republic of Cyprus joined the EU in May 2004. Its government has remained the internationally recognised authority across the whole of the island, and under international law Turkiye is effectively occupying EU territory. The stand-off has continued to bedevil Turkiye's relations with the West; Ankara holds the EU particularly responsible for the paralysis and rejects it as an interlocutor given its structural bias towards its member state, Cyprus. Turkiye has also tried to demonstrate some flexibility over the Cyprus question. During the 2017 Crans-Montana talks it proposed that, as part of an agreement, it would reduce its military presence after an interim period. But since the failure of these talks, along with the 2016 failed attempted coup against Erdoğan and souring relations with the US, Turkiye has grown more adversarial and confrontational, and has supported maximalist demands for a two-state solution on the island.[19]

Despite its public support for the UN-led reunification negotiations, Turkiye has continued its pursuit of social integration with northern Cyprus, including through migration from the Turkish mainland. Universities in the north have become popular destinations for Turkish students and tourism destinations in the TRNC are featured in the 'domestic' section of advertisements. Successive AKP governments have supported the activities of religious-oriented non-governmental organisations in northern Cyprus in the hope that the Muslim population there would become more pious and observant, leading to tensions with the local, less conservative population.

Turkiye generally views Cyprus as a domestic matter, creating a risk of backlash in case of a resolution that results in a reduction of Turkish influence on the island. Turkish nationalist parties, including the ultranationalist Nationalist Action Party (MHP) with which the AKP formed an alliance in 2017, insist that Cyprus is an integral part of the Turkish sphere.

In recent years, the government has increasingly sought to ensure that the TRNC looks to Ankara for leadership rather than pursuing independent policies. In 2020, Ankara vigorously supported the successful presidential election campaign of Ersin Tatar, who is widely regarded as being close to the AKP and has openly called for a two-state solution and the legalisation of the divided status quo on the island.

Turkish battleships parade and helicopters fly overhead in the city of Kyrenia in the self-proclaimed Turkish Republic of Northern Cyprus on 20 July 2024 as part of an event marking 50 years since Turkish troops invaded Cyprus. (Photo: Birol Bebek/AFP via Getty Images)

Cyprus has taken on an added strategic importance for Turkiye since the discovery of substantial natural-gas reserves to the south of the island in 2011. For the AKP, the possibility of securing energy supplies and the necessity to maintain the viability of the TRNC's claims meant that it was worth risking a confrontation with the West, particularly the EU. In 2019, as Turkiye began to conduct natural-gas exploration activities in the area, it also deployed UAVs to its air base on the island – both to increase the protection for Turkish exploration in the region and to serve as an added deterrent against any such activities by others in waters Turkiye claims under the Blue Homeland doctrine.

Turkiye's continued hardline policy on Cyprus and the Blue Homeland doctrine inevitably led to increased tensions with Greece, Cyprus's closest ally. Between 2019 and 2022, the two countries fought an intense war of words accompanied by brinkmanship at sea, with Erdoğan issuing bombastic threats aimed at unsettling Athens. In turn, this led the conservative government of Kyriakos Mitsotakis to cultivate closer political and defence ties with the US and France just as their own relations with Ankara were souring over Syria and other matters. Turkiye also saw Greece's outreach to Saudi Arabia and the UAE and reinforcement of relations with Egypt as part of this strategy.

These crises aggravated tensions in Ankara's often fraught relations with the EU and hindered any progress in the country's own moribund accession negotiations. They also created problems within NATO, of which Greece and Turkiye are members. Turkiye has frequently blocked closer ties between NATO and Cyprus and, since 2004, NATO and the EU. Turkiye has also viewed Cyprus's growing relations with its regional rivals such as Egypt and Israel, but also France and the US, with concern as well as contempt. Ankara sees Cyprus as wanting both to enshrine the status quo on the island without giving the TRNC any breathing room and to leverage its developing relationships to contain Turkish power. Some Turkish officials see France as a behind-the-scenes orchestrator and enabler of Cypriot intransigence, while others see Cyprus as having deftly recruited friends. The growing US–Cypriot and Israeli–Cypriot defence relationships compound these concerns, but Ankara does not perceive a credible military threat emerging.

Successive Turkish governments have long regarded these tensions as a price worth paying for maintaining a foothold in Cyprus and possibly accessing natural gas fields. Until now, they have fallen short of exacting a heavy cost, particularly for the Turkish economy. For Ankara, the potential domestic backlash against relinquishing its claims in Cyprus outweighs the cost of maintaining its presence in the TRNC, including potential sanctions and other measures imposed by external actors.

THE SYRIAN IMBROGLIO

Of the many Arab countries of the Eastern Mediterranean, Syria was, from Erdoğan's perspective, the most promising potential sphere of influence. Prior to the 2011 uprising, the Turkish president had cultivated Assad's government by offering economic incentives and a political lifeline amid its ostracisation by Western and Arab countries. Ankara then became the main supporter of the rebel groups fighting against the government, in the hope that their eventual victory would lead to the establishment of a Muslim Brotherhood-dominated government in Damascus, which would look to it for leadership. As Russian military intervention from 2015 onwards helped tilt the course of the war in the government's favour, Ankara continued to provide funds, equipment and training to groups in the rebel-held areas of northwest Syria. But its focus shifted to containing and weakening the de facto autonomous Kurdish-held swathe of territory in northern Syria which the PKK's Syrian affiliate, the Democratic Union Party (PYD), controlled.

The shift in emphasis played well with both the Turkish security apparatus and the public, enabling Erdoğan to portray Turkiye's increased military involvement in Syria as safeguarding national security. By pushing back the PYD, Ankara also hoped to open up space for the resettlement of some of the 3.6 million Syrian refugees registered in Turkiye, whose continued presence in the country had led to growing public resentment – with a negative impact on Erdoğan's popular support.[20]

The shift also ran parallel to a change in the balance of power inside Turkiye and the increasing concentration of decision-making in Erdoğan's own hands. When the AKP first took office, many in the state apparatus had reservations about Ankara's outreach to the Middle East. Reasons ranged from ideological to more practical considerations, such as the profile of Turkiye's trade, its history of alignment with Western countries, close relations with Israel and the paucity in the bureaucracy of expertise on the region and the relevant language skills. These reservations were widespread in the TGS and became more pronounced when the government began to provide support to the Syrian rebellion.

Although it was prepared to provide military training to Syrian rebels, the TGS remained reluctant to become actively involved in the civil war by deploying Turkish combat troops inside Syria. Senior officers privately expressed their concerns at the potential cost and entanglement of any Turkish military intervention. There was also widespread opposition among the Turkish public to becoming actively involved in what it tended to see as somebody else's war.

As a result, Erdoğan made MİT, which worked closely with the private Turkish military company Sadat, primarily responsible for supporting the rebel forces. The situation changed dramatically after the failed coup attempt of 15–16 July 2016, which enabled Erdoğan to assert his complete control over the state apparatus, including the TGS, and launch limited but effective military operations inside Syria starting that same year (see Chapter Six).

Turkiye now maintains a large and sustainable presence in Syria and has successfully contained the PKK-affiliated People's Protection Units (YPG) Syrian Kurdish militia. However, Erdoğan's Syrian gambit has not delivered the results he had hoped for. He has not managed to enlarge and prepare the safe zone needed to return most of the Syrian refugees in Turkiye to their country, and Syrian refugees remain opposed to a repatriation over fears the Assad government will eventually regain control over the territory. Turkiye's military occupation has come with reputational costs and created geopolitical entanglements. It has not increased Turkish influence in the Eastern Mediterranean but instead validated the sense among critics that Turkiye was an expansionist power. Indeed, Greece and Cyprus have become prominent advocates of Western re-engagement with Damascus.

A forceful ouster of Turkiye by Assad government forces is unlikely in the foreseeable future. So too is a negotiated exit, because of the government's opposition to a comprehensive political settlement that ensures the return of refugees. It is also unlikely that Russia and Iran, the other main foreign powers present in Syria, would risk a confrontation with Ankara over northern Syria. A significant change in Turkiye's posture in Syria will likely have to await political change in Ankara or dramatic alterations in the regional environment.

FROM CONFRONTATION TO CONCILIATION – UNTIL GAZA

The shift in the focus of Turkish policy towards Syria presaged a change in Turkish policy towards the Middle East, including the Eastern Mediterranean, as a whole. The attempt by a large coalition of players (from Greece to the UAE) to contain Turkiye throughout the 2010s failed, in part because of the country's sheer size, power and geographic location, but also because of misalignments in terms of priorities, objectives and risk appetites among its rivals. However, Turkiye has not become the dominant regional power Erdoğan once envisioned, and it has suffered real setbacks. That failure and the country's relative isolation have exposed not only the gap between the AKP's ambitions and capabilities but also the structural limitations of the Turkish state. Tellingly, notwithstanding the now legally challenged agreement with Libya, Turkiye has not yet agreed on maritime borders with any of the other littoral states in the Eastern Mediterranean.

Rather than cowing the other littoral states into acceptance, its aggressive exploratory drilling for natural gas in the Eastern Mediterranean drove them closer together and galvanised opposition to its ambitions from powerful actors such as the US and the EU. The latter even imposed sanctions – and threatened more severe ones unless Turkiye desisted. Domestically, although Erdoğan and the AKP won the May 2023 presidential and parliamentary elections, the results suggested that their popularity was in continuing long-term decline. As the economy faltered, opinion polls indicated that most Turks were primarily concerned with their welfare and security instead of nationalist expansion and aggrandisement, for which levels of support had peaked in the 2010s.[21] Opposition politicians, in the ascendancy since the 2024 municipal elections, have outlined visions for Turkiye that contradict or overlook Erdoğan's grandiose, Middle East-centred plans.

Without publicly renouncing ambitious claims such as the Blue Homeland doctrine or completely abandoning his often fiery rhetoric, Erdoğan gradually began to scale back his aggressive policies, opting instead for engagement and toning down brinkmanship in the Eastern Mediterranean while focusing on exploring the legally uncontroversial waters in the Black Sea. Fidan, the spymaster-cum-strategist, played a central role in recalibrating policy and, starting from June 2023, conducting diplomacy. Turkiye activated diplomatic channels and personal contacts – not least in the hope that rapprochement would lead to an inflow of funds to shore up the ailing Turkish economy and stabilise the high inflation rates that were caused in part by Erdoğan's own maladaptive monetary policies. In 2022, Turkiye's inflation rate hit 80% and 65% in 2023. Tellingly, as soon as Erdoğan began his outreach, the loose regional coalition that sought to contain Turkiye began to lose purpose and cohesion.

In 2020, Turkiye began to establish discreet contacts with Saudi Arabia and the UAE. The process accelerated following the ceasefire in Libya in August 2020 and the Saudi–Qatar agreement in January 2021 that ended Doha's diplomatic isolation. Ankara scaled back its support for nearly all the Muslim Brotherhood affiliates, and stopped in 2022 the trial of the suspects in the 2018 assassination of Saudi journalist Jamal Khashoggi. In return, Saudi Arabia and the UAE undertook to pump money into the Turkish economy. Erdoğan visited Riyadh and Abu Dhabi in 2023, securing pledges for significant investment as well as preparing the ground for a visit to Egypt, which took place in February 2024. One of Erdoğan's objectives was to revive the matter of Turkiye's inclusion in the EMGF, which Cairo has so far made conditional on a Turkish military withdrawal from Libya – something Ankara continues to reject.

The reconciliation with the conservative Gulf monarchies and Egypt was an implicit Turkish admission that its effort to build grassroots and elite support across the Sunni Arab world had failed. This ideological and geopolitical setback raised questions about the viability and post-Erdoğan sustainability of the AKP's regional vision. However, in Ankara's view, failure was not synonymous with defeat and its desire to shape the emerging multipolar world remained intact, requiring engagement with rival powers. In addition to obtaining crucial investment and financial assistance, Turkiye intends its improved relations with the Gulf states to ensure that it is embedded in global connectivity projects. Ankara reacted negatively to the India–Middle East–Europe Economic Corridor – which bypassed Turkiye in favour of a southern route that went into the Eastern Mediterranean through the UAE, Saudi Arabia, Jordan and Israel – instead proposing an alternative route through the Gulf and Iraq into Turkiye.[22]

Ankara's conciliatory moves extended to the Syrian government, hoping that engagement would encourage Damascus to apply pressure on the PYD and facilitate the return home of Syrian refugees in Turkiye. However, despite a meeting among defence and foreign ministers and intelligence heads of both countries, the Assad government insisted that the withdrawal of all Turkish military personnel from Syrian territory was a prerequisite for the normalisation of ties, stopping the process in its tracks.

Absent from Turkiye's outreach was Cyprus, which Ankara continues to ostracise. Turkish officials insist that the failure of Crans-Montana in 2017 and the 2023 election of President Nikos Christodoulides, seen as a hardliner, had effectively ended any possibility of a negotiated solution. Ankara had pivoted to a two-state solution and saw no need to explore compromises that Cyprus would inevitably reject.

Interestingly, Turkiye's hard line on Cyprus did not prevent a marked improvement in relations with Greece (see Table 5.1). Tensions began to subside from the 2017–20 peak in animosity, with fewer reports of maritime and air encroachment on both sides. In 2022, Erdoğan erupted against Mitsotakis after the latter had allegedly lobbied the US Congress against the sale of US military aircraft to Turkiye. 'For me, there is no Mitsotakis. I will never meet with him again', pledged Erdoğan.[23] A year later, the two leaders, both freshly re-elected and thus less vulnerable to domestic criticism, were on speaking terms again, encouraged by US and German officials. Echoing the disaster diplomacy of the 1990s, Greece was the first country to express sympathy and to send aid after the devastating February 2023 earthquake in southern Turkiye. In December 2023, Erdoğan visited Athens and

TABLE 5.1: **RECENT TRENDS IN TURKIYE'S BILATERAL RELATIONSHIPS AS OF MAY 2024**

Country	Trend
Cyprus	No relationship
Egypt	Strengthening
France	Weakening
Greece	Strengthening
Israel	Weakening
Russia	Unchanged
Saudi Arabia	Strengthening
UAE	Strengthening
UK	Unchanged
US	Unchanged

©IISS

↑ Strengthening relationship
= Unchanged
↓ Weakening relationship
⊖ No relationship

Source: IISS analysis

signed a non-binding friendly relations and good-neighbourliness declaration, which covered tourism, trade, migration and regional affairs, among other topics. Importantly, the declaration sidestepped the dispute over the delimitation of the continental shelf and their respective EEZs in the Aegean and Eastern Mediterranean. Mitsotakis reciprocated in May 2024, visiting Ankara to relay similar messages. In Ankara's view, an improved relationship with Greece ameliorates Turkiye's standing in Brussels and, increasingly, in Washington, and does not necessarily require substantive concessions such as a holistic agreement on EEZs. It also telegraphs to Cyprus that Turkiye's relations with the US and Western powers are not contingent on a solution to the Cyprus problem.

Just as spectacular was the meeting between Erdoğan and Israeli Prime Minister Benjamin Netanyahu on the margins of the UN General Assembly in September 2023. A visit to Turkiye by the ceremonial president of Israel, Isaac Herzog, presaged this rapprochement.

Erdoğan and Netanyahu had never met before, and high-level meetings between the two countries had not taken place since 2010 when the *Mavi Marmara* incident took place. The two men discussed trade, technology and energy among other topics, reviving the idea (deemed unrealistic by many experts) of a pipeline that would export Azerbaijani and other oil to Israel and Israeli gas to Turkiye. Erdoğan's outreach was in part motivated by the desire to further divide the loose regional coalition that had opposed him in the previous decade.

This rapprochement with Israel spectacularly ended with the Hamas-led 7 October attacks and the ensuing Israeli offensive in Gaza. Although Erdoğan employed once again a bombastic tone to denounce Israel's conduct of the war, Turkiye was kept on the diplomatic sidelines of this conflict. While foreign minister Fidan was part of the delegation of Organisation of Islamic Cooperation (OIC) ministers who travelled to key capitals to rally support for the Palestinians, the informal Arab contact group of ministers that worked with the US to advance ceasefire and humanitarian proposals notably excluded him. Alongside Turkiye's Qatari ally, Saudi Arabia, Egypt, Jordan and the UAE, all its rivals until recently, have played the leading diplomatic roles. Erdoğan's public embrace of Hamas and vociferous and colourful condemnation of Israel have also revived concerns about his ideological leanings and, among Turkish strategists, about his wisdom. Interestingly, this did not interrupt or stop diplomatic outreach: when they met in December 2023 and May 2024, Erdoğan and Mitsotakis disagreed publicly over Israel and Hamas but managed nonetheless to conduct their affairs. This hardline position on the Israeli–Palestinian conflict, inspired in part by domestic considerations, could result in important regional discussions sidelining Turkiye.

The war in Gaza also has the potential to change the military picture in the Eastern Mediterranean. The region is now crowded with powerful players, including a large US military presence at sea that could remain in place for years to secure Israel and deter Iran. To Ankara's displeasure, its ultimate nemesis Cyprus has emerged as a military, humanitarian and logistical hub for Western powers. Ankara also has to worry about the renewed competition in the Eastern Mediterranean between the US and Russia in the context of the war in Ukraine. While Turkiye competes with these two powers in Syria and Libya, its main interests with them considerably transcend this rivalry. Russia, Turkiye's main Black Sea neighbour, also remains its primary energy partner and is now building its first-ever nuclear-energy plants on the Mediterranean coast in both Egypt and Turkiye.

Whether Ankara perceives these changes as potential challenges, and how it chooses to respond to them, could revive more belligerent policies. The future of Turkish policy in the Eastern Mediterranean will also depend on who rules the country after the 2028 elections. An alternative to Erdoğan's rule appears to be materialising since the municipal elections of 2024, and leading opposition politicians do not share Erdoğan's external orientations. It also remains unclear who within the AKP is best positioned, or being prepared, for the succession.

ENDNOTES

1 Ibrahim Altay, 'Erdoğan Signals Better Ties with Greece, Israel Following Meetings', Daily Sabah, 21 September 2023, https://www.dailysabah.com/politics/diplomacy/erdogan-signals-better-ties-with-greece-israel-following-meetings.

2 See Ahmet Davutoğlu, *Stratejik Derinlik* [Strategic depth] (Istanbul: Kure Yayınları, 2001), translated into English in 2014.

3 The title of Davutoğlu's most famous book; see note 2 above.

4 Behlül Ozkan, 'Turkey, Davutoglu and the Idea of Pan-Islamism', *Survival: Global Politics and Strategy*, vol. 56, no. 4, 2014, pp. 119–40, https://www.tandfonline.com/doi/abs/10.1080/00396338.2014.941570.

5 Abdülkadir Civan et al., 'The Effect of New Turkish Foreign Policy on International Trade', *Insight Turkey*, vol. 15, no. 3, 2013, p. 120, https://repository.bilkent.edu.tr/server/api/core/bitstreams/610df692-105a-4de6-ae0c-7ed8ca717ca6/content.

6 Gil Feiler and Edo Harel, 'Analysis: The Political Logic of Erdogan's Attack on Israel', *Jerusalem Post*, 4 February 2009, https://www.jpost.com/International/Analysis-The-political-logic-of-Erdogans-attacks-on-Israel; and 'What Happened on the Mavi Marmara?', *New York Times*, 11 June 2010, https://www.nytimes.com/2010/06/12/opinion/12sat3.html.

7 'Turkey Downgrades Ties with Israel', Al-Jazeera, 2 September 2011, https://www.aljazeera.com/news/2011/9/2/turkey-downgrades-ties-with-israel.

8 UN Comtrade Database, https://comtradeplus.un.org/.

9 Albayrak has remained influential in Erdoğan's inner circle even after his resignation in November 2020.

10 Diego Cupolo, 'Turkey to Purchase Fourth Drilling Ship to Expand Energy Projects', Al-Monitor, 10 February 2021, https://www.al-monitor.com/originals/2021/02/turkey-purchase-drilling-ship-energy-projects-mediterranean.html.

11 See Chapter Two, page 56.

12 Gürdeniz wrote a weekly column entitled Mavi Vatan ('Blue Homeland') for the nationalist and socialist *Aydınlık* daily newspaper as well as a series of books, including *Doğu Akdeniz: Mavi Vatan'ın Güney Cephesi* [The Eastern Mediterranean: the Blue Homeland's southern front] (Istanbul: Pankuş Yayınları, 2020), and *Anavatandan Mavi Vatan'a* [From the motherland to the Blue Homeland] (Istanbul: Kırmızı Kedi Yayınevi, 2021).

13 IISS, *The Military Balance* 2024 (Abingdon: Routledge for the IISS, 2024), p. 148; and Tayfun Ozberk, 'Analysis: The Future of the Turkish Navy', Naval News, 15 February 2021, https://www.navalnews.com/naval-news/2021/02/analysis-the-future-of-the-turkish-navy/.

14 Tayfun Ozberk, 'Turkish Navy's First Reis-class (Type 214TN) AIP Submarine Begins Sea Trials', Naval News, 7 December 2022, https://www.navalnews.com/naval-news/2022/12/turkish-navys-first-reis-class-type-214tn-aip-submarine-begins-sea-trials/.

15 Emma Helfrich, 'Turkey's "Drone Carrier" Amphibious Assault Ship Enters Service', War Zone, 11 April 2023, https://www.twz.com/turkeys-drone-carrier-amphibious-assault-ship-enters-service.

16 'Letter Dated 29 November 2019 from the Panel of Experts on Libya Established Pursuant to Resolution 1973 (2011) Addressed to the President of the Security Council', UN Security Council, 9 December 2019, https://www.securitycouncilreport.org/atf/cf/%7B65BFCF9B-6D27-4E9C-8CD3-CF6E4FF96FF9%7D/S_2019_914.pdf.

17 Abdulkader Assad, 'Tripoli Court of Appeal Annuls MoU in Hydrocarbons Cooperation with Turkey', *Libya Observer*, 19 February 2024, https://libyaobserver.ly/news/tripoli-court-appeal-annuls-mou-hydrocarbons-cooperation-turkey.

18 IISS, *The Military Balance 2024*, p. 150.

19 Hasan Özertem, 'Back to "the Tradition": Turkey's Changing Position from a Federal to a Two-state Solution to the Cyprus Conflict', Ifri, July 2021, p. 7, https://www.ifri.org/sites/default/files/atoms/files/ozertem_cyprus_conflict_2021.pdf.

20 Bassem Mroue and Suzan Fraser, 'EXPLAINER: What's at Stake in Turkey's New Syria Escalation', AP News, 10 December 2022, https://apnews.com/article/syria-turkey-recep-tayyip-erdogan-government-a61fd4140fa1e2355f158a56f8fa98fb; and Burcu Karakas et al., 'Turkey's Erdogan Faces Struggle to Meet Syrian Refugee Promise', Reuters, 31 May 2023, https://www.reuters.com/world/middle-east/turkeys-erdogan-faces-struggle-meet-syrian-refugee-promise-2023-05-31/.

21 John Halpin et al., 'Is Turkey Experiencing a New Nationalism? An Examination of Public Attitudes on Turkish Self-perception', Center for American Progress, February 2018, https://www.americanprogress.org/wp-content/uploads/sites/2/2018/02/TurkishNationalismPolling-report.pdf.

22 Umang Sharma, '"No Corridor Without Turkey": Erdogan Opposes India–Middle East–Europe Mega Project', Firstpost, 13 September 2023, https://www.firstpost.com/world/no-corridor-without-turkey-erdogan-opposes-india-middle-east-europe-mega-project-13113812.html.

23 'Erdogan Vows Never to Meet Mitsotakis Again', *eKathimerini*, 23 May 2022, https://www.ekathimerini.com/news/1185086/erdogan-vows-never-to-meet-mitsotakis-again/.

Displaced Syrians drive past Turkish military vehicles near the the town of Hazano in Idlib, Syria, on 11 February 2020. (Photo: Aref Tammawi/AFP via Getty Images)

SYRIA HAS BEEN A LABORATORY for the development of coercive Turkish methods combining diplomacy and hybrid instruments such as informational warfare, surrogate militias and direct military intervention. This approach has been fine-tuned and applied in Libya, Iraq and Nagorno-Karabakh.

TURKIYE'S AGGRESSIVE POWER PROJECTION has been driven by changes in its domestic and international context and the national-security fallout from the Syrian conflict, the expansion of Iran and Russia at its doorsteps, the deep rift with NATO allies and competition with Arab states.

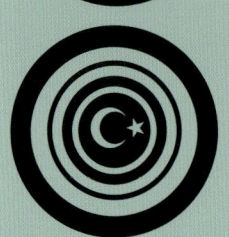

TURKIYE'S PROJECTIONS OF POWER in Libya, Iraq and Nagorno-Karabakh have been more limited than in Syria but have achieved their intended goal. Ankara's ability to iterate and scale this new hybrid toolbox further afield and in theatres like Africa or Asia remains unproven.

CHAPTER SIX

TURKISH COERCIVE DIPLOMACY: SYRIA AND LIBYA AS LABORATORIES

INTRODUCTION

Turkiye has developed, since the mid-2010s, a coercive diplomacy backed by military instruments to advance its strategic goals in the Eastern Mediterranean. It has successfully projected power around the basin in places such as Syria and Libya and adapted this approach further afield in Iraq and Nagorno-Karabakh.

The near-hegemonic nationalist turn of President Recep Tayyip Erdoğan's foreign policy has four main objectives: the thwarting of existential threats, the defence of sovereign rights in the Eastern Mediterranean, the affirmation of Turkiye as an independent regional leader and the development of the Turkish military-industrial complex as an element of strategic autonomy. To that end, Ankara has leveraged its geographical position and its willingness to employ, in an agile way and in small numbers, its armed forces to shape the conflicts in Syria and Libya.

CHARACTERISTICS OF TURKISH COERCIVE DIPLOMACY

As the regional security environment grew increasingly conflictual starting in 2011, Ankara moved away from its initial zero-enemy, diplomacy-based foreign policy and espoused a hard-power strategy backed by coercive instruments (see Figure 6.1).

This development occurred in two phases. The first began in 2011 with substantive Turkish political and organisational support to like-minded Islamist groups in Egypt, Libya, Syria and elsewhere, as well as material support to some in Syria and Libya. It sought to capitalise on the Arab uprisings to build a network of aligned powers, with Ankara as the new regional centre of gravity.

The second was a slow build-up that came into full view in 2016, when Turkiye launched its first military intervention in Syria. This build-up began in 2013, when the United States called off an attack on the Assad government for its use of chemical weapons. It kicked into higher gear in 2015, when the US helped create the Syrian Democratic Forces (SDF), a Kurdish-led rebel alliance dominated by the Kurdistan Workers' Party (PKK) that became the main US surrogate force in Syria. Meanwhile, Russia launched a large-scale military intervention in Syria to prop up the faltering Assad regime. These developments supercharged Turkiye's motivations, including the perception of a national-security threat coming from Syria with the emergence of a Kurdish autonomous area, the need for Turkiye to assert its regional rank and counter Russian and Iranian expansion, and a deepening rift with the US and other NATO allies including France (see Chapter Fifteen).

The 2016 failed coup against Erdoğan was the tipping point. The Turkish president and his Justice and Development Party (AKP) accelerated their consolidation and domination of domestic politics, purging the military, police, media and judiciary of opponents and critics.[1] This gave Erdoğan a quasi-free hand to experiment and project power in ways that members of government agencies (especially in the Turkish General Staff [TGS]) opposed.

THE TURKISH ARMED FORCES' TRADITIONAL ROLE AS THE GUARANTOR OF THE MODERN TURKISH REPUBLIC FOUNDED BY ATATÜRK IS NOW SEVERELY WEAKENED. INSTEAD, IT HAS BECOME AN INSTRUMENT OF POWER PROJECTION, OPERATING BEYOND ITS CORE MANDATE TO DEFEND THE HOMELAND.

FOUR DRIVERS

Türkiye's new coercive diplomacy had four main drivers tied to national security, sovereignty and economics.

The national-security threat posed by the Syrian conflict precipitated the move towards coercive diplomacy as a means to contain it and shape its course. As Syrian protests evolved into an internationalised civil war, the Turkish leadership increasingly perceived transformations there as a core security issue. The conflict strengthened the PKK through the Democratic Union Party (PYD – its Syrian affiliate), its military wing the People's Protection Units (YPG) and later the SDF. The consolidation of a quasi-autonomous zone in northeastern Syria and the Kurds' association with Western powers through the anti-Islamic State (ISIS) campaign was unacceptable to Ankara as it feared this would stir Kurdish separatism at home. The expansion of Iran's and Russia's military power in Syria also heightened the need to assert Türkiye's regional rank.

Ankara's coercive diplomacy became an instrument to foster the Islamist-nationalist brand of the AKP as well as a reaction to Türkiye's changing immediate environment and relationships with allies. Its NATO allies complained that Türkiye had been complacent regarding the rise of ISIS and was not doing enough to combat it, just as the extremist organisation began to carry out unprecedented deadly attacks in Europe, often planned in Syria. For Ankara, Western governments' single-minded focus on defeating ISIS while relying on the SDF became a foundational betrayal which has poisoned the relationship. Several factors cemented this confrontational posture: the 2016 coup, with which Erdoğan accused the US of colluding; the fallout over the US and Germany withdrawing their *Patriot* batteries from Türkiye just as Russia entered the Syrian battlefield; and Ankara's subsequent purchase of Russian S-400 air-defence missiles in 2017.[2]

Türkiye's push for maximalist maritime zones in the Eastern Mediterranean was another powerful driver. Embracing the so-called *Mavi Vatan* ('Blue Homeland') vision enabled the AKP to appeal to the nationalists given the historic Greek–Turkish and Cypriot conflicts (see Chapter Five). Casting it as the defence of the Turkish nation's sovereign rights, unfairly truncated at the end of the Second World War, only increased the appeal of the more coercive posture and helped Erdoğan widen his political base, sealing his alliance with the Nationalist Action Party (MHP).

Türkiye also relied on its growing local military industry as a vital component of power projection, which in turn justified post facto its investment in the defence industry and later facilitated arms sales. These included most prominently domestically produced uninhabited aerial vehicles (UAVs) as well as armoured vehicles, electronic-warfare systems and an array of projectiles.

Türkiye's operational method combined two approaches: surrogate warfare (outsourcing) and compound warfare (cooperation between state and non-state actors).[3] Ankara relied not only on Western-style joint operations with non-state armed groups, which mobilise auxiliaries alongside expeditionary regular forces, but also the Russian use of a private military company composed of mercenaries.

These hybrid operations involved five main actors: the topmost national-security body, the armed forces, its intelligence service, a private military company and non-state armed groups.

The National Security Council (MGK, for Milli Güvenlik Kurulu) is the supreme coordination body for security issues and the main decision-making circle regarding foreign operations. After the 2017 referendum that endorsed a presidential system, the MGK was brought fully under the command of the president by decree in 2018. With its size reduced to ten members,[4] including the president, the ministers in charge of foreign, defence and security policy, and the military chief and force commanders, Erdoğan completed the defanging of the military institution and imposed his control. These changes opened the way for Erdoğan to move forward with direct military interventions in Syria, which the generals had previously refused to do.

The powerful National Intelligence Organization (MİT, for Millî İstihbarat Teşkilatı) was also brought under the control of Erdoğan loyalists and provides a strategic tool to support and direct surrogates abroad. It was initially directly linked to the MGK but has directly reported to the presidency since 2017.[5] The MİT takes a traditional approach to the cycle of intelligence, comprising 'determining the intelligence requirements and orienting the collection activity', 'collecting information', 'processing information' and 'disseminating and using intelligence'.[6] It was headed by Dr Hakan Fidan from 2010 to 2023, when he was appointed foreign minister. He was succeeded by Ibrahim Kalin, who had previously served as the presidential spokesperson and senior adviser to the president from 2014 to 2023.

The Turkish Armed Forces (TSK, for Türk Silahlı Kuvvetleri), headed by the TGS, is the second-largest NATO military and is equipped with significant readiness and capabilities (see Chapter Four, pages 116 and 118). Its traditional role as the guarantor of the modern Turkish Republic founded by Ataturk is now severely weakened. Instead, it has become an instrument of power projection, operating beyond its core mandate to defend the homeland.

SADAT, 'the first and the only Private Military Company' in the country,[7] with close ties to the Turkish ruling circles, has provided Erdoğan with a paramilitary option when the deployment of the TSK is not the ideal option. It was founded by Brigadier General (Retd) Adnan Tanriverdi, who was close to Erdoğan.[8] Named as a chief adviser to the president and a member of the Security and Foreign Policy Committee in the aftermath of the coup in 2016,[9] Tanriverdi was removed in January 2020 after making a controversial religious speech.[10] SADAT emerged on the international stage in the early years of the Syrian civil war. As its website officially explains, it aims

> to provide services in the fields of strategic consultancy, special defense and security training and equipment for the organization of the Armed Forces and Internal Security Forces in the international arena, to create an environment of defense and defense industry co-operation among Islamic countries and to help the Islamic World take its rightful place among the World Super Powers as a self-sufficient military force.[11]

It denies being involved in Turkish-led military operations abroad that have utilised Syrian mercenaries, but US AFRICOM estimated in 2020 that 'Sadat maintains supervision and payment of the estimated 5,000 pro-GNA [Government of National Accord] Syrian fighters in Libya'.[12]

Foreign proxy forces round out the five-pronged toolbox and have become a full component of Turkish strategy. These non-state armed groups are mobilised in foreign theatres. The main ones

Turkish defence minister Hulusi Akar (L), Turkish foreign minister Mevlüt Çavuşoğlu (C) and the chief of Turkiye's National Intelligence Organization Hakan Fidan (R) attend a meeting on efforts to ensure peace and stability in Libya with Russian Foreign Minister Sergei Lavrov and Russian defence minister Sergei Shoigu at the Russian Foreign Ministry's Guest House in Moscow, Russia, on 13 January 2020. (Photo: Cem Ozdel/Anadolu Agency via Getty Images)

are the Free Syrian Army (FSA), a loose rebel coalition composed of military deserters and civilian fighters, and the more inter-operable and projectable Syrian National Army (SNA). The SNA is under the 'near-total control of Turkey's Ministry of Defence and National Intelligence Organisation (MIT)'.[13] The original SNA structure combined several units: Turkmen groups close to Ankara, and former Arab FSA groups. Yet the SNA is not a homogeneous entity and still suffers from internal disputes and chain-of-command issues due to personal and political rivalries.

Relations between MİT, TSK and SADAT remain opaque, complex and ambiguous, as there is no official organisational chart. However, the three entities are essential for the projection of Turkish influence on and through local proxies. Their respective roles depend on their core speciality and the scale of Turkiye's 'prism of cooperation' with local proxies: the more kinetic, the more the army operates; the more political, the more the intelligence services operate; and the 'heavily involved' SADAT operates as a 'facilitator between Ankara and Syrian proxy fighters, complementing the efforts of the Turkish military and security services while affording it opacity and seemingly limitless protections'.[14]

AREAS OF OPERATION AND ASSESSMENTS OF TURKISH PERFORMANCE

SYRIA

Turkiye's approach in Syria evolved to adapt to the changing nature of the conflict. What began between 2011 and 2013 as ad hoc support for the emerging forces challenging Assad's rule in Syria evolved into a more organised and direct intervention by the TSK to contain and push back the PKK affiliate in northeastern Syria.

In the initial years of the uprising, Turkiye worked through the Syrian National Council (SNC) and the National Coalition of Syrian Revolutionary and Opposition Forces, as well as the FSA.

Turkiye hosted the political opposition, helped them organise and provided them with diplomatic support in international fora. This was accompanied by favourable coverage in the state-controlled Turkish news media in Turkish as well as in English or Arabic, such as TRT and Anadolu Agency, and on social media. Humanitarian and aid agencies such as the Humanitarian Relief Foundation and

Turkish flags adorn the streets of the Musiad housing complex for internally displaced Syrians, built with Turkiye's support, near the village of Mashhad Ruhin in the Syrian rebel-held northwestern governorate of Idlib on 13 November 2022. (Photo: Omar Haj Kadour/AFP via Getty Images)

the Turkish Cooperation and Coordination Agency were also deployed.

Despite its influence over the Istanbul-based opposition leadership, Ankara had to contend with intra-Syrian divisions: many exiled opposition politicians were tied to Qatar as well as the United Arab Emirates and Saudi Arabia, which became Turkiye's main regional rivals. The SNC's credibility and effectiveness suffered from being distant and disconnected from military, political and civil-society actors inside Syria. Turkiye adjusted its approach to become the main supporter of FSA fighting units, ostensibly better placed to shape Syria's future. It did so by training, equipping and organising FSA units.[15] In these early days, the TSK did not operate on Syrian soil. This phase of Turkish support, although intense, was limited, as the FSA lacked heavy weaponry, armoured vehicles, main battle tanks, and anti-tank and anti-aircraft systems. Ankara appeared therefore quite prudent in its military support to avoid being dragged into a conventional war against the Syrian regime.

In 2012, the emergence of the al-Qaeda jihadi affiliate Jabhat al-Nusra complicated Ankara's proxy management. New rebel alliances began to form along ideological and opportunistic lines. Faced with an ever-evolving environment, Ankara secured its interests by creating closely allied Turkmen armed groups such as Firqat al-Sultan Murad and Liwa Sultan Mehmed Fatih. Despite intra-Turkmen tensions, these groups were intimately linked to Turkiye.

The environment transformed once again with the battle of Kobane (2014), when the local PKK-backed Kurdish PYD forces fought against the newly formed jihadist ISIS in Syria and Iraq. Turkiye sought to weaken the PKK's new foothold across its border. In 2015, the Suruç bombing in Turkiye and an attack on the Turkish police known as the Ceylanpınar incident broke the negotiations track (known as the 'Solution process' or Çözüm süreci) the Turkish government had with the PKK. The demise of this direct channel allowed Ankara to engage its armed forces in Syria more directly. Prior to that, the TSK had taken limited actions in Syria, such as artillery bombings against the Syrian regime's forces in October 2012, a special-forces operation after the Cilvezoglu terror attack in March 2013, and an operation to relocate the tomb of Suleyman Shah in February 2015.

Ankara decided to act more boldly with a landmark operation. Although limited to two days, the 2015 *Operation Martyr Yalcin* (*Şehit Yalçı*) mobilised the TSK in both Syria and Iraq, and against the YPG and ISIS. Most importantly, in 2016 the TSK launched *Operation Euphrates Shield* (*Fırat Kalkanı*) to prevent the PYD from establishing territorial continuity along Ankara's southern border with Syria, fearing it could serve as inspiration for Turkiye's considerably larger Kurdish minority. The operation was designed to push away from the Turkish border both jihadist groups, primarily ISIS, and the YPG. It was welcomed by some senior Turkish military commanders, who saw it as an opportunity to restore the TSK's domestic prestige, which had been badly damaged by the 2016 coup. Combating 'terrorism' also played well with the Turkish public and boosted Erdoğan's approval ratings.

Turkiye further shaped northern Syria through subsequent large-scale operations such as *Olive Branch* (*Zeytin dalı*) in 2018, *Peace Spring* (*Barış Pınarı*) in 2019 and *Spring Shield* (*Bahar Kalkanı*) in 2020 (see Map 13.1, page 233). Each operation drove the PYD out of an area of northern Syria and each consisted of Turkish-controlled Syrian militias fighting alongside regular Turkish forces. Despite concerns within the TGS about their vulnerability and the risks of escalation, Turkish troops were deployed to Idlib to bolster pro-Turkish militias, to serve as a deterrent against Iran- and Russia-backed Damascus, and to prevent an operation to overrun Idlib that would lead to another influx of refugees into Turkiye.

In parallel, to limit the involvement of the TSK, the reorganisation of Turkiye's proxies produced an integrated, reliable and powerful Syrian auxiliary force: the Jaysh al-Watani al-Suri, or the SNA. Through the SNA, Ankara could fight the PYD, as well as play a role in Idlib. It also enabled it to more directly contain radical Islamist and jihadist groups, such as Tanzim Hurras al-Din and ISIS local cells. In 2018, Ankara added a new entity, the National Liberation Front (NLF), to the SNA, then composed of 80,000 fighters organised into seven corps (three in Aleppo and four in Idlib), and placed it under the authority of the former head of the FSA, Salim Idriss.[16]

TSK–SNA cooperation went further than TSK–FSA cooperation did as the armed forces were not limited to training and structuring but included interoperability, such as joint tactical combat on the ground and firepower support with artillery and air raids. Entirely dependent on Turkiye, the SNA became an auxiliary force deployable in other theatres.

LIBYA

On the southern coast of the Eastern Mediterranean, during and after the turmoil that followed the overthrow of strongman Muammar Gadhafi in 2011, Turkiye was particularly attentive to factions and individuals regarded as being sympathetic to the Muslim Brotherhood. The hope was that Libya would eventually become part of a network of Muslim Brotherhood-affiliated regimes that would look to Ankara for leadership.

Turkiye and its ally Qatar were among the main backers of the Tripoli-based Government of National Accord (GNA), which was formed in 2014 and included elements affiliated with the Muslim Brotherhood. As tensions between the GNA and the rival Tobruk-based parliament and its military branch known as the Libyan National Army (LNA) descended into civil war, Turkiye began clandestine arms shipments by air and by sea to the GNA. The operation was approved by Erdoğan and managed by MİT. After the LNA launched its attack on Tripoli in April 2019, Turkiye provided *Bayraktar* TB2 UAVs that helped the GNA forces recover the city of Gharyan in June and break up a main logistical hub used by the LNA in its offensive. By November, with the GNA's continued need for military and logistical support, Ankara asked for an official framework for its support[17] and a recognition of the southern borders of Turkiye's exclusive economic zone as defined in the Blue Homeland doctrine. On 27 November 2019, the GNA and Turkiye signed a security pact and a memorandum of understanding on the maritime border. Over the following weeks, Turkiye stepped up its military aid to the GNA. On 2 January 2020, the Turkish parliament – in which the AKP and its partner, the MHP, enjoyed a majority – approved a one-year mandate for the deployment of Turkish forces to Libya.

The Turkish government faced practical restraints on the military support it could provide to the GNA. In part to ward off domestic criticism and avoid casualties and in part to maintain deniability, crewed aircraft were ruled out

FIGURE 6.1: MAJOR TURKISH DIPLOMACY AND MILITARY OPERATIONS IN IRAQ, LIBYA, NAGORNO-KARABAKH AND SYRIA, FEBRUARY 2008–FEBRUARY 2024

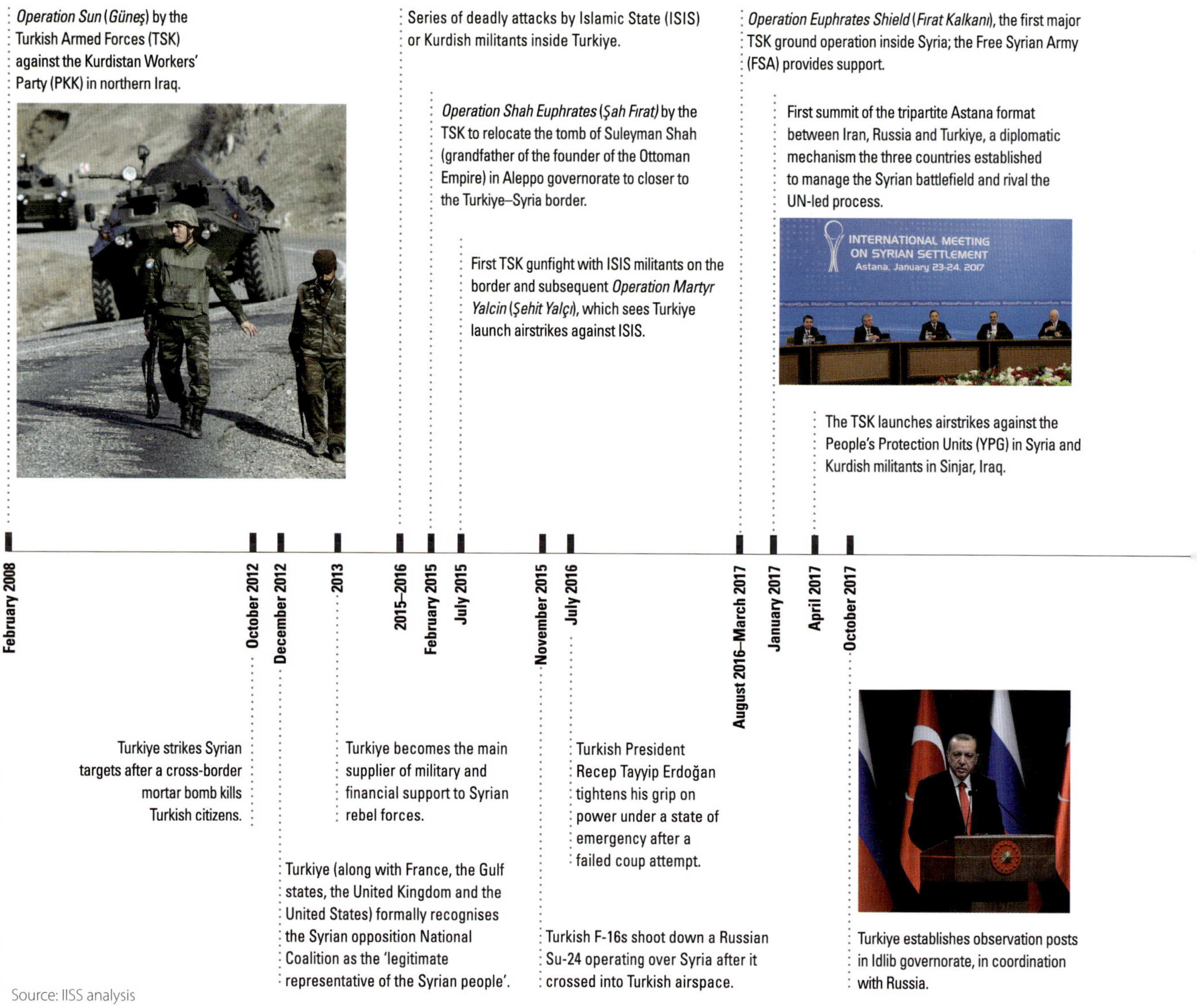

February 2008 — *Operation Sun (Güneş)* by the Turkish Armed Forces (TSK) against the Kurdistan Workers' Party (PKK) in northern Iraq.

October 2012 — Turkiye strikes Syrian targets after a cross-border mortar bomb kills Turkish citizens.

December 2012 — Turkiye (along with France, the Gulf states, the United Kingdom and the United States) formally recognises the Syrian opposition National Coalition as the 'legitimate representative of the Syrian people'.

2013 — Turkiye becomes the main supplier of military and financial support to Syrian rebel forces.

2015–2016 — Series of deadly attacks by Islamic State (ISIS) or Kurdish militants inside Turkiye.

February 2015 — *Operation Shah Euphrates (Şah Fırat)* by the TSK to relocate the tomb of Suleyman Shah (grandfather of the founder of the Ottoman Empire) in Aleppo governorate to closer to the Turkiye–Syria border.

July 2015 — First TSK gunfight with ISIS militants on the border and subsequent *Operation Martyr Yalcin (Şehit Yalçı)*, which sees Turkiye launch airstrikes against ISIS.

November 2015 — Turkish F-16s shoot down a Russian Su-24 operating over Syria after it crossed into Turkish airspace.

July 2016 — Turkish President Recep Tayyip Erdoğan tightens his grip on power under a state of emergency after a failed coup attempt.

August 2016–March 2017 — *Operation Euphrates Shield (Fırat Kalkanı)*, the first major TSK ground operation inside Syria; the Free Syrian Army (FSA) provides support.

January 2017 — First summit of the tripartite Astana format between Iran, Russia and Turkiye, a diplomatic mechanism the three countries established to manage the Syrian battlefield and rival the UN-led process.

April 2017 — The TSK launches airstrikes against the People's Protection Units (YPG) in Syria and Kurdish militants in Sinjar, Iraq.

October 2017 — Turkiye establishes observation posts in Idlib governorate, in coordination with Russia.

Source: IISS analysis

---

because of distance and escalation risks and the deployment of Turkish personnel mostly involved on-the-ground advisers, trainers and intelligence officers rather than combat troops. The Turkish navy escorted merchant ships carrying Turkish military equipment, nearly all of it Turkish-made, to the GNA, while there were regular flights carrying personnel and lighter equipment between Turkiye and Tripoli. The seaborne deliveries included armoured personnel carriers, tanks, artillery, rocket launchers and air-defence systems. These continued in breach of a United Nations-mandated arms embargo and despite the European Union's launch of *Operation Irini* on 1 March 2020, which attempted to enforce the embargo by monitoring incoming cargo into Libya.

In partnership with the Turkish private security company SADAT, MİT oversaw the recruitment of Syrian mercenaries from Turkish-controlled areas of northwestern Syria to fight alongside the GNA and its allies. However, the often poorly trained Syrian mercenaries played only a minor role in *Operation Peace Storm*, which was launched by the GNA in late March 2020 and succeeded in pushing the LNA back from Tripoli and recapturing a large swathe of previously LNA-held territory. More critical to the operation's success were Turkish-supplied equipment, intelligence and expertise deployed with the GNA's own forces (see Map 9.1, page 186).

While this was an objective success for Turkiye's projection of power and shaping of its environment, it also showed Ankara's restraints and limitations. By late June 2020, Egypt, one of the LNA's main backers, threatened to conduct a rare major military operation if the GNA continued its eastward advance. Cairo forced Ankara to stand down by presenting it with the risk of a full-scale war. In August 2020, the GNA and the LNA agreed a ceasefire, which included the stipulation that all foreign fighters should leave Libya within three months. In practice, the stipulation has never been fully implemented and, despite a decline in the levels of violence, a lasting peace settlement has so far proved elusive.

Timeline

January 2018 — *Operation Olive Branch* (*Zeytin dalı*) in Afrin district, the second major TSK ground operation inside Syria; the Syrian National Army (SNA) provides support.

March 2018 — *Operation Tigris Shield* (*Dicle Kalkanı*) by the TSK against the PKK in northern Iraq.

October–November 2019 — *Operation Peace Spring* (*Barış Pınarı*) in Tel Abyad and Ras al-Ain, the third major TSK ground operation inside Syria; the SNA provides support.

November 2019 — Turkiye and Libya (Government of National Accord, GNA) sign a memorandum of understanding (MoU) delineating their maritime border.

January 2020 — *Operation Spring Shield* (*Bahar Kalkanı*) in Idlib, the fourth major TSK ground operation inside Syria.

February 2020 — At least 34 Turkish soldiers are killed in a Syrian/Russian airstrike in Idlib governorate.

February–March 2020 — *Operation Claw-Eagle* (*Pençe Kartal*) and *Operation Claw-Tiger* (*Pençe Kaplan*) by the TSK against the PKK in northern Iraq.

March 2020 — Turkiye launches a military intervention in Libya in support of the GNA.

June 2020 — Turkiye and Russia announce a ceasefire in Idlib. GNA forces, backed by Turkish troops and advisers, break the siege of Tripoli and repel Libyan National Army (LNA) forces eastward.

June–September 2020 — Turkish-backed Syrian mercenaries are sent to Nagorno-Karabakh to support Azerbaijan against Armenia.

September–November 2020 — (continuation)

April 2022 — *Operation Claw-Lock* (*Pençe-Kilit*) by the TSK against the PKK in northern Iraq.

October 2022 — Turkish minister of defence Hulusi Akar and head of intelligence Hakan Fidan meet with Syrian Minister of Defense Ali Mahmoud Abbas and intelligence chief Ali Mamlouk along with Russian minister of defence Sergei Shoigu, to discuss conditions for the normalisation of relations.

December 2022 — Russia proposes a roadmap for Turkish–Syrian normalisation.

May 2023 — Tripoli Court of Appeal annuls energy-exploration MoU. Turkiye and the UN-recognised Libyan government sign an MoU on energy exploration.

February 2024 — (marker)

©IISS

THE EASTERN MEDITERRANEAN AS A LABORATORY: IRAQ AND NAGORNO-KARABAKH

Turkiye applied its model of intervention in two other theatres, though there it rested more on the TSK, rather than surrogates or proxies.

In Iraq, a Turkish-backed force led by Nineveh governor Athil al-Nujaifi's Hashd al-Watani (or Nineveh Guards) failed to contain the PKK. The militia was small and lacking in organisation and experience. Ankara saw no other option than to revert to TSK operations to fight the PKK. Using the army was also a way to prevent Iraq's north from falling under the control of the Hashd al-Shaabi, an Iranian-backed umbrella group of militias, and to counter Tehran's growing influence in the country. Ankara ultimately established a permanent military presence in northern Iraq in order to be able to reach three distant hotspots: Sinjar, Qandil and Kirkuk.[18]

In Nagorno-Karabakh, Ankara's support for Baku consisted mainly in bilateral conventional military cooperation, such as manoeuvres and weaponry (e.g., UAVs). Reports of the deployment of Syrian mercenaries have been denied by both countries.[19] In any case, their limited intervention did not play a significant role in combat operations against Armenia. Instead, it was the hardening and professionalisation of the Azerbaijani force by the TSK that delivered victory.

These two cases demonstrate how Ankara adapts its operating model to different theatres with debatable success.

PROSPECTS FOR DEPLOYMENT OF TURKIYE'S COERCIVE METHODS ELSEWHERE

Despite the success of its evolving assertive diplomacy in the Eastern Mediterranean, Turkiye's diplomatic toolbox has shrunk. Its increased brinkmanship and use of military operations to shape diplomatic outcomes have largely constrained its ability to join or initiate coalitions. Its relations with leading NATO allies like the US and France have been severely damaged, its hegemonic posture has encouraged its regional neighbours to work toward isolating it, and its arrangements with Russia have only been one-offs, not inscribed in the context of deeper cooperation.

There are also questions about how much more it can scale up or expand its current approach to areas of interest in Africa or Central Asia, given its struggling economy and the challenges facing its domestic defence industry in the development of next-stage weapons.

The limits of its approach have also been on display in the current Israel–Hamas war. There, Iran dwarfs any Turkish attempt at establishing control over local armed surrogates, and Erdoğan's bombastic rhetorical attacks against Israel have deprived him of diplomatic credibility in the pursuit of a resolution, in contrast to Qatar and Egypt.

Turkiye's Syrian surrogates have also shown the limits of their capabilities and usefulness. US AFRICOM described the Syrian mercenaries fighting in Libya as 'inexperienced, uneducated, and motivated by promises of considerable salary'.[20] The reprehensible behaviour of the SNA in Libya limited – and probably hurt – the attempt to make Turkish influence accepted in the country, as it is 'likely to further degrade the security situation and generate backlash from the Libyan public'.[21]

A monument of modern Turkiye's founder Mustafa Kemal Atatürk is seen in front of the flags of Azerbaijan and Turkiye and portraits of Turkish President Recep Tayyip Erdoğan and Azerbaijani President Ilham Aliyev on a building in Ankara, Turkiye, on 6 October 2020. (Photo: Altan Gocher/GocherImagery/Universal Images Group via Getty Images)

ENDNOTES

1. 'A Look at Turkiye's Post-coup Crackdown', AP News, 30 August 2018, https://apnews.com/article/dbb5fa7d8f8c4d0d99f297601c83a164.

2. 'Turkey Signs Deal to Get Russian S-400 Air Defence Missiles', BBC, 12 September 2017, https://www.bbc.com/news/world-europe-41237812.

3. Andreas Krieg and Jean-Marc Rickli, *Surrogate Warfare: The Transformation of War in the Twenty-first Century* (Washington DC: Georgetown University Press, 2019); and Thomas M. Huber, *Compound Warfare: That Fatal Knot* (Honolulu, HI: University Press of the Pacific, 2004).

4. Presidency of the Republic of Turkiye – Secretariat-General of the National Security Council, 'About Us', https://www.mgk.gov.tr/en/index.php/secretariat-general/about-us.

5. National Intelligence Organization, 'Mission, Mandate and Responsibilities', accessed 23 April 2023, https://www.mit.gov.tr/english/gorev.html.

6. National Intelligence Organization, 'Intelligence Production', accessed 23 April 2023, https://www.mit.gov.tr/english/isth-olusum.html.

7. Mahmut Hamsici, 'SADAT: Bir Askeri Şirketin Anatomisi', BBC Turkish, 6 July 2022, https://www.bbc.com/turkce/haberler-turkiye-62067169.

8. Jonathan Spyer, 'Erdogan's Shadow Army: The Influence of "Sadat," Turkey's Private Defense Group', The Jerusalem Institute for Strategy and Security, 24 April 2018, https://jiss.org.il/en/spyer-erdogans-shadow-army-influence-sadat-turkeys-private-defense-group/; SADAT, 'Sadat Defense', https://www.sadat.com.tr/en/.

9. SADAT, https://www.sadat.com.tr/en/about-us/news.html.

10. Yayınlanma Tarihi, 'SADAT Nedir, Neden Kuruldu ve Hakkındaki Iddialar Neler?' [What is SADAT, why was it established and what are the claims about it?], Euronews, 18 June 2021, https://tr.euronews.com/2021/06/18/sadat-nedir-neden-kuruldu-ve-faaliyetleri-neler.

11. SADAT, 'Misyonumuz' [Our mission], https://www.sadat.com.tr/tr/hakkimizda/misyonumuz.html.

12. Lead Inspector General Report to the US Congress, 'East Africa Counterterrorism Operation – North and West Africa Counterterrorism Operation', 1 April–30 June 2020, https://media.defense.gov/2020/Sep/02/2002489948/-1/-1/1/LEAD%20IG%20EAST%20AFRICA%20AND%20NORTH%20AND%20WEST%20AFRICA%20COUNTERTERRORISM%20OPERATIONS.PDF.

13. European Union Agency for Asylum, 'Country Guidance: Syria. Anti-Government Armed Groups', September 2020, https://euaa.europa.eu/country-guidance-syria/13-anti-government-armed-groups.

14. Global Security, 'SADAT Defense Consultancy', 4 February 2023, https://www.globalsecurity.org/military/world/europe/tu-sadat.htm; and Matt Powers, 'Making Sense of Sadat, Turkey's Private Military Company', *War on the Rocks*, 8 October 2021, https://warontherocks.com/2021/10/making-sense-of-sadat-turkeys-private-military-company/.

15. Engin Yüksel, 'Strategies of Turkish Proxy Warfare in Northern Syria: Back with a Vengeance', CRU Report, Clingendael, November 2019, https://www.clingendael.org/sites/default/files/2019-11/strategies-turkish-proxy-warfare-in-northern-syria.pdf.

16. Nawar Shaban, 'The Syrian National Army: Formation, Challenges, and Outlook', Syria Transition Challenges Project, The Geneva Centre for Security Policy (GCSP), October 2020, https://dam.gcsp.ch/files/doc/sna-formation-challenges-outlook.

17. 'Libya's GNA Accepts Turkish Offer of Military Support', Al-Jazeera, 19 December 2019, https://www.aljazeera.com/news/2019/12/19/libyas-gna-accepts-turkish-offer-of-military-support.

18. Julien Theron, 'Evolution Stratégique de la Turquie en Syrie et en Irak (2008–2018)' [Turkiye's strategic evolution in Syria and Iraq (2008–2018)], in Clément Steuer and Stéphane Valter (eds), *Le Général et le Politique: Le Rôle Des Armées en Turquie et en Égypte* [The general and the politician: the role of militaries in Turkiye and Egypt] (Paris: L'Harmattan, 2021); and Salim Çevik, 'Turkey's Military Operations in Syria and Iraq', Stiftung Wissenshaft und Politik, 30 May 2022, https://www.swp-berlin.org/publikation/turkeys-military-operations-in-syria-and-iraq.

19. Ed Butler, 'The Syrian Mercenaries Used as "Cannon Fodder" in Nagorno-Karabakh', BBC, 10 December 2020, https://www.bbc.co.uk/news/stories-55238803; Liz Cookman, 'Syrians Make Up Turkiye's Proxy Army in Nagorno-Karabakh', *Foreign Policy*, 5 October 2020, https://foreignpolicy.com/2020/10/05/nagorno-karabakh-syrians-turkey-armenia-azerbaijan/; Hannah Lucinda Smith, Marc Bennetts and Richard Spencer, 'Nagorno-Karabakh Clashes: Turkey Sends Syrian Mercenaries into Combat Against Armenians', *The Times*, 29 September 2020, https://www.thetimes.co.uk/article/nagorno-karabakh-clashes-turkey-sends-syrian-mercenaries-into-combat-against-armenians-wz6cqjc57; and John Lechner and S. Asher, 'Inside the Bloody Business of Turkey's Syrian Mercenaries', *National Interest*, 5 September 2022, https://nationalinterest.org/blog/middle-east-watch/inside-bloody-business-Turkiye's-syrian-mercenaries-204589.

20. Lead Inspector General Report to the US Congress, 'East Africa Counterterrorism Operation – North and West Africa Counterterrorism Operation', 1 April–30 June 2020, https://media.defense.gov/2020/Sep/02/2002489948/-1/-1/1/LEAD%20IG%20EAST%20AFRICA%20AND%20NORTH%20AND%20WEST%20AFRICA%20COUNTERTERRORISM%20OPERATIONS.PDF.

21. *Ibid*.

The Greek HS *Aigaion* frigate during an exercise simulating a humanitarian response to a powerful earthquake and significant movement of IDF and foreign vessels in the Mediterranean Sea on 7 August 2019. (Photo: Jack Guez/AFP via Getty Images)

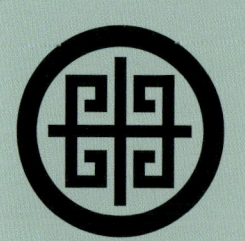

GREECE HAS ORCHESTRATED NETWORKS in the Eastern Mediterranean built on political, defence and energy cooperation with Cyprus, Egypt and Israel. It has done so to contain Turkiye and to position itself as an infrastructure and energy hub between Europe and the Middle East.

THANKS TO US AND FRENCH SUPPORT, and to closer alignment with Western priorities on Russia and China, Greece is quickly modernising its military, reducing the qualitative gap between it and Turkiye.

GREECE'S DIPLOMATIC, POLITICAL and military standing is improving. Athens is now influential in the region, having become able to advocate for regional partners such as Egypt within the EU policymaking process, and to inform part of US thinking on the region. The geopolitical challenges facing the country remain fundamentally unchanged, however.

CHAPTER SEVEN
GREECE: REGIONAL COOPERATION AS GRAND STRATEGY

INTRODUCTION

For Greece, the eastern part of the Mediterranean Sea constitutes, along with the Aegean and Ionian seas, both its historical ecosystem and a strategic arena in which it fends off Turkish revisionism and cooperates with other coastal nations. With 6,000 islands and islets across the two seas and a coastline of over 13,500 kilometres, Greece has a unique regional profile and set of vulnerabilities.

Greece's regional posture revolves around two priorities: firstly, the defence of its territories and maritime zones against Turkish legal and military brinkmanship, which forms the basis of its security and foreign policies; and secondly, as an extension of that concern, its role as Cyprus's guarantor and prime sponsor.

Greece's posture has also been shaped by the transformation of its neighbourhood. Since 2011, the fallout from the Arab uprisings – in terms of migration, the threat of terrorism and Turkiye's more assertive regional ambitions – has tested Athens's resilience and statecraft. High exposure to the second-order effects of Middle Eastern instability has prompted Greece to reach out to its eastern neighbours, aiming to shield itself from crises and gain influence.

These drivers also explain Greece's determined efforts in recent years to modernise its military (see Chapter Four), deepen its strategic relationships with the US and France, join minilateral groupings and position itself as a regional energy hub.

Since its sovereign-debt crisis in 2009, Greece's geopolitical positioning has evolved. It has largely rebounded economically and stabilised its public finances, even if its GDP remains about 20% lower than before the crisis.[1] Doing so has required a repositioning of its foreign, defence, energy and economic orientation. Understanding that financial assistance and geo-economic integration demanded better ties with European Union and NATO countries, Athens has distanced itself from Russia, which had once been a preferred interlocutor, and pursued closer alignment with the United States.

OVERCOMING ECONOMIC CRISIS

Greece's economic crisis, which started in earnest in late 2009, laid bare the mismanagement of the national finances, caused great hardship to the population and nearly led to the country's exit from the eurozone. However, it also prompted Greece to make its first foray into the wider Eastern Mediterranean.

The 2008 global financial crisis, which started in the US subprime market, had a delayed effect on Greece. In October 2009, finance minister Giorgios Papakonstantinou revealed that Greece's budget deficit was 12.5% of GDP, double the official figure, and well above the 3% ceiling stipulated by the EU's Stability and Growth Pact. It was then revised to 15.2%, and within two months the EU, IMF and European Central Bank agreed to provide financing to save the Greek economy, in return for a very harsh austerity package.[2] Over the next eight years, Greece borrowed €256 billion from European institutions.[3] The recessionary effect of the austerity policies dictated by Germany and other frugal European countries in tandem with the IMF cost Greece more than a quarter of its GDP,

FIGURE 7.1: GREECE'S ECONOMIC INDICATORS, 2008–24

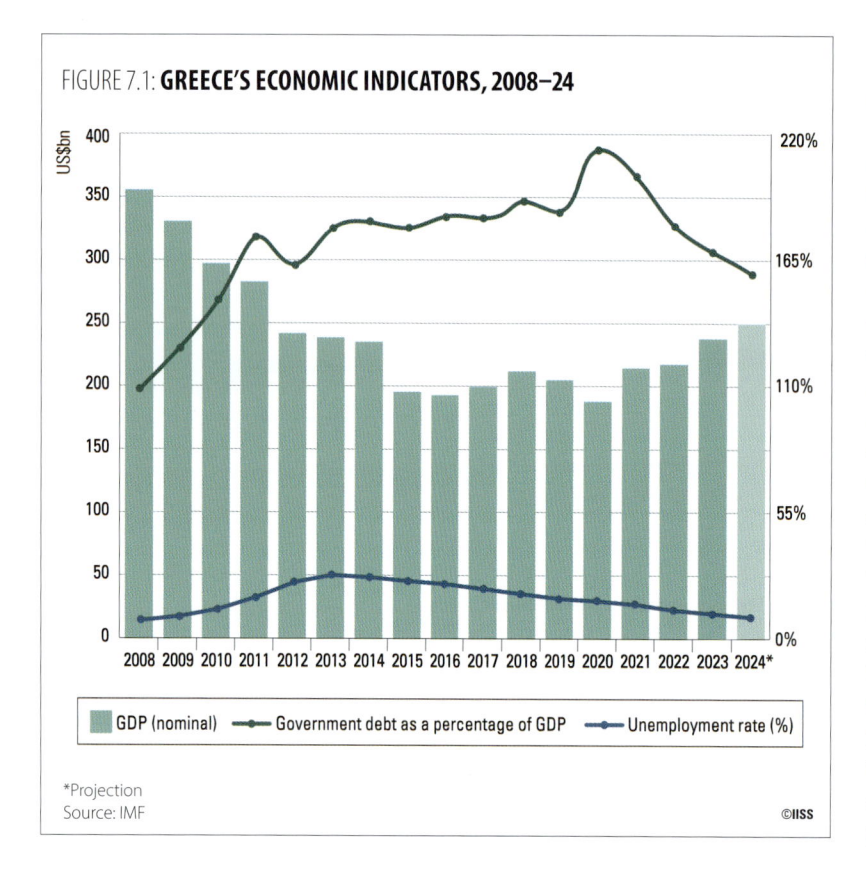

*Projection
Source: IMF

the sharpest contraction of a developed economy since the Second World War (see Figure 7.1).[4]

Despite this dire economic situation, then-prime minister George Papandreou (2009–11) was working on two new policy directions that have proven strategically long-lasting: reviving Greece's efforts to find its own hydrocarbons and advancing relations with Israel.

Greece's role as an energy conduit in southeastern Europe is intimately connected with its Eastern Mediterranean role. It hopes to eventually connect Israeli gas to European markets (a role that puts it at odds with Turkiye and Egypt) and has plans to produce its own gas by 2027. In parallel, it expects to become an electricity hub through three planned 2-gigawatt interconnectors, one running to Israel and two to Egypt.

ENERGY: KERNEL OF A FOREIGN POLICY

Greece established full diplomatic relations with Israel only in 1990, reflecting its long-term alignment with Arab positions on the Israeli–Palestinian conflict. Relations had been constrained by Israel's strong relationship with Turkiye in the 1990s and by Greece's economic and shipping ties with Arab countries. Benjamin Netanyahu became the first Israeli prime minister to visit Athens in August 2010. Netanyahu's visit took place just ten weeks after Israeli commandos boarded the *Mavi Marmara*, the ship at the head of a Turkish flotilla that was attempting to carry humanitarian aid to Gaza to break the naval blockade imposed by Israel. The visit came at a time when Turkish President Recep Tayyip Erdoğan had started hardening his opposition towards Israel, leading to a multi-year rift in relations. In parallel, Greece's relationship with Israel continued to improve under leftist and centre-right governments in Athens. In 2015 the Greek parliament voted in favour of recognising Palestinian statehood, but then-prime minister Alexis Tsipras shelved the matter in order to develop ties with Israel, an approach maintained by his successors.

Besides bilateral benefits, the warming of the Greece–Israel relationship had important carry-over effects, including facilitating an improvement in Greece's relations with the US. In turn, this helped Greece bolster political and defence ties with Washington.

For Israel, gaining an EU partner in its neighbourhood was welcome at a time of geopolitical flux but also energy potential. In 2009 and 2010, US and Israeli oil companies discovered Tamar and Leviathan, Israel's largest offshore-gas fields. This turned Israel overnight into the Eastern Mediterranean's biggest owner of exportable gas. For the Israeli leadership, securing an export path to the EU became a strategic imperative. Greece therefore became a committed supporter of Israel in Brussels and lobbied for EU support for the Eastern Mediterranean Pipeline (EastMed).

This coincided with Greece's development of a framework for its own hydrocarbon exploration, with the creation of the Hellenic Hydrocarbons and Energy Resources Management Authority (HEREMA) in August 2011 and the adoption of legislation, known as the 'Maniatis law' (after the then-energy minister), that reduced corporate tax from 40% to 25% for upstream activities, aiming to attract oil majors to what was still an unproven frontier.[5] In 2014, the Greek government signed concessions with Energean (a British–Greek company) and Hellenic Petroleum for offshore-oil exploration.[6] In 2017, the Greek government approved applications by a consortium of Total (now TotalEnergies), ExxonMobil and Hellenic Petroleum for gas exploration and drilling off the island of Crete, and awarded them the tender in 2018.[7] And in 2019, Spain's Repsol and Hellenic Petroleum signed lease agreements to explore for oil and gas in offshore blocks in western Greece (where Turkiye disputes maritime zones).[8]

The data showed possible gas formations around the Ionian Islands and in the Mediterranean south and west of Crete. Energy finds could potentially stabilise Greece's struggling finances and provide the EU with an alternative source of gas to reduce its dependency on Russia. However, much of the exploration-licence period of seven years that Greece awarded to these companies was eaten up by court injunctions and licensing delays. In 2020, amid the coronavirus pandemic and plummeting oil prices, Repsol pulled out of more than a dozen territories where it had no production, including Greece. Total left in 2022.[9] ExxonMobil was also on the cusp of leaving that same year but stayed at the insistence of the US ambassador to Greece, Geoffrey Pyatt, and US energy officials.[10] This followed a plea from the Greek government and demonstrated the United States' strategic investment in Greece, which is intended partly to keep Russian interests at bay.

The energy crisis caused by the 2022 Russian invasion of Ukraine, and the opportunity to supplement the EU's supply as it reduces its consumption of Russian hydrocarbons, also pushed Greece decisively in favour of drilling for gas after years of delays. The ExxonMobil–Hellenic Petroleum consortium is expected to make a final decision on drilling in the East Crete and South Crete blocks in October 2024.[11] The war has also sharpened competition between Greek-supplied liquefied natural gas and Turkish-supplied Russian pipeline gas. Greece is discussing a separate gas interconnector to North Macedonia with its own import terminal in Thessaloniki. In February 2024 it also added a floating storage and regasification unit (FSRU) in the increasingly strategic port of Alexandroupolis, expanding Greece's export capacity to the Balkans.[12]

However, in addition to the delays and complications in offshore-gas drilling that are related to its maritime-border dispute with Turkiye, Greece's plans to become a gas hub have also faced other headwinds. The EastMed Gas Pipeline it devised with Cyprus and Israel in the 2010s initially received positive EU and US congressional backing despite its high cost. But in 2022, the US State Department expressed reservations about the pipeline's economic viability and environmental impact.[13] Instead, it encouraged Greece to invest in building 'electricity interconnectors that can support both gas and renewable energy sources'.[14]

Indeed, Greece is well placed to make a quick and positive contribution to Europe's energy security in compliance with the EU's Green Deal by supplying stable volumes of electricity from renewable and clean sources in North Africa and the Gulf. When they are completed, Greece will be the key node of the 1,800 kilometre EuroAsia Interconnector (Greece–Cyprus–Israel) and the 950 km GREGY (Greece–Egypt) Interconnector. The EuroAsia Interconnector – the longest and deepest in the world, and backed by partial EU funding – is currently under construction and is expected to be completed by 2026, while the GREGY project is still in the planning phase.[15]

TURKIYE, GREECE'S BÊTE NOIRE

Greece's disputes and conflict with Turkiye define major aspects of its strategic posture. As Turkiye is its main national-security threat, Athens has structured its defence modernisation and cooperation to deter and defend against Ankara. In the past decade, managing Turkiye has been the main driver of Greece's investment in regional partnerships, such as its trilaterals with Cyprus and Israel or with Cyprus and Egypt, and in the East Mediterranean Gas Forum (EMGF). Greece has adeptly capitalised on the deterioration of the United States' and Israel's relationships with Turkiye, improving its own ties and standing with both. It has also upgraded its strategic partnership with France, primarily as a response to Turkiye's assertiveness in the Eastern Mediterranean.

Turkiye and Greece have been rivals for decades and have had open territorial disputes in both the Aegean and Eastern Mediterranean seas that have pushed them to the brink of armed confrontation several times since the end of the Second World War (see Chapter Two). Grievances include the delimitation of continental shelves/exclusive economic zones (EEZs), territorial waters and airspace, and issues of demilitarisation and/or sovereignty concerning several islands. Because of history, geography and now energy, the maritime-border disputes that centre around Crete and Cyprus are the most intractable.

The discovery of gas in the Eastern Mediterranean in 2010 supercharged the existing tensions and grievances (see Chapter Three). The Maniatis law harmonised into Greek law the United Nations Convention on the Law of the Sea (UNCLOS) principle that habitable islands have a continental shelf and EEZ equal to continental coasts, a major point of contention with Turkiye.[16] It set the stage for further confrontation with Turkiye by reaffirming the UNCLOS allowance for up to 12 nautical miles of territorial waters. There have been regular talks aimed at making progress towards resolving the disputes, but these have not produced resolutions because the two countries differ in their legal approaches and appropriate dispute-resolution frameworks. Greece takes the view that international courts must adjudicate all territorial and maritime issues, while Turkiye favours addressing them through a bilateral negotiation.

As a result, brinkmanship and military stand-offs have increased. In 2009, Turkiye violated Greek territorial waters 90 times, as recorded by the Hellenic Armed Forces.[17] But the Greek authorities contend that between 2010 and 2016 there were hundreds of such violations per year, and from 2017, thousands.[18] In 2014, the year Greece discovered natural gas in its Ionian and Mediterranean EEZ, annual violations of Greek airspace by Turkish aircraft nearly quadrupled to over 2,200. The Hellenic Air Force subsequently reported that they rose to over 4,000 in 2019 and to 11,258 in 2022, including overflights of inhabited Greek islands.[19]

Greek officials note that Turkiye has grown emboldened since the US downgraded its presence in the Eastern Mediterranean in the 2010s, with the year 2016 a turning point in the power dynamics between Athens and Ankara. Relations deteriorated sharply after then-prime minister Tsipras refused to hand over eight Turkish officers who had sought asylum in Greece following the failed July 2016 coup against Erdoğan. In the wake of the coup attempt and the failure of the 2017 Crans-Montana negotiations over the Cyprus problem (see Chapter Eight), Turkiye grew increasingly assertive in its projection of power and its expansionist strategy in the Eastern Mediterranean (see Chapter Five), with Ankara viewing Athens's growing defence relations with Egypt, Israel, Saudi Arabia and the United Arab Emirates (UAE) as provocative.

A rapid succession of moves by both sides raised tensions to a boiling point between late 2019 and the end of 2020, bringing them closer to conflict than at any time since 1996. In July 2019, Kyriakos Mitsotakis became prime minister, bringing his centre-right party New Democracy to power. Nikos Dendias, close to New Democracy's nationalist wing and an advocate of closer relations with Turkiye's regional rivals, became foreign minister.

In November 2019, Turkiye signed a memorandum of understanding (MoU) with Libya's Government of National Accord (GNA), carving out a diagonal corridor across what Greece claimed as its own EEZ in the Mediterranean.[20] In response, Greece pressed ahead in January 2020 with its public advocacy for the EastMed Gas Pipeline with Israel and Cyprus, which would cross into waters now claimed by Turkiye.[21] Two months later, in March 2020, Turkiye facilitated the arrival of thousands of asylum seekers at the Greek and Bulgarian borders, creating the biggest migration crisis the EU had faced since its migration deal with Turkiye in the wake of the 2015–16 influx of migrants.[22] In August, Greece delimited its EEZ with Egypt.[23] Shortly afterwards, tensions peaked when a Turkish warship escorted a Turkish exploration ship through the disputed EEZ and collided with a Greek frigate.[24]

Throughout this crisis, Erdoğan threatened to invade Greek islands and repeatedly denounced Mitsotakis, accusing him of reaching out to third parties to strengthen his position, which was a pointed reference to Greece's warming relations with France.[25] The risk that an accident at sea would escalate into an armed confrontation was contained. There were no reports of mobilisation on either side and no outrageous provocation in the air domain either. The crisis

Greek prime minister Alexis Tsipras (L) and Turkish President Recep Tayyip Erdoğan (R) speak during a joint press conference following a meeting at the Presidential Complex in Ankara, Turkiye, on 5 February 2019. (Photo: Adem Altan/AFP via Getty Images)

was ultimately de-escalated through US and German mediation and by direct dialogue between the Greek and Turkish militaries. This was also helped by the general thawing of relations in the Middle East that started in late 2020, and by the discovery of energy resources in Turkish waters in the Black Sea.

Erdoğan and Mitsotakis, bound by their countries' shared membership in NATO, have since met regularly and attempted thaws and resets. In 2023, the devastating earthquake in southeastern Turkiye and the deadly wildfires in Greece provided the two countries with an opportunity to engage in natural-disaster diplomacy, which had successfully de-escalated tensions in the past.

After Erdoğan and Mitsotakis both won re-election in 2023, the Turkish president paid his first visit to Athens in six years on 7 December and met with the Greek prime minister. It was a visit that had been 'designed to succeed', according to a Greek official.[26] Erdoğan hailed a new era of friendship with Athens, expressed hope for the Aegean to become a 'sea of peace' and insisted that a 'glass-half-full perspective' was the best practical approach to talks, while stressing to Mitsotakis that 'there is no issue between us that is unsolvable'. Mitsotakis behaved similarly, stressing the historical responsibility incumbent on both parties to resolve their differences.

The mostly symbolic 'Athens Declaration' that the two countries signed in 2023 included a substantive agreement on migration and called for better deconfliction through enhanced communication. Human trafficking has remained a challenge, given the lucrative revenue streams, but improved cooperation between the Greek and Turkish coastguards reduced illegal migration from Turkiye through the Eastern Mediterranean by about 60% between October and December 2023. The two countries also established a hotline and deployed coastguard-liaison officers in several of each other's ports.

This remarkable change in tone stems from both leaders having a more comfortable domestic political situation and sharing a desire to forge a legacy, and also from economic imperatives. Washington and Berlin are seen as the only effective mediators in the relationship, but in fact Erdoğan and Mitsotakis have established direct communication and now meet without third-party mediation. In contrast, Ankara has spurned the EU, which it sees as obedient to Cypriot interests and unwilling to accommodate Turkish demands for accession, and has particularly shunned France, which it perceives as overly belligerent in the Eastern Mediterranean theatre.

The rapprochement between Ankara and Athens remains fragile and tentative. It is also dependent on mutual goodwill, as the 2023 agreement is not binding. Both sides are therefore proceeding with caution. Yet with Greece still rebuilding its financial health and Turkiye on a painful path to economic recovery, pragmatic motivations compel a more realistic partnership. Mitsotakis has set a 'realistic goal' of increasing annual bilateral trade to US$10.8bn in the next five years, which would be more than double its current level. Increased exports to Turkiye will help mitigate Greece's trade deficit, which stood at US$3.39bn in May 2024.[27]

Both countries are also being urged, particularly by the US, to increase regional cooperation on energy issues, given that the region has a limited window of opportunity to benefit from its recently discovered reserves before the EU completes its transition to green energies. The region's hydrocarbon potential cannot be fully realised, however, as long as Cyprus, Greece and Turkiye do not at least reach an agreement to ring-fence energy matters from the rest of their historic conflict. At their 2023 meeting, Erdoğan and Mitsotakis sidestepped the dispute over the delimitation of their continental shelf and respective EEZs, and over the Cyprus question, instead agreeing to disagree.

THE CYPRUS PROBLEM

Greece has been Cyprus's main sponsor on the international stage and a formal guarantor of the agreements that led to the island's independence (see Chapter Eight). It was an Athens-inspired coup aiming to unite Cyprus with Greece that precipitated the Turkish invasion in 1974 and the resulting division of the island. Greece is its de facto security guarantor, basing troops and equipment on the island and training its military.

> THE REGION'S HYDROCARBON POTENTIAL CANNOT BE FULLY REALISED AS LONG AS CYPRUS, GREECE AND TURKIYE DO NOT AT LEAST REACH AN AGREEMENT TO RING-FENCE ENERGY MATTERS FROM THE REST OF THEIR HISTORIC CONFLICT.

While the political, military and social ties between Greece and Cyprus run deep, their positions are not as aligned as is sometimes believed. At various moments Greece has been much more willing than the Cypriot leadership to engage in negotiations to resolve its outstanding disputes with Turkiye. Greek officials admit feeling constrained by the Cypriot agenda and the high cost of reassuring Nicosia, and consider that Cypriot obstruction exposes Greece to Turkish displeasure and threats. But as much as Greece may want to improve its relationship with Turkiye, it cannot decouple from Cyprus. Doing so would alienate Greek Cypriots and would come at a steep price for any government, given the hardline nationalist constituency who are staunch supporters of Cyprus and permeate Greece's military, business and religious circles but also less politicised Greek citizens. This explains why Turkish officials quip that 'Nicosia decides, Athens supports'.

Helped by the concomitant deterioration in US–Turkiye relations and by Turkiye's increased assertiveness after 2016, the Mitsotakis government deftly leveraged a politically savvy Greek–American lobby in the US Congress to push for the deepening of the relationship. By rallying key members of Congress such as the then-chair of the Senate Foreign Relations Committee, Senator Bob Menendez, the lobby also contributed to delaying Turkiye's bid to modernise its own F-16s.[28]

From the Greek perspective, an enhanced relationship with the US helped to deter Turkiye. Despite their shared membership of NATO, Greece has doubted the Alliance's ability to restrain Turkiye, seeing NATO's leadership and military staff as accommodating Turkiye and as overly favouring it given its geographic location and its large armed forces, only second to the US within the Alliance.

For its part, the US has been keen to strike a balance between Greece and

STRONGER TIES WITH THE US, FRANCE AND ISRAEL; DOWNGRADED TIES WITH RUSSIA

Ironically, Greece's greater Western orientation was put on track by the leftist government of Tsipras, a former communist who governed from 2015 to 2019 and who had vocally criticised the EU's austerity plans for Greece. Once in office, however, seeing no alternative way to rescue Greek finances, Tsipras implemented the austerity agenda supported by Western financial institutions. In October 2017 he met with the United States' then-president Donald Trump in Washington – a trip that crystallised the value of good relations with the US for the entire Greek political spectrum. In April 2018 the government struck a US$1.3bn deal with Lockheed Martin to upgrade 83 F-16 Block 52 fighter jets to *Vipers*, the version used by the US military. The first US–Greece strategic dialogue took place that same year, leading to a broadened Mutual Defense Cooperation Agreement (MDCA) in 2019.

TABLE 7.1: RECENT TRENDS IN GREECE'S BILATERAL RELATIONSHIPS AS OF MAY 2024

Country	Trend
Cyprus	=
Egypt	↑
France	↑
Israel	↑
Russia	↓
Saudi Arabia	↑
Turkiye	↑
UAE	↑
UK	=
US	↑

↑ Strengthening relationship
= Unchanged
↓ Weakening relationship

Source: IISS analysis

Turkiye, signalling that it would not tolerate an attack on Greek territory but at the same time working to keep Turkiye in the Western orbit. This explains the ambiguous positioning Washington has had on the disputed issues between the two capitals, insisting on resolutions through mutual compromise and negotiation backed by the EU and European powers. US officials have been careful not to formally express to Greece any special security guarantee for its territorial integrity beyond the reassurance of NATO's Article 5.

Nevertheless, Greece has become a major security partner for the US, seen by Washington as an important platform from which to protect NATO's southeastern flank in light of the Russian invasion of Ukraine.[29] In December 2019, Congress passed the Eastern Mediterranean Security and Energy Partnership Act, which lifted a 1987 arms embargo on Cyprus and expanded military training and financing for Greece and Cyprus.[30] In 2021, the US and Greece expanded the MDCA, giving the US greater access to the Greek bases at Souda Bay (where the US already had a naval base), Alexandroupolis, Larissa and other locations.

Alexandroupolis, in fact, has become a central hub for US military logistics. It allows military and commercial traffic a route into Bulgaria that bypasses the Bosphorus Strait, thus also providing a land route to Ukraine. The importance of Alexandroupolis has grown ever since Turkiye closed the Bosphorus to the transit of armed forces a few days after Russia invaded Ukraine, in accordance with its responsibilities under the Montreux Convention of 1936.[31] Since 2022 the port has become the second-most important, albeit less publicised, conduit for weapons to Ukraine, after Poland.

This new role has benefitted Greece's quest to modernise its defence capabilities and close the gap with Turkiye. Mitsotakis achieved part of that goal when he delivered a speech to a joint session of the US Congress on 17 May 2022, during which he requested F-35 aircraft and made reference to the Turkish threat. 'The last thing that NATO needs at a time when our focus is on helping Ukraine defeat Russia's aggression is another source of instability on NATO's Southeastern flank. And I ask you to take this into account when you make defense procurement decisions concerning the Eastern Mediterranean', Mitsotakis said.[32]

Greece has been eager to demonstrate its increased willingness to play a security role alongside the US and beyond the Eastern Mediterranean. Since December 2023 it has participated in both the US-led *Operation Prosperity Guardian* and the EU-led EUNAVFOR ASPIDES in response to the attacks on merchant ships in the Red Sea by the Iran-backed Ansarullah (Houthi) militia in Yemen in the context of the Israel–Hamas war.[33]

In January 2024, the US approved the sale of 40 F-35 aircraft to Greece, making it one of only two countries (with Israel) in the Eastern Mediterranean equipped with the fifth-generation fighter jet.[34] In contrast, Egypt's request for F-35 aircraft was denied, while Turkiye was ejected from the programme in 2018 after purchasing the Russian S-400 air-defence system. Upon delivery of the US F-35s and French *Rafale* aircraft (see below), the Hellenic Air Force will have a qualitative edge over Turkiye in the Aegean and Mediterranean theatres.

Among the US drivers for a closer relationship with Greece is the need to contain Russian but also Chinese reach in the Mediterranean. As part of the bailout agreement with the EU and IMF, the Greek state had to privatise major assets as well as critical infrastructure such as airports and ports. By 2016 it had sold a 51% stake of the Piraeus Port Authority to China's COSCO Shipping, which had already been running a major part of Piraeus since 2008.[35] Also in 2016, the State Grid Corporation of China, the biggest electricity-grid operator in the world, purchased 24% of its Greek counterpart, Independent Power Transmission Operator (IPTO/ADMIE).[36] Since the Chinese company took over its operation, Piraeus has become the largest port in the Eastern Mediterranean and the seventh largest in Europe.[37] Greece has since then cooled its partnership with China and invested in economic partnerships with its regional neighbours, EU partners and the US.

FRANCE

Parallel to its rapprochement with Washington, Greece has benefitted from sustained tensions between Turkiye and France since 2010. Two serious naval incidents in rapid succession, pitting a French frigate (June 2020; see Chapter Two) and then a Greek one (August 2020; see above) against Turkish vessels, exemplified the common challenge that Paris and Athens had identified in previous years. Unsurprisingly, the incidents boosted and widened their defence cooperation.

In September 2020, Mitsotakis announced Greece's first increase in defence spending in 12 years. In January 2021, Greece ordered 24 fourth-generation *Rafale* fighter jets from France's Dassault Aviation for US$4.2bn (including missiles and other accompanying systems) to replace its ageing *Mirage* 2000 fighters. The Hellenic Navy also began the process of selecting new frigates and upgrading some of its least antiquated MEKO-type frigates. In March 2022, Greece ordered three frigates from the French company Naval Group for US$3.8bn (including weaponry and other accompanying systems).[38] Greece has dithered on whether to buy a fourth new frigate or three new corvettes that would amplify the range of the first three frigates. The first three are intended to create area denial for Turkish aircraft in the Aegean, while a fourth one would project power in the Eastern Mediterranean by helping to defend Cyprus.

In October 2021, Greece and France signed a strategic partnership that included a mutual-defence clause and pledged to reinforce defence-industrial cooperation. Greece gained a measure of protection it had long sought, especially since the Turkish invasion of Cyprus in 1974. 'Our country has been negotiating since 1974 ... for such a treaty', Mitsotakis said at the signing.

The credibility of the mutual-defence clause is questionable, given France's limited ability to meet its commitment. The agreement is notable in that it is the first intra-NATO mutual-defence pact not to reference NATO as its operating framework, raising eyebrows within the Alliance. For Greece, however, it sent an important strategic signal in its stand-off with Turkiye.

In return, France obtained access to Greek ports and airports for renewable periods of five years, furthering its ambition to project power in the Eastern Mediterranean.

ISRAEL

While Greece has bought defence material from the US for decades and from France since 1989, Israel is a new supplier. This has come as a corollary of the two countries' improved diplomatic relationship, closer defence cooperation (including through the trilateral with Cyprus) and common energy ambitions (see Chapter Four).

Greece's defence relationship with Israel began in 2020. Recognising Turkiye's significant technological advantage thanks to its domestically produced *Bayraktar* uninhabited aerial vehicles (UAVs), Greece sought a rapid stopgap solution to monitor its maritime domain. Accordingly, the Hellenic Air Force leased two Israeli *Heron* UAVs in May of that year. More recently, Greece has procured the *Drone Dome* air-defence system from Israel's Rafael Advanced Defense Systems, along with surveillance-and-reconnaissance UAVs.[39] More recently, Greece has procured training aircraft from Israel's Elbit as well as *Spike* NLOS short-range missile-defence systems and about 500 missiles from Israel's Rafael.

It was notable that Mitsotakis's first overseas trip after the start of the coronavirus pandemic was to Israel in June 2020.[40] During the visit, he signed protocols for cooperation on cyber security with Israeli Prime Minister Netanyahu and invited Israeli investors to use Greece as a base from which to reach the EU single market. Greece and Israel also agreed to establish a joint flight-training centre in the southern Greek town of Kalamata.[41] Israel, which had once benefitted from training in the Turkish airspace, now had access to Athens's vast flight-information region.[42]

The extent of Greece's proximity with Israel became clearer after the beginning of the Israel–Hamas war in October 2023. Mitsotakis was among the Western leaders to fly to Israel, proclaiming on 23 October that 'I come here not just as an ally but as a true friend. […] Greece, from the very first moment, defended and supported the right of Israel to defend itself in line with International Law. […] You can count on our support, on our help.'[43] Soon after, Greece abstained during the first UN General Assembly vote calling for a humanitarian truce in Gaza. If this vote was in line with most EU states, it marked a considerable change given Greece's prior steadfast support for the Palestinian cause. This reflected the weakening of Greece's leftist factions, the western reorientation of the country and the new geo-economic relations.

EGYPT AND THE GULF

As well as bolstering its relations with the US, France and Israel, Greece has strengthened its historic partnership with Egypt (see Table 7.1). The two countries have grown even closer since the Arab uprisings and the tensions between Turkiye and Egypt that followed the 2013 coup in Cairo. Egypt's assertive posture against Turkiye was welcomed in Athens, where partnerships with Arab countries are regarded as having particular political significance.

Athens has become an emphatic advocate of Egypt being too big to fail. For Greece (and Cyprus), the prospect of such a populous and poor country collapsing, and probably triggering the departure towards Europe of tens of millions of people, is a nightmarish one. Cairo's leverage with Athens was enhanced by the migration crisis of 2015–16, which saw more than a million mostly Syrian, Iraqi and Afghan asylum seekers cross the Eastern Mediterranean towards Greece and other EU landing points – primarily from Turkiye, but also, in small numbers, from Egypt. Also, Egypt perceives that in Greece it has a reliable and effective advocate within the EU and among the Western powers.

Greece and Egypt have set up a trilateral with Cyprus and have held eight summits since 2014 to deepen their strategic cooperation on security, energy and economic issues. Greece and Egypt have held twice-yearly *Medusa* joint military exercises since 2015. The two countries also cooperate on energy. Egypt's plans to become a major exporter of renewable energy underpin Greece's electrical-interconnector plans and its own ambition to become an energy hub feeding continental Europe. They are also both founding members of the EMGF and have used it to isolate Turkiye in the region and to attempt to extract concessions in maritime disputes with Ankara in exchange for Turkish accession.

While the relationship with Egypt is valuable to Greece, it also has its limits. Except for the threat of intervention in Libya in mid-2020, Cairo has preferred to manage Ankara and avoid a direct confrontation, maintaining a military-to-military channel throughout the 2010s. Also, although Turkiye's maritime brinkmanship has irked Egypt, Ankara has been careful not to encroach on Egypt's claimed territory. Turkiye's 2019 MoU with Libya was enough of a provocation that it pushed Egypt to pointedly demarcate its own EEZ with Greece the year after, but notably there were no incidents or brinkmanship at sea between Egypt and Turkiye.

This balancing act by Egypt, especially since the thawing of its relations with Turkiye in 2022, shows the limitations of Greece's regional diplomacy. As soon as the de-escalation started, there was less urgency in Cairo to maintain its relations with Greece, though the diplomatic consequences of this were minimal. Cairo has had to balance the importance of Greece as an entry point to the EU with the fact that its trade with Turkiye is three times as large as its trade with Greece.

However, Egypt's regional diplomacy aimed at managing the ongoing Israel–Hamas war has benefitted from Cairo's ties with Athens. Mitsotakis attended the November 2023 meeting in Cairo to push for a diplomatic track, and while Greece abstained on the first vote, it later voted in favour of UN resolutions calling for a ceasefire and a two-state solution, though it has refrained from calling for recognition of Palestinian statehood. In 2024, Mitsotakis has been one of the EU leaders pushing hardest for an assistance package to Egypt to avoid any destabilisation of the country, travelling with an EU delegation to Cairo in March to announce it.

The Mitsotakis government has also turned its attention to deepening Greece's relationships with the UAE and Saudi Arabia, which had previously been limited in scope. As with Greece's other partnerships, a shared rivalry with Turkiye has supercharged these relations. Convergence on Egypt, Libya and other regional matters has evolved into structured diplomacy. In November 2020, in Abu Dhabi, Greece and the UAE signed a strategic alliance that included cooperation on economic matters, tourism and defence. Greek officials describe it as a mutual-defence treaty, but unlike the one with France, its contents have not

Greek Prime Minister Kyriakos Mitsotakis (L) welcomes Egyptian President Abdel Fattah al-Sisi (R) at the Maximos Mansion in Athens, Greece, on 11 November 2020. (Photo: Yorgos Karahalis/POOL/AFP via Getty Images)

been published. Greece's upgraded relations with Saudi Arabia became evident when in February 2021 it lent Riyadh a *Patriot* air-defence battery, complete with its crew, to protect critical facilities from Houthi missile attacks. This gesture was particularly appreciated in Riyadh at a time when it could not secure US *Patriot* batteries.

Also in February 2021, Greece organised the first Philia Forum, a gathering in Athens of the foreign ministers of Bahrain, Cyprus, Egypt, France, Greece and Saudi Arabia, along with the UAE's minister of international cooperation.[44] Conceived as a link between the Eastern Mediterranean and the Gulf, the summit served to display their shared opposition to Turkiye as well as a desire to cooperate on economic, infrastructure and energy projects. However, although pitched as an annual gathering, the Philia Forum has not been convened again, suggesting flagging enthusiasm and momentum for minilateral settings as regional de-escalation took place.

In October 2021, Mitsotakis visited Saudi Arabia and signed with Crown Prince Muhammad bin Salman Al Saud (MBS) an MoU for the establishment of the Greek–Saudi High Level Strategic Cooperation Council. In July 2022, MBS chose to visit Greece for his first trip to an EU country since the 2018 killing of Saudi journalist Jamal Khashoggi, which had caused him to be temporarily ostracised by the West. During that visit, the two countries agreed on a planned joint venture to build an undersea and land data cable linking Asia with Europe, the 'East-to-Med Data Corridor'.[45] As they share an interest in renewable power, they also discussed the possibility of linking their power grids to supply Europe with cheaper green energy.[46]

MARITIME DISPUTES: CREATING FACTS ON THE GROUND

In addition to its expanding military and infrastructure partnerships, Greece has adjusted its approach to its ongoing maritime disputes with Turkiye by making a series of delimitation agreements that translate its theoretical claims into legal realities.

In 2020, it announced an EEZ agreement with Italy and Egypt. The concessions it made were minor. Italian trawlers would have certain fishing rights in Greek waters; and Egypt gained 4,600 square kilometres north of the median line at Greece's expense

– a mere 0.9% of Greece's theoretical half-million square kilometres of EEZ. The point for Greece was to counter the Turkish–Libyan MoU with its own agreement with Egypt.

In addition to these moves, Greece embarked on a global diplomatic campaign to establish the universal application of UNCLOS. This advocacy became a staple of Greek outreach in the region, and the 2021 Philia Forum's final statement affirmed its support for UNCLOS. In 2023, then-foreign minister Dendias visited South Korea and Japan to stress their common cause over the dismissive attitudes of Turkiye and China towards UNCLOS in their respective theatres. The Philippines too were courted, since China has refused to recognise a 2016 decision at the International Court of Justice favouring the Philippines in a dispute over the Spratly Islands.[47]

Turkiye's attempt to create facts on the ground also prompted Greece to begin to establish extended territorial waters. In a tit-for-tat move, Mitsotakis announced in August 2020 – at the height of the Greek–Turkish stand-off in the Aegean – his intention to extend Greek territorial waters in the Ionian Sea, accompanied by a clear message of his intent to do the same in the Aegean. When the extension was voted into law in January 2021, Dendias, a hawk on Turkiye, announced that the next extension would take place south of Crete. But Greece has not yet taken that next step, reportedly due to American pressure to avoid provoking Turkiye.

OUTLOOK

With the Eastern Mediterranean becoming a more porous theatre in recent years, where brinkmanship has returned and more actors are assertively pushing their interests, Greece's more proactive foreign policy has helped it expand its room for manoeuvre. But many of its policies remain reactive, attempting to contain Turkiye's coercive diplomacy while avoiding war. The two countries remain far apart on their core disputes around maritime zones, a fact that will continue to undermine the region's potential as an energy hub.

Greece's partnerships with France, Israel and the US have strengthened its overall posture. However, while the minilaterals it has set up with Israel and

Greek Prime Minister Kyriakos Mitsotakis (R) greets Saudi Crown Prince Muhammad bin Salman Al Saud (L) prior to their meeting at the prime minister's office in Athens, Greece, on 26 July 2022.
(Photo: Louisa Gouliamaki/AFP via Getty Images)

Egypt have added a layer of regional ties, as has the EMGF, they are not alliances with reliable defence clauses, agreed visions, or formal agendas and processes. As such, Greece's position remains vulnerable to Turkiye's threats but also to the possibility that its local partners will accommodate Turkiye if it becomes less aggressive, given the size of its economy and its regional leverage, and thereby downgrade their relationships with Greece.

However, as long as Greece's own thawing of relations with Turkiye maintains momentum, Athens is not at risk of being relegated or isolated. The ongoing improvement in relations looks more promising than during previous periods of rapprochement, and domestically Mitsotakis and Erdoğan are in comfortable enough political positions to be able to engage constructively with each other.

Greece's energy and infrastructure positioning also ensures geopolitical relevance. The country is at present the only viable transit route to Europe for expected renewable energy from the Middle East and is the likely first European continental stop for any connectivity project going through Israel and Cyprus. Greece is well positioned to be one of the beneficiaries of large connectivity projects such as the India–Middle East–Europe Corridor (IMEC) if they materialise.

US diplomacy remains the ultimate instrument of pressure and mediation. Turkish air and sea intrusions diminished considerably after the US intervened and later agreed to modernise Turkiye's air force. However, in Washington, the fatigue caused by seemingly intractable Middle Eastern conflicts and the desire to focus on the Indo-Pacific region mean that Greece likely has limited time to settle its maritime disputes. US officials would prefer a resolution that frees up policy attention and military resources but are unwilling to shepherd a process that might fail.

A confluence of factors, including the Ukraine war and the green transition, is providing Greece with a window of opportunity to become one of Europe's leading nodes for its connectivity with the Mediterranean, North Africa and the Gulf. To fulfil this potential, it will need to resolve the domestic delays in its hydrocarbon explorations and secure the necessary financing for its mega-infrastructure projects, while also keeping tensions with Turkiye in check.

The Greek *Hydra* frigate in the harbour of Thessaloniki, Greece, on 28 October 2018. (Photo: Nicolas Economou/NurPhoto via Getty Images)

ENDNOTES

1. Eric Albert and Marina Rafenberg, 'Greece Painfully Rebuilds Its Economy After 15 Years of Depression', *Le Monde*, 29 October 2023, https://www.lemonde.fr/en/economy/article/2023/10/29/greece-painfully-rebuilds-its-economy-after-15-years-of-depression_6211022_19.html.

2. *Ibid*.

3. Independent Evaluator Appointed by the European Stability Mechanism Board of Governors, 'Lessons from Financial Assistance to Greece', June 2020, https://www.esm.europa.eu/system/files/document/2021-07/lessons-financial-assistance-greece.pdf.

4. Philip Inman and Helena Smith, 'Greek Economy to Shrink 25% by 2014', *Guardian*, 18 September 2012, https://www.theguardian.com/business/2012/sep/18/greek-economy-shrink-great-depression.

5. Interview on 21 March 2023 with Konstantinos Nikolaou, the vice-president of Energean, the company that owns the Eastern Mediterranean's first gas floating production storage and offloading (FPSO) platform, off the coast of Israel, and operates Greece's only productive oilfield, Prinos. He said during the interview that 'Greece is a promising but difficult terrain, so the [reduced] tax rate gave an incentive to companies to invest'.

6. 'Greece to Sign Three Oil, Gas Concession Deals', Reuters, 8 May 2014, https://www.reuters.com/article/markets/commodities/greece-to-sign-three-oil-gas-concession-deals-may-14-idUSL6N0NU51H/.

7. 'Greece Approves Applications by Total-ExxonMobil, Energean for Offshore Oil Exploration', Reuters, 23 June 2017, https://www.reuters.com/article/legal/government/greece-approves-applications-by-total-exxonmobil-energean-for-offshore-oil-expl-idUSL8N1JK2LP/; and 'Greece Awards Exxon, Total Tenders for Crete Oil and Gas Exploration', Reuters, 3 July 2018, https://www.reuters.com/article/idUSL8N1TZ4I3/.

8. 'Repsol, Hellenic Sign Lease Deals to Look for Oil in Western Greece', Reuters, 9 April 2019, https://www.reuters.com/article/breakingviews/repsol-hellenic-sign-lease-deals-to-look-for-oil-in-western-greece-idUSL8N21R1NP/.

9. 'TotalEnergies Pulls Out of Gas Exploration Contracts Off Crete', Reuters, 19 July 2022, https://www.reuters.com/business/energy/totalenergies-pulls-gas-exploration-contracts-off-crete-2022-07-19/.

10. Interview in 2023 with energy-industry officials.

11. Chryssa Liaggou and Costis P. Papadiochos, 'Decision Time for Gas Reserves Off Crete', ekathimerini.com, 25 March 2024, https://www.ekathimerini.com/economy/1234750/decision-time-for-the-gas-reserves-off-crete/.

12. Chryssa Liaggou, 'First Gas Load to Alexandroupoli', ekathimerini.com, 15 February 2024, https://www.ekathimerini.com/economy/1231731/first-gas-load-to-alexandroupoli-fsru/.

13. Lahav Harkov, 'US Informs Israel It No Longer Supports EastMed Pipeline to Europe', *Jerusalem Post*, 18 January 2022, https://www.jpost.com/international/article-693866.

14. US Embassy and Consulate in Greece, 'Statement on East Med Energy Cooperation', 10 January 2022, https://gr.usembassy.gov/statement-on-east-med-energy-cooperation/.

15. Marian Wendt and Eleftherios Petropoulos, 'Energy Region Greece & Eastern Mediterranean – a Region Arises as Europe's Supplier!', Konrad Adenauer Stiftung, 20 March 2023, https://www.kas.de/en/country-reports/detail/-/content/energy-region-greece-eastern-mediterranean.

16. Article 156 of the Maniatis law states: 'Absent a delimitation agreement with neighbouring states whose coasts are adjacent or opposite Greek coasts, the outer limit of the continental shelf and exclusive economic zone (once it is declared) is the line of equidistance.' See Greece, *Official Gazette*, 'NOMOΣ Yp' ARITh. 4001 FEK A 179/22.8.2011 Gia th leitourgía Energeiakών Agorών Hlektrismoύ kai Fysikoύ Aerίou, gia Έreyna, paragwgή kai díktya metaforás Ydrogonanthrákwn kai álles rythmíseis' ΝΟΜΟΣ ΥΠ' ΑΡΙΘ. 4001 ΦΕΚ Α 179/22.8.2011 Για τη λειτουργία Ενεργειακών Αγορών Ηλεκτρισμού και Φυσικού Αερίου, για Έρευνα, Παραγωγή και δίκτυα μεταφοράς Υδρογονανθράκων και άλλες ρυθμίσεις ['Law No. 4001/2011 On the Operation of Energy Markets in Electricity and Natural Gas, on the Exploration, Production and Distribution Networks of Hydrocarbons and Other Regulations 22 August 2011], https://www.kodiko.gr/nomothesia/document/121622/nomos-4001-2011.

17. Hellenic National Defence General Staff, 'Violations', https://geetha.mil.gr/sygkentrotikos-pinakas-paraviaseon-ethnikon-chorikon-ydaton-kata-to-etos-2009/.

18. *Ibid*.

19. *Ibid*.

20. The Government of the Republic of Turkey and the Government of National Accord – State of Libya, 'Memorandum of Understanding Between the Government of the Republic of Turkey and the Government of National Accord-State of Libya on Delimitation of the Maritime Jurisdiction Areas in the Mediterranean', 27 November 2019, https://www.un.org/depts/los/LEGISLATIONANDTREATIES/PDFFILES/TREATIES/Turkey_11122019_%28HC%29_MoU_Libya-Delimitation-areas-Mediterranean.pdf.

21. Angeliki Koutantou, 'Greece, Israel, Cyprus Sign EastMed Gas Pipeline Deal', Reuters, 2 January 2020, https://www.reuters.com/article/business/greece-israel-cyprus-sign-eastmed-gas-pipeline-deal-idUSKBN1Z10R4/.

22. 'Erdogan Warns Europe to Expect "Millions" of Migrants After Turkey Opens Borders', France24, 3 March 2020, https://www.france24.com/en/20200303-erdogan-warns-europe-to-expect-millions-of-migrants-after-turkey-opens-borders.

23. Mahmoud Mourad, 'Egypt and Greece Sign Agreement on Exclusive Economic Zone', Reuters, 6 August 2020, https://www.reuters.com/article/world/egypt-and-greece-sign-agreement-on-exclusive-economic-zone-idUSKCN25222G/.

24. Yaroslav Trofimov and David Gauthier-Villars, 'Turkish, Greek Frigates Collide in the Mediterranean Sea', *Wall Street Journal*, 14 August 2020, https://www.wsj.com/articles/turkish-greek-frigates-collide-in-the-mediterranean-sea-11597414995.

25. 'Erdoğan Threatens Greek Islands with Invasion "at Night"', Euractiv, 5 September 2022, https://www.euractiv.com/section/politics/short_news/erdogan-threatens-greek-islands-with-invasion-at-night/.

26. Interview with senior Greek official, February 2024.

27. Hellenic Statistical Authority, 'Commercial Transactions of Greece: May 2024', https://www.statistics.gr/documents/20181/d27c05c8-4553-5b15-5d8b-9cb57fa29a76#:~:text=pandi%40statistics.gr-,The%20deficit%20of%20the%20trade%20balance%2C%20in%20May%202024%20amounted,in%20euros%2C%20of%2013.6%25.

28. Haley Britzky, 'Senators Call on Biden to Delay F-16 Jet Sale to Turkey Until Finland and Sweden Allowed into NATO', CNN, 2 February 2023, https://edition.cnn.com/2023/02/02/politics/senators-biden-f-16-letter-turkey/index.html.

29. US Department of State, 'Joint Statement on the US–Greece Strategic Dialogue', 9 February 2024, https://www.state.gov/joint-statement-on-the-u-s-greece-strategic-dialogue-2/.

30. US Senate Committee on Foreign Relations, 'Congress Passes Menendez–Rubio Bill Reshaping U.S. Policy in Eastern Mediterranean', 20 December 2019, https://www.foreign.senate.gov/press/dem/release/congress-passes-menendez-rubio-bill-reshaping-us-policy-in-eastern-mediterranean_-.

31. 'Turkey Closes the Dardanelles and Bosphorus to Warships', NavalNews, 28 February 2022, https://www.navalnews.com/naval-news/2022/02/turkey-closes-the-dardanelles-and-bosphorus-to-warships/.

32. Greece, Prime Minister's Office, 'Prime Minister Kyriakos Mitsotakis' Address to the Joint Session of the US Congress', 17 May 2022, https://primeminister.gr/en/2022/05/17/29339.

33. Civil–Military Cooperation Centre of Excellence, 'CIMIC Contribution to Operations in the Bab-el-Mandeb and the Red Sea', https://www.cimic-coe.org/resources/fact-sheets/factsheet-operation-prosperity-guardian-aspides.pdf; and EUNAVFOR Operation ASPIDES, 'Hellenic Frigate Hydra Repels Attack by 2 UAVs', 25 April 2024, https://www.eeas.europa.eu/eunavfor-aspides/hellenic-frigate-hydra-repels-attack-2-uavs_en?s=410381.

34 US Department of Defense, Defense Security Cooperation Agency, 'Greece – F-35 Joint Strike Fighter Conventional Take Off and Landing (CTOL) Aircraft', Transmittal no. 23-01, https://www.dsca.mil/press-media/major-arms-sales/greece-f-35-joint-strike-fighter-conventional-take-and-landing-ctol.

35 'Greek Port of Piraeus Finally Sold', DW, 4 August 2016, https://www.dw.com/en/greece-sells-piraeus-port-to-chinese-bidder/a-19174228; and 'Greece Completes Transfer of 16% Stake in Piraeus Port to COSCO', ekathimerini.com, 7 October 2021, https://www.ekathimerini.com/economy/1169346/greece-completes-transfer-of-16-stake-in-piraeus-port-to-cosco/.

36 'China's State Grid Seals Purchase of Stake in Greek Power Grid', Reuters, 16 December 2016, https://www.reuters.com/article/world/europe/chinas-state-grid-seals-purchase-of-stake-in-greek-power-grid-idUSKBN1451SL/.

37 Kaki Bali, 'In Greece's Largest Port of Piraeus, China Is the Boss', DW, 30 October 2022, https://www.dw.com/en/greece-in-the-port-of-piraeus-china-is-the-boss/a-63581221.

38 Naval Group, 'Naval Group Lays the Keel of HS *Formion*, Third Defence and Intervention Frigate (FDI) for the Hellenic Navy', 24 April 2024, https://www.naval-group.com/en/naval-group-lays-keel-hs-formion-third-defence-and-intervention-frigate-fdi-hellenic-navy.

39 IISS, Military Balance+, accessed 27 August 2024.

40 'Diethnés kéntro ekpaídefsis pilóton stin Kalamáta' Διεθνές κέντρο εκπαίδευσης πιλότων στην Καλαμάτα [International pilot-training centre in Kalamata], Kathimerini, 22 June 2020, https://www.kathimerini.gr/1083825/article/epikairothta/ellada/die8nes-kentro-ekpaideyshs-pilotwn-sthn-kalamata.

41 Derek Gatopoulos, 'Israeli-built Flight School Takes Off in Greece, as Athens Seeks Edge over Ankara', *Times of Israel*, 21 October 2022, https://www.timesofisrael.com/israeli-built-flight-school-takes-off-in-greece-as-athens-seeks-edge-over-ankara/.

42 Richard Weitz, 'Turkey-Israeli Defense Relations Under Strain', Second Line of Defense, 6 September 2020, https://sldinfo.com/2010/06/turkey-israeli-defense-relations-under-strain/.

43 Office of the Prime Minister, Greece, 'Prime Minister Kyriakos Mitsotakis' Meeting with Prime Minister Benjamin Netanyahu', 23 October 2023, https://www.primeminister.gr/en/2023/10/23/32850.

44 Hellenic Republic, Ministry of Foreign Affairs, 'Philia Forum – Joint Statement of the Ministers for Foreign Affairs of the Republic of Cyprus, the Arab Republic of Egypt, the Hellenic Republic, the Kingdom of Bahrain, the French Republic, the Kingdom of Saudi Arabia and the Minister of State for International Cooperation of the United Arab Emirates', 11 February 2021, https://www.mfa.gr/en/current-affairs/statements-speeches/joint-statement-of-the-ministers-for-foreign-affairs-of-the-republic-of-cyprus-the-arab-republic-of-egypt-the-hellenic-republic-the-kingdom-of-bahrain-the-french-republic-the-kingdom-of-saudi-arabia-and-the-minister-of-state-for-international-coopera.html.

45 Telecommunication Telephony Satellite Applications, 'EMC (East-Med Corridor)', 27 July 2022, https://www.ttsa.gr/press-releases/emc-east-med-corridor/.

46 'Greece, Saudi Arabia Seal Deal on Data Cable, Discuss Power Grid Link', Reuters, 26 July 2022, https://www.reuters.com/world/middle-east/saudi-crown-prince-heads-greece-france-tuesday-spa-2022-07-26/.

47 'EU's Statement on South China Sea Reflects Divisions', Reuters, 15 July 2016, https://www.reuters.com/article/southchinasea-ruling-eu/eus-statement-on-south-china-sea-reflects-divisions-idUSL8N1A130Y.

The flags of Greece and Cyprus, and Turkiye and the unrecognised Turkish Republic of Northern Cyprus (TRNC) flying on respective security outposts on opposite sides of the United Nations-controlled buffer zone in Nicosia, Cyprus, on 7 February 2020. (Photo: Amir Makar/AFP via Getty Images)

THE DIVISION OF CYPRUS and the associated threat from Turkiye determine every aspect of Cypriot statecraft and contribute to regional tensions. With no prospect of a negotiated settlement on the horizon, Cyprus has pursued deterrence, while the unrecognised Turkish Republic of Northern Cyprus (TRNC) now advocates for a two-state solution.

CYPRUS IS EMBEDDING ITSELF in Eastern Mediterranean networks linking Turkiye's rivals. To gain strategic depth, Nicosia has expanded its relationships with France, Israel and the United States, strengthened ties with Egypt, and courted the Gulf states. Since the Israel–Hamas war started, it has leveraged its geographic location and infrastructure for humanitarian efforts.

CYPRUS'S REGIONAL PROFILE has risen and its networks have broadened, but these ties remain vulnerable to partners' relations with Turkiye. Fatigue over perceived Cypriot obstructionism and unwillingness to risk a deterioration of relations with Ankara limit European and Arab support for Nicosia.

CHAPTER EIGHT

CYPRUS: PROTRACTED DIVISION, INCREASED STRATEGIC DEPTH AND AN ISRAELI GAMBLE

INTRODUCTION

The division of Cyprus between the internationally recognised Republic of Cyprus[1] and the unrecognised Turkish Republic of Northern Cyprus (TRNC) weighs heavily on regional dynamics despite the island's small size, tiny population and limited natural resources. It is a serious impediment to greater regional cooperation and complicates the European Union's cooperation with both Turkiye and NATO.

Dwarfed by Turkiye's larger economy and military power, Cypriot statecraft is shaped by its conflict with the TRNC and Ankara, which dates back to the division of the island in 1974. Faced with this imbalance of power, Cypriot policymakers have sought to mobilise Western and regional support, becoming adept at leveraging their EU membership and identifying opportunities for regional cooperation.

A member of the EU since 2004, Cyprus has also invested in minilateral groupings with Egypt, Greece and Israel aimed at containing Turkiye and to give itself strategic depth. Helped by Greece, Nicosia's diplomatic activism has been driven by a desire to exploit regional enmity towards Turkiye to increase its own security and bargaining power over Ankara. In the process, it has also elevated its relationships with France, the Gulf states, Israel and the US.

Whether this strategy has been successful is questionable. Nicosia's one-issue focus clashes with the multidimensional agendas of other regional and extra-regional players, including rivals of Turkiye. For them, Cyprus's small economy, weak defence establishment and perceived inflexibility on the matter of reunification of the island do not warrant full alignment. While Cyprus has certainly elevated its profile and diplomatic engagements, the depth and intensity of many of its relationships are clearly limited by others' relationships to Turkiye.

Nevertheless, Cyprus has proven agile, opportunistic and deft in its regional statecraft. It has seized on the Israel–Hamas war to deepen its already expanding ties with Israel and to pitch itself as an invaluable staging ground for both Western contingency planning and humanitarian aid provision.

Cyprus's position on the island's peace process has complicated its diplomatic relationships. Even friendly countries have criticised the Cypriot leadership for having passed up two opportunities for resolution – first during a 2004 referendum on a United Nations reunification plan and then at UN-sponsored talks held in 2017 – and for stalling the issue in order to preserve the status quo. Turkish and Western officials, including from Greece, point to these missed opportunities as having contributed to the hardening of Turkish President Recep Tayyip Erdoğan's Eastern Mediterranean policy. Yet Nicosia may think it has enough international support to resist compromise, except on extremely favourable terms.

Cyprus's prospects were buoyed by the discovery of gas fields in the Mediterranean Sea in 2010. Yet Cypriot gas drilling and exploration activities, seen by Nicosia as a way to assert sovereignty and build political and commercial relationships, have also had a negative impact on relations with the Turkish Cypriots and Turkiye.

FIGURE 8.1: **TIMELINE OF THE CYPRUS PROBLEM**

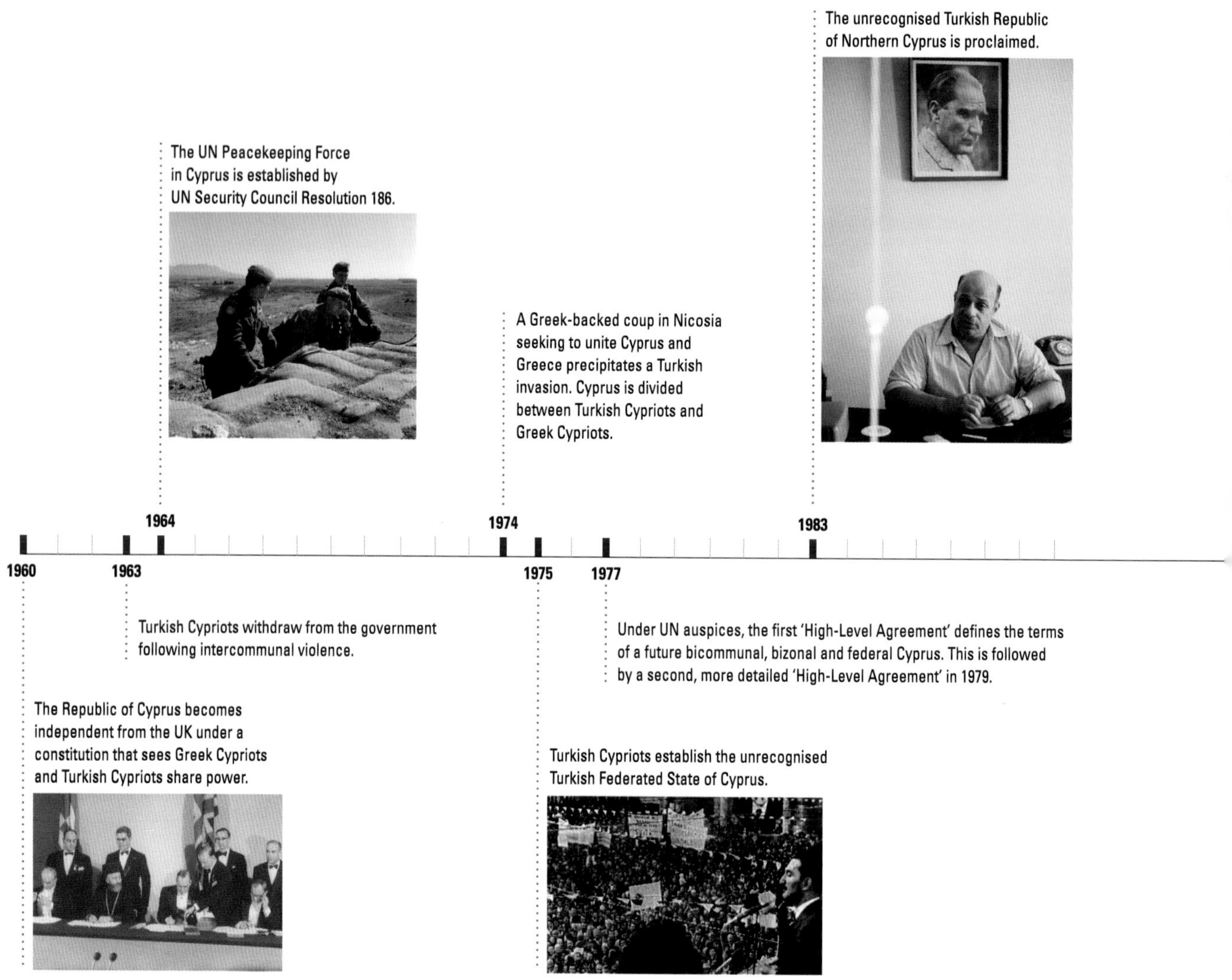

- **1960**: The Republic of Cyprus becomes independent from the UK under a constitution that sees Greek Cypriots and Turkish Cypriots share power.
- **1963**: Turkish Cypriots withdraw from the government following intercommunal violence.
- **1964**: The UN Peacekeeping Force in Cyprus is established by UN Security Council Resolution 186.
- **1974**: A Greek-backed coup in Nicosia seeking to unite Cyprus and Greece precipitates a Turkish invasion. Cyprus is divided between Turkish Cypriots and Greek Cypriots.
- **1975**: Turkish Cypriots establish the unrecognised Turkish Federated State of Cyprus.
- **1977**: Under UN auspices, the first 'High-Level Agreement' defines the terms of a future bicommunal, bizonal and federal Cyprus. This is followed by a second, more detailed 'High-Level Agreement' in 1979.
- **1983**: The unrecognised Turkish Republic of Northern Cyprus is proclaimed.

Source: IISS analysis

'HOSTAGE TO HISTORY': THE CYPRUS PROBLEM

Nicosia's attention is fully focused on what is generally termed 'the Cyprus problem'[2] (see Figure 8.1). In 1974, following years of communal strife and a Greek-sponsored coup in Nicosia, Turkiye invaded and occupied an area of northern Cyprus amounting to 36% of the island's territory.[3] Ankara quickly set about entrenching its control over the territory, including by encouraging mainland Turks to settle there. In 1983, the Turkish Cypriots proclaimed the occupied territory's independence as the TRNC, which is recognised only by Turkiye and dependent on it for access to the outside world. Keeping the TRNC isolated is a core part of Cyprus's international strategy.[4]

As a domestic and external policy challenge, the Cyprus problem shapes Nicosia's strategic calculus.[5] Cypriot officials argue that 'everything is about security'.[6] Conscious of its military inferiority, Nicosia sees diplomacy and international law as the principal means by which to build support for its position and to generate sufficient leverage to force Ankara into concessions or behavioural change. It views Turkiye as an imminent existential threat that constrains Cypriot policymaking at every level: it claims that it has some 40,000 soldiers in Cyprus, in line with Cypriot estimates.[7,8] Informed sources suggest the true number is between 12,000 and 15,000.[9] Turkiye has begun modernising and expanding its military infrastructure in northern Cyprus, including an airfield that could host uninhabited aerial vehicles (UAVs).[10,11]

The UN has run the Cyprus peace process since the 1970s. While Greek and Turkish Cypriot sides had agreed in principle to reunify Cyprus as a bizonal, bicommunal federation (BBF) in what is known as the high-level agreement of 12 February 1977,[12] issues including security guarantees, foreign forces, political representation and property have since removed that agreement. In 2004, Greek

Timeline

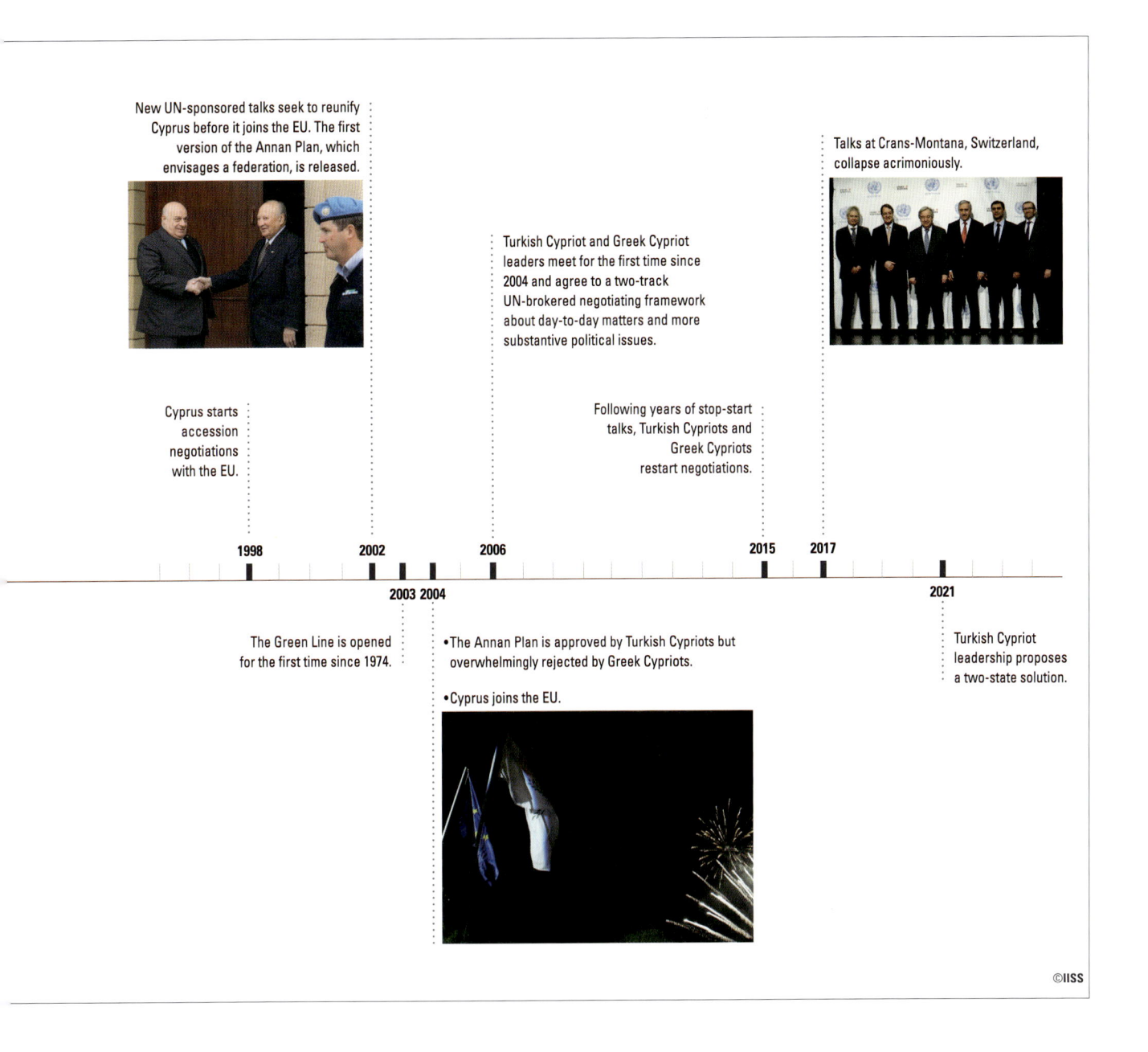

1998 — Cyprus starts accession negotiations with the EU.

2002 — New UN-sponsored talks seek to reunify Cyprus before it joins the EU. The first version of the Annan Plan, which envisages a federation, is released.

2003 — The Green Line is opened for the first time since 1974.

2004 —
- The Annan Plan is approved by Turkish Cypriots but overwhelmingly rejected by Greek Cypriots.
- Cyprus joins the EU.

2006 — Turkish Cypriot and Greek Cypriot leaders meet for the first time since 2004 and agree to a two-track UN-brokered negotiating framework about day-to-day matters and more substantive political issues.

2015 — Following years of stop-start talks, Turkish Cypriots and Greek Cypriots restart negotiations.

2017 — Talks at Crans-Montana, Switzerland, collapse acrimoniously.

2021 — Turkish Cypriot leadership proposes a two-state solution.

©IISS

Cypriot voters overwhelmingly rejected the UN-sponsored Annan Plan for reunification, viewing it as a foreign-designed technocratic imposition – with some officials going as far as claiming it 'would have rendered legal the illegal entity in the north';[13] the majority of Turkish Cypriots voted in favour. Cyprus became an EU member soon after, fuelling Turkish Cypriot and Turkish resentment and disqualifying the EU as a mediator in their eyes. Talks in 2017 in Crans-Montana, Switzerland, collapsed acrimoniously. Most stakeholders now see these failed negotiations as missed opportunities for compromise and resolution that were followed by a hardening of positions and renewed maximalist claims on both sides.

With no prospect of a negotiated settlement on the horizon, both sides have tried to break out. Concerned that EU and regional support has made Cyprus embrace the status quo instead of exploring concessions, the Turkish Cypriots and Turkiye have now rejected the BBF formula in an attempt to shake up perceived Cypriot obstruction and complacency. They have adopted a more aggressive stance and are pushing for recognition for their state, albeit with no success so far. Cyprus, hoping to capitalise on shared animosity towards Turkiye, has looked to Western and Eastern Mediterranean powers to build up leverage and deterrence. It appears to be willing to live with the status quo for the time being, not seeing an opportunity for renewed negotiations. Both sides' moves are designed – in the words of a Turkish diplomat – to push the other 'out of their comfort zone' sufficiently far to make concessions.[14] Neither strategy has worked; instead, frustration and regional tensions have increased.[15]

GOODBYE REUNIFIED CYPRUS?

The 2017 Crans-Montana talks proved to be a critical juncture. Each side has blamed the other (as well as the UN) for the failure of this track, while each recognises that more progress was made than at any time since at least 2004. According to British and Cypriot diplomats present, Turkiye is understood to have verbally offered surprising concessions that included reducing its military presence to 650 soldiers and abolishing the Treaty of Guarantees, through which it has intervention rights in Cyprus.[16,17] Turkish officials maintain that they did not define the numbers they might draw down to. To reduce the chances of a deadlock, the parties negotiated on two tracks simultaneously: one on the governance structure of the island, which was Turkiye's priority, and the other on the security arrangements, on which Cyprus and Greece were more focused, according to Turkish officials involved in the talks. Turkiye, which was represented by then-foreign minister Mevlüt Çavuşoğlu, reportedly made a verbal offer that included an immediate 'significant reduction' of its military presence and a review of the presence of the remaining forces at the end of three election cycles based on the governance negotiation happening simultaneously. They did not specify the number of forces they would initially keep and refused to agree to a sunset clause or commit to a full withdrawal in order to retain leverage to guarantee the rights of Turkish Cypriots. Cypriot diplomats challenge this interpretation, and say that Turkish concessions were vague and conditional (dependent, for example, on Greece making similar concessions). With serious differences still unresolved, then-president of Cyprus Nicos Anastasiades walked away (Turkiye was represented by its foreign minister, Mevlüt Çavuşoğlu). Many Western and UN officials who attended blame Anastasiades for being insufficiently interested in a settlement as he wanted to burnish his nationalist credentials ahead of an upcoming presidential election.[18] Turkish diplomats have stated that an equivalent offer is unlikely to be tabled again.[19]

HARDENING OF THE TURKISH AND TRNC POSITIONS

This failure deflated the peace process and catalysed deep changes in Turkiye's all-round approach to Cyprus, in which it abandoned its support for a BBF in favour of a loose confederal or two-state solution. Ankara also began to intervene more overtly in northern Cyprus's domestic affairs to the benefit of its hardline government.

Within the TRNC, the moderate federalist camp was weakened by the failure at Crans-Montana and Anastasiades's alleged refusal to meet then-president of the TRNC Mustafa Akıncı halfway. Ankara threw its weight behind Ersin Tatar, Akıncı's rival and the National Unity Party (UBP) candidate during the 2020 presidential elections. Since winning that election, Tatar has stated that he wants recognition of Turkish Cypriots' 'sovereign equality' as a precondition for future talks, and advocates for a two-state solution.

This harder TRNC line has manifested on the ground. Immediately after Tatar's election, the Turkish Cypriots symbolically partially reopened fenced-off areas of Varosha, a town abandoned by Greek Cypriot residents in 1974, and which had become a ghost town after the division, a living symbol of what once was. This triggered worries in Nicosia about unilateral changes to the status quo there and at other sites that could deal a 'final blow' to reunification prospects.[20] Turkish steps to upgrade the TRNC's international status and activities within Cyprus's exclusive economic zone (EEZ) further poisoned the atmosphere.

The distance between the two sides was underlined at the most recent talks in Geneva in 2021. Informal 5+1 discussions (Cyprus, Greece, Turkiye, Turkish Cypriots and the United Kingdom, joined by the UN) ended in deadlock. Tatar presented a six-point proposal outlining his 'vision for two-state solution' that demanded recognition of the Turkish Cypriots' 'sovereign equality and equal international status' as a precondition for negotiations.[21] Nicosia, still backing a BBF solution, deemed such demands to be unacceptable.

Whether Turkiye could be coaxed back to serious negotiations is uncertain. Many in Nicosia are watching for signs that a window of opportunity may open, but none has come.[22] Officials in Ankara say that the position has shifted for good, regardless of who holds the Turkish presidency.[23] Meanwhile, Turkiye has begun pushing for international recognition for the TRNC. In September 2022, Erdoğan called at the UN General Assembly for recognition, a move that Turkish diplomats privately admit is unlikely to come. Nicosia has historically maintained a remarkably successful counter-secession strategy based on its EU membership.

Given that Cyprus joined in 2004 on an all-island basis, any recognition risks a punitive response from Brussels and EU member states. Cypriot diplomats are nevertheless 'alarmed' by the new approach.[24]

The TRNC's new approach has created problems for the UN Peacekeeping Force in Cyprus (UNFICYP), which patrols the demilitarised Green Line. The Turkish Cypriots first demanded in September 2022 that the UNFICYP sign a 'Status-of-Forces Agreement' (SOFA) with them. SOFAs regulate the presence of foreign military forces in another state. The Turkish Cypriots issued an ultimatum the following month to the UNFICYP and have submitted a draft SOFA. The UN, for legal reasons, cannot sign a SOFA with the Turkish Cypriots, but is still looking for a way forward.[25] In August 2023, three UNFICYP peacekeepers trying to prevent the construction of a road passing through portions of the Green Line were wounded after being assaulted by Turkish Cypriots. This worrying escalation was followed by Turkish accusations that the UN was abandoning its neutral position in Cyprus.[26]

A STATUS QUO PREFERRED BY THE REPUBLIC OF CYPRUS

There are also serious doubts among foreign officials about the Greek Cypriots' desire for a settlement. Some officials and politicians in Nicosia see the status quo as advantageous: Cyprus's economy is prospering, its regional and international partnerships are strengthening and the cost for Turkiye of forcing a change is prohibitive. In contrast, a minority of officials worry about complacency and widening societal divides between northerners and southerners that would make a settlement impossible.

Nikos Christodoulides, who was elected president of the Republic of Cyprus in 2023, claims that he is still interested in a settlement based on a BBF. Christodoulides was the most hardline candidate during the presidential elections and has expressed reservations about the 'Guterres Framework' that was presented at Crans-Montana, which would be expected to be the starting point of any future BBF-based negotiations.[27] Christodoulides, who served as foreign minister from 2018 to 2022, is also deeply distrusted in Ankara and in northern Cyprus, and is seen as inflexible by foreign partners.

Christodoulides has proposed that the EU takes a greater role through creating a dedicated 'Cyprus Envoy', hoping to create a linkage between Turkiye–EU relations and progress over Cyprus. However, Turkiye and the Turkish Cypriots do not see the EU as an honest broker given the bloc's 2004 decision to admit Cyprus despite its rejection of the Annan Plan. In that vein, they denied observer status to the EU in Geneva in 2021. The EU itself is unwilling to be dragged into this dispute, especially as several EU member states have more important priorities with Ankara. The UK, which ceased being an EU member in 2020, is traditionally the most engaged major external player on the Cyprus problem and has a record of investing significant efforts in trying to bring the sides together in recent years, despite a lack of interest elsewhere. However, distrust of the UK is rife in Nicosia over its perceived proximity to Ankara.

Meanwhile, Turkiye has tightened its grip on northern Cyprus, with its influence having become overt and decisive. In 2022, Turkiye engineered internal UBP dynamics to its advantage, while the space for Turkish Cypriot opposition activists to express dissent has shrunk. Ankara's current ambassador is widely believed to have come with a mission to curb the judiciary, one of the last remaining independent institutions.[28] A controversial protocol signed with Turkiye in April 2022, which was condemned by all parties except those in the ruling coalition, included provisions that introduced significant curbs on civil and political freedoms and have made it easier for mainland Turks who have moved to the island to secure TRNC citizenship.[29] There are no accurate statistics on the number of citizenships handed out each year, but estimates point to a marked uptick; since then, an estimated average of 14 naturalisations took place every day between 2017 and 2021, before jumping to around 50 per day by late 2022.[30] Long-term social, political and demographic transformations ultimately point to the TRNC's de facto integration into Turkiye.

> GAS IS SOMETIMES TOUTED AS A CATALYST THAT COULD CHANGE THE PARAMETERS OF THE CYPRUS PROBLEM. THIS MAY HAVE BEEN THE CASE PREVIOUSLY BUT SEEMS UNLIKELY IN THE CURRENT CLIMATE.

HYBRID WARFARE: MIGRATION

Nicosia accuses Ankara and the TRNC of instrumentalising migration, although this is firmly denied by Ankara.[31,32] Over 90% of asylum-seekers cross the Green Line after arriving in the TRNC – with a brief transit in Türkiye – on poorly regulated student visas.[33] Ankara is likely to be turning a blind eye to the issue as it has no incentive to prevent those with legally valid visas from transiting its territory.

This is a serious problem for Cyprus. In 2022 and 2023, it had the highest percentage of asylum applications per capita in Europe. In 2022, first-time asylum applicants made up 2.4% of Cyprus's population, versus 0.32% in Germany.[34] In 2023, first-time asylum applicants made up 1.3% of the population compared with 0.4% in Germany.[35] In March 2023, Nicosia estimated holders and applicants of international protection made up over 6% of Cyprus's population.[36] Cyprus claims that it is hosting refugees and asylum-seekers at a rate five times higher than other EU front-line states.[37] These migrants see Cyprus as an easy way to get into the EU.

Another migrant route is Lebanon, from where Lebanese, Palestinian and Syrian asylum-seekers depart by boat to reach Cyprus (as well as Greece and Italy). The war in Gaza and worsening conditions in Syria and Lebanon have compelled Nicosia to increase its cooperation with Lebanese security agencies and to enrol EU support to prevent further inflows.

PURSUING INTEGRATION AND BETTING ON THE US

Cyprus has been increasingly active in the Eastern Mediterranean since 2010, deepening its diplomatic ties, participating in trilaterals and delimiting its maritime borders. This growing footprint is tied closely to two developments: the crises in Türkiye's regional relationships and energy discoveries in Eastern Mediterranean waters (see Chapter Three).

What began as opportunistic outreach to Egypt and Israel has since developed into a wider diplomatic tag-team with Greece. Cyprus's intention here is to shape the region through trilateral and multilateral initiatives, in

Israeli defence minister Avigdor Lieberman (L), Cypriot defence minister Savvas Angelides (C) and Greek defence minister Panos Kammenos (R) review an honour guard prior to their meeting at a defence-industry conference in Larnaca, Cyprus, on 22 June 2018. (Photo: Iakovos Hatzistavrou/AFP via Getty Images)

addition to anchoring security and political partnerships that can help balance Türkiye and support Nicosia's positions on the Cyprus problem and maritime disputes. When describing Nicosia's current approach, one senior diplomat said 'If bilateralism is one hand, then trilateralism is the other'.[38] But there are limits to this approach. Cyprus has not succeeded in formalising alliances with any of its partners. Recent trilaterals have deepened relations, but they have not come with mutual commitments. 'There isn't even institutionalised information sharing', one high-level Cypriot official said in 2023, before adding 'there are lots of Cypriot delusions about these relationships, we often take our wishes for realities.'[39]

Despite the absence of formal alliances, Cyprus has intensified its defence and military relationships with Egypt, France, Israel and the US, participating in joint drills amongst other activities (see Table 8.1). Cyprus and the US signed a SOFA in December 2002.[40] In 2022 and 2023, Nicosia signed a raft of first-time agreements: a partnership agreement with the New Jersey Army National Guard, a bilateral defence-cooperation programme with the US, a memorandum of understanding on strategic cooperation with the UK and a bilateral military-cooperation plan with Germany.

Since 2020, it has participated in four military exercises with international partners, including bilateral exercises with France, Israel and the US, and multilateral exercises with France, Greece and Israel, as well as with France, Greece and Italy (see Figure 4.5, page 95).

Since the Hamas-led 7 October attacks against Israel, Nicosia has intensified its already deepening security and intelligence cooperation with Tel Aviv. It has become a haven for thousands of Israelis who sought temporary refuge from the conflict. Simultaneously, it positioned itself as the natural logistical hub for both Western evacuation planning and large-scale operations to deliver humanitarian aid to Gaza. In the immediate aftermath of the Israeli offensive in Gaza, it proposed a maritime corridor to deliver aid. In March 2024 the EU Commission announced the launch of the Cyprus-led Amalthea plan for a maritime corridor to ship aid to Gaza with the backing of Germany, Greece, Italy, the Netherlands, the United Arab Emirates (UAE), the UK and the US.

The US evacuated citizens from Israel to Cyprus in the immediate aftermath of the 7 October attacks. Germany dispatched military personnel to the island to prepare contingencies for potential evacuation plans in case of a wider regional war.[41] The UK has used its sovereign military bases on the island for its air operations to counter Houthi attacks in the Red Sea, in addition to its considerable intelligence, surveillance and reconnaissance capabilities.

CYPRUS AND GREECE – A SPECIAL RELATIONSHIP

The cornerstone of Cyprus's foreign relationships is Greece. Cyprus is not a mere regional matter for Greece, but a domestic one as well. In addition to deep familial and cultural links, Athens is a guarantor power and has a regiment-sized military presence on the island. Defence cooperation is broad and intense. Greece not only voices and amplifies Cypriot concerns within the EU and other fora, but also involves Nicosia when others have not.

Their relationship is, nevertheless, more nuanced than often assumed. Some Greek officials describe Cyprus as a political, diplomatic and military free rider, which automatically expects support from Greece regardless of the inconvenience or cost to Athens. They explain that Greek advocacy for Cyprus is a way to share responsibility for Cypriot stability with other countries, and therefore be less exposed. In turn, there are questions in Nicosia about the strength of the Greek security commitment, as well as concerns that Greek attention could fade. Some Cypriot officials privately question whether Greece would intervene in case of Turkish aggression. Nicosia feels that Greece sometimes prioritises its relationship with Türkiye over Cyprus, with one recent example being Athens's backing for the Turkish General Secretaryship of the International Maritime Organization.

DEEPER REGIONAL TIES

Israel has become, after Greece, Cyprus's closest partner in the Eastern Mediterranean. Israeli officials quietly supported Cyprus's bid to join the EU in the 1990s, but relations blossomed after the Mavi Marmara incident when Israeli commandos killed Turkish activists trying to break the blockade of Gaza in 2010, upending Israeli–Turkish relations. Later that year, Israel and Cyprus delimited their EEZs. The expansion in ties, especially in defence, has since been rapid. The Israel–Cyprus–Greece trilateral started in 2016. It has been the most substantive of the regional minilaterals and has allowed Cyprus to tap into Israel's and Greece's improving relationships with the US, Europe and the Gulf states. Nicosia sees itself as giving Israel regional 'strategic depth', an assessment echoed by some Israeli officials.[42]

TABLE 8.1: RECENT TRENDS IN CYPRUS'S BILATERAL RELATIONSHIPS AS OF MAY 2024

Country	Trend
Egypt	↑ Strengthening
France	↑ Strengthening
Greece	= Unchanged
Israel	↑ Strengthening
Russia	↓ Weakening
Saudi Arabia	↑ Strengthening
Türkiye	⊖ No relationship
UAE	↑ Strengthening
UK	= Unchanged
US	↑ Strengthening

Source: IISS analysis

Cyprus has been an enthusiastic defence partner of Israel, perceiving this relationship as helping to modernise and diversify its own defence capabilities. The two countries signed a SOFA in 2016. Israeli training and military layovers are now regular in Cyprus. In 2022, Israel Defense Forces ground, naval, and air forces were deployed to Cyprus as part of the *Agapinor-2022* exercise, which simulated a war with Iran and Hizbullah.[43] In March 2023, Cyprus and Israel signed further bilateral and trilateral defence agreements and Nicosia has been a regular participant in the *Noble Dina* naval exercise with Greece, Israel and the US. Cyprus has purchased Israeli weaponry, including big-ticket systems such as Iron Dome air-defence system in August 2022 and *Aerostar* tactical UAVs in 2019.[44] Israel is also helping to build a land-monitoring system to monitor asylum-seekers crossing the Green Line. In June 2023 Cyprus reportedly was in advanced talks over the acquisition of Israeli *Merkava* III tanks.[45]

Cyprus calculates that long-term changes catalysed by the Abraham Accords could work to its benefit, especially as the Accords have so far been ring-fenced from fallout from the Israel–Hamas war. Nicosia wants to be included in the Negev Forum, and invitations to Gulf states to participate in multilaterals reflect what Cypriot diplomats dub the 'coalescing' of old and new partnership networks.[46] Among the clearest Cypriot initiatives is the 2021 quadrilateral Paphos Forum of Cyprus–Greece–Israel–UAE and its recent enthusiasm in courting Riyadh.[47] The expectation in Cyprus is that these relationships will strengthen its deterrence vis-à-vis Turkiye.

Egypt is the other key regional relationship for Cyprus. Nicosia was concerned that Muhammad Morsi, Egypt's Muslim Brotherhood president in 2012–13, would embrace Turkish foreign-policy views, so it quickly welcomed his replacement, President Abdel Fattah al-Sisi, even though it was through a coup. The Cyprus–Egypt–Greece trilateral agreement was launched in 2014: the *Medusa* annual air and naval exercises conducted in this format since 2018 have increased search-and-rescue interoperability with Egypt and have allowed Cyprus to interact with Gulf militaries. While Israel has been careful not to antagonise Turkiye by weighing in on legal maritime issues, Egypt has been more supportive of Cyprus's legal posi-

Cypriot president Nicos Anastasiades (L) receives Egyptian President Abdel Fattah al-Sisi (R) during an official ceremony upon the latter's arrival at the presidential palace in Nicosia, Cyprus, on 20 November 2017.
(Photo: Iakovos Hatzistavrou/AFP via Getty Images)

tions on its maritime borders. In return, Cyprus has often echoed Egyptian priorities in EU settings.

In parallel, Cyprus has also had to manage complex relations with Lebanon and Syria. Security and migration risks have dominated the Cypriot agenda. The economic links are small, despite many Lebanese and some Syrians having settled on the island due to its proximity, stability and ease of doing business. While there have been some defence and intelligence exchanges with Lebanon, political instability in Beirut, as well as concerns about Iranian influence, have limited this relationship. Cypriot security agencies are indeed worried about possible attacks against Israeli soft targets conducted by Iranian-backed groups. However, Nicosia has actively lobbied the EU to support Lebanese institutions, notably to stop the influx of refugees.

Refugees, as well as a shared animosity towards Turkiye, also shape Cypriot views on Syria. Cypriot officials quietly confide their preference for resuming relations with the Assad regime, which have been frozen since 2011. However, Cyprus's relations with Syria are constrained by EU policy and its lack of leverage in Damascus. In addition to other priorities, this means it is not well positioned to change EU priorities.

As for its maritime borders, Cyprus has not delimited its border with Syria, though it is not a contentious situation. An agreement was reached with Lebanon in 2007, although it has still not been ratified by the Lebanese parliament. Cyprus and Lebanon are expected to adjust their agreement to reflect the 2022 agreement between Lebanon and Israel, which would move the common maritime-border point between Cyprus, Israel and Lebanon southwards, giving Lebanon more territory.

RECALIBRATING INTERNATIONAL RELATIONSHIPS

Central to Cyprus's offering is a self-proclaimed role as a bridge between Europe and the Eastern Mediterranean. Nicosia casts itself as an honest interpreter and broker that can mediate and moderate criticism of Middle Eastern partners within the EU and influence the European Neighbourhood Policy.[48] Leveraging EU membership, Cypriot diplomats admit, is fundamental.[49] There is evidence that it has been successful. President Sisi has thanked Cyprus for its role in voicing Egyptian concerns in Brussels.[50] Cypriot parliamentary speaker Yiannakis Omirou, on a visit to Cairo in 2016, said that Cyprus was 'ready to be the representative of Egypt and its ambassador in European organisations'.[51] Cyprus has also raised Israeli, Jordanian and Lebanese issues in European fora, while Saudi Arabia has said it sees Cyprus as a 'bridge'.[52,53] Cyprus, in exchange, expects support for its position on the division of Cyprus and maritime disputes with Turkiye, which it does receive. For example, Egypt 'holds the flag' for Cyprus at the Organisation of Islamic Cooperation, a rare forum where the Turkish Cypriots are represented.[54]

In addition to its perch within the EU, Cyprus has worked on recalibrating its international ties, downgrading its relations with Russia while promoting those it has with the US and Gulf countries.

After a period of proximity with Russia, which peaked in the early 2010s before and during the banking crisis of 2012–13, Cyprus seems to have finally downgraded this relationship. Instead, Anastasiades invested in building ties with Paris and Washington. Cyprus has made serious progress over the past five years with the US in particular, with the 3+1 grouping of Cyprus–Greece–Israel–US gaining relevance. Washington has also sought to reward Nicosia for scrapping an agreement with Moscow that permitted port calls by Russian vessels in Cyprus and for tightening anti-money-laundering efforts and regulation and oversight of its banking sector.[55] In 2023, Washington removed remaining elements of its long-standing arms embargo on Cyprus, which had pushed Nicosia towards Soviet and then Russian suppliers.[56,57] It represented a significant boost to Nicosia's international standing. 'The US embargo was an albatross for a long time, it affected how countries saw us and [they] refused to deal with us', one Cypriot official said.[58] Its removal has facilitated Cyprus's shift towards other weapons suppliers – including Israel – and away from Russia. Because Nicosia has lost technical support for its many Russian-manufactured weapons systems, it was forced to look elsewhere.

Cyprus's shift away from Russia and towards alignment with Europe and Washington is also visible through its participation in the training of Ukrainian soldiers in Germany under the EU's Military Assistance Mission. Ukrainian personnel are also being trained by Cypriot, Irish and US personnel in demining activities in Cyprus itself.[59]

The March 2023 Partnership Agreement with the New Jersey Army National Guard will involve cooperation and training across a range of areas, including cyber defence, communications and maritime security. Given that NATO membership is a near impossibility, integration into the web of US security partnerships serves as an important long-term hedge for Cyprus, even if it does not affect the on-the-ground security picture on the island. Instead, the Cypriot leadership 'sees a tripwire US presence' in the Eastern Mediterranean and wants to 'anchor' Cyprus to the US by building closer security ties and proving its credibility as a partner.[60] While Cyprus has high expectations of the relationship with the US, US policy remains non-committal. The US is not seeking to increase its footprint in the Eastern Mediterranean. Important voices in the US State Department and the Pentagon are keen on maintaining good relations with Turkiye, a prickly ally in the eyes of Washington, but one that has the second-largest army in NATO and a pivotal geographic location. Officials in Nicosia have therefore seen Cyprus's role as the logistical hub for Western military and humanitarian efforts during the Israel–Hamas war as potentially changing US perspectives on the position of the island in its regional defence posture.

Finally, Cyprus has also begun to look towards the Gulf more strategically. For decades, Gulf states chose to align with Turkiye on Eastern Mediterranean issues, partially out of Muslim solidarity. More recently, Bahraini, Emirati and Saudi ties with Cyprus have grown out of a common desire to contain Turkiye and to encourage investment and tourism. In May 2020, the UAE (and France) joined the Cyprus–Egypt–Greece trilateral as the 3+2 issued a strong statement condemning Turkish drilling activities in Cyprus's claimed EEZ. Cyprus has shown interest in joining the French-led patrolling initiative, the European Maritime Awareness in the Strait of Hormuz.[61]

While Cyprus is now visible internationally beyond the Cyprus problem, critics charge that the agreements that Cyprus has struck are political theatre and are sometimes not implemented. Another criticism is that the trilaterals are marriages of convenience that are overly centred on Turkiye. 'There is nothing to keep them together when Turkiye's relationships with Israel and Egypt improve', commented one Cypriot expert.[62] Despite fervent denials, Cypriot officials are clearly nervous about Turkiye's current efforts to patch up its relations with Egypt and the Gulf states, although the Israel–Hamas war complicates a potential rapprochement between Turkiye and Israel.

Another illustration of that gap is Cyprus's keenness to institutionalise its partnerships, while many of its partners want to retain political and strategic flexibility. Cyprus has set up a Permanent Secretariat for the Trilateral Mechanism with Greece and Israel with the intention of formalising these relationships and monitoring agreement implementation. Christodoulides had previously floated an idea for a regional organisation in the Eastern Mediterranean, which has found little support among relevant countries.

CYPRUS AND GAS: PIPE DREAMS?

Hydrocarbons have been heralded as a potential game-changer for Cyprus, both politically and economically. In the early years after the discovery of the first gas fields in Cypriot waters in 2011, the thinking went that, in the best case, gas production could catalyse progress on the Cyprus problem or even lead to a settlement. However, given Turkiye's uncompromising stance towards exploration and drilling activities within Cypriot waters and intra-communal disagreement about revenue sharing between Cyprus and the TRNC, Cyprus's energy hopes have faced strong headwinds.

Cyprus's two biggest discovered fields (Aphrodite/Yishai and Glaucus) are estimated to have up to 240 billion cubic metres (bcm) of remaining reserves combined (see Table 3.1, page 64). Once Cyprus's five discoveries to date become productive, the Center on Global Energy Policy expects the island's gas output to reach a maximum of around 32 bcm per year.[63] The gas in these discoveries lies in areas that are contested by Turkiye – Cyprus has licensed out 13 blocs, of which only two are completely uncontested by either Turkiye or the TRNC (Blocks 10 and 11). These gas discoveries were crucial in kick-starting Cypriot ties to Egypt and Israel, but as of March 2024, Nicosia has not yet overseen the start of gas production because of Cyprus's small market, commercial-contractual disagreements and enduring questions about export options (see Chapter Three). The most realistic near-term energy project is currently not gas-based, but rather the EuroAfrica Interconnector and the Great Sea Interconnector projects that will link the electricity grids of Cyprus, Egypt and Greece, and Cyprus, Greece and Israel, respectively.[64]

Cyprus's gas potential has been undermined, unsurprisingly, by the unresolved Cyprus problem and Turkiye. Ankara, which had already become increasingly alienated by Nicosia's approach, took a sharply aggressive turn after the collapse of the Crans-Montana talks in 2017. Turkish behaviour within Cyprus's EEZ, especially in 2018 and 2019, has made Cypriot gas a geopolitical risk for energy companies and financial institutions.[65] In 2018, Turkiye prevented Eni from drilling at the Cuttlefish prospect in Block 3 in the most serious escalation of the dispute. In retaliation, in 2020 Christodoulides, then foreign minister, held up EU sanctions on Belarus until they were extended to Turkiye in response to drilling in Cyprus's EEZ. This came at a political cost for Cyprus and Christodoulides (since then elected president) as many EU countries perceived them as willing to obstruct EU priorities for their own interests, but this move nevertheless may have induced caution on Turkiye's part. Turkiye has not sent a drilling ship into Cyprus's EEZ since 2020.

Gas is sometimes touted as a catalyst that could change the parameters of the Cyprus problem. This may have been the case previously but seems unlikely in the current climate. Nevertheless, moderate Cypriots on both sides speak of gas as retaining the potential to change the calculus of both sides of the conflict. Nicosia's current offer to the Turkish Cypriots is that if exploitation begins before a final settlement, then a share of revenues would be deposited in escrow pending a settlement, but that this would be conditioned on a delimitation agreement between Ankara and Nicosia. The Turkish Cypriots' position is for a joint committee that could decide on hydrocarbon activities, including revenue sharing. Ironically, such gas-sharing agreements may undermine further prospects for a two-state solution by creating vested interests in the status quo.

Brinkmanship is seen as needed to change the other side's view. In 2011, Turkiye and the TRNC agreed to their own delineation agreement and exploration licences were granted to the Turkish Petroleum Corporation (TPAO).[66] The areas licensed overlap with seven blocks already licensed by Cyprus. Mustafa Ergün Olgun, a powerful Turkish Cypriot negotiator, wrote in 2019 that he believed hydrocarbons had 'aggravated' the Cyprus problem and 'fuelled maritime and territorial disputes'. He added that 'fear of disaster' and pushing the Greek Cypriots out of their 'comfort zone' was the best approach to stimulate 'win-win solutions'.[67] This idea is increasingly echoed in Ankara and the TRNC.

SEARCHING FOR STRATEGY

Cyprus's division and its hostile relationship with Turkiye structure Nicosia's strategy in the Eastern Mediterranean. Cyprus is confident that it can play a weak hand well, but risks falling prey to unrealistic expectations about its relationships with its neighbours and the US. With the focus in Europe and Washington on Ukraine, China and economic challenges, the Cyprus problem has fallen ever lower down the West's priority list, something which could leave Nicosia vulnerable and isolated were Turkiye to rebuild successfully its foreign relationships.

Confident in its new partnerships and standing and pessimistic about peace prospects, Nicosia itself may no longer prioritise solving the Cyprus problem. But the problem will continue to curtail Cyprus's stability, diplomacy and long-term economic prospects. Neither side is likely to return to the negotiating table in the near future with the willingness to make the necessary compromises, despite the rising costs of not doing so.

Instead, Christodoulides is likely to continue what he calls Cyprus's 'extroversion' in the Eastern Mediterranean, since the TRNC's efforts to gain support for a two-state solution are finding no traction internationally and have not reshaped the domestic politics of the south.

It is unlikely that Turkiye's diplomatic progress with both Egypt and Greece since 2023 will weaken Cypriot links to both countries. Likewise, Nicosia's growing ties with the US and Israel appear solid, but contrary to what some Cypriot officials would like, the US shows no desire to increase its footprint in the region, let alone to join or replace the British Armed Forces operating from sovereign bases on the island.

Nicosia will have to balance its rapprochement with Israel with its ties with its Arab neighbours. Since 7 October 2023 it has showed solidarity with Israel but also voted for UN General Assembly resolutions supporting Palestinian self-determination and aligning with mainstream European and Arab positions.

Cyprus's gas reserves can become a boon for the country, but only if Nicosia resolves the outstanding issues holding back the development of its fields, including approving development plans submitted by the international oil companies and reaching a profit-sharing deal with Israel. This will require finding a modus vivendi with Turkiye that ensures a minimum level of calm.

Nicosia's initial gamble on the Eastern Mediterranean (EastMed) Gas Pipeline, which it once saw as geopolitically transformative, will need to be revised. The pipeline now looks unlikely to be built, with floating liquid nitrogen gas facilities appearing to be the most cost-effective route to export gas. Despite its advantageous geographical position, Cyprus's fate remains dictated by its small size.

ENDNOTES

1. In this chapter and throughout this Strategic Dossier, the Republic of Cyprus is referred to as Cyprus.
2. Christopher Hitchens, *Hostage to History: Cyprus from The Ottomans to Kissinger* (London: Verso, 1997), p. 1.
3. James Ker-Lindsay, 'Great Powers, Counter Secession, and Non-Recognition: Britain and the 1983 Unilateral Declaration of Independence of the "Turkish Republic of Northern Cyprus"', *Diplomacy and Statecraft*, vol. 28, no. 3, p. 433.
4. James Ker-Lindsay, 'The Four Pillars of a Counter-Secession Foreign Policy: Lessons from Cyprus', in Eckhart Woertz and Diego Muro (eds), *Secession and Counter-secession: An International Relations Perspective* (Barcelona: CIDOB, 2017), pp. 85–90.
5. Alexandros Zachariades and Petros Petrikkos, 'Balancing for Profit: The Republic of Cyprus' Grand Strategy in the Eastern Mediterranean Sea', *The Cyprus Review*, vol. 32, no. 1, Spring 2020, pp. 89–136, https://cyprusreview.org/index.php/cr/article/view/725/588.
6. Interview with senior diplomat at the Ministry of Foreign Affairs of Cyprus, April 2023.
7. Anna Koukkides-Procopiou, 'All the President's Decisions: Foreign Policy in the Republic of Cyprus After 2004', in Zenonas Tziarras (ed.), *The Foreign Policy of the Republic of Cyprus: Local, Regional, and International Dimensions* (London: Palgrave Macmillan, 2022), p. 55.
8. 'Turkiye to Re-inforce Military Presence in Northern Cyprus – Erdogan', Reuters, 28 September 2022, https://www.reuters.com/world/Turkiye-re-inforce-military-presence-northern-cyprus-erdogan-2022-09-28/.
9. Interview with former UK diplomatic advisor with expertise on Cyprus, April 2023.
10. Neither include figures for the TRNC's own Security Forces Command.
11. Interview with ex-European diplomat and analyst in Nicosia, March 2023; on Turkish military infrastructure expanding in northern Cyprus, see Hasan Selim Özertem, 'Back to "the Tradition": Türkiye's Changing Position From a Federal Position to a Two-State Solution to the Cyprus Conflict', Ifri, July 2021, https://www.ifri.org/en/publications/notes-de-lifri/back-tradition-Turkiyes-changing-position-federal-two-state-solution; see also Dorothee Schmid and Yasmina Dahech, 'Turkey's Method in the Mediterranean: The Hold Over Northern Cyprus', Ifri, July 2021, https://www.ifri.org/en/publications/briefings-de-lifri/turkeys-method-mediterranean-hold-over-northern-cyprus.
12. Republic of Cyprus, Ministry of Interior, 'High-Level Agreement of 12 February 1977', https://www.pio.gov.cy/en/agreements-high-level-agreement-of-12-february-1977.html.
13. Interview with Cypriot official, April 2023.
14. Interview with Turkish official, April 2023.
15. Interview with senior Turkish diplomat, April 2023.
16. The Treaty of Guarantees is one of three treaties under which Cyprus became independent. Greece and the UK are the other guarantors.
17. Interview with diplomat who attended the Crans-Montana talks, April 2023.
18. This is widely stated, but see Alexandra Novosseloff, 'Assessing the Effectiveness of the United Nations Peacekeeping Mission in Cyprus (UNFICYP) and the Office of the Special Adviser to the Secretary-General on Cyprus (OSASG)', Norwegian Institute for International Affairs, 2021, https://effectivepeaceops.net/publication/assessing-effectiveness-of-unficyp-and-osasg/.
19. Interview with senior Turkish diplomat, June 2023.
20. Interview with senior government official of the Republic of Cyprus, March 2023.
21. Turkish Republic of Northern Cyprus, Ministry of Foreign Affairs, 'Our Vision for Two-state Solution', 2021, https://mfa.gov.ct.tr/cyprus-negotiation-process/our-vision-for-two-state-solution/.
22. Interview with Cypriot officials and foreign diplomats, November 2022 and April 2023.
23. Interview with senior Turkish diplomat, March 2023.
24. Interview with senior diplomat at the Ministry of Foreign Affairs of the Republic of Cyprus, April 2023.
25. Interview with UNFICYP figure, November 2022.
26. 'Turkey Accuses UN Security Council of Losing Its Neutrality in Cyprus After Assault on Peacekeepers', AP News, 22 August 2023, https://apnews.com/article/turkey-accuses-un-abandoning-neutrality-81bf820116a093b0337705a6e6609c0f#:~:text=ANKARA%2C%20Turkey%20(AP)%20%E2%80%94,condemned%20their%20assault%20on%20U.N.
27. Alexandros Zachariades, 'Elections and the Cyprus Problem: Change or Continuity', LSE, January 2023, https://blogs.lse.ac.uk/greeceatlse/2023/01/31/elections-and-the-cyprus-problem-change-or-continuity/.
28. Interview with think tanker in Cyprus, November 2022.
29. Esra Aygin, 'Ankara Asserting "Absolute Authority" Over Northern Cyprus', *Cyprus Mail*, 29 May 2022, https://cyprus-mail.com/2022/05/29/ankara-asserting-absolute-authority-over-north/.
30. Esra Aygin, 'Türkiye's Trojan Horse Policy', *Cyprus Mail*, 19 June 2022, https://cyprus-mail.com/2022/06/19/Turkiyes-trojan-horse-policy/; and Esra Aygin, 'Legal Action to Stop North Handing Out Citizenships', *Cyprus Mail*, 30 October 2022, https://cyprus-mail.com/2022/10/30/legal-action-to-stop-north-handing-out-citizenships/.
31. Interview with senior Cypriot government official, April 2023. See also 'Cyprus Claims Turkiye Exploiting Migrant Crisis', *Financial Mirror*, 28 March 2022, https://www.financialmirror.com/2022/03/28/cyprus-claims-Turkiye-exploiting-migrant-crisis/.
32. Interview with senior Turkish diplomat, March 2023.
33. '18.5 Thousand Irregular Migrants Crossed the Green Line This Year', KNews, 2 December 2022, https://knews.kathimerini.com.cy/en/news/18-5-thousand-irregular-migrants-crossed-the-green-line-this-year.
34. 'Eurostat: First-time Asylum Applicants Up 64% in 2022', Eurostat, 23 March 2023, https://ec.europa.eu/eurostat/web/products-eurostat-news/w/ddn-20230323-2#:~:text=Compared%20with%20the%20population%20of,and%20Luxembourg%20(3%20711).
35. 'Eurostat: First-time Asylum Applicants Up 20% in 2023', Eurostat, 25 March 2023, https://ec.europa.eu/eurostat/web/products-eurostat-news/w/ddn-20240325-1#:~:text=Compared%20with%20the%20population%20of,applicants%20per%201%20000%20people.
36. 'Asylum Applications up by 480% since 2016', KNews, 24 March 2023, https://knews.kathimerini.com.cy/en/news/asylum-applications-up-by-490-since-2016.
37. Michele Kambas, 'Cyprus Calls for EU Rethink on Syria Migration as Refugee Numbers Rise', 14 December 2023, https://www.reuters.com/world/europe/cyprus-calls-eu-rethink-syria-migration-refugee-numbers-rise-2023-12-14/.
38. Interview with senior official at the Ministry of Foreign Affairs of Cyprus, April 2023.
39. *Ibid.*
40. US Department of State, 'Agreement Between the United States of America and Cyprus', 5 December 2002, https://www.state.gov/wp-content/uploads/2020/04/02-1205-Cyprus-Defense-TIMS-44877.pdf.
41. US Embassy in Israel, 'Security Alert #10', 15 October 2023, https://il.usembassy.gov/security-alert-10/.
42. Interview with senior diplomat at the Ministry of Foreign Affairs of Cyprus, April 2023.
43. Anna Ahronheim, 'Israel to Simulate War with Hezbollah in Cyprus', *Jerusalem Post*, 29 May 2022, https://www.jpost.com/israel-news/article-707968; 'Israel Forces Largest Drill With Neighbour Cyprus', *Financial Mirror*, 31 May 2022, https://www.financialmirror.com/2022/05/31/israel-forces-largest-drill-with-neighbour-cyprus/; for the Israeli perspective, see Yanatan Brander, 'A Strategic Friendship: Israeli Perceptions of the Israel-Cyprus Relationship', PRIO Centre Cyprus, 2022, https://www.prio.org/publications/13020.
44. Emmanuel Fabian, 'Cyprus Set to Buy Iron Dome From Israel – Report', *Times of Israel*, 21 August 2022, https://www.timesofisrael.com/cyprus-set-to-buy-iron-dome-from-israel-report/; and 'Cyprus Stocking Up on Drones', KNews 3 October 2019, https://knews.kathimerini.com.cy/en/news/cyprus-stocking-up-on-drones.
45. Amir Tibon and Oded Yaron, 'Israel Plans to Sell Its Merkava Tanks to Cyprus', *Haaretz*, 22 June 2023, https://www.haaretz.com/israel-news/security-aviation/2023-06-22/ty-article/israel-cyprus-plans-to-sell-its-merkava-tanks/00000188-e278-d7f8-abbb-e6ff5f2c0000.

46 Interview with senior diplomat at the Ministry of Foreign Affairs of Cyprus, April 2023.

47 Eleonora Ardemagni, 'Why the Gulf Monarchies Have Laid Eyes on Cyprus', ISPI, 2019, https://www.ispionline.it/en/publication/why-gulf-monarchies-have-laid-eyes-cyprus-24045.

48 Tziarras (ed.), *The Foreign Policy of the Republic of Cyprus: Local, Regional, and International Dimensions*.

49 Interview with senior diplomat of the Republic of Cyprus, April 2023.

50 'President Sisi Thanks Cyprus for Its Contribution to Establishment of EU–Egypt Relations', In-Cyprus, 24 February 2019, https://in-cyprus.philenews.com/news/local/president-sisi-thanks-cyprus-for-its-contribution-in-the-establishment-of-eu-egypt-relations-pics/.

51 'Cyprus Ready to "Represent Egypt" in Europe: Cypriot Parliamentary Speaker', *Ahram Online*, 12 April 2016, https://english.ahram.org.eg/NewsContent/1/64/199356/Egypt/Politics-/Cyprus-ready-to-represent-Egypt-in-Europe-Cypriot-.aspx.

52 Tziarras (ed.), *The Foreign Policy of the Republic of Cyprus: Local, Regional, and International Dimensions*.

53 'Saudi Sees Cyprus as Bridge Between Europe, Middle East', AP News, 13 February 2022, https://apnews.com/article/european-union-houthis-middle-east-europe-cyprus-59bd874fb3ad704a985ae0f56666e65f.

54 Interview with senior Cypriot diplomat, April 2023.

55 'Cyprus Denies Russian Ships Access to Ports', KNews, 5 March 2022, https://knews.kathimerini.com.cy/en/news/cyprus-denies-russian-ships-access-to-ports.

56 *Ibid*.

57 US Department of State, 'Lifting of Defense Restrictions on the Republic of Cyprus for Fiscal Year 2024', Press Statement, 18 August 2023, https://www.state.gov/lifting-of-defense-trade-restrictions-on-the-republic-of-cyprus-for-fiscal-year-2024/.

58 Interview with Turkish official, March 2023.

59 Menelaos Hadjicostis, 'Ukrainian Deminers Get Training in Cyprus from US, Irish Experts', AP News, 12 May 2023, https://apnews.com/article/cyprus-ukraine-demining-minefields-ireland-us-0bafda54e28cfe92defea5e1c979dffb.

60 Interview with senior diplomat at the Ministry of Defence of Cyprus, April 2023.

61 Interview with senior diplomat at the Ministry of Foreign Affairs of Cyprus, April 2023.

62 Interview with academic in Nicosia, November 2022.

63 Dr Shangyou Nie and Robin Mills, 'Eastern Mediterranean Deepwater Gas to Europe: Not Too Little, But Perhaps Too Late', Center on Global Energy Policy, March 2023, https://www.energypolicy.columbia.edu/wp-content/uploads/2023/03/East-Med-Gas-CGEP_Report_030923-2.pdf, p. 29.

64 Interview with Charles Ellinas, Atlantic Council, March 2023.

65 *Ibid*.

66 Ayla Gürel, Fiona Mullen and Harry Tzimitras, 'The Cyprus Hydrocarbons Issue: Context, Positions and Future Scenarios', PRIO Cyprus Centre, 2013, https://www.prio.org/publications/7365.

67 Mustafa Ergün Olgun, 'Can Hydrocarbons Catalyse New Out of the Box Thinking on Cyprus? A Turkish Cypriot Perspective', Istituto Affari Internazionali, 23 February 2019, https://www.iai.it/en/pubblicazioni/can-hydrocarbons-catalyse-new-out-box-thinking-cyprus.

Soldiers opposed to Libya's United Nations-recognised government ride a truck near the Zueitina oil terminal on 14 September 2016. (Photo: Abdullah Doma/AFP via Getty Images)

LIBYA IS AN ARENA FOR COMPETITION in the Eastern Mediterranean. Its polarised domestic politics, overall stability and prosperity are intimately linked to regional dynamics.

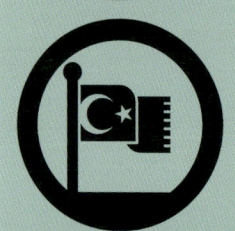

TURKIYE'S INFLUENCE IN LIBYA has grown through the controversial 2019 maritime-boundary agreement and its successful military intervention there in 2020. In response, Cyprus, Egypt and Greece further coalesced to contain Ankara. This dynamic established a structural linkage between the Libyan crisis and other disputes in the Eastern Mediterranean.

RUSSIA HAS CULTIVATED A RELATIONSHIP with Libya's eastern authorities, giving it a military foothold on NATO's southern flank. Western powers have been divided over their priorities and approaches towards energy, migration, terrorism or political influence.

CHAPTER NINE
LIBYA: INTERNAL DIVISIONS, FOREIGN INTERVENTION AND OIL

INTRODUCTION

Libya has historically been a minor player in the Eastern Mediterranean, dwarfed by Egypt and mostly focused on the Sahel region. Things started to change in 2011 when an uprising unseated the regime of Muammar Gadhafi, turning Libya into an arena for geopolitical competition. A civil war that started in earnest in 2014 has drawn in regional players, extremist groups and international attention. Major Eastern Mediterranean powers, including Egypt and Turkiye, have been keen to shape the politics of the country. In doing so, Libya has been pulled into the basin's complex politics.

ENDURING DIVISIONS

Libya has been split between rival authorities since 2014 and mired in political deadlock that has defeated multiple attempts to reunite the country and hold elections. Corruption, criminality and political dysfunction have flourished as a result of this institutional limbo. Libya is now divided between two governments: one in Tripoli, currently headed by Abdul Hamid Dbeibah, which is internationally recognised and known as the Government of National Unity (GNU), and another in Sirte known as the Government of National Stability (GNS), currently headed by Osama Hammad and supported by the Benghazi-based strongman General Khalifa Haftar. Many militias operate in parallel, with loose affiliations with the central governments.

Rival groups exacerbate these divisions as they compete to control Libya's vast oil resources. Though it has the ninth-largest proven crude-oil reserves in the world, periodic attacks on hydrocarbon infrastructure by different factions have severely curtailed Libya's ability to utilise its energy resources.[1]

Many foreign actors, including Western and Middle Eastern powers, have played into these divisions. Western countries have mostly focused on countering terrorism, containing migration and securing energy resources, while Middle Eastern states have prioritised ideological and geopolitical competition. Turkiye and Qatar, which supported Islamist organisations during and after the 2011 uprising, have mostly backed the GNU, while Egypt, Russia and the United Arab Emirates (UAE) have backed the GNS and Haftar, who claims to be fighting extremism instigated by the Muslim Brotherhood (see Map 9.1).

A key episode in the country's recent history has been the siege of Tripoli (2019–20). Major fighting commenced when Haftar launched an attack on the capital in April 2019 with the support of Russian mercenaries and acquiescence from the UAE. For its part, Egypt showed more caution, being apprehensive that such an action could further destabilise Libya and decrease border security, the latter being Cairo's main concern. In January 2020, Turkiye intervened militarily upon the request of the Tripoli authorities and pushed Haftar's forces back east. Both Russia and Turkiye have since consolidated their in-country military presence, giving them significant influence not only over domestic politics but also over regional dynamics.

Efforts to manage the conflict have been unsuccessful and controversial. The United Nations Security Council (UNSC) imposed an arms embargo in 2011. Ten years later, a UN expert

MAP 9.1: TERRITORIAL CONTROL AND FOREIGN MILITARY PRESENCES IN LIBYA AS OF MAY 2024

THE POLITICISATION OF THE ENERGY SECTOR

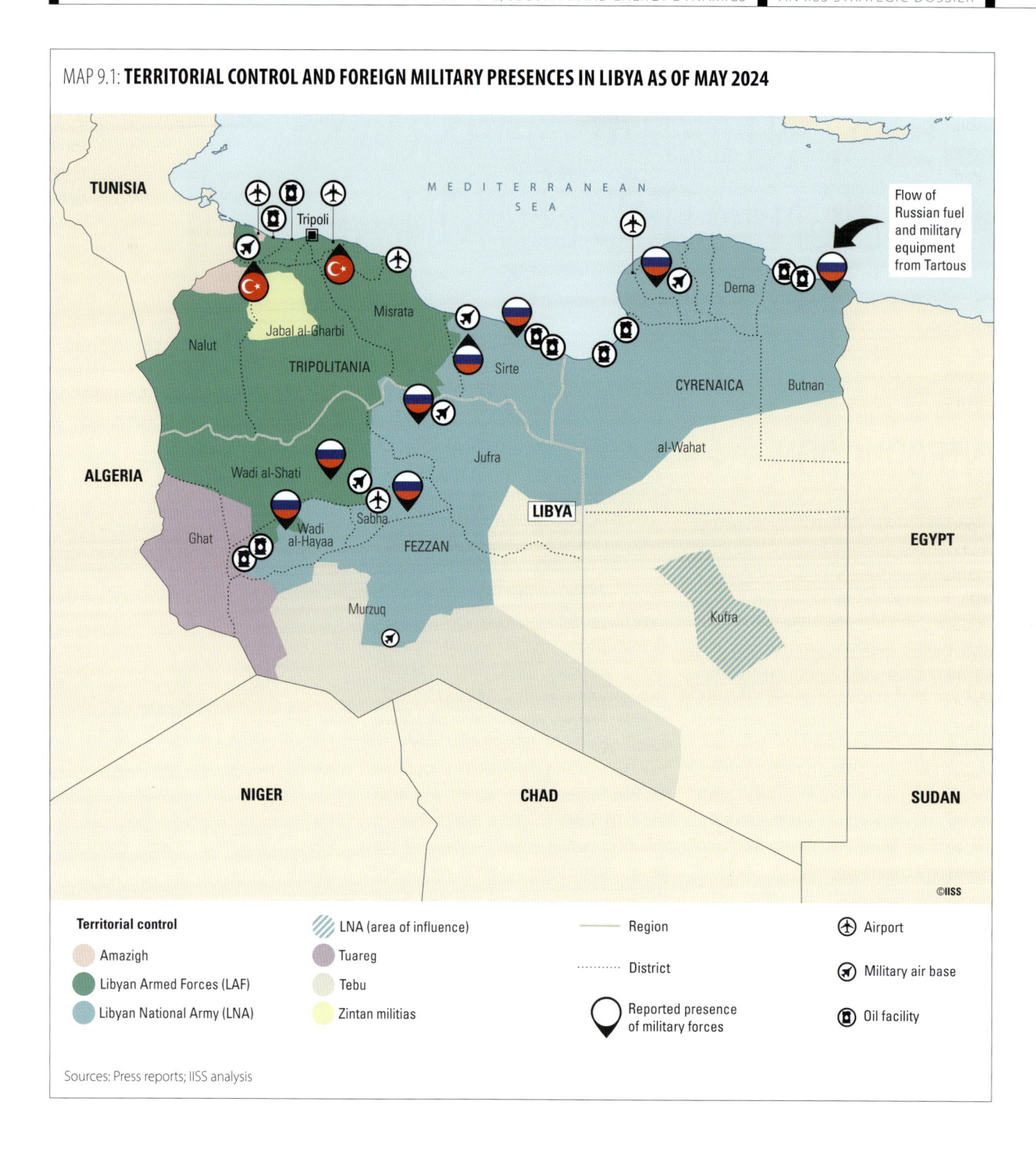

panel called it 'totally ineffective'.² The European Union established *Operation Irini* in 2020 with the core task of implementing the UN arms embargo, with a UNSC mandate to do so that has continued to be renewed yearly.³ However, Turkiye has accused the operation of focusing solely on Turkish naval shipments to Tripoli, while not interdicting weapons shipments to the east, by air and over land, from Egypt, Russia or the UAE. In 2020, in the last months of the Trump administration, the United States levelled similar criticism against *Operation Irini*.⁴

Control over Libya's large oil and gas reserves has been a key driver of violent competition. Competing militias have tried to capture oil facilities but have also blockaded and attacked them. In January 2020, Haftar's advancing forces imposed a blockade on the oilfields and terminals in a bid to extract a more favourable profit-sharing arrangement from the Tripoli authorities.⁵ When the blockade ended eight months later, the cost was enormous, with Libya only able to export that year half of its average annual exports between 2011–19 (see Figure 9.1).⁶

The weaponisation of oil has favoured different factions over time. Dbeibah's clout grew once western factions asserted their control over oil facilities in Tripolitania but not enough to give him the upper hand in the whole of Libya. Facing him, Haftar maintained control over Cyrenaica and Fezzan and has not shied away from using economic warfare, issuing repeated threats of new blockades to pressure Tripoli. The weaponisation of oil resources also exacerbated pre-existing socio-economic grievances that culminated in widespread protests against the political establishment and the ransacking of the House of Representatives in early July 2022.

Since Russia's invasion of Ukraine, the scramble to diversify European energy sources has further intensified the competition among rival internal factions over natural resources. In 2022, Libya was the fifteenth-largest exporter of crude oil in the world, generating an annual revenue of US$30.3 billion. Italy was by far the biggest importer of Libyan crude, importing 20% of Libya's exports, nearly twice as much as the next country, Spain.[7] During Italian Prime Minister Giorgia Meloni's visit in January 2023, Italy's energy company Eni signed an US$8bn, 25-year gas-production deal with Libya's National Oil Corporation.[8] But such megadeals remain vulnerable to continuing domestic divisions and the crises of legitimacy they engender as well as to pressures from regional powers involved with the rival Libyan factions.

Oil and gas reserves have indeed drawn the country into the fault lines of Eastern Mediterranean competition. The controversial 2019 demarcation of Turkish–Libyan maritime zones[9] ignored the Greek island of Crete and has been contested by Greece and Egypt ever since (see Map 2.2, page 47).[10] In October 2022, Turkiye signed a memorandum of understanding (MoU) with the Tripoli authorities to explore for hydrocarbons on Libya's soil and in territorial waters off of Tripoli.

The dispute over the maritime borders and, by extension, over offshore-gas exploration between Turkiye and the GNU on the one hand, and Egypt and Greece on the other, negatively affected GNU–Greek as well as GNU–Egyptian relations. Egypt sought to counter it by declaring a unilateral maritime border and by intensifying its support for the GNS. Athens had less influence, though it tilted towards the GNS. In November 2022, the Greek then-minister for foreign affairs Nikos Dendias, a hardliner who had vigorously developed Greek outreach to Egypt and Israel, refused to disembark from his plane in Tripoli because he was being greeted by his GNU counterpart Najla al-Mangoush, whom he considered illegitimate. He raised no similar objections when he landed in the east, meeting with Haftar and the speaker of the House of Representatives. In May 2024, the GNU sent a letter to the Greek ambassador protesting seismic surveys Greece was conducting in the west and southwest of the island of Crete in waters that both Libya and Greece consider to be their own.[11]

Illustrating the volatility of the legal environment, in February 2024 the Tripoli Court of Appeal annulled the 2022 energy MoU with Turkiye.[12] A group of lawyers had argued that the MoU violated Libyan laws governing energy resources and the granting of energy concessions, as well as going against the interests of Libya and the UN-backed reconciliation process, given the Greek and Egyptian contentions.[13] Such uncertainty increases the potential legal risks to international energy companies operating in Libya.

COMPETITION AMONG REGIONAL POWERS

The 2024 Court of Appeal's ruling showed the ripple effect of Libya's political fragmentation, not just on the proper governance and security of the country, but also on its relations with regional and global actors. The considerable sway that Turkiye holds in Tripolitania following its military intervention has not shielded it from this judicial setback. Nevertheless, Turkish influence has proven resilient and durable. Through its military presence in western Libya, Ankara has consolidated ties with important stakeholders in Misrata and Tripoli. Turkiye's military foothold is expected to last as it tries to influence the Eastern Mediterranean space from the mainland and the unrecognised Turkish Republic of Northern Cyprus, as well as from Syria and now Libya. Libya is also a springboard for Turkiye's projection of power into Africa at a time of upheaval in the Sahel and a growing Russian presence there.

Egypt, which has supported the eastern forces, has not welcomed Turkiye's expansion of power in Libya. As Turkish forces pushed Haftar's forces back in 2020, Cairo took the extremely unusual step of issuing red lines and threatening to intervene if Turkish forces advanced further east than Jufra and Sirte. Egypt has, however, generally been cautious. Reluctant to intervene and become entangled in Libya, it has prioritised the security of its western borders. Since then, relations between Turkiye and Egypt have

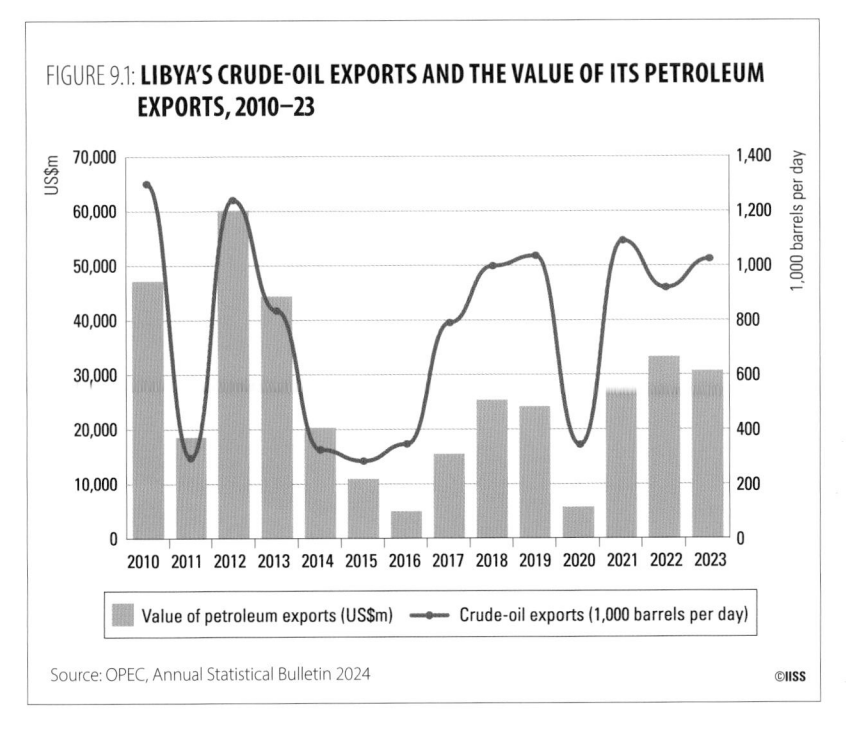

FIGURE 9.1: **LIBYA'S CRUDE-OIL EXPORTS AND THE VALUE OF ITS PETROLEUM EXPORTS, 2010–23**

Source: OPEC, Annual Statistical Bulletin 2024

warmed, even if they remain at odds over Libya. Egyptian officials assert in private that obtaining the departure of Turkish forces from Libya is their top national-security priority and allude to the possibility of holding up Turkish accession to the East Mediterranean Gas Forum until this goal is met.

The resulting military stalemate has largely frozen the armed conflict in Libya, which has resulted in a softening of the Emirati position as well. From 2011, the UAE's main policy in Libya was focused on the political and military defeat of Turkiye-aligned Islamist and revolutionary militias and what it saw as a complacent political class in Tripoli. The maximalist Emirati agenda culminated in 2019–20, when Abu Dhabi supported Haftar's attempt to seize Tripoli by force. His failure, alongside the changing international landscape, reduced Abu Dhabi's risk appetite. The UAE has since de-escalated with Turkiye and initiated a rapprochement with the Tripoli government, though it remains aligned with Cairo on the issue of the Turkish military presence in Libya.

Improved relations between Ankara and Abu Dhabi have so far helped to preserve the ceasefire that was reached in 2020 between the Tripoli authorities and Haftar's forces, but this has not been enough to begin a comprehensive political settlement of the conflict. Libyan actors remain intransigent and entrenched in their maximalist positions. Before resigning from his position in April 2024, the UN's Libya envoy, special representative to the secretary-general Abdoulaye Bathily, said that Libyan stakeholders met his efforts to mediate a political process with 'stubborn resistance, unreasonable expectations and indifference to the interests of the Libyan people'.[14]

Egypt has also played a central role by supporting and propping up Haftar. For Cairo, containing the externalities of the ongoing Libyan conflict, be they terrorism- or migration-related, is a matter of national security. Ankara's 2019 maritime-zones MoU and its decisive support for the GNU were read through this prism and deemed a security and strategic problem for Cairo. This has brought Greece and Egypt closer; they share the same policy objectives and coordinate their positions, with Greece being a de facto advocate for Egypt inside the EU. In response to the 2019

Turkish defence minister Hulusi Akar (R) attends a graduation ceremony at a military academy in Tripoli, Libya, on 26 December 2020. (Photo: Arif Akdogan/Anadolu Agency via Getty Images)

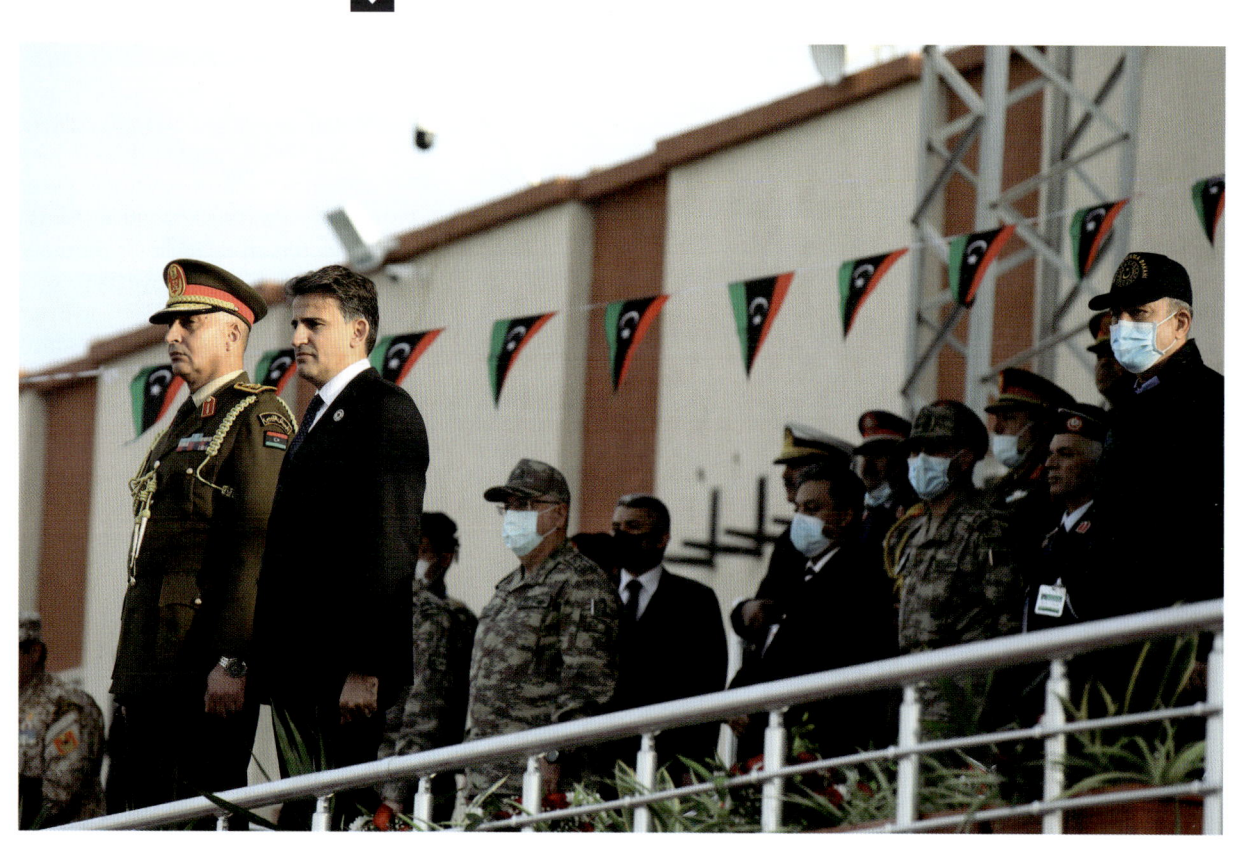

MoU, Greece and Egypt delimited their maritime zones and Egypt unilaterally delimited its maritime border with Libya.

Cairo's enduring intransigence contrasts with the flexibility of its main partner, the UAE, which is making inroads with Tripoli. This divergence between Haftar's two closest supporters has further complicated efforts to revive the political process to reunify Libyan institutions and hold elections. It has also opened more space for Russian influence.

GEOPOLITICAL FLUX FUELLING DOMESTIC INSTABILITY

Indeed, Russia has been steadily growing its presence and influence in eastern Libya. In the immediate aftermath of the 2014 civil war and the ensuing split, Russia had instructors working with Haftar's forces. By the time Haftar launched his attempted takeover of Tripoli in 2019, 2,000 Russian Wagner Group mercenaries were assessed to be in the country, actively supporting Haftar's operations, according to the US military's Africa Command (AFRICOM). They laid landmines and improvised explosive devices in and around Tripoli and all the way down to the city of Sirte. Moreover, AFRICOM reported that 'at least 14 Mig-29s' were flown from Russia to Libya through Syria, and that Russia had also sent military armoured vehicles and air defences.[15]

For Russia, Libya has strategic value as a foothold on NATO's southern flank and in the Mediterranean's warm waters, as well as being an anchor in Africa for its geopolitical and influence activities on the continent, especially in the Sahel. Since Russia invaded Ukraine, it has continued to invest in expanding its role in Libya. High-level Russian officials have paid regular visits to Haftar, including after Wagner Group leader Yevgeny Prigozhin died and the Russian Ministry of Defence took over the mercenary group. In 2024, Russia was estimated to have at least 1,800 military personnel in the country[16] and, in mid-April 2024, two Russian landing ships reportedly docked in the deep-water port of Tobruk to move military equipment from the Russian naval base in Tartous in Syria.[17]

Russia's relationship with Haftar and deepening foothold

Forces loyal to Libya's United Nations-recognised Government of National Unity (GNU) parade a Russian-made *Pantsir* air-defence system in Tripoli, Libya, on 20 May 2020, after its capture at al-Watiya air base from forces loyal to General Khalifa Haftar. (Photo: Mahmud Turkia/AFP via Getty Images)

in Libya were facilitated by divisions among Western powers, as well as US disengagement following the attacks on its Benghazi consulate in 2012. Despite Libya's strategic location at the southern border of Europe, European stakeholders including France, Germany, Italy and the United Kingdom have largely failed to agree on a common approach that would combine their strength and influence. Instead, they have pursued narrow interests that have sometimes pitted them against each other. For example, for many years, France's approach to Libya was dominated by a counter-terrorism focus and was shaped by its close partners Egypt and the UAE; as a result, it lent considerable support to Haftar until late 2020 to early 2021. Italy's approach has mainly been driven by a desire to limit migration and to advance Italian energy giant Eni's interests. Unlike the hard confrontations between France and Turkiye, Turkiye and Italy have long shared similar strategic interests in Libya, where they have shored up support for the authorities in Tripoli. However, they are now in competition in Tripolitania, while Rome's position has evolved in part because of political proximity between Meloni, the far-right Italian prime minister, and Haftar.

European countries' scattered political efforts and dwindling ability to shape the behaviour of Libyan actors were evident in the contrast between the 2019 and 2021 Berlin conferences, which were called to provide comprehensive answers to the conflict. While the first conference gathered heads of government and state from the main stakeholders and initiated the formation of the GNU, the latter only gathered foreign ministers and struggled to produce an effective road map towards intra-Libyan reconciliation, holding elections or reunifying state institutions.

In contrast, China has avoided political entanglements, instead pursuing economic interests while engaging with both Tripoli and Benghazi and subsequently growing more influential. China was among the political and economic losers from the fall of the Gadhafi regime, and thus essentially reduced its profile in subsequent years. However, authorities in Tripoli signed up in 2018 to join China's Belt and Road Initiative, Beijing's global campaign of overseas lending and investment.[18] Since then, China has been either the highest or second-highest exporter to Libya, alternating with Turkiye.[19] In May 2024, Tripoli and Beijing agreed to initiate the reopening of the Chinese embassy in Tripoli during a meeting in China between Dbeibah and the Chinese minister of foreign affairs, Wang Yi.[20]

OUTLOOK: THE GEOPOLITICISATION OF THE ENERGY SECTOR

The politicisation of the oil sector has made Libya even more vulnerable to the geopolitical competition in the Eastern Mediterranean. Moreover, the Libyan conflict is now intrinsically linked to the Eastern Mediterranean maritime disputes, with three of its major actors – Egypt, Greece and Turkiye – deeply invested in its affairs, with high stakes attached.

It is too early to tell whether the recent warming of the Egyptian–Turkish and the Greek–Turkish relationships will be reflected in the Libyan theatre. Libya may even turn out to be one of the real litmus tests for regional detente and potential cooperation. So far, positions have remained mostly entrenched. Turkiye sees its expanded influence and military presence in the country as a part of its regional projection of power. Egypt views Libya as a core national-security issue, and Libya is now involved in the deadlocked, decades-long Greek–Turkish maritime dispute.

All attempts at breaking the political deadlock and uniting government institutions have failed. While levels of violence have decreased in recent years, there is no visible promising path at the time of writing. The EU and US appear willing to accept the status quo as long as migration and terrorist threats emanating from Libya-based groups remain under control. But Russia's and China's growing influence, if left unchecked, may deal strategic setbacks to Western powers, while confirming Arab countries' increasing hedging of their international partnerships.

ENDNOTES

1. Organization of the Petroleum Exporting Countries, 'OPEC Share of World Crude Oil Reserves', https://www.opec.org/opec_web/en/data_graphs/330.htm.

2. United Nations, 'Libya Arms Embargo "Totally Ineffective": UN Expert Panel', 17 March 2021, https://news.un.org/en/story/2021/03/1087562.

3. Operation *Irini*, 'About Us', https://www.operationirini.eu/about-us/; United Nations, 'Security Council Renews Authorization to Inspect Vessels Suspected of Violating Libya Arms Embargo, Adopting Resolution 2684 (2023)', 2 June 2023, https://press.un.org/en/2023/sc15303.doc.htm.

4. Humeyra Pamuk, 'US Senior Diplomat Complains Europe Not Doing Enough in Libya', Reuters, 16 July 2020, https://www.yahoo.com/news/u-senior-diplomat-complains-europe-173108538.html?guccounter=1&guce_referrer=aHR0cHM6Ly93d3cuZ29vZ2xlLmNvbS8&guce_referrer_sig=AQAAAFuBuDAr9WNP1-vHoQzEyAfu9iiDD7_uXdl0O3ajhd_VB5UdAkZRDOxc_JggN9QWtr1OgSSBw_IRXWcC3rFahyuTFG2y3zbFPS0lwZ2790Ex93bNPU7T0zOCRLmiCw1k-FkFWQy4UizfyxwqdjqXbWOLSTe97rX1CsXFhT1GfszM.

5. 'Libya: Haftar Plans to Lift 8-month Oil Blockade', DW, 18 September 2020, https://www.dw.com/en/libya-haftar-plans-to-lift-8-month-oil-field-blockade/a-54981299.

6. CEIC, 'Libya Crude Oil: Exports', https://www.ceicdata.com/en/indicator/libya/crude-oil-exports.

7. OEC, 'Crude Petroleum in Libya', https://oec.world/en/profile/bilateral-product/crude-petroleum/reporter/lby.

8. Gavin Jones, 'Italy's Eni Signs $8 Billion Libya Gas Deal as PM Meloni Visits Tripoli', Reuters, 29 January 2023, https://www.reuters.com/world/italys-meloni-expected-sign-major-gas-deal-she-starts-libya-visit-2023-01-28/.

9. The Government of the Republic of Turkey and the Government of National Accord – State of Libya, 'Memorandum of Understanding Between the Government of the Republic of Turkey and the Government of National Accord-State of Libya on Delimitation of the Maritime Jurisdiction Areas in the Mediterranean', United Nations, 27 November 2019, https://www.un.org/depts/los/LEGISLATIONANDTREATIES/PDFFILES/TREATIES/Turkey_11122019_%28HC%29_MoU_Libya-Delimitation-areas-Mediterranean.pdf.

10. 'Turkey and Libya Sign Maritime Hydrocarbons Deal', France 24, 3 October 2022, https://www.france24.com/en/live-news/20221003-turkey-and-libya-sign-maritime-hydrocarbons-deal-1.

11. Vassilis Nedos, 'Tripoli Protests Prospecting South of Crete', *Kathimerini*, 22 May 2024, https://www.ekathimerini.com/politics/foreign-policy/1239318/tripoli-protests-prospecting-south-of-crete/?utm_source=dlvr.it&utm_medium=twitter.

12. Abdul Kaderassad, 'Tripoli Court of Appeal Annuls MoU in Hydrocarbons Cooperation With Turkey', *Libya Observer*, 19 February 2024, https://libyaobserver.ly/news/tripoli-court-appeal-annuls-mou-hydrocarbons-cooperation-turkey.

13. 'Lawyer Thuraya Al-Tuwaibi Reveals to the "Witness". How Did the Dbeibah and Turkey Agreement Violate Libyan Law?', Al Shahed, 15 January 2023, https://www.libyaakhbar.com/libya-news/2055540.html#google_vignette.

14. United Nations, 'Rival Actors' Stubborn Resistance, Unreasonable Expectations Impeding Political Progress, Elections in Libya, Special Representative Tells Security Council', 16 April 2024, https://press.un.org/en/2024/sc15666.doc.htm.

15. United States Africa Command, 'Russia, Wagner Group Complicating Libyan Ceasefire Efforts', 15 July 2020, https://www.africom.mil/pressrelease/33008/russia-wagner-group-complicating-libyan-cease; US Department of Defense, 'Russia, Wagner Group Continue Military Involvement in Libya', 24 July 2020, https://www.defense.gov/News/News-Stories/Article/Article/2287821/russia-wagner-group-continue-military-involvement-in-libya/.

16. 'A Big Mess Is Brewing: Thousands of Russian Fighters Are Flooding Into Libya, Raising Concerns Over What the Kremlin Might Be Planning', Meduza and Verstka, 16 May 2024, https://meduza.io/en/feature/2024/05/16/a-big-mess-is-brewing.

17. Tom Kington, 'Russia Funneling Weapons Through Libyan Port, Eying Gateway to Africa', *Defense News*, 19 April 2024, https://www.defensenews.com/global/europe/2024/04/19/russia-funneling-weapons-through-libyan-port-eying-gateway-to-africa/.

18. IISS, 'IISS China Connects', https://chinaconnects.iiss.org/.

19. See 'IMF Direction of Trade Statistics', IMF, https://data.imf.org/?sk=9d6028d4-f14a-464c-a2f2-59b2cd424b85&sid=1514498277103.

20. 'China to Reopen Embassy in Libya', Libya Review, 30 May 2024, https://libyareview.com/44662/china-to-reopen-embassy-in-libya/.

An aerial view of Egypt's New Administrative Capital on 11 September 2023. (Photo: Fareed Kotb/Anadolu Agency via Getty Images)

EGYPT IS DIVERSIFYING ITS INTERNATIONAL PARTNERSHIPS, maintaining traditional ties with Western countries while deepening its relations with the Gulf states as well as Russia and China. But its dependency on foreign support, limited power projection and enduring economic crisis constrain its yearning for external influence.

EGYPT HAS INCREASED ITS POLITICAL, MILITARY AND ECONOMIC PROFILE in the Eastern Mediterranean. It has partnered with Greece and Cyprus, reconciled with Turkiye and solidified ties with Israel, and aims to become a regional energy hub despite considerable challenges.

EVEN AS SECURITY AND GEOPOLITICAL THREATS SURROUND IT, Egypt has failed to shape decisively or resolve any of the challenges in its immediate neighbourhood. The ongoing Israel–Hamas war highlights its enduring regional role but also exposes its limited leverage and its exposure to the externalities of conflict.

CHAPTER TEN
EGYPT: REGIONAL AMBITIONS AND DOMESTIC WEAKNESS

INTRODUCTION

Egypt's significant activism in the Eastern Mediterranean since 2014 has been an imperative to shape a particularly volatile neighbourhood as well as an attempt to regain regional leadership and reverse the country's economic slump. Cairo's regional policy has aimed to manage security and geopolitical challenges and establish new relationships that can help it better hedge in an increasingly transactional strategic context. This approach has been essential in successfully rallying regional and international support for the country's post-2013 authorities, pushing back against Turkiye's regional ambitions and containing the external effects of the Israeli–Palestinian, Syrian, Libyan and Sudanese conflicts, and has been sustained by the country's once-growing role as a natural-gas exporter.[1] Despite its efforts, the Israel–Hamas war and its potential expansion illustrate how vulnerable Egypt remains to its weak economy and unstable immediate environment. This crisis has already tested the strength and value of its regional relations.

GLOBAL AND REGIONAL AMBITIONS

While Egypt no longer has the power attributes that once made it the leader of the Arab world, it maintains clout in regional affairs and is seeking more influence, especially in the Eastern Mediterranean. Egyptian officials fear potential spillover from fragile or failed states and prefer state-centric solutions to nearby conflicts.[2] They portray Egypt as a moderate, measured linchpin whose stability – and potential instability – ripples far beyond its borders. External actors have bought into this framework, making Egypt a pillar of their regional strategies, establishing strategic partnerships with it, and turning a blind eye to endemic corruption and mismanagement on the basis that the 115-million-strong country is 'too big to fail'. As a result, Cairo has not implemented reforms the IMF and World Bank say are necessary (including reducing the role of the military in the economy), has responded to criticisms of its human-rights abuses by raising the spectre of terrorism and instability, and has extracted geopolitical and financial support by highlighting its role in managing migration towards Europe.

Egypt's priorities have centred around security and the economy. Following the 2011 uprising that overthrew the government of Hosni Mubarak and the rise to power of the Muslim Brotherhood, the Egyptian military seized power in a 2013 coup led by General Abdel Fattah al-Sisi, who subsequently became president. The military has since continuously heralded the primacy of order and security at home and in the region. An uptick in armed violence in Egypt, including activity by jihadi and criminal groups in the Sinai Peninsula, enabled the military to highlight this role and to expand its powers not only in security affairs but also in the political and economic realms. The Sisi government has seen popular movements in the Arab world as intrinsically destabilising, and prone to being manipulated and dominated by Islamist factions and their state sponsors Qatar and Turkiye but also Iran. It has blamed civil wars in Iraq, Libya and Syria, as well as the rise of Hamas in Gaza and the resulting regional turbulence, on these forces. In response, it has supported incumbent governments and joined regionwide counter-Islamist coalitions. Power vacuums in neighbouring countries have also motivated Egypt's emphasis on defence modernisation.

To legitimise his rule, Sisi has embraced a statist–nationalist rhetoric that emphasises restoring Egypt's lost glory as a regional leader and counters perceptions that Egypt is punching below its weight. This has entailed prioritising large-scale mega-projects, particularly in the sectors of infrastructure, energy and construction. Military personnel and army generals have been involved in the planning and implementation of these projects as well as in the economy more broadly.[3] This empowerment of security-oriented bodies and institutions, meant to reward and consolidate his loyalist base, has come at the expense of other institutions.

Sisi has sought to diversify the country's partnerships, giving it more leeway to challenge the United States despite the continuing long-standing partnership between the two. Cairo has vehemently rejected US critiques of its domestic policies, such as restrictions on political activity and large-scale alleged abuses of human rights, and decried the suspension of parts of US military assistance in 2013 (which were restored later). Broadening its partnerships has been a way for Egypt to try to assert itself as an essential middle power with more freedom of manoeuvre, independence and autonomy. Sisi has consequently forged close relations with US rivals Russia and China, which emphasise stability and overlook domestic issues like political repression, culminating in Egypt's invitation to join the BRICS grouping in 2023. This policy has been somewhat successful at fending off critics in Western governments who no longer possess the leverage they once had over Egypt. Yet, rather than abandoning Egypt altogether, they have proved willing to work with the military leaders, particularly on security issues, as they fear further upheaval and exposure to its externalities, notably migration. In 2024, at the height of the Israel–Hamas war, the European Union provided €7.4 billion (US$8.1bn) in financial assistance to Cairo over concerns about Egypt's stability, exposure to regional conflicts and migration trends.[4]

In diversifying its partnerships, Cairo plays a delicate balancing game in an increasingly multipolar order. Contrasting with its previous caution, it has shown a willingness to exploit geopolitical tensions to achieve its own objectives. It maintains a nominal alignment with the US and continues to receive up to US$1.3bn per year in US military aid.[5] But it increasingly engages in strategic hedging. It has upheld its warm political and economic relations with Moscow, even after the Russian invasion of Ukraine.[6] This collaboration has deepened in the past decade, with Egypt becoming Russia's largest trading partner in the Middle East and Africa.[7] Russia has signed several arms deals and is also building Egypt's first nuclear-power plant.[8] Egypt, accordingly, has little to gain and much to lose from alienating Russia. However, Cairo is also cognisant of the limited value and reliability of the relationship: Russia indefinitely suspended the delivery of Su-35 combat aircraft to Egypt after the 2022 invasion of Ukraine, and has not been responsive to Egypt's twin food and energy crises during the COVID-19 pandemic and post-invasion. A weakened Russia is therefore unlikely to be a reliable partner for the foreseeable future.

Egypt has simultaneously intensified relations with China. The significant rise in Chinese investments has caused concern in the US, which cautioned Cairo over the involvement of Chinese firms in developing Egypt's 5G network.[9] China is also a key player in the ongoing construction of Egypt's New Administrative Capital. Yet, despite Western misgivings, Egypt has accelerated cooperation with China, including on its Belt and Road Initiative. Egypt purchased armed *Wing Loong* uninhabited aerial vehicles and is in talks to buy more weapons from China.[10]

Egypt's ties with the Gulf states resemble a patron–client relationship, although Cairo retains autonomy and has played on differences among them. Relations have fluctuated, with Egypt expecting that its sheer size and regional importance would suffice to bridge disagreements and misalignments, while the Gulf states have moved away from unconditional financial support. If Egypt and the United Arab Emirates (UAE) had largely cooperated over Libya from 2014, tensions have risen since 2020; they have also sat on opposite sides of the Sudanese divide since the coup there in 2021. Similarly, Egypt competes with Saudi Arabia for influence in the Red Sea region. A 2022 visit by Sisi to Qatar, once reviled for its support of the Muslim Brotherhood, suggested a willingness to explore new avenues for Gulf investment and to reduce its dependency on Saudi Arabia and the UAE.

IISS research shows that, between 2011 and 2022, the Gulf states provided Egypt with around US$50bn in aid, including direct deposits to the country's central bank, fuel assistance and other forms of support.[11] Bailouts mostly came from Saudi Arabia and the UAE. Despite these sizeable investments, the Gulf states received limited returns, resulting in increasing exasperation. They accordingly started demanding economic reforms and suggested they were no longer willing to simply provide unconditional financial assistance.[12] However, concerns over the ripple effects of the Israel–Hamas war and Egypt's mounting financial problems contributed to an Emirati announcement in February 2024 of a massive US$35bn investment deal by the UAE-owned ADQ conglomerate to develop the Ras al-Hekma peninsula. This aid was ultimately not conditioned on legal and regulatory reforms, curbing the influence of military-owned or military-run companies or downsizing costly mega-projects, as had been the expectation just before the start of the Israel–Hamas war. Nonetheless, at the time of writing, the extent to which the deal may have ceded Egypt's sovereign rights to the UAE remained unclear, though it validated Cairo's view that external partners still perceived Egypt as being too big to fail. The Emirati investment paved the way for further assistance from the EU, the IMF and the World Bank (see Figure 10.1).

GROWING PROFILE IN THE EASTERN MEDITERRANEAN

Egypt's complex relationship with the Gulf states influences the country's growing outlook towards, and investment in, the Eastern Mediterranean region. To mitigate its economic vulnerability, Egypt aims to anchor itself within new networks and make itself indispensable in other security arrangements and political blocs. Cairo has played a central role in reviving, creating or orchestrating regional networks. The East Mediterranean Gas Forum (EMGF) ranks highest in this regard, but the strategy extends to other formats: the current secretary-general of the Union for the Mediterranean is a former senior Egyptian diplomat, and Egypt has deployed its international influence through lobbying, cultural and academic channels.

Cairo has been particularly active in the Eastern Mediterranean region through naval modernisation. Egypt boasts the most modern navy in the Eastern Mediterranean basin and has inaugurated three new naval bases since 2019, two of which are on the Mediterranean: one in Jarjub on the northwestern coast and one in Port Said on the Suez Canal. But its equipment purchases have mirrored its hedging diplomacy, with ships procured from France, Italy, South Korea and the United Kingdom, raising questions about its operational ability to integrate, sustain and coordinate complex naval operations (see Table 4.2, page 102).

Cairo intends the Eastern Port Said Naval Base to boost security near offshore-gas resources. This expanded military presence is an indication of the significance Sisi has attached to the Mediterranean. New vessels – such as the ENS *Anwar El Sadat* (a French *Mistral*-class ship) and *Al-Aziz*-class frigates (German MEKO A200 frigates) – are stationed at Alexandria's naval base. This naval presence is a form of power projection useful for signalling and defence cooperation. Turkiye is Egypt's main (albeit distant) naval competitor, while Cyprus, Greece and Israel are partners, and its navy has a greater patrolling capability than those of its neighbours.[13] There have been no attacks on gas infrastructure in the Mediterranean thus far, including in the first eight months of the Israel–Hamas war. Islamic State (ISIS)-affiliated militants attacked an Egyptian naval vessel in the Mediterranean in 2015, but there have been no attacks since.

Egypt's four nuclear-power plants are also being built on the Eastern Mediterranean, at al-Dabaa, 170 kilometres west of Alexandria. Alexandria is Egypt's second-largest city, with over 6m inhabitants, as well as an important seaport. Smaller cities such as Port Said on the Suez Canal's Mediterranean end are strategic for Egypt's economy and security, with 19,000 ships using the canal in 2019.[14] Egypt also has significant trade with other Eastern Mediterranean states (see Figure 10.2): trade with Greece and Cyprus has increased significantly in recent years and, even during the long-standing diplomatic rift with Ankara, Egypt and Turkiye continued to be active trading partners.[15] Cairo and Ankara signed a free-trade agreement in 2007, since when the volume of trade between them has tripled. The trade surplus generally works in Turkiye's favour, but the agreement has also benefitted Egyptian manufacturers in need of foreign markets.[16] Egypt's balance-of-payments deficit vis-à-vis Turkiye during most of the 2010s was a restraining factor in their geopolitical rivalry. In recent years, Egypt has exported slightly more to Turkiye than the other way around.

Regional integration has emerged as a key strategy for Cairo in the Eastern Mediterranean. It has strengthened bilateral ties with Greece and Cyprus, which it sees as gateways to the EU and to

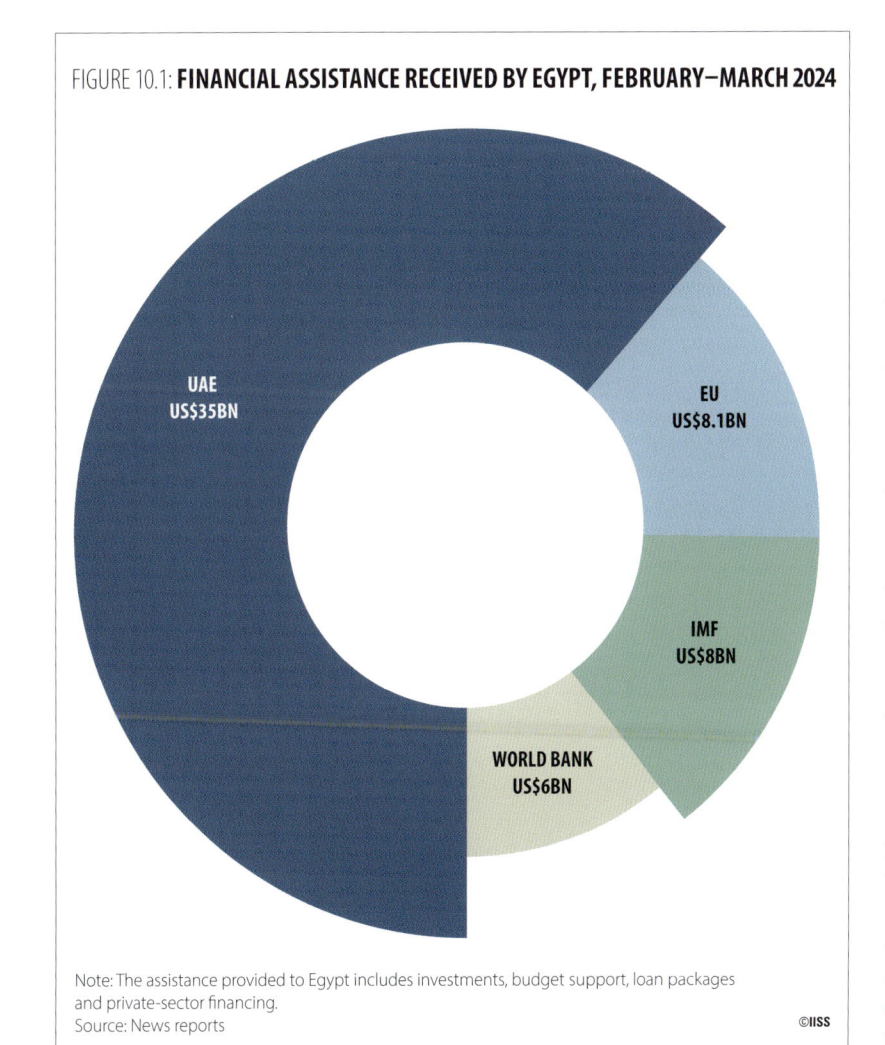

FIGURE 10.1: **FINANCIAL ASSISTANCE RECEIVED BY EGYPT, FEBRUARY–MARCH 2024**

- UAE US$35BN
- EU US$8.1BN
- IMF US$8BN
- WORLD BANK US$6BN

Note: The assistance provided to Egypt includes investments, budget support, loan packages and private-sector financing.
Source: News reports
©IISS

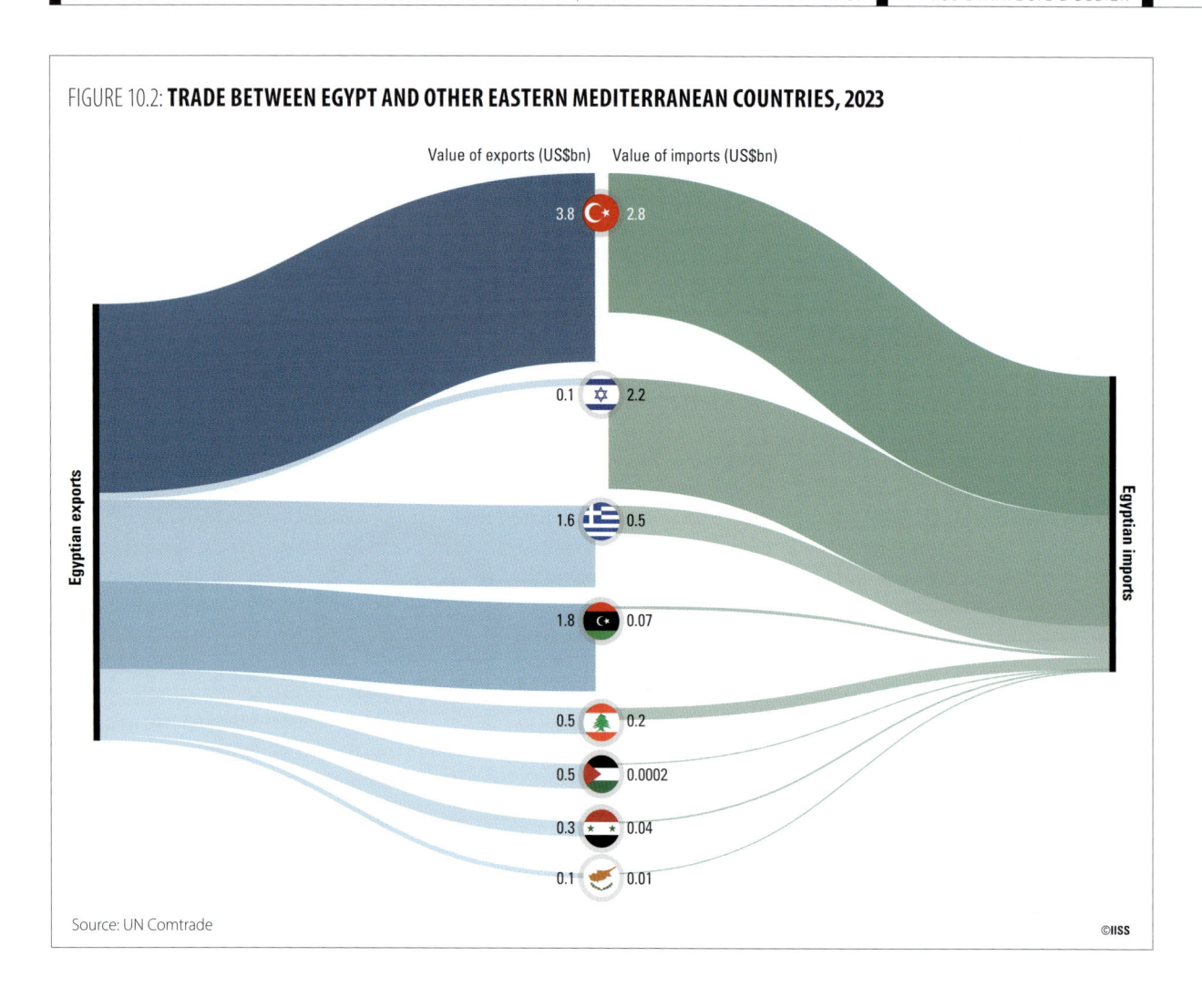

FIGURE 10.2: **TRADE BETWEEN EGYPT AND OTHER EASTERN MEDITERRANEAN COUNTRIES, 2023**

Value of exports (US$bn)   Value of imports (US$bn)

Country	Exports	Imports
Turkiye	3.8	2.8
Israel	0.1	2.2
Greece	1.6	0.5
Libya	1.8	0.07
Lebanon	0.5	0.2
Palestine	0.5	0.0002
Syria	0.3	0.04
Cyprus	0.1	0.01

Source: UN Comtrade

European markets. Egypt has correctly assessed that Athens and Nicosia, which embraced Sisi in 2013 out of relief that the coup had checked Turkiye's influence in Cairo, would be effective advocates in Brussels for its interests. Egypt, Greece and Cyprus sought to become a power bloc in the region, with an eye to isolating Turkiye. Egypt severed relations with Turkiye after Ankara's refusal to recognise the 2013 coup. Among the concerns of the Egyptian military in 2013 was the fear that a Muslim Brotherhood-led government would make maritime concessions to Turkiye or deepen the bilateral defence relationship. The two actors have been on opposing sides in Libya, and Egypt considers Turkiye's military role there a major national-security concern. Tellingly, the only time it threatened to deploy its own forces in Libya was during an advance eastward by Turkish-backed forces in 2020: it effectively deterred them from advancing further.

However, after a decade of heightened tensions, relations between the two countries started thawing in 2022, and Turkish President Recep Tayyip Erdoğan's visit to Cairo in 2024 was the culmination of this rapprochement. This de-escalation was an indication that both had seen the limits of their maximalist positions and acknowledged the economic necessity of patching up their relations. They resumed bilateral ties and stated that they would cooperate more closely, especially on Libyan security – though Cairo's wish for a Turkish withdrawal remains a major point of friction. Nevertheless, the two countries have maintained defence relations throughout their dispute.

Meanwhile, Egypt's dependence on Israeli gas and the revenues it derives from exporting this to Europe have further cemented the Israeli–Egyptian partnership and preserved their energy cooperation despite the ongoing Israel–Hamas war. Egypt's energy minister visited Israel in February 2021, the first senior Egyptian government official to visit Israel in five years. Working in conjunction with Israel, Egypt presented itself as an alternative to Russian gas in the aftermath of the invasion of Ukraine.

Some European capitals perceive Egypt as a short- and medium-term source of reliable energy that can help the EU as it embarks on its energy transition.[17] However, the European appetite for increased reliance on autocratic countries, including Egypt, is limited and there are questions about the reliability of its energy potential given its growing domestic consumption and dwindling reserves (see Chapter Three, page 75).

Israel is a consequential regional power for Egypt despite their complicated bilateral relationship. Cairo resents its military superiority but has worked with it rather than against it, in part to accommodate the US. The two countries have enjoyed warm relations since Sisi's rise to power. Egyptian officials have conducted quiet top-level security and intelligence collaboration with their Israeli counterparts, and the two countries appear content with the parameters of a 'cold peace'.[18] This has remained the case despite the Israeli offensive in Gaza, even if it has created tensions. For Cairo, the peace agreement remains an essential part of its regional posture. Competition in the maritime domain has been limited, and the two countries have invested in maritime cooperation. Egypt has a larger maritime presence, but Israel is building up its own navy and has a superior air force plus better intelligence, surveillance and reconnaissance (ISR) capabilities and technological depth.

Cairo has been concerned about being diplomatically relegated after the 2020 Abraham Accords between Israel and the UAE and Bahrain, and about the way these sidelined and possibly shelved the Israeli occupation of the Palestinian territories from international attention. This amplified Cairo's fears that it could become an observer rather than a shaper of regional politics. For example, the then-foreign minister Sameh Shoukry was the last invitee to the March 2022 Negev Summit where Israel's then-foreign minister also hosted counterparts from Bahrain, Morocco, the UAE and the US.[19]

Indeed, the Israeli–Palestinian conflict is one of the few theatres where Egypt retains diplomatic and coercive influence. Egypt's role as an intermediary in Israeli–Arab relations is central to its geopolitical standing; Cairo has therefore been concerned that new formats could render this historical role and other minilaterals it has designed redundant.

EGYPT AND THE ISRAEL–HAMAS WAR

The ongoing Israel–Hamas war has both allayed and amplified these concerns. The conflict has re-established Egypt's regional centrality, making Cairo's diplomatic and intelligence networks key to the management and possible resolution of the crisis. Egypt has leverage over – and a unique understanding of the dynamics within – Hamas, as well as solid intelligence coordination with Israel. In its eyes, its insistence (together with Jordan) on maintaining focus on the necessity of Israeli–Palestinian peace has been vindicated. The crisis has temporarily rendered irrelevant non-Egypt-centric gatherings such as the Negev Forum, and accelerated reconciliation with Turkiye (see Table 10.1).

As the US and European countries scrambled to contain the fallout from the Israel–Hamas war, they unblocked significant financial assistance in 2024 which they had previously held up hoping to extract reforms from Egypt, further reinforcing Cairo's sense of self-importance. The concern shown for Egypt's stability by Brussels as well as Greece and Cyprus contributed to the EU's decision to elevate their relationship to a Strategic and Comprehensive Partnership in March 2024 alongside its US$8.1bn package.

However, the risks of the Israel–Hamas war to Egyptian national security significantly outweigh these short-term benefits. It has compounded an already dire situation in Egypt's immediate neighbourhood, with ongoing wars in Sudan and Libya, a geopolitical rivalry with Ethiopia and complex relations with the Gulf states.

The Israel–Hamas war poses even greater political and reputational risks for Sisi's government. The possibility of a protracted conflict on Egypt's borders with immense humanitarian consequences that could trigger domestic political upheaval has unnerved Egyptian officials. They have decried Israel's tactics and objectives, and resented perceptions that they have been willing enforcers of the Gaza Strip's siege since 2007. The risk that Israel would intentionally and forcibly transfer some or all Gazan civilians into the Sinai Peninsula has also featured prominently in Egyptian minds. Such a violation of Egyptian territorial sovereignty would damage the standing of the government and the military and could revive instability on the already restless peninsula. Likewise, Egypt is wary of the prospect of taking charge of the stabilisation and governance of the devastated Strip, after Israel has reshaped the Gazan landscape enough to use reconstruction as a method of population control.

Should any of these scenarios play out, the risks of a direct confrontation with the Israeli government and military would increase. Egypt's military has deployed along the border, leading – despite increased communication with US and Israeli interlocutors – to incidents. Israel by mid-2024 had not publicised any governance plan for Gaza, but instead was in the process of redrawing its geography and announcing its desire to control the border between Egypt and Gaza, which the Israeli military calls the Philadelphi Corridor. Such a prospect would place Israel between Egypt and its

TABLE 10.1: RECENT TRENDS IN EGYPT'S BILATERAL RELATIONSHIPS AS OF MAY 2024

Country	Trend
Cyprus	↑
France	↑
Greece	↑
Israel	↓
Russia	↑
Saudi Arabia	↑
Turkiye	↑
UAE	↑
UK	=
US	=

↑ Strengthening relationship
= Unchanged
↓ Weakening relationship

Source: IISS analysis

Palestinian interlocutors, severing direct contact. Seeking to respond indirectly, Egypt has signalled its discontent by supporting South Africa's case of genocide against Israel at the International Court of Justice.[20]

Underlying Egypt's concerns is the Egyptian population's enduring perception of Israel as an enemy state, despite the peace treaty that the Egyptian political and security elite are determined to protect. Officials in both countries had been keen not to let various security incidents jeopardise their cooperation, purposely shielding its extent. This led to accusations that the government had secretly cultivated ties and even aligned with Israel. Popular outrage since the Israeli offensive in Gaza began in October 2023 has surpassed previous episodes of solidarity with the Palestinians, compelling the government both to repress such movements and to adopt a harsher tone against Israel in public.

But various factors also constrain Egypt from adopting a truly hardline position towards Israel. It is increasingly dependent on Israeli gas for both domestic consumption and exports: a breakdown in the relationship could therefore jeopardise both and encourage Israel to opt for non-Egyptian export options, depriving Egypt of precious foreign-currency access (even if, in the short term, Israel does not have a better option for its gas). Additionally, Cairo is concerned that the US could retaliate should Egypt take more determined action against Israel, suspending aid, denying IMF assistance or disregarding Egypt's views on regional matters. This has left Cairo with limited escalatory and retaliatory options. Additionally, the crisis's second-order effects have harmed Egypt, most notably the disruption of maritime traffic in the Red Sea due to Yemeni Ansarullah (Houthi) attacks on commercial and military vessels to show solidarity with Hamas in Gaza. In addition to immediate loss of revenue of around US$4.5bn, a key concern in Cairo is any long-term adjustment in the shipping industry away from the Suez Canal.

ENERGY AND EXPORT MARKETS

A key plank of Egypt's development and regional strategy has been its positioning as a regional energy hub in the Eastern Mediterranean. Egyptian officials describe this as a short-term focus on gas,

Egyptian President Abdel Fattah al-Sisi (C) addresses a plenary session during an emergency-aid summit for Gaza hosted by Jordan on 11 June 2024. (Photo: Alaa al-Sukhni/POOL/AFP via Getty Images)

a medium-term focus on electricity and a long-term focus on renewables.

Gas has been the primary vehicle of Egyptian ambitions. These have aimed to capitalise on the country's geographic location, its existing infrastructure, its first-mover advantage as well as the ongoing transition away from oil. Its investment in liquefied natural gas (LNG) facilities and infrastructure built in the early 2000s makes this possible. Egypt has two LNG-export terminals: one that Italian energy firm Eni operates in Damietta (60 km west of Port Said), and a larger one that Shell operates in Idku (50 km east of Alexandria). While the liquefaction plants have proved useful today, the facilities have not been functioning continuously and have generally operated well below capacity because of shortages in production and declining reserves. Following political upheaval in Egypt, Damietta was taken offline in 2012, which led to an array of legal disputes between gas firms and the Egyptian government over the disruption. Following international arbitration, Egypt was ordered to pay compensation. Liquefaction at Idku slowed down significantly in 2013 and 2014 but the plant remained operational.

Eni's 2015 discovery of the giant offshore Zohr gas field was a significant boost to Egypt's ambitions. Operating at full capacity, the country can export 1.6bn cubic feet per day and produce between 6.5bn and 7bn cubic feet per day according to its energy ministry.[21] Given Egypt's growing ambitions in this sector, there has been talk of building additional facilities. To that end, Egypt has signed an agreement with Chevron to explore developing further infrastructure for gas liquefaction and export.[22] But concerns about political and economic risk and contractual and commercial terms have dampened investor interest.

Cairo has pursued this role not only to obtain additional – and desperately needed – foreign-currency revenue from exports but also to become an influential actor in global energy markets.[23] Record-high natural-gas exports in 2022 represented around 16% of all Egypt's exports for that year, with around 80% of them going to Europe, but they have since slumped. Exports in April 2023 had decreased by more than 75% compared to April 2022.[24] Alongside dwindling reserves, gas production has also declined as a result of high domestic consumption, especially in the hot summer months. The government has sought unsuccessfully to reduce this: it introduced in 2022 initiatives like dimming the lights, rationing electricity, and using fuel oil in power plants.[25]

Egypt has hoped that further discoveries would strengthen its claim to be an energy hub. In December 2022, Eni and Chevron made gas discoveries in an offshore field, but not enough to maintain the exports levels Egypt desires. Other exploration efforts since then have been unsuccessful. Officials continue to express optimism about future oil and gas explorations, and the government approved a bill for the Ministry of Petroleum and Mineral Resources to contract a subsidiary of Eni for further oil and gas exploration in the Eastern Mediterranean.[26] But such exploration is far from certain, and LNG production in 2023 was mostly flat. In June 2023, Egypt was unable to export any LNG due to domestic demand. Energy minister Tarek El-Molla nevertheless announced plans to increase LNG exports by 40% in 2025, most of which is slated to go to Europe.[27] Egypt, however, missed its targets in the following months.

Israel has become a crucial component in Egypt's plans to become an energy hub, making continued cooperation a prerequisite for the realisation of Egypt's visions. Egypt imports gas from Israel that is cheaper than LNG spot prices, thereby allowing Egypt to make a profit. Egypt has sought to depict gas deals with Israel as a private-sector transaction through firms closely associated with the General Intelligence Service: Dolphinus Holdings and East Gas.[28] In so doing, the government has sidestepped questions and criticisms of the deal. Gas imports from Israel reached 5.81bn cubic meters in 2022, a record level and a quarter of Israel's gas exports.[29] They grew a further 17% in 2023.

In its quest to embed itself in region-wide networks, Cairo seeks to export Israeli gas via Egyptian LNG facilities to the EU. Egypt, Israel and the EU signed a memorandum of understanding (MoU) outlining a nine-year agreement in June 2022, which offers the EU an alternative to Russian energy. Egypt stands to make significant profits from this project, which will see tankers transport gas to European shores.[30] This route would be a substitute for

THERE IS A SIGNIFICANT GAP BETWEEN EGYPT'S AMBITIONS AND ITS CAPABILITIES. DESPITE ITS INVESTMENT IN THE EASTERN MEDITERRANEAN THEATRE, THIS HAS NOT TRANSLATED INTO DOMINANT INFLUENCE.

the Eastern Mediterranean Pipeline (EastMed) project, a plan that energy analysts and Western government officials have deemed logistically complicated, expensive, politically unwise and not viable in the long term.[31] Egypt and Israel instead have sought to link Israel's Leviathan gas field directly to Egyptian LNG terminals, from where it can be exported to Europe.

An additional gas pipeline is scheduled to be built from Israel's Leviathan field, which can supply Egypt with gas.[32] Currently, Israeli gas flows via a pipeline intersecting with the 1,200-km-long Arab Gas Pipeline, which connects Egypt with Jordan, Syria and Lebanon. The pipeline has been controversial, as it embodied Egyptian–Israeli normalisation, and has been subject to numerous attacks in the north of the Sinai Peninsula. Questions arose in 2022 after the announcement of a deal for Egypt to export natural gas to Lebanon through the Arab Gas Pipeline. The project ultimately stalled due to terms the World Bank set for reforms in Lebanon's power sector and to concerns about US sanctions on Syria.[33]

Cairo has also pursued energy-centric mechanisms for regional economic integration. The Cairo-based EMGF was established in 2019 to invigorate a regional gas market and coordinate natural-resource development. Egypt played a central role in founding the forum with support from the US and the EU, and it also includes Cyprus, France, Greece, Israel, Italy, Jordan and the State of Palestine. The forum has evolved into a membership organisation, and is widely seen as an Egyptian-influenced diplomatic instrument rather than a mechanism of economic cooperation. So far, its main success has been its ability to serve as a multilateral platform: it has not yet resulted in major joint projects. Apart from having excluded Turkiye from regional gas-cooperation discussions, the EMGF has still not produced tangible achievements even though it proclaims to be proactively shaping the future architecture of the region.

High hopes for 'gas diplomacy' – attempts to leverage energy interests to resolve political disputes – have thus far failed to materialise.[34] Successive US administrations have sought to motivate regional actors towards conflict resolution by highlighting the windfall more cooperation could produce in energy and other fields. And Egypt has acted as an intermediary between Israeli and Palestinian officials to encourage natural-gas production off the coast of the Gaza Strip, and encouraged Lebanese–Israeli talks on the demarcation of their maritime border.[35] But even before the 2023 Israel–Hamas war, Egypt struggled to influence these disputes, due to its own increased alignment with and dependency on Israel and because its regional clout had diminished.

Geopolitical and energy drivers have accelerated Egypt's search for maritime-demarcation agreements. In November 2019, Turkiye and Libya signed an MoU on maritime borders in the Mediterranean, followed by a maritime-hydrocarbons deal.[36] Both Athens and Cairo saw this as a provocation, even though it only infringed on Greek maritime rights and not Egyptian ones. In response, Egypt and Greece signed a maritime-demarcation agreement in August 2020.[37] In December 2022, Egypt's president announced the unilateral demarcation of its western maritime border with Libya, a move that Libya's Government of National Unity rejected.[38] Egypt signed similar agreements with Cyprus and Saudi Arabia as well.

Egyptian officials insist that gas is merely a short-term energy solution and that it is investing in renewable energy, including green hydrogen, as part of its long-term strategy.[39] Egypt's agreements for hydrogen projects have not yet materialised. As part of a shift to more sustainable energy, it has sought to increase solar- and wind-power generation, but these have proceeded at a slower pace than initially anticipated. The government missed its goal to have 20% of its electricity from renewable sources by 2022, only achieving 10%.[40] A large solar complex in Benban in Aswan Governorate in the south has been touted as the world's biggest solar park.[41] The project is still not complete, but Egypt hopes that it will allow the country to export energy to other states in Africa – though the infrastructure to connect to their electricity grids does not yet exist. The country received backing from the US and major European powers for investments that would facilitate its transition towards clean energy.[42]

As part of its comprehensive energy policy, Egypt is also working on building a nuclear-power plant in al-Dabaa on its

FIGURE 10.3: EGYPT'S REAL GDP GROWTH, 2010–24

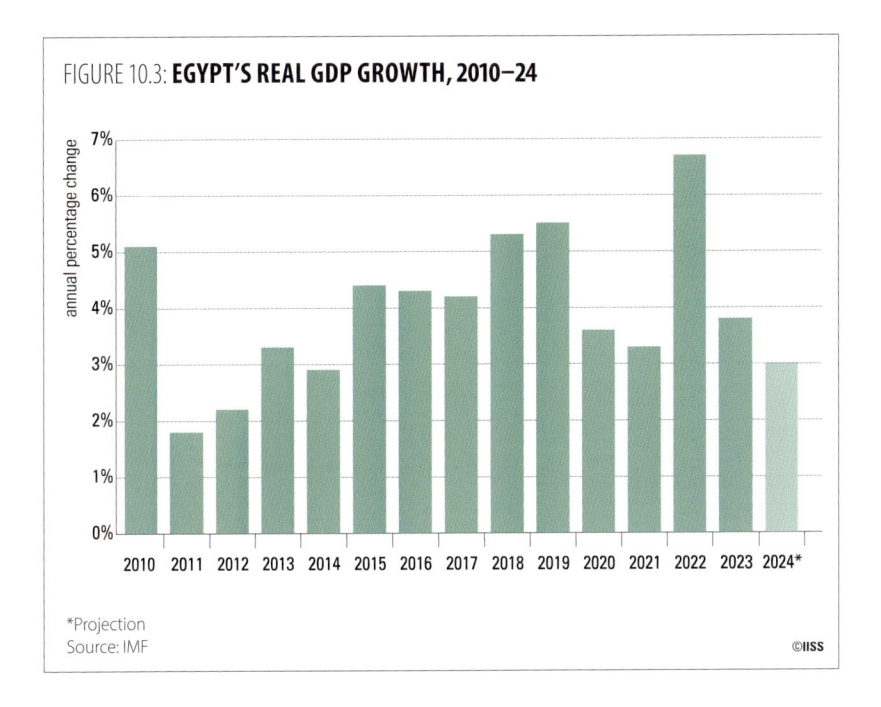

*Projection
Source: IMF

northern coast. Dubbed a 'long-awaited dream for more than half a century' by the Egyptian state, critics see it as a vanity mega-project to promote techno-nationalism rather than an effective economic-industrial project.[43] Cairo chose Russia to build and finance the project through a US$25bn loan, yet in 2022, Moscow reportedly subcontracted part of the work to a South Korean company.[44]

The viability of this overall vision also depends on linking the Egyptian grid to European ones: a submarine EuroAfrica Interconnector connecting Egypt, Cyprus and Greece has been in the planning stages since 2017, but implementation has fallen behind announcements.

LIMITATIONS AND DOMESTIC WEAKNESS

There is a significant gap between Egypt's ambitions and its capabilities. Despite the country's investment in the Eastern Mediterranean theatre, this has not translated into dominant influence. Egypt is struggling to shape actively the politics of this region, behaving mostly in reactive, opportunistic ways.

Severe economic crisis is a major factor limiting Egypt's ambitions in the Eastern Mediterranean. Many of the projects the state has outlined seem fundamentally disconnected from the reality of economic distress. In 2022–23 alone, real GDP growth decreased from 6.7% to 3.8%, while the Egyptian pound lost more than 50% of its value compared to the US dollar (see figures 10.3 and 10.4).[45] Prices for necessities such as food have skyrocketed.[46] The government's approach to alleviating the crisis has been to sell assets or borrow money, rendering itself perpetually dependent on foreign actors to rescue it from collapse. Egypt's ambitions for a greater role and credibility in the Eastern Mediterranean are ultimately contingent upon its ability to stabilise its economy.

Its foreign-policy hedging will serve it well in the short term, as the international order that has previously prevailed is in upheaval. However, without greater coherence and inter-operability for its military forces, and without greater regional cooperation on energy, climate and conflict resolution (even if some rivalries and disagreements are bound to persist), Egypt will struggle to return to its diplomatic heyday, instead having to resort to opportunistic manoeuvring when crises arise.

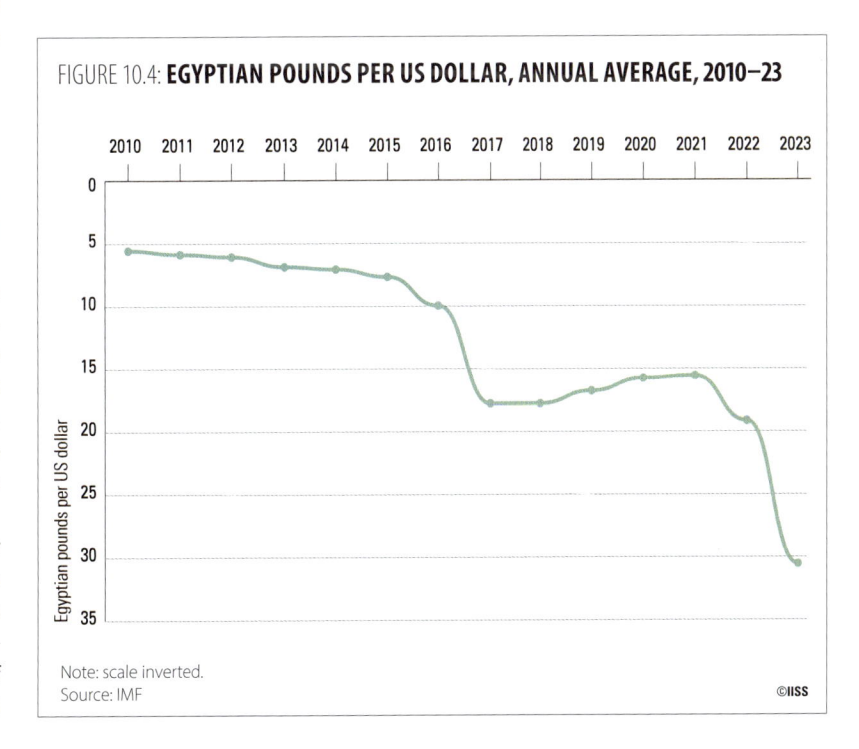

FIGURE 10.4: EGYPTIAN POUNDS PER US DOLLAR, ANNUAL AVERAGE, 2010–23

Note: scale inverted.
Source: IMF

ENDNOTES

1. Karim Elgendy, 'Egypt as an Eastern Mediterranean Power in the Age of Energy Transition', Middle East Institute, 18 July 2022, https://www.mei.edu/publications/egypt-eastern-mediterranean-power-age-energy-transition.

2. Mohamed Kamal, 'The Middle East According to Egypt', *Cairo Review of Global Affairs*, Spring 2018, https://www.thecairoreview.com/wp-content/uploads/2018/05/cr29-kamal.pdf.

3. Yezid Sayigh, 'Owners of the Republic: An Anatomy of Egypt's Military Economy', Carnegie Middle East Center, 18 November 2019, https://carnegieendowment.org/research/2019/12/owners-of-the-republic-an-anatomy-of-egypts-military-economy?lang=en&center=middle-east.

4. Lisa O'Carroll, 'EU Seals €7.4bn Deal With Egypt in Effort to Avert Another Migration Crisis', *Guardian*, 17 March 2024, https://www.theguardian.com/world/2024/mar/17/egypt-eu-deal-refugees-mediterranean.

5. Jeremy M. Sharp, 'Egypt: Background and U.S. Relations', Congressional Research Service, 30 September 2021, https://crsreports.congress.gov/product/pdf/RL/RL33003/116.

6. Ahmed Elleithy, 'Egypt, Russia Find Opportunity in Crisis', Al-Monitor, 3 March 2023, https://www.al-monitor.com/originals/2023/02/egypt-russia-find-opportunity-crisis.

7. Khalil Al-Anani, 'Growing Relations Between Egypt and Russia: Strategic Alliance or Marriage of Convenience?', Arab Center Washington DC, 27 September 2021, https://arabcenterdc.org/resource/growing-relations-between-egypt-and-russia-strategic-alliance-or-marriage-of-convenience/.

8. Dimitar Bechev, 'What's Behind the Partnership Between Russia and Egypt?', Tahrir Institute for Middle East Policy, 17 December 2021, https://timep.org/2021/12/17/whats-behind-the-partnership-between-russia-and-egypt/.

9. Khalid Hassan, 'US Warns Egypt to Avoid Chinese Companies on 5G Connections', Al-Monitor, 3 November 2020, https://www.al-monitor.com/originals/2020/11/egypt-china-us-war-5g-networks-boycott.html; and 'Egypt–China Relations Strengthen With $2 Billion Factory Deal', Al-Monitor, 24 March 2023, https://www.al-monitor.com/originals/2023/03/egypt-china-relations-strengthen-2-billion-factory-deal.

10. Jon Lake, 'Egypt Inducts Armed Chinese Drones', Times Aerospace, https://www.timesaerospace.aero/features/defence/egypt-inducts-armed-chinese-drones; and 'Egypt, China, on the J-10C Fighter', Tactical Report, 22 May 2023, https://www.tacticalreport.com/daily/61893-egypt-china-on-the-j-10c-fighter.

11. Hasan T Alhasan and Camille Lons, 'Gulf Bailout Diplomacy: Aid as Economic Statecraft in a Turbulent Region', IISS, October 2023, https://www.iiss.org/globalassets/media-library---content--migration/files/research-papers/2023/10/gbd/iiss_gulf-bailout-diplomacy.pdf.

12. Summer Said and Chao Deng, 'Saudi Arabia, Gulf Countries Want Better Returns for Bailing Out Egypt', *Wall Street Journal*, 7 April 2023, https://www.wsj.com/articles/saudi-arabia-gulf-countries-want-better-returns-for-bailing-out-egypt-e6e8b047.

13. Emmanuel Karagiannis, 'The Coming Naval Arms Race in the Eastern Mediterranean', RUSI, 22 July 2021, https://www.rusi.org/explore-our-research/publications/commentary/coming-naval-arms-race-eastern-mediterranean.

14. Suez Canal Authority, 'Navigation Statistics', https://www.suezcanal.gov.eg/English/Navigation/Pages/NavigationStatistics.aspx.

15. 'Egypt's Exports to Cyprus Hike 69% in 2022', Zawya, 10 April 2023, https://www.zawya.com/en/economy/north-africa/egypts-exports-to-cyprus-hike-69-in-2022-ykloj2pv.

16. Amr Adly, 'How Egypt and Turkey Trade Amid Tensions', Carnegie Middle East Center, 19 October 2021, https://carnegieendowment.org/research/2021/11/how-egypt-and-turkey-trade-amid-tensions?lang=en&center=middle-east.

17. 'Egypt Is Establishing Itself as a Natural Gas Hub, Petroleum Minister Says', CNBC International YouTube channel, 23 May 2022, https://www.youtube.com/watch?v=SzgbdyTxDrs.

18. David D. Kirkpatrick, 'Secret Alliance: Israel Carries Out Airstrikes in Egypt, With Cairo's O.K.', *New York Times*, 3 February 2018, https://www.nytimes.com/2018/02/03/world/middleeast/israel-airstrikes-sinai-egypt.html.

19. Amr Hamzawy, 'The Negev Summit's Participants Had Wildly Different Goals', Carnegie Endowment for International Peace, 6 April 2022, https://carnegieendowment.org/posts/2022/04/the-negev-summits-participants-had-wildly-different-goals?lang=en.

20. 'Egypt Says It Will Join South Africa's Genocide Case Against Israel at ICJ', Al-Jazeera, 12 May 2024, https://www.aljazeera.com/news/2024/5/12/egypt-says-it-will-join-south-africas-genocide-case-against-israel-at-icj.

21. Ahmed Ismail, 'Egypt's LNG Exports at Full Capacity After Gas Price Surge – Minister', Reuters, 2 December 2021, https://www.reuters.com/markets/commodities/egypts-lng-exports-full-capacity-after-gas-price-surge-minister-2021-12-02/.

22. 'Egypt and Chevron Agree to Explore New East Med Gas Deal', Reuters, 21 June 2022, https://www.reuters.com/world/middle-east/egypt-chevron-sign-mou-concerning-east-med-gas-petroleum-ministry-statement-2022-06-20/.

23. David Butter, 'Egypt's Energy Ambitions and Its Eastern Mediterranean Policy', in Michaël Tanchum (ed.), *Eastern Mediterranean in Uncharted Waters: Perspectives on Emerging Geopolitical Realities* (Ankara: Konrad-Adenauer-Stiftung Derneği Türkiye Temsilciliği, 2020), pp. 69–79, https://www.kas.de/documents/283907/10938219/Eastern+Mediterranean+in+Uncharted+Waters_KAS+Turkey.pdf/6f554da1-93ac-bba6-6fd0-3c8738244d4b?version=1.0&t=1607590823989.

24. Noha El Hennawy, 'Egypt's Lucrative Natural Gas Exports May Be Over: Experts', Zawya, 10 July 2023, https://www.zawya.com/en/business/energy/egypts-lucrative-natural-gas-exports-may-be-over-experts-wzhcmcjo; and 'Egyptian Oil and Gas Exports Drop 28.1% in First Two Months of 2023: CAPMAS', *Egypt Today*, 7 May 2023, https://www.egypttoday.com/Article/3/124200/Egyptian-oil-and-gas-exports-drop-28-1-in-first.

25. 'Egypt to Ration Electricity to Boost Gas Exports', Reuters, 12 August 2022, https://www.reuters.com/business/energy/egypts-cabinet-approves-plan-ration-electricity-save-gas-export-2022-08-11/; Jennifer Holleis and Mohamed Farhan, 'To Solve Economic Woes, Egypt Turns Off City Street Lights', Deutsche Welle, 16 August 2022, https://www.dw.com/en/to-solve-economic-woes-egypt-turns-off-city-street-lights/a-62823634; and Sarah El Safty, 'Egypt Burns More Heavy Fuel Oil to Free Gas for Export', Reuters, 13 December 2022, https://www.reuters.com/business/energy/egypt-burns-more-heavy-fuel-oil-free-gas-export-2022-12-13/.

26. 'Parliament Approves 3 Bills on Oil Exploration', *Egypt Today*, 19 March 2024, https://www.egypttoday.com/Article/1/131107/Parliament-approves-3-bills-on-oil-exploration.

27. Abdel Latif Wahba and Anna Shiryaevskaya, 'Egypt Plans to Resume LNG Exports in Autumn, Minister Says', Bloomberg, 19 July 2023, https://www.bloomberg.com/news/articles/2023-07-19/egypt-plans-to-resume-lng-exports-in-autumn-minister-says; and Salma El Wardany and Paul Wallace, 'Egypt Sees 2025 as Earliest It Can Boost LNG Exports to Europe', Bloomberg, 15 February 2023, https://www.bloomberg.com/news/articles/2023-02-15/egypt-sees-2025-as-earliest-it-can-boost-lng-exports-to-europe.

28. Hossam Bahgat, 'Who's Buying Israeli Gas? A Company Owned by the General Intelligence Service', *Mada Masr*, 23 October 2018, https://madamasr.com/en/2018/10/23/feature/politics/whos-buying-israeli-gas-a-company-owned-by-the-general-intelligence-service/.

29. Peter Stevenson, 'Egypt: Record November Israeli Gas Imports as Domestic Output Continues Descent', *MEES*, vol. 66, no. 3, 20 January 2023, https://www.mees.com/2023/1/20/oil-gas/egypt-record-november-israeli-gas-imports-as-domestic-output-continues-descent/297df9d0-98bf-11ed-96e6-6bb22a5b665f.

30. Sarah El Safty and Ari Rabinovitch, 'EU, Israel and Egypt Sign Deal to Boost East Med Gas Exports to Europe', Reuters, 15 June 2022, https://www.reuters.com/business/energy/eu-israel-egypt-sign-deal-boost-east-med-gas-exports-europe-2022-06-15/.

31 'Rethinking Gas Diplomacy in the Eastern Mediterranean', International Crisis Group, 26 April 2023, https://www.crisisgroup.org/middle-east-north-africa/east-mediterranean-mena-turkiye/240-rethinking-gas-diplomacy-eastern.

32 'Leviathan Partners in Israel to Invest $568 Million in Third Gas Pipeline', Reuters, 2 July 2023, https://www.reuters.com/business/energy/leviathan-partners-israel-invest-568-million-3rd-gas-pipeline-2023-07-02/.

33 Will Todman, 'The Politics of Lebanon's Gas Deal With Egypt and Syria', Center for Strategic and International Studies, 23 June 2022, https://www.csis.org/analysis/politics-lebanons-gas-deal-egypt-and-syria; and Khaled Yacoub Oweis, Nada Homsi and Ellie Sennett, 'Power Vacuum: Why a Regional Deal to Supply Energy to Lebanon Has Faltered', National, 25 November 2022, https://www.thenationalnews.com/mena/2022/11/25/power-vacuum-why-a-regional-deal-to-supply-energy-to-lebanon-has-faltered/.

34 'Rethinking Gas Diplomacy in the Eastern Mediterranean'.

35 Adel Zaanoun, 'Egypt Mediates Talks to Develop Gaza Offshore Gas', Al-Monitor, 14 October 2022, https://www.al-monitor.com/originals/2022/10/egypt-mediates-talks-develop-gaza-offshore-gas.

36 'Turkey and Libya Sign Maritime Hydrocarbons Deal', France24, 3 October 2022, https://www.france24.com/en/live-news/20221003-turkey-and-libya-sign-maritime-hydrocarbons-deal.

37 Salwa Samir, 'Egypt Eyes More Economic Benefits After Signing Maritime Demarcation Deal With Greece', Al-Monitor, 19 October 2020, https://www.al-monitor.com/originals/2020/10/egypt-greece-agreement-maritime-borders-demarcation-energy.html.

38 'Libyan GNU Government Refuses Egypt's Move on Maritime Borders' Demarcation', Reuters, 17 December 2022, https://www.reuters.com/world/libyan-gnu-govt-refuses-egypts-move-maritime-borders-demarcation-statement-2022-12-16/.

39 Sergio Matalucci, 'Egypt to Announce Ambitious Hydrogen Strategy', Deutsche Welle, 18 October 2022, https://www.dw.com/en/hydrogen-economy-egypt-to-announce-ambitious-h2-strategy/a-63466879.

40 Samy Magdy and Jack Jeffery, 'In Egypt, Host of COP27, a Small Step Toward Green Energy', Associated Press, 12 November 2022, https://apnews.com/article/health-africa-business-middle-east-egypt-80a7303cea21c34f9ba9b0679192820d.

41 Andrew Raven, 'A New Solar Park Shines a Light on Egypt's Energy Potential', International Finance Corporation, 29 October 2017, https://www.ifc.org/en/stories/2010/benban-solar-park-egypt.

42 Nibal Zgheib, 'Egypt's NWFE Energy Pillar Gathers International Support', European Bank for Reconstruction and Development, 11 November 2022, https://www.ebrd.com/news/2022/egypts-nwfe-energy-pillar-gathers-international-support.html.

43 'El Dabaa Nuclear Energy Plant Project', Egypt State Information Service, 4 February 2023, https://www.sis.gov.eg/Story/176389/El-Dabaa-Nuclear-Energy-Plant-Project?lang=en-us.

44 Kim Tong-hyung, 'S Korea Signs $2.25 Billion Deal With Russia Nuclear Company', Associated Press, 25 August 2022, https://apnews.com/article/russia-ukraine-middle-east-africa-349bf2b3eb2551bdea5ec886855dea92.

45 Netty Idayu Ismail, 'Egypt Pound Hedging Frenzy Unmasks Growing Devaluation Angst', Bloomberg, 13 April 2023, https://www.bloomberg.com/news/articles/2023-04-13/egypt-pound-hedging-frenzy-unmasks-growing-devaluation-anxiety.

46 Kamal Tabikha, 'How Egyptians Are Changing Their Diets to Cope With Higher Food Prices', National, 15 March 2023, https://www.thenationalnews.com/mena/egypt/2023/03/15/how-egyptians-are-changing-their-diets-to-cope-with-higher-food-prices/.

An Israeli Navy vessel passes by the Tamar gas field's production platform during an exercise off the coast of Israel on 27 May 2013. (Photo: Uriel Sinai via Getty Images)

UNTIL OCTOBER 2023, Israel's grand strategy in the Eastern Mediterranean consisted of containing and sidelining the Palestinian question and maintaining military dominance over its immediate neighbourhood (Lebanon and Syria) while developing relations with other regional powers through energy and security cooperation.

HAMAS'S OCTOBER 2023 ATTACK and the war that followed have upended Israeli assumptions and strategic thinking. Rebuilding Israel's security and deterrence is now the priority of Israeli officials, who are evaluating regional relationships in terms of their contribution to Israel's security requirements.

ISRAEL'S DIPLOMATIC RELATIONSHIPS with Cyprus, Greece and the United Arab Emirates (UAE) have withstood the war, while its relations with Egypt, Jordan and Turkiye have deteriorated. Israel's ability to partake in regionwide connectivity projects will depend on its general strategic orientation once the conflict ends.

# CHAPTER ELEVEN

ISRAEL: BETWEEN THE AMBITION OF REGIONAL INTEGRATION AND THE REALITY OF CONFLICT

INTRODUCTION

Until Palestinian Islamist movement Hamas's attacks against civilian and military targets in Israel on 7 October 2023, the country had seemingly developed and refined a successful strategy for regional integration that extended from the Eastern Mediterranean to the Arabian Peninsula. By maintaining and fuelling a split among Palestinian factions and effectively boxing them in politically and militarily since the mid-2000s, successive Israeli governments delayed – indefinitely, they hoped – any prospect of Palestinian statehood. In turn, this impasse led to the downgrading of interest in the issue across the region.

Simultaneously, Israel began to think differently about its immediate neighbourhood. It identified a convergence of interests with states from southern Europe to the Gulf region over the ideological and security challenges from Iran, Turkiye and populist Islamist movements. It sought to translate this into new regional alignments and to embed itself in burgeoning regional diplomatic, energy and infrastructure networks. Over time, the Abraham Accords, the upgrading of relations with Cyprus and Greece and the tantalising possibility of normalisation with Saudi Arabia turned Israel into a node in every major infrastructure and connectivity project, however aspirational, in the Eastern Mediterranean. In addition to its prized geographic location which allowed the bypassing of the Red Sea, an increasingly volatile space given the growth of threats to maritime traffic from Yemen's Ansarullah (Houthis), piracy and regional competition, Israel could provide capital, technology and talent. An additional benefit would be the certain Western approval of and investment in ambitious plans which participants to these projects presented as benefitting everyone except Iran-aligned countries and the Palestinians. Potential access to Israeli cyber and defence technologies was another driver of integration. The apparent success of this strategy contributed to the political and policy blind spots that the 7 October attacks exposed fully.

ISRAEL'S CHANGING STRATEGIC ENVIRONMENT

Israel's strategic situation had markedly improved in the years prior to the Hamas-led attacks of 7 October 2023. It had defeated the second Palestinian intifada, which ran from 2000 to 2005. The Palestinian Authority (PA), in charge of parts of the West Bank after losing control over Gaza to Hamas in 2007, had become a mostly quiescent entity whose legitimacy among Palestinians and credibility regionally and internationally was shrinking. The division between the PA and Hamas and between the West Bank and Gaza debilitated Palestinian politics and ability to articulate a national agenda. Crucially, it allowed Israel to postpone indefinitely any serious discussion about ending its occupation and about Palestinian statehood by arguing that there was no credible, unified Palestinian counterpart for such an effort. Israel's success in doing so allowed for an unimpeded growth in Israeli settlements in the West Bank, further shrinking the prospects of peace. The dominant belief in Israeli political and national-security circles was that Hamas in Gaza was effectively contained. Coercion, made possible by superior military and intelligence capabilities, combined with tactical rewards (such as working permits or looser import rules) and financial enticements (Qatar providing the latter as part of an agreement with Israel and the United States), ensured that Hamas was focused on governance of the Gaza Strip rather than fighting Israel. From this perspective, conflicts in Gaza in 2008, 2012, 2014 and 2021 were merely Hamas's attempts to improve marginally its position in both domestic politics and international bargaining. As a result, Israel did not feel pressured or compelled to seek political agreements, let alone engage in serious talks about a two-state solution.

The main strategic threat from Israel's perspective has been Iran's emergence as a regional player. Israel had previously not seen Iran as a conventional military challenge given its weak economy, limited capabilities and difficulties in procuring weapons systems. However, the convergence of its growing network of partners across the Middle East, its broad arsenal of uninhabited aerial vehicles (UAVs) and missiles, and its nuclear programme posed an unacceptable

A member of the Israeli Air Force (IAF) (R) and a member of the United States Air Force (L) stand near the Israel Defense Forces' military system *David's Sling* at Hatzor IAF Base in central Israel on 25 February 2016. (Photo: Gil Cohen-Magen/AFP via Getty Images)

threat to the Jewish state. Israel's failure to defeat Hizbullah in Lebanon during a 33-day war in 2006 showed the limitations of its military and technological superiority against the resilience of a disciplined and well-supplied militia with popular support. Iran has supported and enabled militias that the US and Arab rivals of Iran have struggled to contain. These have included the Badr Organisation and Kataib Hizbullah among others in Iraq, the Houthis in Yemen and an array of groups operating across Syria since 2012. In contrast, Israel as well as analysts saw Hamas as a smaller organisation, less aligned ideologically and politically with Iran than the others, and in control of more limited resources.

Iran's nuclear programme has presented the most serious challenge because of the Islamic Republic's deep commitment to endanger, or at the very least challenge, Israel's very existence. Much of Israeli defence planning since the 2000s has focused on how not only to deter and delay Iran but also to destroy its nuclear infrastructure if required. The immense difficulty of this military mission, as well as the opposition of the US and many other countries to it, led Israel to resort to sabotage, assassinations and other means to disrupt and delay Iran's nuclear advances. Israel remained the main proponent of a total international isolation of Iran through sanctions and political pressure, with Prime Minister Benjamin Netanyahu publicly opposing the 2015 Joint Comprehensive Plan of Action (JCPOA), which temporarily stopped Iran's nuclear progress in exchange for sanctions relief. Israel welcomed the Trump administration's decisions to withdraw from the JCPOA, impose a sanctions regime of maximum pressure and assassinate in 2020 Major-General Qasem Soleimani, the head of Iran's Quds Force and architect of Iran's regional strategy.

Regionally, however, Israel's emergence as an economic and technological powerhouse and the discovery of gas reserves changed domestic perceptions about the country's place in the region as well as regional perceptions of Israel. Israel's economic growth since the 2000s has led its GDP to surpass vastly those of its direct geographical neighbours: in current prices, its GDP grew from US$147 billion in 2005 to US$509bn in 2023, whereas Egypt's for example went from US$94bn to US$394bn during the same period and Lebanon's stagnated at US$22bn.[1] Israel's high-tech sector made a particular contribution to this success, with the country ranking 14th worldwide on the 2023 Global Innovation Index and 1st in the region.[2] Other technologies, such as water desalination, also made

Palestinians destroy a section of the Israel–Gaza border fence on 7 October 2023. (Photo: Stringer/Anadolu Agency via Getty Images)

Israel an attractive partner in a region increasingly dependent on them.

The deliberate Israeli strategy to harness its economic and technological power to improve regional relations proved successful with the 2020 Abraham Accords and improvement of relations with several neighbours. Crucially, the US Department of Defense moved Israel in 2021 from European Command's (EUCOM's) to Central Command's (CENTCOM's) Area of Responsibility, facilitating its defence cooperation with willing neighbours.

THE REPERCUSSIONS OF THE 7 OCTOBER ATTACKS

The Hamas-led 7 October attacks against Israel have had a systemic and still unfolding impact on state and society alike. They have altered the relationships between citizens, the military and security services and the political leadership, aggravating existing divides but also creating new ones. They have shaken Israel's sense of invincibility and belief that technological and military superiority guarantee security. Crucially, regional partnerships have not necessarily translated into tangible security and diplomatic alignments.

At the time of writing, Israel's military is fighting a brutal war against Hamas in Gaza, which has imposed great costs on Gaza's civilian population and infrastructure (see Map 11.1). A debate over Israeli intentions in this war has opposed those who accuse Israel of committing genocide or at least large-scale war crimes to punish and eventually expel the entire Gazan population against others who argue that the devastation reflects urban warfare and the nature of Hamas, an extremist guerrilla group that uses terrorism against Israel and manipulates Palestinian suffering. Given its unquestioned military superiority, Israel's campaign was able to significantly degrade Hamas throughout Gaza by May 2024. Israel had succeeded in reducing Hamas's firing of rockets, ability to mount large attacks and to train and organise new recruits, and had killed many of the movement's top commanders. Hamas had effectively lost any ability to reach into Israeli territory, was at risk of losing access into Egypt as Israel sought to occupy the Philadelphi corridor and faced difficulties moving fighters across the Strip. However, Hamas displayed resilience by evolving into an insurgency and preventing Palestinian competitors from emerging. Having made Gaza essen-

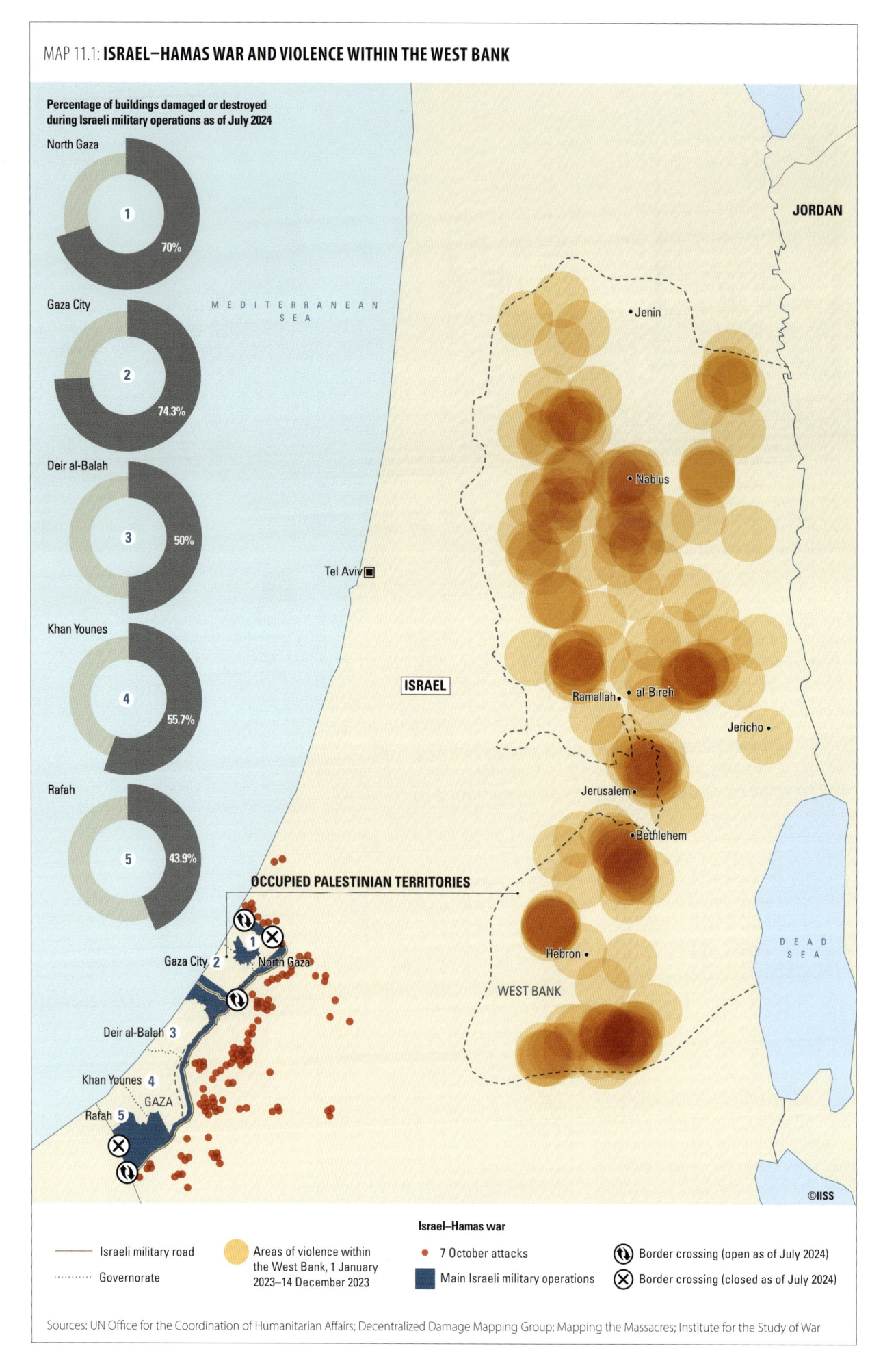

TURBULENCE IN THE EASTERN MEDITERRANEAN: GEOPOLITICAL, SECURITY AND ENERGY DYNAMICS ■ AN IISS STRATEGIC DOSSIER

MAP 11.1: ISRAEL–HAMAS WAR AND VIOLENCE WITHIN THE WEST BANK

Percentage of buildings damaged or destroyed during Israeli military operations as of July 2024

- North Gaza — 1 — 70%
- Gaza City — 2 — 74.3%
- Deir al-Balah — 3 — 50%
- Khan Younes — 4 — 55.7%
- Rafah — 5 — 43.9%

Israel–Hamas war

- — Israeli military road
- ⋯ Governorate
- Areas of violence within the West Bank, 1 January 2023–14 December 2023
- • 7 October attacks
- Main Israeli military operations
- ↻ Border crossing (open as of July 2024)
- ⊗ Border crossing (closed as of July 2024)

Sources: UN Office for the Coordination of Humanitarian Affairs; Decentralized Damage Mapping Group; Mapping the Massacres; Institute for the Study of War

tially unliveable, the Israeli campaign appeared to lack a realistic and sustainable political and governance endgame for the Strip. An endless de facto occupation of Gaza in which the Israel Defense Forces (IDF) preserves the ability to intervene at will is more likely than other scenarios considered, such as an international force or the empowerment of the PA. Israel has in parallel pursued a more aggressive strategy in the West Bank despite Western advice, Arab protestations and PA condemnations. There it sought to dismantle Hamas cells as well as those of other Palestinian armed groups but also expanded its settlement activities, fuelling the possibility of the war expanding to the West Bank.

Domestically, Israel's political and societal challenges have been exacerbated by the war. The suspicion among many Israelis that the war was being prolonged to serve Netanyahu's political goals has amplified pre-war concerns about the judicial reforms he introduced and his reliance on a political alliance with the extremist right. In parallel, Israelis have been torn between their support for the war and assigning the responsibility for the failures that led to the 7 October 2023 attacks to the leadership of the IDF and the security agencies conducting that war. The cost has also been economic. In May 2024, the head of the Israeli central bank estimated the cost of the war to be US$67bn between 2023 and 2025, including military and related civilian spending, and growth will likely diminish.[3]

In parallel, Israel's international standing has suffered considerably because of the IDF's conduct of the war, its immense human and infrastructure cost and concerns about the intentions of the Israeli government. In January 2024, South Africa, supported by other nations, introduced a case claiming that Israel was conducting genocide in Gaza in front of the International Court of Justice (ICJ). While the ICJ has not yet ruled on the matter, it still agreed to examine the motion and issued provisional measures intended to limit the harm done to Palestinians during this war. In May 2024, the prosecutor of the International Criminal Court asked that arrest warrants be issued for war crimes and crimes against humanity against the Israeli prime minister and defence minister, as well as the top three Hamas leaders. Israel has had to rely on a small

THE ISRAEL–HAMAS WAR AND THE FUTURE OF PALESTINIAN STATEHOOD

By the time of the Hamas-led 7 October 2023 attacks against Israel, the prospects for an end to the Israeli occupation of Palestinian territories and for Palestinian statehood were as remote as they had ever been.

Israel's crushing of the second intifada (2000–05), and the division between the West Bank (including East Jerusalem) and Gaza that took place between 2005 and 2007, debilitated Palestinian politics. This split over legitimacy, authority and resources between the two governing entities (the Fatah-dominated Palestinian Authority or PA in the West Bank, and Hamas in Gaza) made it harder for the various Palestinian factions to articulate and pursue a national agenda. Instead, it fuelled factionalism, corruption, brutality and misgovernance. The widespread perception among Palestinians that the PA no longer represented their national aspirations benefitted Hamas. An Islamist Palestinian armed movement affiliated with the Muslim Brotherhood and backed militarily and financially by Iran, Hamas sought to supplant the PA by posing as the true defender of Palestinian rights. It was torn, however, between its governance responsibilities in Gaza and its *muqawama* (resistance) ethos, with senior commanders worried that the former eroded the latter.

Combined with a successful Israeli strategy to maintain this division and delay indefinitely any political resolution of the conflict, this situation led to a gradual decline in interest for the Palestinian cause and diplomatic apathy among Arab and Western leaderships. The last serious diplomatic effort to broker peace was a short-lived United States effort in 2013–14, notwithstanding the so-called 'Deal of the Century' in 2019–20 by the administration of the then-president Donald Trump, which would have required significant Palestinian concessions in return for limited sovereignty. In parallel, the Arab and Israeli focus on containing Iran and Turkiye throughout the 2010s led to a dramatic convergence of interests and intensified key Arab states' intelligence and political relations with Israel.

The marginalisation of the PA grew as international attention and aid decreased and Israeli pressure in terms of withholding tax revenues, security operations and land seizure increased. Aside from the East Mediterranean Gas Forum (EMGF), which the State of Palestine joined thanks to Egyptian and Jordanian insistence, regional connectivity projects have excluded the PA. The 2020 Abraham Accords showed several Arab states' readiness to overlook the Palestinian cause in pursuit of the political, security, economic and technological benefits from normalisation with Israel. Traditional supporters of the Palestinian cause such as Cyprus and Greece prioritised security, energy and economic relations with Israel, an economic powerhouse and a close partner of the US.

Pre-7 October, the Gaza Strip, a densely populated area of about 365 square kilometres bordering Israel and Egypt, appeared relatively marginal in the broader geopolitics of the Eastern Mediterranean. The pre-war status of Gaza was, nevertheless, complex. Although Israel dismantled its settlements there and withdrew its ground troops in 2005, it still maintained effective control over the area through its control of borders, air and maritime space, and water and electricity among other necessities. Internally, however, Hamas ruled the area and Egypt controlled the southern border (which Israel calls the Philadelphi Corridor) and the key Rafah border crossing. Between 1 January 2008 and 6 October 2023, two high-intensity wars and four medium-intensity rounds of clashes took place, killing a total of 5,365 Palestinian civilians and combatants as well as 52 Israelis.[1] Despite these events, Israel and many other states believed that Hamas was effectively contained and the Gazan population quiescent. They did not see Gaza's status as an obstacle to regional cooperation plans.

The Hamas-led 7 October attacks against Israel and the ensuing Israel–Hamas war put Gaza and its long-term fate squarely at the centre of the

---

1   United Nations Office for the Coordination of Humanitarian Affairs (OCHA), 'Data on Casualties', accessed 6 September 2024, https://www.ochaopt.org/data/casualties.

region's attention. The gruesome nature of the attacks, which killed around 1,200 Israeli civilians and soldiers and led to the kidnapping of over 240,[II] aimed not only to shake Israel's psyche, self-confidence and security assumptions but also to widen fractures that were already emerging in Israeli society. Further, Hamas aimed to upend the status quo, including grandiose regional normalisation and integration projects, and force the issue of Palestine back onto the regional and international agenda. Importantly, the Hamas leadership in Gaza sought to draw its allies in Iran and Lebanon into the war, but failed as their risk appetites and priorities differed significantly. It focused on securing the organisation's survival rather than a conventional victory: by holding Israeli hostages and operating from a vast tunnel network, it played for time to try to win the narrative battle.

The ongoing war has dramatic repercussions for the future of Gaza. The human and material toll of the Israeli campaign surpasses any devastation suffered during previous Israeli–Palestinian conflicts, with nearly 35,000 civilian and combatant deaths by May 2024.[III] Without substantive long-term external assistance, Gaza risks becoming a near-uninhabitable place because of the destruction of housing, infrastructure, basic services and means of livelihood. An Israeli-engineered expulsion of Gazan residents or a slow outward trickle due to intolerable living conditions are major concerns among Palestinian civil society and leadership as well as for neighbouring countries.

The nature of the Israeli military posture in Gaza will also shape the area's future. The various Israeli security corridors and 'safe zones' that the Israel Defense Forces (IDF) has built, as well as its aim to control the Gaza–Egypt border, endanger Gaza's geographical viability. Rather than a direct and comprehensive occupation, the IDF appears to prefer a model where it occupies only some areas while retaining the ability to intervene throughout the Strip at will. This precludes any deployment of foreign troops or even non-Hamas Palestinian security forces. Without an international mandate (which Israel is likely to resist) and a clear Palestinian consensus, any external force would appear, to Palestinian citizens in Gaza and to Hamas, to be an IDF proxy. External troops operating alongside the IDF would find themselves in violent conflict with Hamas insurgents and at risk of clashing with or being obstructed by Israeli forces. Likewise, although no new governance model can emerge without Israeli consent and facilitation, Israel has remained both vague and maximalist about its requirements. Israeli conditions for post-war reconstruction include the 'destruction' of Hamas, Gaza being 'demilitarized' and the 'deradicalization' of Palestinian society as well as the dismantlement of the United Nations Relief and Works Agency for Palestine Refugees in the Near East (UNRWA), and would devolve only a limited level of autonomy to an undefined local authority.[IV] The US has publicly urged Israel to refrain from occupying Gaza and forcibly displacing Palestinians, but its ability to shape Israeli policies has been minimal.

Another important aspect of Gaza's future is its relationship with the West Bank (including East Jerusalem). Israel, as well as some other states, has proceeded on the basis that the West Bank's fate is separate from that of Gaza. While linkages between the two territories have weakened, the sense of shared identity remains strong. In the West Bank, the expansion of Israeli settlements, rising settler violence against Palestinians, Israeli designs on Jerusalem and the formal annexation of parts or all of this area have the potential to ignite large-scale armed resistance and possibly a third intifada. In such a scenario, the resulting damage to the

---

[II] Cassandra Vinograd and Isabel Kershner, 'Israel's Attackers Took About 240 Hostages. Here's What to Know About Them', *New York Times*, 20 November 2023, https://www.nytimes.com/article/israel-hostages-hamas-explained.html; and Linda Dayan and Maya Lecker, 'How Haaretz Is Counting Israel's Dead from the October 7 Hamas Attack', *Haaretz*, 23 November 2023, https://www.haaretz.com/haaretz-explains/2023-11-23/ty-article-magazine/.premium/how-haaretz-is-counting-israels-dead-from-the-october-7-hamas-attack/0000018b-d42c-d423-affb-f7afe1a70000.

[III] OCHA, 'Hostilities in the Gaza Strip and Israel | Flash Update #164', 10 May 2024, https://www.unocha.org/publications/report/occupied-palestinian-territory/hostilities-gaza-strip-and-israel-flash-update-164.

[IV] Benjamin Netanyahu, 'Benjamin Netanyahu: Our Three Prerequisites for Peace', *Wall Street Journal*, 25 December 2023, https://www.wsj.com/articles/benjamin-netanyahu-our-three-prerequisites-for-peace-gaza-israel-bff895bd.

number of Western partners to face these legal and political challenges.

The war has had immediate regional dimensions, compelling Israel to operate on several fronts simultaneously for the first time since 1973. Israel has sought to degrade the capabilities of Iran and Hizbullah, Hamas's close partners, which have conducted many operations to show solidarity with their Palestinian associates while striving to avoid an all-out conflict. Nevertheless, the risks of an all-out regional conflict that could engulf Lebanon and Syria and possibly Iran have also remained high. In April 2024, Iran mounted a large retaliatory air attack against Israel for the first time ever: a coalition of international partners and Israel's air force and air-defence systems intercepted incoming UAVs and missiles. The attacks nevertheless illustrated Israel's vulnerabilities and external dependencies.

There are also long-term strategic considerations. The crucial Israeli assumption of US support in times of war has been validated. However, having already lasted nine months at the time of writing, Israel's war against Hamas, which lacks any advanced weapons system, is the longest-ever high-intensity war the IDF has fought. This has tested Israel's doctrine that seeks to fight short wars on the enemy's territory. Israel's reliance on US deterrence, intelligence, logistics and weapons delivery throughout the war has also tested Israel's preference for strategic and operational autonomy. The prospect of a multifront war, once distant, has also risen, with Israel attacked regularly from Lebanon, Syria, Iraq and Yemen since 2023. In prior years, Israel had conducted a campaign to degrade Iranian capabilities in the region as Iran made regional inroads by enabling allied militias. Despite superior technology, Israel's hard geography, the limited availability and high cost of air-defence systems, and the risk that Iran and its partners could overwhelm its defences could limit Israel's responsive effectiveness.

Israel's new partners in the region have also hedged their positions. While there are no signs that countries that have signed peace treaties with Israel are considering ending them, tensions with Egypt and Jordan are at an all-time high since their respective treaties, and even Greece and Cyprus have joined calls for a de-escalation and pushed for diplomacy

PA's credibility, morale and ability to operate would effectively render impotent its security forces, which were central to the pacification of the West Bank after the second intifada. Hamas, weaker in the West Bank than in Gaza, has sought to increase its presence there, and has benefitted from Iranian support through arms smuggling from Jordan and Syria. For the PA to play a credible and constructive role, a series of reforms, a broadening of the Palestinian political representation inside the Palestine Liberation Organization (PLO) and new elections appear to be necessary.

The key factor deciding whether a peace process leading to Palestinian statehood will emerge once the war ends will be Washington's willingness and ability to jump-start it. Although President Joe Biden's administration has publicly announced its intention to do so, it has yet to articulate a specific approach. Further, there is no sign that Israel is ready for such a compromise. Resistance within Israeli society against Palestinian statehood, already high since 2000, has significantly increased since the 7 October attacks and many Israeli politicians have claimed that granting Palestinian statehood would be tantamount to rewarding Hamas for its atrocities. Similarly, Palestinian opposition to peace with Israel has increased, with many accepting Hamas's argument in favour of armed resistance regardless of the cost while others consider that Israeli-settlement activities have rendered a two-state solution impossible. Biden's officials themselves have been divided over the merits and risks of such a high-stakes, high-profile diplomatic effort with limited chances of success, while some Republican foreign-policy advisers have called for greater US support for Israel in its military campaign and the rejection of a Palestinian state. In any case, the Israeli government will likely now closely monitor and circumscribe, on security grounds, the amount of sovereignty Gaza or a wider Palestinian entity can exercise in dealing with other regional actors.

However, the war has been a significant setback to Israel's ambitions for regional integration. Its relations with Egypt and Jordan have deteriorated significantly. While signatories to the Abraham Accords have shown no desire to suspend or cancel normalisation, they have expressed concerns about Israeli political and strategic wisdom and dismissal of their advice. Most importantly, Saudi Arabia has articulated clearly the need for credible and irreversible steps toward Palestinian statehood before it would consider normalising relations with Israel. Prime Minister Benjamin Netanyahu's hardline government is hoping that a decisive victory in Gaza, a regionalised war implicating Iran, or a Trump administration taking office from January 2025 will contain or end such pressure.

Palestinians have taken some comfort from the international support and solidarity they have received during the conflict, as well as from legal cases against Israel and its leaders at the International Court of Justice and the International Criminal Court. Western states such as Ireland, Norway and Spain have recognised Palestinian statehood, bringing the total that do to 143 out of 193 UN member states. In Palestinian eyes, seeking international legitimacy by courting rising non-Western powers is designed to balance Western political and military support for Israel. However, Global South solidarity has not translated into tangible political and economic benefits.

How Hamas emerges from Israel's offensive in Gaza will depend on how much military strength, territorial control and especially popular support it retains in Gaza by the time of a potential ceasefire. The Islamist movement is unlikely to be able, in the foreseeable future, to mount a quasi-conventional challenge to Israel as it did on 7 October 2023. Only when the fighting ends might Hamas face sustained criticism from the Gazan population about the wisdom of the 7 October attacks, its lack of readiness for a predictable Israeli response as well as its neglect of civilian suffering.

Regionally, Hamas already faces complex dynamics. Its dogged fight against Israel has improved its regional standing but its actions have created serious risks and damage to its partners in Iran and Lebanon. Rebuilding its armed strength in Gaza will be much harder than in the past, as the IDF will remain deployed aggressively against it. As it reconstitutes itself, Hamas could expand regionally with a greater presence in Lebanon and Syria and begin to develop a presence in Jordan. There, it could recruit, organise and plan with Iranian and Hizbullah support, albeit while becoming more dependent on its sponsors and risking becoming a mere proxy.

to reach Palestinian statehood. Importantly, several countries – such as Saudi Arabia – have seen Israel as operationally effective but politically divided and strategically misguided, and have as a result maintained good relations with Iran to avoid any entanglement in a regional war.

For Israel, many of the assumptions that drove its regional integration strategy now appear fragile and possibly misguided. It is also not clear that, as it seeks to heal internally and rebuild its image externally, Israel will be able to devote as much political attention and skill to nurture its regional relations as it did in the past. At the same time, Israel's position as the energy superpower of the Eastern Mediterranean is not in question. The energy sector has not faced any meaningful interruption from the war and countries that import Israeli gas are even more dependent on it than in the past. This could still change if the conflict turns into a regional explosion that exposes Israeli infrastructure to attack. Contrary to Hamas's reduced means, Hizbullah's large arsenal can endanger Israeli energy facilities and pipelines. This would harm energy supply to Egypt and Jordan and push them to diversify their energy relationships away from Israel.

Another danger is that partners may freeze Israel out of regional connectivity projects such as the India–Middle East–Europe Economic Corridor (IMEC), which assumed that goods arriving through the Arabian Peninsula could be exported to Europe from Haifa and other Israeli ports. While the economic incentives for such projects remain high, Arab countries' political willingness to enter such agreements has diminished for the foreseeable future.

ENERGY AS A POLICY DRIVER

For an 'energy island' like Israel, the discoveries in 2009 and 2010 of the Tamar and Leviathan offshore gas fields triggered a transformative process in Israeli strategic thinking. They presented a rare opportunity to reduce the country's dependence on imported fossil fuels and engage in regional energy cooperation. In parallel, Israel began to prioritise the maritime domain, in which it had underinvested in previous decades.

Pursuing its interests in the Eastern Mediterranean has demanded the development of both domestic policies to handle the transition from full energy dependence to significant energy independence as well as foreign policies to become an energy exporter and influential actor within the region.

For most of its history, Israel was an energy island surrounded by a sea of oil- and gas-producing states. Bereft of its own domestic energy supply and with Arab League members boycotting the country since its establishment in 1948, Israel had to cast a wide net to meet its energy needs. Under those conditions, consecutive Israeli governments prioritised the security and reliability of supply over its affordability. Israel's conflict with the Arab states was not about energy, and yet energy-security concerns were a dominant feature. Both the 1956 Suez Crisis and the 1973 Arab oil embargo highlighted the relationship between global trade, the Arab–Israeli conflict and international politics. This made energy security a national-security issue, often determined at the highest levels of office and with limited transparency. As Israel's standing in the international community improved (largely due to the Oslo peace process), so too did its network of partnerships with energy-exporting states. However, the goals of energy independence and energy security remained elusive.

The path towards realising Israel's potential as an energy exporter would shake up not only Israeli politics but regional politics as well. The most significant natural-gas discoveries in Israel's waters were the Tamar and Leviathan offshore fields, in 2009 and 2010 respectively, by US-based Noble Energy (later acquired by Chevron) and Israel's Delek Group. Tamar and Leviathan combined held an estimated 736bn cubic metres (bcm) of natural gas, far exceeding Israel's domestic needs. These fields established the Levant Basin as a region rich in fossil-fuel reserves and Israel as a potential regional energy exporter. Israel's success is best reflected by the evolution of its energy mix. In 2000, imported oil and coal represented respectively 61% and 35% of that mix.[4]

In 2022, domestically produced natural gas represented 40.7% of the mix; crude oil and other petroleum products amounted to 37.6%, with Azerbaijan, Brazil, Gabon and Kazakhstan as top exporters; imported coal 15.9%; and renewable energy 5.8%.

Due to the Israeli market's limited size, Noble and Delek advocated for exporting the majority of Tamar and Leviathan's natural gas. A debate ensued over the country's energy strategy. It was settled when, in a statement in February 2016 to the Supreme Court of Israel, Netanyahu presented the discovery of offshore natural-gas reserves as a unique opportunity to foster cooperative regional relationships, enhance Israel's security and deliver an economic boon to the national economy. 'If we reverse course', he argued, 'we will fall into the chasm once and for all'.[5]

Netanyahu's decision to rely on a national-security argument fitted the traditional understanding of energy within Israeli policy discourse. Since 1948, national-security interests developed and executed by the Prime Minister's Office, the Ministry of Defense and the National Security Council have driven Israeli foreign policy and energy policy. The contours of the strategy were to rely on the US, the global superpower, to guarantee Israel's energy interests while continuously working to diversify the supply of energy imports.

Now that an energy bonanza had arrived, it was time for Israel to improve its regional standing by exporting natural gas as well. Energy diplomacy became a key pillar of Israel's regional outreach. It explored several potential export arrangements with its neighbours. While not all of these endeavours produced meaningful partnerships, Israel's energy partnerships with Egypt and Jordan were significant achievements which political and commercial drivers made possible and which required technical cooperation.

Egypt–Israel energy relations dated back to the 1979 peace treaty. At the time of Tamar's and Leviathan's discoveries, Egypt was supplying Israel with around 40% of its annual needs.[6] The energy relationship encountered difficulties: the Sinai pipeline that carried gas to Israel came under attack from tribal and jihadi elements in the 2010s, and the Muslim Brotherhood government that ruled Egypt between 2012 and 2013 criticised the arrangement but did not stop it. Both countries understood that the then-upcoming delivery of Israeli natural gas – which Egypt could use domestically or export to the global market via its liquefied natural gas (LNG) terminals in Idku and Damietta – was a win–win proposition. Egypt's interest in Israeli natural gas intensified following its 2015 discovery of the giant Zohr field, holding an estimated 850 bcm.[7] The combination of Zohr and additional natural gas from Israel would quickly allow Egypt to become an energy hub. In 2018, the two countries signed a US$15bn export arrangement, deepening their strategic partnership and their interdependency.[8] At the deal's signature, then Israeli energy minister Yuval Steinitz told reporters: 'The export of gas to Egypt, from Leviathan and Tamar, is the most significant economic cooperation between Israel and Egypt since the signing of the peace treaty between the countries.'[9] Israeli gas exports to Egypt began in 2020.

In parallel, Israel pursued an arrangement with energy-poor Jordan, although the conditions were different to those with Egypt. The Tamar-field partners and Jordanian-owned companies Arab Potash and Jordan Bromine signed a deal in 2014 to sell US$500 million of gas over 15 years, and an additional deal in 2018.[10] In 2016, Delek and Noble Energy signed an export deal worth US$10bn with Jordan's National Electric Power Company (NEPCO) that would deliver approximately 45 bcm of natural gas over 15 years.[11]

These arrangements came under political scrutiny in Jordan due to the public's sympathy for the Palestinian cause and its resistance to further normalising relations with Israel. During the negotiation process, regular protests took place in Amman and members of Jordan's parliament called for the process to be halted. These efforts compelled Jordan to demand that commercial actors rather than governments sign the export agreements. Ultimately, the combination of shared security and economic interests proved too compelling for the Hashemite Kingdom to reject cooperating with Israel, and the arrangement has paved the way for discussions on future energy projects.[12]

> WHILE THERE ARE NO SIGNS THAT COUNTRIES THAT HAVE SIGNED PEACE TREATIES WITH ISRAEL ARE CONSIDERING ENDING THEM, TENSIONS WITH EGYPT AND JORDAN ARE AT AN ALL-TIME HIGH, AND EVEN GREECE AND CYPRUS HAVE JOINED CALLS FOR A DE-ESCALATION.

Israel's natural-gas exports to Egypt and Jordan benefitted from pre-existing relationships with these Arab neighbours. They also benefitted from the technical feasibility of modifying existing energy infrastructure – as was the case with Egypt – or developing new pipelines to Jordan. The parties designed these export contracts primarily to serve the interests of the natural-gas companies; however, they also furthered Israeli strategic interests, creating greater interdependence with neighbouring states that had suffered from recent economic and political distress. While Israel would pursue other diplomatic initiatives in the Eastern Mediterranean, few produced the same tangible economic and strategic achievements.

The 7 October attacks and their aftermath cast a shadow over this optimistic outlook. Operationally, the consequences were limited for Israel. In coordination with Israeli authorities, Chevron and its partners suspended the pipeline to Egypt and production at Tamar for a month out of concern that Hamas could target the field. Tamar is, however, smaller than Leviathan, and Hamas showed no ability to disrupt its operations. The practical impact was minor, and production resumed quickly.

However, the political baggage of the relationship became heavier, especially for Jordan. Responding to popular outrage and frustrated by Israel's disregard for its advice in its conduct of the war, Amman suspended a 2021 water-for-energy memorandum of understanding (MoU). Because it had not been implemented, this was seen as a signal of anger rather than a redirection. A separate water agreement was renewed in 2024. Nevertheless, the episode illustrated the entanglement of energy with politics. In parallel, Egypt's worsening economic and energy situation became a source of concern. As Egypt's gas production declined and reliance on importing Israeli gas for domestic consumption grew, questions grew about its ability to meet its financial obligations and to maintain its viability as an export hub. Israeli officials have been keen to accommodate Egypt's energy needs to ensure stability in the relationship. At present, Israel lacks a gas-exporting alternative to Egypt, although Cyprus's own export ambitions may present opportunities in the medium term.

ENERGY AND CONFLICT

While Israel managed to achieve export contracts with Egypt and Jordan, the discovery of offshore resources exacerbated maritime tensions with other Eastern Mediterranean neighbours. It was only when international energy companies started to explore along the Levantine coast in the mid-2000s that policymakers understood that an undefined maritime boundary between Israel and Lebanon, two states formally at war, could be problematic. Israel and Lebanon used different demarcation methods to map out their respective claimed exclusive economic zones.[13] These differences produced a disputed area of roughly 860 square kilometres.

Over the course of a decade, the US mediated several efforts to produce a peaceful resolution to the dispute. From 2010 to 2012, American officials shuttled between the parties and presented a proposal that would divide the disputed waters in a ratio of 55 to 45 in Lebanon's favour (commonly called the 'Hof Line'), but talks eventually collapsed. After a decade's worth of on-again, off-again mediation, Israel and Lebanon reached terms in October 2022 that enabled Israel to continue exploiting resources undisturbed, allowed foreign companies to feel comfortable exploring Lebanon's waters, and did not require the two parties to normalise relations (a non-starter for Beirut).

A confluence of events created uniquely conducive circumstances for Israel and Lebanon to reach an agreement. Worsening economic conditions in Lebanon since 2019 compelled the Lebanese government and Hizbullah to set aside temporarily their opposition to Israel for the sake of brokering a deal that could potentially unlock valuable gas deposits and avoid open conflict. But this was not the only geopolitical development that made the agreement possible. The Gulf states, two of which normalised relations with Israel in 2020, were in favour of a peaceful resolution, especially if discoveries made Lebanon less expecting of foreign aid. The Western interest in alternative oil and gas supplies for Europe, especially after the 2022 Russian invasion of Ukraine, also contributed to the determination of US President Joe Biden's administration to push for an agreement. The timing of domestic political developments was also fortuitous. Due to then-upcoming elections in Israel, Lebanon and the US, each of the negotiating parties as well as the mediating party hoped that a deal would help their standing at the ballot box.

Between August 2020 and October 2022, negotiators shifted their emphasis from addressing each party's international legal arguments towards Israel's and Lebanon's core interests. For Israel, this meant emphasising national-security concerns such as achieving de facto Lebanese recognition of the buoy line Israel installed after its 2006 war with Hizbullah, enabling the safe development of the Karish gas field and establishing a deconfliction mechanism along its northern maritime boundary. For Lebanon, this required delinking maritime negotiations from its enduring conflict with Israel in order to convince international oil and gas companies to explore and develop its own waters. Lebanon also believed the potential of future development would help improve its position with the IMF and court foreign investments.

This period of relative calm and optimism lasted only a year. The Israel–Hamas war since October 2023 has exposed the frailty of the diplomatic edifice. While the 2022 maritime delineation deal has survived the war at the time of writing, it has not prevented a significant escalation of violence between Israel and Hizbullah. Violent incidents at sea in the case of an Israel–Hizbullah war could test its durability. Hizbullah's missile and UAV arsenal is large and sophisticated enough to pose a threat to Israel's energy infrastructure, notably in Haifa and Karish.

Additionally, the disappointing results of French energy company TotalEnergies' early exploration efforts in Block 9 (awarded also to Eni and QatarEnergy) in October 2023 were sobering for the Lebanese government and people. Enthusiasm for the deal in Lebanon had rested in part on the potential for significant discoveries. The failure to find exploitable gas could lead to internal recriminations over the merits and terms of the maritime deal with Israel as the regional context worsens.

Interestingly, however, Amos Hochstein – the lead US negotiator of the 2022 deal and a senior adviser to Biden – became the lead US mediator between Israel and Lebanon to avoid an escalation post-October 2023. This demonstrated the expertise and fragile trust that he had built on both sides. Hochstein proved able to avoid all-out confrontation for the first eight months of the crisis, although his ability to deliver a deal remained uncertain at the time of writing. The contours

↑

Amos Hochstein (L), Senior Advisor for Energy and Investment to US President Joe Biden, meets with Israeli Prime Minister Benjamin Netanyahu (R) in West Jerusalem, Israel, on 17 June 2024. (Photo: Amos Ben-Gershom (GPO)/Handout/Anadolu via Getty Images)

of a potential agreement include a withdrawal of Hizbullah forces from the regions bordering Israel and the deployment of Lebanese military units and a beefed-up United Nations force. Hizbullah, however, has increasingly questioned his trustworthiness and has conditioned a cessation of hostilities on a prior ceasefire between Hamas and Israel in Gaza.

Another aspect of this complex picture is the Occupied Palestinian Territories' dependency on Israeli-provided energy, including electricity. As an occupying power, international law requires Israel to meet the needs of the Palestinian people, and there are multiple grievances over natural resources between the two sides. About 94% of the electricity supply to the West Bank is produced in Israel and supplied through the state-owned Israel Electric Corporation via local Palestinian retailers. A small percentage of Palestinian electricity originates in Jordan and is supplied to a specific area within Jericho, and an even smaller portion is produced on small solar farms. In 2022, all fuel and cooking gas in the West Bank (a market estimated at US$1bn annually) originated in Israel and was supplied by two private Israeli fuel companies (Paz and Dor Alon) under contracts with the Palestinian Fuels Authority. Buying electricity third-hand translates into high prices, forcing households to reduce their consumption and resort to biomass as a cheaper alternative. These conditions were even worse in the Gaza Strip pre-October 2023, where infrastructure is even more outdated, resources more limited and dependence on Israel greater. Announcing the Israeli military response to the 7 October attacks, Israeli Defense Minister Yoav Gallant said he had 'ordered a complete siege on the Gaza Strip. There will be no electricity, no food, no water, no fuel, everything is closed.'[14]

The discovery of offshore natural gas in the Eastern Mediterranean rekindled ongoing disputes between Israel and the Palestinian Authority over access to Gaza Marine field, first discovered in 2000 by British Gas. Although a small field – estimated to hold up to 30 bcm – its successful development could provide significant relief to the Palestinian economy. For years, Israel rejected these proposals out of concern that revenues would end up in the wrong hands. But in June 2023 Israel quietly approved Egypt and the Palestinian Authority developing Gaza Marine provided that this met Israeli security needs.[15] Another project was the 'Gas for Gaza' initiative, which Qatar and the Palestinian Authority advanced in 2021 to construct a pipeline that would deliver Israeli natural gas to Gaza's only electric power station.

A successful development of Gaza Marine would have been a rare win–win for Israeli–Palestinian relations and reinforced Egypt's role as a regional energy hub.[16] The ongoing Israel–Hamas war will, at a minimum, delay considerably these already speculative projects, and possibly even put an end to them. The extensive destruction of Gazan infrastructure and the changes in its geography, demography and governance make any talk of energy development superfluous. Much will depend on 'day after' scenarios, themselves dependent on Israeli decisions. Additionally, establishing a framework for gas production and attracting investors and producers has become considerably more complex and risky, especially given the small size of the Gaza Marine field. Notably, however, Hochstein has stressed that Gaza Marine would remain a Palestinian asset and that future exploitation of the field would generate revenues to fund reconstruction and development.[17]

The rising significance of Israel's energy reserves – as well as the persistent tensions between Israel and its immediate neighbours – has coincided with a more intentional Israeli investment in the maritime domain and a growing naval presence in the Eastern Mediterranean. Israel's navy conducted a significant number of naval cooperation exercises with Greece and Cyprus prior to October 2023: these activities are currently paused because of the war, and whether they resume and in what format will be an indication of the health of Israel's regional relations. Israel's inclusion in US CENTCOM has also reinforced links with the Bahrain-based US Fifth Fleet, whose naval assets also patrol the Red Sea and the Bab el-Mandeb Strait.

Concerned over the physical security of its offshore investments, the Israeli government also expanded the navy's and air force's mission to protect natural-gas infrastructure (as well as other vulnerable coastal infrastructure). Israel invested in four German-made corvettes specifically for this task.[18] Both in 2021 and 2022, Hamas and Hizbullah independently tested the Israeli navy's preparedness by operating UAVs near offshore natural-gas platforms. However, at the time of writing, Hamas has failed to conduct any successful attack at sea during its war with Israel due to non-existent capabilities to do so. Hizbullah, however, demonstrated in 2006 its ability to target Israeli vessels when it hit an Israeli corvette with a Chinese C-802 anti-ship missile. The Lebanese militant group has invested significantly in its maritime-domain capabilities, becoming able to fly armed UAVs and having formed a unit equipped with speedboats to attack facilities and vessels at sea.

THE GREECE–CYPRUS–TURKIYE TRIANGLE

Although Israel's agreements with Egypt and Jordan provided reliable export routes for its hydrocarbons, natural-gas companies and Israeli officials have hoped to find an additional export route towards Europe. They have periodically considered two: a pipeline to Turkiye, and the Eastern Mediterranean (EastMed) Gas Pipeline via Cyprus and Greece.

One of the earliest proposed routes was via Turkiye, already in the process of turning itself into an energy hub and reliable natural-gas transit state between the region and Europe. But Israel–Turkiye relations took a dramatic turn in May 2010 following the Gaza flotilla affair. As Israeli and Turkish officials tried to resolve their issues, Noble Energy and Delek lobbied for an undersea pipeline between the two countries. The purely commercial logic was sound and the estimated US$2–4bn cost relatively inexpensive.[19] When Israel and Turkiye reached a reconciliation agreement in 2016, Netanyahu emphasised the potential energy cooperation: 'This agreement opens the way for cooperation on economic and energy matters, including the gas issue.'[20]

There were, however, significant obstacles to an Israel–Turkiye pipeline. Firstly, the drop in global energy prices reduced the appeal of a costly pipeline project. Secondly, the proposed pipeline faced geopolitical complications. It would have passed through Lebanon and Syria, carrying legal and security risks that were deal-breakers for Israel. Another option had it going through Cypriot waters which Ankara contested. Israel did not want to be exposed to the Turkiye–Cyprus dispute, especially as it was investing in strengthening its relationships with Cyprus and Greece. By the time Israel and Turkiye normalised ties in June 2016 and then again in 2023 (before the Israel–Hamas war), the nature of the bilateral relationship – as well as the regional geopolitics and economic calculus surrounding a possible pipeline – had changed such that the two sides deemed the project no longer feasible.

Israel also explored the possibility of the EastMed pipeline via Cyprus and Greece. However, this faced its own feasibility issues. The proposed 1,900 km undersea pipeline would cost an estimated US$8–10bn. While the European Commission listed the EastMed pipeline as a Project of Common Interest in 2013, industry experts questioned whether gas delivered through such an expensive route would ever be competitive on the European market. And despite Greek, Cypriot and Israeli officials continuing to advocate the project's promising future, few industry players take it seriously. Instead, they primarily see it as a political tool designed to keep Turkiye out of the regional energy game. In 2022, the US publicly withdrew its support for the project and essential European Union funding never materialised.

Although the EastMed pipeline faded from the headlines, Israel used the prospect of energy cooperation to deepen its strategic ties with Nicosia and Athens (see Table 11.1). In January 2016, Cyprus hosted the first trilateral meeting between the countries' heads of state. They held five additional trilateral summits between 2016 and 2019, eventually incorporating US participation in what became known as the 3+1 cooperation framework. Other energy projects, most notably the EuroAsia Interconnector – now known as the Great Sea Interconnector, a high-voltage cable that would link the electricity systems of Greece, Cyprus and Israel and enable the countries to trade excess power between themselves – have gradually replaced the EastMed pipeline as feasible trilateral projects that could connect Israeli and European energy interests.[21]

Israel's warming towards Greece and Cyprus is not limited to energy diplomacy: enhanced security cooperation has been an additional pillar of the relationship over the past decade. In April 2021, Israel and Greece agreed to a US$1.6bn deal that would enable Elbit Systems, a leading Israeli defence company, to develop a flight training programme and centre for the Hellenic Air Force.[22] Joint military exercises, as well as the sharing of training facilities and methodologies, became frequent. From Israel's perspective, Cyprus's and Greece's ports could theoretically offer strategic depth in the event of a major conflict.[23]

The development of ties with Cyprus and Greece served multiple purposes. Firstly, it helped Israel balance out the loss of its strategic partnership with Turkiye. Secondly, it helped strengthen Israel's relationship with the EU. Finally, Israeli partnerships with Cyprus and Greece developed in parallel with Egypt's, the UAE's and Saudi Arabia's significantly greater diplomatic engagement with the two countries, helping to cement regionwide understanding about the challenges Turkiye and Islamist movements posed.

TABLE 11.1: RECENT TRENDS IN ISRAEL'S BILATERAL RELATIONSHIPS AS OF MAY 2024

Country	Trend
Cyprus	↑
Egypt	↓
France	=
Greece	↑
Russia	↓
Saudi Arabia	↓
Turkiye	↓
UAE	=
UK	=
US	=

↑ Strengthening relationship
= Unchanged
↓ Weakening relationship

Source: IISS analysis

Constant scepticism in Israel regarding security and energy cooperation with Ankara as long as the Justice and Development Party (AKP) remained in power helped the development of relations with other countries. Israeli national-security and foreign-policy circles are adamant that the country's energy security should not depend on Turkiye. Rather, they believe Israel should continue to pursue a middle path between cooperation with Ankara and upgrading its relationships with Athens and Nicosia. Navigating the complexities of the Turkiye–Greece–Cyprus triangle has not always been easy for Israel, but both pipeline routes' lack of feasibility has compelled Israel to develop diplomatic agility. However, Turkiye remains central to Israel's oil security: Azerbaijan, Turkiye's closest partner, is one of Israel's major crude-oil suppliers and its oil has been shipped to Israel from the Turkish port of Ceyhan.

The Israel–Hamas war has magnified many of these challenges. Turkiye's political support for Hamas before 7 October and Hamas leaders' visits to Ankara since then have amplified in Israeli eyes a sense of Turkish perfidy. The merits of dealing with Turkish President Recep Tayyip Erdoğan have declined significantly among Israeli decision-makers. In contrast, the relationship with Cyprus has become even more important as it has played a strategic and logistical role for Israel during the war. Even if the prospect is distant and the economic argument weak, Cyprus remains the best alternative for Israeli gas exports should a political or operational disruption affect the Egypt route. While Nicosia itself has proved an eager defence and economic partner, it has yet to become an energy player that Israel can depend on.

OUTLOOK

Post-7 October Israel is undergoing profound transformations, the extent and magnitude of which are still unclear. This current war has unique political, legal and reputational dimensions for Israel. The manner in which it ends militarily and the perceptions in Israel and elsewhere about which party managed to prevail will be a part of the overall assessment. Much will depend on Israeli society: whether it stays cohesive, whether it can absorb the human, economic and political cost of the war, whether trust in the political and security leadership is restored, and whether there is interest in a negotiated settlement.

Israel's relationships with its immediate neighbourhood will likely remain troubled for years, if not decades, dictating greater defence investments and readiness. Whether the Israeli polit-

Thousands of Israelis, including the families of hostages held by Hamas, attend the '50 Days of Hell' rally in support of the hostages outside 'The Hostages Square' near the Tel Aviv Museum of Art in Tel Aviv, Israel, on 25 November 2023. (Photo: Gili Yaari/NurPhoto via Getty Images)

ical leadership will show the appetite and ability to pursue an ambitious regional strategy will depend on the security requirements and priorities it perceives when this conflict abates. Much of the pre-7 October regional agenda appears salvageable and remains relevant, unless relations with Egypt and Jordan deteriorate so drastically that their governments suspend their peace agreements or a war with Hizbullah and/or Iran brings about massive destruction in Israel. The speed at which this agenda can get back on track will depend on how the war in Gaza ends and whether Israel is willing to engage in good faith in a political process leading to Palestinian statehood.

Becoming an energy exporter has transformed the way Israel interacts with its immediate neighbourhood, creating new pathways for future collaboration. At the same time, some of the basic principles that have dictated Israeli policy since before the country's founding – reliance on its allies' support, adopting an integrationist approach, maintaining relations with major energy actors and using diplomacy to create new energy partnerships – today remain as critical as ever to ensuring Israel's energy security. While Israel's global standing has improved since 1948, it still operates as a partial island – limited in specific ways due to lacking both formal diplomatic ties with the world's largest oil and natural-gas producers and the infrastructure that would allow it to connect with greater energy systems such as Europe's and the Gulf's. What has changed is the way that Israeli policymakers and the general public discuss energy issues. Hidden for decades in a shroud of secrecy, energy security is now a topic of public debate.

From the perspective of Israeli officials, offshore hydrocarbons transformed the country's standing in the Eastern Mediterranean and positioned it to both shape and contribute to the region's future geopolitical architecture. The establishment of the East Mediterranean Gas Forum (EMGF) in 2019 was one such attempt. The EMGF offered Israel a unique platform to engage in technical discussions alongside four European and three Arab actors (including, notably, the State of Palestine). While Israel has enjoyed bilateral relations with all EMGF member states in the past, the forum established a structured mechanism for regional dialogue that had previously been absent. Israeli officials had hoped to take this further, using the momentum generated by oil and gas discoveries to position Israel as a hub between European, Mediterranean and Gulf investments. However, the EMGF may not stay immune from the tremors of the Israel–Hamas war. Egypt, Jordan and the Palestinian Authority are too dependent on Israeli energy to rupture the relationship with Israel, but they are unlikely to help it improve its regional standing

Palestinian youths attend a rally at the Gaza City seaport, Palestine, to demand Israel and the international community recognise Palestinian rights to gas from the Gaza Marine gas field and the opening of a sea passage from Gaza on 13 September 2022. (Photo: Ahmed Zakot/SOPA Images/LightRocket via Getty Images)

while the conflict rages and before the establishment of a Palestinian state. Even if Israel considers the EMGF format too restrictive and frustrating in the post-7 October context, it is unlikely to abandon a rare regional format.

Regardless of the conflict, Israel's role as an energy exporter remains somewhat unclear. At a regional level, its gas fields are significant and continue to attract investors, yet international energy companies are reluctant to invest in additional export options. Commercial, technical and financial considerations when gas arrives in Egypt limit Israel's cooperative ties with Cairo: shortages in Egyptian gas supply often result in the domestic consumption of Israeli gas instead of its export. At the same time, Israel remains dependent on Egypt's LNG export facilities, which constrains its own leverage over Cairo. Many geopolitical actors around the world – most importantly in Europe – are pushing for greater investment in green energy. Israel's interest in European markets depends on European energy and security calculations. In June 2022, in the aftermath of the Russian invasion of Ukraine, Israel, Egypt and the EU signed an energy-export MoU, though this is now subject to considerations linked to the Israeli–Palestinian conflict. Faced with these contradictory short- and long-term interests, Israel will continue to explore various export routes.

Since the mid-2000s, Israel has tried to establish itself as both a central actor within the region and a bridge between different regional spaces. Participation in inter-regional activity between Europe, Africa and the Middle East potentially offered significant long-term benefits for Israel as a hub for commercial and strategic activity. The Abraham Accords and possible normalisation with Saudi Arabia amplified these prospects. This dynamic, combined with a decade's worth of diplomatic activity in the Eastern Mediterranean, allowed Israel to start linking conversations and interests stretching from Europe to Asia through the Gulf, diversifying Israel's set of potential partners. Israel hoped that its advanced port facilities in the Mediterranean could offer an alternative transportation route to the Suez Canal. This project became part of the IMEC announced in September 2023 at the G20 Summit. In addition to the ongoing work on the EuroAsia Interconnector (which will link the grids of Greece, Cyprus and Israel), potential Israeli import of Gulf solar energy and green hydrogen through regional grids in the medium term would also serve to cement its regional position. But some of these connectivity projects are now on hold, given the conflict and the realisation among Gulf and other actors of the enduring political risk.

Israeli Prime Minister Benjamin Netanyahu holds up a map of 'The New Middle East' as he addresses the United Nations General Assembly in New York, United States, on 22 September 2023. (Photo: Michael M. Santiago via Getty Images)

ENDNOTES

1. 'Israel: Datasets', IMF, April 2024, https://www.imf.org/external/datamapper/profile/ISR.

2. Soumitra Dutta et al. (eds), 'Global Innovation Index 2023', World Intellectual Property Organization, 2023, https://www.wipo.int/edocs/pubdocs/en/wipo-pub-2000-2023-en-main-report-global-innovation-index-2023-16th-edition.pdf.

3. Sharon Wrobel, 'Bank of Israel Chief Warns War Against Hamas Will Cost $67 Billion in 2023–2025', Times of Israel, 30 May 2024, https://www.timesofisrael.com/bank-of-israel-chief-warns-war-against-hamas-will-cost-67-billion-in-2023-2025/.

4. International Energy Agency, 'Israel', https://www.iea.org/countries/israel/energy-mix.

5. Steven Scheer, 'Israel's Netanyahu Defends Gas Deal in Rare Supreme Court Visit', Reuters, 14 February 2016, https://www.reuters.com/article/world/israel-s-netanyahu-defends-gas-deal-in-rare-supreme-court-visit-idUSKCN0VN0RW/.

6. Hirak Jyoti Das, 'Israel's Gas Diplomacy with Egypt', Contemporary Review of the Middle East, vol. 7, no. 2, June 2020, https://doi.org/10.1177/2347798920901877.

7. 'Eni Discovers 850 bcm Giant Gas Field Offshore Egypt', Enerdata, 31 August 2015, https://www.enerdata.net/publications/daily-energy-news/eni-discovers-850-bcm-giant-gas-field-offshore-egypt.html.

8. 'Geo-economics and Israel's Gas Exports in the Eastern Mediterranean', IISS Strategic Comments, vol. 26, no. 6, October 2020, https://www.tandfonline.com/doi/full/10.1080/13567888.2020.1841938.

9. 'In Milestone, Israel Starts Exporting Natural Gas to Egypt', Times of Israel, 15 January 2020, https://www.timesofisrael.com/in-milestone-israel-starts-exporting-natural-gas-to-egypt/.

10. 'Noble Energy Signs 15-year Gas Sale Agreement with Jordan Customers', Enerdata, 21 February 2014, https://www.enerdata.net/publications/daily-energy-news/noble-energy-signs-15-year-gas-sale-agreement-jordan-customers.html.

11. Yossi Abu, 'Israel's Leviathan Signs $10bn Gas Deal with Jordan's Nepco', Financial Times, 26 September 2016, https://www.ft.com/content/0cbeecda-3712-3889-89e8-a38173a96b67.

12. Sue Surkes, 'Israel, Jordan, UAE Sign New MOU on Deal to Swap Solar Energy for Desalinated Water', Times of Israel, 8 November 2022, https://www.timesofisrael.com/israel-jordan-uae-sign-new-mou-on-deal-to-swap-solar-energy-for-desalinated-water/.

13. Israel marked the border as being at a 90-degree angle from the coastline. Lebanon marked it as a continuation of the land border. To further complicate the situation, the two parties disagreed about the point on land from which the maritime boundary should be drawn.

14. Emanuel Fabian, 'Defense Minister Announces "Complete Siege" of Gaza: No Power, Food or Fuel', Times of Israel, 9 October 2023, https://www.timesofisrael.com/liveblog_entry/defense-minister-announces-complete-siege-of-gaza-no-power-food-or-fuel/.

15. Dean Shmuel Elmas, 'Israel Consents to Palestinian Gas Field Development', Globes, 18 June 2023, https://en.globes.co.il/en/article-israel-consents-to-palestinian-gas-field-development-1001449748.

16. Ambassador Hesham Youssef, 'How a Gaza Marine Deal Could Benefit Palestinians, Israelis and the Region', United States Institute of Peace, 3 August 2023, https://www.usip.org/publications/2023/08/how-gaza-marine-deal-could-benefit-palestinians-israelis-and-region.

17. Mina Al-Oraibi, 'US Envoy Hochstein Says Offshore Gas Belongs to the Palestinian People', National, 19 November 2023, https://www.thenationalnews.com/mena/palestine-israel/2023/11/19/us-envoy-hochstein-tells-the-national-offshore-gas-belongs-to-the-palestinian-people/.

18. Sue Surkes, 'Navy Doubling Up on Seaborne Iron Dome Batteries to Thwart Hezbollah', Times of Israel, 28 March 2017, https://www.timesofisrael.com/navy-doubling-up-on-seaborne-iron-dome-batteries-to-thwart-hezbollah/.

19. By 2010, Turkiye consumed 50 bcm of natural gas per year, with its domestic demand projected to increase in the coming decades. A pipeline from Israel could potentially deliver some 8–10 bcm per year.

20. 'PM Netanyahu's Statement at His Press Conference in Rome', Embassy of Israel to the United States, 27 June 2016, https://embassies.gov.il/washington/NewsAndEvents/Pages/PM-Netanyahus-statement-in-Rome-27-June-2016.aspx.

21. Gabriel Mitchell, 'Supercharged: The EuroAsia Interconnector and Israel's Pursuit of Energy Interdependence', Israeli Institute for Regional Foreign Policies, February 2021, https://mitvim.org.il/wp-content/uploads/2021/02/Gabriel-Mitchell-The-EuroAsia-Interconnector-and-Israels-Pursuit-of-Energy-Interdependence-February-2021.pdf.

22. Judah Ari Gross, 'Israeli Firm Inks NIS 5.4 Billion Flight Training Deal with Greece', Times of Israel, 18 April 2021, https://www.timesofisrael.com/israeli-firm-inks-nis-5-4-billion-flight-training-deal-with-greece/; and Seth J. Frantzman, 'Israel, Greece Sign $1.7 Billion Deal for Air Force Training', Defense News, 6 January 2021, https://www.defensenews.com/training-sim/2021/01/05/israel-greece-sign-17-billion-deal-for-air-force-training/.

23. Eran Lerman, 'Israel's Priorities in the Eastern Mediterranean: The Tango with Turkey Has Limits', Jerusalem Institute for Strategy and Security, 30 July 2023, https://jiss.org.il/en/lerman-israels-priorities-in-the-eastern-mediterraneanthe/.

A demonstrator holding a Lebanese flag with black stripes stands atop the Martyrs' Statue at the Martyrs' Square in the centre of Beirut, Lebanon, during an anti-government demonstration on 1 September 2020. (Photo: AFP via Getty Images)

REGIONAL ATTENTION for Lebanon's eroding governance and declining economy has rebounded due to concerns over the possible extension of the Israel–Hamas war to Lebanon and the involvement of Iran, now a de facto power in the Eastern Mediterranean through its sponsorship of Hizbullah.

THE PROSPECT OF FINANCIAL WINDFALLS from potential gas discoveries in Lebanese waters motivated the 2022 maritime-demarcation agreement between Israel and Lebanon. However, the moderating impact of these commercial incentives is waning, as Lebanon has still not found gas, while the state is paralysed and bankrupt and Hizbullah is prioritising its conflict with Israel.

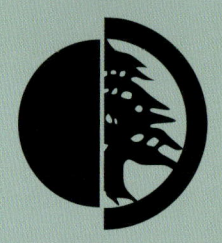

LEBANON'S PROTRACTED POLYCRISIS has frustrated external powers and has produced negative effects for the Eastern Mediterranean and beyond: it has become a departure point for irregular migration to Europe and a ripening environment for radicalisation and conflict. Lebanese actors perversely expect that they can derive geopolitical benefits by offering to contain such effects.

CHAPTER TWELVE

LEBANON: ENDURING POLYCRISIS AND ON THE BRINK OF WAR

INTRODUCTION

Lebanon went from being a small but consequential state in the Eastern Mediterranean in the 1940s to becoming the region's perennial 'problem child' by the 1970s. Exposed to regional turmoil but also producing its own instability, today the country is simultaneously on the periphery of the region's central dynamics and at the centre of another potentially catastrophic conflict.

MORE THAN A DECADE OF POLYCRISIS

Lebanon has hopscotched from political crises to economic and financial collapse since 2005, against the backdrop of a military build-up between the Iran-backed non-state armed group Hizbullah and Israel, which now threatens to turn into an all-out war. In this time, Lebanon has been subject to a war in 2006; Hizbullah taking over Beirut in 2008; the effects of the Syrian civil war (including a major refugee influx that puts immense pressure on the country's resources and has alienated the population); three protracted periods of rule by caretaker governments without an elected president; two major protest movements; an explosion of historic proportions that devastated Beirut; and one of the worst national economic collapses that the world has known in centuries.

The magnitude of Lebanon's dysfunction is remarkable. It took the ruling political parties two and a half years between April 2014 and October 2016 to elect a new president.[1] During that time, the country's already dysfunctional political institutions were paralysed. In 2015, mass protests erupted but failed to produce change. In 2019, with Lebanon on the cusp of what would end up being the worst economic crisis the country has known, mass protests erupted again, demanding economic and political reforms, but were similarly unable to bring about change. By August 2020, following the massive explosion at Beirut's port that killed at least 218 people and devastated large parts of Beirut, costing billions in damage, the country's economy was experiencing one of the worst crises globally since the mid-nineteenth century.[2]

A liquidity crisis became apparent in September 2019, when banks, having placed client deposits into the central bank (which in turn loaned the money to an insolvent state), severely limited access to dollar deposits. This boiled over when, in March 2020, Lebanon defaulted on its Eurobonds payments.[3] By 2022, general government gross debt had ballooned to 283.2% of GDP, up from 172.3% in 2019 at the beginning of the crisis (already the sixth highest in the world). Real GDP had contracted 34% since the beginning of the crisis, wiping out more than 15 years of post-war economic growth, while the Lebanese pound has lost more than 98% of its value against the US dollar (see figures 12.1 and 12.2).[4] The Lebanese parliament has been unable to elect a new president since October 2022 due to deep political polarisation. This has resulted in a caretaker government ever since and has further complicated attempts to enact the difficult financial and political reforms demanded by international financial institutions

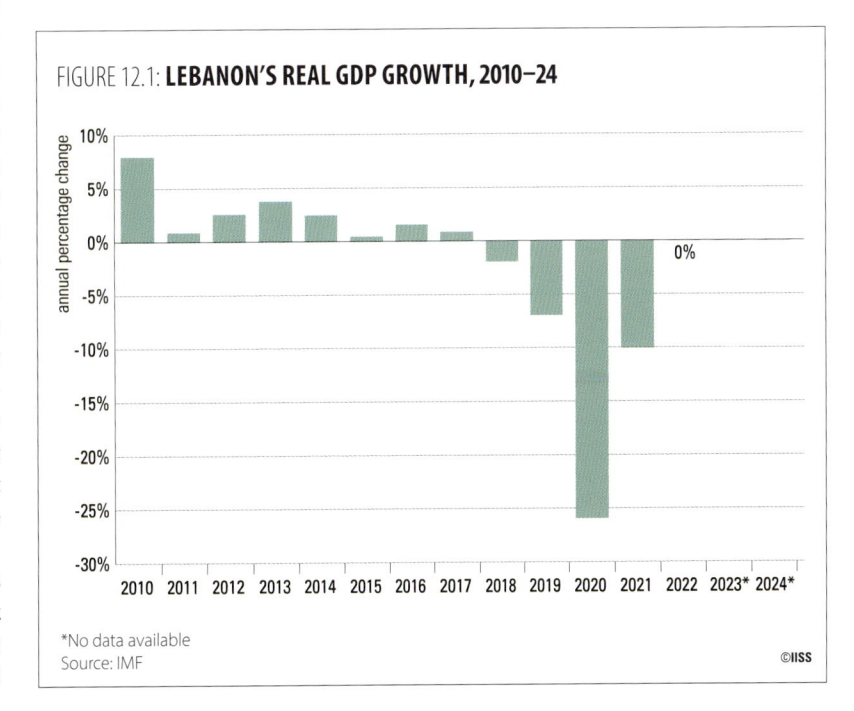

FIGURE 12.1: **LEBANON'S REAL GDP GROWTH, 2010–24**

*No data available
Source: IMF
©IISS

to provide necessary aid. By 2024, no structural-reform plan had been put in place. The impact has been devastating on Lebanon's middle and working classes.

These difficulties have affected the Lebanese Armed Forces (LAF), with soldiers struggling to feed their families and some taking second jobs, eroding the force's readiness. There have also been strains on the cohesion of the force, with heightened fears of a collapse akin to the ones that occurred during the country's civil war from 1975–90. This has prompted France, the United Kingdom, the United States and key Arab states to increase their financial support for the LAF, despite the lack of political reforms they have been seeking for over a decade. At an international conference convened by France in June 2021 to coordinate foreign aid and raise funds to support the LAF, the chief of the armed forces, General Joseph Aoun, underlined the urgency: 'The situation is critical. If unmitigated, the economic and financial crisis will inevitably lead to the collapse of all state institutions including the Lebanese Armed Forces.'[5] Despite having consistently ranked as the most trusted institution in Lebanon, the LAF's image has also suffered as a result of its repeated role in protecting the political system against the 2015 and 2019 protest movements, in addition to charges of corruption levelled in December 2020 against the former army chief and former high-ranking security officials.[6]

While Lebanon's chronic crises and instability have been priced into the Eastern Mediterranean landscape, supporting the LAF is also increasingly seen as important in controlling migration and refugee flows from Lebanon into Cyprus and the European Union, as well as countering Islamist jihadist threats. The only military battles the LAF has waged since the end of the Lebanese civil war were fought against Islamist militants, including Fatah al-Islam at a Palestinian refugee camp in northern Lebanon in 2007, and the Islamic State (ISIS) near the Lebanese–Syrian border from 2014–17. In May 2024, the EU announced a €1 billion assistance package to Lebanon to stop refugee flows into Cyprus.

In contrast, the LAF's continued inability and unwillingness to restrain Hizbullah has drawn increasing criticism from within. The Lebanese Shia militant organisation has grown in power and reach since the 1990s, becoming Iran's ultimate instrument of deterrence and defence, as well as the mentor of Iran-aligned armed groups throughout the region. It fought wars against Israel in 1993, 1996 and 2006, successfully preventing Israel from achieving its aims. Israel ended its occupation of southern Lebanon in 2000 and suffered a strategic failure in 2006, turning Hizbullah into a regional power enjoying popular backing across the region, even though public opinion in Lebanon remained sharply divided. Hizbullah's military capabilities are currently estimated to include over 150,000 guided rockets and missiles, as well as armed uninhabited aerial vehicles, with these supplied by Iran (transported via Syria), as well as indigenous production facilities. Its fighting force, estimated to be around 50,000, has become battle-hardened in Syria, where it was an essential component of the coalition that ensured the survival of the regime of Syrian President Bashar al-Assad.

In addition to dominating the LAF in terms of military capabilities, Hizbullah has consolidated its domination of Lebanese politics since 2005. That year marked a turning point for the country following the assassination of former prime minister Rafik Hariri and Hizbullah's participation in the Lebanese government for the first time. The move was meant to ensure that its strategic and operational autonomy remained immune from domestic pressure, gaining significant political power in the process but generating opposition across the political spectrum. The group grew more emboldened in asserting its domination, including through the threat of the use of force when its militants occupied the centre of Beirut in a showdown with the government in 2008. In 2011, the United Nations-backed special court investigating Hariri's death issued an indictment against four Hizbullah commanders; while they were never arrested, one was found guilty and sentenced in absentia in 2020,[7] followed by two others in 2022. Hizbullah has also expanded its military operations outside Lebanon since the 2010s, not only intervening to prop up the regime of Assad (despite the divisions this caused in Lebanon) but also providing support for Yemen's Ansarullah (Houthis).

Successive US administrations have maintained their financial support for the LAF despite US congressional criticism. In spite of its shortcomings, outside powers

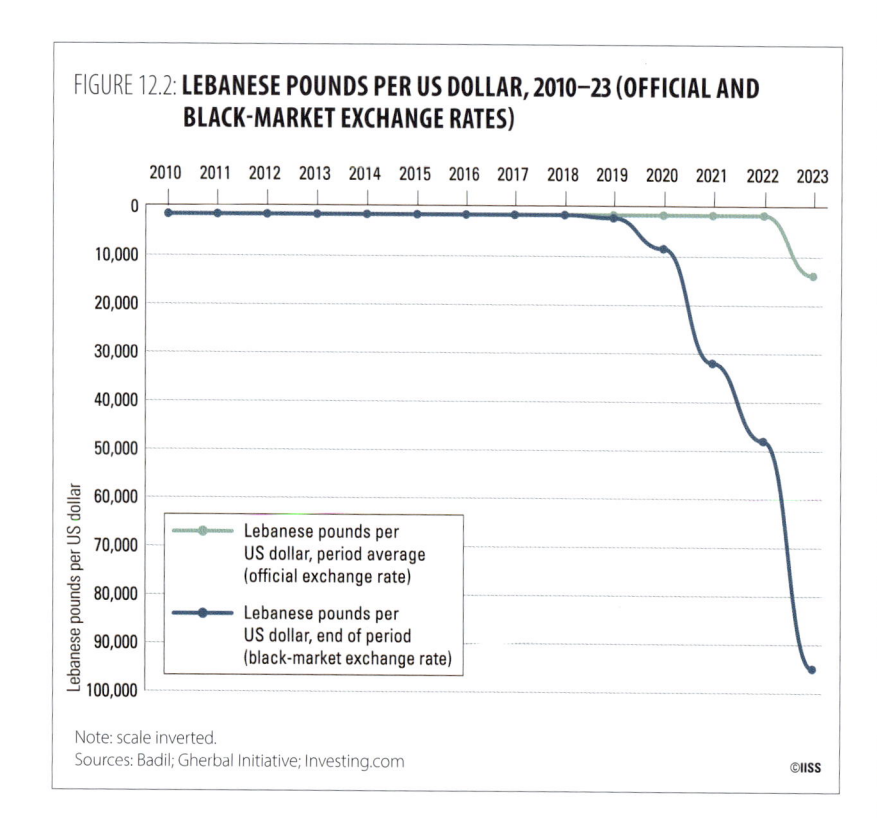

FIGURE 12.2: LEBANESE POUNDS PER US DOLLAR, 2010–23 (OFFICIAL AND BLACK-MARKET EXCHANGE RATES)

- Lebanese pounds per US dollar, period average (official exchange rate)
- Lebanese pounds per US dollar, end of period (black-market exchange rate)

Note: scale inverted.
Sources: Badil; Gherbal Initiative; Investing.com

such as the US and France still perceive the LAF to be the only institution that could play a role in the resolution of the conflict with Israel. It was through the LAF that the 2022 maritime-border agreement was operationally achieved, and it has been a central part of American and French efforts to find a diplomatic off-ramp to end the escalation between Israel and Hizbullah after the 7 October Hamas-led attacks against Israel. But doubts persist over the LAF's ability to take over southern Lebanon from Hizbullah and restore the state's sovereignty over all its territory.

A HISTORIC, BUT FRAGILE, MARITIME-BORDER DELIMITATION DEAL

In October 2022, Lebanon and Israel signed a US-brokered maritime-border demarcation agreement ending their decades-long dispute.[8] The two countries are enemies and concluded the deal without having established diplomatic relations, but the potential economic windfall from gas exploitation, especially given Lebanon's economic crisis, convinced the stakeholders to take this historic step. Notably, the two countries have yet to demarcate their land border, a move that would be more politically sensitive and consequential, especially as doing so would contradict Hizbullah's stated opposition to the recognition of Israel.

Lebanon and Israel have had competing official claims over their adjacent maritime zones since Israel delineated its maritime boundary with Cyprus in 2010. Lebanon submitted a competing claim in 2011 (see Chapter Two, page 51). Lebanon's economic crisis in 2019, which occurred just as Israel began to develop the Karish gas field across the maritime border, gave new impetus for a resolution. Lebanese players understood that without a deal, international energy companies would never risk investing and operating in Lebanese waters. The first drilling exploring for gas fields started after the agreement was sealed but has not discovered any exploitable gas to date.

Despite its historic nature, the agreement has three major vulnerabilities. Lebanon may not find a viable field to exploit and benefit from, taking away one of the major rationales for the deal. Exporting the gas is the second challenge, given the severe political and technical constraints. Finally, the ongoing military confrontation between Hizbullah and Israel in light of the war in Gaza could spill over

Lebanese protesters take part in a rally affirming Lebanon's right to its offshore-gas wealth on 4 September 2022. (Photo: Mahmoud Zayyat/AFP via Getty Images)

MAP 12.1: ATTACKS AND FORCED INTERNAL DISPLACEMENT IN ISRAEL AND LEBANON SINCE 8 OCTOBER 2023

Legend:
- Air/drone strike
- Intercepted attack
- Shelling/artillery/missile attack
- Displacement flow
- Litani River
- Governorate

Number of internally displaced people (IDPs) in Lebanon: 1–50, 51–100, 101–500, 501–4,860

Note: The International Organization for Migration (IOM) does not record the number of IDPs in Israel.
Sources: IOM – DTM Mobility Snapshot; American University of Beirut

---

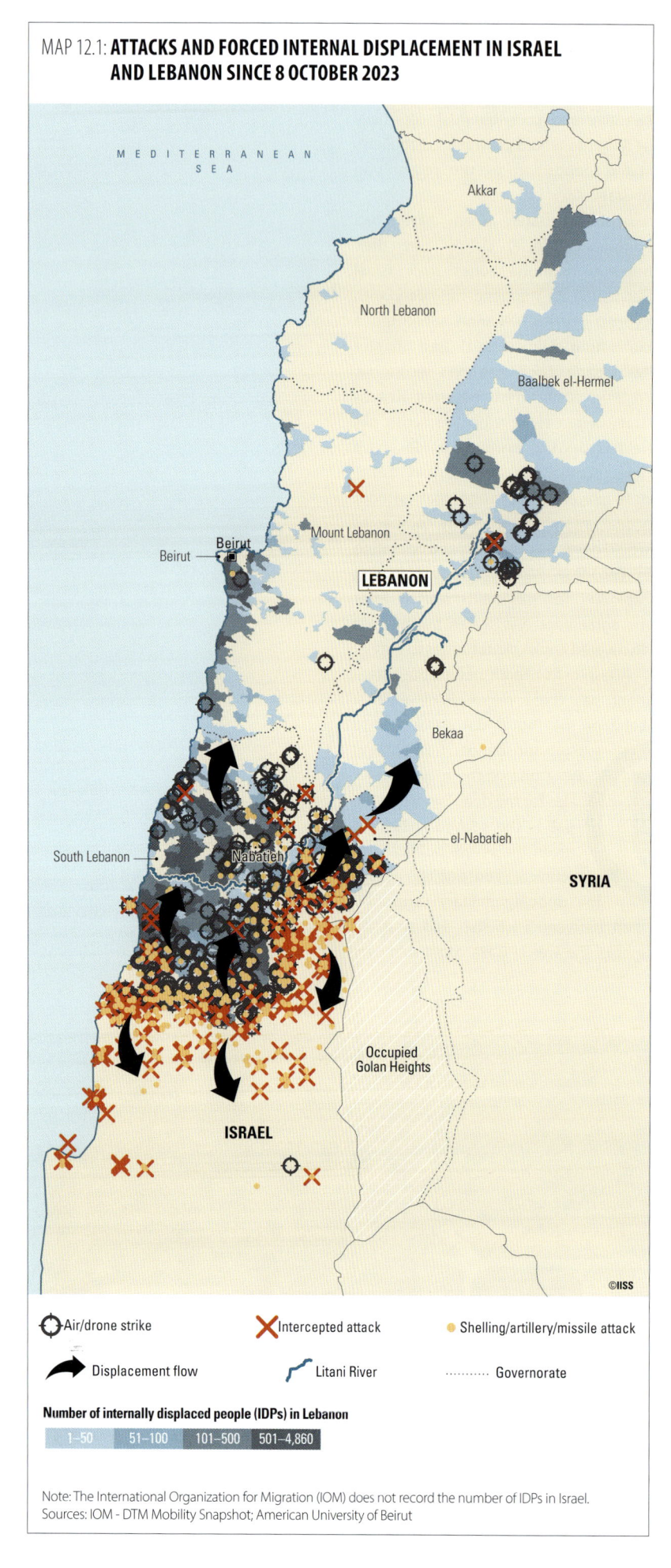

into an all-out war that jeopardises the deal. This tenuous situation is a reminder that in the Eastern Mediterranean, if the geopolitical stakes are high enough, they trump economic and financial dynamics.

Lebanon also has an open maritime dispute with Syria and is in the process of adjusting its 2007 demarcation agreement with Cyprus to reflect the border delineation it agreed with Israel in 2022 (see Chapter Two, pages 51 and 53). Yet these two disputes do not carry the risks of geopolitical destabilisation that the one with Israel does.

ESCALATING ARMED CONFLICT

At the time of writing, the survival of the maritime-border agreement, despite the escalation between Israel and Hizbullah, has emboldened its architect, Amos Hochstein, a senior adviser to US President Joe Biden, to design a diplomatic off-ramp aimed at preventing an all-out conflict between the two sides. US mediation is predicated on a demarcation of the land border, resolving a dispute over three border villages and implementing UN Security Council Resolution 1701, which calls for the withdrawal of Hizbullah to north of the Litani River, the deployment of the LAF to the border with Israel, and the cessation of Israeli violations of Lebanese sovereignty.

By May 2024, the confrontation between the two sides had not yet tipped into a high-intensity war, but the risk remained elevated. The forced displacement of tens of thousands of Israelis from their towns close to the Lebanese border for the first time since 1948, and the failure of the Israeli state to prevent an unprecedented deadly attack within its 1967 borders, have made the status quo ante with Hizbullah no longer acceptable for a majority of Israelis.[9] Polling by the Israel Democracy Institute has consistently shown that a plurality of Israelis support an all-out Israeli attack against Hizbullah.[10]

In the days following the Hamas-led attacks, Hizbullah's posture was deterred by the swift deployment of US carrier strike groups into the Eastern Mediterranean along with a US warning not to attack Israel. The group's restraint has largely held, even as Israel's attacks in Gaza have grown more intense and despite growing pressure from within Hizbullah's ranks and a part of its constituency to escalate its responses to Israeli attacks on its commanders and infrastructure. The Iran-backed group appears to have assessed that it is better off managing the escalation rather than risking consequential losses and large-scale destruction in a full-fledged war. The preservation of its status as Tehran's ultimate deterrence tool has trumped other goals, though the long-term effects on its credibility remain unclear. The dire socio-economic context in Lebanon since 2019 has also played a moderating role, with many Lebanese opposed to a destructive war.

This has allowed Israel to maintain escalation dominance, dictating the tempo and geographic spread of the war. It created a de facto uninhabitable buffer zone four kilometres within Lebanese territory, forcibly displacing more than 93,000 civilians (see Map 12.1).[11] The Israel Defense Forces (IDF) has claimed that it has killed more than 300 Hizbullah fighters, including both rank and file and middle and senior commanders, while at least 73 civilians have also been killed.[12] Hizbullah has not provided an overall tally of its losses, but based on its public announcements, which may not be an exhaustive account, more than 270 of its fighters had been killed by the end of April 2024. Israeli attacks since the beginning of the war in Gaza have degraded Hizbullah's fighting capabilities, having targeted its command-and-control centres, its missile launch pads, its weapons depots, and medium- to high-level commanders, but Hizbullah claims to have adapted and maintained its readiness and capabilities, conducting air operations into Israel to expose Israel's own vulnerabilities.

TENUOUS NORMAL THAT CAN EXPLODE AT ANY TIME

At the time of writing, Israeli attacks on Hizbullah and Iranian interests do not seem to have crossed the threshold that warrants an all-out war. When the Islamic Revolutionary Guard Corps, Iran's powerful paramilitary force, attacked Israel directly on 13 April 2024, Hizbullah played a notably minor role despite being the tip of its defence spear against Israel. This calculus in favour of restraint could nevertheless change in the coming

Smoke billows during an Israeli bombardment on the village of Khiam in southern Lebanon near the border with Israel on 19 June 2024. (Photo: Rabih Daher/AFP via Getty Images)

months, depending on how the rest of the Israel–Hamas war unfolds and the tempo and targets of Israeli attacks in Lebanon and Syria. Hizbullah is militarily prepared for a new war with Israel, having sufficiently increased its arsenal so that it is now able credibly to threaten all of northern Israel and having built ground defences across southern Lebanon. A satisfactory solution to the Lebanese crisis would have to compel Hizbullah to relinquish its armed status, restore state authority and pacify relations with Israel. It appears highly unlikely that this war would garner enough international attention to force such a comprehensive solution.

With no credible path out of its economic crisis, or for reforms – political, governance or economic – Lebanon is set to continue with its ad hoc coping mechanisms, with simmering social tensions that could boil over at any time, including rising anti-refugee and anti-migrant sentiments. There is also increased concern about armed clashes between Lebanese parties, especially in the event of mass displacement of Shia communities from southern Lebanon towards Sunni- and Christian-majority areas due to a war with Israel.

This multitude of crises has exasperated commercial partners as well as external powers. It may dissuade international energy companies from shouldering more risk to explore for gas fields, despite the active political investment of the US administration in this arena. In the past, Lebanon maintained good relations with most Eastern Mediterranean countries, but this is no longer the case. For example, should gas be found, exporting through Cyprus would have been a plausible option. However, Nicosia's growing ties with Israel and perception of Lebanon as a problem-ridden country now appear to preclude that. Today, Lebanon does not feature on a single regional connectivity or cooperation project. It is not a member of the East Mediterranean Gas Forum as Israel is a member, and it is bypassed by all large infrastructure plans, such as the India–Middle East–Europe Economic Corridor. This exclusion from regional integration only compounds the country's woes and reflects Lebanon's dire straits.

Lebanon seems set to continue to be perceived by its closest Western and Arab neighbours as a problem to contain and a crisis to avert, rather than as a country in which to rebuild and invest.

Hizbullah's Secretary-General Hassan Nasrallah meets acting Foreign Minister of Iran Ali Bagheri Kani in Beirut, Lebanon, on 4 June 2024. (Photo: Lebanon Hezbollah Press Office/Anadolu via Getty Images)

ENDNOTES

1. 'Lebanese MPs Fail to Elect New President in First Vote', BBC, 23 April 2014, https://www.bbc.com/news/world-middle-east-27124574; and 'Lebanon: Michel Aoun Elected President, Ending Two-year Stalemate', BBC, 31 October 2016, https://www.bbc.com/news/world-middle-east-37821597.

2. Bassem Mroue and Lujain Jo, '3 Years After Beirut Port Blast, Political Intrigue Foils Prosecutions and Even the Death Toll Is Disputed', PBS News, 4 August 2023, https://www.pbs.org/newshour/world/3-years-after-beirut-port-blast-political-intrigue-foils-prosecutions-and-even-the-death-toll-is-disputed#:~:text=4%2C%202020%20explosion.,billions%20of%20dollars%20in%20damages; and 'Lebanon Sinking Into One of the Most Severe Global Crises Episodes, Amidst Deliberate Inaction', World Bank Group, 1 June 2021, https://www.worldbank.org/en/news/press-release/2021/05/01/lebanon-sinking-into-one-of-the-most-severe-global-crises-episodes.

3. '"The Banks Don't Care": Lebanese Scream for Their Dollars', France 24, 31 December 2019, https://www.france24.com/en/20191231-the-banks-don-t-care-lebanese-scream-for-their-dollars; and 'Lebanon to Default on Debt for First Time Amid Financial Crisis', Guardian, 7 March 2020, https://www.theguardian.com/world/2020/mar/07/lebanon-to-default-on-debt-for-first-time-amid-financial-crisis.

4. IMF, 'General Government Gross Debt', https://www.imf.org/external/datamapper/GGXWDG_NGDP@WEO/LBN?zoom=LBN&highlight=LBN; and 'Lebanon: New World Bank Project to Restore Basic Fiscal Management Functions in Support of Public Service Delivery', World Bank Group, 15 February 2024, https://www.worldbank.org/en/news/press-release/2024/02/15/lebanon-new-world-bank-project-to-restore-basic-fiscal-management-functions-in-support-of-public-service-delivery.

5. 'International Powers Promise to Help Lebanon's Crisis-hit Army', Al-Jazeera, 17 June 2021, https://www.aljazeera.com/news/2021/6/17/world-powers-promise-to-help-lebanons-army-amid-economic-crisis.

6. Timour Azhari, 'Lebanon Ex-army Boss, Intelligence Heads Charged With Corruption', Al-Jazeera, 2 December 2020, https://www.aljazeera.com/news/2020/12/2/lebanon-ex-army-boss-intelligence-heads-charged-with-corruption.

7. 'Court Indicts Hezbollah Members Over Hariri Killing', France 24, 17 August 2011, https://www.france24.com/en/20110817-lebanon-justice-un-hague-court-indicts-hezbollah-over-hariri-assassination; and 'Special Tribunal for Lebanon Sentences Merhi and Oneissi to Life in Prison', L'Orient Today, 16 June 2022, https://today.lorientlejour.com/article/1302886/special-tribunal-for-lebanon-sentences-merhi-and-oneissi-to-life-in-prison.html.

8. Maya Gebeily and Maayan Lubell, 'Israel, Lebanon Finalise Maritime Demarcation Deal Without Mutual Recognition', Reuters, 27 October 2022, https://www.reuters.com/world/middle-east/lebanon-israel-set-approve-maritime-border-deal-2022-10-27/.

9. Maayan Lubell and Dan Williams, 'How Hezbollah Attacks Displace 60,000 Israelis, Six Months On', Reuters, 4 April 2024, https://www.reuters.com/world/middle-east/six-months-hezbollah-fire-keeps-uprooted-israelis-limbo-2024-04-04/; and 'Israel, Hezbollah Trade Fire, Israeli Minister Warns of "Hot Summer" at Lebanon Border', Reuters, 9 May 2024, https://www.reuters.com/world/middle-east/israel-hezbollah-trade-heavy-fire-violence-escalates-2024-05-08/.

10. Tamar Hermann and Yaron Kaplan, 'Most Israelis: An "Absolute Victory" to the War Is Unlikely', The Israel Democracy Institute, 20 February 2024, https://en.idi.org.il/articles/52976.

11. Relief Web, 'Lebanon: Flash Update #17 – Escalation of Hostilities in South Lebanon, as of 2 May 2024', OCHA, 8 May 2024, https://reliefweb.int/report/lebanon/lebanon-flash-update-17-escalation-hostilities-south-lebanon-2-may-2024.

12. Emanuel Fabian, 'IDF Says Some 4,500 Hezbollah Targets Hit, 300 Operatives Killed Since Start of War', Times of Israel, 12 March 2024, https://www.timesofisrael.com/idf-says-some-4500-hezbollah-targets-hit-300-operatives-killed-since-start-of-war/#:~:text=According%20to%20the%20IDF's%20estimates,daily%20skirmishes%20along%20the%20border.

Syrian regime soldiers in the previously rebel-held Jobar in Eastern Ghouta on 2 April 2018. (Photo: Louai Beshara/AFP via Getty Images)

SYRIA HAS BEEN AN ARENA for geopolitical competition since the 2011 Arab uprisings. With five foreign militaries operating on its territory, the divided and broken country has little agency and a limited ability to articulate and pursue interests other than the survival of the government of President Bashar al-Assad.

DESPITE SYRIA'S RETURN TO THE ARAB LEAGUE in 2023, its tense relationships with its neighbours preclude any involvement in regional cooperation initiatives. Instead, foreign engagement with Damascus focuses on containing the negative effects that the conflict generates, such as transnational terrorism, migration and drug trafficking.

SYRIA IS AN ARENA FOR THE CONFLICT between Israel on the one hand and Iran and its partners on the other. It risks being engulfed in another expanded war it does not want and has no agency in, given its weak state and dependence on Iran.

CHAPTER THIRTEEN
SYRIA: A BROKEN STATE AND AN ARENA FOR COMPETITION

INTRODUCTION

Syria has historically behaved and seen itself as a shaper of dynamics in the Eastern Mediterranean through its involvement in Lebanon, support for non-state armed groups and balancing game between Arab states, Western powers and Iran. Syria has dominated the Arab Levantine agenda, notably vis-à-vis Israel, with which it has been at war since 1948. This role ended with the devastating internationalised civil war that started in 2011, which has shattered its geographic coherence and political reach. Today, despite its enviable location, Syria is an arena for geopolitical competition to which the ruling government of Bashar al-Assad is a bystander.

FROM ACTOR TO ARENA

Despite weaker attributes of power than its neighbours and regional rivals, under Hafez al-Assad, Syria succeeded in being a regional shaper due to Assad's ability to use Syria's geography and to manipulate loose relationships to its benefit. Its power relied not on economic or military qualities but on autocratic stability, as well as its dominance over Lebanon from 1976 to 2005 and its support for Palestinian rejectionist factions. However, it failed against more powerful regional players. Syria lost on the battlefield against Israel in 1973 and 1982, failed to prevent Egypt from signing its peace treaty with Israel in 1979, and stood down against Turkiye in 1998. Its domestic-oriented, quasi-autarkic economy and meagre natural resources, as well as the government's distrust of external engagement (including foreign investment), meant that it remained marginal in nascent regional cooperation efforts.

Yet Western and Arab engagement remained strong until 2011, owing to Syria's geographic centrality, the outsourcing by Arabs and Westerners of the handling of troubled Lebanon to Damascus and the hope that involving it in regional diplomacy would lead to peace with Israel and split Syria from Iran, its only ally since the 1980s.

For Damascus, a prospective peace with Israel contained as many dangers as opportunities. Key for Assad was the return of the Golan Heights, whose loss he played a role in while defence minister during the 1967 Six-Day War. The risk was that peace would end Syria's self-proclaimed role as the Arab stalwart, jeopardise its relationship with Iran and possibly force it to relinquish control over Lebanon. It would also expose its economic weakness compared to Israel. On the other hand, peace would generate foreign investment and Arab and Western attention and reduce the need for a large defence budget. The last attempt to negotiate a peace treaty with Assad floundered in 2000, when then-president of the United States Bill Clinton conveyed in person an Israeli offer for less than a full withdrawal from the Golan Heights, which was rejected.

Bashar al-Assad inherited power in 2000, generating hope that his youth and limited Western experience would transform and moderate Syria. He was courted by the European Union, which extended generous terms to conclude an Association Agreement; by Turkiye, which sought stronger economic and political ties; and by Gulf states, which sought to obtain limited political concessions in return for investment. Instead, his almost 25-year rule has proved considerably more tumultuous, repressive and violent than his father's 30-year tenure. In 2005, his government was compelled to end its occupation of Lebanon. Starting in 2011, it lost significant authority and territorial control over the country as well as autonomy vis-à-vis Iran and standing vis-à-vis militias it once supported, and alienated all its neighbours. Although the ruling clique has proven resilient to these setbacks, it has lost considerable power, reach and credibility in the process.

Indeed, the civil war exposed Syria's myriad fault lines, which had been either hidden from or ignored by other governments. The explosion of sectarian, urban–rural and class divides led to a multidimensional conflict that has ruined its human and economic resources. More than 12 million Syrians – almost half of the population – are either internally displaced or living abroad as refugees.[1]

Several cities have largely been destroyed, including Aleppo, once the country's most important economic centre. The government made decisions during the war that have had long-term repercussions on both Syrian society and governance. If its core military maintained its cohesion, it also proved weak and ineffective on the battlefield. It was only able to hold onto power thanks to the enduring military interventions of Iran and Russia – both of which now exercise considerable control over Syrian territory – and the reluctance of the rebellion's foreign sponsors to match this investment. Loyalist militias were allowed to form, which has further aggravated corruption, misgovernance and repression, precluding the emergence of cohesive central governance. As a result, the Assad government and its allies lack the resources as well as the political power and will to reunite and rebuild the country, which would require governance and power-sharing reforms that threaten their very survival.

Syria's inward focus has come at the expense of its regional power projection. This loss of influence was most remarkable in Lebanon, where a large number of political parties and citizens from various communities firmly oppose Syrian meddling and influence. A further sign of the Assad government weakening was the relative disinterest of once-loyal partners such as the Lebanese Shia Amal Movement. Hizbullah, the Lebanese Islamist armed group, came to the rescue of the government out of concern for its own interests in Syria (notably the strategic depth it provides in terms of facilities, logistics and social links to Iran and Iraq) but less so out of allegiance to Assad himself. Once the kingmaker in Beirut, Damascus saw its erstwhile allies define and pursue their political interests with scant regard for its own preferences.

The Assad government also lost influence with Hamas, the most prominent Palestinian Islamist group it hosted. It had supported Hamas in obstructing the Palestinian Authority to ensure that it would not reach agreements with Israel that might be detrimental to Syrian interests. In 2011, Hamas sided with the Syrian rebellion out of sectarian and ideological solidarity. Its leadership left Damascus for Qatar while some of its fighters fought alongside rebel militias. While smaller Palestinian factions, such as Palestinian Islamic Jihad, remained loyal, the split with Hamas further demonstrated Syria's weakening hold. In 2017, after Assad gained the upper hand in the war, Iran and Hizbullah encouraged a reconciliation between Assad and Hamas. By then, the Palestinian movement had grown closer to both of the former. However, Assad proved unwilling to forgive and reconcile, maintaining a chilly attitude towards all Palestinian groups.

FOREIGN POWERS IN SYRIA

In 2011, in addition to major urban centres, all of Syria's peripheral areas revolted against the central government. Today, except for regions bordering Lebanon, they operate outside its authority and instead are either exposed to external influences or under foreign occupation.

Indeed, in 2024 five foreign militaries have a significant presence in the country (see Map 13.1). The Assad government invited Iran and Russia to intervene to rescue it against the rebellion and, at a later stage, from the Islamic State (ISIS)

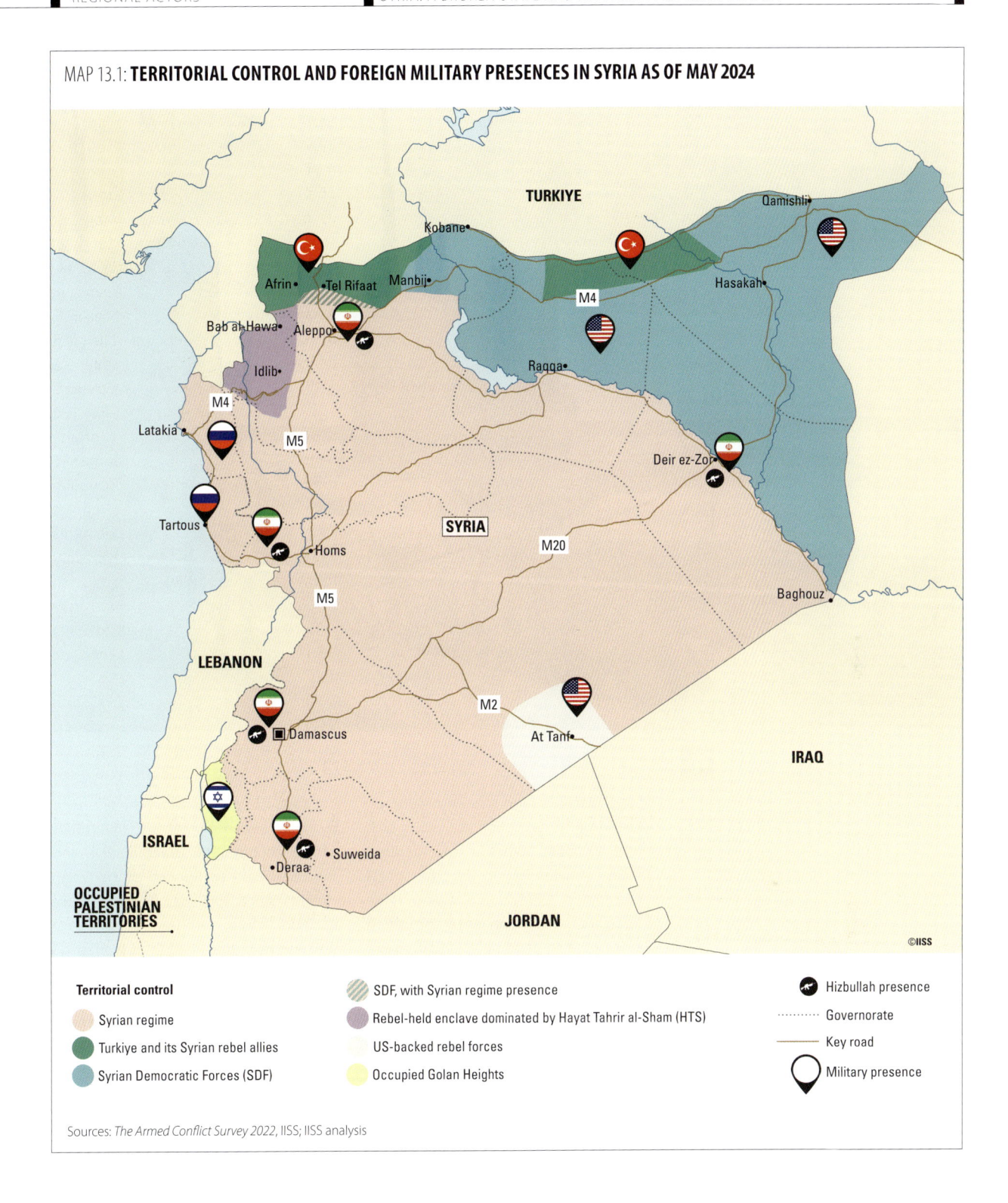

REGIONAL ACTORS — SYRIA: A BROKEN STATE AND AN ARENA FOR COMPETITION

MAP 13.1: TERRITORIAL CONTROL AND FOREIGN MILITARY PRESENCES IN SYRIA AS OF MAY 2024

Territorial control
- Syrian regime
- Turkiye and its Syrian rebel allies
- Syrian Democratic Forces (SDF)
- SDF, with Syrian regime presence
- Rebel-held enclave dominated by Hayat Tahrir al-Sham (HTS)
- US-backed rebel forces
- Occupied Golan Heights
- Hizbullah presence
- Governorate
- Key road
- Military presence

Sources: *The Armed Conflict Survey 2022*, IISS; IISS analysis

and other extremist organisations. It continues to be dependent on both for its survival.

Although it had a small presence in Syria pre-2011, Iran developed an extensive network of militias once the war started. It saw an opportunity to extend its reach into the Eastern Mediterranean, to open a new front against Israel and to secure logistical and supply lines with Hizbullah. Iran's pervasive and country-wide presence – consisting of a combination of senior Islamic Revolutionary Guard Corps (IRGC) commanders overseeing bases, weapons depots and production facilities, and local partner militias – makes it difficult for the Assad government to dislodge or even manage it. Iran's and Hizbullah's presence in Syria has also opened it up to regular Israeli aerial attacks targeting IRGC and Hizbullah commanders in an attempt to contain their deepening presence on the border with the occupied Golan Heights.

The other invited foreign presence in Syria is Russia. Assad invited Russia to intervene in the conflict in 2015, and Moscow has since opened two bases: a naval facility in the port of Tartous and an air base in Hmeimim. At their peak, Russian forces numbered 6,000, but that number is believed to have dropped to an estimated 2,000 since 2022.[2] Russia has greater influence than Iran over the Syrian officer corps, but it has not built the extensive militia network that Iran has.[3]

A Russian soldier stands next to submarines at the Russian naval base in the Syrian port of Tartous on 26 September 2019.
(Photo: Maxime Popov/AFP via Getty Images)

Russia places a high strategic value on expanding its presence in Syria, which offers valuable access to the Mediterranean Sea, adding to its other ports in occupied Crimea and giving it an important foothold on NATO's southern flank. It also compels engagement from Israel, Jordan, Turkiye and other Arab states.

Beyond the survival of the government, Iran's and Russia's interests have at times diverged in Syria. Russia has privileged relations with the government's armed forces and has sought to accommodate Israel; in contrast, Iran has favoured the nurturing of militias and has built capabilities to confront Israel. Their rapprochement over Ukraine since 2022 has improved the relationship. Neither has shown interest in rebuilding Syria's economy and infrastructure; Russia, for example, has invested little capital and provided only meagre humanitarian help since 2017.[4] Both see Syria primarily as a window onto the Mediterranean and they share a similar distaste for the United States' military presence. However, it remains unlikely that they would cooperate militarily should a regional war start.

Parts of Syria's territory are occupied by three countries that are adversaries of the government: Israel, Turkiye and the US. Israel's occupation of the Golan Heights since 1967 has been a source of humiliation for Damascus. Peace discussions in the 1990s (and the last US mediation in early 2011) had focused on an Israeli withdrawal, but as of 2024, no peace track seems viable and Israel is even more embedded on the Heights. In 2019, the Trump administration recognised Israel's annexation of the Golan Heights, a move endorsed by the Biden administration in 2021. Israel deems the Heights to be vital to its security and its ability to monitor southern Syria, where Iranian forces and partners are stationed, thus allowing for a third front alongside Gaza and southern Lebanon.

Turkiye is another well-entrenched enemy of the Assad government. Relations between the two countries have been contentious since the 1930s, when France ceded the region of Antioch (Antakya) to Turkiye. Turkiye carried out four major military interventions in Syria, starting in 2016, to contain Kurdish separatists and, to a lesser extent, ISIS. Since then, Turkiye has seized territory across the border, in part to settle Syrian refugees, in addition to having built a civilian infrastructure that is linked to Turkish government agencies. Turkiye also finances and equips a network of militias that are remnants of the rebellion to secure this area alongside its own military. Assad has been keen to expel Turkish forces, but his military has suffered significant losses against the superior Turkish Armed Forces. Russian-mediated diplomatic efforts have so far failed to bring Syria and Turkiye closer. Under President Recep Tayyip Erdoğan, Ankara is unlikely to agree to fully normalise relations with Damascus should they be conditioned on a prior withdrawal of its forces and without a political settlement that secures the return of refugees and reverses Kurdish autonomy. Turkiye is, therefore, embedded in Syria for the time being.

The last major force in Syria is the US. Washington's presence is a legacy of the fight against ISIS. The US first cultivated the People's Protection Units (YPG), a Kurdish militia, as its local partner to defeat the extremist movement, starting in 2014. That initial cooperation was successful and the US ramped up its involvement, starting in 2015, by providing airpower, intelligence, training and weapons to the YPG. It also deployed special forces in forward-operating bases across the northeast of Syria in the battle to oust ISIS from Raqqa and the surrounding area.

Washington designed an operation with a small footprint to minimise risks of entanglement and expectations. However, despite several Trump administration announcements that US forces would be withdrawn, the US remains in eastern and northern Syria, stuck in an uncomfortable position between Iran, Russia, Turkiye and the Syrian government. America's lasting presence serves several purposes: to monitor remaining ISIS forces, to contain Iran and Russia, and to provide support for the YPG, without which it would be vulnerable to Turkish or Assad predation. Importantly, the YPG's fate depends on US policy choices. The Kurdish militia has initiated discussions with the Assad government and Russia in order to hedge a potential US withdrawal prompted by US fatigue and frustration, but also by Iranian harassment.

'STABILISATION' AND NORMALISATION

While Assad has survived the war, there was no victory dividend to stabilise the country on his terms. The EU, the United Kingdom and the US have heavily sanctioned his government and foreign investors have assessed that Syria's potential and myriad risks do not warrant interest. Syria now sits outside regional trading and financial networks and is excluded from regional infrastructure and connectivity plans.

After years of ostracisation, Assad's survival, regional fatigue with the crisis and the necessity to contain the adverse effects of the conflict have prompted new thinking among Middle Eastern ruling elites. The desire to check Iranian influence remains an important driver, but the main concerns relate to transnational terrorism, migration and refugee flows, as well as the smuggling of Captagon (fenethylline), a drug manufactured in Syria for consumption in Europe and the Gulf. An additional concern has been the flow of weapons from Syria, which has reportedly increased since 2023,[5] with Iran seeking to supply Hamas in the West Bank but also Islamist cells in Jordan.

Starting in 2018, the United Arab Emirates, followed by Jordan and Saudi Arabia in 2023, normalised relations with Damascus, hoping to extract concessions for the region. In 2023, Riyadh pushed for the return of Syria to the Arab League and a committee of foreign ministers was formed to reintegrate Syria in exchange for gradual concessions related to refugees, drug trafficking and border control. As of early 2024, results were meagre, with Syria sliding down the regional agenda and superseded by the Israel–Hamas war. Additionally, Assad's primary objective has been the lifting of Western sanctions, which relevant powers refused to do. These sanctions, notably the US Caesar Act, greatly complicate Syria's attempts to attract foreign investors, including for its onshore oilfields, and have stood in the way of the revival of the Arab Gas Pipeline, which would link Egypt to Lebanon through Jordan and Syria. Syria is also not party to the East Mediterranean Gas Forum, which it refuses to join because it includes Israel.

Arab states have prioritised the return of refugees, but Assad's refusal to contemplate a political settlement and provide guarantees for their safe settlement has complicated the matter. Likewise, they have raised the matter of Captagon production and trafficking with Damascus, which has not been responsive. Drug trafficking has become Syria's main export, overseen by the government and conducted by its militias, as well as Iran's.

The Assad government has counted on divisions among European states to mollify the EU position on Syria. It has offered to share intelligence with several EU states. Some countries, including neighbouring Cyprus and, to a lesser extent, Greece, have lobbied for a gradual re-engagement with Damascus, arguing that their security interests and concerns about migration require it. Both have also shown concerns for the fate of Syria's Orthodox Christian community. However, more powerful EU states have resisted such moves, citing Damascus's political obstructionism, while Western sanctions remain an obstacle to Western engagement. Additionally, Cyprus and Greece are unwilling to risk their strengthening ties with the US and Israel over Syria.

Looking eastward for options, the government has hoped that China would play a key role in Syria's rebuilding and reintegration. In January 2022, Syria joined the Belt and Road Initiative (BRI), yearning to be a recipient of Chinese investment. Damascus has presented its Mediterranean ports as particularly viable for China's expansion strategy. However, Beijing has adopted a cautious approach, seeing Syria as too risky and too difficult to navigate. No major Chinese investment has materialised as of 2024 and Syria remains absent from BRI connectivity projects.

Syria's borders with its Mediterranean neighbours are all undemarcated, further complicating prospects for pacifying its regional relations and its participation in energy cooperation. Syria does not recognise Israel and continues to ask for the return of the Israeli-occupied Golan Heights. Its land and maritime borders with Lebanon are contentious and purposely undelineated as part of the leverage Damascus wants to maintain against its smaller neighbour.

OUTLOOK

In 2023, Assad perceived the Arab League summit as a good chance to reintegrate into the Arab world without making significant concessions and to be protected from further Western pressure. The war that started in October 2023 between Israel and Hamas has, at the very least, delayed this expectation.

Now a weak country, Syria is de facto party to this conflict as Iranian forces use Syrian territory against Israel without the Syrian government having the means, or intent, to partake in the war. Furthermore, Israel has conducted numerous operations inside Syria. In 2007, Israeli aircraft destroyed Syria's secret nuclear plant; in 2008, Israeli commandos killed Imad Mughniyeh, the most senior Hizbullah security chief at the time, in Damascus and, later that same year, General Muhammad Suleiman, the architect of Syria's special defence projects. Israel has also targeted Syria since 2015 as part of its 'mowing the grass' strategy, regularly violating Syrian airspace to destroy key facilities and military installations and kill Iranian and Syrian military personnel. More recently, Damascus was the scene of the April 2024 Israeli attack on an Iranian consular annex that killed General Mohammed Reza Zahedi, the highest-ranking IRGC commander assassinated since Qasem Soleimani in 2020. The April 2024 attack triggered Iran's first direct attack on Israel.

This has made Syria particularly vulnerable to the risk of expansion of the Israel–Hamas war. Assad has tried to stay out of this conflict, concerned that Israel could target his country's infrastructure, humiliate him to the point that he is compelled to intervene, or target him directly. Syria's extreme weakness and dysfunction make it unlikely that any regional player will see it as more than an arena in which to pursue their own interests.

Its maritime borders with Cyprus and Turkiye are also likely to remain undelineated as long as the conflict persists.

Iranian foreign minister Hossein Amir Abdollahian (L), Russian Foreign Minister Sergei Lavrov (2nd L), Syrian Foreign Minister Faisal Mikdad (2nd R) and Turkish foreign minister Mevlüt Çavuşoğlu (R) attend the quadripartite foreign ministerial meeting between Iran, Russia, Syria and Turkiye in Moscow, Russia, on 10 May 2023.
(Photo: Sefa Karacan/Anadolu Agency via Getty Images)

ENDNOTES

1. UN High Commissioner for Refugees, 'Syria Situation', 2024, https://reporting.unhcr.org/syria-situation-global-appeal-2024.
2. Estimate based on author's analysis.
3. See IISS, 'Iran's Networks of Influence in the Middle East', Chapter Three, p. 85.
4. Jonathan Robinson, 'Five Years of Russian Aid in Syria Proves Moscow is an Unreliable Partner', Atlantic Council, 8 June 2021, https://www.atlanticcouncil.org/blogs/menasource/five-years-of-russian-aid-in-syria-proves-moscow-is-an-unreliable-partner/.
5. Clara Hage, 'Arms Trafficking Accelerates, Fueling Jordan-Syria Border Tension', *L'Orient Today*, 15 January 2024, https://today.lorientlejour.com/article/1364430/arms-trafficking-accelerates-fueling-jordan-syria-border-tension.html.

India-Middle East-Europe Economic Corridor

GLOBAL ACTORS

GLOBAL ACTORS

CHAPTER FOURTEEN	UNITED STATES: BETWEEN RETRENCHMENT AND ENTANGLEMENT	240
CHAPTER FIFTEEN	FRANCE: HIGH AMBITIONS, REDUCED INFLUENCE	252
CHAPTER SIXTEEN	THE SOUTHERN FLANK: A CHALLENGE FOR NATO AND THE EU	260
CHAPTER SEVENTEEN	THE GULF STATES IN THE EASTERN MEDITERRANEAN: FROM GEOPOLITICS TO GEO-ECONOMICS	270
CHAPTER EIGHTEEN	RUSSIA: MAXIMISING THE POLITICAL RETURNS OF ITS INTERVENTIONS	284
CHAPTER NINETEEN	CHINA IN THE EASTERN MEDITERRANEAN: SMALL BUT GROWING PRESENCE	296

↑

(top to bottom) The French ship *Dixmude*, which between 27 November 2023 and 27 January 2024 served as a field hospital for wounded Palestinians who had crossed into Egypt from Gaza, at the port of al-Arish, Egypt, on 31 December 2023; Saudi Crown Prince Muhammad bin Salman Al Saud (L), Indian Prime Minister Narendra Modi (C) and US President Joe Biden (R) attend a session at the G20 Summit in New Delhi, India, on 9 September 2023; Syrians wave Russian flags and a portrait of Syrian President Bashar al-Assad during a rally in support of Russia in Damascus, Syria, on 25 March 2022. (Photos: Khaled Desouki/AFP via Getty Images; Evelyn Hockstein/POOL/AFP via Getty Images; Louai Beshara/AFP via Getty Images)

TURBULENCE IN THE EASTERN MEDITERRANEAN: GEOPOLITICAL, SECURITY AND ENERGY DYNAMICS ■ AN IISS STRATEGIC DOSSIER

USS *Gerald R. Ford* and USS *Dwight D. Eisenhower* operate together in the Eastern Mediterranean on 3 November 2023. (Photo: US Navy Janae Chambers/Handout/Anadolu via Getty Images)

VIEWING INVOLVEMENT IN LOCAL CONFLICTS and rivalries as costly and distracting entanglements, successive presidential administrations have attempted to recalibrate US diplomatic engagement and military investment in the Eastern Mediterranean. Geopolitical competition and the Israel–Hamas war's regional repercussions have reversed this trend.

THE US HAS ENCOURAGED REGIONAL DEFENCE and energy cooperation and connectivity so as to develop local networks, integrate Israel into the region, manage Turkish ambitions and contain Iranian reach. It has upgraded its relations with Cyprus and especially Greece, and facilitated their rapprochements with Egypt and Israel.

STILL MILITARILY DOMINANT, the United States' credibility and influence are being tested by both its partners and its rivals. Unable to win or solve conflicts, the US has lowered its own and its partners' expectations, seeking small wins rather than risking larger undertakings. It brokered the 2022 Israel–Lebanon maritime deal but has settled for conflict management elsewhere.

GLOBAL ACTORS | UNITED STATES: BETWEEN RETRENCHMENT AND ENTANGLEMENT

CHAPTER FOURTEEN

UNITED STATES: BETWEEN RETRENCHMENT AND ENTANGLEMENT

INTRODUCTION

The United States is deeply involved in the geopolitical and security dynamics of the Eastern Mediterranean region. Omnipresent and powerful yet often ineffective and denounced, the US has increasingly shown reluctance to shoulder the role of security balancer and diplomatic troubleshooter it has played for decades. This reflects a growing consensus in Washington that two decades of military intervention and political entanglements have distracted the US from more important strategic priorities elsewhere. The slow retrenchment that began during Barack's Obama presidential administration continued throughout Donald Trump's and Joe Biden's.

Washington has moved from an expansive definition of its regional interests, which required significant attention and resources, to a narrower and more transactional one. The 2022 National Security Strategy (NSS) states that 'in the Middle East, [the US has] worked to enhance deterrence toward Iran, de-escalate regional conflicts, deepen integration among a diverse set of partners in the region, and bolster energy stability'.[1]

Such a shift in strategic thinking has faced numerous challenges. The legacy of the United States' 2003 invasion of Iraq has proven costly for all, with its consequences remaining central to the region's dynamics. By action and omission, the US has shaped the region while rarely obtaining its desired outcomes. Events such as the expansion of the Islamic State (ISIS) in 2014, the resurgence of Russia's regional influence since 2015 and the Israel–Hamas war since 2023, as well as tensions among its local partners, have compelled the US to deploy diplomatic attention and military resources that it would otherwise have preferred not to. The region houses the two NATO members the most at odds (Greece and Turkiye) and the top two recipients of US military assistance (Israel and Egypt), as well as several countries and factions reliant on US military assistance (the Lebanese Armed Forces, the Syrian Democratic Forces in northeast Syria and the Free Syrian Army units on the Syrian–Jordanian border, and the Palestinian Authority's security forces). It also includes Libya and Syria: two countries in which the US intervened during the 2010s against their sitting governments and later against jihadi insurgencies, and whose future US policy continues to affect. Finally, it comprises the Occupied Palestinian Territories, whose lack of sovereignty imposes serious reputational and political costs on the US and in whose fate the US plays a determining role through its support for Israel.

The US government does not recognise the 'Eastern Mediterranean' as a geographical and policy concept. The 2022 NSS mentions 'Eastern Mediterranean' only once (in a reference to the East Mediterranean Gas Forum) and the 'Middle East' nine times. Israel is cited four times, Syria thrice, the Palestinians twice, and Turkiye and Libya once each. Cyprus, Egypt, Greece and Lebanon do not feature. Meanwhile, distant Iran appears six times and 'the Iranian people' once. Reflecting Washington's strategic priorities, China is mentioned 51 times and Russia 67 times. Three US combat commands share responsibility for the region's nine countries (see Map 14.1): Cyprus, Greece and Turkiye fall under European Command (EUCOM); Egypt, Israel, Lebanon, Syria and the Occupied Palestinian Territories under Central Command (CENTCOM); and Libya under Africa Command (AFRICOM). The US 6th Fleet, based in Naples, Italy under EUCOM, has purview over the Mediterranean alongside the 5th Fleet, based in Bahrain under CENTCOM. These bureaucratic divisions extend to the State Department. Importantly, these bureaucratic structures generate policy biases and preferences that influence the articulation and pursuit of US interests. For instance, while EUCOM has traditionally accommodated Turkiye as a powerful NATO member, CENTCOM's focus on theatres like Iraq and Syria has made it distrustful of and even confrontational toward Ankara.

CAUSING AND MANAGING INSTABILITY

Since 1990, when it intervened to repel the Iraqi invasion of Kuwait, the US has been a pervasive and overwhelming player in the Middle East, with an ambition to create a regional security architecture. The scope and intensity of its political and military involvement increased even more from 2003, when the US became a de facto Middle Eastern state by invading and occupying Iraq, upending an already fragile geopolitical order. The ripple effects and second-order consequences of that war have shaped the Eastern Mediterranean in several ways. These include the acceleration of Iran's rise to regional prominence, with Tehran able to extend and solidify its influence in Lebanon, Syria and the Occupied Palestinian Territories. A burgeoning Sunni jihadi movement,

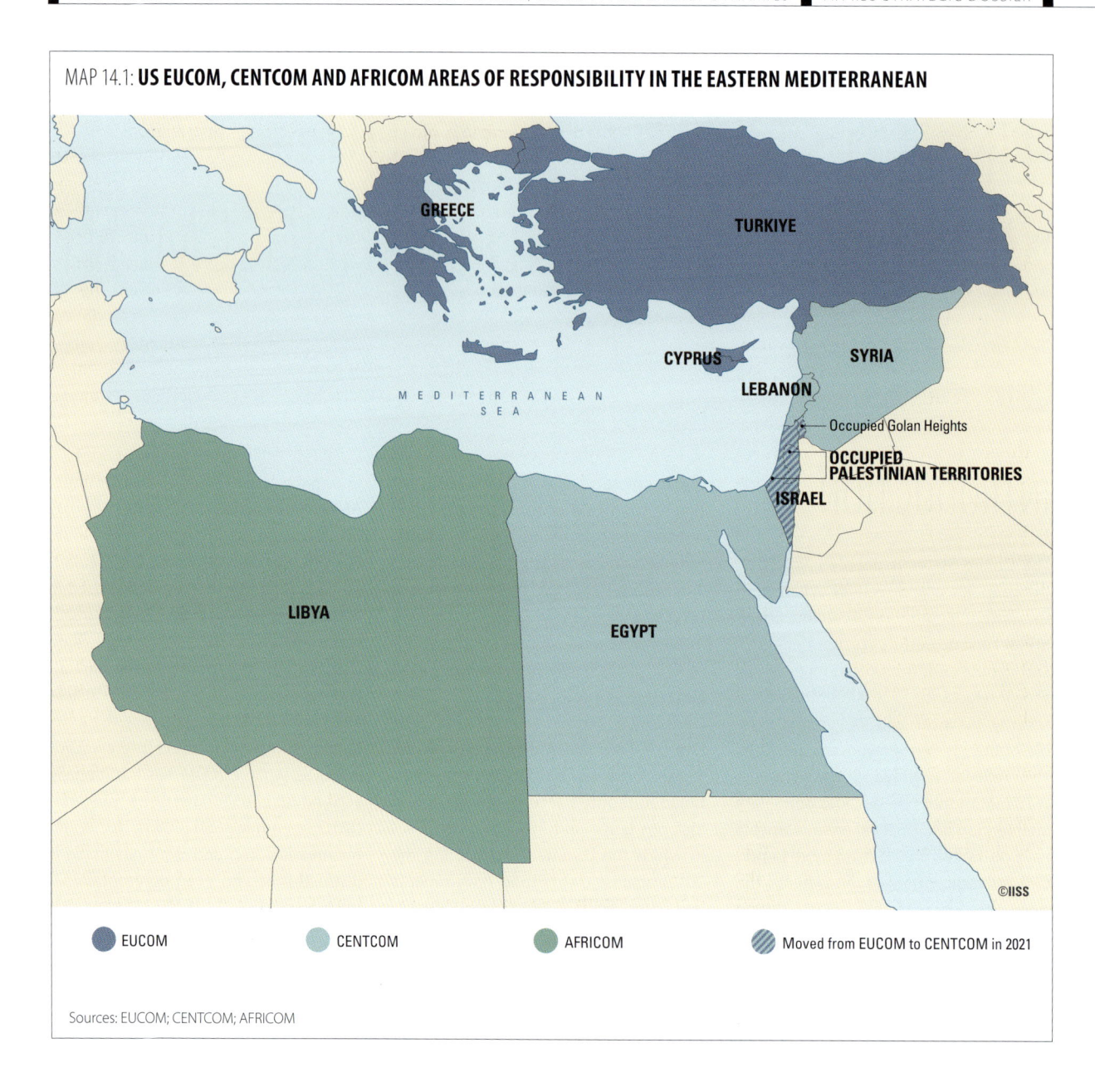

MAP 14.1: US EUCOM, CENTCOM AND AFRICOM AREAS OF RESPONSIBILITY IN THE EASTERN MEDITERRANEAN

- EUCOM
- CENTCOM
- AFRICOM
- Moved from EUCOM to CENTCOM in 2021

Sources: EUCOM; CENTCOM; AFRICOM

boosted by the invasion of Iraq, has since operated across North Africa, the Levant and Turkiye. The Arab–Israeli conflict, whose resolution in the 1990s was a high priority for Washington, has also been relegated on the international and regional agenda. Importantly, the opposition of Turkiye's then-new conservative government to the Iraq War began a long period of distrust and drift between the once-close NATO allies.

Washington's record of engagement in the Eastern Mediterranean has been a mostly unhappy one. It has failed to reach peace agreements between Israel, the Palestinian Authority, Lebanon and Syria, and has had to manage several rounds of conflicts between Israel and these actors that have made any resolution an even more distant prospect. Its 2011 intervention in Libya under NATO auspices delivered the military outcome it sought (the ouster of Muammar Gadhafi), but Libya's own divisions, regional competition and Western reluctance to engage in stabilisation produced instability that continues to this day. In contrast, frustration and dithering over Syria, where the US hesitated to back the Syrian rebellion for fear of a sudden collapse of President Bashar al-Assad's government and subsequent Islamist takeover, marred US credibility in the region.

Alongside this instability, and partly resulting from the weakness and crisis of legitimacy of many Arab states, the rise of Islamist extremist movements such as al-Qaeda and later the Islamic State has compelled the US to mount large, sustained counter-terrorist campaigns.

Its own role in exacerbating the drivers of jihadi mobilisation, and its concern that regional governments would succumb to extremist violence, also motivated the US. As a result, the US and its Western allies engaged in various levels of counter-terrorism operations in and cooperation with all the Eastern Mediterranean countries. During the 2000s, this had included security assistance and military training for Lebanese and Palestinian security forces as well as intelligence sharing with Libyan and Syrian intelligence agencies. This support delivered operational outcomes, such as the Lebanese Armed Forces defeating ISIS in 2017 or the Palestinian Authority's security forces stabilising the West Bank. However, the overall result was more mixed: the prioritisation of counter-terrorism generated political short-sightedness and led to costly entanglements. Importantly, the security achievements had no flow-on effects in terms of broader political stability and governance.

The campaign against the Islamic State illustrated this dilemma. The necessity to defeat ISIS's caliphate, an outgrowth of militant groups that had fought the US in the 2000s, led the US to design a battle plan that relied on local partners to which the US offered intelligence, training, resources and calibrated direct military support. The campaign was successful in defeating the caliphate territorially, but ISIS's endurance as well as the desire to contain Iran compelled the US to maintain a military presence in Syria (as well as Iraq), which alienated the Syrian government as well as Russia and Iran. US counter-terrorism goals conflicted with Ankara's own interests in Syria, leading to an adversarial coexistence in the country's northeast. The US today remains entangled in Syria: its military presence prevents the return of active conflict and competition without creating conditions for a diplomatic breakthrough, while its departure would benefit all its geopolitical adversaries and expose its remaining partners.

Another source of frustration in Washington has been its largely futile attempts to shepherd and shape political change and transitions across the Arab world. The US has tried in several regional countries to shape political processes, alternating between neutrality and picking sides without ever being able to determine or control outcomes. After his 2004 re-election, George W. Bush's administration had elaborated a broad concept entitled 'The Greater Middle East Initiative' based on the need for democracy, but it fell victim to its own failure in Iraq and contradictions elsewhere.[2] In the Occupied Palestinian Territories, Hamas's 2006 election victory led the US to denounce the outcome of a contest it had insistently called for. In Lebanon, its bet on political forces opposed to Iran and Hizbullah failed when the latter two proved willing to use coercion to defeat the former in 2008. The Obama administration faced similar disappointments during the Arab transformations that started in 2011. A mere 18 months after Obama's powerful speech in Cairo to promote democracy, the US was surprised by Egypt's revolution and then struggled to adapt to its political fluctuations. The US moved from celebrating democratic change in 2011 to endorsing military rule in 2013. By then, it had effectively abandoned any pretence of a freedom-and-reform agenda, instead accepting autocratic modernisation in Egypt and other countries.

This cynical pragmatism has continued throughout the Trump and Biden administrations. Both have set lower expectations and tried to reduce their involvement in the region, but this has been met with limited success. The Trump administration's major achievement was the 2020 Abraham Accords that normalised relations between Israel and the Gulf states of Bahrain and the United Arab Emirates (UAE) as well as Morocco. The US also encouraged the launch of multilateral regional forums such as the Negev Forum and jump-started discussions about regional defence cooperation.

Extricating the US from conflicts proved harder. Trump's dual attempts to withdraw US troops from Syria in 2018 and 2019 were resisted by his own government as well as regional governments over concerns about ripple effects on counter-terrorism and Iran policy. Trump's 2020 plan to resolve the Israeli–Palestinian conflict, which required significant Palestinian concessions over territory and sovereignty, was roundly rejected by the Palestinian Authority as well as many other countries in the region.[3] The Biden administration formulated no initiative to resolve the Israeli–Palestinian conflict, instead pursuing it as part of its efforts to normalise Israeli–Saudi relations.

Instead, in Libya and Syria, the US has offered rhetorical support for United Nations-led mediation processes without backing them with political muscle, or has joined contact groups in which it played no leadership role. On Libya, the US supported German efforts through the Berlin process, and asked Egypt, Turkiye and the UAE to ease their competition, but did not exert direct influence on the various Libyan players. In Syria, the US neither challenged the Astana process led by Iran, Russia and Turkiye nor orchestrated its sanctions strategy to punish and incentivise the parties to engage in the beleaguered UN process. Overall, the US approach has remained one of crisis management and containment.

The Biden administration's biggest success has been the 2022 demarcation of the maritime border between Israel and Lebanon, one made possible by the specific political circumstances in Israel and especially Lebanon. The year-long effort by Amos Hochstein, the most senior energy official at the White House, built on previous US attempts over more than a decade. However, the US administration's hope that the deal would have a flow-on effect on regional stability was shattered after the Hamas-led 7 October 2023 attacks against Israel and the subsequent regionalisation of that conflict.

MANAGING REGIONAL COMPETITION

The Eastern Mediterranean has been throughout the 2010s an arena of intense competition, often pitting Washington's closest partners against one another across theatres. The region has been split along two fault lines: one over political Islamism and another over Iran's influence. The first one has rallied Egypt, the UAE, Saudi Arabia, Greece and Cyprus against Turkiye, Qatar and their local partners in Libya and Syria. The second one has pitted Iran, Syria and their Iraqi, Lebanese and Yemeni partners against Egypt, the Gulf states and other countries. In Lebanon, Iraq and especially Syria, these two fault lines existed concurrently, making the formulation of policy considerably more complex.

The US has invested significant diplomatic capital in managing these tensions, even devoting presidential attention. Strategically, the US has settled for lower ambitions, intervening not to determine or force outcomes but to defuse tensions. This has nonetheless allowed space for regional competition to unfold at higher intensity than in previous decades. In 2013, facing a possible opportunity to intervene directly in the Syrian conflict, the Obama administration demurred, allowing regional players (as well as Russia) to fill the resulting vacuum. The US oversaw military and financial assistance to the Syrian rebellion in part to manage tensions between Turkiye, Qatar, Saudi Arabia and the UAE. A similar dynamic played out in Libya, with the US effectively stepping back after the 2012 attack on the US consulate in Benghazi.

The United States' most vexing challenge has been Recep Tayyip Erdoğan's Turkiye, whose regional and global ambitions have proved hard to manage. The risk of a rupture with a NATO ally, which displayed an increasingly authoritarian and nationalist orientation and geopolitical hedging, constrained US options. Thanks to its geography, Turkiye has a unique ability to manoeuvre in several arenas of critical interest for the US, being simultaneously a prized ally in one and a prickly rival in another. If the US saw Turkiye's role negatively in Syria, it valued it in Ukraine. Washington itself is divided over Turkiye's geopolitical utility. While many officials and analysts value its role as a regional balancer against Russian influence, others consider that its hedging and clear preference for a multipolar world create more problems than strategic advantages.

Tensions have built up ever since 2010, when Erdoğan both criticised Israel harshly over its occupation of the Palestinian territories and maintained relations with Iran even as it pressed ahead with its nuclear programme. They increased throughout the decade over important regional matters such as Syria policy, where Washington and Ankara disagreed over Assad's fate and over the design of the campaign to defeat the Islamic State (which included tensions over the US Air Force using Incirlik Air Base). They culminated in Turkish allegations of US connivance in the 2016 coup against Erdoğan and Ankara's 2018 procurement of the Russian S-400 air-defence system.

Washington expelled Turkiye from the F-35 combat-aircraft programme in 2019, setting back Turkish airpower modernisation. Washington additionally imposed sanctions in 2020 on select Turkish individuals and entities under the Countering America's Adversaries Through Sanctions Act (CAATSA).[4] A crisis in 2019 over a Turkish campaign in northeast Syria against Kurdish partners of the US, which could have resulted in firefights between US and Turkish troops, required then-vice president Mike Pence to visit Ankara and de-escalate the tensions.

In contrast, US criticism of Turkiye on Libya, including during the Trump years, was less pronounced. While Paris aligned with Egyptian and Emirati policy, which provided active support for the Libyan National Army (LNA) of Khalifa Haftar, Washington refrained from doing so, working instead with the UN-recognised Government of National Accord (GNA) in Tripoli. The US offered only superficial support for France during its diplomatic spat with Turkiye over alleged Turkish weapons supplies to the GNA. This reflected in part concerns over Russia's support for the LNA and strategies of influence in North Africa and the Sahel. Turkiye's intervention in Libya in 2020 elicited limited criticism from the US government, which months before had loudly protested its operations in northeast Syria.

Another aspect of US involvement in the region has been its behind-the-scenes management of Greek–Turkish tensions during their peak in 2019 and 2020. The US has been reluctant to push for an elusive resolution of the Greek–Turkish crisis over maritime claims, calling instead for restraint and for the parties to manage the crisis through established conflict-management mechanisms. It has supported multilateral efforts, including military-to-military dialogue under the NATO umbrella and political dialogue with the European Union and Germany. Similarly, the US played a subdued role during the 2017 Crans-Montana talks to resolve the Cyprus question, backing the UN efforts without exerting direct influence on the parties and without leading a new approach once they had failed. A former US official described the attitude as one of resignation and a desire to minimise involvement and exposure.[5] At the height of Turkish–Cypriot tensions in 2019 and 2020, Washington's position was noticeably more muted than the EU's, which publicly sided with its member state Cyprus and threatened to impose sanctions. In contrast, the US imposed no sanctions on Turkiye over Cyprus.

Even as it struggled to manage Turkish ambitions, geopolitical and political factors have produced remarkable improvements in US relations with Cyprus and Greece during the 2010s. The US had been unpopular among the Greek public, in part due to US support for the Greek military junta that held power until 1974. Turkiye's sheer size and proximity to the Soviet Union and then Russia made Ankara rather than Athens the preferred US partner. In turn, Greece and Cyprus maintained cosy relations with the Soviet Union and later Russia, which until the 1990s sold them weapons and invested in their banking and real-estate sectors. US support during Greece's near economic collapse between 2009 and 2018 contributed to the improvement in relations and over time has improved the Greek population's perception of the US. It was notable that this process continued even during the tenure of leftist prime minister Alexis Tsipras during the Trump presidency (see Figure 14.1). Initially seeking backing from Russia and potentially China to counter Western conditionalities, Tsipras came to understand that only Western support would stabilise his country's finances.[6] His successor since 2019, US-educated right-of-centre politician Kyriakos Mitsotakis, has accelerated this shift.

Rapid changes in the Eastern Mediterranean landscape contributed to altering US preferences. Strategic and political differences between Turkiye and many NATO allies diminished the former's reliability and the value of its geographic position for the US. Following its invasion of Ukraine in 2014, Russia's interventions in Syria and Libya propelled Moscow into the Mediterranean, compelling the US to

---

FIGURE 14.1: **TIMELINE OF US–GREECE RELATIONS, MAY 2010–JANUARY 2024**

2010 — Greece is bailed out by the IMF and the European Union, which agree to a package totalling €110 billion (approximately US$145bn).

2016 — The US and Greece launch the first iteration of their annual Strategic Dialogue.

2017 — Greek prime minister Alexis Tsipras meets US president Donald Trump at the White House, during which an agreement to upgrade Greece's fleet of F-16 fighter jets is announced. The US also announces its desire to expand its key naval base in Souda Bay, Crete.

2018 — In a sign of growing US–Greece ties, the US appoints Geoffrey Pyatt, a senior diplomat with energy expertise who was previously posted in Kyiv during the first Russian invasion of Ukraine, as its ambassador in Athens.

2019
- The '3+1' partnership arrangement between Cyprus, Greece, Israel and the US is established to improve regional security and economic growth.
- US-educated Kyriakos Mitsotakis is elected prime minister of Greece.

2021
- The US Congress approves a National Defense Authorization Act (NDAA) that paves the way for an increased military presence in the Balkans and Eastern Mediterranean.
- An amendment to the Mutual Defense Cooperation Agreement (MDCA) between the two countries gives the US increased access to Greek naval bases, including Alexandroupolis.

2022 — Greece takes part in *Operation Prosperity Guardian* alongside the US and other Western allies in response to Houthi attacks on shipping in the Red Sea, and later also hosts the headquarters of the EU's *Operation Aspides* to secure the Red Sea.

2023 — Mitsotakis becomes the first Greek leader to address the US Congress.

2024 — The US Department of State approves the sale of US$8.6bn worth of military equipment to Greece, including 40 F-35 fighter jets.

Source: IISS analysis

©IISS

monitor and contain its activities. Three other dynamics facilitated the improvement in US relations with Greece. Firstly, the latter (joined by Cyprus) had begun to enhance relations with Israel in the 1990s; these grew spectacularly in the 2010s over energy cooperation and shared regional perceptions. Closer ties with Israel improved perceptions of Greece in the US, notably in Congress, at a time when views on Turkiye had soured. Secondly, a Congressional Hellenic Caucus, formed in 2006, championed Greek and Cypriot causes. Simultaneously, the Greek American community became more active in US politics, advocating for better terms for Greece and Cyprus and tougher US positions on Turkiye. In doing so, it found allies among other advocacy groups, including Jewish American and Armenian American ones. Cyprus benefitted from Hellenic solidarity and advocacy conducted by organisations such as the American Hellenic Educational Progressive Association and the Hellenic American Leadership Council. This activism also intersected with growing Egyptian, Emirati and Saudi government lobbying in Washington against Turkiye and its partners (notably Qatar). Thirdly, Greece and to a lesser degree Cyprus began to distance themselves from Russia, notably after the 2014 Russian annexation of Crimea. Greek reliance on Russian energy as well as political and historic ties between their Orthodox communities had glued the countries together, but Russia's declining standing among Western powers and its perennial economic weakness made it an increasingly inadequate partner.

By the mid-2010s, a strong bipartisan consensus in favour of stronger ties with Greece had formed, facilitating Washington's plans to expand political, military and economic ties. Mike Pompeo, Trump's secretary of state, was a major architect of this shift, while another key proponent was Robert Menendez, the powerful Democratic chairman and ranking member of the US Senate Committee on Foreign Relations. In contrast, Turkiye had no similar bottom-up advocacy support and instead relied exclusively on relations with the executive branch and the US military, which had become increasingly fraught.

Helping Greece and Cyprus recover from their respective crises by supporting EU and IMF efforts was key to this shift.

The US also sought to facilitate Greek and Cypriot access to non-Russian energy and weapons to wean them off Moscow. The consecutive selections as US ambassador to Greece of Geoffrey R. Pyatt (from 2016 to 2022), a senior diplomat previously posted in Kyiv, and George J. Tsunis (since 2022), a US political appointee of Greek descent, demonstrated elevated US interest in Greece.

For US planners, Cyprus's position in the Eastern Mediterranean and Greece's proximity to the Black Sea at a time of Russian resurgence and Turkish unreliability makes them strategically and logistically valuable. The US Naval Support Activity (NSA) in Souda Bay on the island of Crete has acquired renewed importance. The Trump administration agreed with Tsipras in October 2017 a deal to upgrade Greece's F-16 fighter jets and to expand the NSA Souda Bay, and with Mitsotakis in 2019 an upgraded Mutual Defense Cooperation Agreement (MDCA) which 'enabled [the US] to expand bilateral activities at Larissa and Stefanovik[e]io, to sustain increased cooperation at Naval Support Activity Souda Bay, and to receive assured access at the Port of Alexandroupoli'.[7] The defence dimension of the relationship became prominent. In 2021, US Secretary of State Antony Blinken claimed that the 'US–Greece relationship is stronger than ever' after an amendment to the MDCA.[8] The amendment further expanded US military access in the port of Alexandroupoli, the air base of Stefanovikeio and two other bases. Greece's popularity in Washington culminated in Mitsotakis's 2022 address to a joint session of Congress, a rare occurrence for foreign leaders.

In parallel, Washington began to strengthen ties with Cyprus, a country it had long overlooked. Several US officials had seen the EU's 2004 decision to allow a divided Cyprus to join it as wrong-headed and as complicating a path to resolution. In following years, the US wanted to avoid any entanglement in the Cyprus question, relying instead on the UN, EU and the United Kingdom to manage the frozen conflict. The US viewed with suspicion Cypriot ties with Russia, including the Russian navy's access to Cypriot ports (negotiated in 2015 prior to the Russian intervention in Syria) and the country's historical ties with the Cypriot National Guard.[9] For the US, the island's main value was the pres-

> FOR US PLANNERS, CYPRUS'S POSITION IN THE EASTERN MEDITERRANEAN AND GREECE'S PROXIMITY TO THE BLACK SEA AT A TIME OF RUSSIAN RESURGENCE AND TURKISH UNRELIABILITY MAKES THEM STRATEGICALLY AND LOGISTICALLY VALUABLE.

ence of the two UK Sovereign Base Areas of Akrotiri and Dhekelia, which facilitated the regional operations of its closest ally and allowed US intelligence gathering and air operations. In 2020, the US began relaxing arms-sales restrictions imposed on Cyprus since 1987, expanding and extending this decision since 2022 on an annual basis. While Cyprus has yet to buy US systems and lacks the financial capacity to do so, this decision enraged Turkiye, which protested that such moves could upend the status quo and jeopardise a resolution to the conflict.[10] The main outcome from this rapprochement has been the curtailing of Russian access to Cypriot ports and increased US access to these ports.[11] Just as with Mitsotakis in Greece, the 2023 election as Cypriot president of Nikos Christodoulides, a right-of-centre politician who as foreign minister previously had taken a hard line on the Cyprus question and explored relations with both Russia and the US, intensified his country's cooperation with the US. Capping ties further deepened during the Israel–Hamas war, in which the US has used the island for logistics, intelligence and operational purposes, the two sides launched a US–Cypriot strategic dialogue in 2024.

CHAMPIONING REGIONAL INTEGRATION

The US has championed regional integration to lessen its own commitments. The 2022 NSS posited that 'a more integrated Middle East that empowers our allies and partners will advance regional peace and prosperity'. The US has hoped since the 1990s that the EU's political and economic power could help stabilise the region economically and in terms of governance and integration through the Barcelona Process, while its own military power would deter state and non-state threats and maintain regional peace when needed. Enduring instability, the EU's inability to achieve its goals and new geopolitical thinking in Washington have led the US to define less ambitious integration objectives and to embrace regional minilateralism.[12] Washington has moved away from trying to create a friendly regional security architecture toward supporting regionwide networks among local US partners based on diplomatic, defence and energy cooperation with a view to making them self-sustaining. A key plank of this approach has been US-facilitated defence cooperation through joint military exercises and defence diplomacy (see Chapter Four).

A paramount objective of US strategy has been to embed Israel in regional networks. The US has viewed positively Greek and Cypriot outreach to Israel as a way of tying its closest Middle Eastern partner to other Mediterranean powers. As a result, the US has actively encouraged regional diplomatic and defence cooperation. Since 2019, it has backed the trilateral cooperation mechanism that brought together Cyprus, Greece and Israel.[13] It has also viewed positively the trilateral cooperation group between Cyprus, Egypt and Greece that has been in place since 2014.[14] The ultimate step was the normalisation of relations between Israel and two Gulf states (Bahrain and the UAE) in 2020, which paved the way for active US diplomacy toward normalising relations between Israel and Saudi Arabia, a potential prize which would be seen as the real game changer in regional politics.

The proliferation of bilateral visits and minilateral meetings in subsequent years was notable even if they produced few concrete outcomes. The main effect sought was political signalling toward, and isolation of, respective rivals: Turkiye in the case of the Greece-hosted Philia Forum in 2021, and Iran and the Palestinians in the case of the Israel-hosted Negev Forum in 2022. Other minilaterals include the I2U2 grouping that has brought together since 2021 India, Israel, the UAE and the US.

The US has also supported the development of the East Mediterranean Gas Forum as a platform to encourage regional energy cooperation, reduce countries' reliance on Russian energy and help Israel's energy-export objectives. However, several US officials have privately criticised its transformation into a membership organisation that excludes Turkiye, concerned that this antagonises Ankara, drives it closer to

Moscow and hardens its position on Cyprus rather than anchoring it among regional partners. Similarly, the Biden administration has been relatively sceptical about the EastMed pipeline that would have transported Israeli gas to Europe through Cyprus and Greece, over geopolitical, feasibility and economic concerns.[15] This contrasts with the Trump administration's support for the project. That the Biden administration has expressed its concerns quietly shows a desire to placate its local partners and allow them to remain publicly in the lead.

In September 2023, at the G20 summit in New Delhi, the US unveiled its most ambitious connectivity project. The India–Middle East–Europe Economic Corridor (IMEC) is designed to link through cable, pipeline, road, rail and ship some of the world's largest economies.[16] The signatories of the memorandum of understanding (MoU) that set IMEC's principles include the EU, France, Germany, India, Italy, Saudi Arabia, the UAE and the US. From a US perspective, although a main benefit of IMEC was to dilute China's geo-economic reach and Belt and Road Initiative projects across Asia and into Europe, it also linked important US partners together into a US-backed architecture.

There was no signatory among the Eastern Mediterranean coastal states, but the MoU mentions Israel and Jordan (two countries not present in New Delhi for the summit). Indeed, as designed, the corridor would pass through the Eastern Mediterranean and would rely heavily on Israel, notably the port of Haifa, as well as Jordan and Greece (Cyprus's role is unclear but would be limited). IMEC would ship Indian goods from UAE ports to Haifa through Saudi Arabia and Jordan (as is already the case, albeit outside a formal framework) and could link up Gulf and European electricity grids through the Euro-Asia Interconnector, an ongoing project to connect the electricity grids of Cyprus, Greece and Israel. For some, IMEC could even revive the fortunes of the EastMed pipeline if it could be rethought to transport Gulf-produced gas and in the future green hydrogen to Europe. It is notable that the lead US architect of IMEC is Hochstein, the senior official who not only negotiated the Israel–Lebanon maritime-demarcation agreement but is also central to US–Saudi talks about normalisation with Israel. Such was the promise of IMEC that Israeli Prime Minister Benjamin Netanyahu celebrated its announcement. In his September 2023 speech to the UN General Assembly, he heralded the advent of a 'New Middle East', physically drawing the corridor on a map that represented Israel without any mention of the Occupied Palestinian

(L-R) Bahraini Foreign Minister Abdullatif bin Rashid Al Zayani, Egyptian foreign minister Sameh Shoukry, Israeli foreign minister Yair Lapid, US Secretary of State Antony Blinken, Moroccan Foreign Minister Nasser Bourita and UAE Foreign Minister Sheikh Abdullah bin Zayed Al Nahyan at the Negev Forum in southern Israel on 28 March 2022. (Photo: Israeli Government Press Office/ Handout/Anadolu Agency via Getty Images)

Territories and included the annexed Golan Heights.¹⁷

Despite the enthusiasm that greeted IMEC, it still faces considerable geopolitical and geo-economic obstacles in the Middle East.¹⁸ It supposes that Saudi Arabia and the UAE, currently geo-economic competitors, would collaborate on such an ambitious project. It also assumes that normalisation between Israel and Saudi Arabia is inevitable, presenting IMEC as both an incentive for and a benefit of such a normalisation. Additionally, key members of IMEC such as Saudi Arabia and the UAE have good relations with China and would be unlikely to commit fully to either the US or China.

Importantly, IMEC excludes two major Eastern Mediterranean powers: Egypt and Turkiye. The latter has criticised the project and instead proposed a Turkiye-centric route that passes through Gulf ports and Iraq.¹⁹ Egypt, meanwhile, would stand to lose considerable revenues and standing if trade were to bypass the Red Sea and the Suez Canal in favour of a land route.²⁰ Iran too has criticised the project for its US inspiration and integration of Israel. The unsurprising exclusion of Lebanon and Syria despite their favourable geographical position reflects their political isolation given their de facto alignment with Iran, dire political and economic straits, high security risk and lack of sufficient infrastructure to sustain such a project.

Finally, the Israel–Hamas war beginning just a month after IMEC's signature has highlighted the political risk that such connectivity projects carry. If Israel–UAE relations have withstood the conflict, Saudi Arabia has signalled that normalisation with Israel would require more substantive concessions toward Palestinian statehood than was the case in September 2023. Jordan is particularly exposed: while keen to be included in regionwide projects for its own economic viability, the country has taken a very critical view of Israel's offensive in Gaza and its repercussions on the West Bank. Accordingly, the prospect of greater economic cooperation with Israel is deeply unpopular among the general Jordanian public. Jordanian absence from or obstruction of IMEC would lead to significant changes in the project.

Israel has also emerged as a risk. Its critical infrastructure is vulnerable: Hizbullah has repeatedly threatened the port of Haifa and Yemen's Ansarullah (Houthi) movement has targeted the port of Eilat. Despite its considerable advantages, many countries perceive Israel as a liability, worrying about linking their infrastructure and prosperity to a state constantly facing and engaging in war. The lack of active follow-up on IMEC since

A US military convoy in Deir ez-Zor governorate, Syria, on 13 August 2023. (Photo: Omer Al Diri/Anadolu Agency via Getty Images)

the war began reflects this: a meeting among the relevant countries, which the founding MoU had called for within 60 days of its signature, has not occurred.

Relevant leaders have been keen to insulate IMEC from conflict and geopolitical turmoil. Greek Prime Minister Mitsotakis insisted in February 2024 that, although 'the war in Gaza and turmoil in the Middle East is undoubtedly destabilising … it does not undermine the powerful logic behind IMEC. Nor should it weaken our resolve to work towards realising it.'[21]

OUTLOOK

Seeking to escape predicaments in the Middle East, the US has found itself perennially entangled in complex dynamics which its volatile approach, as well as factors outside its control, have exacerbated. If Eastern Mediterranean states have had to adjust to 'benign US neglect', the US has struggled to align expectations, policies and resources.[22]

Treating the Eastern Mediterranean as a geopolitical backwater where it can manage competition and contain conflict at arm's length is no longer a sustainable approach. After dismissing Russia as a fading power in 2012,[23] Obama watched as it rapidly increased its standing across the region by establishing bases in Syria and Libya and building political, energy and defence relationships with Egypt and Turkiye. Containing Russian influence has since required significant US attention, resources and capital. Although it is far from being a significant competitor in the region, China too has made inroads through calibrated, patient and opportunistic moves to exploit US weaknesses and setbacks, most recently during the Israel–Hamas war.

Moderating and adjusting to changing Turkish attitudes has been particularly demanding for the US. With Turkiye behaving increasingly as a power no longer constrained by Western policy preferences, the US must figure out if promoting integration of Turkiye into its regional schemes can work, or if it will jeopardise them. After Russia's full-scale invasion of Ukraine in 2022, the US made facilitating Finnish and Swedish accession to NATO a priority. Yet Turkiye stalled the process for almost two years, linking their accession to reversals of their policies on Kurdish issues. Ultimately, lifting Turkish opposition required US concessions, with Washington agreeing to modernise Turkish F-16 aircraft. In turn, the US has had to make sure that the regional minilaterals it encouraged did not exacerbate regional divides or create undue expectations about Washington's role. Mindful of Turkish perceptions, US officials have been keen to stress that increased defence cooperation with Greece and Cyprus did not amount to security guarantees.

The Israel–Hamas war since October 2023 has shown how quickly and deeply the US can be pulled back into the Eastern Mediterranean. During the war's first six months, the US maintained a considerable military footprint to defend and supply Israel and to deter Iran and its partners. It increased its presence in Cyprus, readied naval capabilities to evacuate civilians and worked to support humanitarian assistance. It positioned at least one carrier strike group (CSG), several ballistic-missile-defence destroyers and guided-missile submarines for much of the conflict, surging to two CSGs at critical junctures. These capabilities were central to defending Israel against the first-ever direct Iranian air attack against it in April 2024. As of June, this greater military involvement had succeeded in deterring a regional war.

Importantly, the regional ties with Israel that the US has encouraged in previous years have withstood the conflict. The Abraham Accords and the peace treaties with Egypt and Jordan have held up, even though all these states have criticised Israeli policies and asked for greater US involvement to help end the war. Greece and Cyprus have been, on the whole, supportive of Israel and of US policies, even though they voted in favour of resolutions several times against US preferences at the UN General Assembly (see Figure 1.3, page 20). For Cyprus in particular, the war has been an opportunity to deepen relations with the US. However, the activities and consultations of US-backed minilaterals such as I2U2, the various trilaterals and the Negev Group have been suspended for the time being.

The overall reputational and political costs for the US have been significant. Despite being the only player able to orchestrate a diplomatic track, the US had yet to deliver a ceasefire in Gaza ten months into the war or to provide a credible road map for its future or Israeli–Palestinian peace. This ineffectiveness contrasts with US performance during every other high-intensity Israeli–Palestinian and Israeli–Lebanese war since 1991. From Arab states' perspectives, the US has a greater responsibility to deliver a political resolution to the Israeli–Palestinian conflict than for any other in the world. But instead, the US has vetoed three UN Security Council resolutions calling for a ceasefire and Palestinian self-determination within the first six months of the war, doing so alone during the last such vote in February 2024.[24] The US has also had to try to reassure its close partners Egypt and Jordan about Israeli objectives and to moderate Israeli behaviour and rhetoric. The war has also threatened the US position in fragile countries such as Syria and Iraq: Iranian-backed militias have repeatedly attacked US bases and political pressure to force the US out has increased.

The US has also had to sustain crucial initiatives, such as the prospect of Israeli–Saudi normalisation, and watch the freezing of grandiose plans such as IMEC. In these circumstances and despite the clear geo-economic and geopolitical interests of the relevant parties, realising the potential of IMEC will require significant US political commitment.

Ultimately, the US faces difficult decisions in the region. Several factors plead in favour of a reassessment of the US defence posture in the Eastern Mediterranean, so that it centres on larger facilities and expanded access in Cyprus and Greece. Issues include the likelihood of continued tensions between Israel and Iran and its partners, the amount of expensive naval resources it has deployed in support of Israel during the war, the limitations on the use of US bases in the Gulf for such contingencies because of local sensitivities, and the possibility that the US may withdraw from Syria and Iraq. However, a larger and more permanent US footprint would be likely to increase tensions with Erdoğan's Turkiye and to lead Washington to take a more active role in managing regional tensions and conflicts. For the US, escaping one set of entanglements seems necessarily to lead to entering a new one.

ENDNOTES

1 White House, 'National Security Strategy', October 2022, p. 18, https://www.whitehouse.gov/wp-content/uploads/2022/10/Biden-Harris-Administrations-National-Security-Strategy-10.2022.pdf.

2 Condoleezza Rice, 'Transforming the Middle East', *Washington Post*, 7 August 2003, https://www.washingtonpost.com/archive/opinions/2003/08/07/transforming-the-middle-east/2a267aac-4136-45ad-972f-106ac91e5acd/.

3 White House, 'Peace to Prosperity: A Vision to Improve the Lives of the Palestinian and Israeli People', January 2020, https://trumpwhitehouse.archives.gov/wp-content/uploads/2020/01/Peace-to-Prosperity-0120.pdf.

4 Michael R. Pompeo, 'The United States Sanctions Turkey Under CAATSA 231', US Department of State, 14 December 2020, https://2017-2021.state.gov/the-united-states-sanctions-turkey-under-caatsa-231/.

5 Interview with former senior US official, August 2023.

6 Mehreen Khan, 'Isolated Greece Pivots East to Russia, China and Iran. But Will It Work?', *Telegraph*, 5 April 2015, https://www.telegraph.co.uk/finance/economics/11511653/Isolated-Greece-pivots-east-to-Russia-China-and-Iran.-But-will-it-work.html.

7 US Department of State, 'Secretary Pompeo Travels to Greece to Advance Security, Peace, and Prosperity', 27 September 2020, https://gr.usembassy.gov/secretary-pompeo-travels-to-greece-to-advance-security-peace-and-prosperity/.

8 Antony J. Blinken, 'Signing of Protocol of Amendment to the Mutual Defense Cooperation Agreement with Greece', US Department of State, 14 October 2021, https://gr.usembassy.gov/statement-by-secretary-antony-j-blinken-signing-of-protocol-of-amendment-to-the-mutual-defense-cooperation-agreement-with-greece/.

9 'Russia, Cyprus Sign Military Deal on Use of Mediterranean Ports', Reuters, 27 February 2015, https://www.reuters.com/article/world/russia-cyprus-sign-military-deal-on-use-of-mediterranean-ports-idUSKBN0LU1EW/.

10 Turkiye, Ministry of Foreign Affairs, 'Press Release Regarding the Extension of the U.S. Decision to Lift the Arms Embargo on the Greek Cypriot Administration', 19 August 2023, https://www.mfa.gov.tr/no_-200_-abd-nin-gkry-ye-yonelik-silah-ambargosunu-kaldirma-kararinin-uzatilmasi-hk.en.mfa.

11 'US Lifts Embargo on Cyprus but with Russian Caveat', KNEWS, 17 September 2022, https://knews.kathimerini.com.cy/en/news/us-lifts-embargo-on-cyprus-but-with-russian-caveat.

12 That is, 'small international groups assembled to achieve limited if significant strategic objectives, as opposed to broader, larger or more formal bilateral or multilateral alliances or institutions'. See IISS, 'Changing Alliance Structures', December 2021, https://www.iiss.org/globalassets/media-library---content--migration/files/research-papers/2021/alliances-report.pdf.

13 US Embassy in Greece, 'Joint Declaration Between Cyprus, Greece, Israel, and the U.S. After the 6th Trilateral Summit', 21 March 2019, https://gr.usembassy.gov/joint-declaration-between-cyprus-greece-israel-and-the-u-s-after-the-6th-trilateral-summit/.

14 Egypt State Information Service, 'The 9th Tripartite Summit Between Egypt, Greece, and Cyprus in Athens', 19 October 2021, https://www.sis.gov.eg/Story/159635/The-9th-Tripartite-Summit-between-Egypt%2C-Greece%2C-and-Cyprus-in-Athens?lang=en-us.

15 'U.S. Voices Misgivings on EastMed Gas Pipeline – Greek Officials', Reuters, 11 January 2022, https://www.reuters.com/business/energy/us-voices-misgivings-eastmed-gas-pipeline-greek-officials-2022-01-11/.

16 India, Ministry of External Affairs, 'Memorandum of Understanding on the Principles of an India–Middle East–Europe Economic Corridor', 2023, https://www.mea.gov.in/Images/CPV/Project-Gateway-Multilateral-MOU.pdf.

17 'Full Text of Netanyahu's UN Address: "On the Cusp of Historic Saudi–Israel Peace"', *Times of Israel*, 22 September 2023, https://www.timesofisrael.com/full-text-of-netanyahus-un-address-on-the-cusp-of-historic-saudi-israel-peace/.

18 Hasan Alhasan and Viraj Solanki, 'Obstacles to the India–Middle East–Europe Economic Corridor', IISS, 16 November 2023, https://www.iiss.org/online-analysis/online-analysis/2023/11/obstacles-to-the-india-middle-east-europe-economic-corridor/.

19 Sinan Tavsan, 'Turkey Pushes $25bn Iraq Transport Route Over India–Europe Corridor', *Nikkei Asia*, 20 October 2023, https://asia.nikkei.com/Politics/International-relations/Turkey-pushes-25bn-Iraq-transport-route-over-India-Europe-corridor.

20 Amr Emam, 'Egypt's Suez Canal Faces Alternative Spots on Trade Map', *Al Majalla*, 18 November 2023, https://en.majalla.com/node/304581/business-economy/egypts-suez-canal-faces-alternative-spots-trade-map.

21 Suhasini Haidar, 'Let's Proceed with IMEC Despite Gaza War, Says Greek PM Kyrios Mitsotakis', *Hindu*, 22 February 2024, https://www.thehindu.com/news/national/india-greece-agree-to-expand-cooperation-in-diverse-areas/article67870320.ece.

22 Interview with former senior US official, March 2024.

23 Glenn Kessler, 'Flashback: Obama's Debate Zinger on Romney's "1980s" Foreign Policy', *Washington Post*, 20 March 2014, https://www.washingtonpost.com/news/fact-checker/wp/2014/03/20/flashback-obamas-debate-zinger-on-romneys-1980s-foreign-policy/.

24 'US Vetoes Another UN Security Council Resolution Urging Gaza War Ceasefire', Al-Jazeera, 20 February 2024, https://www.aljazeera.com/news/2024/2/20/us-vetoes-another-un-security-council-resolution-urging-gaza-war-ceasefire.

The French aircraft carrier *Charles de Gaulle* deployed off the eastern coast of Cyprus in support of *Operation Inherent Resolve* (*Chammal*) on 10 February 2020. (Photo: Mario Goldman/AFP via Getty Images)

FOR FRANCE, THE EASTERN MEDITERRANEAN is an essential area of power projection and for European stability and sovereignty – where it rivals Russia and Turkiye and attempts to match the United States. Despite its military presence, strategic partnerships and historic role, it has increasingly struggled to shape outcomes.

COUNTERING TERRORISM AND MIGRATION as well as preserving trade, defence markets and diplomatic influence drive France's posture. It uses its NATO and European Union memberships as well as other forms of minilateralism to compensate for its waning influence.

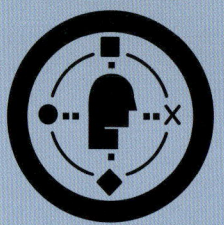

FRANCE'S BIGGEST CHALLENGE in the Eastern Mediterranean has become Turkiye's assertive policies. Ankara is perceived in Paris as a major national-security problem, with repercussions on domestic cohesion as well as peace and stability in the Mediterranean. In response, France has aligned with Egypt, Greece and others across battlefields.

CHAPTER FIFTEEN
FRANCE: HIGH AMBITIONS, REDUCED INFLUENCE

INTRODUCTION

A former colonial power in the region, France is a central actor of the Eastern Mediterranean, enabled by one of the world's top navies and a vast diplomatic network as well as considerable commercial and socio-economic ties.

The Mediterranean is France's 'mare nostrum', a quintessentially strategic theatre for Paris. It was therefore not surprising that in 2008, Nicolas Sarkozy announced a flagship initiative called Union for the Mediterranean. This, he hoped, would reinvigorate Mediterranean relations, but to his dismay there was limited enthusiasm and significant scepticism from coastal states. An organisation was established but the initiative ultimately lost political momentum and relevance, a victim of its contradictions, suspicions about French designs and broader geopolitical dynamics.

Nevertheless, the sheer ambition reveals how the Mediterranean is a concentrate of most of France's guiding imperatives and enduring dilemmas. It is one of the key arenas where Paris wants to preserve its influence and assert an independent French and European foreign policy vis-à-vis the United States, but where its own power still depends on US strategic and operational enablers and where other European states question and even challenge French policy. The region is also a site of competition with Iran, Russia and Turkiye, although France is not able to commit as many assets as durably and deeply. It is where it fights Islamist jihadism and tries to contain the migration flows that have upended politics at home and across the European Union but ends up entangled. The Eastern Mediterranean has a permanent presence in the French public sphere due to France's historical and cultural role in the Levant as well as large French–Lebanese and French–Israeli communities.

With the regional balance deeply disrupted since the Arab uprisings of 2011, Paris has attempted to preserve its standing and counter threats through increasingly limited means. It did so by projecting military power through its flagship aircraft carrier *Charles de Gaulle*, participating in military exercises and operations, deepening its strategic relationship with Greece and developing defence cooperation with Egypt and Cyprus (see Map 15.1). It also immersed itself in the region's minilaterals such as the East Mediterranean Gas Forum (EMGF).

French President Emmanuel Macron, in a 2020 speech, stated: 'The Mediterranean will be the challenge of the coming years … Europe must define its role and place in it … We are talking about our neighbourhood, our security, our stability.'[1] He then listed the many challenges it presents: maritime disputes, confrontations between littoral countries, destabilisation of Libya, migration, trafficking, access to resources and competition between powers.

LEVERAGING MILITARY, STRATEGIC TIES AND INTERESTS

Since 2011, and under three different presidents, France has deployed its military and joined multilateral operations to shape outcomes in the Mediterranean at five key junctions. In 2011, it was a leading power behind the United Nations Security Council-sanctioned and NATO-led armed intervention in Libya to protect civilians from the repressive campaign of then-leader of Libya, Muammar Gadhafi, who was ultimately ousted.[2] In 2013, it once again advocated for military strikes against the Assad government in Syria in retaliation for its use of chemical weapons, only to be undercut when the US chose not to intervene at the last minute. In 2014, it joined the US and the United Kingdom in *Operation Inherent Resolve* (*Chammal*), a large counter-Islamic State (ISIS) operation in Iraq and Syria. In 2017 and 2018, it participated with the US and the UK in limited strikes against Syrian chemical-weapons facilities in response to repeated chemical-weapons use by Assad. In 2020, at a moment of heightened tension in the Eastern Mediterranean over Turkish maritime brinkmanship with Greece and Cyprus, a French frigate deployed in NATO's *Operation Sea Guardian* was involved in a heated stand-off with Turkish naval assets suspected of carrying an illegal shipment of weapons destined for Libya and had to stand down. France later left the NATO operation.

None of these operations led to decisive gains for France. Instead, they revealed France's waning influence and limited ability to act unilaterally. For example, its attempt to shape the course of the Syrian uprising-turned-internationalised-civil-war suffered from lack of political will and limited capabilities, despite France's high exposure to the fallout of the conflict. The coordination of the support for the Syrian rebellion was left to the US, while France struggled to align its Gulf partners behind a common strategy and

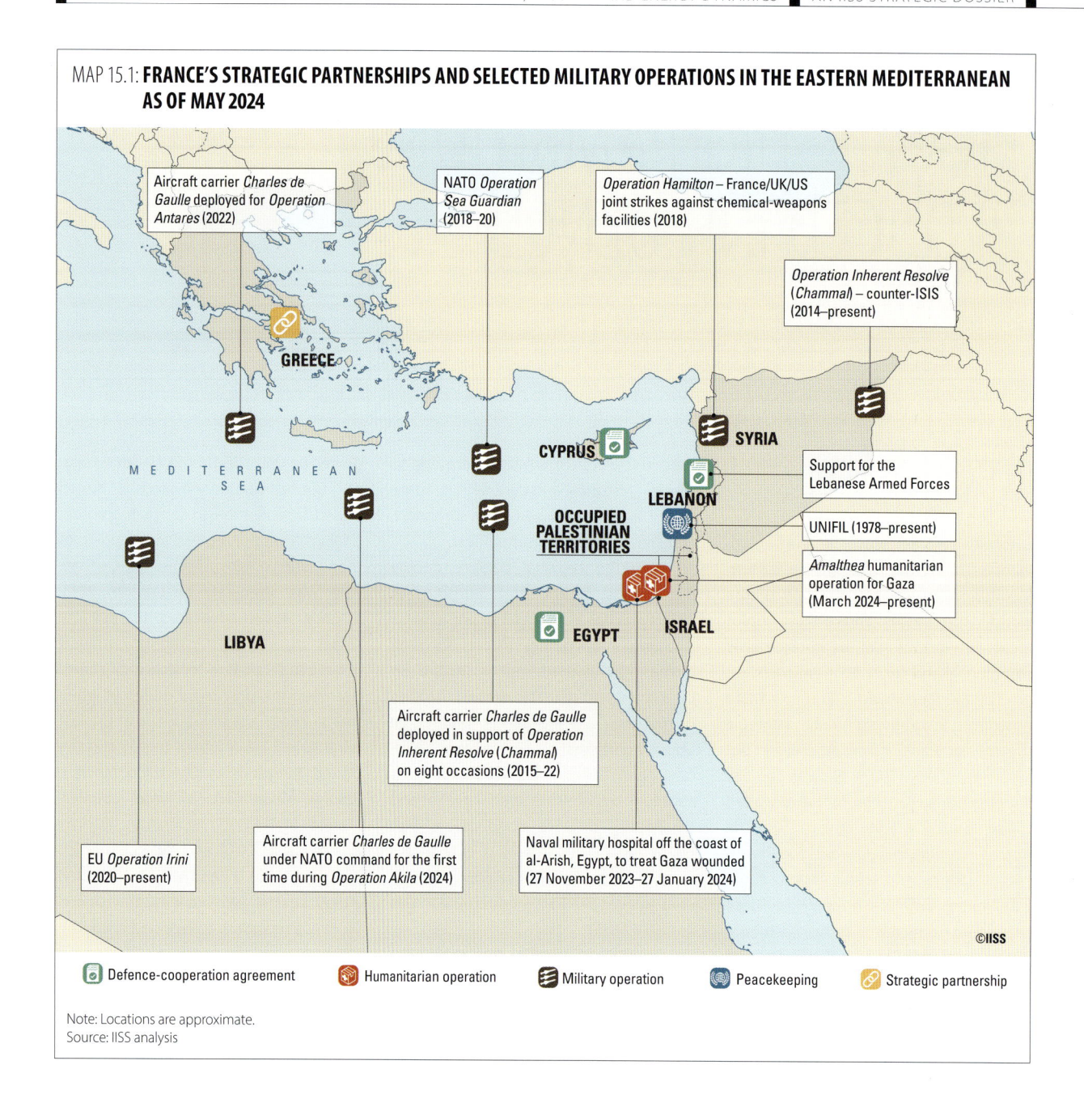

MAP 15.1: **FRANCE'S STRATEGIC PARTNERSHIPS AND SELECTED MILITARY OPERATIONS IN THE EASTERN MEDITERRANEAN AS OF MAY 2024**

- Aircraft carrier *Charles de Gaulle* deployed for *Operation Antares* (2022)
- NATO *Operation Sea Guardian* (2018–20)
- *Operation Hamilton* – France/UK/US joint strikes against chemical-weapons facilities (2018)
- *Operation Inherent Resolve* (*Chammal*) – counter-ISIS (2014–present)
- Support for the Lebanese Armed Forces
- UNIFIL (1978–present)
- *Amalthea* humanitarian operation for Gaza (March 2024–present)
- Aircraft carrier *Charles de Gaulle* deployed in support of *Operation Inherent Resolve* (*Chammal*) on eight occasions (2015–22)
- EU *Operation Irini* (2020–present)
- Aircraft carrier *Charles de Gaulle* under NATO command for the first time during *Operation Akila* (2024)
- Naval military hospital off the coast of al-Arish, Egypt, to treat Gaza wounded (27 November 2023–27 January 2024)

Legend: Defence-cooperation agreement · Humanitarian operation · Military operation · Peacekeeping · Strategic partnership

Note: Locations are approximate.
Source: IISS analysis

---

local partners. While Paris correctly assessed the regional implications of a loss in Syria, it could not commit enough resources or convince Western partners to increase their own investment. It was ultimately outmanoeuvred and eclipsed by Iran, Russia and Turkiye, which intervened decisively and now shape post-conflict Syria.

The relationship with the US has been particularly complex and frustrating for Paris. The authors of the 2013 White Paper on Defence and National Security noted the decreasing US commitment to the Mediterranean space and in turn the expectation for an increased European and French role.[3] However, France has depended heavily on US enablers to operate both in Libya and in Syria. Yearly deployments of its nuclear-powered aircraft carrier *Charles de Gaulle* in the Eastern Mediterranean since 2015 have increased France's deterrence, operational, intelligence and overall diplomatic profile, but have also exposed the limits of French capacity when compared with the US. In turn, when the US reduced its engagement in the region, France's also suffered. The fluctuations in US policy have been particularly problematic for France. In 2013, the US called off planned joint strikes against Assad government targets without informing Paris. Even as the US showed frustration with Ankara, it did not back Paris in its escalating feud with the Turkish government. In Lebanon, where Paris makes a claim of parity, US policy at times differed significantly from French policy, leading to frustration, tensions and miscommunication on important matters.

Nevertheless, France remains able to leverage strategic ties and interests in the region. Paris was quick to embrace the government of Abdel Fattah al-Sisi in Egypt despite Western criticism of the 2013 coup, paving the way for a strong relationship based on defence cooperation despite the absence of an official partnership. The French presidency directly handles the strategic and military aspects of this relationship and has shielded it from media and political criticism. French defence sales to Egypt, including ships and advanced aircraft, can be credited to French cultivation of Cairo's willingness to diversify away from the US.

SPECIAL TIES TO LEBANON, SYRIA AND PALESTINE?

Through its 700-strong participation in the United Nations Interim Force in Lebanon (UNIFIL) since 1978, which is deployed at the border with Israel,[4] France has been involved in the complex dynamics between Hizbullah, Iran, Israel and Syria. This military role makes it an interlocutor of the Lebanese, Israeli and US governments, and supports its ambition to mediate the conflict.

The development since the mid-2010s of the relationship with Greece and Cyprus, two countries which until then had limited historical and political engagement with France, deserves particular attention. Rooted in shared animosity towards Turkiye, it shows how France has sought to insert itself in attempts to contain Ankara. Paris has sided with both countries on all aspects of their disputes with Turkiye. In 2017 it concluded a military-cooperation agreement with Cyprus and in 2021 upgraded its strategic partnership with Greece to include a mutual-defence clause.[5]

Even France's relations with Israel improved significantly in the past two decades. They had reached a low point during the presidency of Jacques Chirac (1995–2007), who was critical of Israel's expansionist policies in the Occupied Palestinian Territories and US policies that led to the invasion of Iraq. The shift occurred during the presidency of Nicolas Sarkozy and under the impetus of a new cadre of strategic thinkers who saw limited returns on France's investment in the Arab world, prioritised addressing Iran's nuclear challenge and espoused a more Atlanticist outlook. If defence cooperation has remained limited (France has not sold major systems to Israel, nor has it bought any from it), the political relationship has improved significantly, including during Macron's presidency. France has been an active contributor to naval exercises in the Eastern Mediterranean, and is second only to the US in the number of its engagements with regional navies. This has also elevated France's profile. Hosting the world's second-largest Jewish community after the US as well as large Muslim and Arab-origin populations, France has proven particularly exposed to the second-order effects of Middle Eastern conflicts.

France has sustained these strategic ties through its defence, energy and shipping industries. The deep-seated relations between the French state and its private sector have explicit as well as implicit impacts on foreign expectations of France. Major players like shipping and port operator CMA CGM, Dassault Aviation (producer of the *Rafale* fighter jet), MBDA, Naval Group (producer of FREMM frigates), Safran, Thales and TotalEnergies have major interests in the Eastern Mediterranean (see Map 15.2) and have pursued them in sync with French political direction.

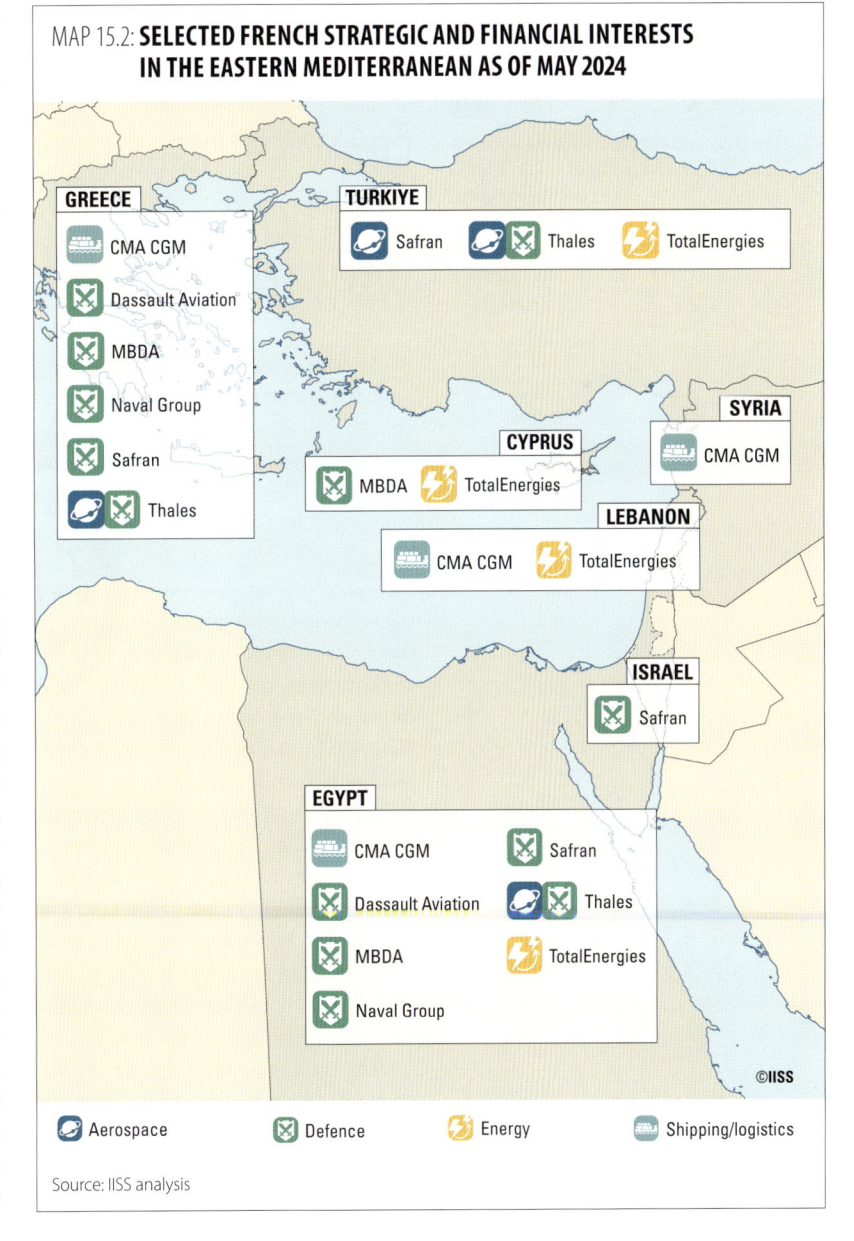

MAP 15.2: SELECTED FRENCH STRATEGIC AND FINANCIAL INTERESTS IN THE EASTERN MEDITERRANEAN AS OF MAY 2024

GREECE: CMA CGM, Dassault Aviation, MBDA, Naval Group, Safran, Thales
TURKIYE: Safran, Thales, TotalEnergies
CYPRUS: MBDA, TotalEnergies
SYRIA: CMA CGM
LEBANON: CMA CGM, TotalEnergies
ISRAEL: Safran
EGYPT: CMA CGM, Dassault Aviation, MBDA, Naval Group, Safran, Thales, TotalEnergies

Legend: Aerospace, Defence, Energy, Shipping/logistics

Source: IISS analysis

French President Emmanuel Macron (L) greets Turkish President Recep Tayyip Erdoğan (R) during a bilateral meeting as part of the NATO summit in Vilnius, Lithuania, on 11 July 2023. (Photo: Ludovic Marin/AFP via Getty Images)

FRANCE'S DIFFICULT RELATIONS WITH TURKIYE

While Russia's expansion into the warm seas of the Mediterranean is of strategic concern to France, Turkiye has been its most significant challenge in the region in recent years. Turkiye was described in France's 2013 defence white paper as a 'first-tier ally', but the two countries have since clashed over Libya's domestic dynamics, the campaign against the Islamic State, Syria's future and the fate of the Kurds, Turkiye's brinkmanship in the Eastern Mediterranean as well as more distant topics such as the Armenian genocide, French secularism, human rights in Turkiye and the conflict in Nagorno-Karabakh. Paris's closest partners in the Middle East, Egypt and the United Arab Emirates (UAE), share a similar distrust of Turkiye, which has informed and influenced its own views.

The two countries appear to be on irreconcilable paths. They each see themselves as rightfully dominant Mediterranean powers with expansive interests. The clash has also taken on an ideological dimension since the conservative Justice and Development Party (AKP) has come to dominate Turkish politics since 2002. French politicians had developed an appreciation for the Kemalist imposition of secularism in Turkiye and have bemoaned its rolling back under the AKP. They have been among the most vocal opponents of Turkiye's potential accession to the EU. French criticism of Turkiye's human-rights record and treatment of the Kurdish community has been met with Turkish efforts to challenge French secularism, including through its network of cultural organisations and anti-France online disinformation campaigns.[6] The personal, acrimonious nature of the rivalry between Macron and his Turkish counterpart, Recep Tayyip Erdoğan, has made it more difficult to ease tensions. During his 2020 address to the UN General Assembly, Macron said: 'In the Eastern Mediterranean, we must resume effective and clarified dialogue to avoid a new area of confrontation and the undermining of international law. … We respect and are prepared to dialogue with Turkey, but we expect Turkey to respect European sovereignty, international law and to provide clarification concerning its activities in Libya and Syria. Insults are ineffective.'[7]

Strategically, their already complex relationship deteriorated significantly when they chose two clashing approaches to the Syrian conflict, based on their different national-security prerogatives. For Turkiye, the British, American and French failure to enforce their joint red line in Syria in 2013 undermined their credibility, allowed Iran and Russia to fill the vacuum and operate on Turkiye's border and fuelled the rise of Kurdish ambitions and of jihadi extremism.

In response, Turkiye ramped up its unilateral policy in Syria, focusing on boosting Islamist factions to prevent the Syrian Kurdish militia from establishing autonomous governance in the northeast and along the Turkish border. France assessed that Turkiye wilfully ignored the expansion of the Islamic State and the arrivals of radicalised European nationals crossing into Syria to join it. This jihadi threat, which culminated in the massive 2015 ISIS attacks in Paris, quickly became a top national-security priority for France and its driving focus in Syria. There, alongside the US and the UK and notwithstanding Turkish opposition, it supported the formation of the Syrian Democratic Forces, made up of the Kurdistan Workers' Party's (PKK) offshoot in Syria, as the main surrogate for *Operation Inherent Resolve* (OIR) in northeastern Syria.

The French counter-terrorist mission in Syria had mixed results. French special forces deployed in Syria did manage to hunt down and eliminate a sizeable number of ISIS militants. By 2019, OIR achieved its goal of defeating the territorial caliphate that ISIS had established. Yet France and the ultimate sustainability of the approach remained dependent on US policy. In 2019, then-president of the United States Donald Trump announced in a surprise move that he would withdraw US forces from northeastern Syria.[8] As in 2013, France had not been consulted and scrambled to plan its contingency as it would have been unable to sustain its presence unilaterally. Ultimately, the US only reduced its presence but this episode fully exposed French vulnerabilities vis-à-vis Turkiye and other rivals like Iran and Russia.

At the same time, France's risky gambit in Libya had failed. The start of the Libyan civil war in 2014 coincided with an increasing terrorist threat level from the Middle East and the Sahel, where French troops had intervened to avoid a jihadi takeover of Mali. France's overriding counter-terrorism priority led it to work with the eastern factions of General Khalifa Haftar, who posed as the rampart against non-state Islamist militias. In 2017, the embrace of Haftar was accelerated by the newly elected president Emmanuel Macron, who saw an opportunity for a diplomatic success in Libya despite caution from his diplomats. After a failed peace conference, Macron doubled down on his support for Haftar against the UN-recognised government in Tripoli. In doing so, he aligned with the preferences of his regional partners, Egypt and the UAE, and, to a lesser extent, Greece but also, embarrassingly, Russia. This, however, put him at odds with Italy, Germany, the UK and the US. In 2019, France supported Haftar's assault against Tripoli but in doing so, it overplayed its hand. Once again, it faced greater Turkish commitment in the Eastern Mediterranean. In 2020, Ankara's military intervention decisively stopped and repelled Haftar's forces.

France's attempt to stand up to Turkiye produced mixed results. Its enforcement of the international arms embargo on Libya was seen as politicised because of its rivalry with Ankara. When the aforementioned Turkish warship became involved in an armed stand-off with the aforementioned French frigate patrolling in the Eastern Mediterranean, the Alliance tried to quickly move past the incident, with some allies blaming France for being too forceful. Vocal French support for Greece and Cyprus in the face of Turkish brinkmanship raised criticism inside the EU and NATO, in contrast with the more measured German, Italian and British positions. Even then, Paris has also had to contend with Athens and Nicosia also showing greater interest in their relationships with the US. Tellingly, Paris and Ankara have been unable to find a transactional basis on which to mend their relationship as Turkiye has done with Egypt, the UAE and Saudi Arabia.

France faced setbacks in other arenas as well. France has arguably its greatest leverage in Lebanon. Yet, its efforts to shape Lebanese politics have failed, with Paris left with little leverage to push for political reform and forced to accommodate Hizbullah's political interests. Its effort to reform the Lebanese economy since the 2019 collapse failed to sway or force the hand of

> WHILE RUSSIA'S EXPANSION INTO THE WARM SEAS OF THE MEDITERRANEAN IS OF STRATEGIC CONCERN TO FRANCE, TURKIYE HAS BEEN ITS MOST SIGNIFICANT CHALLENGE IN THE REGION IN RECENT YEARS.

the Lebanese political and economic elites. Despite this setback, France has not imposed sanctions on relevant Lebanese actors. French restraint and contradictions have been shared across presidencies, exposing both the limits of French influence and the fear that pushing Lebanese politicians too hard would either collapse the system or lead to war. In August 2020, with the country reeling from political paralysis, financial collapse and the explosion of the Beirut port, France was presented an opportunity to disrupt the country's power dynamics. Even then, despite being the only world leader to devote energy and attention to the country, Macron failed to extract significant concessions from the ruling political class and ended up reinforcing the dominance of Hizbullah and its allies, which was the opposite of his intended outcome.

France's relative weakening was also on display as the US conducted a mediation to demarcate the maritime border between Israel and Lebanon, which resulted in an agreement in 2022. France's absent leverage in Israel and inability to provide guarantees made it a secondary player, supporting US diplomacy without being able to shape it. That subordinate role extends to diplomatic efforts to prevent the expansion of the Israel–Hamas war to Lebanon or to end the political crisis in Beirut. In contrast, France had played prominent roles in the agreements and UN resolutions that ended the 1996 and 2006 wars between Israel and Lebanon and was central to several internal mediation efforts in the past. Today, Paris's role focuses on avoiding worst-case outcomes such as a war that would require evacuating European nationals from Lebanon and Israel.

Despite all these setbacks, France has managed to play an effective role in the minilateral effort to contain Turkiye. It is a member of the EMGF and an associate to the Greece–Cyprus–Egypt trilateral. It upgraded its strategic partnership with Greece in 2021 to include a mutual-defence clause and to deepen defence-industrial ties.[9] The pact is primarily strategic signalling aimed at Turkiye but also a way for France to emerge as a security provider in a region where the US has been intent on reducing its footprint. For Greece, this relationship is a way to diversify its Western relations as it distances itself from Russia, a long-time partner. The partnership with France will enable Greece to modernise its ageing fleet with three new frigates and, with 21 *Rafale* aircraft on order, to boast a modern air force surpassing Turkiye's.

Yet the defence clause was met with scepticism from some European and NATO partners which questioned its relevance given the pre-existing NATO Article 5 and the EU Treaty's Article 42.7 – both of which provide for mutual defence. There are also doubts about France's political willingness and military capability to implement the clause if it were invoked, including within the ranks of the French military.

But nowhere has France's shrunken leverage been more dramatic than in the Israel–Hamas war. Paris has traditionally attempted to have a balanced approach to the conflict, both as a staunch supporter of Israel's right to exist and defend itself (it assisted it in its development of nuclear weapons in the 1950s and equipped the Israel Defense Forces), and as a supporter of Palestinian self-determination and a two-state solution. This stance had previously given it a regional role despite the dominance of the US. However, the double effect of the US-led Abraham Accords normalisation between Israel and some Arab Gulf states and Macron's initial disinterest in the Palestinian issue sidelined France. Since the outbreak of the war in Gaza, however, Macron has been the first head of a major Western state to call for a ceasefire and France was the only one of the three Western permanent members of the UN Security Council to vote in favour of Palestinian statehood in 2024. Whether this reflects a desire to return to a more balanced position or the concern that the internal polarisation due to the war could threaten domestic security remains unclear. However, French influence on both Israeli and Palestinian dynamics, already limited, has further receded.

OUTLOOK

France's standing in the Eastern Mediterranean as a power able to shape this environment has diminished. In addition to limited defence and intelligence capabilities, this is in large part owing to its choice either to follow the lead and preferences of its local partners even on ineffective policies, or to attempt to contain malign actors instead of attempting to roll them back. Iran's reach through its powerful network of influence and Turkiye's assertive animosity will continue to challenge Paris's interests. Russia and China are also benefitting from key Middle Eastern countries' desire to diversify away from traditional Western partners.

It is therefore likely that the influence of France, along with other Western powers like the US and the UK, will continue to diminish. The political and strategic fallout of the Israeli offensive in Gaza, including the Western inability to enforce the rules of the international order, has undermined their standing and made other countries less observant of Western advice and guidance.

Nevertheless, France still retains strategic assets and remains well placed to benefit from the regional desire for hedging. Its ability to stabilise and rebuild its power in the region will depend on whether it presents a unique and distinguishable offering, with the resolve to get involved in long-term diplomatic, political, geo-economic and military manoeuvring. It will also have to find a way to articulate and pursue a more common strategy and approach with allies and partners like the EU, Germany, Italy, the UK and the US to reduce the headwinds it could face in the region.

ENDNOTES

1. See 'Discours en l'Honneur des Défilants du 14 Juillet 2020 Depuis l'Hôtel de Brienne' [President Emmanuel Macron's speech in honour of the military parade from Hotel Brienne on 14 July 2020], speech given by Emmanuel Macron, Paris, 13 July 2020, https://www.elysee.fr/emmanuel-macron/2020/07/13/discours-en-lhonneur-des-defilants-du-14-juillet-2020-depuis-lhotel-de-brienne.

2. See NATO, 'NATO and Libya', 9 November 2015, https://www.nato.int/cps/en/natohq/topics_71652.htm.

3. France, Ministry of Defence, 'Livre Blanc Défense et Sécurité Nationale' [White paper: defence and national security], 2013, https://www.vie-publique.fr/files/rapport/pdf/134000257.pdf.

4. See France, Ministry of the Armed Forces, 'Opération DAMAN', https://www.defense.gouv.fr/operations/operations/operation-daman#:~:text=Pr%C3%A9sente%20depuis%201978%20au%20Liban,fran%C3%A7aise%20%C3%A0%20la%20force%20internationale.

5. See France, Ministry of Europe and Foreign Affairs, 'France and Cyprus', https://www.diplomatie.gouv.fr/en/country-files/cyprus/france-and-cyprus-65023/#:~:text=Cooperation%20between%20France%20and%20Cyprus,jointly%20with%20other%20European%20navies. France and Cyprus have a defence-cooperation agreement that was signed in 2017 and came into effect in 2020 at the height of the resurgent Turkish brinkmanship at sea. The agreement aims to deepen an already well-established military relationship with Nicosia. Indeed, it has been a backstop for French troops operating within OIR since 2015, and for contingency evacuation planning in case of an Israel–Lebanon war; for the strategic partnership with Greece, see Légifrance, 'Décret n° 2022-180 du 14 février 2022 portant publication de l'accord entre le Gouvernement de la République française et le Gouvernement de la République hellénique pour l'établissement d'un partenariat stratégique de coopération en matière de défense et de sécurité, signé à Paris le 28 septembre 2021 (1)' [Decree No. 2022-180 of February 14, 2022 publishing the agreement between the Government of the French Republic and the Government of the Hellenic Republic for the establishment of a strategic partnership for cooperation in defence and security matters, signed in Paris on 28 September 2021 (1)], https://www.legifrance.gouv.fr/jorf/id/JORFSCTA000045174545.

6. After a major speech Macron gave on the integration of immigrants and the need to organise Islam in 2020, and after the assassinations of school teachers by Islamist jihadis in 2020 and 2023.

7. See France, Ministry of Europe and Foreign Affairs, 'Emmanuel Macron Speaks at UN General Assembly (22 Sept. 2020)', https://www.diplomatie.gouv.fr/en/french-foreign-policy/france-and-the-united-nations/news-and-events/united-nations-general-assembly/unga-s-75th-session/article/emmanuel-macron-speaks-at-un-general-assembly-22-sept-2020.

8. See Julian E. Barnes and Eric Schmitt, 'Trump Orders Withdrawal of U.S. Troops From Northern Syria', *New York Times*, 13 October 2019, https://www.nytimes.com/2019/10/13/us/politics/mark-esper-syria-kurds-turkey.html.

9. See Légifrance, https://www.legifrance.gouv.fr/jorf/id/JORFSCTA000045174545.

NATO heads of government attending the NATO Summit in Madrid, Spain, on 29–30 June 2022. (Photo: Celestino Arce/NurPhoto via Getty Images)

THE EASTERN MEDITERRANEAN IS THE BACKDROP for the war in Ukraine and the Black Sea, making it a highly strategic arena for NATO and the European Union in which Russia's profile is growing. Both organisations have, however, struggled to exert geopolitical power and devote appropriate resources to the region.

INTERNAL DIVISIONS AND POLITICAL TENSIONS among member states and allies, as well as their inability or unwillingness to put in place appropriate capabilities, have limited the effectiveness of EU and NATO operations in the region.

EU AND NATO POLICIES IN THE EASTERN MEDITERRANEAN have predominantly centred on fighting terrorism and countering migration, with limited results, while the EU's chequebook diplomacy and externalising of its border controls have opened it up to costly quid pro quos.

CHAPTER SIXTEEN

THE SOUTHERN FLANK: A CHALLENGE FOR NATO AND THE EU

INTRODUCTION

The Eastern Mediterranean is a vital space for both the European Union and NATO. The EU has two member states in the region (Cyprus and Greece), and a geographic and demographic proximity that have made it vulnerable – politically and on the security level – to the second- and third-order effects of the multiple conflicts and crises in the Eastern Mediterranean. For NATO, whose Eastern Mediterranean members are Greece and Turkiye, the basin is the beginning of its southern flank and an area where Russia has deepened its foothold in both Syria and Libya, as well as the source of internal tensions over the Cyprus question (see Chapters One and Eight).

The last time NATO directly intervened in the basin was in 2011 in the operation that ousted Libyan leader Muammar Gadhafi. Since then, its standing has been tarnished in the area, with accusations – pushed by Russian disinformation – that it went beyond its initial United Nations mandate in order to effect regime change which resulted in regional instability. The EU, for its part, has moved away from the association-agreement framework to an approach based on chequebook diplomacy aimed at preventing migration flows and countering terrorism, through economic assistance, border security and security-capacity building and assistance for migrants and refugees. This has made it vulnerable to quid pro quos by autocratic leaders in the region.

Despite, however, their respective weight and leverage, the deployment of military missions and their considerable financial packages, both organisations have struggled in the past decade to maintain cohesion among their members and to shape their immediate strategic environment. Intra-EU disagreements on the missions of both of its operations in the Mediterranean (*Operation Sophia* and *Operation Irini*),[1] coupled with Turkiye's explicit opposition to this perceived intrusion into its own sphere, have hamstrung the EU's naval operations, as well as NATO's *Operation Sea Guardian*. Cooperation between the EU and NATO operations remains stunted at best.

NATO

While NATO has primarily focused on its eastern flank in recent years, devoting less strategic attention to the Mediterranean Sea, its recognition of the increasing risks to its strategic interests there is growing.

The ongoing Israel–Hamas war and its possible wide-ranging fallout, as well as the enduring conflict in Libya and increased military activity from Russia and China in the region, have heightened security concerns and increased the need to ensure a visible NATO presence at sea. Yet members' divergence on priorities, friction between allies, the enduring Cyprus problem and the Russian invasion of Ukraine have limited the bandwidth for NATO's presence and impact in the south.

Within NATO, countries such as Estonia, Lithuania and Poland prioritise attention on the eastern flank, while others including France, Italy and Spain prioritise the southern flank. Advocates of a more effective NATO presence and engagement in the Eastern Mediterranean have pointed out that the Eastern Mediterranean is the strategic hyphen between the two theatres.² It is also the backdrop for the war in Ukraine and the Black Sea. Part of the Russian Black Sea Fleet had been moved to the Mediterranean prior to the 2022 invasion of Ukraine, to ensure its safety and conserve an ability to navigate, and Russia's naval facilities and access to ports in Syria and Libya have become strategically significant.³

At the Madrid Summit in June 2022, NATO allies agreed to take steps to improve the Alliance's maritime posture.⁴ They have since been working on upgrading capabilities in the basin in response to maritime-security developments, including the increased Russian presence.

The United States is indisputably the dominant military in the region, with essential operational, monitoring, signalling and deterrence roles played by its Naples-based Sixth Fleet and its Bahrain-based Fifth Fleet. Aside from the national military capabilities deployed either permanently or on rotation by France, Germany, Italy, the United Kingdom and the US – which are there to occupy the space, obstruct a larger Russian footprint and carry out essential intelligence, surveillance and reconnaissance operations – NATO runs several initiatives in the Mediterranean. These include its standing immediate-reaction naval forces, Standing NATO Maritime Group 2 (SNMG2) and Standing NATO Mine Countermeasures Group 2, which operate directly under NATO operational command.⁵ It also carries out maritime and joint exercises as well as capacity-building projects with partners in the southern neighbourhood.⁶ Signifying NATO's renewed interest in the region, its secretary-general commissioned an expert report on NATO's role in its southern neighbourhood in October 2023 and appointed a special representative in July 2024.

Operation Sea Guardian has also been a main component of NATO's Mediterranean presence since its inception in 2016 (see Figure 16.1 and Map 16.1). This non-Article 5 crisis-management maritime-security operation was initially primarily focused on counter-terrorism (CT). While maintaining its CT function, it has added supporting maritime situational awareness – focusing on information-sharing between allies – and contributing to maritime-security capacity-building to its mission. As of May 2024, it stood ready to expand its maritime-security operations to include upholding freedom of navigation, conducting maritime interdiction, fighting the proliferation of weapons of mass destruction and protecting critical infrastructure.⁷ At the time of writing, however, it has yet to receive the approval of the North Atlantic Council to do so.

Operation Sea Guardian has suffered from infighting among allies and limited asset availability. In order to enhance its capabilities, NATO has been seeking a deeper level of operational cooperation with outside actors in recent years.⁸ The Royal Australian Air Force's P-8A *Poseidon* maritime patrol aircraft participated in *Sea Guardian* for the first time in 2022,⁹ a move which was described as a 'natural step-up … on responding to today's global security challenges' by the country's chief of joint operations.¹⁰ In addition to Australia and New Zealand, Georgia also gained operational-partner status after a four-year evaluation programme.¹¹ Israel was in the process of obtaining the same status,¹² but the ongoing war between Israel and Hamas appears to have halted that discussion.

With maritime-security threats continuing to evolve, allies agreed at the Vilnius Summit in 2023 to establish the Maritime Centre for the Security of Critical Undersea Infrastructure within NATO's Maritime Command (MARCOM), which was launched in May 2024.¹³ In the Mediterranean, the Alliance does not plan to expand *Operation Sea Guardian*, but rather intends to enhance its vigilance activities using its standing maritime forces and increase its capabilities in the area by showing flexibility in transferring authority and capability under NATO command and structure. Whether that will enhance capabilities and effectiveness remains to be seen.

This new strategy is built on NATO's 2022 deterrence and defence concept.¹⁴ The plans allow the Supreme Allied Commander Europe to coordinate national activities in pursuit of NATO

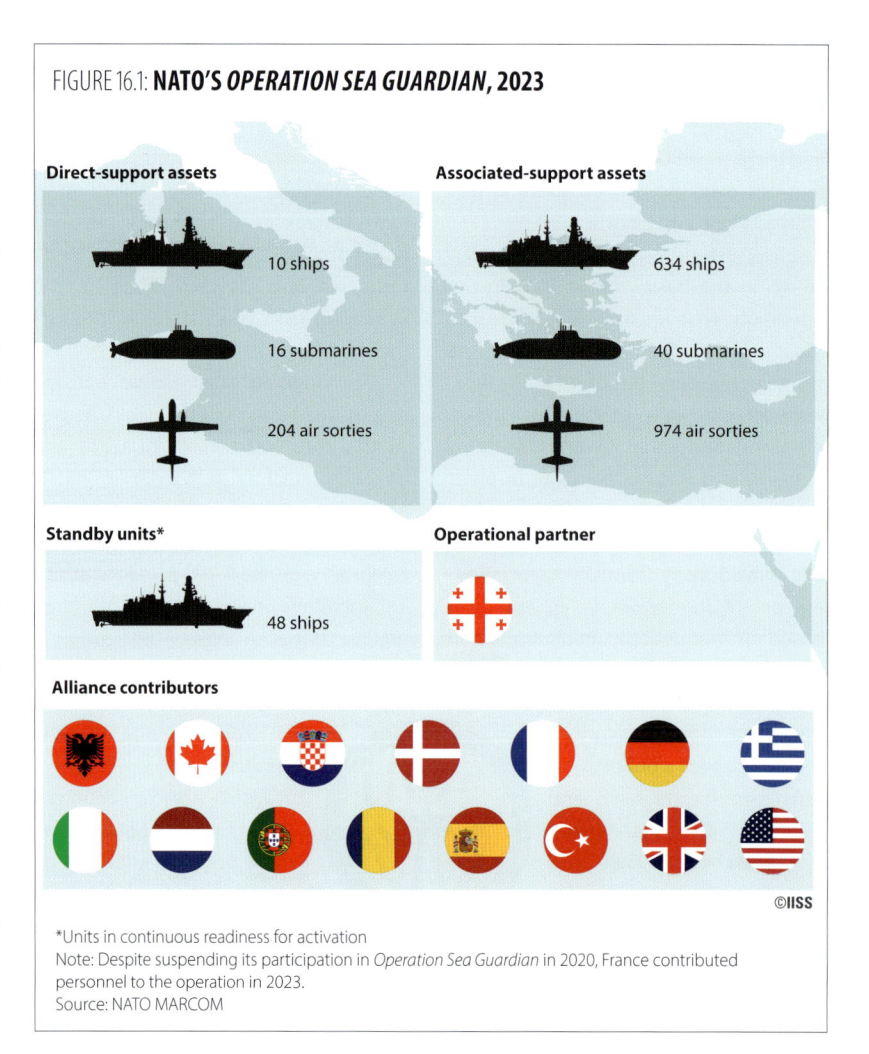

FIGURE 16.1: NATO'S *OPERATION SEA GUARDIAN*, 2023

Direct-support assets
- 10 ships
- 16 submarines
- 204 air sorties

Associated-support assets
- 634 ships
- 40 submarines
- 974 air sorties

Standby units*
- 48 ships

Operational partner
- Georgia

Alliance contributors
Albania, Canada, Croatia, Denmark, France, Germany, Greece, Italy, Netherlands, Portugal, Romania, Spain, Turkey, United Kingdom, United States

*Units in continuous readiness for activation
Note: Despite suspending its participation in *Operation Sea Guardian* in 2020, France contributed personnel to the operation in 2023.
Source: NATO MARCOM

objectives, which is intended to boost inter-operability significantly.[15] The Alliance has also recently increased the size and frequency of its maritime drills in the basin, with a renewed emphasis on preparing NATO for high-intensity and multi-domain operations.[16] Since 2022, France, the UK and the US have also stepped up strategic signalling in the Mediterranean by transferring aircraft carriers, their most powerful and symbolic assets, under NATO command for exercises.[17]

As strategic competition in the Mediterranean intensifies, NATO is using training and associated activities to simulate and prepare for armed conflict and sub-threshold activity. The Alliance is holding more tactical trainings, with submarine-warfare and anti-submarine war-fighting exercises like *Dynamic Manta* and *Mongoose*, and avoiding exercises that would pull capabilities out of the area without a strictly tactical purpose.[18]

Despite the overlap in membership and the importance of the Eastern Mediterranean for both the EU and NATO, greater cooperation between the two has been difficult to achieve. Security and defence relations are dominated by rivalry and suspicion. Issues like the Turkish–Cypriot conflict, which affects NATO's internal workings and taints Ankara's relationship with the EU, and disagreements between NATO-first and EU-first allies over the balance between the development of more EU military capabilities and the primacy of NATO and the transatlantic relationship, remain thorny. This has weakened their respective abilities to contain and counter effectively the common threats they face.

A near-confrontation in the Mediterranean Sea between France and Turkiye in 2020 was a turning point for intra-Alliance tensions. A French frigate patrolling under *Operation Sea Guardian* got into a stand-off with a Turkish warship when it was denied permission to board a Tanzanian-flagged civilian ship being escorted by Turkish vessels, which was suspected of involvement in arms trafficking with Libya. The French contend that the Turkish warship trained its arming laser on it and that Turkish sailors had taken position behind their machine guns, while the Turkish warship says it simply gave a warning to stand down. This confrontation has haunted *Sea Guardian* ever since, with France suspending its participation in the operation and redirecting its resources to the EU's *Irini* mission, which did not involve Turkiye as it was designed to be impartial, with no third-party involvement.[19] And though NATO's deconfliction mechanism has continued to act as a safety net between Greece and Turkiye, the brinkmanship at sea also led to a breakdown of structured cooperation with the EU's *Operation Irini*. A technical-cooperation agreement between *Sea Guardian* and *Irini* was proposed after *Irini*'s inception but never approved by NATO due to Turkish objections. However, although constraints remain and NATO–EU coordination in the basin has decreased over time since the end of *Sophia*, an information-sharing agreement has been established between NATO and Frontex (with SNMG2 supporting anti-migrant-trafficking efforts). Furthermore, *Sea Guardian–Irini* informal cooperation operates at the staff-to-staff level and through the joint EU–NATO conference, Shared Awareness and de-Confliction in the Mediterranean (SHADE MED), as well as indirectly due to the dual membership of some countries.

THE GEOPOLITICS OF THE EU IN THE EASTERN MEDITERRANEAN

The EU's posture in the Eastern Mediterranean is hamstrung by the Cyprus problem and shaped by three imperatives: to contain and repel migration; to counter terrorism; and, since Russia's invasion of Ukraine in 2022, to secure energy supplies.

Migration became a challenge for the cohesion of the EU and a major domestic political problem for its member states

MAP 16.1: NATO'S *OPERATION SEA GUARDIAN* PORT CALLS IN THE EASTERN MEDITERRANEAN, 2022–23

Port calls in 2022   Port calls in 2023

Source: NATO MARCOM

in 2015, when more than one million refugees and migrants from war-torn Afghanistan, Iraq and Syria crossed from Turkiye's Mediterranean coast into Greece and other countries to settle in Western Europe. In recent years, Cyprus has seen a significant rise in migrant and refugee numbers coming either through the Green Line buffer zone via the unrecognised Turkish Republic of Northern Cyprus or by sea from Lebanon. Given deep divisions among its member states on how best to manage migration, including on issues such as rescues at sea and migrant quotas, and straightforward opposition to any migration from the Middle East in several countries, such as Hungary, the EU has failed to come up with an effective functioning migration policy. As a result, it has resorted to externalising its border control through hefty assistance packages, which include migration-related conditions and support, with Turkiye (2016, an initial €6 billion, with an additional €3bn in 2023),[20] Egypt (2024, €7.4bn),[21] Lebanon (2024, €1bn)[22] and Tunisia. This migration-first approach has fuelled concerns that the EU's leverage over its neighbourhood is eroding. Its border agency Frontex, which supports local border forces in Cyprus and other countries along key migration routes, has also been accused by human-rights organisations of being 'complicit in the abuse' of migrants through its provision of aerial surveillance to the Libyan coastguard, enabling the interception of migrant boats and the return of migrants to 'systemic and widespread abuse' on shore in Libya.[23]

Energy is another source of internal discord. Even though securing alternative energy sources has become a strategic imperative for the EU, it is still an issue largely driven by member states at the national level. Member states such as Italy and France have competed against each other to secure gas supplies from Algeria and Libya. The EU has not managed to push the Eastern Mediterranean (EastMed) Gas Pipeline – a planned subsea pipeline meant to connect Israeli and Cypriot gas fields to Greece and mainland Europe – beyond the feasibility-study stage, reflecting internal differences over the economic and political merits of the project, and reluctance to invest in a long-term natural-gas project as the EU conducts its energy transition. The pipeline project was further undercut by the US in 2022 when the Biden administration expressed its misgivings about it (in part motivated by a desire to stabilise relations with Turkiye).[24]

Turkish–EU relations have also been in turmoil. Ankara's EU-accession track is stuck in decades-long limbo over Ankara's

Migrants and refugees are transferred from the *Topaz Responder*, a ship run by the Maltese non-governmental organisation Moas and the Italian Red Cross, to the Italian Coast Guard's ship CP906, on 4 November 2016, after rescue operations off the Libyan coast. (Photo: Andreas Solaro/AFP via Getty Images)

lagging delivery on required reforms (namely on rule of law and fundamental rights) and especially because of the opposition to Turkiye's EU membership from populist European governments on civilisational, religious and economic grounds. It is possible that upgrading the EU–Turkiye customs union or liberalising the visa regime would improve the relationship, but this would fall short of the expectations of the Turkish economic and liberal elite. Another enduring source of tension has been Cyprus's accession in 2004, which ensured that Brussels could not be a mediator in the conflict and crystallised Turkiye's conviction that Cyprus, with French backing, has the power to determine EU policy or at least has a veto right. This, as well as geopolitical tensions over Turkiye's Middle Eastern policies, has resulted in hostility between Turkiye and EU member states such as France and Greece in recent years.

Nevertheless, Turkiye has savvily turned the power dynamic to its advantage, leveraging its geopolitical position to extract concessions. The need to keep Turkiye on board given Russian aggression and for the management of conflicts in the Middle East has made several key EU countries more accommodating and willing to offer political and economic incentives. The EU remains – by far – Turkiye's top trading partner, accounting for nearly one-third of its trade.[25] The migration agreement with Ankara was the pilot programme in the EU's strategy of externalising its migration controls starting in 2016, though the deal has fallen short of the expectations of many member states. It has been instrumentalised by Turkiye to secure political gains from the EU and more burden-sharing by EU countries, most notably in 2020.[26] Despite these challenges, EU countries including Germany, Hungary and Italy have worked on smoothing over relations for their own domestic political considerations.

In contrast, EU officials in Brussels have viewed the strategic nature of Greek and Cypriot relations with Israel and Egypt – as well as France and the US – as 'neutral to problematic',[27] needlessly inflaming relations with Ankara. EU officials have sought to differentiate between EU policies and national ones in order to allay Turkish concerns that it is being isolated. Regardless, this gap further weakens Europe's overall power and credibility in the region.

EU MILITARY OPERATIONS IN THE EASTERN MEDITERRANEAN

As the EU has been supercharging its common security and defence policy, with the adoption of the EU Global Strategy (2016)[28] and Strategic Compass (2022), it has worked on expanding its military capabilities and missions. The Eastern Mediterranean has posed a particular security and cohesion challenge since the Arab uprisings. Member states have disagreed over the best course of action in Libya; how to manage the migration trails from the Sahel and North Africa, the Levant and further afield through the Mediterranean; how to counter terrorism in the region; and how to chart the relationships with NATO and Turkiye.

The EU has attempted to be a security player in the Mediterranean,

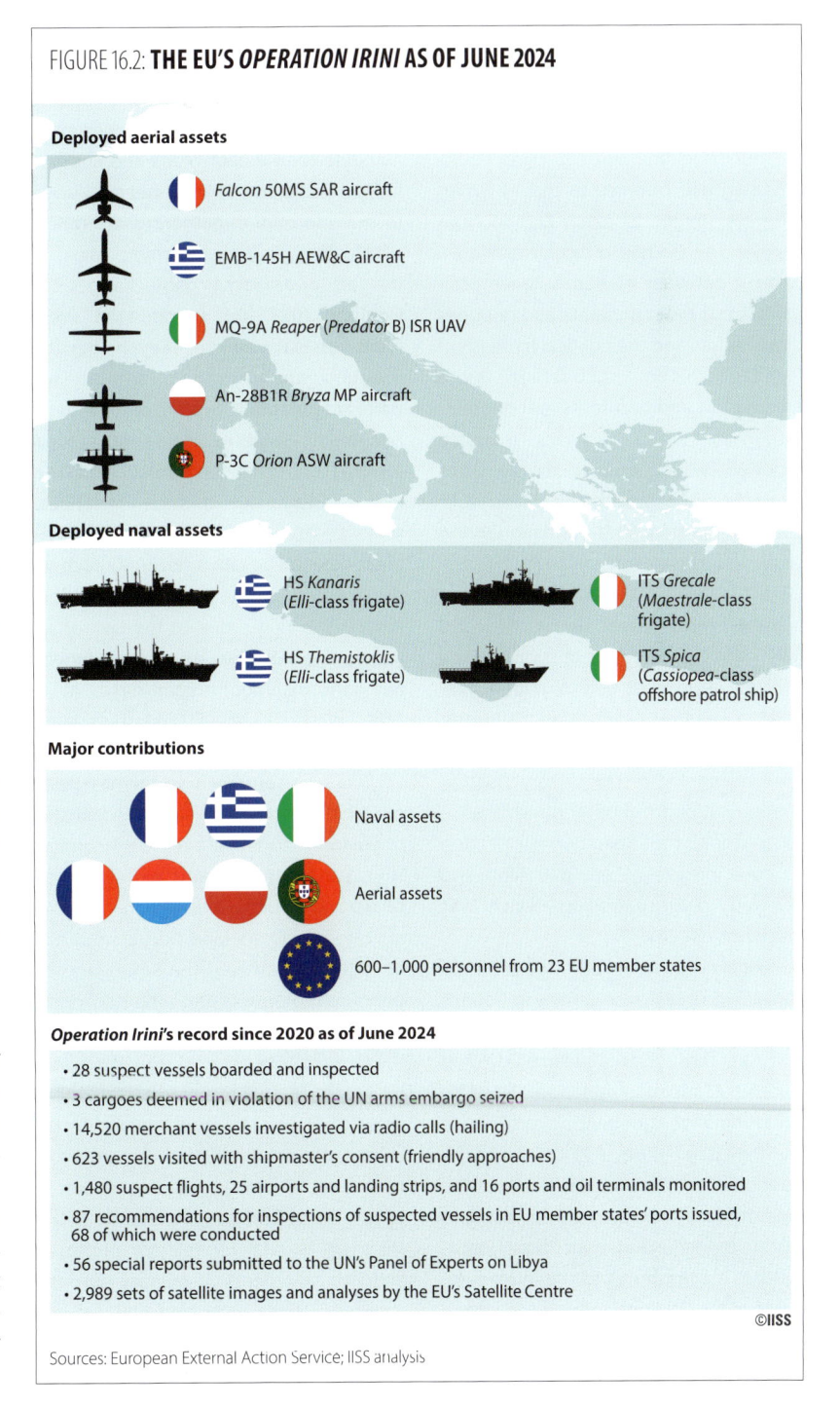

FIGURE 16.2: THE EU'S *OPERATION IRINI* AS OF JUNE 2024

Deployed aerial assets

- 🇫🇷 *Falcon* 50MS SAR aircraft
- 🇬🇷 EMB-145H AEW&C aircraft
- 🇮🇹 MQ-9A *Reaper* (*Predator* B) ISR UAV
- 🇵🇱 An-28B1R *Bryza* MP aircraft
- 🇵🇹 P-3C *Orion* ASW aircraft

Deployed naval assets

- 🇬🇷 HS *Kanaris* (*Elli*-class frigate)
- 🇮🇹 ITS *Grecale* (*Maestrale*-class frigate)
- 🇬🇷 HS *Themistoklis* (*Elli*-class frigate)
- 🇮🇹 ITS *Spica* (*Cassiopea*-class offshore patrol ship)

Major contributions

- 🇫🇷 🇬🇷 🇮🇹 Naval assets
- 🇫🇷 🇳🇱 🇵🇱 🇵🇹 Aerial assets
- 🇪🇺 600–1,000 personnel from 23 EU member states

Operation Irini's record since 2020 as of June 2024

- 28 suspect vessels boarded and inspected
- 3 cargoes deemed in violation of the UN arms embargo seized
- 14,520 merchant vessels investigated via radio calls (hailing)
- 623 vessels visited with shipmaster's consent (friendly approaches)
- 1,480 suspect flights, 25 airports and landing strips, and 16 ports and oil terminals monitored
- 87 recommendations for inspections of suspected vessels in EU member states' ports issued, 68 of which were conducted
- 56 special reports submitted to the UN's Panel of Experts on Libya
- 2,989 sets of satellite images and analyses by the EU's Satellite Centre

©IISS

Sources: European External Action Service; IISS analysis

mainly through its EUNAVFOR MED operations. The operations have struggled to be effective, however, due to their limited mandates and member states' contributions, as well as disagreements among member states. Although the operations have remained primarily focused on the Tunisian and Libyan coasts, their mandates have undergone critical changes, reflecting the shifting priorities of EU external migration policy.

Established at a European Council summit in June 2015, Operation Sophia was launched in October of that year in response to the rising death toll among migrants and refugees trying to reach Europe on dinghies. Despite the emphasis on anti-migrant-smuggling operations, including through aerial surveillance, it struggled to disrupt the lucrative migrant-trafficking business that had boomed as mainly Syrian refugees sought to reach Europe from Turkiye. The EU had difficulty striking a balance between its humanitarian obligations not to let migrants and refugees drown at sea and the political backlash in member states against EU refugee-quota schemes. In addition to its anti-migrant-smuggling duties, Sophia's mandate included helping enforce the UN arms embargo on Libya in the high seas – but not from the air or land – and monitoring illegal trafficking of Libyan oil.[29]

Ultimately, tensions between member states – especially Germany and Italy – undercut Sophia's mission. Matteo Salvini – a populist anti-migration politician – became Italy's interior minister in 2019 and refused to take in people from search-and-rescue ships, attracting condemnation from other governments. As a result, the operation suspended its core mission of sea patrolling and reverted to air patrolling, which was much less effective.[30]

Sophia was replaced by Operation Irini ('peace' in Greek) in a European Council decision in March 2020 with a mandate that runs through to 31 March 2025.[31] It involves 23 member states and is led by a rotating force commander from Greece and Italy (see Figure 16.2). In light of the position of the Italian government at the time, it was given a narrower mandate that no longer included maritime rescue. Instead, it contributes to the implementation of the UN arms embargo on Libya[32] and was given aerial, satellite[33] and maritime assets.[34]

Irini almost immediately raised tensions with Turkiye. Ankara contended that the disproportionate focus on intercepting maritime arms shipments to Tripoli (which were supported by Ankara), in the absence of any mandate or capability to intercept aerial and ground shipments, favoured General Khalifa Haftar's Libyan National Army – which was supplied by Russia, the United Arab Emirates (UAE) and Egypt, among others, and favoured by France and Greece – over the Tripoli-based, Turkish-backed Government of National Accord.

Besides its core mission, Irini's secondary objectives include carrying out maritime-security tasks, such as monitoring human-trafficking and smuggling activities, as well as illicit exports of oil and petrol.[35] However, without a mandate to intercept boats and combat human trafficking, Irini has been reduced to an information-gathering operation which, though it has intrinsic value, is not an operational gamechanger. In October 2023, EU Commission President Ursula von der Leyen backed boosting the mission's anti-human-trafficking mandate in a letter to leaders, but member states have not moved forward on this.[36] As evidence of the EU's halting answer to such challenges, projects under the EU Border Assistance Mission in Libya (EUBAM) such as the training of the Libyan coastguard have yet to begin due to the lack of an agreement with the Libyan government and concerns about human-rights violations voiced by some EU members, such as Germany.[37]

Irini's performance so far has been mixed. It has failed to stem the transfer of weapons to Libya because incoming ships can deny its teams permission to board and because it lacks a mandate to operate on Libya's land borders.[38] It has nevertheless reduced the smuggling of petroleum products and recorded violations of the arms embargo.[39]

Over its four years of operation, Irini has boarded and inspected 28 suspect vessels but seized cargo deemed to be in violation of the UN arms embargo only three times – including twice in 2022.[40] The seized goods were one illegal shipment of fuel for military purposes and two shipments of military-purpose vehicles.[41] While Operation Irini did not identify the exporting country or party in its announcements of the seizures,[42] the final report of the UN panel of experts on the embargo on Libya identified one shipment as being transported on a vessel owned by a Turkish operator and another from the UAE.[43] But not all ships and their flag countries have cooperated with Irini inspections: Turkish-flagged ships have denied permission to board and inspect on 11 occasions. The operation has also investigated 1,480 suspect flights. With limited means, however, Irini has not managed to seize any weapons shipments by air.

The US had been critical of Irini under the Trump administration, but the Biden administration has been more positive. In 2020, then-assistant secretary of state of the United States David Schenker expressed doubts about the operation, upholding the Turkish claim that Irini was overly focused on intercepting Turkish military equipment over Russian military equipment.[44] In 2022, however, Ambassador Richard Mills, Deputy US Representative to the United Nations, praised Irini for providing 'a deterrent to would-be arms smugglers' and for 'help[ing] the UN Panel of Experts on Libya and others gather critical information'.[45] This change in attitude was further demonstrated by another US official who applauded Operation Irini for its diversions of vessels transporting illegal arms.[46] The shift in the US position towards Irini recognised the operation's contribution to the prevention of the flow of arms to Libya, and opened the way for a more structured cooperation between Irini and the US.[47]

OUTLOOK

The EU and NATO face considerable challenges in the Eastern Mediterranean. Instability in the Middle East and the Sahel region, Russia's expanding and deepening footprint, China's increasing interest in the basin and Turkiye's assertive posture are all enduring threats. Despite increased awareness of their strategic importance, both struggle to find effective operational responses. Both organisations' own internal divisions and the inadequate resources dedicated to the area are the primary impediments.

For NATO and EU crisis-management and defence planners, the Eastern Mediterranean has a medium to high potential for inter-state conflict and produces events that generate destabilising second- and third-order effects on EU and NATO member states and allies. Yet both organisations are ill-equipped to provide pre-emptive or responsive solutions. Cooperation among members is also limited by a host of political misalignments, not least because of the built-in hurdles tied to Cyprus and Turkiye.

Their current military operations have shown their limits. *Irini* in particular is vulnerable to a new migration crisis. If one were to occur, it would test the resilience and coherence of the operation. Should it buckle as *Operation Sophia* did, it would require the EU to decide whether to change its mandate again, at a time of increased opposition to migration from EU states and citizenry.

Some EU officials believe that *Operation Irini* in its current format will serve as a placeholder for potentially broader maritime-security tasks within the bloc. For that to be possible, there will need to be political support for potentially expanding the operation's responsibilities and redefining it as a permanently available force for defending EU interests.[48] Given the current fatigue generated by the effort needed to support Ukraine, and the pressure on national budgets, this seems unlikely in the immediate future. Without a significant increase in military assets, Europe will be unable to maintain a viable maritime posture in the Eastern Mediterranean.[49] Countries have consistently underinvested in military vessels and skills, and challenges persist in terms of coherence and synergies, at both the operational and strategic levels.[50]

Irini embodies the EU's difficulty in becoming a geopolitical actor. The EU prioritises proving *Irini*'s impartial implementation of the arms embargo over the efficacy of its operation, shaping its strategic environment and publicly targeting those who harm its interests the most.

With the pervasiveness of geopolitical tensions, however, the EU's weak power, recourse to chequebook diplomacy and externalisation of migration controls have made it more vulnerable to blackmail and quid pro quo instead of increasing its leverage and security.

Vice-President of the European Commission and EU High Representative for Foreign Affairs and Security Policy Josep Borrell holds a press conference during a visit to the headquarters of the EU's *Operation Irini* in Rome, Italy, on 18 March 2021. (Photo by Tiziana Fabi/AFP via Getty Images)

ENDNOTES

1 Formally, *European Union Naval Force Mediterranean* (EUNAVFOR MED) and EUNAVFOR MED IRINI, respectively.

2 Interview with NATO official in Brussels, February 2023.

3 Based on interviews with European naval officers, March 2023 and March 2024.

4 NATO, 'NATO Allies and Partners Discuss Maritime Security', 6 December 2022, https://www.nato.int/cps/en/natohq/news_209324.htm.

5 The NATO Standing Naval Forces carry out operational missions and provide a deterrent presence and offshore and undersea installation situational awareness. See NATO Supreme Headquarters Allied Powers Europe (SHAPE), 'NATO Standing Naval Forces', https://shape.nato.int/about/aco-capabilities2/nato-standing-naval-forces.

6 The Alliance has also recently established the NATO Strategic Direction-South HUB (NSD-S HUB) in Naples, Italy, designed to increase NATO's understanding of the regional dynamics of the Middle East, North Africa, the Sahel, Sub-Saharan Africa and adjacent areas. See NSD-S HUB, 'About the NATO Strategic Direction-South HUB', https://thesouthernhub.org/about.

7 NATO, 'Operation Sea Guardian', 26 May 2023, https://www.nato.int/cps/en/natohq/topics_136233.htm.

8 Ukrainian operational-partner status has been pending for some time. See Mission of Ukraine to NATO, 'Ukraine's Participation in Alliance-led Operations, Missions, NATO Response Force and Exercises', 16 June 2021, https://nato.mfa.gov.ua/en/ukraine-and-nato/nato-ukraine-cooperation-peace-support-operations.

9 NATO Allied Maritime Command, 'MARCOM at a Glance', March 2023, https://mc.nato.int/resources/site1/General/at-a-glance/marcom_at_a_glance.pdf.

10 Australian Government Department of Defence, 'Defence Builds Closer Ties With NATO in the Mediterranean', 4 October 2022, https://www.defence.gov.au/news-events/releases/2022-10-04/defence-builds-closer-ties-nato-mediterranean.

11 Civil Georgia, 'Georgian Coast Guard Officers Join NATO's "Sea Guardian" Operation', 12 September 2023, https://civil.ge/archives/558838#:~:text=Following%20a%20successful%20four%2Dlevel,the%20Mediterranean%20Sea%20in%202022.

12 Information provided by NATO officials, February 2023.

13 NATO, Vilnius Summit Communiqué, 11 July 2023, https://www.nato.int/cps/en/natohq/official_texts_217320.htm; and NATO, 'NATO Officially Launches New Maritime Centre for Security of Critical Undersea Infrastructure', 28 May 2024, https://mc.nato.int/media-centre/news/2024/nato-officially-launches-new-nmcscui#:~:text=Northwood%2C%20UK%20%E2%80%93%20NATO%20has%20established,global%20communications%20and%20economic%20activity.

14 The Concept for Deterrence and Defence of the Euro-Atlantic Area (DDA, or Deter and Defend) is a set of prearranged plans, interconnected in all domains, and linked with national military plans to ensure NATO commands and troops have clear guidance and objectives and can detect and respond to threats rapidly and collectively. See NATO SHAPE, 'Deter and Defend', 29 September 2022, https://shape.nato.int/news-archive/2022/deter-and-defend-an-overview.

15 Even with a significant portion of activities remaining national.

16 NATO, 'Major Exercises Demonstrate NATO Allies' Readiness', 15 March 2023, https://www.nato.int/cps/en/natohq/news_212791.htm?selectedLocale=en.

17 The USS *Harry S. Truman* aircraft-carrier strike group was placed under NATO command twice in 2022 for the *Neptune Shield* exercise in the Mediterranean, marking only the second transfer of a US carrier group to NATO since the end of the Cold War. See NATO, 'US Carrier Group, Amphibious Assault Ship Placed Under NATO Command', 18 May 2022, https://www.nato.int/cps/en/natohq/news_195495.htm?selectedLocale=en#:~:text=In%20the%20Mediterranean%2C%20the%20US,end%20of%20the%20Cold%20War. In 2022, operational control of the UK nuclear submarine HMS *Audacious* was transferred to NATO authorities for the first time in NATO history. See George Allison, 'British Nuclear Sub Completes NATO Patrol in Mediterranean', *UK Defence Journal*, 2 September 2022, https://ukdefencejournal.org.uk/british-nuclear-sub-completes-nato-patrol-in-mediterranean/. In 2024, France's nuclear-powered aircraft carrier *Charles de Gaulle* was deployed under NATO command for the first time. See Rudy Ruitenberg, 'In First, France's Aircraft Carrier to Deploy Under NATO Command', *Defence News*, 11 April 2024, https://www.defensenews.com/global/europe/2024/04/11/in-first-frances-aircraft-carrier-to-deploy-under-nato-command/.

18 *Dynamic Manta* is an annual MARCOM-led live exercise held in the Mediterranean Sea to exercise submarine-warfare and anti-submarine war-fighting (ASW) capabilities for submarines, ASW surface units and maritime aircraft. In 2023 it involved assets from Canada, France, Germany, Greece, Italy, Spain, Turkiye, the United Kingdom and the United States, and took place near Italy's coasts. See NATO MARCOM, 'NATO's Advanced Anti-submarine Warfare Exercise Dynamic Manta Underway in Italy', 27 February 2023, https://mc.nato.int/media-centre/news/2023/nato-advanced-antisubmarine-warfare-exercise-dynamic-manta-underway-in-italy; and IISS, Military Balance+ database, accessed February 2023.

19 Xavier Vavasseur, 'France Pulls Out of NATO Operation Sea Guardian Amid Tensions With Turkey', Naval News, 3 July 2020, https://www.navalnews.com/naval-news/2020/07/france-pulls-out-of-nato-operation-sea-guardian-amid-tensions-with-turkey/.

20 European Parliament Legislative Train Schedule, 'EU–Turkey Statement & Action Plan', 20 June 2024, https://www.europarl.europa.eu/legislative-train/theme-towards-a-new-policy-on-migration/file-eu-turkey-statement-action-plan; and Nicolas Bourcier, 'EU–Turkey Migration Deal: Four Million Refugees, €9 Billion in Aid and a Mixed Record', *Le Monde*, 25 April 2024, https://www.lemonde.fr/en/international/article/2024/04/25/eu-turkey-migration-deal-four-million-refugees-9-billion-in-aid-and-a-mixed-record_6669474_4.html.

21 'EU and Egypt Sign 7.4bn Euro Deal Focussed on Energy, Migration', France24, 17 March 2024, https://www.france24.com/en/live-news/20240317-eu-egypt-agree-7-4-bn-euro-deal-focussed-on-energy-migration.

22 European Commission, 'President von der Leyen Reaffirms EU's Strong Support for Lebanon and Its People and Announces a €1 Billion Package of EU Funding', 2 May 2024, https://neighbourhood-enlargement.ec.europa.eu/news/president-von-der-leyen-reaffirms-eus-strong-support-lebanon-and-its-people-and-announces-eu1-2024-05-02_en.

23 Human Rights Watch, 'EU: Frontex Complicit in Abuse in Libya', 12 December 2022, https://www.hrw.org/news/2022/12/12/eu-frontex-complicit-abuse-libya.

24 'U.S. Voices Misgivings on EastMed Gas Pipeline – Greek Officials', Reuters, 11 January 2022, https://www.reuters.com/business/energy/us-voices-misgivings-eastmed-gas-pipeline-greek-officials-2022-01-11/.

25 Council of the European Union, 'EU–Turkiye Trade Relations', 2024, https://www.consilium.europa.eu/en/infographics/eu-turkiye-trade-relations/#:~:text=The%20EU%20is%20by%20far,reached%20almost%20%E2%82%AC200%20billion.

26 Dorian Jones, 'Inside Europe: Turkey Opens Border for Migrants', DW, 3 June 2020, https://www.dw.com/en/inside-europe-turkey-opens-border-for-migrants/audio-52651447.

27 Interview with EU official in Brussels, February 2023.

28 Formally, the Global Strategy for the European Union's Foreign and Security Policy.

29 For more information on EUNAVFOR MED *Operation Sophia*, see https://www.operationsophia.eu/.

30 Jennifer Rankin, 'EU to Stop Mediterranean Migrant Rescue Boat Patrols', *Guardian*, 27 March 2019, https://www.theguardian.com/world/2019/mar/27/eu-to-stop-mediterranean-migrant-rescue-boat-patrols.

31 Council of the European Union, 'EU Launches Operation IRINI to Enforce Libya Arms Embargo', 31 March 2020, https://www.consilium.europa.eu/en/press/press-releases/2020/03/31/eu-launches-operation-Irini-to-enforce-libya-arms-embargo/; and Council of

the European Union, 'Council Extends Mandate of EU Military Operation IRINI in the Mediterranean Until 2025', 20 March 2023, https://www.consilium.europa.eu/en/press/press-releases/2023/03/20/council-extends-mandate-of-eu-military-operation-Irini-in-the-mediterranean-until-2025/.

32   As established by UN Security Council Resolution 1970 in 2011. See UN Security Council, 'Security Council Committee Established Pursuant to Resolution 1970 (2011) Concerning Libya', February 2011, https://www.un.org/securitycouncil/sanctions/1970.

33   The European Union Satellite Centre's (SATCEN) support to EU missions and operations, including *Irini*, has increased more than five times in the last two years. See Sorin Ducaru, 'EU SATCEN 30th Anniversary: Supporting EU Security and Defence Policy, With a Look at the Future', *EU Military Forum*, European Union Military Committee, January 2023, https://www.eeas.europa.eu/sites/default/files/documents/EUMC-Forum%231_23.pdf.

34   EUNAVFOR MED *Operation Irini*, 'Assets', https://www.operationIrini.eu/media_category/assets/.

35   Council of the European Union, 'EU Launches Operation IRINI to Enforce Libya Arms Embargo'.

36   Eleonora Vasques, 'EU Mulls Whether to Boost Anti Human Trafficking Mandate of Mediterranean Military Mission', Euractiv, 26 October 2023, https://www.euractiv.com/section/migration/news/eu-mulls-whether-to-boost-anti-trafficking-mandate-of-mediterranean-military-mission/.

37   Safa Alharathy, 'IRINI: Training Plan for Libyan Coast Guard Awaiting Green Light From EU', *Libya Observer*, 31 March 2022, https://libyaobserver.ly/news/Irini-training-plan-libyan-coast-guard-awaiting-green-light-eu; and Frank Jordans, 'Germany Won't Train Libyan Coast Guard Due to Alleged Abuse', AP News, 30 March 2022, https://apnews.com/article/europe-middle-east-germany-migration-european-union-ed724be5068d95e9da907754c7e18c4c.

38   The UN Panel of Experts on Libya's 2021 and 2022 reports, released before the arms seizure of 2022, indicated that the arms embargo remained 'ineffective'. See UN Security Council (UNSC), 'Final Report of the Panel of Experts on Libya Established Pursuant to Security Council Resolution 1973 (2011)', S/2021/229, 8 March 2021.

39   *Ibid*.

40   EU External Action Service, 'EUNAVFOR MED IRINI Activity Report for May 2024', 6 June 2024, https://www.eeas.europa.eu/eeas/activity-report-eunavfor-med-Irini-may-2024_en.

41   UNSC, 'Report of the Secretary-General on the Implementation of Resolution 2684 (2023)', S/2024/352, 30 April 2024.

42   EUNAVFOR MED *Operation Irini*, 'EU Operation IRINI Found a Cargo in Breach of the UN Arms Embargo on Libya During the Inspection of a Ship Off the Coast of Libya', 20 July 2022, https://www.operationirini.eu/eu-operation-Irini-found-cargo-breach-un-arms-embargo-libya-inspection-ship-off-coast-libya/; and EUNAVFOR MED *Operation Irini*, 'Operation IRINI Seizes Illegal Cargo', 9 November 2022, https://www.operationirini.eu/operation-irini-seizes-illegal-cargo/#:~:text=The%20boarding%20team%20discovered%20dozens,European%20port%20for%20further%20inspection.

43   UNSC, 'Final Report of the Panel of Experts on Libya Established Pursuant to Security Council Resolution 1973 (2011)'.

44   Humeyra Pamuk, 'U.S. Senior Diplomat Complains Europe Not Doing Enough in Libya', Reuters, 16 July 2020, https://www.reuters.com/article/us-libya-security-usa-idUSKCN24H2V2.

45   US Mission to the UN, 'Remarks at a UN Security Council Briefing on UN–EU Cooperation', 16 June 2022, https://usun.usmission.gov/remarks-at-a-un-security-council-briefing-on-un-eu-cooperation-2/.

46   UN, 'Successful Elections in Libya Hinge on All Citizens' Voices Being Heard, Special Representative Tells Security Council', 18 April 2023, https://press.un.org/en/2023/sc15261.doc.htm.

47   Interviews with EU officials, March 2023.

48   Matteo Bressan, Daniele Giorgini and Manuel Moreno Minuto, 'Operation IRINI: Long Term Perspectives of an Enduring EU Presence in a Troubled Region', *EU Military Forum*, European Union Military Committee, January 2023, https://www.eeas.europa.eu/sites/default/files/documents/EUMC-Forum%231_23.pdf.

49   Some EU members are already utilising EU defence-policy frameworks to build the necessary naval capability, for example, through the Permanent Structured Cooperation (PESCO) and European Defence Fund. Some, such as France and Italy, are also increasing defence spending to account for more naval vessels. See Daniel Fiott, 'Europe and the South: The Maritime Dimension', *Confluences Méditerranée*, vol. 123, no. 4, April 2022, pp. 111–21.

50   Fiott, 'Europe and the South: The Maritime Dimension'.

Saudi Crown Prince Muhammad bin Salman Al Saud (R) and Egyptian President Abdel Fattah al-Sisi (C) inspect investment projects in Ismailia, Egypt, on 5 March 2018. (Photo: Bandar Algaloud/Saudi Kingdom Council/Handout/Anadolu Agency via Getty Images)

SAUDI ARABIA AND THE UNITED ARAB EMIRATES (UAE) have opportunistically operated in the Eastern Mediterranean to counter Turkiye, Qatar and Islamist movements, stabilise Egypt and improve connectivity with Europe. However, they have not invested enough political capital to substantively shape outcomes and have differed on priorities, interests and local partnerships.

SAUDI ARABIA AND THE UAE are attempting to avoid entanglements in Levantine conflicts, including the Israeli–Palestinian conflict, which could threaten their geo-economic priorities. Instead, the UAE has ring-fenced its normalisation agreement with Israel, while Saudi Arabia remains open to such an agreement even if the prospect has become less likely.

CHAPTER SEVENTEEN
THE GULF STATES IN THE EASTERN MEDITERRANEAN: FROM GEOPOLITICS TO GEO-ECONOMICS

INTRODUCTION

In the past few years, the Gulf states have moved from half-hearted attempts at geopolitical competition in the Eastern Mediterranean to more determined projections of geo-economic power: investing in energy and connectivity projects towards Europe, and using their financial heft to stabilise Egypt and pacify once-tense relations with Turkiye. Although the Gulf states have managed to insert themselves into the Eastern Mediterranean space at relatively low cost, their overall impact on the zone's geopolitical dynamics has remained small.

Between 2011 and 2021, Saudi Arabia and the UAE increased their involvement in the Eastern Mediterranean. They did so to counter Turkiye's power projection, prevent the Muslim Brotherhood from taking power in Syria, Libya or Egypt and limit any negative impacts on their security. They shifted from an initially defensive posture aimed at containing Turkiye's influence in the Arab world to a more aggressive strategy of building partnerships with its Eastern Mediterranean rivals – Cyprus, Egypt, Greece and Israel – to encircle it.

The Eastern Mediterranean's geostrategic relevance to Gulf states has been receding since 2021, in large part because they have begun prioritising their own prosperity and economic agendas. The normalisation of Saudi and Emirati relations with Ankara since 2021, Syria's gradual re-entry into the Arab world and the UAE's shrinking involvement in Libya have all contributed to this diminishing importance. The Gulf states, except for Qatar, have also shunned any effective role in the resolution of the ongoing Israel–Hamas war, even though it has momentarily derailed their efforts to expand their geo-economic footprints in the region.

The Gulf states have not invested enough political and economic capital to shape the region's geopolitical dynamics. Other than in Egypt and Turkiye, their economic leverage in the region remains limited, and their political engagement with Greece and Cyprus is too recent and opportunistic to be influential. Despite the billions of dollars Gulf states have injected into Egypt's economy over the past decade, Cairo has pushed back on their political and economic advice and has conducted an autonomous foreign policy that has often resulted in frictions with Gulf capitals.

The Gulf states have been even less successful at their military interventions in the region. The UAE's involvement in the Libyan conflict since 2014 has failed to turn the tables on the Islamist-leaning Tripoli government, leaving Turkiye as the only regional player to have successfully projected power and maintained its influence in the Libyan theatre. In Syria, after their initial support for the revolutionary factions in 2011, Qatar, Saudi Arabia and the UAE struggled to work effectively together. Divided over objectives and approaches, they failed to unseat the government of President Bashar al-Assad. They have since largely deprioritised resolving the Syrian conflict or shaping its future. Their inability to influence Lebanese politics and contain Hizbullah despite considerable political and economic investment has also led to frustration and disinterest.

PROJECTING REGIONAL RIVALRIES AND FORGING NEW PARTNERSHIPS

The Gulf states' interest in the Eastern Mediterranean is a relatively recent phenomenon (see Figure 17.1). Up until 2017, their political and economic influence in the region remained focused on the southern shore of the Eastern Mediterranean, mainly looking at it through the lens of Middle Eastern politics. They had channelled financial aid to 'frontline' Arab states confronting Israel during the 1970s and 1980s. Saudi Arabia proposed the 1981 Fahd Peace Plan and the 2002 Arab Peace Initiative to resolve the Israeli–Palestinian conflict, but Israel ignored and ultimately rejected these initiatives. Saudi Arabia's biggest diplomatic achievement was the 1989 Taif Agreement, which provided the political infrastructure that later ended the Lebanese civil war. Nevertheless, the Gulf states had focused primarily on threats closer to home post-1979, notably a revolutionary Iran, a belligerent Iraq and later al-Qaeda. Threats in their immediate neighbourhood have since occupied a more central place in their strategic calculus than developments further away in the Arab world.

The 2011 Arab uprisings increased the region's strategic importance as it became a major battleground for Saudi Arabia and the UAE's emerging competition with Turkiye and Qatar. This rivalry was a struggle for regional clout and ideological supremacy.

The downfall of Egyptian president Hosni Mubarak, Islamist parties winning elections in Egypt and Tunisia, and the eruption of civil wars in Libya and Syria provided Turkiye and Qatar with openings to project their influence on the southern shores of the Eastern Mediterranean. In turn, Saudi Arabia and the UAE perceived the Muslim Brotherhood and the growing role of Turkiye and Qatar as a threat to their own internal stability and regional influence.

The Gulf states' own divisions weakened their ability to shape outcomes. The competition over Egypt's political transition between 2011 and 2013 was among the most intense. Saudi and Emirati backing was critical in allowing General Abdel Fattah al-Sisi to lead the military in overthrowing president Muhammad Morsi, who enjoyed Turkish and Qatari support. In Libya, following the fall of Muammar Gadhafi, Turkiye and Qatar supported the United Nations-recognised government in Tripoli, whereas the UAE-backed General Khalifa Haftar and the Tobruk-based parliament. In Syria, Saudi Arabia, the UAE, Turkiye and Qatar all supported the Syrian opposition during the initial phase of the Syrian civil war but often backed competing groups. By 2016, their interests there had completely diverged, with the UAE accommodating Assad, Saudi Arabia showing disinterest and Qatar maintaining its support for the rebellion. The rivalry spread to other countries and regions such as Tunisia, Yemen and the Horn of Africa. Importantly, the Israeli–Palestinian conflict became peripheral to Gulf calculations, though Qatar served as a conduit to Hamas in coordination with the United States and Israel.

Saudi and Emirati relations with Turkiye deteriorated following the 2016 coup attempt against President Recep Tayyip Erdoğan, which he accused them of supporting. Relations worsened further when Turkiye sent economic and military support to Qatar after Bahrain, Egypt, Saudi Arabia and the UAE ruptured ties with Doha in 2017. The following year, Ankara revealed the murder of Saudi journalist Jamal Khashoggi at the Saudi consulate building in Istanbul, bringing its relationship with Riyadh to a new low. The two Gulf states condemned Turkiye's military operations in northeastern Syria in 2018 and 2019 and countered them by supporting the Syrian Kurds and re-engaging with Assad. In January 2020, the deployment of Turkish troops changed the dynamics of the Libyan civil war, repelling the UAE-backed forces of General Haftar. By that point, containing Turkiye's influence in the region had become an explicit Saudi and Emirati foreign-policy objective. The UAE's then-minister of state for foreign affairs Anwar Gargash publicly and repeatedly called for standing up to Turkiye's expansionist agenda in the Arab world.[1]

Riyadh and Abu Dhabi exploited the fact that Turkiye's aggressive posture in the Eastern Mediterranean had fostered distrust and hostility towards Ankara among its neighbours. Its *Mavi Vatan* ('Blue Homeland') doctrine and its border-demarcation agreement with Libya's

GLOBAL ACTORS — THE GULF STATES IN THE EASTERN MEDITERRANEAN: FROM GEOPOLITICS TO GEO-ECONOMICS

FIGURE 17.1: SELECTED POLITICAL, SECURITY AND ECONOMIC DEVELOPMENTS BETWEEN THE GULF STATES AND THE EASTERN MEDITERRANEAN, JULY 2016–FEBRUARY 2024

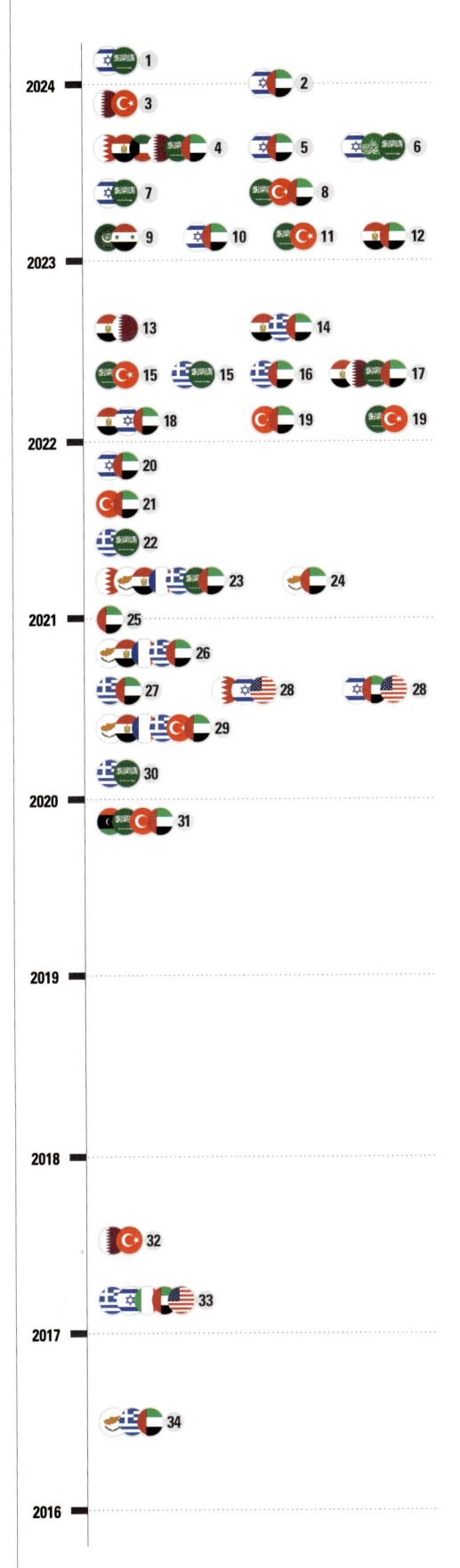

1. Saudi Arabia's foreign ministry issues statement stating the country will not open diplomatic relations with Israel before the recognition of a Palestinian state on 1967 borders.

2. The United Arab Emirates' (UAE) presidential diplomatic adviser Anwar Gargash affirms the UAE's strategic decision to establish warmer relations with Israel amid the Israel–Hamas war.

3. Ninth Qatar–Turkiye High Strategic Committee meeting takes place with 12 agreements signed in the presence of Turkiye's President Recep Tayyip Erdoğan and Qatar's Emir Sheikh Tamim bin Hamad Al Thani.

4. Egypt hosts Cairo Peace Summit amidst the Israel–Hamas war, attended by some Gulf Cooperation Council (GCC) heads of state.

5. Israeli Prime Minister Benjamin Netanyahu speaks to UAE Crown Prince Mohammed bin Zayed Al Nahyan on 15 October in the first phone call between Netanyahu and an Arab leader since the start of the Israel–Hamas war.

6. Israel–Hamas war begins. Saudi Arabia pauses normalisation talks with Israel.

7. Israeli delegation led by the country's tourism minister makes first public visit by an Israeli cabinet minister to Saudi Arabia to attend UNESCO meeting.

8. Erdoğan visits Saudi Arabia and the UAE, signing agreements with the latter worth over US$50 billion.

9. Syrian President Bashar al-Assad arrives in Saudi Arabia in his first visit since the start of the Syrian civil war to attend the Arab League's summit.

10. UAE and Israel sign a Comprehensive Economic Partnership Agreement.

11. Saudi Arabia deposits US$5bn into Turkiye's central bank.

12. Egypt's President Abdel Fattah al-Sisi visits the UAE.

13. Sisi visits Qatar, following a visit by Al Thani to Egypt.

14. Al Nahyan visits Egypt and Greece.

15. Saudi Crown Prince Muhammad bin Salman Al Saud visits Turkiye and Greece.

16. The UAE and Greece create a US$4.2bn investment initiative to invest in infrastructure, logistics, renewables, healthcare and agriculture in Greece.

17. Qatar, Saudi Arabia and the UAE pledge US$22bn in financial support to Egypt.*

18. Summit at Sharm al-Sheikh, Egypt, sees trilateral talks between Al Nahyan, Sisi and Israel's prime minister Naftali Bennett.

19. Erdoğan visits the UAE, followed by Saudi Arabia.

20. Bennett makes the first visit by an Israeli prime minister to the UAE, followed by the first Israeli presidential visit to the UAE.

21. Al Nahyan visits Turkiye and announces the creation of a US$10bn investment fund.

22. Greece loans *Patriot* missile battery to Saudi Arabia to protect it from Houthi attacks.

23. Philia Forum in Greece attended by Bahrain, Cyprus, Egypt, France, Saudi Arabia and the UAE.

24. The UAE and Cyprus sign their first military-cooperation agreement.

25. The UAE joins the Cairo-based East Mediterranean Gas Forum as an observer.

26. Egypt hosts the regular *Medusa* maritime exercise, which includes Cyprus and Greece and, for the first time, the UAE and France.

27. Greek Prime Minister Kyriakos Mitsotakis visits the UAE and signs strategic partnership and defence agreement.

28. Abraham Accords and normalisation of diplomatic relations agreed between Israel and Bahrain, and Israel and the UAE.

29. Joint Cyprus–Egypt–France–Greece–UAE statement condemns Turkish drilling activity in Cyprus's exclusive economic zone.

30. Mitsotakis visits Saudi Arabia.

31. Turkiye–Libya maritime-border-delineation agreement signed, triggering criticism from Saudi Arabia and the UAE.

32. Start of GCC crisis. Turkiye agrees to deploy 3,000 troops to Qatar.

33. First participation of Israel, Italy, the UAE and the United States in joint military exercises hosted by Greece.

34. The UAE officially inaugurates an embassy in Cyprus and new embassy headquarters in Greece.

*This number includes investment pledges.
Source: IISS analysis

©IISS

Government of National Accord (GNA) in 2019 prompted wide concern in the Eastern Mediterranean, providing Saudi Arabia and the UAE with an opportunity to join and orchestrate an anti-Turkiye coalition in its own neighbourhood.

Within a few years, the two Gulf states built political, defence and economic partnerships with Turkiye's main rivals in the Eastern Mediterranean. The UAE joined the East Mediterranean Gas Forum (EMGF) – comprising Cyprus, Egypt, France, Greece, Israel, Italy, Jordan and the State of Palestine but purposely excluding Turkiye from energy cooperation in the Eastern Mediterranean – as an observer in 2020.[2] The 2020 Abraham Accords that normalised Emirati and Bahraini relations with Israel further facilitated the deepening of the Gulf states' political presence in the Eastern Mediterranean. Saudi Arabia too improved its relations with Israel by allowing Israeli airlines to overfly Saudi territory from 2022.[3] Moreover, Saudi Arabia and the UAE upgraded their political relations with Greece and, to a lesser extent, Cyprus, exchanging high-level visits and signing strategic-partnership agreements.

Building on this political momentum, Saudi Arabia and the UAE expanded defence cooperation with Turkiye's neighbours. Between 2020 and 2021, the two Gulf states signed cooperation agreements with Greece and Cyprus.[4] They also took part in multiple joint military exercises with Eastern Mediterranean states. Since 2017, the UAE has dispatched F-16 fighter aircraft to Greece to participate in annual Greek-led military drills alongside Cyprus, Egypt, Israel, Italy and the US. In 2020, Cyprus, Egypt, France, Greece and the UAE held their first joint aeronautical exercise in Alexandria. In February 2021, Bahrain, Saudi Arabia and the UAE participated in the Greek-led Philia Forum, alongside Cyprus, Egypt and France, with the clear objective of developing an anti-Turkish front. In 2021 and 2022, Saudi Arabia dispatched F-15 fighter jets to Greece to participate in joint drills. Despite this intensification of defence cooperation, the various countries refrained from formalising it or offering mutual-security guarantees. As soon as the de-escalation with Turkiye began in 2021, attention waned, and momentum weakened though the political relationships remained solid.

Bahraini Foreign Minister Abdullatif bin Rashid Al Zayani, Cypriot foreign minister Nikos Christodoulides, Egyptian foreign minister Sameh Shoukry, Greek foreign minister Nikos Dendias, Saudi Foreign Minister Prince Faisal bin Farhan Al Saud and Emirati Minister of State for International Cooperation Reem Ebrahim Al Hashimy hold a joint press conference on 11 February 2021 in Athens, Greece, during the Philia Forum. (Photo: Petros Giannakouris/POOL/AFP via Getty Images)

The specific, limited nature of this cooperation became even clearer after the beginning of the Israel–Hamas war in 2023. Despite Israel being included in various regional minilaterals, the Gulf states have adopted a defensive posture and have not contributed directly to regional defence efforts. Saudi Arabia did participate in the US-led integrated air- and missile-defence network in the region, intercepting Ansarullah (Houthi) missiles overflying its territory and reportedly passing on intelligence to forewarn the US of Iran's missile and uninhabited aerial vehicle (UAV) attack on Israel. But beyond that, the Gulf states except for Bahrain have participated in neither the US-led *Operation Prosperity Guardian* in the Red Sea nor the strikes against Houthi targets in Yemen, and have reportedly asked the US not to use their territories or airspaces to launch direct attacks on Iran.[5] They seem to be calculating that their interests lie in preserving the truces that the UAE in 2022 and Saudi Arabia in 2023 reached with Iran, however temporary they may prove to be. Although the Gulf states have protected their airspaces and allowed the US to position military assets on their territories, they have avoided projecting any offensive message to Iran. Importantly, their relationships with Turkiye continued to improve despite Erdoğan's strident criticism of Israel and embrace of Hamas, which both Saudi Arabia and the UAE view as an ideological and security threat.

THE COOPERATIVE TURN IN THE GULF STATES' PRIORITIES

Recent years have seen a shift in the Gulf states' priorities in the Eastern Mediterranean. The economic repercussions of the COVID-19 pandemic and the war in Ukraine, the weakening of US–Gulf relations and perceptions of a growing threat coming from Iran encouraged Saudi Arabia, the UAE, Turkiye and Qatar to de-escalate geopolitical tensions among themselves in the region.

In January 2021, the Gulf states ended the four-year rift between Saudi Arabia, the UAE, Bahrain and Qatar at a summit in al-Ula, Saudi Arabia.[6] The UAE then dispatched National Security Advisor Sheikh Tahnoun bin Zayed Al Nahyan to Ankara in August, paving the way for the restoration of diplomatic relations and resumption of high-level visits.[7] The UAE's gesture followed the scaling back of its involvement in the Libyan civil war since 2020, which led to the easing of frictions with Turkiye. Abu Dhabi had significantly downgraded its support for General Haftar following military setbacks, especially as a result of the decisive Turkish military intervention, and even aligned itself more closely with Turkiye by backing the Government of National Unity's (GNU) Prime Minister Abdul Hamid Dbeibah.[8] Saudi Arabia and Turkiye have also fully normalised relations; President Erdoğan visited Riyadh in April 2022, a gesture that Saudi Crown Prince Muhammad bin Salman Al Saud returned two months later.[9] In the span of two years, Turkiye went from being one of the Gulf states' main regional competitors to becoming one of their key regional partners.

One of the drivers of this radical shift is economics. The COVID-19 pandemic had severe repercussions for Turkiye's economy, leaving Ankara in need of foreign loans and investments.[10] In contrast, rising oil prices in the aftermath of the pandemic and the Russian invasion of Ukraine flushed the Gulf states' coffers with revenues, increasing their attractiveness as economic partners. In late 2021, following the diplomatic rapprochement, the UAE announced the creation of a US$10 billion investment fund and in January 2022 signed a credit-swap agreement for US$4.9bn with Turkiye's central bank to buttress its dwindling foreign-currency reserves.[11] Saudi Arabia also placed a US$5bn deposit in Turkiye's central bank in March 2023.[12]

Security also drove the Gulf states' recalibration in the Eastern Mediterranean. The breakdown in nuclear diplomacy with Iran, and concerns about its embedded regional reach in Iraq, Lebanon, the Occupied Palestinian Territories, Syria and Yemen, shifted the Gulf states' security priorities back to their eastern flanks. Bahrain, Saudi Arabia and the UAE have taken a dual approach on Iran, de-escalating tensions and diplomatically engaging with Tehran while seeking deeper security partnerships with Israel. The 2020 Abraham Accords opened the door to growing security cooperation, including through

> THE GULF STATES HAVE LONG BEEN MAJOR ECONOMIC PLAYERS IN THE EASTERN MEDITERRANEAN AND ARE THEREFORE WELL POSITIONED TO ACCESS AND INVEST IN STRATEGIC ECONOMIC ASSETS.

participation in joint military exercises and the sharing of intelligence and technologies. Emerging defence relations with Greece and Cyprus also opened new possibilities. In September 2021, Greece delivered a battery of *Patriot* missiles and 120 Greek personnel to Saudi Arabia to help the Kingdom defend against airborne threats from Iran and Yemen.[13] The United States' concurrent withdrawal – to Riyadh's displeasure – of *Patriot* missiles from Saudi Arabia made the Greek gesture even more significant.[14]

Interestingly, Saudi Arabia and the UAE increasingly see Turkiye itself as an attractive partner in their strategies towards Iran and in other arenas. In addition to being a regional balancer of Iranian reach, Turkiye is a significant supplier of military equipment to the Gulf states, including armed UAVs, which Western states refuse to supply. Even at the height of political tensions between Turkiye and the two Gulf states, Ankara continued to provide military equipment to Saudi Arabia and the UAE and did not suspend licences issued to the UAE for producing infantry fighting vehicles. Subsequent diplomatic rapprochements allowed this cooperation to develop further. In September 2022, the Turkish defence firm Baykar delivered 20 *Bayraktar* armed UAVs to the UAE. The company has begun talks with Saudi Arabia for a similar sale.[15] In 2020–21, Turkish arms exports accounted for 13% of the UAE's total arms imports by value, according to some estimates.[16] According to official Turkish figures for the 'defence and aviation industry' sector (including dual-use items), Turkiye exported US$332 million in 2022 and US$650m in 2023 to the UAE, while the UAE exported just US$1m in each of those years to Turkiye.[17] As Saudi Arabia and the UAE seek to localise their defence spending and develop their defence-industrial bases, Turkiye is well positioned to be a top candidate for jointly developing and manufacturing weapons systems. In 2021, two Saudi manufacturers started producing a Turkish-made UAV, the *Karayel*-SU, and the Kingdom has since expressed interest in manufacturing other Turkish UAVs as well.[18]

The *Bayraktar* TB3 uninhabited aerial vehicle developed by Baykar on display at the UMEX Exhibition in Abu Dhabi, United Arab Emirates, on 23 January 2024.
(Photo: Waleed Zein/Anadolu via Getty Images)

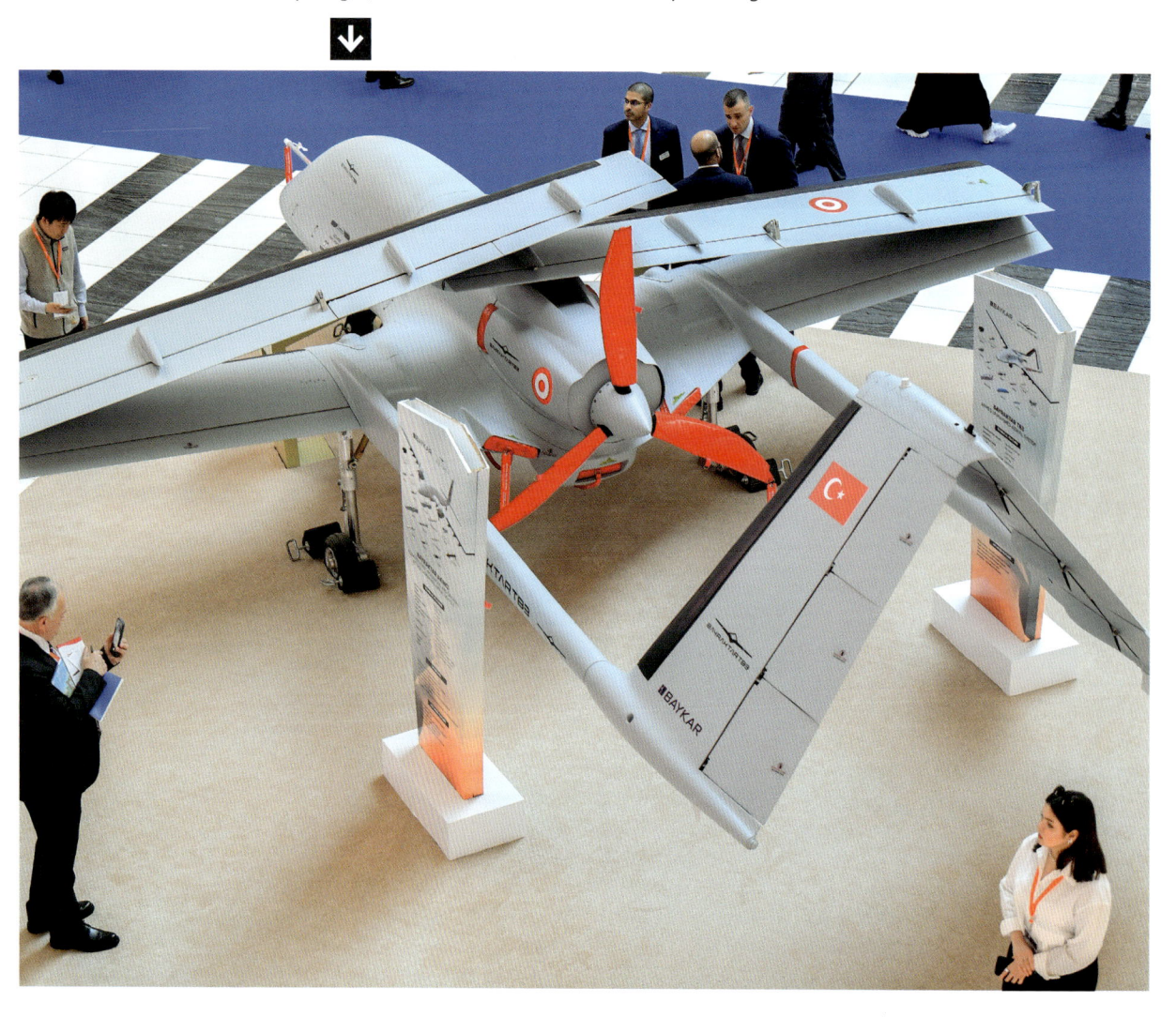

THE GULF STATES AS CONNECTIVITY AND ENERGY PLAYERS AT EUROPE'S DOORSTEP

While the Gulf states are toning down competition dynamics in the Eastern Mediterranean, they are increasingly shifting to a more geo-economic approach to the region. Saudi Arabia and the UAE are using their massive financial reserves and political openings in the Eastern Mediterranean to carve out a role for themselves in Europe's connectivity projects, notably in energy (see Map 17.1). The Russia–Ukraine war reignited (if momentarily) global interest in the region's energy reserves, providing the Gulf states with an opportunity to position themselves as indispensable partners for the European Union's energy-diversification strategy. As a result, energy cooperation became a prominent feature of the strategic partnership that the EU and the Gulf Cooperation Council (GCC) launched in May 2022.[19]

The Gulf states have long been major economic players in the Eastern Mediterranean and are therefore well positioned to access and invest in strategic economic assets. Their trade volumes with Eastern Mediterranean states began to rise in 2012, sustained mainly by increased economic exchange with Egypt, Turkiye, Lebanon and Libya. The Gulf states' economic heft is concentrated on the southern shores of the Eastern Mediterranean, where they appear among the top trading partners of Egypt, Lebanon, Syria and Libya. The Gulf states channelled around 44% of their bailout aid – which is estimated at US$363bn in total – to the Arab states of the Eastern Mediterranean between 1963 and 2022.[20] They have become some of Egypt's largest creditors, collectively accounting for 28% of Egypt's external-debt stock, including half of its short-term debt, in December 2023. They are also major sources of overseas development assistance (ODA) to the Eastern Mediterranean, though they channelled over 90% of that aid towards Egypt according to 2021 data. Gulf denial of economic assistance is another form of statecraft. In 2016, Saudi Arabia suspended a US$3bn military package to Lebanon, a longtime recipient of Gulf largesse, to signal its displeasure with Lebanon's failure to contain Hizbullah and a sense that no amount of aid could deliver the expected political benefits. Since then, Gulf countries have reduced their assistance to Lebanon and disengaged politically.

The UAE and Qatar have also secured an energy foothold by investing in Israel's and Lebanon's gas sectors. In 2021, UAE state-owned firm Mubadala Energy acquired a 22% stake in Israel's Tamar gas field for US$1bn, the largest deal that the UAE and Israel have concluded since the 2020 Abraham Accords.[21] In January 2023, QatarEnergy joined TotalEnergies and Eni in a consortium to develop two blocks of Lebanon's offshore oil and gas fields, replacing Russia's Novatek.[22] Mubadala also expressed interest in Egyptian gas fields in the Eastern Mediterranean and offshore Nile Delta, although investments have yet to materialise.[23]

The Gulf states' European ambitions have motivated their investments in Eastern Mediterranean gas infrastructure. If political drivers have contributed to the UAE's and Qatar's involvement in Israeli and Lebanese gas fields, they also give them a stake in Europe's energy future as it seeks non-Russian sources of natural gas.[24] Turkiye has stated its ambition to work with Saudi Arabia to become an 'energy corridor' for natural gas and oil to Europe, though it faces competition in this regard from Egypt and Greece.[25]

The Gulf states also see the Eastern Mediterranean as a potential gateway for electricity connectivity with Europe. In 2022, Saudi Arabia stated its willingness to use Greece as a gateway for the export of cheaper electricity and hydrogen to Europe, including through the linking of the two countries' electricity grids.[26] Riyadh is already planning the construction of a 3 gigawatt (GW) Saudi–Egyptian electricity interconnector.[27] Given Egypt's own planned EuroAfrica Interconnector project, the Saudi–Egyptian electricity interconnector could link the GCC's electricity grid to the EU's via Egypt in the coming years.

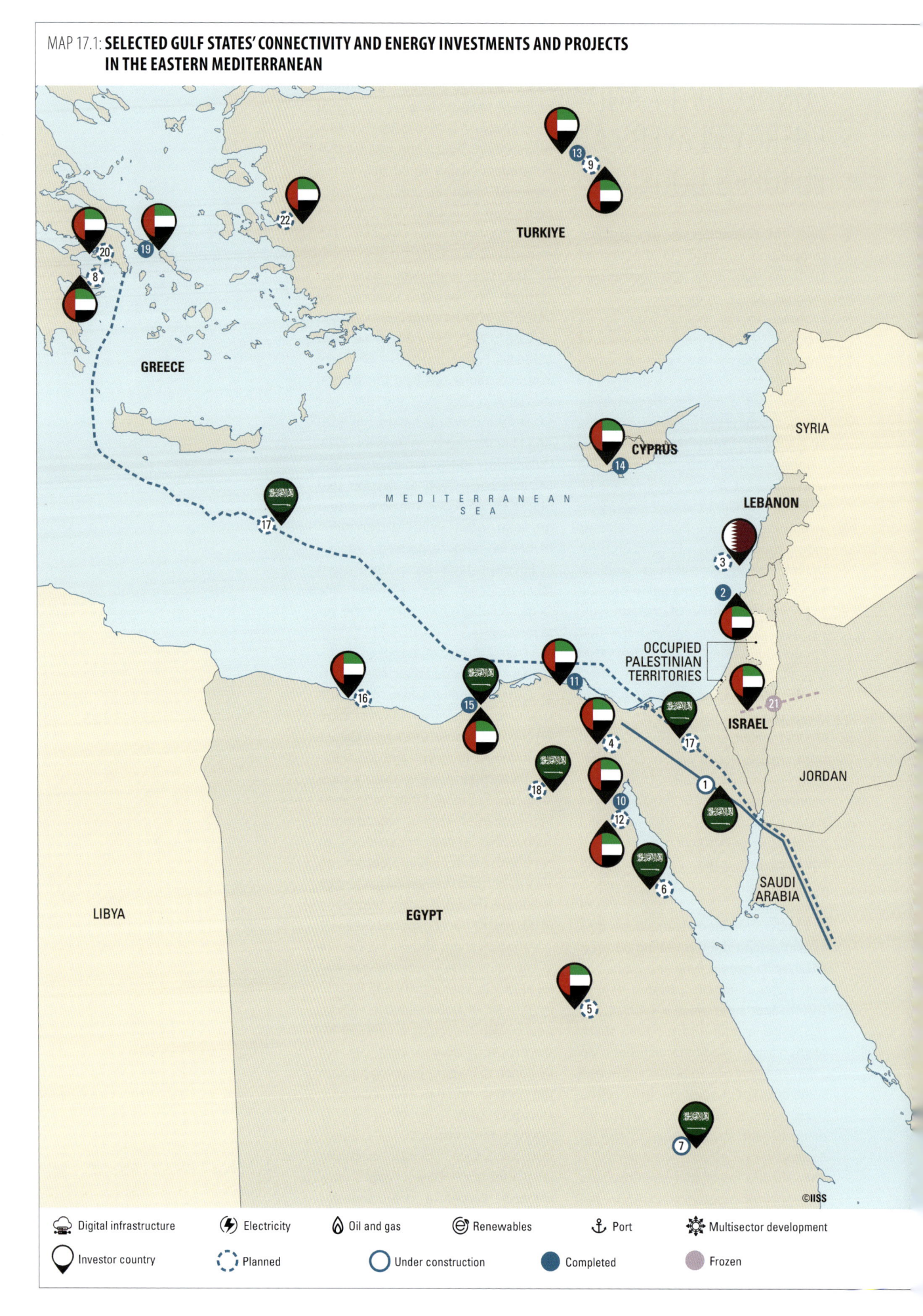

MAP 17.1: SELECTED GULF STATES' CONNECTIVITY AND ENERGY INVESTMENTS AND PROJECTS IN THE EASTERN MEDITERRANEAN

Legend:
- Digital infrastructure
- Electricity
- Oil and gas
- Renewables
- Port
- Multisector development
- Investor country
- Planned
- Under construction
- Completed
- Frozen

The goal of interconnectivity has also motivated greater Gulf investments in renewable-energy projects in Eastern Mediterranean countries. While these investments are primarily aimed at satisfying local demand for renewable power, European markets could also absorb production. The UAE's Masdar is leading a consortium to build two green-hydrogen facilities in the Suez Canal Economic Zone and on Egypt's Mediterranean coast and a 10 GW onshore wind farm in Egypt, while Saudi state-owned ACWA Power is developing a 1.1 GW wind farm at an estimated cost of US$1.8bn and a 200 megawatt solar plant in the Egyptian city of Kom Ombo.[28] The UAE's Abu Dhabi National Oil Company (ADNOC) and Masdar signed agreements in 2021–22 to develop solar-photovoltaic and offshore wind farms in Greece.[29] Further, in 2021, the UAE's ADQ signed an agreement with the Turkish presidency's investment office to explore renewable-energy projects with a total capacity of up to 3 GW in Turkiye.[30] Since Egypt, Greece and Turkiye are or will soon be connected to the EU power grid, renewable-energy projects in these countries could help generate electricity surpluses for sale to the EU market.

The Gulf states have also sought to broaden their footprint in Eastern Mediterranean states' ports and logistics sectors. They derive geo-economic power and prestige from their position as key players in transregional connectivity networks that are vital for the circulation of goods and commodities in the global economy. In November 2021, the UAE's DP World completed a US$520m expansion of Ain Sokhna Port, the main port it operates in Egypt, and expressed interest in building a second port on Egypt's Mediterranean coast. In 2022, Abu Dhabi Ports (ADP) acquired stakes in two Egyptian cargo companies and bid for contracts to develop a terminal at Ain Sokhna Port, a river port in Minya and the new Tenth of Ramadhan dry port, winning the first two. ADQ, which owns a majority stake in ADP, has shown interest in Greece's logistics sector, notably Heraklion Port in Crete.[31] The Qatar Investment Authority, the country's sovereign-wealth fund, is in talks with the Egyptian transport

---

1. 3 gigawatt (GW) Saudi–Egyptian electricity interconnector
2. Mubadala Energy's 2021 acquisition of a 22% stake in Israel's Tamar gas field. Value: US$1 billion
3. Eni–QatarEnergy–TotalEnergies consortium bidding to explore two blocks of Lebanon's offshore oil and gas fields
4. Masdar 4 GW green-hydrogen facilities
5. Masdar 10 GW wind farm
6. ACWA Power 1.1 GW wind farm
7. ACWA Power 200 megawatt (MW) solar plant
8. Masdar and Abu Dhabi National Oil Company (ADNOC) to sponsor solar-plant and wind-farm projects
9. Strategic-cooperation agreement for ADQ to invest in renewable-energy projects of up to 3 GW capacity
10. DP World expansion and operation of Ain Sokhna Port. Value: US$520 million
11. Abu Dhabi Ports finalises an agreement in 2022 to manage and operate warehouses in Damietta Port
12. Preliminary agreement for AD Ports Group to oversee the development and operation of Ain Sokhna Port
13. Strategic-partnership agreement between AD Ports Group and Turkiye's sovereign-wealth fund
14. DP World awarded 25-year concession to operate Limassol terminal in April 2016
15. ADQ and Saudi Egyptian Investment Company's (SEIC's) acquisition of shares in Alexandria Container and Cargo Handling Company
16. ADQ-led consortium to invest in Egypt's Ras al-Hekma coastal region. Value: US$35bn
17. Saudi Arabia and Greece establish special purpose company to explore feasibility of an electricity interconnector between the two countries
18. ACWA Power signs framework agreement for green-hydrogen project in Egypt with capacity of 600,000 tonnes/year of green ammonia. Value: US$4bn
19. Mubadala and Hellenic Development Bank of Investments expand partnership. Value: US$219m
20. UAE–Greece MoU focusing on investments in data centres in Greece with a collective capacity of 500 MW
21. Masdar and Jordan sign water-for-energy MoU with Israel
22. AD Ports Group set to buy stake in Port of Izmir. Value: US$500m

Note: locations and routes are approximate
Source: IISS analysis

ministry and the Egyptian Group for Multipurpose Terminals for a 25-year contract to manage Safaga Port, and is conducting feasibility studies for other port projects including West Port Said container terminal.[32] Similarly, AD Ports Group's agreement with Türkiye Varlık Fonu, Turkiye's sovereign-wealth fund, may allow the UAE to gain a foothold in Turkiye's ports and logistics sector.[33] In 2016, Cyprus awarded DP World a 25-year concession to operate Limassol multipurpose terminal. And in 2021, it showed interest in the privatisation of the Israeli port of Haifa before pulling out of the bid.

ISRAEL–HAMAS WAR: A SPOILER

The Israel–Hamas war that started in October 2023 has derailed aspects of the Gulf states' geo-economic designs in the Eastern Mediterranean that involve Israel. Despite the disruption of merchant shipping through the Red Sea due to the Houthis' attacks having rekindled interest in overland trading routes that bypass the Suez Canal, any upsurge in connectivity projects between the Gulf states or Jordan and Israel now seems politically impossible for the foreseeable future. In marked contrast with Saudi Crown Prince Muhammad bin Salman Al Saud's statement in September 2023 that Riyadh and Tel Aviv were getting closer 'every day' to establishing formal relations, Saudi Arabia, as the war has unfolded, has explicitly made any normalisation of diplomatic relations with Israel conditional on there being a credible and irreversible pathway towards a Palestinian state.[34]

The Israel–Hamas war has led to a general hardening of positions among the Gulf states towards Israel. It has paralysed, at least temporarily, minilateral cooperative constructs such as I2U2 that had brought together India, Israel, the UAE and the US, or the Negev Forum that had convened Abraham Accords signatories Israel, the UAE, Bahrain, Morocco and the US. Another temporary casualty of the war has been the India–Middle East–Europe Economic Corridor announced at the September 2023 G20 meeting. This major project would have transported goods from Gulf ports inland through Saudi Arabia to Israel, consolidating the Gulf's global connectivity, but the political and security ramifications of the war preclude any progress on this in the foreseeable future. Instead, the UAE and Qatar have partnered with Iraq and Turkiye to develop an alternative route that would bypass the Eastern Mediterranean altogether, although the viability of this project depends on stability in Iraq. Similarly, talks between BP and ADNOC to acquire 50% of Israel's NewMed Energy, a major stakeholder in a large gas field, were paused in March 2024 'due to the uncertainty created by the external environment', a reference to the increased risk linked to the war.[35]

Nevertheless, the war has not led to a complete overhaul of the Gulf states' approaches to the Eastern Mediterranean. Besides providing humanitarian aid, the Gulf states have limited their involvement in the war to either mediation (Qatar) or diplomatic activism through the UN Security Council (UAE) or the Arab League and the Organisation of Islamic Cooperation (Saudi Arabia). Meanwhile, the Abraham Accords remain formally intact. Saudi Arabia is seizing the opportunity to upgrade defence ties with the US by bargaining for a binding defence treaty and for access to nuclear-energy technology in exchange for normalising relations with Israel. Resorting to its 'bailout diplomacy' playbook, the UAE has stepped in massively to help Egypt stabilise its economy and make up for a shortfall in revenues from tourism and transit through the Suez Canal by injecting US$24bn in investments and converting US$11bn of Egyptian debt owed to the UAE into investments, in return for developing the Ras al-Hekma peninsula on Egypt's Mediterranean coast. Although the Israel–Hamas war could delay the implementation of the Gulf states' connectivity projects in the Eastern Mediterranean, Masdar's June 2024 acquisition of a majority stake in Greece's clean-energy firm Terna Energy illustrates the enduring geo-economic interest of these states in the region.[36]

CONCLUSION

Saudi Arabia and the UAE have taken a versatile approach to the Eastern Mediterranean. They have moved away from their initial interests in containing Turkiye and now focus on expanding their geo-economic presence in the Eastern Mediterranean's energy and logistics sectors. Where possible, the Gulf states have opportunistically capitalised on the Middle East's arguably fragile de-escalatory momentum since 2021 to expand their economic and political influence in the Eastern Mediterranean. They no longer see the Eastern Mediterranean uniquely through the lens of Middle Eastern rivalries, but also as a gateway for closer economic and energy integration with Europe.

For the Gulf states, the Eastern Mediterranean is a zone of opportunity, not one of strategic necessity. Notwithstanding the possibility of all-out war involving Israel, the US and Iran, the limited impact of the Israel–Hamas war on the economic and security prospects of the Gulf states illustrates the disconnect between the two sub-regions.

But this disconnect is also contingent on factors the Gulf states do not control and have not invested much in trying to shape. So long as Egypt is stable, Iran's reach is limited to small, marginal, war-torn countries, and Turkiye's influence in the Arab world is contained, the Gulf states' political and geo-economic ambitions in the Eastern Mediterranean remain marginal to their core interests. In fact, they often intend their engagement with the region to serve their ambitions in other areas, notably to preserve their influence in the Arab world and strengthen their relations with European partners. This is evident from the limited diplomatic and political capital they have been willing to invest in the region's most enduring conflicts and crises like Lebanon, Libya, Palestine or Syria. Their stakes in the region's energy landscape, though growing, also remain relatively limited.

The Gulf states' geo-economic ambitions in the Eastern Mediterranean are under constant threat from resurgent geopolitical tensions, however. The Gulf states will have to carefully calibrate their role in the Israeli–Palestinian conflict and address difficult questions, including the future of their relations with Hamas and Israel, the extent of their involvement in reforming the Palestinian Authority, the scope of reconstruction aid, and whether to contribute to a peacekeeping force in a post-conflict scenario in Gaza. Although every Gulf state remains wary of costly entanglements in the protracted Israeli–Palestinian conflict, some impacts are unavoidable: it not only disrupts their interests and reveals the limits of their influence in their near abroad but also exposes them to second-order repercussions such as potential instability in Egypt and Jordan.

(L-R) Bahraini Foreign Minister Abdullatif bin Rashid Al Zayani, Israeli Prime Minister Benjamin Netanyahu, US president Donald Trump and Emirati Foreign Minister Abdullah bin Zayed Al Nahyan participate in the signing ceremony of the Abraham Accords at the White House on 15 September 2020 in Washington DC, United States. (Photo: Alex Wong via Getty Images)

ENDNOTES

1. 'UAE: The Arab World Will Not Be Led by Iran and Turkey', *National*, 27 December 2017, https://www.thenationalnews.com/world/mena/uae-the-arab-world-will-not-be-led-by-iran-and-turkey-1.690879; and 'UAE's Gargash: Turkey Sees Strategic Space for Historical Dreams in the Arab World', *Arab News*, 20 June 2020, https://arab.news/ja95s.

2. 'Egypt Says UAE Joins East Mediterranean Gas Forum as an Observer', Reuters, 16 December 2020, https://www.reuters.com/article/egypt-emirates-gas-int-idUSKBN28Q29M.

3. 'Saudi Arabia to Open Airspace to All Airlines, Including from Israel', CNBC, 15 July 2022, https://www.cnbc.com/2022/07/15/saudi-arabia-to-open-airspace-to-all-airlines-including-from-israel.html; and Alexander Cornwell and Dan Williams, 'Saudis Open Airspace to More Flights Serving Israel', Reuters, 4 August 2022, https://www.reuters.com/world/middle-east/saudis-open-airspace-more-flights-serving-israel-2022-08-04/.

4. Republic of Cyprus Presidency, 'Joint Statement at the Conclusion of the Cypriot President's Visit to the Kingdom of Saudi Arabia', 2 March 2022, https://www.presidency.gov.cy/cypresidency/cypresidency.nsf/All/200AA56EC7DAD4EBC22587F9002C9516?OpenDocument; 'UAE Signs Joint Defense Agreement with Cyprus', Al-Monitor, 13 January 2021, https://www.al-monitor.com/originals/2021/01/uae-cyprus-defense-turkey-mediterranean.html; Safiye Karabacak, 'Saudi Arabia, Greece Sign Defense Cooperation Agreement', Anadolu Agency, 21 April 2021, https://www.aa.com.tr/en/europe/saudi-arabia-greece-sign-defense-cooperation-agreement/2215357; and 'Greece, UAE Sign Political, Defense Agreements', Al-Monitor, 18 November 2020, https://www.al-monitor.com/originals/2020/11/greece-prime-minister-uae-emirates-mbz-turkey-mediterranean.html.

5. Michael R. Gordon, Nancy A. Youssef and Gordon Lubold, 'Iranian-backed Militias Mount New Wave of Attacks as U.S. Supports Israel', *Wall Street Journal*, 24 October 2023, https://www.wsj.com/world/middle-east/iranian-backed-militias-mount-new-wave-of-attacks-as-u-s-supports-israel-d51364d4; Sean Mathews, 'Gulf States Warn US Not to Launch Strikes on Iran From Their Territory or Airspace', Middle East Eye, 12 April 2024, https://www.middleeasteye.net/news/exclusive-gulf-states-warn-us-not-launch-strikes-iran-territory-airspace; David S. Cloud et al., 'How the U.S. Forged a Fragile Middle Eastern Alliance to Repel Iran's Israel Attack', *Wall Street Journal*, 15 April 2024, https://www.wsj.com/world/middle-east/how-the-u-s-forged-a-fragile-middle-eastern-alliance-to-repel-irans-israel-attack-4a1fbc00; and Nancy A. Youssef, Gordon Lubold and Michael R. Gordon, 'U.S. Shuffles Military Assets in Middle East After Gulf Pushback', *Wall Street Journal*, 3 May 2024, https://www.wsj.com/politics/national-security/u-s-shuffles-military-assets-in-middle-east-after-gulf-pushback-e728e357.

6. Tuqa Khalid, 'Full Transcript of AlUla GCC Summit Declaration: Bolstering Gulf Unity', Al Arabiya English, 6 January 2021, https://english.alarabiya.net/News/gulf/2021/01/06/Full-transcript-of-AlUla-GCC-Summit-Declaration-Bolstering-Gulf-unity.

7. 'Turkish President Receives Emirati Delegation Led by Tahnoun Bin Zayed', WAM, 18 August 2021, https://wam.ae/en/details/1395302961597; and Nasser Karimi and Jon Gambrell, 'Top UAE Adviser Makes Rare Trip to Iran Amid Nuclear Talks', Associated Press, 6 December 2021, https://apnews.com/article/middle-east-iran-israel-dubai-united-arab-emirates-509050c8e4cf18b02dfda9c9b9bd3f5e.

8. Emadeddin Badi, 'The UAE Is Making a Precarious Shift in Its Libya Policy. Here's Why', Atlantic Council, 27 October 2022, https://www.atlanticcouncil.org/blogs/menasource/the-uae-is-making-a-precarious-shift-in-its-libya-policy-heres-why/.

9. Orhan Coskun, 'Erdogan Visits Saudi Arabia Hoping for New Era in Ties', Reuters, 29 April 2022, https://www.reuters.com/world/middle-east/turkeys-erdogan-travel-saudi-arabia-thursday-2022-04-28/; and '"A New Era": Saudi Arabia's MBS in Turkey as Nations Mend Ties', Al-Jazeera, 22 June 2022, https://www.aljazeera.com/news/2022/6/22/saudi-crown-prince-mbs-visits-turkey-as-countries-normalise-ties.

10. 'OECD Economic Surveys: Turkey 2021', OECD, January 2021, https://doi.org/10.1787/2cd09ab1-en.

11. 'UAE Announces $10B Investment Fund in Turkey as Erdogan, MBZ Meet', TRT World, 24 November 2021, https://www.trtworld.com/turkey/uae-announces-10b-investment-fund-in-turkey-as-erdogan-mbz-meet-51981; and Onur Ant, 'Turkey Signs $5bn Swap Deal with UAE, Boosting Foreign Reserves', Al-Jazeera, 19 January 2022, https://www.aljazeera.com/economy/2022/1/19/turkey-signs-5bn-swap-deal-with-uae-boosting-foreign-reserves.

12. 'Saudi Arabia Deposits $5 Bln in Turkey's Central Bank – Statement', Reuters, 6 March 2023, https://www.reuters.com/world/middle-east/saudi-arabia-deposits-5-bln-turkeys-central-bank-statement-2023-03-06/.

13. Derya Gulnaz Ozcan and Tevfik Durul, 'Greece Delivers Patriot Battery to Saudi Arabia', Anadolu Agency, 15 September 2021, https://www.aa.com.tr/en/europe/greece-delivers-patriot-battery-to-saudi-arabia/2365514.

14. 'US Pulls Missile Defenses in Saudi Arabia amid Yemen Attacks', Voice of America, 11 September 2021, https://www.voanews.com/a/6222846.html; and Abigail Ng, 'Saudi Prince Says the U.S. Should Not Withdraw Patriot Missiles from Saudi Arabia', CNBC, 9 September 2021, https://www.cnbc.com/2021/09/09/saudi-prince-us-should-not-pull-patriot-missiles-from-saudi-arabia.html.

15. Orhan Coskun, 'Exclusive: Turkey Sells Battle-tested Drones to UAE as Regional Rivals Mend Ties', Reuters, 21 September 2022, https://www.reuters.com/world/middle-east/exclusive-turkey-sells-battle-tested-drones-uae-regional-rivals-mend-ties-2022-09-21/.

16. Data extracted from SIPRI's Arms Transfers Database, expressed in trend-indicator values (TIVs): see http://www.sipri.org/databases/armstransfers/sources-and-methods/.

17. Türkiye İhracatçılar Meclisi [Turkiye Exporters Assembly], 'BAE: Ülke Bilgi Notu' [UAE: country information note], July 2024, https://tim.org.tr/files/downloads/Ulke_Bilgi_Notları/BAE_Ülke%20Bilgi%20Notu.pdf.

18. Burak Ege Bekdil, 'Two Saudi Companies to Produce Turkish Drones', *Defense News*, 22 March 2021, https://www.defensenews.com/unmanned/2021/03/22/two-saudi-companies-to-produce-turkish-drones/.

19. European Commission, 'GCC: EU Unveils Strategic Partnership with the Gulf', 18 May 2022, https://ec.europa.eu/commission/presscorner/detail/en/IP_22_3165.

20. Hasan T. Alhasan and Camille Lons, 'Gulf Bailout Diplomacy: Aid as Economic Statecraft in a Turbulent Region', IISS, October 2023, pp. 13, 16, https://www.iiss.org/globalassets/media-library---content--migration/files/research-papers/2023/10/gbd/iiss_gulf_bailout-diplomacy.pdf.

21. Alisa Odenheimer, 'UAE–Israel Ties Deepen as Mubadala Buys Gas Stake for $1 Billion', Bloomberg, 2 September 2021, https://www.bloomberg.com/news/articles/2021-09-02/uae-israel-ties-deepen-as-mubadala-buys-gas-stake-for-1-billion.

22. Bassem Mroue, 'Qatar Replaces Russian Company in Lebanon Gas Exploration', Associated Press, 29 January 2023, https://apnews.com/article/israel-italy-qatar-lebanon-business-a216289f83f4da47542c1d56665e8a85.

23. 'UAE's Mubadala Intends to Inject New Investments in Egyptian Energy Field', *Egypt Today*, 1 November 2022, https://www.egypttoday.com/Article/3/120277/UAE-s-Mubadala-intends-to-inject-new-investments-in-Egyptian; and Fatma Ahmed, 'Egypt Examines Cooperation Opportunities with Mubadala Petroleum', Egypt Oil & Gas, 19 June 2022, https://egyptoil-gas.com/news/egypt-examines-cooperation-opportunities-with-mubadala-petroleum/.

24. Daniel Avis, 'Israel Plans Gas Exports to Europe as Output Surges by 22%', Bloomberg, 24 August 2022, https://www.bloomberg.com/news/articles/2022-08-24/israel-eyes-gas-exports-to-europe-as-production-surges-by-22.

25. 'Türkiye Seeks Saudi Coop as It Plans to Be Energy Hub to Europe', *Daily Sabah*, 31 October 2022, https://www.dailysabah.com/business/energy/turkiye-seeks-saudi-coop-as-it-plans-to-be-energy-hub-to-europe.

26. 'Saudi Arabia, Greece Issue Joint Statement at Conclusion of HRH Crown Prince's Visit to Greece', Saudi Press Agency, 27 July

27 'Misr Tastahdif Bad' Alrabt Alkahrabayiyi Ma' Al-Saoudiyyah Muntasaf 2025' "مصر تستهدف بدء الربط الكهربائي مع السعودية منتصف 2025 – اقتصاد الشرق مع بلومبرغ"، [Egypt aims to start the electrical connection with Saudi Arabia in mid-2025], Asharq Business, 19 October 2022, https://www.asharqbusiness.com/article/43023/%D9%85%D8%B5%D8%B1-%D8%AA%D8%B3%D8%AA%D9%87%D8%AF%D9%81-%D8%A8%D8%AF%D8%A1-%D8%A7%D9%84%D8%B1%D8%A8%D8%B7-%D8%A7%D9%84%D9%83%D9%87%D8%B1%D8%A8%D8%A7%D8%A6%D9%8A-%D9%85%D8%B9-%D8%A7%D9%84%D8%B3%D8%B9%D9%88%D8%AF%D9%8A%D8%A9-%D9%85%D9%86%D8%AA%D8%B5%D9%81-2025/.

28 'Masdar-led Consortium Strengthens Partnership to Advance Landmark 4 GW Green Hydrogen Program in Egypt', PR Newswire, 16 November 2022, https://www.prnewswire.com/news-releases/masdar-led-consortium-strengthens-partnership-to-advance-landmark-4-gw-green-hydrogen-program-in-egypt-301680393.html; and 'Egypt's Largest Solar Plant, Kom Ombo, Receives US$ 114 Million Financing Package', ACWA Power, 22 April 2021, https://www.acwapower.com/news/egypts-largest-solar-plant-kom-ombo-receives-us-114-million-financing-package/.

29 'Masdar, Taaleri Energia to Build 65 MW Solar Plant in Greece', Balkan Green Energy News, 7 May 2021, https://balkangreenenergynews.com/masdar-taaleri-energia-to-build-65-mw-solar-plant-in-greece/; and 'Memoranda of Understanding Between MORE, MASDAR and ADNOC for Investment Opportunities in Greece', Motor Oil Group, 10 May 2022, https://www.moh.gr/en/news/memoranda-of-understanding-between-more-masdar-and-adnoc-for-investment-opportunities-in-greece/.

30 Presidency of the Republic of Türkiye Investment Office, 'Invest in Türkiye', December 2021, https://www.invest.gov.tr/en/news/newsletters/lists/investnewsletter/investment-office-dec-2021-newsletter.pdf.

31 'ADQ Announces 4 Billion Euros Investment Partnership with Greece', ADQ, 9 May 2022, https://adq.ae/media/news/adq-announces-4-billion-euros-investment-partnership-with-greece; and Ilias Bellos, 'UAE Funds Looking to Invest in Greece', Kathimerini, 29 August 2022, https://www.ekathimerini.com/economy/1191979/uae-funds-looking-to-invest-in-greece/.

32 'Masadir Li "Alsharq": "Qatar Lil-Istithmar" Yatafawad 'ala Tatwir Mina' Safaja Fi Misr' "مصادر لـ"الشرق": "قطر للاستثمار" يتفاوض على تطوير ميناء سفاجا في مصر"، [Sources for "Al-Sharq": "Qatar investment" Is negotiating the development of Safaga Port in Egypt], Asharq Business, 24 November 2022, https://www.asharqbusiness.com/article/44439/%D9%85%D8%B5%D8%A7%D8%AF%D8%B1-%D9%84%D9%80%D8%A7%D9%84%D8%B4%D8%B1%D9%82-%D9%82%D8%B7%D8%B1-%D9%84%D9%84%D8%A7%D8%B3%D8%AA%D8%AB%D9%85%D8%A7%D8%B1-%D9%8A%D8%AA%D9%81%D8%A7%D9%88%D8%B6-%D8%B9%D9%84%D9%89-%D8%AA%D8%B7%D9%88%D9%8A%D8%B1-%D9%85%D9%8A%D9%86%D8%A7%D8%A1-%D8%B3%D9%81%D8%A7%D8%AC%D8%A7-%D9%81%D9%8A-%D9%85%D8%B5%D8%B1/; and 'Qatar Eyes Investment in Egypt's Container Terminals', Enterprise, 19 September 2022, https://enterprise.press/stories/2022/09/19/qatar-eyes-investment-in-egypts-container-terminals-81460/.

33 'AD Ports Group Signs Strategic Partnership Agreement with Turkiye Varlik Fonu', Abu Dhabi Media Office, 25 November 2021, https://www.mediaoffice.abudhabi/en/economy/ad-ports-group-signs-strategic-partnership-agreement-with-turkiye-varlik-fonu/.

34 Matt Spetalnick and Eric Beech, 'Mohammed bin Salman Says Saudi Arabia Is Getting "Closer" to Israel Normalization', Reuters, 21 September 2023, https://www.reuters.com/world/middle-east/saudi-crown-prince-says-getting-closer-israel-normalization-fox-interview-2023-09-20/; and Jack Dutton, 'Saudi FM: No Israel Normalization Without "Irreversible Path" to Palestinian State', Al-Monitor, 22 January 2024, https://www.al-monitor.com/originals/2024/01/saudi-fm-no-israel-normalization-without-irreversible-path-palestinian-state.

35 NewMed Energy, letter to Israel Securities Authority and Tel Aviv Stock Exchange Ltd, 13 March 2024, TS, https://newmedenergy.com/wp-content/uploads/2024/03/NewMed-IR-10.3.24-שגגונת.pdf.

36 'Masdar and GEK TERNA Strike Landmark €3.2bn Deal. UAE Renewables Champion to Acquire Greece's TERNA ENERGY', Masdar, 20 June 2024, https://masdar.ae/en/news/newsroom/uae-renewables-champion-to-acquire-greeces-terna-energy.

TURBULENCE IN THE EASTERN MEDITERRANEAN: GEOPOLITICAL, SECURITY AND ENERGY DYNAMICS ■ AN IISS STRATEGIC DOSSIER

↑
(L–R) Russian President Vladimir Putin, Iranian president Ebrahim Raisi and Turkish President Recep Tayyip Erdoğan pose for a photo before a trilateral meeting on Syria in Tehran, Iran, on 19 July 2022.
(Photo: Sergei Savostyanov/Sputnik/AFP via Getty Images)

RUSSIA HAS EXPANDED ITS FOOTPRINT in the Eastern Mediterranean since 2015, establishing a military presence in Libya and Syria and building defence and energy relationships with Egypt and Turkiye. These ties have positioned Moscow on NATO's and the European Union's southern flank and helped it counter Western efforts to isolate it.

RUSSIAN POLICY aims to achieve gains to leverage elsewhere, not to dominate the region. As a result, many Eastern Mediterranean countries do not see it as a threat to their own security. In contrast, Western powers have worried about Russian inroads and ability to challenge their regional influence at low cost.

RUSSIA'S ECONOMIC WEAKNESS prevents it from playing a geo-economic role and from designing and pursuing regionwide connectivity projects that regional governments would be keen to join. As such, Russia remains a disrupter rather than an architect of a new regional order.

CHAPTER EIGHTEEN

RUSSIA: MAXIMISING THE POLITICAL RETURNS OF ITS INTERVENTIONS

INTRODUCTION

While Russia lacks an explicit strategy for the Eastern Mediterranean, its historical relationships and the region's proximity to Eastern Europe, Eurasia, the Middle East and Africa have meant it has always received significant attention in Moscow. Kremlin decision-makers and Russian policy strategists have long seen the Eastern Mediterranean as key to Moscow's ability to protect sea routes from the Black Sea through the Dardanelles and the Aegean Sea to the Atlantic and Indian oceans, to influence and project power in these regions and to maintain a presence on NATO's and the EU's southern flank.[1] While retaining substantial military power and diplomatic reach there, Russia's technological, geo-economic and soft-power weaknesses limit its overall influence. As a result, Russia has remained a reactive player in the region, adjusting its relationships and policies in line with economic and security priorities instead of trying to shape it along its preferred lines.

Eager to maintain appearances and retain a say in regional diplomatic dynamics, Russia acts as a would-be great power in the Eastern Mediterranean. Since his return to the presidency in 2012, Vladimir Putin has sought to impress his own agenda and appear decisive in the region. Indeed, Russia has shown staying power and resilience in the face of significant challenges and pushback. Most notably, its full-scale invasion of Ukraine since February 2022 has not reversed the vast expansion of its influence in the region that began a decade prior. While Russia's regional political, economic and security influence remains far below that of the United States, its willingness to show its muscles and take risks differentiates it from China and puts it on par with major secondary powers such as France and the United Kingdom.

Regional players have not treated Russia as the power it claims to be, but they have accommodated Russian interests when necessary and pandered to the Kremlin when convenient without any expectation that Russia would emerge as a transformational power in the region or that it would align with and promote their interests fully. Russia has benefitted from the desire of key Middle Eastern states to diversify their relations away from their traditional Western partners, creating entanglements which compel them to remain engaged with Moscow into the future.

RUSSIA'S RESURGENCE

Vladimir Putin's first decade in power saw little Russian activism in the Middle East. He focused his attention on domestic consolidation, economic recovery and relations with Western countries and Russia's near abroad. His opposition to the Iraq War did not translate into active obstruction of US policy there. Russia voted in favour of several US- and French-drafted United Nations Security Council (UNSC) resolutions on Syria and Lebanon which were inimical to Syrian and Iranian interests, including Resolution 1701 that ended the 2006 Israel–Hizbullah war. Notably, Russia supported the Western sanctions strategy to obtain concessions from Tehran regarding Iran's nuclear programme. During that period, Russia maintained legacy ties with Cyprus and Greece, and improved relations with Israel. Overall, however, Russia remained a minor player. Its arms exports to the region had drastically reduced since the peaks reached during the Soviet era and its sole export commodity was oil. In his foundational speech at the 2007 Munich Security Conference, in which he warned about the risks of NATO's enlargement, Putin mentioned the Middle East only once, as he did with Iran's nuclear programme, and Iraq (then the dominant international issue) never.[2]

A series of political tremors in Russia's immediate neighbourhood and further afield, plus Russia's improved economic prospects and new ambitions in reaction to shifting geopolitical dynamics, changed Moscow's perspectives on the Eastern Mediterranean. Russia saw political transitions in Georgia and Ukraine, countries previously included in the Soviet Union, as reflecting a Western strategy of encirclement and as encroaching upon Russia's self-proclaimed sphere of influence. Moscow interpreted the uprisings that shook the Middle East from 2011 through the same prism. It saw the Western states as uniquely manipulative and powerful in steering political change, dangerously misguided about their relations with Islamist political movements and naive about the risks of instability. Then-placeholder president Dmitry Medvedev's 2011 decision not to veto a UNSC resolution authorising a NATO-led intervention against Libyan leader Muammar Gadhafi has generated debate over whether it motivated Putin's return to the presidency.[3] Putin had criticised Medvedev's decision at the time, and while Russia had some economic interests in Libya, Putin's opprobrium came more from opposing presumed Western intentions and designs than from promoting his own agenda. With Russia's influence waning throughout the northern

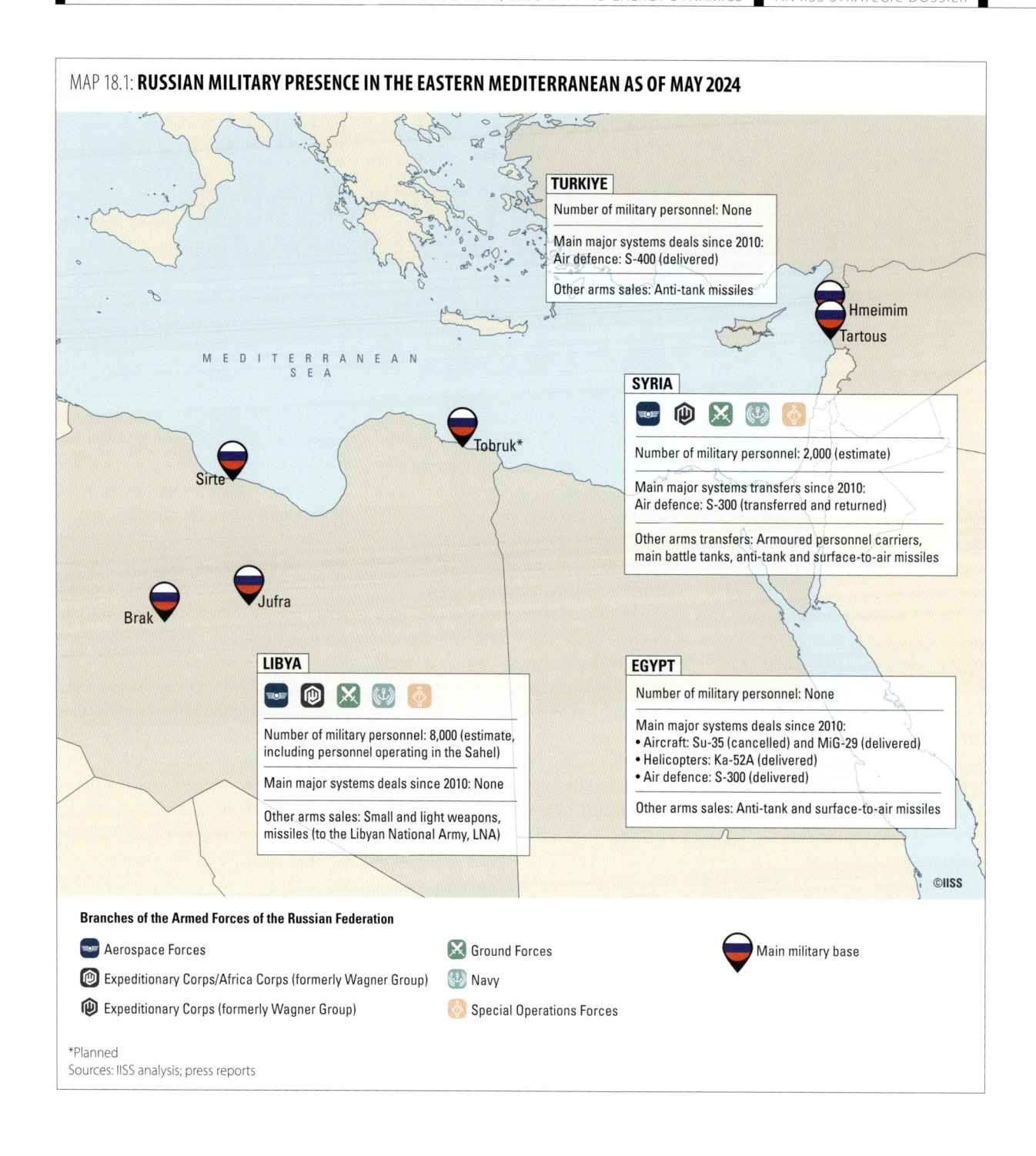

MAP 18.1: RUSSIAN MILITARY PRESENCE IN THE EASTERN MEDITERRANEAN AS OF MAY 2024

TURKIYE
Number of military personnel: None
Main major systems deals since 2010:
Air defence: S-400 (delivered)
Other arms sales: Anti-tank missiles

SYRIA
Number of military personnel: 2,000 (estimate)
Main major systems transfers since 2010:
Air defence: S-300 (transferred and returned)
Other arms transfers: Armoured personnel carriers, main battle tanks, anti-tank and surface-to-air missiles

LIBYA
Number of military personnel: 8,000 (estimate, including personnel operating in the Sahel)
Main major systems deals since 2010: None
Other arms sales: Small and light weapons, missiles (to the Libyan National Army, LNA)

EGYPT
Number of military personnel: None
Main major systems deals since 2010:
• Aircraft: Su-35 (cancelled) and MiG-29 (delivered)
• Helicopters: Ka-52A (delivered)
• Air defence: S-300 (delivered)
Other arms sales: Anti-tank and surface-to-air missiles

Locations marked: Hmeimim, Tartous (Syria); Tobruk*, Sirte, Jufra, Brak (Libya)

Branches of the Armed Forces of the Russian Federation
- Aerospace Forces
- Expeditionary Corps/Africa Corps (formerly Wagner Group)
- Expeditionary Corps (formerly Wagner Group)
- Ground Forces
- Navy
- Special Operations Forces
- Main military base

*Planned
Sources: IISS analysis; press reports

Mediterranean (including in the Balkans), preserving and developing its reach in the southern and eastern Mediterranean became more urgent. Although Algeria remained a solid partner in the western Mediterranean, Moscow saw a risk of losing its foothold in the east. This fuelled Putin's subsequent determination to at least complicate further Western military and political projects in the region, but also to find and build new relationships there.

Russia's Syria policy is arguably the pinnacle of its successes in the Eastern Mediterranean, and one where precisely such dynamics were on display. The Kremlin has long had strong relations with Syria's government – under both President Bashar al-Assad and his father and predecessor Hafez al-Assad – and supported the incumbent authorities in the aftermath of the outbreak of the Syrian revolution in 2011. Russia offered limited material support early on; it also obstructed diplomatic efforts by the various UN envoys and protected Syria against Western pressure at the UNSC.[4]

Russia's formal intervention in the Syrian conflict, starting in September 2015, came as a surprise. The Kremlin formally stated that it intervened because the Assad government was at risk of falling to the Islamic State (ISIS), but it prioritised during the first 18 months the targeting of the loose coalition of secular and Islamist militias that controlled large swathes of territory across Syria. The Kremlin described its intervention as limited, seeking to avoid domestic ire over sending soldiers to a conflict in which few Russians were invested.[5] But it deployed significant air assets as well as ground troops, and cooperated with the Assad government forces, Iranian conventional and Islamic Revolutionary Guard Corps troops, and Lebanese Hizbullah militiamen as well as an array of local militias. In subsequent years, Russia turned to the Wagner Group – a paramilitary group founded in 2014 to support its intervention in Ukraine – to take charge of many of the highest-risk operations and give it plausible deniability (at least in Russia's tightly controlled media) of increasing involvement in the conflict, even after high-profile incidents such as the February 2018 clash with US special forces in Syria.[6]

Even as the Assad regime consolidated control over most of the country in the following years, the Kremlin remained entrenched there, securing in 2019 a deal to allow a Russian company to manage the port of Tartous, the country's largest, for 49 years (see Map 18.1).[7] It maintained a military presence in the country, deploying military police in unstable areas in the south and the northwest, and conventional forces across the northeast in proximity with US and Turkish forces. Russian artillery and aircraft took part in a multitude of operations alongside Syrian government forces in the northwest. Importantly, the small size of the Russian presence remained financially and politically manageable for the Kremlin. Although refraining from investing in the country's reconstruction or providing any meaningful humanitarian assistance, Russia facilitated fuel and food trade that contravened US and EU sanctions. Russia's greatest vector of influence was the Syrian military, whose officer corps preferred Russia over Iran, and which relied on Moscow to contain Iranian-backed militias. Russia achieved limited success in reforming the Syrian military: the lack of domestic resources and Moscow's unwillingness to invest in it ensured that the armed forces would remain an internal security force based on loyalty to Assad and brutality against its domestic enemies.

When it intervened, Russia also noted that domestic security concerns were a factor.[8] Russia had inadvertently helped fuel the conflict by allowing hundreds, and likely thousands, of Islamist militants from the North Caucasus to travel to Syria in the preceding years – permitting even those wanted by Russian authorities to depart the country to join the fight.[9] As ISIS activity brought additional Western intervention in the conflict, the Kremlin also increased its rhetoric around confronting supposed Western-led 'regime change'.[10]

Russia's success in Syria surprised Western policymakers who had predicted a quagmire, and impressed Arab governments for its ruthlessness, resolve and cunning. It proved a turning point for Russia's standing and influence in the region. It consolidated the burgeoning relationship with Egypt and allowed Moscow to re-engage with the Gulf states from a position of strength. It compelled Turkiye to modify its Syria policy and to accept managing the conflict in coordination with Russia and later Iran. It entangled Israel in cooperation mechanisms over Syria. Russia also attracted plaudits in Greece and Cyprus: religious solidarity with Orthodox Christians (a sizeable minority in Syria) and suspicion of Turkish intentions in Syria had made them sceptical about the Western policy of supporting Assad's rebel enemies.

Putin sought to recreate the successful Syria playbook in Libya, which slid into civil war following the NATO-led intervention in 2011 as domestic militias jockeyed for power and derailed attempts at establishing democratic institutions. The Kremlin, which was close to Gadhafi's government and had economic interests in the country, bided its time before intervening. It waited for a suitable partner to establish itself as a potential ally, settling on General Khalifa Haftar by January 2017 and increasing support after he consolidated control over the country's eastern oil ports and second city of Benghazi in the summer of 2017.[11] The first reports of Russian security forces arriving in the country began to appear later that year, although Russian involvement increased significantly after Wagner arrived in October 2018.[12]

Russia's support helped establish Haftar as one of the country's key power brokers. However, contrary to what it did in Syria, it did not enable him to win decisively. It refrained from intervening directly in his subsequent efforts to take the capital Tripoli in 2019, even as Turkiye and Qatar moved to support his rivals in the Government of National Accord (GNA).[13] When Turkiye signed an agreement with the GNA on maritime boundaries in November 2019 that encroached on waters also claimed by Greece and Cyprus, Moscow stayed put. Russia deployed aircraft to Libya in May 2020, but these came too late and did not take part in the siege of Tripoli, which ultimately failed.[14]

Russia has expanded and entrenched its presence in Libya, notably using the port of Tobruk to transfer equipment and supplies.[15] Moscow has proved not only discreet but also politically agile, returning its ambassador to Tripoli in mid-2023 and cultivating relationships beyond Haftar. The assassination of Wagner head Yevgeny Prigozhin in August 2023 had a minor effect on Russia's posture. A senior Russian military delegation visited Haftar on the eve of Prigozhin's death, an indication that the Kremlin was seeking a more direct and active role in the country.[16] In the months following, Moscow rebranded Wagner and integrated it into a newly established Africa Corps. It became clearer that Libya served as an entry point and logistical base for Russia's expansion efforts in the Sahel.

In both Libya and Syria, Russia provided little support for international mediation efforts beyond rhetorical backing for UN-led processes. Instead, it created parallel mechanisms such as the Astana process to manage the Syrian battlefield. It also provided no significant humanitarian relief, state-led economic reconstruction or management of internally displaced people and refugees. In doing so, it avoided taking responsibility for comprehensive stabilisation and governance. Instead, it sought to shift these responsibilities onto the UN, Western states and regional powers, advocating for the lifting of sanctions and the relaxation of conditions on its local partners.

COOPERATION AND TENSION WITH REGIONAL POWERS

Russia has had to manage the impact of its interventions in Libya and Syria on its relations with other Eastern Mediterranean countries. It has leveraged them to secure its interests but has struggled to reconcile its conflicting relationships or to achieve breakthroughs given its diminished economic position and isolation.

ISRAEL

Russia and Israel maintain ambivalent relations which have a strong and dangerous military dimension because of Russia's presence in Syria. In September 2018, Syrian air defences mistakenly shot down a Russian military aircraft in Syrian airspace during an Israeli air attack, killing 15 aboard. Russia blamed Israel, alleging that Israel's 'irresponsible actions' had caused the incident, and that its aircraft had 'deliberately created a dangerous situation for surface ships and aircraft in the area'.[17]

Israel's desire to preserve operational autonomy in Syrian skies to operate against Iran and its partners there has required it to accommodate Moscow. Most notably, Israel refused to join Western sanctions against Russia in both 2014 and 2022 and limited its support for Kyiv to avoid alienating Russia. While the Kremlin positioned itself as a Palestinian ally for most of the Soviet era and retained strong ties with the Palestinian Authority subsequently, it largely refrained from any direct involvement in Israeli–Palestinian relations, instead using the diplomatic paralysis to castigate the US. This, as well as the large Russian-origin community in Israel, helped to improve Russia's relations with Israel under Putin, with Benjamin Netanyahu particularly eager to cosy up to him. However, Israel's close ties to the US continued to constrain economic and military cooperation with Russia.[18] Total Israeli trade with Russia amounted to just over US$1 billion in 2022, while total trade with the US amounted to US$35.2bn in 2023.[19] While Russia was unhappy with the US role in facilitating the Abraham Accords, it cautiously welcomed them to placate its Israeli and Gulf partners.

The rapid succession of its full-scale invasion of Ukraine since February 2022 and the Israel–Hamas war since October 2023 has compelled Moscow to make new geopolitical calculations. It has prioritised countering Western policies and narratives that seek to contain and isolate Russia, making greater political and defence alignment with Iran a necessity. It also hosted Hamas leaders after the 7 October attacks, and Putin called the war a 'vivid example of the failure of the United States' policy in the Middle East'.[20] Only a decade earlier, Russia had championed a hardline approach to all Islamist groups and rejected Hamas as part of its outreach to Israel. Understanding that it had no diplomatic leverage to mediate the conflict, and still focused on Ukraine, Russia chose to use the war to promote a narrative of Western hypocrisy and failure.

In turn, this aggravated relations with Israel, which has watched with concern the development of Iran–Russia defence cooperation and technology transfers. As Moscow becomes dependent on Iranian provision of missiles and uninhabited aerial vehicles, Israel worries that it will gradually side with Iran on regional issues and its nuclear programme. Israel is also concerned that Russia might help Iran modernise its own armed forces, a prospect that UN sanctions and restrictions (which Russia had contributed to putting in place during the 2010s) had previously complicated.

TURKIYE

Turkiye is another country that Russia has had to cultivate and pressure simultaneously. It is arguably the most important country in the region for Russia, given its control over the Black Sea's sole route into the Mediterranean (and thus international seas) as well as its influence in the Caucasus, which checked Moscow's own in the Armenia–Azerbaijan theatre. Russia has seen Turkiye's deteriorating relations with key Western powers and its complex membership in NATO over the last decade as reasons to engage Ankara constantly despite profound divergences in the Eastern Mediterranean. Russian–Turkish relations hit a nadir in November 2015 after Turkiye shot down a Russian Su-24 attack plane that had crossed into Turkish airspace while operating in Syria. The incident did not lead to a triggering of NATO's consultative self-defence mechanism, Article 4, though Ankara had done so that July over terrorism threats emanating from the Syrian conflict. The incident came as NATO–Turkiye relations were already under strain, with the Alliance withdrawing a *Patriot* air-defence system from the country despite Ankara's earlier Article 4 invocation.[21]

This incident ironically sped up Putin's attempt to use Turkish President Recep Tayyip Erdoğan's lukewarm approach to the West to advance his interests. Eschewing military options, Russia retaliated by imposing broad sanctions and other measures on Turkiye.[22] Within a few months, Russia's coercive power against Turkiye and airpower in Syria compelled Ankara to drop its previous Syrian policy and embrace a new one more compatible with Russian interests. In turn, Russia sought to partner with Turkiye, leading to entanglements that would both constrain Turkish policy and facilitate the pursuit of its own strategic objectives.

In December 2014, Putin announced during a visit to Turkiye that he was cancelling efforts to build a new gas pipeline under the Black Sea to Bulgaria. This project had encountered substantial Western opposition which escalated in the aftermath of Russia's annexation of Crimea and intervention in eastern Ukraine earlier that year. Alongside Erdoğan, Putin announced that Russia would instead build a new underwater pipeline to Turkiye, dubbed TurkStream, and that Eastern European countries could receive Russian gas through that route instead. The two presidents also announced plans for Russia's Rosatom to build Turkiye's first nuclear-power plant, in Akkuyu (see Table 18.1). Although Erdoğan had offered rhetorical opposition to the annexation of Crimea, he refused to join Western sanctions on Russia.[23] The Su-24 crisis was surprisingly short-lived as the two leaders saw each other as useful for countering the West. When Erdoğan survived a coup attempt in July 2016, which he explicitly blamed on the US and its failure to extradite his former ally and political Islamist thinker Fethullah Gülen as he had demanded,[24] Erdoğan once again turned to Moscow to demonstrate that his partnership options were not limited to the West.

Turkiye and Russia would subsequently expand cooperation significantly, despite continuing to back opposite sides in the Syrian conflict. Construction of the TurkStream pipeline began in May 2017 and work on Akkuyu was launched in yet another meeting between the Turkish and Russian presidents in April 2018.[25] The two countries announced their most explicitly anti-Western move in December 2017, when Ankara agreed to buy Russia's S-400 air-defence system

TABLE 18.1: NUCLEAR PROGRAMMES IN THE EASTERN MEDITERRANEAN AS OF MAY 2024

Country	Location	Status of programme and expected date of completion	Nature of programme	Provider	Financing and commercial model	Current or potential challenges
Egypt	al-Dabaa, northwestern coast	Under construction. Claimed completion date at full-capacity operation of 2030 but delays are likely	Civil-energy programme	Rosatom (Russia)	Build-own-operate (BOO) model. Cost of programme currently US$30 billion. 85% financing from Russia, 15% from Egypt. Loan repayable over 22 years. First instalment due in October 2029	Initial model was build-operate-transfer (BOT) but morphed into BOO model due to Egypt's financial situation and sovereign-debt risk. Potential Western sanctions on Rosatom
Israel	Dimona reactor, Negev Desert	Ongoing	Military programme	Indigenous, with French help at inception	Not known	Believed to possess nuclear weapons. Not party to the Non-Proliferation Treaty (NPT) and not under International Atomic Energy Agency (IAEA) safeguards
Libya	N/A	Dismantled following 2003 agreement. No current programme	Military programme	Indigenous	N/A	N/A
Syria	Deir ez-Zor governorate	Destroyed by Israel in 2007	Suspected military programme	Believed to have received North Korean and possibly Iranian assistance	Not known	IAEA investigation has not fully established the facts
Turkiye	Akkuyu, Mersin province	Under construction since April 2018. First unit to be commissioned by end of 2024 and all four units to be completed by 2028	Civil-energy programme	Rosatom (Russia)	BOO model at an estimated cost of US$25bn	Potential Western sanctions on Rosatom
Turkiye	Likely sites include Sinop and Thrace	Under negotiation. China, Russia and South Korea are in separate negotiations with Turkiye on Sinop, while China is in negotiations on Thrace	Civil-energy programme	Under negotiation	Under negotiation	Potential Western sanctions on Rosatom if Russia wins the Sinop contract

Source: IISS analysis

rather than the US-made *Patriot* system it had previously sought. Although Erdoğan would have been well aware that the deal violated US sanctions legislation passed earlier that year, he repeatedly rebuffed US demands to reconsider it.[26] The US ultimately enacted sanctions in the waning weeks of Donald Trump's presidential administration, though they were relatively limited, comprising just asset bans and visa freezes on Turkish Presidency of Defence Industries (SSB) officials and denials of export licences to the SSB.[27] While the US had earlier suspended Turkish participation in its F-35 fighter programme over the move as well, Russia was eager and willing to position itself as an alternative partner for Turkiye, pitching it its own fifth-generation Su-35 aircraft instead.[28]

Although such a sale has not come to fruition, Russia's approach to the Erdoğan government brought it dividends when it launched its full-scale invasion of Ukraine in February 2022. Although Turkiye closed the Black Sea to non-littoral warships in the aftermath, meaning Russia could not add to its Black Sea Fleet based in occupied Crimea, the closure also prevented NATO from deploying additional ships to project force in the area or protect Ukrainian shipping.[29] Ankara also continued to refuse Western entreaties to join the expanded sanctions programme against Russia, and has since become a route for the Kremlin to mitigate trade sanctions and put Russia's hard-currency reserves to use.[30] Further, Russia agreed to Turkiye mediating and then serving as an observer on the Black Sea Grain Initiative between July 2022 and July 2023.

EGYPT

Russia has employed a similar playbook in Egypt as it has in Turkiye. Its opposition to the Arab uprisings made it a natural partner for the military-backed government that came after the 2013 coup. Abdel Fattah al-Sisi (then commander of the armed forces) made his first foreign visit after the coup to Russia, and his first official trip as president was to Russia as well.[31] Weapons dealings with Moscow had been limited under the pre-2011 Hosni Mubarak government; but after the US suspended some exports following the 2013 coup, the Russian–Egyptian defence relationship expanded significantly.[32] When Putin made his own visit to Egypt in February 2015, he agreed to have Rosatom build Egypt's first nuclear-power plant, in al-Dabaa, much as he had done in Turkiye.[33] Political relations were

Russian President Vladimir Putin (L) and Egyptian President Abdel Fattah al-Sisi (R) visit the Black Sea Fleet's guards missile cruiser *Moskva* in the sea port of Sochi, Russia, on 12 August 2014. (Photo: Alexei Druzhinin/Ria Novosti/AFP via Getty Images)

relatively unaffected by the October 2015 bombing of a Russian commercial airliner bringing tourists from Sharm al-Sheikh back to Russia, although the subsequent cancellation of Russia–Egypt flights significantly impacted tourism numbers, which fell from 3.16 million visits in 2014 to 53,800 in 2016, a 98% decline.[34] The two countries only agreed to resume flights after another visit by Putin in December 2017, when they also agreed contracts for al-Dabaa.[35] Putin further lobbied for additional arms contracts and in October 2018 agreed to a landmark US$2bn sale of the fifth-generation Su-35s, with Egypt similarly ignoring concerns about US sanctions.[36] However, this deal would prove the limitations of Russia's Egypt outreach, as Cairo reportedly scuppered the deal in the face of growing US sanctions threats after the full-scale invasion of Ukraine,[37] and as Cairo increasingly depended on US support not just for its military budget but also for approving IMF financial support to address a severe economic crisis. Nevertheless, Egypt appears poised to remain in an intermediate position vis-à-vis the Russia–US rivalry: documents leaked online in early 2023 claimed that Sisi ordered covert shipments of rockets to Russia to support its war against Ukraine, though US officials said they do not believe Egypt ultimately executed the plan.[38]

Russia has courted Egypt to drive a wedge among its traditional Western partners. Moscow has advocated for Egyptian membership in the BRICS grouping and has diplomatically supported Cairo's positions on conflicts in Libya, Sudan, Syria and other countries. In turn, having the Arab world's most populous nation as a partner has helped Russia deflect accusations about its domestic repression of Chechens and other Muslim minorities. Egypt has also refrained from criticising Russia over its invasion of Ukraine.

However, Russia has been of limited help in addressing Egypt's greatest challenge, its faltering economy. Russia's economic weakness has led Egypt to see the limits of its hedging, ultimately turning to Western and Gulf governments for essential economic assistance. Egypt's dire finances have been an issue for Russia: the two countries settled on a 'Build-own-operate' model for the al-Dabaa nuclear project instead of the more typical 'Build-operate-transfer' because of Egypt's debt exposure. While this gives Moscow influence over Egypt's energy and economic security, it also represents additional risks and responsibilities for Moscow. Further, Egypt has been particularly exposed to the second-order effects of the invasion of Ukraine. The invasion has jeopardised its food imports from Ukraine, leading to rising food prices that have aggravated an already dire economic situation. It was therefore not surprising that Russia announcing the suspension of the Black Sea grain-export deal in July 2023 led to rare criticism from Egypt.[39] Finally, the highly personalised nature of the Egyptian–Russian relationship limits its depth. Besides the presidency, the senior military cadre and the security services, Russia has little access to Egyptian society, including the economic elite.

CYPRUS AND GREECE

Russia has also tried to pull Cyprus and Greece into intermediate positions vis-à-vis its rivalry with the West. Banking on historical, religious and economic ties, Moscow has tried to keep them in its circle of partners in the Eastern Mediterranean. The relationship with Cyprus was sufficiently symbiotic that Russia even loaned it €2.5bn (US$3.1bn) in 2012 to help alleviate its banking crisis.[40] Cypriot banks have long been key hubs for Russian money to move abroad while limiting ownership disclosures and seeking tax advantages, and in turn be reinvested in Russia. Russia has also secured greater access for its military ships to Cypriot ports. To Cyprus's displeasure, however, the Kremlin has broadly stayed out of its dispute with the unrecognised Turkish Republic of Northern Cyprus. For Russia, the need to accommodate Ankara but also to ensure that Western–Turkish relations remain tense prevailed over Cypriot pleas.

Russia's efforts in Cyprus have failed, primarily because only Western countries could provide the economic assistance to stabilise and restart its economy. The EU conditioned its help in part on cleaning up and reforming Cyprus's banking system, of which Russia had taken advantage. Moscow misjudged the extent to which Cyprus would prioritise its position in and good relations with the EU, which provided a far larger bailout less than a year after Moscow had extended its own support. In January 2023, Russian Foreign Minister Sergei Lavrov bitterly observed that: 'I don't know what Greece and Cyprus are suffering more from, we were always very close friends with the Greeks and Cypriots and those transformations – in the leadership of those countries, it's only natural that we've noted this'.[41]

Wealthy Russians who had acquired Cypriot passports under the country's investment-by-citizenship programme were stripped of the documents in the aftermath of the 2022 invasion of Ukraine.[42] Cyprus has also received outsized attention from the US and European powers for its improving relations with Israel. EU officials even viewed its gas potential favourably as part of a strategy to move away from Russian gas.[43] In 2022, Cyprus agreed to curtail Russian access to its ports at the request of the US, which had also linked the lifting of its arms embargo to reduced defence ties between Cyprus and Russia.

Russia has had a similarly mixed track record in Greece. Since Putin first came to power, Russia's public diplomacy has emphasised their shared Orthodox ties.[44] These efforts reached their peak in 2016 when he visited Mount Athos, one of Orthodox Christianity's holiest sites. They ultimately failed to align Greece with Russian preferences after the Greek Orthodox Church recognised in 2018 an autocephalous (self-governing) status for the Orthodox church in Ukraine; in retaliation, the Russian Orthodox Church split from the Greek.[45] Russia also used more traditional methods of economic diplomacy to build influence in Athens, particularly when the left-wing Syriza government clashed with Brussels between 2015 and 2019. It floated a bid for its natural-gas company DEPA although no official offer was ever announced.[46] And while then-prime minister Alexis Tsipras did engage in public criticism of the sanctions against Russia, Greece never seriously opposed them, preferring not to expend its already limited political capital in Brussels.[47] Greece has viewed with concern Russia's rapprochement with Turkiye since 2016 and sale of advanced weapons systems. This has led to several diplomatic disputes, including Greece recalling its ambassador from Moscow in 2018.[48]

Another declining vector of influence has been defence relations. Greece procured several Russian systems for its land forces as well as its air defence in the aftermath of the collapse of the Soviet Union. It also conducted maritime exercises with the Russian navy in the Aegean and Mediterranean seas. However, the Greek economic crisis froze its defence modernisation and the stabilisation of Greek finances oriented the country firmly westward. By the time Greece was able to invest again in its defence capabilities, it turned to France, Israel and the US, while Russia was undergoing isolation by the West and selling weapons to Turkiye instead.

Russia's strongest leverage over Greece has been the latter's significant dependence on Russian energy, among the highest in Europe.[49] In 2005, Russia provided 85% of Greece's total energy needs. The International Energy Agency notes that 'in 2021, Russia accounted for 96% of hard coal imports, 41% of natural gas imports, 21% of crude oil imports and a small share of oil products imports', remaining Greece's main energy partner.[50] The TurkStream pipeline transports Russian gas to Greece, crossing Turkish territory. In the aftermath of the 2022 invasion of Ukraine, European countries made deliberate efforts to reduce this dependency. Conveniently for Greece, a new liquefied natural gas terminal was completed and became operational in the summer of 2022, allowing Greece to halve the amount of gas imported from Russia. Nonetheless, Greek imports of Russian gas rebounded in 2023 and doubled in early 2024, amounting to 44% of Greece's total imports.[51]

The government of Greek Prime Minister Kyriakos Mitsotakis has taken a firm westward approach that has riled Russia, providing political and military support for Kyiv although refraining from sending much-needed air defences. With Greece now embedded in US-backed networks in the Eastern Mediterranean and developing defence relationships with both Washington and Paris, Moscow appears effectively sidelined.

However, support for Russia persists in the nationalist and leftist camps in Greece. More recently, Russia has found some indirect support from Greece's more conservative-leaning traditional business elite in the shipping industry, with which the Kremlin has long had dealings given its importance for Russia's oil industry – US officials estimate 70% of Russia's oil exports travel by sea.[52] Greek shipping magnates helped Russia manage initial sanctions on its shipping industry by supporting a fire sale of some of the fleet of ships sold by its state shipping company Sovcomflot after its designation following the full-scale invasion.[53] They subsequently sold dozens of ships to Russia, forming the base of its 'shadow fleet' that seeks to mitigate or dodge other sanctions, including the G7 oil-price cap introduced in December 2022.[54] Such dealings are the latest evidence of Russia's ability to find and develop ties with partners in the Eastern Mediterranean, even under strained circumstances.

In addition, by being a key partner of some of Greece's closest interlocutors in the Eastern Mediterranean such as Egypt, Russia remains relevant to Greek interests. In Libya, Greece and Cyprus prefer the Kremlin's favourite Khalifa Haftar, and in Syria they seek a relaxation of Western sanctions and re-engagement with the Assad government, which Russia supports.

LEBANON

Lebanon is among the countries where Russia has had the least influence, in part because of disinterest and its marginal impact on Russian interests. Russia's close ties to the Assad government and Iran mean that Lebanese political factions see it as a biased actor. Importantly, Russia is unable to offer financial support as Lebanon faces a debilitating crisis, and does not see commercial opportunities there. Its failure to understand Lebanese politics led the Kremlin to express surprise when Lebanon's government formally criticised the full-scale invasion of Ukraine in February 2022.[55] Hizbullah, and politicians from various minor parties, subsequently defended Russia. Russia's interest in Lebanon's gas potential has been limited despite the possible foothold it could offer in the developing Eastern Mediterranean gas market. The nominally private Russian firm Novatek agreed in 2017 to explore for gas along with Western energy firms in two offshore Lebanese blocks, but withdrew in September 2022.[56] This appears to have been an economic decision rather than one forced by sanctions, given Novatek is only subject to so-called sectoral sanctions that do not affect such operations abroad.

OUTLOOK

Russia has had notable policy successes in the Eastern Mediterranean under Putin, even if it has not prioritised the region. By positioning itself to take advantage of changing geopolitical alignments and to enter spaces vacated or ignored by Western rivals, and by proving flexible in the partners it is willing to work with, Moscow has significantly expanded its regional influence. Russia's defence and energy ties with Egypt and Turkiye and military presence in Libya and Syria give Moscow an outsized role, and it can easily sustain them. Throughout the region, Moscow's ability to align with popular and elite sentiments on matters such as the Israel–Hamas war has translated into sympathy for Moscow over its own adventures such as the invasion of Ukraine. Regional players harbour no illusions, understanding that Russian policy aims to achieve gains to leverage elsewhere rather than to dominate the region or solve its conflicts. As a result, many Eastern Mediterranean countries do not see Russia as a threat to their own security. In contrast, Western powers have worried about Russian inroads in the region and ability to disrupt and challenge their influence at low cost.

Russia has made missteps along the way: its limited resources have enabled warlords and failed to stabilise countries. It remains unable to make any significant geo-economic offer to its regional partners, and Western sanctions limit prospects for economic cooperation. It is excluded from all the major regional energy, infrastructure and geo-economic projects.

Moscow is, however, eager to present realistic and limited proposals rather than extend improbable security and economic guarantees. In the Eastern Mediterranean, Putin is content despite not being in the driver's seat, seeking instead to score incremental successes when opportunities arise. As a rare area of foreign-policy success, and given the supreme significance for Putin of seeking any advantages in the conflict in Ukraine, it is likely that Russia will continue to dedicate outsized resources to the region. Policymaking has been, and will continue to be, dictated by a mix of occasional interventions from the highest levels of the Kremlin and entrepreneurial efforts by government and quasi-state actors, though the international sanctions regime targeting Russia since 2022 may limit the latter.

The Russian Navy's Kremi-class aircraft carrier *Admiral Kuznetsov* offshore Limassol, Cyprus, on 8 April 2014. (Photo: Andrew Caballero-Reynolds/Bloomberg via Getty Images)

ENDNOTES

1 Zaur Gasimov, 'Russia under Putin in the Eastern Mediterranean: The Soviet Legacy, Flexibility, and New Dynamics', *Comparative Southeast European Studies*, vol. 70, no. 3, 11 October 2022, pp. 464–5, https://doi.org/10.1515/soeu-2021-0061.

2 Kremlin, 'Speech and the Following Discussion at the Munich Conference on Security Policy', 10 February 2007, http://en.kremlin.ru/events/president/transcripts/24034.

3 Philip Short, *Putin: His Life and Times* (London: The Bodley Head, 2022), pp. 526–8.

4 Roy Allison, 'Russia and Syria: Explaining Alignment with a Regime in Crisis', *International Affairs*, vol. 89, no. 4, July 2013, pp. 795–823, https://www.jstor.org/stable/23479395.

5 Levada Center, 'Russian Participation in the Syrian Military Conflict', 6 November 2015, https://www.levada.ru/en/2015/11/06/russian-participation-in-the-syrian-military-conflict/.

6 Kyle Atwell and Daphne McCurdy, 'Russia's Wagner Group and the Rise of Mercenary Warfare', Modern Warfare Institute at West Point, 4 December 2020, https://mwi.westpoint.edu/russias-wagner-group-and-the-rise-of-mercenary-warfare/.

7 'Syria Parliament Okays Russian Lease of Tartus Port: State Media', France24, 12 June 2019, https://www.france24.com/en/20190612-syria-parliament-okays-russian-lease-tartus-port-state-media.

8 Samuel Charap, Elina Treyger and Edward Geist, 'Understanding Russia's Intervention in Syria', Rand Corporation, 31 October 2019, p. 4, https://www.rand.org/pubs/research_reports/RR3180.html.

9 Maria Tsvetkova, 'How Russia Allowed Homegrown Radicals to Go and Fight in Syria', Reuters, 13 May 2016, https://www.reuters.com/investigates/special-report/russia-militants/.

10 'Minister: Russian Operation in Syria Stopped Chain of Color Revolutions in Middle East', TASS, 21 February 2017, https://tass.com/politics/932137.

11 'By Supporting Marshal Haftar, Russia Marks Its Territory in Libya', France24, 24 January 2017, https://www.france24.com/en/20170124-supporting-marshal-haftar-russia-marks-its-territory-libya; and Ayman Al-Warfalli, 'Libya's Eastern Commander Declares Victory in Battle for Benghazi', Reuters, 6 July 2017, https://www.reuters.com/article/us-libya-security-benghazi/libyas-eastern-commander-declares-victory-in-battle-for-benghazi-idUSKBN19Q2SK.

12 Thomas Arnold, 'Exploiting Chaos: Russia in Libya', Center for Strategic and International Studies, 23 September 2020, https://www.csis.org/blogs/post-soviet-post/exploiting-chaos-russia-libya; and 'Wagner, Shadowy Russian Military Group, "Fighting in Libya"', BBC, 7 May 2020, https://www.bbc.com/news/world-africa-52571777.

13 Ahmed Helal, 'For Turkey, the Libyan Conflict and the Eastern Mediterranean Are Inextricably Linked', Atlantic Council, 28 October 2020, https://www.atlanticcouncil.org/blogs/menasource/for-turkey-the-libyan-conflict-and-the-eastern-mediterranean-are-inextricably-linked/.

14 'US Says Russia Sent Jets to Libya "Mercenaries"', BBC, 26 May 2020, https://www.bbc.co.uk/news/world-africa-52811093.

15 Tom Kington, 'Russia Funneling Weapons Through Libyan Port, Eyeing Gateway to Africa', Defense News, 19 April 2024, https://www.defensenews.com/global/europe/2024/04/19/russia-funneling-weapons-through-libyan-port-eying-gateway-to-africa/.

16 'Russian Army Officials Visit Libya After Haftar Invite', *Moscow Times*, 22 August 2023, https://www.themoscowtimes.com/2023/08/22/russian-army-officials-visit-libya-after-haftar-invite-a82219.

17 'Russia Blames Israel After Military Plane Shot Down Off Syria', BBC, 18 September 2018, https://www.bbc.co.uk/news/world-europe-45556290.

18 Mark N. Katz, 'Russia and Israel: An Improbable Friendship', in Nicu Popescu and Stanislav Secrieru (eds), *Russia's Return to the Middle East: Building Sandcastles?* (Paris: EU Institute for Security Studies, 2018), pp. 103–8, https://www.jstor.org/stable/resrep21138.15.

19 UN Comtrade Database, 2024, https://comtradeplus.un.org/.

20 Ivan Nechepurenko, 'Hamas Leaders Arrive in Moscow as the Kremlin Attempts to Showcase Its Clout', *New York Times*, 26 October 2023, https://www.nytimes.com/2023/10/26/world/middleeast/hamas-russia-moscow.html; and Laura Hülsemann, 'Putin Blames US for Israel–Hamas Conflict', Politico, 10 October 2023, https://www.politico.eu/article/vladimir-putin-russia-blames-us-over-isreal-hamas-conflict/.

21 Jim Townsend and Rachel Ellehuus, 'The Tale of Turkey and the Patriots', War on the Rocks, 22 July 2019, https://warontherocks.com/2019/07/the-tale-of-turkey-and-the-patriots/.

22 Kremlin, 'Executive Order on Measures to Ensure Russia's National Security and Protection of Russian Citizens Against Criminal and Other Illegal Acts and on the Application of Special Economic Measures Against Turkey', 28 November 2015, http://en.kremlin.ru/events/president/news/50805.

23 'Crimean Tatar Leader Receives Turkey's Highest State Order', Radio Free Europe/Radio Liberty (RFE/RL), 16 April 2014, https://www.rferl.org/a/crimean-tatar-leader-receives-turkeys-highest-state-order/25335329.html; and Balkan Devlen, '"Don't Poke the Russian Bear": Turkish Policy in the Ukrainian Crisis', Norwegian Peacebuilding Resource Centre, May 2014, https://www.files.ethz.ch/isn/180832/a5fa13f65a0a0fcece44339be2957279.pdf.

24 Victor Kotsev and John Dyer, 'Turkey Blames U.S. for Coup Attempt', *USA Today*, 18 July 2016, https://www.usatoday.com/story/news/world/2016/07/18/turkey-blames-us-coup-attempt/87260612/.

25 'Turkey Embarks on New Energy Strategy with First Nuclear Plant Built by Russia', *Daily Sabah*, 4 April 2018, https://www.dailysabah.com/energy/2018/04/04/turkey-embarks-on-new-energy-strategy-with-first-nuclear-plant-built-by-russia-1522800356.

26 Tom Karako, 'Coup-proofing? Making Sense of Turkey's S-400 Decision', Center for Strategic and International Studies, 15 July 2019, https://www.csis.org/analysis/coup-proofing-making-sense-turkeys-s-400-decision.

27 Michael R. Pompeo, 'The United States Sanctions Turkey Under CAATSA 231', US Department of State, 14 December 2020, https://2017-2021.state.gov/the-united-states-sanctions-turkey-under-caatsa-231/.

28 Karen DeYoung, 'U.S. Suspends Turkey's Participation in F-35 Fighter Program Over Ankara's Purchase of Russian System', *Washington Post*, 1 April 2019, https://www.washingtonpost.com/world/national-security/us-suspends-turkeys-participation-in-f-35-fighter-program-over-ankaras-purchase-of-russian-system/2019/04/01/c38a16be-54b6-11e9-8ef3-fbd41a2ce4d5_story.html; and Burak Ege Bekdil, 'Russia Pitches Turkey the Su-57 Fighter Jet if F-35 Deal with US Collapses', Defense News, 6 May 2019, https://www.defensenews.com/global/europe/2019/05/06/russia-pitches-turkey-the-su-57-fighter-jet-if-f-35-deal-with-us-collapses/.

29 Raul (Pete) Pedrozo, 'Closing the Turkish Straits in Times of War', Lieber Institute at West Point, 3 March 2022, https://lieber.westpoint.edu/closing-turkish-straits-war/.

30 Humeyra Pamuk and Daphne Psaledakis, 'US Sanctions 5 Turkish Firms in Broad Russia Action on Over 150 Targets', Reuters, 14 September 2023, https://www.reuters.com/world/us-sanction-five-turkey-based-firms-broad-russia-action-2023-09-14/; and Ragip Soylu, 'Russian State Firm Signs $9.1bn Loan Deal to Fund Nuclear Plant in Turkey', Middle East Eye, 16 September 2022, https://www.middleeasteye.net/news/russia-turkey-gazprombank-akkuyu-plant-loan-fund.

31 Joel Gulhane, 'Al-Sisi, Putin Seek Stronger Ties in Sochi', *Daily News Egypt*, 12 August 2014, https://www.dailynewsegypt.com/2014/08/12/al-sisi-putin-seek-stronger-ties-sochi/.

32 Mark N. Katz, 'The Russia Factor in the Egyptian–American Relationship', Atlantic Council, 15 November 2013, https://www.atlanticcouncil.org/blogs/menasource/the-russia-factor-in-the-egyptian-american-relationship/; and Tatiana Kondratenko, 'Why Russia Exports Arms to Africa', Deutsche Welle, 29 May 2020, https://www.dw.com/en/russian-arms-exports-to-africa-moscows-long-term-strategy/a-53596471.

33. 'Russia to Help Build Egypt's First Nuclear Power Plant', France24, 10 February 2015, https://www.france24.com/en/20150210-russia-help-build-egypt-first-nuclear-power-plant-putin-sisi.

34. Said El Atiek and Stéphane Goutte, 'Impacts, Sustainability, and Resilience on the Egyptian Tourism and Hospitality Industry After the Russian Airplane Crash in 2015', HAL Portal SHS, 2023, p. 2, https://shs.hal.science/halshs-03917358.

35. Patrick Markey and Maria Tsvetkova, 'Putin, Egypt's Sisi Discuss Restart of Flights, Sign Nuclear Deal', Reuters, 11 December 2017, https://www.reuters.com/article/us-egypt-russia/putin-egypts-sisi-discuss-restart-of-flights-sign-nuclear-deal-idUSKBN1E51BR.

36. Ali Dizboni and Karim El-Baz, 'Understanding the Egyptian Military's Perspective on the Su-35 Deal', Washington Institute for Near East Policy, 15 July 2021, https://www.washingtoninstitute.org/policy-analysis/understanding-egyptian-militarys-perspective-su-35-deal.

37. Tim Martin, 'Suspected Collapse of Su-35 Deal Sees US Agree Egyptian F-15 Order', Shephard Media, 18 March 2022, https://www.shephardmedia.com/news/air-warfare/collapsed-su-35-deal-sees-us-agree-f-15-order-with/.

38. Evan Hill et al., 'Egypt Secretly Planned to Supply Rockets to Russia, Leaked U.S. Document Says', Washington Post, 10 April 2023, https://www.washingtonpost.com/national-security/2023/04/10/egypt-weapons-russia/.

39. Abdel Latif Wahba, 'Egypt Criticizes Russia for Ending Ukraine Grain-export Deal', Bloomberg, 20 July 2023, https://www.yahoo.com/news/egypt-talks-400-million-uae-102251608.html/.

40. Dan Bilefsky, 'For Rescue Line, Cyprus Prefers a Russian Loan', New York Times, 18 June 2012, https://www.nytimes.com/2012/06/19/world/europe/cyprus-counts-on-its-close-ties-to-russia.html.

41. 'Russia Has "Noted" Transformation in Cyprus' Leadership', Cyprus Mail, 18 January 2023, https://cyprus-mail.com/2023/01/18/russia-has-noted-transformation-in-cyprus-leadership/.

42. 'Four More Russian Billionaires Blacklisted by EU to Lose Cypriot Citizenship', RFE/RL, 21 April 2022, https://www.rferl.org/a/cyprus-russian-billionaires-passports/31814484.html.

43. Paul Tugwell and Georgios Georgiou, 'Cyprus Gas Discoveries Boosted by EU's Shift from Russia Supplies', Bloomberg, 25 July 2022, https://www.bloomberg.com/news/articles/2022-07-25/cyprus-gas-discoveries-boosted-by-eu-move-from-russia-supplies.

44. Alexander Baunov, 'Putin and the Greeks: The Limits of Orthodox Diplomacy', Carnegie Endowment for International Peace, 6 June 2016, https://carnegiemoscow.org/commentary/63729.

45. Kadri Liik, Momchil Metodiev and Nicu Popescu, 'Defender of the Faith? How Ukraine's Orthodox Split Threatens Russia', European Council on Foreign Relations, 30 May 2019, https://ecfr.eu/publication/defender_of_the_faith_how_ukraines_orthodox_split_threatens_russia.

46. Paul Stronski, 'A Difficult Balancing Act: Russia's Role in the Eastern Mediterranean', Carnegie Endowment for International Peace, 28 June 2021, https://carnegieendowment.org/2021/06/28/difficult-balancing-act-russia-s-role-in-eastern-mediterranean-pub-84847.

47. Helena Smith, 'Alexis Tsipras Calls Western Sanctions Against Russia "Road to Nowhere"', Guardian, 31 March 2015, https://www.theguardian.com/world/2015/mar/31/alexis-tsipras-greece-russia-relations.

48. 'Recalled Greek Ambassador to Leave Moscow in Late September – Source', TASS, 15 August 2018, https://tass.com/politics/1017295.

49. Georgia Nakou, 'Energy Without Russia: The Case of Greece', Friedrich-Ebert-Stiftung, 2023, https://library.fes.de/pdf-files/bueros/budapest/20476.pdf.

50. 'Greece 2023: Executive Summary', International Energy Agency, 2023, https://www.iea.org/reports/greece-2023/executive-summary.

51. 'Greece Doubles Pipeline Gas Imports from Russia', Energy Intelligence, 17 April 2024, https://www.energyintel.com/0000018e-ebec-d9cc-abce-fffe59b10000.

52. David Wessel, 'The Story Behind the Proposed Price Cap on Russian Oil', Brookings, 5 July 2022, https://www.brookings.edu/articles/the-story-behind-the-proposed-price-cap-on-russian-oil/.

53. Elisabeth Braw, 'How Greek Companies and Ghost Ships Are Helping Russia', Foreign Policy, 23 November 2022, https://foreignpolicy.com/2022/11/23/how-greek-companies-and-ghost-ships-are-helping-russia/.

54. Elisabeth Braw, 'Greece Is Making a Killing Selling Ships to Russia', Foreign Policy, 11 September 2023, https://foreignpolicy.com/2023/09/11/greece-russia-tankers-oil-sanctions/.

55. 'Russia Says It Is Surprised by Lebanon's Condemnation of Invasion', Reuters, 25 February 2022, https://www.reuters.com/world/russia-says-it-is-surprised-by-lebanons-condemnation-invasion-2022-02-25/.

56. Bassem Mroue, 'Qatar Replaces Russian Company in Lebanon Gas Exploration', Associated Press, 29 January 2023, https://apnews.com/article/israel-italy-qatar-lebanon-business-a216289f83f4da47542c1d56665e8a85.

An Israeli flag flies in front of shipping containers on the dockside at the Port of Haifa, Israel, on 5 November 2020. (Photo: Kobi Wolf/Bloomberg via Getty Images)

CHINA HAS INCREASED ITS INFLUENCE in the Eastern Mediterranean over the past decade. It has taken advantage of the region's vast financial needs, interest in joining connectivity projects, and political frustration with Western partners and hedging behaviour among Arab states partners to gain a foothold in Europe's immediate neighbourhood.

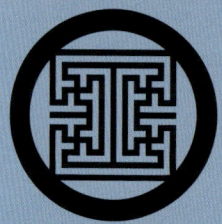

BEIJING HAS NOT ARTICULATED a comprehensive strategy towards the region, has kept its relations mainly transactional and has cautiously set low expectations. If its diplomatic, economic and military footprint remains modest, it has opportunistically sought to capitalise on Western failures and entanglements, including the Israel–Hamas war.

IN A CONTEXT OF INTENSIFYING great-power competition, China's investments in strategic infrastructure and technology companies at the doors of Europe are now seen as challenging Western countries' interests. In response, China's geopolitical rivals have designed new connectivity projects to entice Eastern Mediterranean and Gulf countries.

CHAPTER NINETEEN
CHINA IN THE EASTERN MEDITERRANEAN: SMALL BUT GROWING PRESENCE

INTRODUCTION

In recent years, China has showed interest in playing a more overt political and security role in regions located far from its direct neighbourhood. It opened its first overseas base in Djibouti in 2017, conducted naval exercises in the Eastern Mediterranean and successfully mediated the Saudi–Iranian rapprochement in March 2023. In 2022–23, the launch of China's Global Development, Global Security and Global Civilization initiatives signalled Beijing's ambition to play a normative leadership role. Its alignment with Russia in challenging the Western-led global order also adds a new geopolitical dimension to its presence in the Eastern Mediterranean, in which China is a discreet player. This is not a priority theatre for Beijing, whose stakes in the region's energy resources are minimal and whose investments – except in Israel – remain relatively limited. Consistent with its traditional foreign-policy principle of non-interference, China has long been cautious to avoid entanglements in the Middle East's complex geopolitics.

Nevertheless, over the past decade, along with broader shifts in its foreign policy and rising global ambitions, Beijing has gradually deepened its economic, political and security footprint in the Eastern Mediterranean. Taking advantage of the region's vast financial needs and of political frustrations towards Western partners, China is slowly gaining a foothold in a fragile but strategic region in the direct neighbourhood of Europe. The Eastern Mediterranean offers several points of interest for Beijing. Egypt's Suez Canal is a key maritime choke point on global trade routes linking Europe to Asia. Israel is well positioned in the global race for emerging technologies. Syria and Turkiye are important partners in Beijing's counter-terrorism and repression efforts against Uyghur fighters and other dissidents. The Eastern Mediterranean also represents a useful door into European markets and NATO's southern flank.

However, China has yet to articulate a coherent and comprehensive strategy for the Eastern Mediterranean and has kept its relations with the region mainly transactional. Chinese media, academic articles and government websites rarely define the Eastern Mediterranean as a coherent region, rather approaching each subregion separately – Europe, West Asia and North Africa.[1] In many Eastern Mediterranean countries, the hopes generated by China's Belt and Road Initiative (BRI) led to disappointment and frustrations. In the context of the conflict in Ukraine, some of them have realigned themselves more closely with the United States and Europe, shrinking the space for China's influence.

A DISCREET BUT EMERGING PLAYER

China's connections with Eastern Mediterranean countries are not recent. In the 1950s, Beijing already enjoyed good relations with Egypt, Libya, the Palestine Liberation Organization and Syria within the framework of the Non-Aligned Movement. It was also a notable arms provider to Egypt and Israel in the 1980s. However, relations always remained in the shadow of European and US influence. China has traditionally been reluctant to get involved in the politics of a region considered complex, dangerous and remote from Chinese core interests.

Over the past two decades, China's economic boom and the launch of the BRI in 2013 gave new impetus to Beijing's engagement with the region. For China and Chinese companies, the primary objective of the BRI is to promote the export of Chinese-manufactured goods and excess industrial capacity to the developing world. Countries like Turkiye and Egypt, with large populations and infrastructure-development needs, stand as interesting export markets. But more importantly, they serve as useful entry points into broader regional markets such as Africa for Egypt[2] or Europe for Greece. For most Eastern Mediterranean countries, which struggle with recurring economic difficulties, the BRI represents an opportunity to attract much-needed Chinese loans and investments.

The Eastern Mediterranean is located at the crossroads of land and maritime trade routes connecting Asia to Europe. Beijing has identified the Suez Canal in Egypt, through which 12% of global seaborne trade passes, as being of particular strategic importance to its Maritime Silk Road (see Map 19.1). Sixty per cent of Chinese exports to Europe pass through the canal, and Chinese ships account for around 10% of the annual traffic volume.[3] Over the past 15 years, Chinese companies, supported by Chinese bank loans, took part in multiple infrastructure and industrial projects around the Suez Canal economic zone and in key Mediterranean ports. In 2008, the Chinese municipality of Tianjin established the China–Egypt TEDA Suez Economic and Trade Cooperation Zone,

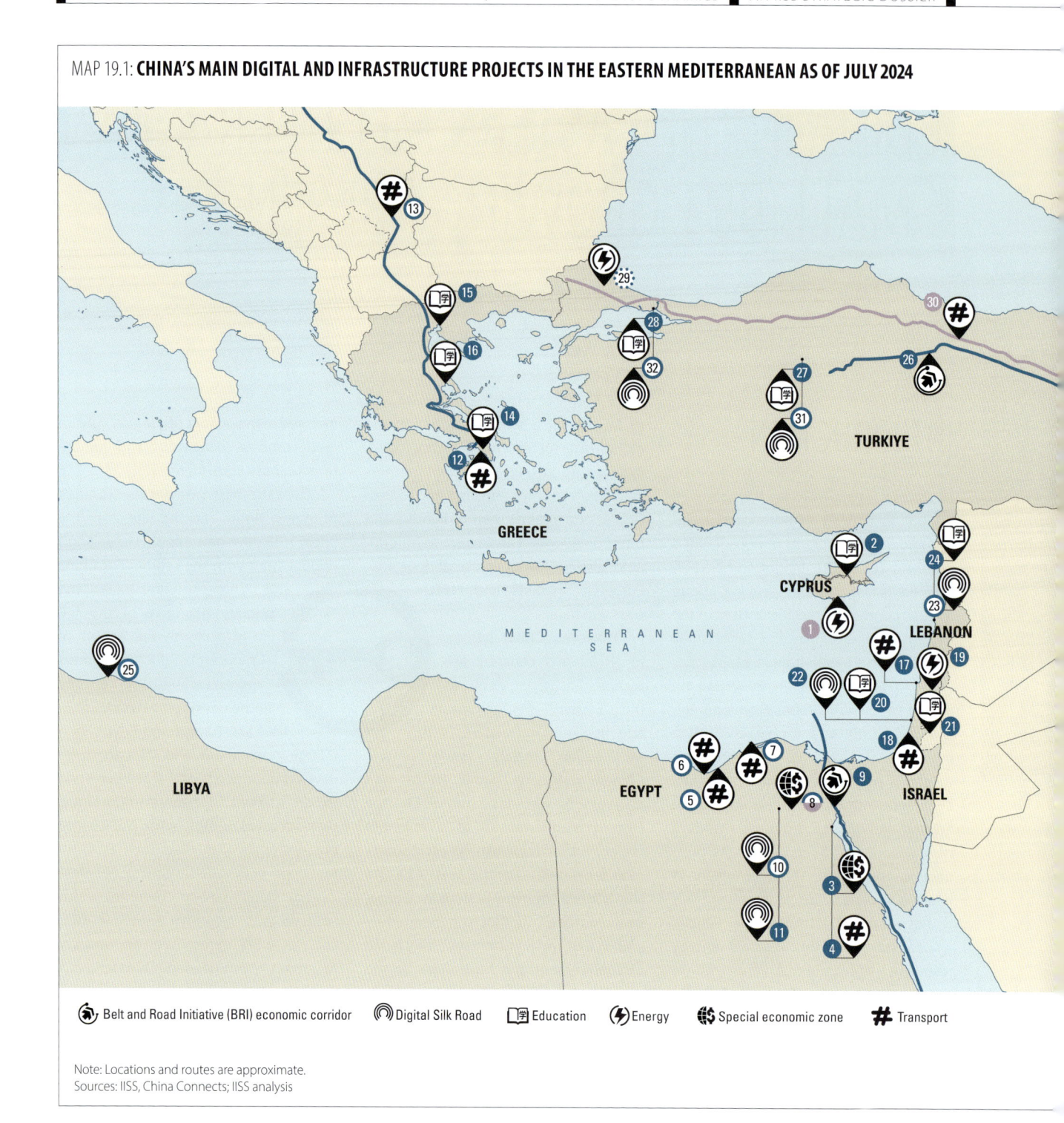

MAP 19.1: **CHINA'S MAIN DIGITAL AND INFRASTRUCTURE PROJECTS IN THE EASTERN MEDITERRANEAN AS OF JULY 2024**

Belt and Road Initiative (BRI) economic corridor | Digital Silk Road | Education | Energy | Special economic zone | Transport

Note: Locations and routes are approximate.
Sources: IISS, China Connects; IISS analysis

which benefitted from strong Chinese government backing and funding. The project, which became a flagship BRI initiative in the region, aimed to attract up to US$5 billion in industrial investments around the Suez Canal. By the end of 2020, the cooperation zone had attracted 96 enterprises, with combined investments of over US$1.25bn,[4] and in March 2023, a new industrial agreement worth US$5bn was pledged.

Chinese companies have been involved in other key infrastructure and port projects across the Eastern Mediterranean, such as the Piraeus Container Terminal in Greece, the Alexandria and El-Dekheila ports in Egypt, and the Ashdod and Haifa ports in Israel. In Greece, the China Ocean Shipping Company (COSCO) obtained in 2009 a 35-year concession to operate two piers at the Piraeus Container Terminal following Greece's financial crisis. It continued investing in the port's development, purchased a majority stake in 2016, and bought a 60% stake in the

1	Liquefied natural gas (LNG) terminal		15	Confucius Institute at Aristotle University of Thessaloniki
2	Confucius Institute at the University of Cyprus		16	Confucius Institute at University of Thessaly
3	Tianjin Economic-Technological Development Area (TEDA), Suez Canal Economic Zone		17	Construction and operation of Bayport by Shanghai International Port Group
4	New container terminal constructed by China Harbour Engineering Company (CHEC) (US$520 million)		18	Construction of South Port by subsidiary of CHEC
5	Development of new container terminal by Hutchinson Ports		19	373 MW oil-fired power plant, partially owned by subsidiary of CHEC
6	Operation of container terminal by Hutchinson Ports		20	Confucius Institute at Tel Aviv University
7	Development and operation of container terminal by Hutchinson Ports in partnership with the Egyptian Navy (US$730m joint investment)		21	Confucius Institute at Hebrew University of Jerusalem
			22	US$300m smart-city fund launched by tech company Kuang-Chi
8	New Administrative Capital (Cairo) • Phase 1: US$3 billion, contracted by China State Construction Engineering Corporation • Phase 2: estimated US$20bn, contracted by China Fortune Land Development Company; cancelled in 2018		23	Development of 5G network with Huawei
			24	Confucius Institute at Saint Joseph University of Beirut
			25	Development of 4G network with Huawei
			26	China–Central Asia–West Asia economic corridor
9	Maritime Silk Road		27	Confucius Institute at Middle East Technical University
10	Development of 5G network with Huawei		28	Confucius Institute at Bogazici University, Istanbul Okan University and Yeditepe University
11	Launch of Huawei's OpenLab		29	Nuclear-power plant
12	Operation and majority ownership of port by COSCO Shipping		30	High-speed rail route
13	Planned rail route from Budapest to the Port of Piraeus, as part of the China–Europe Land–Sea Express Route		31	Development of 5G network with Huawei
14	Business Confucius Institute at Athens University of Economics and Business		32	Smart City infrastructure project involving Huawei

○ Under negotiation   ○ Under development   ● Operational   ● Cancelled

and the Beirut–Tripoli railway in Lebanon, never materialised.[9]

Between 2010 and 2021, trade volumes between China and the Eastern Mediterranean more than doubled from US$45.9bn to US$96.5bn, mainly led by growing trade with Egypt, Israel and Turkiye (see Figure 19.1).[10] But this trade remains largely unbalanced in favour of China, with the volume of Chinese exports towards the region more than four times bigger than imports.

The country attracting the most Chinese investments in the region is Israel. Between 2010 and 2017, Chinese FDI stocks in Israel jumped from US$22 million to over US$4bn, mainly directed at Israel's start-up ecosystem and technology companies.[11] According to a report by Israel's IVC Research Center, Chinese companies invested between US$500m and US$600m per year in Israeli technology start-ups in 2015–17, representing around 12% of all capital raised by Israeli start-ups during that period.[12] In a context of growing global competition for emerging technologies, China's objective is to foster the transfer of technologies and accelerate its own emergence as a technological power. In recent years, however, those investments declined slightly after the US put significant pressure on Israel to limit the risk of transferring sensitive technologies to China.

From a political perspective, China sees in the Eastern Mediterranean an opportunity to make headway at a relatively low cost in a region where the most powerful states (Egypt, Israel and Turkiye) have been traditionally close to the West and are located in Europe's immediate neighbourhood. The Eastern Mediterranean, which includes weak countries such as Lebanon, Libya, Syria and the Palestinian Territories, is Europe's soft underbelly and an arena for geopolitical competition. Migrant flows and terrorist threats coming from the southern shore of the Mediterranean directly impact Europe's internal politics and have created friction between Europe and its Eastern Mediterranean partners. Some countries in the region are close security partners of the West. Egypt, Israel and Turkiye receive advanced US and European weapons. Turkiye is a NATO member and has shown during the conflict in Ukraine how it could leverage its membership

Greek railway company Piraeus Europe Asia Rail Logistics (PEARL) in 2019. In 2014, then-premier of China, Li Kenqiang, declared that China saw Greek ports as a 'gateway to Europe'.[5]

Beyond a few flagship projects, Chinese foreign direct investments (FDI) in the Eastern Mediterranean have generally remained low, limited by the region's economic difficulties and political instability (see Figure 19.2). In 2021, China accounted for only 1% of the total FDI entering Eastern Mediterranean economies.[6] Chinese loans, despite a sharp increase over the past decade, appear marginal when compared to loans coming from other key lenders. In Turkiye, Egypt and Syria, Chinese loans represented respectively only 0.4%, 3.2% and 1.5% of their total external debts in 2022.[7] In 2024, Egypt's debt to China amounted to US$8.8bn, or 5.5% of the country's total stock.[8] In highly unstable countries such as Lebanon, Libya and Syria, hopes that China would invest in local industries and infrastructure, such as the port of Tripoli

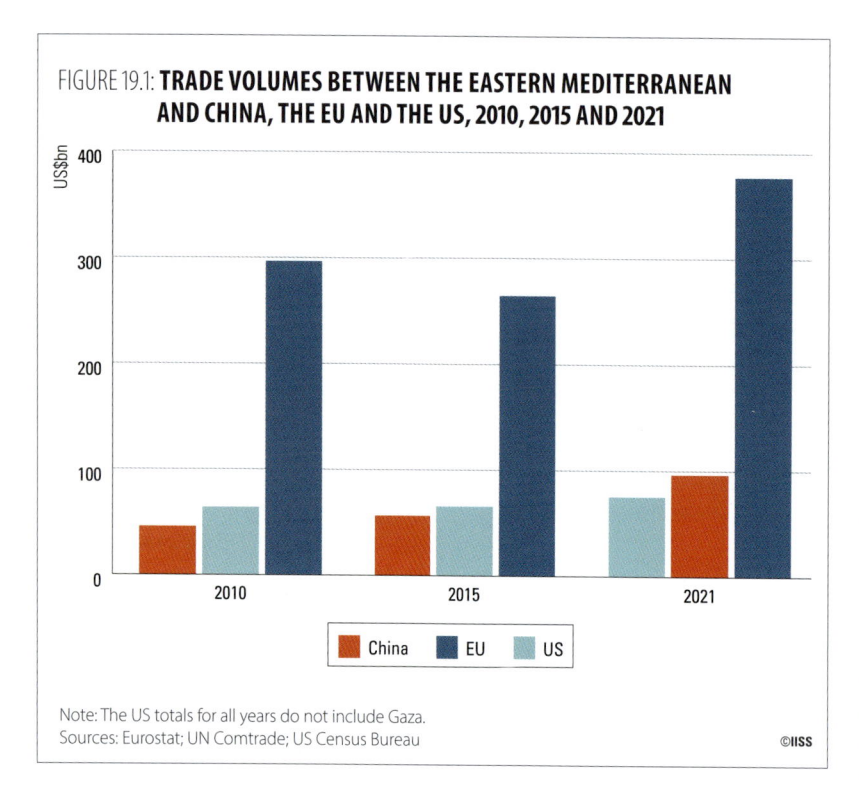

FIGURE 19.1: TRADE VOLUMES BETWEEN THE EASTERN MEDITERRANEAN AND CHINA, THE EU AND THE US, 2010, 2015 AND 2021

Note: The US totals for all years do not include Gaza.
Sources: Eurostat; UN Comtrade; US Census Bureau

GEOSTRATEGIC AND SECURITY IMPLICATIONS OF CHINA'S PRESENCE

China's emergence in the Eastern Mediterranean has been met with suspicion in Western capitals. The growing naval presence of the People's Liberation Army Navy (PLAN) and the involvement of Chinese companies in strategic infrastructure projects in this busy maritime space raises questions about Beijing's intentions in the region.

Recent Chinese policies have blurred the line between commercial and military activities abroad, creating concerns that China's strategic investments could be weaponised in case of a future escalation with the US. China has passed laws such as the 2010 National Defence Mobilisation Law and the 2016 National Defence Transportation Law, which require Chinese transportation companies located abroad to provide logistical support to People's Liberation Army (PLA) operations overseas.[15] The 2018 National Intelligence Law legally obliges Chinese citizens, organisations and organs to comply with national intelligence work.[16]

As a result, Western experts and officials have debated whether the involvement of Chinese companies in the development and management of critical port infrastructures could present a risk of espionage, access denial or leverage for the use of the facilities by the PLAN.[17] The port of Haifa, for instance, which regularly hosts the US Fifth and Sixth fleets, became a point of friction between the US and Israel after China's state-owned Shanghai International Port Group (SIPG) was granted in 2015 a tender to operate a terminal.[18] In early 2020, the US intervened to make Israel decline a Chinese bid for a highly strategic desalination plant that was planned to be built near a military base.[19] Washington also convinced Israel to create a foreign-investment screening system, designed to give particular attention to Chinese investments.

Similar concerns have been raised about the growing presence of Chinese technology companies in the

to push its interests against the majority view within NATO.[13]

Eastern Mediterranean countries have in turn seen in China an opportunity to balance their relations with their traditional European or US partners, and to increase their political margin of manoeuvre, especially in times of economic crisis. They have been particularly proactive at developing their ties with China in the past decade. Greece's then-prime minister Alexis Tsipras and Turkiye's President Recep Tayyip Erdoğan attended the first Belt and Road Forum in Beijing in 2017 in person, and Egypt's President Abdel Fattah al-Sisi attended the second forum in 2019. Over the past ten years, Erdoğan has paid four visits to China, and Sisi six since his election in 2014.

Egypt, Turkiye and other countries have been particularly keen to display their emerging ties with Beijing when Western countries have pressed them over their human-rights records or on their economic situation. Egypt's President Sisi has cultivated China when faced with US and European criticism of domestic repression and calls for the suspension of military assistance. Greece courted China after the 2009 debt crisis put considerable strain on its relations with Brussels. In 2018, the injection of Chinese investments into the Turkish market helped alleviate the devaluation of the Turkish lira.[14]

development of the region's digital infrastructure. ZTE and Huawei have signed 4G or 5G agreements with telecoms operators in all Eastern Mediterranean countries, except Israel. They have cooperated on smart-city projects, developed data centres and submarine cables, and provided surveillance technologies. China's 'Digital Silk Road' raised concerns in Western policy circles that widespread Chinese technological equipment could be used for intelligence-gathering purposes. In 2020, the US reportedly stipulated that the basing of a major US Navy ship in Greece was conditional on the banning of Huawei from the country's 5G networks, and pressured Athens to join its 'Clean Network Initiative'.[20] In Israel, where Chinese companies have invested significantly in technology start-ups, the close military relationship between Israel and the US and the porosity between the technology and defence ecosystems have caused alarm in Washington over the risk of digital espionage from Chinese entities and the potential access to dual-use US technologies.[21] The US, however, has had limited success in constraining Israel's technological cooperation with China. China has even shown interest in selling nuclear-energy technology in the region. Turkiye is in discussions with China National Nuclear Corporation Overseas and State Power Investment Cooperation regarding a potential nuclear plant in the region of Thrace.[22]

In the meantime, China has slowly expanded its conventional military presence in the region to protect its economic assets and secure passage around the strategic maritime route. In 2006 and 2011, Chinese civil naval assets conducted the first overseas repatriation missions of Chinese nationals in the region, from Lebanon and Libya respectively. The PLAN began anti-piracy operations in the Gulf of Aden in 2008 to escort merchant ships through the Suez Canal. Supported by the opening of its first overseas base in Djibouti in 2017, it gradually expanded its footprint in the region, conducting bilateral naval drills with Egypt and Russia in May and September 2015, live-fire drills in the Mediterranean in July 2017, and anti-piracy exercises with Egypt in August 2019.

The PLA also takes part in a few multilateral security operations around the Eastern Mediterranean. It has contributed 400 troops to the UN peacekeeping force in Lebanon since 2006 and supported the dismantlement of the Syrian chemical-weapons programme in 2014. A major Chinese interest has been the monitoring of several thousand Chinese Uyghur foreign fighters in Syria and Iraq.

While local and Western countries initially encouraged this enhanced military presence as providing an additional layer of security – for instance, the PLAN took part in anti-piracy exercises with NATO in the Gulf of Aden in 2015[23] – they now increasingly view it in the context of the growing US–China rivalry. The use of China's naval presence in the Eastern Mediterranean and the Red Sea remains very calibrated: PLAN naval assets present in theatre were not deployed to protect maritime traffic when Ansarullah (Houthi movement) began to disrupt it in October 2023. This reflects China's reluctance to take on regional security responsibilities and to raise the expectations of its local partners that it may do so, but gradually builds up Beijing's ability to project power around strategic global maritime choke points far from its territory.

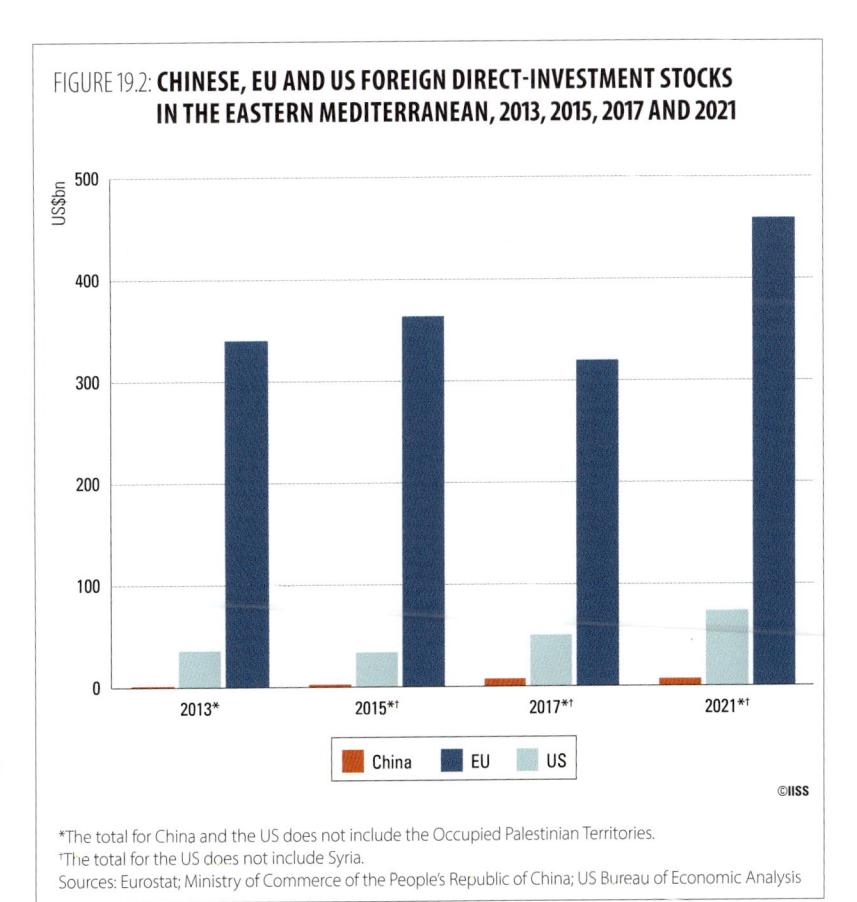

FIGURE 19.2: **CHINESE, EU AND US FOREIGN DIRECT-INVESTMENT STOCKS IN THE EASTERN MEDITERRANEAN, 2013, 2015, 2017 AND 2021**

*The total for China and the US does not include the Occupied Palestinian Territories.
†The total for the US does not include Syria.
Sources: Eurostat; Ministry of Commerce of the People's Republic of China; US Bureau of Economic Analysis

On a few occasions, the PLAN's presence in the Eastern Mediterranean even took a more political turn. In 2012, the passing of a PLAN escort fleet through the Suez Canal, just as Russia dispatched 11 warships to the Mediterranean, was interpreted as a quiet sign of support from Beijing to Russia's operations in Syria.[24] Three years later, China's joint naval exercises with Russia in the Mediterranean took place at a time when Russia was stepping up its military involvement in Syria and China was backing Russia's vetoes of United Nations Security Council (UNSC) resolutions on Syria. However, such displays of alignment in the Eastern Mediterranean have not yet led to much deeper security cooperation in the region between China and Russia.

A PATIENT, CAUTIOUS AND GRADUAL APPROACH

Despite this growing footprint in the region, Beijing has so far refrained from articulating a comprehensive strategy. It has chosen a patient, cautious and gradual approach to avoid entanglements or creating undue expectations about its role. China has been reluctant to get involved in regional politics beyond diplomatic facilitation to escape any military obligation. As elsewhere, China has viewed regional issues through the lens of its own priorities rather than the larger public good and the specific interests of its interlocutors. For example, while it has vocally supported the government of Bashar al-Assad during the Syrian civil war and provided political cover at the UNSC, China has avoided investing in Syria because of the unfavourable conditions and high risk of doing so. This has disappointed Damascus, which expected greater economic and humanitarian assistance and viewed its geographical position as appealing to Beijing.

The Israeli–Palestinian issue is the only regional file on which Beijing has expressed relative interest. It proposed a Four-Point Peace Plan in 2013 and hosted talks in Beijing in 2017. In April 2023, it offered again to play a mediation role.[25] However, these initiatives never led to any tangible result and Beijing showed no readiness to invest the necessary diplomatic capital in the process. But its interest grew considerably after the start of the Israel–Hamas war in October 2023. China has been

(Front row, L-R) Chinese Politburo Standing Committee member Cai Qi, Bahraini King Hamad bin Isa Al Khalifa, Egyptian President Abdel Fattah al-Sisi, Chinese President Xi Jinping, UAE President Sheikh Mohamed bin Zayed Al Nahyan, Tunisian President Kais Saied and Chinese Foreign Minister Wang Yi pose ahead of the opening ceremony of the 10th Ministerial Meeting of the China–Arab States Cooperation Forum at the Diaoyutai State Guesthouse in Beijing, China, on 30 May 2024. (Photo: Jade Gao/Pool via Getty Images)

diplomatically active, vocally denouncing Israel's campaign in Gaza and clashing with the US at the UN Security Council. It also hosted several meetings of Palestinian factions, including Hamas and Palestinian Islamic Jihad, with the ostensible aim of promoting unity. In doing so, China has insisted it was a mere facilitator rather than a mediator or an architect. This light touch is in line with its main Middle Eastern diplomatic achievement, the de-escalation of tensions between Iran and Saudi Arabia; China hosted the parties for talks but declined to monitor or enforce their agreement. In May 2024, China hosted an international conference with Arab leaders during which President Xi Jinping called for the establishment of a Palestinian state and announced a 500m-yuan (US$69m) humanitarian-assistance package.[26] Nevertheless, Israel remains one of China's main interlocutors and investment destinations in the region. Despite its strident criticism of Israel, Beijing has refrained from suspending diplomatic relations or introducing sanctions. In the long term, Israel itself may decide to relegate the relationship and limit Chinese investments in its economy as payback for China's support for the Palestinians. The conflict appears to have primarily provided an opportunity for China to highlight and criticise Western policies as tensions intensify over a number of issues unrelated to the Palestinian cause, and, importantly, to assert its leadership of the Global South by promoting a narrative of Western hypocrisy.

Beyond this, China has remained strikingly absent from recent debates around gas disputes in the Eastern Mediterranean and on Turkish–Greek tensions. Beijing views the Cyprus question primarily through the lens of its own Taiwan issue. While its position in favour of the Republic of Cyprus aligns with that of the international community, the issue also gives China an opportunity to oppose revisionist, pro-independence tendencies, echoing Taiwan's claim for independence.[27]

On many occasions, Beijing has leveraged its economic and political influence to secure support from Eastern Mediterranean countries on issues such as Taiwan or the Uyghurs. In the 2000s, for example, the development of China–Cyprus relations was immediately followed by public expressions of support for China by Cyprus and Greece on the Taiwan issue and on the European Union's arms ban,[28] suggesting that Beijing had imposed this as a condition for the rapprochement. On the Uyghurs issue, in 2019 Egypt, the State of Palestine and Syria – all of whose relations with China were improving while those with the US were deteriorating – were among the signatories of a letter of support for China's policies in Xinjiang addressed to the UN Human Rights Council.[29] Conversely, when Turkiye criticised China for its treatment of the Uyghurs, Beijing retaliated immediately by condemning Ankara over the Kurdish issue.[30] After a period of stormy relations with Ankara, China finally obtained the signature in 2017 of an extradition treaty with Turkiye, which is still pending ratification. It later invested more money in Turkiye to buy Turkish silence on Xinjiang in future. In Cyprus, a similar deal went into effect in 2020,[31] and in Egypt, increasing crackdowns on the Uyghur minority have been reported by Human Rights Watch.[32]

Despite the reiterated 'win–win cooperation' narrative surrounding the BRI, the overall figures of Chinese investments in the Eastern Mediterranean are disappointing, and their impact on regional countries' development very questionable. In Egypt, the Chinese-funded US$59bn New Administrative Capital is decried by many observers as a vanity project that will neither benefit the population nor boost the economy.[33] Due to the tendency of Chinese companies to employ their own migrant workers, Chinese investments in infrastructure projects have had a limited impact on local job creation and transfer of know-how to the region. After a rapid growth between 2013 and 2017, China's economic involvement in the Eastern Mediterranean has slowed down in recent years, and even contracted in certain countries. This follows a trend of declining BRI financing around the globe, further accelerated by the COVID-19 pandemic.

Recently, the repercussions of the COVID-19 pandemic and the war in Ukraine have further eroded China's influence in the Eastern Mediterranean. Meanwhile, the united response of the US and the EU to the war in Ukraine trumped the narrative of a Western decline. The willingness of European powers to invest in Eastern Mediterranean gas solutions to alleviate the loss of Russian energy created a new impetus. China's desire to regain the initiative partly explains why it has been particularly vocal in its condemnation of Western support for the Israeli campaign in Gaza.

Finally, escalating tensions between Greece and Turkiye pushed Greece to reprioritise its security partnership with the US, to the detriment of its relationship with China. In September 2020, then-secretary of state of the US Mike Pompeo visited Greece to state his support for Athens and announce the expansion of the US naval presence in Greece; he also demanded guarantees from Greece that it would ban Huawei from its 5G networks.[34] The two countries upgraded their Mutual Defense Cooperation Agreement the following year. While Greece is cautious not to close the door to China, Chinese investments will have little weight in comparison with hard security guarantees from the US.

OUTLOOK

Despite its increased profile, Beijing is not a major player in the Eastern Mediterranean. But as its global ambitions continue to grow and global competition intensifies, the Eastern Mediterranean may feature more prominently on its list of priorities.

China benefits from the local powers' keenness to hedge and diversify away from traditional Western partners. Countries such as Egypt and Turkiye have welcomed the advent of a multipolar world, and see China as a demanding and inevitable interlocutor on a wide range of issues. China was an advocate of the expansion of the BRICS grouping, which Egypt was invited to join in 2023 and in which Turkiye has shown some interest. By expanding soft competition and information warfare to regions where the US is entangled and on the back foot, China secures local support at low cost. It will consider carefully whether to align more with Russia in the Eastern Mediterranean:

Russia's influence in the region's troubled countries such as Libya and Syria but also in Turkiye and Egypt surpasses that of China at present. Russia is also more at risk of an accidental confrontation with the US given their concomitant presence in Syria and greater Iranian–Russian security cooperation. In contrast, Beijing remains eager to avoid any such risk.

The key concern for Beijing has been the management of local expectations. China has shown no appetite for acting as a guarantor of security arrangements and has not proposed alternative local or regional governance structures. Local players have so far accepted this approach, focusing their demands on the US. But as the US reorients its attention and resources, expectations of China may grow.

There are also dangers that China will have to manage. The disruption of maritime traffic in the Red Sea due to Houthi attacks on vessels since October 2023 could in the long term increase the cost of trade between China and Europe. In addition to providing escorts to Chinese ships, China has communicated through Iran to the Houthis that targeting them should be avoided. Its efforts have been solely focused on Chinese interests, not on securing maritime trade for all.

China will also face greater geo-economic competition in the broader Middle East. While appealing, China's offer is in competition with others and Eastern Mediterranean countries have looked favourably at projects that either exclude or overlap with China's. The US, India and several European states have described the India–Middle East–Europe Economic Corridor (IMEC), unveiled in September 2023, as a geo-economic response to China's BRI. While currently frozen due to the Hamas–Israel war, IMEC represents ways rivals of China such as India and partners of China such as Saudi Arabia can pursue projects alongside Chinese interests. Whether China will in turn invest in competing routes will reveal its appetite for greater involvement in the region.

ENDNOTES

1 The countries fall between different departments of the Ministry of Foreign Affairs and belong to various regional cooperation platforms. Greece is part of the 16+1 cooperation group focused on Central and Eastern European countries; Egypt, Libya, Lebanon, Palestine and Syria are grouped into the China–Arab States Cooperation Forum (CASCF); and Egypt and Libya also belong to the Forum on China–Africa Cooperation (FOCAC).

2 'Know About Major Trade Agreements Linking Egypt with Africa', EgyptToday, 23 August 2021, https://www.egypttoday.com/Article/3/107171/Know-about-major-trade-agreements-linking-Egypt-with-Africa.

3 'Suez Canal Blocking Could Hike Freight Fees Between China and Europe if Not Cleared Soon: Analyst', *Global Times*, 24 March 2021, https://www.globaltimes.cn/page/202103/1219372.shtml.

4 Li Kun, Song Rui and Wu Danni, 'Five Years On, Suez Flagship Project Tells Story of Dynamic China–Egypt Cooperation', Xinhua, 24 January 2021, http://www.xinhuanet.com/english/2021-01/24/c_139693564.htm.

5 'Greece Seeks Role as China's Gateway to Europe', Reuters, 20 June 2014, https://www.reuters.com/article/greece-china-assets-idCNL6N0P14DW20140620.

6 UN Trade & Development (UNCTAD), Statistics, https://unctadstat.unctad.org/datacentre/dataviewer/US.GDPTotal; and People's Republic of China, Ministry of Commerce, 'Statistical Bulletin of China's Outward Foreign Direct Investment', 2022.

7 World Bank, 'International Debt Statistics', https://datatopics.worldbank.org/debt/ids/.

8 Central Bank of Egypt, 'External Position of the Egyptian Economy', July/March 2023/2024, https://www.cbe.org.eg/-/media/project/cbe/listing/research/position/external-position-85.pdf.

9 'China Interested in Lebanon's Infrastructure Projects', *Global Times*, 3 March 2019; A. Ghiselli and M. Al-Sudairi, 'Syria's "China Dream": Between the Narratives and Realities', King Faisal Center for Research and Islamic Studies, 15 September 2019; and C. Cornish and A. Zhang, 'Lebanese Port Eyes China as It Sells Itself as Hub for Syria', *Financial Times*, 3 January 2019, https://www.ft.com/content/386b3fd2-01db-11e9-99df-6183d3002ee1.

10 UN Comtrade Database, https://comtradeplus.un.org/.

11 People's Republic of China, Ministry of Commerce, 'Statistical Bulletin of China's Outward Foreign Direct Investment', 2022.

12 Gil Press, 'China and Israel: A Perfect Match, Growing Steady', Forbes, 26 February 2018, https://www.forbes.com/sites/gilpress/2018/02/26/china-and-israel-a-perfect-match-growing-steady/#10ff8a345ec9.

13 Aslı Aydıntaşbaş, 'Turkiye, NATO, and the Ukraine War: Why Erdogan's Grievances Are About More than Sweden and Finland', European Council on Foreign Relations, 16 May 2022, https://ecfr.eu/article/turkey-nato-and-the-ukraine-war-why-erdogans-grievances-are-about-more-than-sweden-and-finland/.

14 Matt Clinch, 'China Backs Turkiye to Overcome Its Economic Crisis', CNBC, 17 August 2018, https://www.cnbc.com/2018/08/17/china-backs-Turkiye-to-overcome-its-economic-crisis.html.

15 Conor M. Kennedy, 'China Maritime Report No. 4: Civil Transport in PLA Power Projection', CMSI, December 2019, https://digital-commons.usnwc.edu/cmsi-maritime-reports/4/; and 'Law of the People's Republic of China on National Defense Transportation', Chinalawinfo Database, http://lawinfochina.com/display.aspx?lib=law&id=22581.

16 The National People's Congress of the People's Republic of China, '中华人民共和国国家情报法', 中国人大网' [National Intelligence Law of the People's Republic of China], 12 June 2018, http://www.npc.gov.cn/npc/c30834/201806/483221713dac4f31bda7f9d951108912.shtml.

17 US House of Representatives, 'Hearing: China's Maritime Silk Road Initiative: Implications for the Global Maritime Supply Chain', 17 October 2019, https://docs.house.gov/Committee/Calendar/ByEvent.aspx?EventID=109805.

18 Arie Egozi, 'US Presses Israel on Haifa Port amid China Espionage Concerns: Sources', Breaking Defense, 5 October 2021, https://breakingdefense.com/2021/10/us-presses-israel-on-haifa-port-amid-china-espionage-concerns-sources/.

19 Felicia Schwartz, 'Amid U.S. Pressure, Israel Rejects Chinese Bid for Major Infrastructure Project', *Wall Street Journal*, 26 May 2020, https://www.wsj.com/articles/amid-u-s-pressure-israel-rejects-chinese-bid-for-major-infrastructure-project-11590502529.

20 Giannis Seferiadis, 'Greece Joins "Anti-Huawei Camp" as US Seals Stronger Ties', Nikkei Asia, 5 October 2020, https://asia.nikkei.com/Spotlight/Huawei-crackdown/Greece-joins-anti-Huawei-camp-as-US-seals-stronger-ties.

21 David Gordon and Meia Nouwens (eds), *The Digital Silk Road: China's Technological Rise and the Geopolitics of Cyberspace* (Abingdon: Routledge for the IISS, 2022).

22 'Turkey, China Discuss Mining, Nuclear, Renewable Energy During Minister's Visit', Reuters, 21 May 2024, https://www.reuters.com/markets/commodities/turkey-china-discuss-mining-nuclear-renewable-energy-during-ministers-visit-2024-05-21/.

23 'China Navy Holds First Joint Anti-piracy Drill with NATO', Reuters, 27 November 2015, https://www.reuters.com/article/us-china-nato-idUSKBN0TG08H20151127.

24 J. Michael Cole, 'China's Navy in the Mediterranean?', *Diplomat*, 30 July 2012, https://thediplomat.com/2012/07/whys-chinas-navy-in-the-mediterranen/.

25 Guy Burton, 'China's Offer to Mediate in the Israel–Palestine Conflict Is Overstated – For Now', *Diplomat*, 26 April 2023, https://thediplomat.com/2023/04/chinas-offer-to-mediate-in-the-israel-palestine-conflict-is-overstated-for-now/.

26 'Xi Pledges More Gaza Aid at Chinese Summit with Arab Leaders', PBS News, 30 May 2024, https://www.pbs.org/newshour/world/xi-pledges-more-gaza-aid-at-chinese-summit-with-arab-leaders.

27 Kadir Temiz, 'An Illustration of Sino-Turkish Relations: The Cyprus Question', *Insight Turkiye*, vol. 20, no. 1, 1 January 2018, pp. 81–98, https://doi.org/10.25253/99.2018201.06.

28 Ibid.

29 United Nations, 'Joint Letter to the President of the Human Rights Council', 12 July 2019, https://digitallibrary.un.org/record/3853509#record-files-collapse-header.

30 Nurettin Akcay, 'Amid Tensions with Turkey, China Is Putting the Kurdish Issue in Play', *Diplomat*, 4 December 2021, https://thediplomat.com/2021/12/amid-tensions-with-Turkiye-china-is-putting-the-kurdish-issue-in-play/.

31 Safeguard Defenders, 'China Expands System of Extradition Treaties', 25 January 2023, https://safeguarddefenders.com/en/blog/china-expands-system-extradition-treaties.

32 Human Rights Watch, 'Egypt: Don't Deport Uyghurs to China: Muslim Minority Face Jail, Torture if Forcibly Returned', 7 July 2017, https://www.hrw.org/news/2017/07/08/egypt-dont-deport-uyghurs-china.

33 Grady McGregor, 'China Emerges as Lead Funder for Egypt's New Administrative City', Al-Monitor, 20 December 2022, https://www.al-monitor.com/originals/2022/12/china-emerges-lead-funder-egypts-new-administrative-city.

34 Seferiadis, 'Greece Joins "Anti-Huawei Camp" as US Seals Stronger Ties'.

Strategic Dossiers (Print ISSN 2837-7710, Online ISSN 2837-7729) is published annually for a total of one issue per year by Taylor & Francis Group, 4 Park Square, Milton Park, Abingdon, Oxon, OX14 4RN, UK.

Send address changes to Taylor & Francis Customer Services, Informa UK Ltd., Sheepen Place, Colchester, Essex CO3 3LP, UK.

Subscription records are maintained at Taylor & Francis Group, 4 Park Square, Milton Park, Abingdon, OX14 4RN, UK.

Subscription information: For more information and subscription rates, please see tandfonline.com/pricing/journal/tstd). Taylor & Francis journals are available in a range of different packages, designed to suit every library's needs and budget. This journal is available for institutional subscriptions with online only or print & online options. This journal may also be available as part of our libraries, subject collections, or archives. For more information on our sales packages, please visit: librarianresources.taylorandfrancis.com.

For support with any institutional subscription, please visit help.tandfonline.com or email our dedicated team at subscriptions@tandf.co.uk.

Subscriptions purchased at the personal rate are strictly for personal, non-commercial use only. The reselling of personal subscriptions is prohibited. Personal subscriptions must be purchased with a personal check, credit card, or BAC/wire transfer. Proof of personal status may be requested.

Back issues: Please visit https://taylorandfrancis.com/journals/customer-services/ for more information on how to purchase back issues.

Ordering information: To subscribe to the Journal, please contact: T&F Customer Services, Informa UK Ltd, Sheepen Place, Colchester, Essex, CO3 3LP, United Kingdom. Tel: +44 (0) 20 8052 2030; email: subscriptions@tandf.co.uk.

Taylor & Francis journals are priced in USD, GBP and EUR (as well as AUD and CAD for a limited number of journals). All subscriptions are charged depending on where the end customer is based. If you are unsure which rate applies to you, please contact Customer Services. All subscriptions are payable in advance and all rates include postage. We are required to charge applicable VAT/GST on all print and online combination subscriptions, in addition to our online-only journals. Subscriptions are entered on an annual basis, i.e., January to December. Payment may be made by sterling check, dollar check, euro check, international money order, National Giro or credit cards (Amex, Visa and Mastercard).

Disclaimer: The International Institute for Strategic Studies and our publisher Taylor & Francis make every effort to ensure the accuracy of all the information (the "Content") contained in our publications. However, The International Institute for Strategic Studies and our publisher Taylor & Francis, our agents (including the editor, any member of the editorial team or editorial board, and any guest editors), and our licensors make no representations or warranties whatsoever as to the accuracy, completeness, or suitability for any purpose of the Content. Any opinions and views expressed in this publication are the opinions and views of the authors, and are not the views of or endorsed by The International Institute for Strategic Studies and our publisher Taylor & Francis. The accuracy of the Content should not be relied upon and should be independently verified with primary sources of information. The International Institute for Strategic Studies and our publisher Taylor & Francis shall not be liable for any losses, actions, claims, proceedings, demands, costs, expenses, damages, and other liabilities whatsoever or howsoever caused arising directly or indirectly in connection with, in relation to, or arising out of the use of the Content. Terms & Conditions of access and use can be found at http://www.tandfonline.com/page/terms-and-conditions.

All Taylor & Francis Group journals are printed on paper from renewable sources by accredited partners.